SAM PHILLIPS

ALSO BY PETER GURALNICK

Dream Boogie: The Triumph of Sam Cooke

Careless Love: The Unmaking of Elvis Presley

Last Train to Memphis. The Rise of Elvis Presley

Searching for Robert Johnson

Nighthawk Blues

Sweet Soul Music: Rhythm and Blues and the Southern Dream of Freedom

Lost Highway: Journeys and Arrivals of American Musicians

Feel Like Going Home: Portraits in Blues and Rock 'n' Roll

SAM PHILLIPS

THE MAN WHO INVENTED

ROCK 'N' ROLL

PETER GURALNICK

LITTLE, BROWN AND COMPANY

NEW YORK | BOSTON | LONDON

Little, Brown and Company
Hachette Book Group
1290 Avenue of the Americas, New York, NY 10104
littlebrown.com

FIRST EDITION: November 2015

PAGE I: Acetate "Rocket 88." *Courtesy of Jerry Gibson and Jim Cole*
TITLE PAGE: Elvis, Bill Black, and Scotty Moore, February 1955, through the control room window. *Courtesy of the Sam Phillips Family*
PAGE VIII: Sam and Becky with Knox and Jerry, May 1949. *Courtesy of the Sam Phillips Family*
PAGE 1: "Mystery Train" tape box with instructions for mastering. *Courtesy of Ernst Jorgensen*
PAGE 662: *Courtesy of the Sam Phillips Family*

Lyrics from "I Walk the Line" written by John R. Cash. © 1956, renewed, BMG Bumblebee/House of Cash, Inc. All rights reserved. Reprinted by permission.

All photographs are copyrighted by the photographer and/or owner cited, all rights reserved.

Little, Brown and Company is a division of Hachette Book Group, Inc.
The Little, Brown name and logo are trademarks of Hachette Book Group, Inc.

The publisher is not responsible for websites (or their content) that are not owned by the publisher.

The Hachette Speakers Bureau provides a wide range of authors for speaking events. To find out more, go to hachettespeakersbureau.com or call (866) 376-6591.

Library of Congress Cataloging-in-Publication Data
Guralnick, Peter.
  Sam Phillips : the man who invented rock 'n' roll / Peter Guralnick.—First edition.
    pages cm
  Includes bibliographical references and index.
  ISBN 978-0-316-04274-1 (hc)
  1. Phillips, Sam, 1923-2003. 2. Sound recording executives and producers—United States—Biography. I. Title.
  ML429.P54G87 2015
  781.66092—dc23
  [B]   2015024690

RRD-C

Designed by Susan Marsh

10 9 8 7 6 5 4 3 2 1

Printed in the United States of America

For Knox Phillips

And for Ava, Anastasia, and Frances

Contents

In which SAM PHILLIPS *addresses the* AUTHOR: *excerpted from a real-life* PLAY IN ONE SCENE

It's a great story, and it will go down in history. I don't know how great the book will be—but it's a great story. Peter, look, let me just tell you like I told all of my children, like I told every artist that walked in the door. Don't be afraid of it. No matter what I say to you, don't be afraid of it. But be frightened to death of not giving your best judgment to everything. Don't let history down. Fuck Sam Phillips. Fuck anything that goes. It's an important era—you got so much more responsibility to that than you got to any one person, including my ass.

The AUTHOR *acknowledges that this is so. The* AUTHOR *suggests that if he doesn't come in for criticism, in Sam's terms he will have fucked up.*

If you don't, you're just another one of the motherfuckers that are using this thing to the detriment of the beautiful changes it wrought. That's not right. If you let that happen, you ain't a very conscientious, dedicated, devoted person. It ain't for you to put me in a good light. Just put me in the focus that I'm supposed to be in. Man, I don't give a damn if you say one good thing about me. Your charge is to put all of it in focus and ferret out the bullshit. There's been enough of that. I'm going to tell you, Peter, Ferret it out, for God's sake. Look, and tell your damn publisher, "Hey, if it takes me forever to write it, it's going to be the most authentic thing that has ever emanated from this era. With all the contradictions to the contrary." You read me?

AUTHOR: *I do. (And he does.)*

"From this, he took a lesson: value the original, fragile, and rough. That's the art." —HOLLAND COTTER *on the art of Henri Matisse*

"To us, their less tried successors, they appear magnified . . . pushing out into the unknown in obedience to an inward voice, to an impulse beating in the blood, to a dream of the future. They were wonderful; and it must be owned they were ready for the wonderful." —JOSEPH CONRAD, *Lord Jim*

Author's Note

IT WAS A HEAVY CHARGE, as I think should be evident from the dramatic reconstruction on the opposite page — but one from which I never felt I could shrink.

I met Sam Phillips in a flood (see chapter 9), and as I wrote at the time, from that first meeting his words had all the weight of vatic truth. He seemed like an Old Testament prophet to me, in both looks and manner. Or, as singer-songwriter John Prine said, in describing his own first meeting with Sam: his eyes would grow wide, "like fire and brimstone. It looked like his eyebrows and his eyes themselves were on fire — they were just wild — you'd swear that his hair would kind of get curly, and his hands moved like a preacher's."

I mean, it was *something!*

But that wasn't it — not really. At least not all of it. I suppose I should confess at the start what I am sure will become immediately apparent to the reader: this is a book written out of admiration and love. Nor will it be any less evident that this book is different from the two other biographies I have written, on Elvis Presley and Sam Cooke. Not that there was any less admiration or love in those books. But I *knew* Sam Phillips, I knew him for almost twenty-five years, I was with him through good times and bad, and while I might not necessarily have chosen to have my responsibilities read to me by my subject, they are the same responsibilities felt by any other biographer (ferret out the truth, don't be afraid of it, and, in the end, "Fuck anything that goes") — they are the self-imposed responsibilities taken on by every writer, of fiction or nonfiction, for better or worse.

In that spirit perhaps I should also add that Sam would have disclaimed the subtitle of this book — well, to be perfectly honest, he would have both claimed and disclaimed it, as he frequently did, more often than not in the same elongated sentence. "I didn't set out to revolutionize the world," he said one time. Instead, what he wanted to do was to test the proposition that there was something "very profound" in the lives of ordinary people, black and white, irrespective of social acceptance. "I knew the physical separation of the races—but I knew the integration of their souls." That was what he set out to capture when he first opened his studio in January of 1950, "when Negro artists in the South who wanted to make a record," he declared early on, "just had no place to go." It went against all practical considerations, it went against all well-intended advice. He considered himself not a crusader ("I don't like crusaders as such") but an *explorer.* To Sam, "Rock and roll was no accident. Absolutely not an accident at all." "You can say," he told me, "he had the light coming on, and it spotted the possum. *Right there.*"

Well, I guess that's one way of putting it. Let's just say Sam was the man who *discovered* rock 'n' roll. But more to the point, he considered it his mission in life "to open up an area of freedom within the artist himself"—whether that artist was Elvis Presley or Howlin' Wolf or B.B. King or Johnny Cash—"to recognize that individual's unique quality and then to find the key to unlock it." That is what he sought to do with every artist who entered his studio, whether or not they ever achieved worldly success, whether or not they were ever likely to achieve it.

It might have seemed sometimes to an outsider as if the musicians were just fumbling around, and the producer (a term that did not even exist then, and that Sam to some extent would always disdain: I think he might have preferred to be called a practicing psychologist) was just letting things go to rack and ruin. But he wasn't. He was simply trying to pare things down to their most expressive essence. Michelangelo said: "In every block of marble I see a statue as plain as though it stood before me, shaped and perfect in attitude and action. I have only to hew away the rough walls that imprison the lovely apparition to reveal it to the other eyes as mine see it." That was what Sam Phillips saw not in marble but in untried, untested, unspoken-for people: an eloquence and a gift that sometimes they did not even know they possessed. Like other celebrated American artists—like Walt Whitman, who sought to encompass the full range of the American experience in his poetry; like William Faulkner, who could see past prejudice to individual distinctions; like Mark Twain, who celebrated the freedom of the river and a refusal to be civilized — Sam was driven by a creative vision that left him with no alternative but to persist in his determination to give voice to those who had no voice. "With the belief that I had in this music, in these people," he said, "I would have been the biggest damn coward on God's green earth if I had not."

From the day I first met him in 1979, Sam Phillips began telling me the story of his life. Not in so many words, of course. But then, given his discursive nature, it may well have *been* so many words. To Sam his life was epic, mythic, intimate, and instructive by turns, and the tone he used to describe it was casual, colloquial, lyrical, thundering, and eloquently collusive. All of which pretty much ruled out any hope of linearity. What you were going for, in Sam's terms, was "just another swinging day at the fair."

He saw himself as a teacher and a preacher. That was the motivation that drove him to expound his message to the world, long after he had stopped making records. But in a very real sense the persona that he created in later life to convey that message did a disservice to the watchful, reactive role he had fashioned for himself when all of his attention was focused on no more than "to bring out of a person what was in him . . . to help him express what he believed his message to be." To Sam every session was meant to be like "the making of *Gone with the Wind*," with all its epic grandeur — but at the same time every session had to be fun, too. If it wasn't fun, it wasn't worth doing, he said, and if you weren't doing something different, of course, then you weren't doing anything at all. As far as failure went, there could be no such thing in his studio, because in the end, Sam insisted, it was all about individuated self-expression, nothing more, nothing less.

"Perfect imperfection" was the watchword — both in life and in art — in other words, take the hand you're dealt and then make something of it. If Ike Turner's guitarist's amp fell off the car on the way up to Memphis to cut "Rocket 88," well, stuff some paper where the speaker cone was ruptured, and THEN YOU HAD AN ORIGINAL SOUND! If a telephone went off in the middle of a session, well, you kept that telephone in — just make sure it's THE BEST-SOUNDING DAMN TELEPHONE IN THE WORLD.

You can see how this could affect a person — and by "person," in this instance I mean me. Meeting Sam for me was a life-changing event — but for all of the impact of his message, and for all of the fact that in retrospect

I think I can say he hit virtually every point in his narrative at that first meeting, I soon discovered that it was a message that could all too easily be misunderstood. When Sam referred to his mental breakdown and electroshock treatment, for example, not long after opening the studio (he even called his wife, Becky, to verify the dates of his hospitalization), I thought it represented a triumph over darkness once and for all. But that wasn't quite what Sam meant, although there would have been no telling that at the time. (He didn't mean the opposite either.) So many of the conclusions I came to, after that first immersion in the Book of Sam, the conclusions to which Sam was pointing, in a sense was *always* pointing, were so much more nuanced than the supremely confident language in which they were clothed. I mean, it wasn't that they didn't hold up over the years. They did. They were, if anything, reinforced. But they were *modified,* as all of our truths are modified, by the life that was lived. They were like the family anecdotes that we all tell one another, a neat summation that encapsulates a far deeper and more complex reality.

Since that time I have continued to be engaged in a running dialogue with Sam, as I'm sure will escape the notice of no one who reads this book. The conversation is never anything less than lively — it is thought-provoking, engaging, frequently as challenging as it was in real life. The difference is, simply, that in real life, there was no shut-off valve. Now, more than ten years after his death, I can simply take my leave of Sam after three, four, maybe even five hours, and go on to other pursuits. It is, I suppose, more civilized — but given the choice, I'm not sure with Sam polite discourse would ever be the preferred mode.

How many times have I wanted to ask him questions of both fact and opinion? I study the transcripts of our conversations, I pore over other interviews and try to read between the lines, attempting to gauge what his vocal and facial expressions must have been — I torture my brain sometimes trying to interpret Sam's Ciceronian syntax or, in many instances, guess at the periodic conclusion at which he never quite arrived.

Occasionally — well, *more* than occasionally — I think of Sam's reaction. More than once I've hesitated momentarily at revealing some of the things he appeared to have kept secret. Or at least that I didn't know about. Which, of course, are by no means the same thing, though often one is tempted to conflate the two. But in the end I hope I've kept faith with Sam's charge of total honesty ("I don't want any accolades. I just want the truth. And, God believe me, Peter . . . if you fuck it up, then you're a goddamn crook as far as I'm concerned, and I'll tell you to your teeth"), tempered with the same consideration for people that Sam so often showed, in his own way, particularly in his creative endeavors. I've also tried to hold up as an example to myself his inextinguishable faith in humanity. Not *soppy* inextinguishable faith. What I'm talking about is the broad framework that would banish forever the exclamation "That's disgusting" with reference to behavior with which we're not familiar or of which we do not approve, and substitute instead the recognition *That's human.* There was nothing, in other words, in Sam's cosmogony that could make us less than human, even if it didn't conform to the more convenient tale we would like to tell about ourselves.

Sam always made it plain—not just to me but to everyone around him—that he wanted hard, unvarnished truths, and I never doubted for a moment that he did. As Jerry Phillips said at one point while pondering whether or not to tell a particularly uncomfortable story about his father, "Sam would just say, 'Tell the goddamn truth'"—and that is what he and every other member of Sam's family was committed to. Not so much in the sense of, Let the chips fall wherever they fucking may (his wife, Becky, was too kind for that, his older son, Knox, too devoted, and his longtime companion, Sally Wilbourn, underneath a fiercely protective outer shell, perhaps in the end too fragile), but there was never any sense on anyone's part, least of all Sam's, of hiding his humanity under a neatly formed construct, of sacrificing the truth at any point to an invitingly colorful legend.

There were so many crazy times, so many two-fisted drinking dinners (I'm speaking here of Sam's two fists)—Knox and I discussed all the time the wreck of all our well-conceived plans and expectations. ("That was a weird interview with Sam," Knox might say. "I mean, weird *good.*") But without meaning in any way to equate my own outsider status with Knox's own indissoluble bond with his father—I mean, *close* doesn't even begin to describe it—there was not, we always hasten to agree, there was not one single moment either of us would not give everything to have back. As Sam would certainly say, they were all great, they were all to be prized—because they were all, each and every one of them, indubitably *real.* R-E-A-L.

As you can see, nearly everyone who loved Sam has contributed to this book. Not all of them understood Sam. In fact, outside the immediate family, most — with the notable exception of self-proclaimed-and-proud-of-it "nuts" like Jack Clement and Sputnik Monroe or more reserved wisemen like Roland Janes — probably did not. Some preferred to think of him as a kind of high-achieving "rodeo clown" — and permitted themselves to be, simply, amused by some of his more outrageous pronouncements or actions (cf. his appearance on the *David Letterman* show). But there was no one that I encountered who was untouched, or was not in some way inspired, by Sam. There was no one who failed to recognize his unique — well, if they wouldn't give him "genius," every one of them was ready to concede they had never met anyone else even remotely like Sam.

Which brings me back to my role in this book. Because, of course, like everyone else in Sam's life, I was assigned a role, however small — and like everyone else, as should be clear from just a smattering of our dialogue, *I was expected to carry it out.* In writing the book I felt I had to take advantage of that role, not to enlarge myself but to give the kind of firsthand insight that however well I might feel I knew Elvis or Sam Cooke, I simply was not afforded by personal experience. It's not that the events that I witnessed were magnified in any way by my presence — but they were no less colorful or characteristic either, and it was, of course, a rare opportunity to report from the front lines.

Occasionally (*very* occasionally) I was a witness to history, more often to the unfettered expression of personality — but, most important, I was afforded a glimpse, whether advertent or inadvertent, as Sam might say, of some of the dramedy of real life. Sitting with Sam just before (and just after) he delivered his paean to Johnny Cash and Jesus and the Hotel Peabody at a NARAS celebration in Memphis that shocked and offended half the audience while raising Sam up even higher in the shockabilly esteem of the rest. Private moments of desolation and despair (well, perhaps despair is too big a word for his feelings — *doubt* maybe?), when he might unburden himself of his frustrations, then castigate himself for giving in to negative thinking, against all of his strongly held beliefs. Those times when he would call up a long-since-forgotten past and summon up unsung heroes (unsung even in the body of this book) like Alex "Puddin'" Beck, an African-American plumber's assistant, who was as brilliant as any advanced-degree sanitary engineer, Sam said, and could emerge from the messiest and smelliest job as clean as a whistle. "Hey," said Sam without a smidgen of irony, "are you gonna tell me people like that are not brilliant?" And then there were those rare exposed moments when all pretense was cast aside and Sam stood, like Lear upon the heath, raging at unseen cataracts and hurricanoes.

One thing that for me can be difficult about many biographies — well, about so many stories in general — is the predictable spinning out of the tale. With Elvis Presley and Sam Cooke that issue never really presented itself — they both died so young. But Sam Phillips lived to the age of eighty, and to all intents and purposes he had by then been retired from any active engagement in the record business for over forty years. Sam was never boring — at least not to me — but a recitation of all his accolades and honors would have been. I have done my best to avoid that recitation. Instead, I have attempted to write a book that conforms to Sam's definition of what a recording session ought to be, as epic as, well, take your pick of epics, but as intimate as sexual relations. That tells a story that, like most stories, can be both heroic and tragic at the same time, in its own mortal way.

Sometimes in the middle of the night he arrives unbidden. He even sets me riddles. In one dream he said to my bewilderment (both then and now), "I am nothing if not an idealist. . . . I am everything but an idealist. . . . The boy cannot fully understand." I dream of Sam. I dream of my grandfather. I dream of Solomon Burke and the songwriter Doc Pomus. All gone. They come around less frequently now. But whenever Sam arrives, as often as not rattling at the window in the midst of a torrent of conflicting concerns, I always listen.

SAM PHILLIPS

"SCOTCH Magnetic Tape"

BRAND · PATENTED UNDER U.S. PATENT NO. 2,654,681

REEL NO._____

TRACK NO._____ DATE_____ SPEED_____
TITLE _____ ARTIST

Bill: — Give Me "Hot" based on
Both 78 + 45's And as much presence
Peak + Bass as possible !
Forward Acetate Masters To:
    S. J. Shaw Plating Co.
    2604 Glendora Ave. Cincinnati, Ohio
Return To: Memphis Recording Serv.
    706 Union Ave
    Memphis, Tenn,

NOTICE: Buyers shall determine that contents are proper kind for intended use. If defective in the manufacture, labeling, or packaging, contents will be replaced. There are no other warranties, expressed or implied.

● The term "SCOTCH" and the plaid design are registered trade marks for Magnetic Tape made in U.S.A. by Minnesota Mining and Manufacturing Company. ●

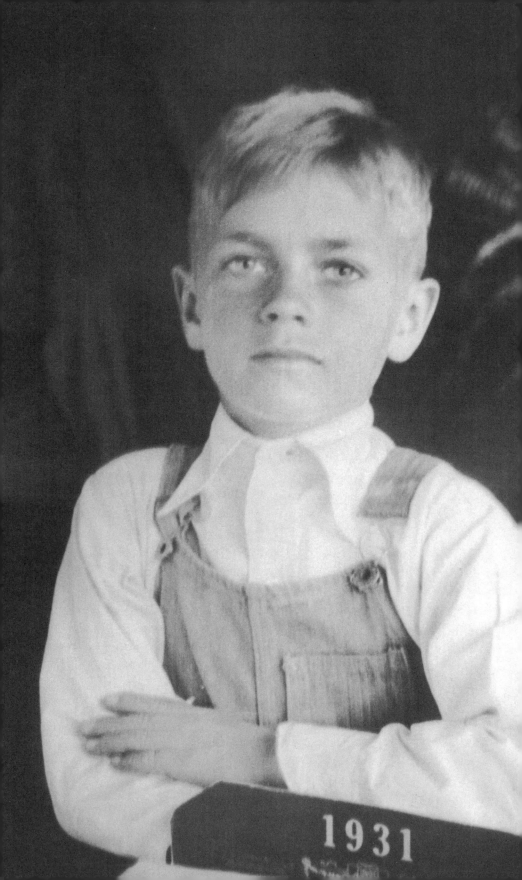

1931

*Nothing passed my ears. A mockingbird or a whippoorwill — out in
the country on a calm afternoon. The silence of the cottonfields, that
beautiful rhythmic silence, with a hoe hitting a rock every now and
then and just as it spaded through the dirt, you could hear it. That was
just unbelievable music: to hear that bird maybe three hundred yards
away, the wind not even blowing in your direction, or no wind at all.
But it carried, it got to my ears. I would hear somebody speak to a mule
harshly, I heard that. I mean, I heard everything. It wasn't any time
until I began to observe people [too], more by sound — I certainly didn't
know what to do with everything I heard, but I knew I had something
that could be an asset if I could just figure out what to do with it.*

I N   L A T E R   Y E A R S   Sam Phillips would always refer to the moment of
his arrival on this earth with a wonderment not altogether free of
caustic amusement. "You take my ass dying when I was born, and
you take a drunk doctor showing up — man, he didn't even make it till
I was born — and my mama being so kind she got up out of bed and put
him to bed until he sobered up, and then the midwife comes and Mama
feels so sorry for Dr. Cornelius she named me after him!"

Nobody ever took more pleasure in his own story than Sam Phillips.
It was, in his telling, a poetic as much as a realistic vision, a mythic
journey combining narrative action, revolutionary rhetoric, Delphic
pronouncements, and the satisfaction, like that of any Old Testament
god, of being able to look back on the result and pronounce it "good."

Sam at eight. *Courtesy of the Sam Phillips Family*

He would return again and again to the same themes over the years, with different details and different emphases, but always with the same underlying message: the inherent nobility not so much of man as of *freedom,* and the implied responsibility — no, the *obligation* — for each of us to be as different as our individuated natures allowed us to be. To be different, in Sam's words, *in the extreme.*

But it always started out with a slight, sickly looking tow-headed little boy looking out at the world from the 323-acre farm at the Bend of the River, about ten miles outside Florence, Alabama. His daddy didn't own the farm, just rented it, and by the time Sam was eight years old, his two oldest brothers and older sister had all married, leaving him at home with his seventeen-year-old sister, Irene, his fifteen-year-old-brother, Tom, and the next youngest, ten-year-old J.W. (John William, later to be known as Jud), who was, like Sam, something of an afterthought for parents who were forty-four and nearly forty by the time their youngest child was born.

He and his family worked the fields with mules, along with dozens of others, black and white sharecroppers, poor people — his daddy was a *fair* man, he treated them all the same. His daddy didn't say much; the one thing that really made him mad was if someone told him a lie — it didn't matter who it was, he would stand up and tell them to their face. Daddy had a feel for the land, he grew corn, hay, and sweet sorghum, and the cotton rows were half a mile long. His mama was kind to everyone, believed wholeheartedly in all her children, and worried a lot — there was nothing she wouldn't do for any of them, and nothing she couldn't do as well as any man. Sometimes at night she might dip a little snuff and pick the guitar, old folk songs like "Barbara Allen" and "Aura Lee," the guitar took on all the properties of a human voice, but she didn't sing, it was almost as if she were quilting the music together.

Just like Daddy, she taught them how to work, by her example. She taught them responsibility by the kindness she and Daddy showed to others less fortunate, including relatives, passing strangers, and, by the presence in their own home, her sister Emma, blinded in one eye and made deaf and mute by Rocky Mountain spotted fever when she was

The Phillips Family, 1916 (before J.W. and Sam were born). Left to right: Charles, Irene, Horace, Madgie, and Tom. Standing at back: Mary and Turner. *Courtesy of the Sam Phillips Family* three. Sam observed Aunt Emma closely and, in order to communicate with her (she was a well-educated woman, a graduate of the internationally renowned Alabama Institute for Deaf and Blind at Talladega), learned to sign almost before he could read. He was the only one in the family who could communicate fully with her except for Mama and his sister Irene, who wanted to become a nurse. Even when he was working (and there was seldom a time that he wasn't), he was watching, listening, observing: the interactions of people, the scudding of the clouds across the sky, the communication of crickets and frogs (he was convinced that he could talk to them—and not just as a little boy either), the flow of the beautiful Tennessee River. He couldn't understand why all the little black boys and girls he worked and played with couldn't go to the same little country school that he did; he registered the unfairness of the way in which people were arbitrarily set apart by the color of their skin, and he thought, What if I had been born black? And he admired the way they dealt with adversity—he envied them their power of resilience, their ability to maintain belief in a situation in which he doubted he could have sustained belief himself. But, for the most part, knowing how different his feelings were even from those closest to him, from his very family, and knowing how much more different he intended to *be*, he kept his thoughts to himself and listened to the a cappella singing that came from the fields, testament as he saw it, whether sacred or secular, to an invincible human spirit and spirituality.

> They found a way to worship. You could hear it. You could feel it.
> You didn't have to be inside a building, you could participate in a cotton patch, picking four rows at a time, at 110 degrees! I mean, I saw
> the inequity. But even at five or six years old I found myself caught
> up in a type of emotional reaction that was, instead of depressing—I
> mean, these were some of the astutest people I've ever known, and
> they were in [most] cases almost totally overlooked, except as a beast
> of burden—but even at that age, I recognized that: Hey! The backs
> of these people aren't broken, they [can] find it in their souls to live
> a life that is not going to take the joy of living away.

SAMUEL CORNELIUS PHILLIPS (remember Dr. Cornelius) was born on January 5, 1923, in the only home that his father would ever own, in a tiny hamlet six or seven miles north of Florence called Lovelace

Sam and J.W. (Jud). *Courtesy of the Sam Phillips Family*

Community, named for his mother's family and populated with musically talented Lovelaces and practical, hardworking Phillipses. When he was just nine months old, the house burned down, and the family moved in and out of town, then to the old Martin place on Chisholm Highway and then further out in the country to the old Pickens place in Oakland, which was an eight-year-old's (and later a seventy-eight-year-old's) 323-acre vision of Eden. His overwhelming impression, his overwhelming *experience*, was of hard work—his mama and his daddy never stopped, and his brother Horace, older by fourteen years, was, everyone acknowledged, a "mechanical genius," who would make a career in heavy equipment. The sensibility of the two youngest, though, Sam and his brashly self-assured brother J.W., was different in type if not in kind. J.W. possessed the sort of robust personality to which everyone, adults and children alike, was inevitably drawn. He was confident, articulate, outgoing, a natural leader, even if Sam sometimes mistrusted just where his leadership might be taking them. He was warmhearted and trustful just like their daddy, but unlike Daddy there was no holdback in his speech: he proclaimed his views eloquently and convincingly, although his younger brother occasionally questioned whether J.W. really knew what he was talking about.

Sam saw himself as set apart and wasn't about to apologize for it. He prized independence and artistry, even when he was too young to put a name on them. He saw Daddy as an artist of the soil, he saw music as an expression of innate spirituality. He was a delicate child, "a runt that really had a rough time surviving," as he frequently said, but for all of that, he was determined to go his own way. "I got impatient with children doing the same things other children did. I had the ability to love other people, but I also had the ability to tell them what I thought, even at an early age. I wasn't a spoiled person, but for some reason or another I was totally an independent cat, and to be that, and be as sickly as I was and not be screaming for Mama must have signified something." What it signified, Sam firmly believed, was that he had his own eyes and ears to assess things with, and they were going to lead him to the greater goal he had in mind, even if he couldn't say precisely what it was. It was not lost on him, however, what he sacrificed in terms of popularity. It was impossible not to like J.W., as his younger brother was well aware, and for J.W. the approval of others was the greatest authenticator. As for himself, despite all his bravado, he couldn't help but regret the absence of that same easy camaraderie. He was, he recognized with some asperity, "the greenest persimmon on the tree. If you took a bite of me, you didn't like me too much."

Growing up, he was surrounded by music — square dances, round dances, once a month, at a neighbor's, a relative's, sometimes at home. On those occasions you pushed all the furniture out of the room and everybody would sing and play — fiddle, banjo, ukulele, guitar — sometimes his sober-sided daddy might even call. His sister Irene made sure to take him and J.W. along, from the time they were no more than four or five years old, and he would sit in a corner, just watching all of his grown-up brothers and sisters and all the others, hardworking farmers and their wives, dancing and having a good time. When he was six, just before the October stock market crash, they got a Graphophone record player at Kilgore Furniture Store — they set it on the floor and wound it up and played the one record they were able to afford with their initial purchase, Jimmie Rodgers' "Waiting for a Train," over and over. Though

Rodgers has come to be universally invoked as the "Father of Country Music," the song was a blues, profound in its portrait of loss and displacement and uncanny in its foreshadowing of the Great Depression that hovered unseen just over the horizon. "'All around the water tank,'" Sam would quote sixty, seventy years later at the drop of a hat, "'Waiting for a train/A thousand miles away from home/Sleeping in the rain...' And then he walks up to a brakeman 'to give him a line of talk'—you know, he was trying to get in that boxcar—and this brakeman says, 'Well, you got any money, I'll see that you don't walk.' But Jimmie didn't have any money, and 'he slammed the boxcar door.' If you can just visualize that—Depression, hard times, won't be another train for a long time. Let me tell you something, Jimmie Rodgers didn't waste a word."

THE DEPRESSION didn't hit the Phillips family as hard as some, but it hit hard enough to inalterably change the pattern and outcome of their lives. Charlie Phillips was able to hold on for the first few years, but then in 1933, when cotton was down to five cents a pound, he recognized that he could no longer make a living off the land, and the family moved to town. It was like being cast out of paradise.

Sam's daddy's first job off the farm was flagging on the old L&N railroad bridge, which had a single lane for vehicular traffic, working from six in the evening till six in the morning seven days a week for thirty dollars. He moved the family in and out of town over the next few years, keeping the job as the salary increased to thirty-five and then forty dollars a week but continuing to farm simply because of his love of the land. He grade contracted for others, he terraced the Florence State Teachers College amphitheater with mules and sodded it with Bermuda grass ("He was," said Sam, "the greatest sculptor of the soil I've ever seen"), he grew an experimental vegetable garden for Dr. Willingham, the president of the college, he held out a helping hand to others when he could barely afford the rent himself—and his youngest son took it all in. The way he was with people, the way he was with animals, the kindness he showed to others, the expectations he had of himself. "My daddy didn't do things I didn't see. He didn't know I was looking at him, I wasn't *staring*—but my daddy never ceased to amaze me. He knew the soil. He knew mules. I mean, he *knew* mules! My daddy never used a stick or a whip or anything. Mules would work for him, people would work for him—and they would rise and achieve above their normal capacity." His

Sam and Aunt Emma, late 1955 or early 1956. *Courtesy of the Sam Phillips Family*

daddy was never truly happy in town, the little boy felt. Even as a small child he saw his father fueled by an agrarian vision — though he certainly couldn't have named it at the time. There was an idealism, he believed, that fed his father beyond faith and hard work. His daddy would never have chosen to make a *living* off the land if he hadn't had to. "There was something clean about the soil, there was something clean about plowing a mule — he could just take the soil in his hands and watch it produce for him." It was the purity of a dream.

He was a frail but determined child. Even though his brother was twice his size, and much more physically commanding, he and J.W. fought like cats and dogs — but they always got together again afterward. You just couldn't help but love J.W., but it was his aunt Emma who truly fascinated him for her refusal to be intellectually inhibited by her inability to hear or speak. He was well aware of the example of Helen Keller, across the river in Tuscumbia, and he had long, animated signing discussions with his aunt, who read the newspaper cover to cover every day and irritated some members of the family with her strong opinions and behavior that could just as easily be described as willful as strong-willed. Only Sam and his mother were able to calm Aunt Emma down, and of all the nephews and nieces he was clearly her favorite.

When he was in the sixth grade, the family moved to Royal Avenue in North Florence, directly behind the cotton gin where they had once brought their cotton. When the circus came to town, it passed right by their house, with the elephants at the head of the parade, before pitching tent by the railroad track in East Florence, a mile and a half away. The carnival set up in back of the store right across the alley from them. And any children in the neighborhood could ride for free.

It was in the sixth grade, too, that he had his first drum lesson, on the kind of "field" drum that you wore around your neck, from the city music director, Mr. D. Γ. Stuber. Sam had been begging his mama and daddy for music lessons, beating on pots and pans till he like to drove his mama crazy, and he had to rake leaves and mow Mr. Stuber's yard while his daddy grew a garden for Mr. Stuber to help pay for the lessons. He wasn't the best drummer in the world, he knew, but he was diligent in his application, and with sufficient practice, Mr. Stuber assured him, he could join the marching band the following year when he entered junior high school.

It was during this time that Uncle Silas joined the Phillips household. According to the official Phillips Family Reunion book, Charlie and Madgie Phillips "never turned anyone away who needed food, clothing, shelter, comfort, love, and affection." They raised three children in addition to their own, and many others, including Aunt Emma, lived with them, so that there were frequently as many as "nineteen or twenty . . . around the Phillips supper table." In this case it was Silas Payne, a poor black sharecropper, originally from Louisiana, who had worked on the old Pickens place and was, said Sam, a "genius with chickens" even after he went blind from syphilis. Another family had taken him in after the Phillipses moved to town, but when the Miles family could no longer afford to care for him, Charlie Phillips borrowed the cotton gin manager Mr. Wiggins' 1929 Chevrolet and moved Uncle Silas in with them.

The story of Uncle Silas is at the epicenter of everything that Sam

Phillips ever believed both about himself and the "common man," in that most uncommon narrative that became the lodestar for his life. It was not sympathy for this old black man's plight that drew him to Silas Payne — far from it, Sam Phillips always insisted. Rather, it was admiration for those same qualities of imagination, creativity, and invincible determination that he had first noted in the black fieldworkers on his father's farm — that and the kind of emotional freedom, the unqualified generosity and kindness that he himself would have most liked to be able to achieve.

He recognized that even for his father, just like for nearly everyone else who lived nearby, while there may have been no overt prejudice, whites were still whites, niggers niggers — for all of his daddy's fair-mindedness (who else took a colored man into his house?), that was simply the way he had been taught and raised. For the young boy, though, there was something almost magical about Uncle Silas, with the hundreds of chickens he kept out back, every one of whom he could distinguish by name, and the Bible stories he rhymed up, the songs he sang, the stories he told of an Africa he had never known, with batter-cake trees and a Molasses River that took a twelve-year-old boy away to a world in which he was freed from all the emotional and physical bonds by which he felt so constricted in his day-to-day existence.

Not long after Uncle Silas came to live with them — right after graduating sixth grade in June of 1936 — Sam became ill, so ill, in fact, that old Dr. Duckett was just about ready to give up on him. He had two bouts of double pneumonia, and his lungs were weakened by pleurisy to the point where it almost hurt too much to breathe. The doctor, a gruff old-timer with flowing hair and a long white beard, knew the family's limited resources and brought his patient oranges to build up his strength, but one day after the doctor's visit, Sam heard his mother and Mrs. Reynolds, the lady who lived right behind them on North Royal, talking about him, and he suddenly sensed that he might be about to die. He didn't tell his mother that he had overheard their conversation, but he experienced a sudden and almost overwhelming sense of panic at the thought of the world going on without him, at the thought of all the things he would not get to do, all the ongoing narratives, his own and everyone else's, whose outcome he would never learn. That panic returned from time to time, but it was soothed as much as anything not just by his mother's reassurances and ministrations as by Uncle Silas' constant reiterations that not only was he going to get better, he was going to be able to achieve the kind of things he could scarcely formulate in words or even dream of now.

"He liked to sit in the kitchen and put me on his knee, grab me by my bony shoulder and say, 'Samuel, you're going to grow up and be a great man someday.' I mean, I was just a sickly kid—physically, I don't know, maybe mentally, too—but somehow, as much as I didn't believe him, I did believe him. Because he sounded so confident. And he was a great storyteller—but [what I got from his stories] is that, number one, you must have a belief in things that are unknown to you, that what you see and hear is really not all that important, except for the moment. I mean, Africa was just another way of him pointing to the things that were all over and available to us one way or another. Africa was a state of mind that he hoped everybody could see and be a part of or participate in." Most of all, rather than moralize, he just tried to teach the sickly little boy, as much by example as anything else, "how to live and be happy, no matter what came along, [that] even when you're feeling bad, you're feeling good."

This enforced isolation only served to underscore the privations that Silas and Sam's aunt Emma had had to learn to put up with and endure and further sharpened his own powers of observation. He sat out on the porch swing watching the world go by, he listened for different cadences of speech without even heeding the words, he studied movement and demeanor, and he grew to believe, for all of his fears and insecurities, that he had been granted a God-given gift, the ability to read people in the same way that other people read books.

When he was finally able to return to school, the insight that he had gained was mixed somehow with a resentment of the experience that he had missed—it was almost as if he saw things in too sharp a focus and didn't know what to do with his new clairvoyance. He was a "mean little bastard" in the seventh and eighth grades by his own unapologetic description ("I was just very, very convinced of things"), until his favorite homeroom teacher, Mrs. Mary Alice Lanier, spanked the hell out his hand with a ruler. It was the first and last time he was ever physically reprimanded in school, but it evidently shocked him back to his senses. He was no more "likable" after that, according to his own lights—that was for J.W.—but he was finally starting to put things in the proper perspective, and as he finished the eighth grade at sixteen, working five

afternoons a week plus Saturdays at J. Will Young's grocery store to help out the family, he made up his mind to seek the mantle of leadership that he believed to be both his gift and his destiny.

I first came through Memphis in 1939 on the way to Dallas to hear Dr. George W. Truett, the famous pastor of the First Baptist Church, preach. It was five of us boys, including my brother J.W. and myself, all of us members of Highland Baptist Church, and we left Florence between midnight and one o'clock, drove to Memphis on a gravel road by way of Savannah, Tennessee. Well, I'd heard about Beale Street all my life, pictured it in my mind what it was — I could not wait! We arrived at four or five o'clock in the morning in pouring down rain, but I'm telling you, Broadway never looked that busy. It was like a beehive, a microcosm of humanity — you had a lot of sober people there, you had a lot of people having a good time. You had old black men from the Delta and young cats dressed fit to kill. But the most impressive thing to me about Beale Street was that nobody got in anybody's way — because every damn one of them wanted to be right there. Beale Street represented for me, even at that age, something that I hoped to see for all people. That sense of absolute freedom, that sense of no direction but the greatest direction in the world, of being able to feel, I'm a part of this somehow. I may only be here a day or two, but I can tell everybody when I get back home what a wonderful time I had.

The trip to Memphis was probably the most significant event not just of Sam's life to date, but very likely of his entire life. It fused all of the elements that he had come to believe represented his unique makeup as a human being and set his future course as well. But it came about not entirely coincidentally as the result of another kind of quest that J.W., by now a full-grown man of eighteen, had set out upon with increasing determination over the past couple of years.

While Sam was being a bad boy ("I do think by having a little devil in you, you define the devil — and, you know, he can be a great teacher!"), J.W. had discovered religion. Religion had occupied only a small role for

Beale Street. *Courtesy of Preservation and Special Collections, University Libraries, University of Memphis* the Phillips family, traditional Methodists who dutifully attended North Wood Avenue Methodist church just two blocks from the house. They were God-fearing people who lived their faith, though for J.W. and Sam, now the only children left at home, it was not a particularly uplifting form of worship. But when the Highland Baptist Church dedicated its sprawling new edifice in 1936 and subsequently committed itself to a dynamic youth program under the leadership of Pastor F. L. Hacker, J.W. jumped right in, declaring that he had found his calling, he was going to be a preacher, and persuading his scrawny younger brother that here was an opportunity for the Phillips brothers to make their mark.

With his motivating, infectiously upbeat personality, his charismatic presence, and the seeming effortlessness of his soaring oratorical skills, J.W., everyone agreed, was born to preach, and soon he and Sam were holding services in the garage out behind the house on North Royal, packing the modest structure with young people brought together under the banner of their own DeMolay Council, an interfaith Christian youth group founded in Kansas City in 1919 that by now had hundreds of chapters across the country. J.W. held the little congregation spellbound, while Sam enrolled in the church's BYPU (Baptist Young People's Union) study course and formed a gospel quartet, in which he sang bass, to back up J.W.'s preaching.

Nobody could outdo his brother, Sam felt proudly, he could deliver a fire-and-brimstone message if the occasion demanded it, even if he didn't particularly lean in that direction, and he was a devoted student of the Bible. But Sam had his own ideas about the Bible, his version was always a little different, and they had a great time debating abstruse biblical points on which each was equally well-informed and equally convinced that he was right. Sam taught Sunday school at Highland Baptist—a year or two later he would become the youngest Sunday school superintendent ever elected in Lauderdale and Colbert Counties—and J.W. tried to persuade him that maybe he, too, should become a preacher. But Sam recognized that he was as much drawn to the drama as the ritual, that he could never be constrained to espouse what he didn't truly believe by the requirements of a particular denomination—and besides, he was absolutely convinced that life had something more to offer.

Sometimes it called out to him in ways he was not fully prepared to evaluate. For example, when church let out punctually at noon at Highland Baptist and everyone hurried home for their big Sunday meal,

Sam was drawn inextricably by the sounds of the black church just half a block away. Armstead Methodist Chapel sat in proud and incongruous isolation in the midst of a white neighborhood to which most of its parishioners had to walk from all over the city. For sixteen-year-old Sam Phillips, fresh from his brother's impassioned preaching and his own enthusiastic participation as a 110-pound bass singer in the Highland Baptist choir, not to mention the spirited renderings from the Stamps-Baxter hymn book offered up by his little quartet, Armstead Methodist was simply something he could not pass by. More often than not alone, occasionally with a girl if he could persuade her to lag behind with him after the Highland service, he stood on the sidewalk soaking up the sounds of joyous affirmation so similar in language but so different in effect from his own church ceremony. Particularly in summer, with the windows folded out and the heat only inspiring ever-greater fervor from both pastor and congregation, it seemed almost as if the life force had entered his soul. It was the purity of human endeavor, the raw beauty of the human voice, that the preacher's words proclaimed, the congregation's testimony echoed, the music *celebrated* — it was the individuated nature of spiritual and musical and *creative* expression, as he had first glimpsed it as an eight-year-old on the farm in Oakland at the Bend of the River.

I T WAS J.W. who first conceived of the idea of driving to Dallas to hear Dr. Truett preach. They had all heard of George W. Truett, he was one of the most celebrated orators of the day, past president of the Southern Baptist Convention, present head of the Baptist World Alliance, at one time an ambassador for President Wilson for world peace, and for the past forty-two years pastor of the First Baptist Church in Dallas, which under his guidance had become the largest church in the world. Through his work with the Southern Baptist Convention, Dr. Truett had helped foster the growth of the Southwestern Baptist Theological Seminary in Fort Worth, and it was Southwestern Baptist on which J.W., after speaking with his hometown minister, Pastor Hacker, about his desire to be ordained, had set his heart, with the trip to Dallas to hear Dr. Truett preach intended as a first step toward that goal. For Sam, though, it was the route they took that was of at least equal importance.

They set out from Florence around midnight, the five of them, in Joe LaBaugh's cramped 1937 Dodge coupe, with Sam, the youngest, sitting excitedly in the rumble seat. Joe was the old man of the group — he was close to twenty-five, while all the others, even J.W., were still in their teens — and with the help of their mothers they had loaded up the car with enough canned goods and Vienna sausage for a ten- or eleven-day adventure. All of the boys were faithful church members, all were, as Sam said, "of excellent moral character," but at the same time they were all intrigued by the idea of seeing the storied sights of Beale.

And yet, as Sam quickly came to realize, "I think my conception was a little different than theirs." Beale Street to them was "a place where all the niggers went on Saturday night to get drunk. In their minds there was absolutely no prejudice or bias [in this view], they were just looking at 'the niggers' in their place."

To Sam on the other hand, drawn not just by the stories he had heard from Uncle Silas but by the true facts and life of fellow Florentine and "Father of the Blues" W. C. Handy, who had arrived in Memphis some twenty-five years earlier looking to make his way as a professional musician ("Look at the courage that man showed when he came to Memphis, a black man trying to make a name for himself in the white man's world"), Beale Street represented the sum total of everything he had ever yearned for or imagined. For a boy who had never even been as far as Birmingham, Beale Street and the Mississippi River were nothing less than the spelling-out of his dreams and his destiny.

But, save for his brother J.W., who knew all about his views and shared them to a considerable degree, he was not about to reveal his feelings to anyone else in the packed little car, just as he was not about to challenge directly the assumptions of nearly everyone else he had ever known in the world in which he had grown up. As they drove up and down the rain-slicked street, the roughly five blocks that made up what was for Sam "the most famous street in America," gawking and laughing like sin-seeking tourists, he took in the sights in silent wonderment. He saw one man strumming a guitar and another beating on a lard can with a broomstick, he saw falling-down drunks and men proceeding toward their goal with absolute sobriety. He saw so much pain and so much pleasure and so much life, and suddenly he had a vision, "almost diametrically opposed to everything I had been taught at Highland Baptist Church, of a world in which somehow sin did not exist," in which sin *could* not exist, "because Beale Street was heaven, in so many ways. And I knew I was going to live in Memphis someday."

T HEY CROSSED THE RIVER, "that wonderful, untamable uncon-
trollable water — I mean, they can mess around with my beautiful
Tennessee River, and that's fine, but there are just some things that
are not going to be tamed" — and camped out on the other side. The
ground was soaked, but they found some rotten wood that would light
and cooked their eggs and boiled some coffee, and nothing they had ever
eaten in their lives had tasted any better. Then they grabbed a little sleep
and set off for Dallas, a distance of some four hundred miles. They had
to get in that night so they could find a hotel room, the only time they
would sleep indoors the entire trip, and clean up.

They had hardly reached the outskirts of Dallas when a policeman
stopped them for speeding. They were taken aback — Joe LaBaugh was
the kind of driver who wouldn't ordinarily have gone over the speed
limit, if only out of concern for his tire wear — but when they explained
to the policeman why they had come to Dallas, how far they had come,
and how excited they were not only to hear the great Dr. George W
Truett preach but to see if this boy here, J.W., could find some way to
work his way through Southwestern Baptist Theological Seminary, the
policeman had them pull a little farther off the road and said, "Boys, let
me pray with you." Then they checked into a little ma-and-pa motel and
cleaned up and got a good night's sleep and showed up at First Baptist
the next morning bright and early.

There to meet them at the door was a well-dressed man with a big
smile on his face who greeted each and every one of the thousands who
had come to attend service that day with an outstretched hand. That
turned out to be the church's world-famous music director Robert Coleman, the compiler, Sam knew, of the standard Baptist hymnal, the very
one that they employed at Highland Baptist, and what struck Sam even
more than the fact of his presence outside the church was his contagious
enthusiasm for the job. He made every single soul who turned out that
day feel comfortable, far from acting high and mighty, he made every
one of them feel as if they belonged there just as much as he did himself.
Then they heard Dr. Truett preach, and to Sam's surprise he turned
out to be an unprepossessing-looking little man in his seventies who
you would never think to be capable of commanding multitudes. But
when he opened his mouth to speak, he held his congregation of four
thousand spellbound, and at the same time, he made every one of them
feel as if he was speaking directly to them. Afterward they got a chance

to speak for a few minutes with Dr. Truett, and he warmly encouraged J.W. to pursue his theological studies at Southwestern. It was, for Sam, an unforgettable experience. Dr. Truett possessed the kind of glowing personal magnetism that you could never summon up on a whim, and it was a breathtaking experience to hear him speak, almost as inspiring as some of the black preachers he had heard through the Armstead Methodist windows. But for all of his recognition that "Who *wouldn't* want to sound like Dr. Truett from a stately pulpit," he knew he was never going to be a preacher. For Sam the unquestionable highlight of the trip, its one true source of enchantment and allure, was Beale Street, with all of its irreducible radiance, its irresistibly beckoning glow.

S AM WAS ELECTED president of the ninth grade, the graduating class of the junior high school, that October, in the fall of 1939. He wasn't able to be present for the election because he was working that afternoon. It seemed like he had been working constantly ever since his return to health some two years earlier, six days a week, first at the grocery store on North Seminary, then at the Corner Drug Store just down the street. He had even had his own seasonal business for a while, selling more than a dozen different types of drinks from a stand in front of the house. It was so successful that after a while he hired some help, whom he supervised from the swing on the front porch. His sister Mary's son Phillip, not quite five years younger and more a brother than a nephew, teased him that he wouldn't leave the porch, not even to go to the bathroom, for fear of missing a single transaction. "Uncle J.W. was the type, if he made a dollar, he'd spend two. If Uncle Sam made one, he'd save two. That was the difference in them!" He and J.W. worked at the post office, too, during the Christmas rush — he got permission to make special deliveries at night from the superintendent of schools, Mr. Powell. It seemed like everybody wanted to help them because they were so poor.

Mr. Powell was less happy to see him when Sam approached him in his capacity as a member of the combined junior and senior Coffee High School band. As one of its most junior members and by no means one of its more accomplished players, Sam was almost astonished at himself, but it was all part of his growing sense of civic responsibility, of responsibility to himself, really, and his own increasing belief that if he didn't take the reins, who would? He made an appointment to see Mr. Powell, a dour, imposing figure whom few were inclined to address, to demand why it was that little Sheffield High School, across the river, had four sousaphones, braided uniforms, and gold belts, when Coffee High School, more than twice Sheffield's size, had nothing but one beat-up old tuba and no uniforms whatsoever. Mr. Powell, six foot four and rail-thin, looked at Coffee's second-string marching drummer as if he had been deliberately affronted. And who, he asked, was going to play that great big sousaphone — assuming the money was available and Mr. Stuber was willing to support this harebrained scheme. Not little Thomas Mitchell, certainly, the current tuba player (and a highly accomplished musician, who Mr. Powell noted was *not* making the request) — surely you couldn't expect him to tote a thirty-nine-pound horn around on his back. No, Sam agreed calmly, once again surprising himself, he wouldn't want to impose that on Thomas; he would give up drums and take on the sousaphone himself.

He still had to fight like the devil to make the case, but in the end he did, and before the sousaphone even arrived, he practiced assiduously on the tuba while contributing a new drum cadence for the band. He loved the marches of John Philip Sousa, every one subtly different in its own way, he loved being part of the band — with the sound swelling all around him it functioned as a kind of elixir, giving him that reassuring sense of being part of something bigger than himself whenever his mood was down. He never had any illusions about his musicianship — he never imagined that this was anything he might want to pursue in later life. He knew he wasn't good enough, for one thing, but more than that, it didn't satisfy his inchoate yearning for something more, something he couldn't quite put his finger on but that took greater advantage of his innate gift for observation and decisive action, his sense of himself in a grander role that had yet to reveal itself to him.

At the end of that year, his leadership qualities were officially recognized for the first time when, just before graduation, he was presented with a copy of a little red leatherette book called *I Dare You!*, on behalf of the principal and the entire faculty. Written nearly ten years earlier and limited at first to a private edition for friends and family by its author, Ralston Purina founder William Danforth, it was a can-do (in fact, almost a *must*-do) collection of aphorisms, epigrams, and advice on the development of self, written in the heady, inspirational style of Dale Carnegie's *How to Win Friends and Influence People*. Perhaps as a result of the runaway success of Carnegie's all-time best seller from the time of its first publication in 1936, Danforth gave the copyright of his little book to the American Youth Foundation, and the Foundation, which he had cofounded a decade earlier, published the book more widely to encapsulate its own stated aims — the physical, mental, moral, and social betterment of American youth. (Its motto was, "My own self, At my very best, All the time.") *I Dare You!*, however, became a phenomenon in its own right as a result of both its giveaway in schools across the nation and its passionate adoption by businessmen, educators, church leaders, and impressionable youth alike.

It offered any number of different homiletic lessons — including the call to treat the body as a temple ("Good health makes happiness"), but its overall message could be boiled down to one central tenet: Dare to be different, dare to be great, dare to take on the challenges that life hands you without flinching. ("If you face problems aggressively, they are half solved already.")

To live, in other words, was to dare. And Sam Phillips, who would cherish the book to the end of his life, as much for what it seemed by its presentation to recognize about him as for its articulated message, was fully determined to take that dare.

SAM ENTERED HIGH SCHOOL with a new self-assurance, and a new acceptance of both his strengths and his limitations. He was well aware that he was never going to enjoy the kind of popularity that J.W., or even the boy he'd beaten for class president in the ninth grade, Bobby Arello, possessed. If it were a popularity contest, they'd win hands down any day of the week — but that no longer mattered so much to him. It was his leadership skills, his self-certainty, his willingness to put his neck on the line for what he believed, without overly concerning himself with the possibility of rejection or defeat ("I Dare You, young man," William Danforth wrote, "you who come from a home of poverty — I dare you to have the qualities of a Lincoln") — that was all that really mattered. ("You can cure your weakness by vigorous action. Start something! Break a window, if necessary.") At seventeen he had gone from a "bony," nice-looking boy with an unusually penetrating gaze to a lean young man with the dashing good looks of a Hollywood matinee idol — not the dominating man's-man Clark Gable appearance that his ruggedly handsome brother cultivated, more the sensitive, windswept appeal of a rising young star like Alan Ladd. He was voted "Best Looking Boy" in the sophomore class, and, Sam said with relish, his classmates often referred to his "lean and hungry look."

He was no more conventional about his appearance, though — and no less meticulous — than he was about any other aspect of his self-presentation. He wore a coat and tie to school, the same belted corduroy sports coat every day, because he couldn't afford a more extensive wardrobe, but he kept it scrupulously clean, and, with the open-toed sandals that he wore winter and summer ("I set myself out to be a little bit different"), he was confident that he made a sufficient impression. Sam was so particular about his appearance, according to J.W., that when their mother starched Sam's pants in keeping with his specific instructions, he would stand on a chair and step into them to avoid wrinkling the crease. If Sam didn't like the look of his eggs, Uncle J.W. told their nephew Phillip, their mother would give the eggs to J.W. and fry Sam some more.

Between band rehearsals and work six days a week, there wasn't much time for play, but baseball was the one sport in which Sam maintained an abiding interest, not just listening to re-creations of the big league games on the radio but participating in the sandlot games that went on at Monumental Park down by the old Florence City Cemetery. He was drawn not so much by the heritage and history of the game, in which every other boy shared, as by the grace and elegance with which it was played, and, not surprisingly, he developed his own style of throwing, catching, and batting, some intricate little twist that he would build upon his study of the game's finer points. He adopted much the same approach working for Dr. Babson at the Corner Drug Store, where he took particular pride in the flair with which he carried out not only his duties as a soda jerk but the free ice-cream-cone delivery that Dr. Babson promised his customers and for which Sam developed furious bicycle-pedaling skills.

At school he was introduced to the dapper new band director, twenty-six-year-old Floyd McClure, who wore spats and a homburg, drove a black 1937 Ford, had played tuba with the Tiny Hill dance band in Chicago, and possessed just as passionate a commitment to the band as Sam did. Perhaps even more so, because Mr. McClure was summarily fired for his fiery outbursts by the superintendent, Mr. Powell, several times in his first year — though each time he was rehired, and eventually the two men seemed to come to an uneasy accommodation.

Coffee High School days. *Courtesy of the Sam Phillips Family*

Although Sam was only a sophomore, his collaboration with the new band director was from the beginning a partnership of equals. "Sam was the backbone of the band," said McClure. "Everybody looked up to him because he was a gentleman, because he was different, and because he did what he was supposed to do and didn't make fun of people. I never will forget one time these two big boys fighting, and I was just standing there watching, and Sam looked perturbed at me, because I was the teacher, and [then] he got up and broke up the fight."

With McClure's seriousness of purpose and Sam's growing confidence in his own abilities ("It's tough for me to say I was somebody of real substance, but I demanded of myself a kind of orderly manner"), he was able to mobilize the by now seventy-two-piece band for rehearsals and special tasks alike, packing down the sod on the brand-new football stadium by marching back and forth for two days solid and, for the first time in their history, electing a band captain.

As captain, one of Sam's first acts was to lobby Mr. Powell once again for new uniforms — they had their sousaphones, they had their full-size band, but they were still marching in what amounted to hand-me-downs, no match for Sheffield High's pomp and glory. Times were tough, Mr. Powell said sensibly, just how did Sam propose to raise the money? Sam had been thinking about this for a good while, and he said he thought maybe they could get the John Daniel gospel quartet, who broadcast on WSM from Nashville every morning at daybreak and even performed on WSM's Grand Ole Opry, to come in and do a show for a fifteen- or twenty-five-cents price of admission.

Mr. Powell was against it. On any number of grounds. To begin with, none of the churches would stand for it. Samuel knew very well that his own Highland Baptist Church was adamantly opposed to professional gospel singing, the Methodists felt the same way — it was simply too close to popular entertainment. Then there was the question of smoking. Mr. Powell was a ferocious foe of smoking in any and all of its forms, he would have nothing to do with an event that permitted smoking, or with a group that smoked themselves. Having no idea of the facts, but convinced that he could mediate any situation that might arise, Sam assured Mr. Powell that there was not a single smoker in the John Daniel Quartet, in fact they were adamantly opposed to it themselves. As for the churches, he was sure he could persuade them that these were good Christians, strong in the expression of their faith.

The day of the show he organized a parade. He got Mr. Goodman, who had a Model A Ford with a PA system and was hired to advertise every public event that came to town, to drive up and down Court Street, with the full marching band accompanying him. Mr. Goodman insisted that Sam sit beside him in the car and then surprised the boy by handing him the microphone. At first he was taken aback. He knew he couldn't do as good a job as Mr. Goodman — this was what Mr. Goodman did for a living, and he was well aware that he didn't have the voice or the diction of the older man — but he got the hang of it as they drove up and down the street, and the only thing Mr. Goodman told him was to hold the mike still and slow his tempo down, otherwise he was doing a wonderful job.

The concert itself was a great triumph. The John Daniel Quartet drove up in their elegant 1939 gray Packard, the first aerodynamically contoured touring car, and the group's performance could not have been better, with old John himself on first tenor, not a great voice but he could really sell a song, his brother Troy on second tenor, and Sam's favorite, Clyde Roach, singing bass. With the proceeds, the band was finally able to get its uniforms, nothing fancy, just cape uniforms that showed off their black-and-gold colors when you turned them out, kind of like that new comic-book hero, Batman, and they proudly marched up and down Court Street every three or four weeks for several months thereafter.

J.W. WAS PREACHING in earnest by now. He would substitute sometimes for Pastor Hacker, when Pastor Hacker was called out of town, and he would preach on occasion at the Pleasant Hill Methodist Church in Lovelace Community, too. If you walked past the house, you could catch him almost every afternoon sitting out on the porch in an old rocking chair, his feet propped up, studying his Bible. He continued his efforts to persuade his brother to give preaching a try, but Sam remained adamant that it didn't suit him, and if J.W. got under his skin enough, he might accuse his brother of the one thing that concerned him about J.W.'s ministry, of not truly believing the words that he was preaching. But mostly the brothers got along. He and J.W. got up early on Sunday to stoke the coal-burning furnace at Highland Baptist in the wintertime. Both of them worked part-time at the Brown-Service Funeral Home, with J.W. for the most part serving as a highly effective "greeter" and Sam working the graveyard shift on weekends, occasionally sleeping at the funeral home and going out in the country with the regular driver to pick up a body.

One time they had to go all the way to Russellville, more than twenty miles away, to collect the body of a small child, and the mother simply wasn't prepared to give her up. The driver, an older man who was good at his job but whose job was driving, deferred to Sam, and he never forgot the sense of obligation and accountability it taught him. It took him an hour and a half to reassure the mother; he told her he would sit in back with her baby, and if she wanted to come along she could, but he'd rather that she didn't, and if for some reason he sensed that she needed to see her child again, they would just turn around and drive all the way back on that long dusty road. "I didn't say everything's going to be all right—I joined in [her] grief. Maybe I cried, maybe I didn't, but I never rushed a person—because she would have picked up instantly if I was in a hurry [to] take her baby away from her."

His other jobs were decidedly more prosaic. He went out on a bread truck at four in the morning and set bread out in front of all the little stores that took their delivery, then was home in time for Mama to fix him breakfast and to go to school. In the summer he made three runs a week for the G. S. Dowdy Candy Company — start out Monday mornings at 5 A.M. to load up the Mars bars, Baby Ruths, every type of candy you could think of, then roll across the countryside for two days to Iron City, Collinwood, Waynesboro, Linden, and Clifton, Tennessee, and get back Tuesday night to load up again Wednesday morning.

There was never any question in his mind that life was made up of hard work — but it needed to be work you cared about, something that was brought home to him when he would go to visit his father flagging the few cars still crossing the bridge to Colbert County in the early evening hours, at the start of his shift, after everyone had gone home to have their supper.

> I couldn't figure out how in the world my daddy could stay here and be so lonesome all night. I knew he didn't want to be there. He wanted to be a part of nature. But he could not make a living on [the farm]. So he came there and worked twelve hours a day seven days a week, and the only consolation that he felt was this Tennessee River. It made him feel a little closer to what he loved, which was the soil, the water, trees, land. So I'd stay with him and wait until the last bus ran from Burns Transportation, which was the inner-city bus line then, and he had a pass because he was a flagman and I could ride to North Florence free. I did that many nights, then get up early, go to school the next morning.

As much as he felt for his daddy, as much as he recognized the role that external forces could play in anyone's life, Samuel C. Phillips was not about to write off this earthly existence as nothing but drudgery and solitude. People were just too damn interesting — and there were just too many interesting avenues to pursue.

In the fall, when criminal court was in session, he would go down to the Lauderdale County Courthouse and plant himself on one of the hard oak benches just to listen to the defense oratory of George Barnett and George Jones every time he got a chance. They were the most eloquent speakers he had ever heard outside of the kind of preacher who could convince you against all the evidence that the world was about to come to an end so long as you didn't happen to just look out the door — but, like Clarence Darrow, they were speaking up for the rights of the common man, for the weak and defenseless, for justice. It was the drama that captured him at first, but then he thought, What had led these people to become criminals? Was it the Depression? And it came to him in that moment that this could be his calling: not just the righting of wrongs but the study of humanity, in all of its diversity, in all of the multitude of its manifestations.

He felt much the same way when he visited Kate Nelson's whorehouse on South Seminary on a Saturday afternoon. It was located right behind the big mule barn where they had the farmers' auctions, and he observed every detail of its operation with delight, from the satisfaction of his own needs to how much the farmers "absolutely loved the idea of being down in the red-light district but not getting caught. I mean, nobody could deny a farmer the right to go to an auction!" And he watched with admiration the way Kate Nelson ran her business, not just the way she handled the men ("She was a master handler of men") but the way she treated her girls.

"You have to keep in mind that this was during the Depression, when a lot of girls had to leave home because there wasn't enough to eat. Now Kate Nelson could have made a living doing anything she wanted to—she was the best businessperson that I ever met in my life—but she chose to do that, and she took those girls in and nobody abused them and lot of them got married [out of] there, and I know that in her heart she was in that profession to help them as well as, of course, to help herself." She didn't go out of her way to encourage young men like Sam, but, recognizing the realistic nature of human need, Sam felt, neither did she turn them away. In fact, "she felt so sorry for some young people that didn't have two dollars, that most of them—I know I speak for myself—got a discount."

What probably tickled him most was the broad perspective the experience afforded him on the human comedy. Hanging around the adjacent pool hall afterward, he concluded that the men probably got more pleasure out of talking about the experience than they did from the experience itself. He felt no sense of guilt or hypocrisy. It was all grist for the exploration of human nature to which, in one way or another, he was determined to dedicate his life. From his point of view, "Kate Nelson was an exceptional person, an extremely decent person," and a genuine asset to the community in any number of ways. "I mean, I was going to church, I was deeply *dedicated*, but the Bible says, Better to spill your seed in the belly of a whore than it is on the ground—and I took that to heart!" If others chose to interpret the Scriptures differently, well, let him who was without sin cast the first stone.

H E FORMED a kind of dance band the summer after sophomore year, the summer of 1941. There were so many great musicians in the marching band, it would have been a crime just to let all that spirit and enthusiasm go to waste, so he put out a call for volunteers — not for anyone who was just idly curious but for band members who were genuinely *committed* (the criterion was "not [so much] your great prowess as a musician but your dedication to it") — and, lo and behold, he got solid interest from about fifteen band members who promised to attend at least two rehearsals a week, no matter what demand their other work put on them. They quickly developed a repertoire that included swing standards, a crude attempt at Tommy Dorsey's "Boogie Woogie," the very first record that came close to capturing some of the excitement he took from the music he had heard in the cotton fields, the Sammy Kaye novelty number "The Hut Sut Ralston," and pop treatments of familiar compositions by Bach, Beethoven, and Tchaikovsky. They had scarcely played in public, though they were gaining a little bit of a reputation from the reaction of some of the parents who attended their rehearsals, when he got a call from the commander of the American Legion Post, Harold May: would they be willing to play the Post awards ceremony at the Teachers College outdoor amphitheater? Sam may have felt a certain amount of trepidation, but he wasn't going to let it show. Instead, he accepted with the same alacrity that he encouraged in the band, acknowledging that while they might have no business playing the ambitious repertoire they were attempting, that was no excuse for holding back. "If you're going to hit a wrong note," he said, "hit it like you mean it!"

When they showed up at the amphitheater that his daddy had helped to build, though, he was surprised to discover that the show was going to be broadcast on the radio. Mr. Connolly, the general manager of local station WMSD, across the river in Sheffield, asked if he would be willing to announce the program, give the titles and composer of each number that they played, and he responded with a mix of confidence and not altogether disguised unease that he would certainly like to try. At the conclusion of the program, Mr. Connolly asked if he might like to do a regular program on the air — it wouldn't pay anything, not even

Jimmy Connolly on WMSD in Sheffield (soon to become WLAY), mid- to late 1930s. *Courtesy of Dot Connolly West and the Sam Phillips Family*

Opposite: WLAY. *Courtesy of the Sam Phillips Family*

bus fare — and without hesitation he accepted. "I don't know why. I had never thought about being in radio until that night. I said, 'I could do it maybe two days a week.' He said, 'No I would have to have you five days a week if I put you on a program,' and, God, it went through my mind, I have *got* to do this. I might even get our band on this radio station. Hey, I ain't turning it down, no matter what. So I worked it out, and I did 'Hymn Time' on a part-time basis five days a week from five to five-thirty in the afternoon, for the Corner Drug Store, [where] I had worked when I was younger."

He loved the music of the old quartets, Stamps-Baxter, the Speer Family, the Chuck Wagon Gang, the Rangers, and, despite being scared to death at first, he knew he could put it across, even with — perhaps because of — all that "South in my mouth." In any case his old boss, Dr. Babson, was more than satisfied with his new announcer: he told Jimmy Connolly this boy put it across much better than the regular announcer, with his highfalutin "radio" voice suggesting that he obviously didn't give a damn. Dr. Babson liked the records he played and the conviction with which he introduced them. So after a brief trial period, his position was secure, and once school started up again, he would get out of band

practice, catch the bus, wait forty-five minutes at the transfer point, and arrive just in time to go on the air at five.

In October he was elected president of the junior class, once again beating out Bobby Arello, the boy he had defeated two years earlier, who was recognized in the yearbook as the "Most Popular Boy" in the class. Probably the single most significant achievement of his term in office was gaining recognition for the students of East Florence, poorer even than the North Florence neighborhood in which he lived, which was in turn substantially below the standard of North Court Street or North Wood Avenue, where all the big homes were. Whether by intention or design, the East Florence students had always been left out of official functions like Junior Night, and Sam argued vociferously with the faculty adviser Miss Rogers that it simply wasn't right and, when every practical objection to their inclusion, *at least for this year,* had been raised, managed to overcome them all one by one.

H E AND UNCLE SILAS listened to the war news from Europe with mounting concern. Uncle Silas' favorite was Bob Burlingame, who broadcast every night on WHO, a 50,000-watt clear channel out of Des Moines. Uncle Silas, an inveterate news devotee, would sit in the kitchen, paying close attention to the detailed reporting, then give a word-by-word summary, if called upon by any member of the Phillips family who might have missed something. "You listen, Samuel," he would say, "this guy will tell you more about what's going on in fifteen minutes than you will hear a lot of times in a whole day." Now, with U.S. involvement clearly on the horizon, they listened every night to Gabriel Heatter's commentary on the Mutual network, too. It seemed to Sam that in his blindness the old black man could picture the world better than any of them, but in a way, he had come to believe, this could be attributed to radio's special properties as well. Just as Uncle Silas' stories had carried him away when he was a young boy, the capacity of a broadcaster's voice to paint a picture, the way in which music — not just in the fields but *across the airwaves* — was able to set the soul free, was something he would never have thought to articulate before. He found his own radio work more and more gratifying — it wasn't just a matter of playing the records, it was the way in which you presented them, in a certain rhythm, in a certain order, with a certain *sound,* that opened up new possibilities in both the material world and the imagination.

And it only added to all the ideas he was turning over in his mind about *communication* — about the way he hoped to utilize all these lessons in defense of the common man once he was able to enter his chosen profession of the law.

One thing he had learned: there was no room for self-doubt if you wanted to convey to others the essence of what was important to you. The previous year a girl named Mary Lois Crisler had moved to town from Moulton, thirty-five miles away — her father repaired old woodstoves at the smallest hardware store in town, and the family was extremely poor. There were mock-trial cases every week in a course he took in commercial law, and every week, Sam beat everybody, whether for the prosecution or the defense — unless he happened to run up against Mary Lois Crisler. "Now, she didn't have as many friends in the class as I did, but when she got through with her case, she whipped my ass every time — but that taught me something. Now, here was the woman that I just absolutely wanted to whip more than the rest of the class put together, but probably I got afraid. And didn't know it. I got frightened to death that this woman was going to win and couldn't admit it [to myself]." The lesson was clear: "You can't let anybody get a hold of you and make something out of you that is not instinctively yours." The result was "Mary Lois Crisler was about the only girl at that time that I reckon I ever thought I was in love with."

One time he took her to a John Daniel Quartet show that J.W. was promoting for the DeMolay society, going out to Lovelace Community to borrow his brother Horace's 1937 Dodge for their date and impressing Mary Lois with his knowledge not just of the music but his personal acquaintance with some of the members of the quartet. The highlight of the concert was Troy Daniel reciting an old poem called "Would Anybody Care?"

"If I had heavy burdens," Troy recited with feeling, "That I must bear alone

If I had grief and troubles
That others had not known
If I in my heart's deep sorrow
And nothing to compare
Would anybody comfort me,
Would anybody care?

If my life had been a failure
And I tried but could not win
If I became discouraged
And said, I'll never try again
If my heart is sad and lonely
Filled with sorrow and despair
Would anybody cheer me,
Would anybody care?

It was a rich, full, and constantly engaging life, which he was confident would soon expand to an even greater engagement with the world, with his graduation from high school in another year and his subsequent apprenticeship to the law. His father had fallen seriously ill, and he and J.W. spent a good deal of time shuttling him back and forth to the doctor and making sure that their mother knew things were going to be all right, but he could see no serious impediment to his future so long as he kept his nose to the grindstone. Then on December 7 Pearl Harbor was bombed, and one week later, in the early-morning hours, after he and J.W. had stoked the furnace and gone home to change into their church clothes, Highland Baptist Church burned down. Everything was lost in the fire, but they had church that afternoon at Gilbert Elementary School, from which Sam had graduated five years earlier, and they started raising funds on the spot for the rebuilding.

Not three weeks later his father died, just days before Sam's nineteenth birthday, and in rapid succession J.W., twenty-one now and no doubt eager to be out on his own, married a local nurse, an older woman he had recently met, and then, not long after, in the summer, inexplicably joined the Marines. He and his new wife were living in the Phillips family home, and after his enlistment his wife continued to live there, where she got her husband's monthly check, leaving Sam the sole support of his widowed mother, his deaf-mute aunt, and Uncle Silas.

Sam was furious at his brother — and for a brief time despondent, too, at the way his own world had shrunk in a moment. He had never told his mother how much he wanted to be a criminal defense lawyer, and he didn't tell her now, with no chance of even being able to complete high school, let alone go on to college. Instead, he went in and had a talk with Mr. H. A. Bradshaw, the head of the draft board and an old friend of the family as well as attorney for the Florence City Schools, explaining that he was going to have to quit school and in the end getting a hardship deferment that he didn't feel quite right about. He turned J.W.'s actions over and over in his mind and felt nothing but bafflement at what he considered to be the irresponsibility of his choices. It was, quite simply, a betrayal, not just of Sam, but of everything they had ever worked for together. But J.W. was still his brother, and he recognized that if life had given him some hard knocks, there were others who had it much harder. He was not going to let himself be ruled by anger or disappointment. He was not going to let adversity defeat him. Somehow, he was determined, he would take up life's dare and forge a destiny of his own.

TWO | Radio Romance

He had just come in out of the rain the day we first met. His hair was windblown and full of raindrops. He wore sandals and a smile unlike any I had ever seen before. He walked into the small radio station studio where I worked, sat down on the piano bench, and began to talk to me. He was so young, so handsome with a gentle compelling [demeanor] that was so overpowering. I told my family that night I had met the man I wanted to marry.

— Becky Burns Phillips

S AM MET BECKY BURNS in September of 1942. He was still working only part time at the radio station, still doing his gospel records show every day, along with all his other jobs, and he and the demure but outgoing seventeen-year-old, a Sheffield High School senior, barely five feet tall, fell into conversation immediately. Mostly they talked about radio, the one thing they clearly had in common, but before long the ideas, the plans, the dreams, and ambitions that Sam had harbored for so long seemed to come pouring out of him. For Becky, attractive, engaging, with a quick wit and a ready smile, it was as if her whole life changed in an instant. She had wanted to be an entertainer for as long as she could remember, but now her focus shifted to what life could offer her as a helpmeet, as a person dedicated to bringing other people's dreams — her husband's, her family's — to fruition.

Courtesy of the Sam Phillips Family

Becky Burns had been performing with her older sister Earline on WMSD (the "Muscle Shoals District" station, which had only recently changed its call letters to WLAY) from the age of nine. They had started out on a children's talent show. Earline, who was ten years older, played the piano, and Becky sang and played the ukulele while standing on a box so she could reach the microphone. Then their older sister, Erin, married Jimmy Connolly, the dapper Birmingham native who had originally hired Sam, shortly after his arrival at the station in 1935. Jimmy was a big fan of his wife's kid sisters, and he gave them their own program, *Dear Diary*, which evolved into a scripted show, with an intro written by Earline and read by Becky leading into their performance of each song. The songs were love songs mostly, like Bob Crosby and Kay Kyser's 1940 hit, "With the Wind and the Rain in Your Hair," which, once she had met Sam, for obvious reasons she claimed as their own. She and Earline were paid in movie tickets at first, and the girls and their mother went all the time—they especially loved the Busby Berkeley musicals—and sometimes they would take Becky's father after he got off work if they thought it was the kind of movie he might like.

Mr. Burns worked for the railroad, in the roundhouse, where they repaired the engines and freight and passenger cars, and with his brother he owned the intercity bus company, Burns Transportation, for which Sam's brother Tom, who was married to Becky's cousin Lucille, worked. It was a somewhat sheltered world, in which, as Becky herself realized, they were barely touched by the Depression. They had a player piano, a Victrola, and a Silvertone cabinet radio, and both parents played the piano themselves while encouraging their daughters' ambitions. Erin and Jimmy Connolly had a little girl of five, but Erin took on a job at the station anyway and proved herself to be a whiz-bang salesperson. In addition to her radio work, Earline gave piano lessons, and because of the manpower shortage due to the war, Becky started announcing various nonmusical programs, even though she was still in high school.

For Sam it was a glimpse into a whole other world, a world that was by and large free from want—and free perhaps from the kind of burning ambition that came with it. It was Becky Burns' voice, actually, that first drew him to her. His brother's wife, the nurse, who was living with them by herself now that J.W. was off in the Marines, heard her on the radio and thought she was adorable, and Sam practically fell out of his seat when he heard the natural graciousness and confidence of her delivery. "She could pick up and sight-read anything and make you think she wrote it, she never did anything that sounded like it was being read, ever." He envied the ease with which she was able to communicate, and when he met her not long afterward, he found that she was able to put him at ease in much the same way.

He and Becky started going out right away in the black 1937 Dodge coupe he had recently purchased. He was so proud of that car, he kept it like new, spit shining it out beside the house every time he got the chance. It seemed like he and Becky would never run out of things to talk about — they had such a common bond of radio, of music, of *communication,* but most of all they talked about the future. For Becky it was, for the most part, their future together, Sam's and her future, but for Sam it was something larger. Sometimes they talked about Memphis. She knew how much that city meant to Sam, and she talked about its wide, clean streets, the civility with which people went about their business to the point where an anti-noise ordinance prevented them from even blowing their horns. Because of his job, her father got free railroad passes, and the whole family had been to Memphis many times — they had even stayed at the elegant Hotel Peabody, where Becky's sister, Earline, asked, and was granted, permission to play the piano in the hotel lobby for all the cotton planters and people of quality. For Sam, "All the things she said about that beautiful city, how clean it was, no horns and — you know, I thought, that's wonderful, but I believe Becky's missed the whole point. I didn't dare tell her that. But I [knew] the gravitational pull that I felt for Memphis." And he knew that *his* Memphis was not confined to the lobby of the Hotel Peabody.

Becky had never met anyone like Sam before. She had never met anyone so sensitive but with so much belief in himself, too. "Well, you never knew exactly what Sam was thinking. He was a spiritual person, but his thoughts about God were so personal that he just didn't talk about that at all, and you never really knew exactly what he believed, but he did think about it, I knew that he did." She also knew how insecure he could be. On one of their early dates, he had to stop the car and pull over, because, he said, he was having a nervous attack. "He became ill, he thought he was dying — and he lay his head in my lap, and I tried to comfort him." Dr. Duckett had reassured him that it was nothing serious, he told her afterward, but it only endeared him to her all the more — that he might actually need someone to take care of him. Because in every other way he was the most self-confident person she had ever met. "I don't believe he ever questioned himself. I was always amazed at how Sam knew how to do everything, from the simplest to the most complicated — and I wondered where all that knowledge came from. It seemed he had an inner sense of being led." On the other hand, if he didn't know something, he'd go to whatever source he needed to find out. And, of course, he invariably had his own way of doing things — "he had his own way of putting a screw into the wall. He thought he was right about everything — and maybe he was. He was about a lot of things!"

Becky herself was an intensely religious person who had been brought up Lutheran but was leaning toward her brother-in-law's Catholic Church — and it bothered her sometimes that Sam didn't choose to share more of his own beliefs. He could have made a great minister, she felt, and part of her may have regretted that this was not the path he had chosen, but she never doubted his deep spirituality. She met his mother, his deaf-mute aunt, and Uncle Silas, and thought she could see where Sam got not just his sense of confidence but his sense of mission. "His mother nursed him through a lot of hard times when he was young, but she always made him believe that he was going to be all right and that his life was going to be good — he always needed someone to encourage him that way." As for his aunt Emma, "they could just joust back and forth [in] sign language, and *laugh* . . . Sam was her favorite, and he could do no wrong, but she had a temper, and if anybody was giving Sam a hard time, they had to deal with Emma!" She might have been even more surprised by Uncle Silas, the blind Negro sharecropper who had lived with the Phillipses all these years, if Sam hadn't told her so much about him — and if she weren't as aware as she was of Sam's determinedly democratic principles, his ability to "communicate with everyone, no matter if they were rich or poor, no matter what race." There was no question of his closeness to Uncle Silas, or of the pride the talkative old man took in Sam, and she could see how Sam could very well have taken the lesson that he always said he had learned from Uncle Silas when he was young: "Whatever he believed, he could do."

Becky began to use her program to send love messages to Sam. She made it hard on her sister Earline, because now "everything she wrote had to be about my love for Sam. We didn't call any names, but each [song

Sam and Becky. *Courtesy of the Sam Phillips Family*

introduction had] to say the things that I felt in my heart for him. She worked so hard trying to get it like I wanted it, but it was difficult." Soon she and Sam had another song of their own, Woody Herman's "There Will Never Be Another You," whose title Becky immediately embraced, even as she chose to ignore its bittersweet tone of nostalgic regret.

Sam went to work full-time for the station when he got the *SSL Hillbilly Jamboree*, one of the station's most popular programs, from 11:15 to noon every day. Jimmy Connolly asked if he thought he could handle it, and while he knew he didn't have the smooth delivery or practiced diction of someone like Becky, he never hesitated for a minute. He was confident at this point that he was believable, that he could put the music across in a way that he knew people would respond to it, and he flung himself into it, the sequencing, the pacing, and making those worn-out old records — pressed with war-issue "shellac and mud" — sound as good as they possibly could. "Man, I made those records come alive! And when I got through doing that show, the cards and letters they would send in — then I knew I was on my way, I knew I wouldn't be in the courtroom, but I could be talking to my courtroom out there. And getting people to forget maybe about some of the things that were difficult for them for a while." He was reminded, too, of what radio had meant to him as a kid, hearing the Grand Ole Opry and the Stamps-Baxter program coming in on 50,000-watt KRLC out of Dallas, clear as a bell, or even listening to the gathering storms of war with Uncle Silas. "Radio took me away, not necessarily the location, it took my *mind,* and it traveled for me — let me tell you something, music will take you anywhere you want to go."

With an eye to furthering his career, he took an Alabama Polytechnic Institute (later to be known as Auburn University) extension course offered at Florence State. It was given five nights a week, three hours a night, for six weeks, and was aimed primarily at certifying electrical engineers for the war effort, but it would permit him to get his Class C permit, something he needed in order to be able to engineer as well as announce his own programs. He knew he was in a little over his head, with all these highly qualified students, but he peppered the instructor, John Smith, the chief engineer at WLAY, with questions until he just about wore him out. Then when he got enough money for a bus ticket, he rode a Dixie Liner to Atlanta, where he took the third-class "phone ticket" exam that qualified him as a Class C engineer at the beginning of May.

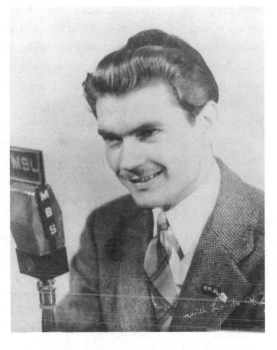

Decatur, Alabama, 1944.
*Courtesy of the Sam
Phillips Family*

At the same time, he secured a variety of personal references from some of his old employers and longtime family friends. ("I have known Sammie Phillips for the past fifteen years," wrote Charles Edgar Young, circuit court clerk of Lauderdale County. "He comes from one of the best families of Lauderdale County.") Jimmy and Erin Connolly had left for Nashville some six months earlier when Jimmy got a job at WLAC, a 50,000-watt "clear channel" station and a big step up in his career. Sam plainly thought that he could do better, too. In November he moved to radio station WMSL in Decatur, like Florence a town of fifteen to sixteen thousand, some forty miles upriver and situated on a high plateau. The station was another 250-watter, but it offered a five-dollars-a-week raise with the opportunity for advancement, and indeed Sam was soon promoted to production manager. In the staff picture taken around this time, Sam stands out from the others (four dark-suited older men, an apprentice engineer, and a businesslike-looking woman, also in a dark suit) with his upswept hair, his two-tone jacket, and his Ronald Colman mustache and jaunty smile.

Becky was still on the air in Sheffield, and with a little ingenuity on Sam's part they set up a line between the two stations so they could send messages and records back and forth over the air. Every weekend Becky would ride the bus to Decatur, and she would even do a little announcing on Sam's station. She knew they were going to get married soon, but she didn't know when ("Boy, do I need a wife?" Sam wrote to her on November 17. "The answer is YES."), and almost right away Earline and her mother started making a pretty new dress for her every weekend just in case Sam made up his mind. He had already picked out the minister, he had bought the ring at a little jewelry store in town, but, despite the increasingly desperate tone of his letters, he didn't seem able to decide on a date.

In the end they got married on December 13, 1943, a Monday, with only her daddy in attendance and none of Sam's family. Sam's best man was John Slatton, the chief announcer, musical director, and news editor at the station, and Becky's matron of honor was John Slatton's wife, whom she barely knew. They spent one night at the Cornelian Hotel in town and then moved in with an old lady and her daughter. They had a big open room with their own bath, plus kitchen privileges. Becky had never done much cooking at home, but she did her best to cook everything just the way Sam liked it, exactly the way his mother made it. He was very particular about his food, and he tried to instruct her about the value of things when they went shopping together, how much more economical it was to buy the larger Number Two can of corn, which you could get two meals out of, than the Number One—he understood she had never had to worry about things like that. They traded out a lot of their meals—Becky wrote the copy for the two-spot-a-day ads for the G&W Cafe, and in return they got "regular cafe meals"—and before long they were practically running the station by themselves. When Becky's announcing shift was up, she almost invariably stayed around, because what better did she have to do than listen to her brilliant, handsome, gifted, ambitious young husband's program?

Then in the late spring of 1944 disaster unexpectedly struck. Sam had been exhibiting more and more of his "nervous" symptoms, he just couldn't seem to turn his mind off, he told her, he felt like he was going to either die or go crazy. But he knew he needed help, and somehow or another—she was never sure quite how—he became convinced that he needed to go to Hill Crest Sanitarium in Birmingham, run by a man named Dr. Becton. This was the one place, he insisted, that would be able to deal with his problem. Becky was frightened, but even in his diminished state Sam expressed himself with such firmness and such certainty that she, too, became convinced that Hill Crest was the answer to their prayers.

So they traveled to Birmingham, where Becky arranged to stay with Jimmy Connolly's brother Paul and his family, who lived just on the other side of the woods that adjoined the sanitarium grounds, and Dr. Becton persuaded Sam that what he needed was a brand-new form of treatment known as electroshock. Sam had no reservations about the treatment — he had read a lot about it since its therapeutic introduction in the United States and Britain in 1940 — but, he told Becky, he just couldn't stand to be by himself in the hospital. So when visiting hours were over, Becky rolled under the bed and pulled the bedspread down to hide herself, then, with the coast clear, stayed with Sam all night, climbing out the window and taking the path through the woods to Jimmy's brother's house in the early hours of the morning.

After eight shock treatments and several weeks of hospitalization, Sam was pronounced fit to go home and reported back to work by the end of the summer, only to be told by the station owner, after what appears to have been a trial period of which he was unaware, that as of the first of the year he would no longer have a job, because, as Sam put it, he was "supposed to be crazy." It was an injustice that remained with him all his life. He was firmly convinced that mental illness was no different from any other kind of illness, but the man who owned the damned station wouldn't give him a chance. He was utterly crushed and uncertain as to how to proceed — he'd be goddamned if he would go back to Florence with his tail between his legs — but then he spoke with Jimmy Connolly, who said there might be an opening at his station in Nashville, WLAC, if Sam wanted to come in for an audition. Sam told him that, as much as he appreciated the tip, he thought he would try WSM, the home of the Grand Ole Opry, first. He knew he wasn't the world's greatest announcer, but he was sure he could do a damn good job on the Opry if given the chance.

True to his belief that you could fail only if you failed to dare, he did get his audition at WSM — he met with Artist Service Bureau head Jim Bulleit, with whom he had corresponded to book the John Daniel Quartet in Decatur the previous year, and with acting program director Ott Devine, who politely reinforced what Sam already knew: they had a stack of acetates from some of the greatest announcers in the country (with its clear-channel signal, the station reached virtually all of the continental United States at night, while the Opry, known throughout the world as the shrine of country music, had been broadcasting for more than five years now over the NBC network), and there was no chance of anything opening up in the near future. It was only then that he went over to WLAC, where Jimmy Connolly introduced him to the program director, Paul Oliphant, and F. C. Sowell, the general manager — and got the job.

WLAC, a CBS affiliate with the same broad reach as WSM, turned out to be a dream come true. Set atop the Third National Bank Building downtown, it afforded a spectacular view of all of Nashville from its twelfth-floor offices. The lobby alone was bigger than any radio station Sam had ever seen, and the elevator ride turned out to be a thrill in itself, while the control rooms were better equipped than anything he could ever have hoped for. At first he was confined primarily to doing news and station IDs in between the half-hour network-affiliated shows that made up much of the programming, but soon his role expanded into the same kind of announcing, deejaying, and engineering duties he had had in both Florence and Decatur.

He and Becky moved in with Jimmy and Erin Connolly and their seven-year-old daughter, Dot, to start off with. Sam and Jimmy went fishing all the time and stayed up long after everyone else had gone to sleep, playing checkers and talking about the dream they had of one day starting their own radio station. One time they played poker with some of the guys from the station, and when they came back, Sam had money sticking out of all of his pockets and from under the band of his hat. It was all good fun — Sam didn't drink, he had, in fact, never touched a drop of liquor, and Becky didn't worry about him in any way, except for his nervous condition, which so far, pretty much as the doctor had predicted, had given no indication of coming back. She and Erin fixed Sam and Jimmy's lunch every day, and one day the lunch boxes got mixed up, and Sam discovered that he preferred Jimmy's, and from then on Becky always fixed Sam vanilla wafers with peanut butter, Jimmy's favorite. For the two of them it was almost like a storybook adventure. When one of the announcers went on vacation, Jimmy got Becky a job introducing records while he ran the board, and he thought he might be able to get her a job singing with one of the big bands in town, her lifelong dream.

Then Becky got pregnant, and they couldn't have been happier. By now they had a little place of their own on Scott Avenue in East Nashville, and Becky fixed Sam biscuits every morning, just like his mother did. Sam loved everything about the busy, raucous atmosphere of the station — he particularly enjoyed Gene Nobles, a bent-over little man from Hot Springs, Arkansas, who suffered from rheumatoid arthritis and followed the horses with such passion that when his luck was running right, he was likely to take off for days at a time. He was thirty-one years old, a hard-drinking, eccentric ex-carny, who used carny doubletalk, speaking, as he said, "from the heart of my bottom," both to skirt the edge of propriety and to communicate with those in the know in his own "slanguage." Within a couple of years he would make his real mark by introducing "race records" on his 10:15-to-midnight show, mixing in spirituals with swing at first and then adding to the mix, thus initiating the revolution for which WLAC would soon become known: the presentation of unfiltered r&b late at night to a national audience, both black and white.

There was probably nothing about his work that Sam didn't enjoy, but, still, he knew it was only a stopgap solution, both because of the uncertainty of the position (he had been made well aware by Mr. Oliphant from the start that John Richbourg, the erudite announcer for whom he was filling in, was entitled to his old job when he got out of the service) and because, when you got right down to it, as great as Nashville was, Nashville was not the place he wanted to be. Besides, Jimmy made no secret of his own desire to move on — he was going back to Birmingham as soon as he got the chance. So when the opportunity arose, Sam jumped at it.

It came when Ray Mueller, a fellow announcer who had been at WMSD in Sheffield when Sam first started out, returned from his annual June vacation by way of Memphis, where he discovered there was an opening at WREC, one of Memphis' premier stations and a fellow CBS affiliate. He knew how much Sam had always wanted to go to Memphis, and the position, he said, was made to order for him — they were looking for a part-time announcer and part-time engineer. Within days, Sam flew over for a job interview. It was his first airplane ride, and he was so nervous that another friend from work, a board engineer named Ira Trotter, accompanied him, ostensibly to visit the Memphis zoo — but with or without Ira Trotter, he was determined to go after this job with every fiber of his being.

H IS INITIAL MEETING was with Mr. Wooten, Mr. Hoyt Wooten, the station founder and owner, one of the pioneers in Memphis radio, who had built his own battery-operated transmitter for the first station he had put on the air, a little 10-watter he had begun operating out of his home in Coldwater, Mississippi, in 1921. Elegant, well-spoken, mustachioed, a fifty-one-year-old authoritarian figure disinclined to dispense either small talk or compliments lightly, Wooten grilled Sam on his engineering experience and was pleased to learn that in Sam he had found someone nearly as fanatic about sound as he was himself. Then Sam met Hoyt's brother Roy, who was the program director, and another brother, S.D., who was the chief engineer. After going through a battery of tests, he was offered a job on the spot.

He didn't hesitate for a moment. It didn't matter to him in the slightest that it would mean going from a 50,000-watt powerhouse whose reach extended all across the country to a 5,000-watt station whose signal, however prestigious it might be, was confined to the mid-South. It didn't matter that the studios were not quite as big as WLAC's — they were just as up-to-date, with an integrated RCA system in all three of their control rooms in the basement of the Hotel Peabody. Everything was immaculate, everything was first-class — it was clear that Mr. Wooten was a perfectionist in everything that he did. And as for the Peabody, Sam thought it was the most beautiful hotel he had ever seen, you walked in the lobby and it just suggested the kind of Southern gentility and charm that couldn't help but be entrancing to a young man of twenty-two from Florence, Alabama. But at the same time, with full acknowledgment of the duality on which he had always prided himself, he recognized that it was in fact just a block from Beale Street, even if to some that might have seemed like a world away.

H E STARTED WORK on June 26, 1945, uncharacteristically oversleeping on his first day. But, he wrote to Becky with cheerful abandon, his boss, Roy Wooten "just laughed — he seems swell." Becky was still stuck in Sheffield at her parents'. As much as Sam kept pushing, her doctor wouldn't allow her to travel until Sam found them a place to live. It embarrassed Becky a little the way Sam was with her doctor, the same way he was with his own, even with the doctors at the sanitarium, his habit of addressing them by their first names, not disrespectfully but with the familiarity of a longtime colleague — but in this case on

Hoyt Wooten, 1944.
Courtesy of Preservation and
Special Collections, University
Libraries, University of Memphis

behalf on their unborn child he just accepted the verdict. He was living temporarily at the Hotel Peabody, until he could locate an apartment, and Mr. Wooten even let him advertise his search on the air. It was hard to find someone willing to rent to a young couple expecting a child — it was still wartime, and housing was in short supply. But then, after two weeks, he found this gracious lady — she was actually from Sheffield and knew some of Becky's family, and she had a place out near the Kennedy veterans' hospital on Shotwell (when the hospital went in, the street had been renamed Getwell, but everyone still called it Shotwell), "and she called and said, 'Look, if you want to bring your wife, we got just a small house, two bedrooms, and I've got two children and a husband'— and I just couldn't believe it, and I went out to see her and I just couldn't accept it — but I did, until we could find [a place of our own]."

He went back and collected Becky and all their things, and they moved in with the nice lady and her family, and for the first time Becky could see what Memphis actually meant to him. It was almost like his eyes lit up every morning, sparkling with the possibility of something she couldn't even imagine, and yet she could — because she could see how it touched Sam. It was the city of his dreams; she understood that much. Nashville had only been a stepping-stone.

Sam's duties at the station rapidly expanded. He started out doing much the same sort of thing he had been doing in Nashville, putting on his best announcer's voice to give the station ID in between network broadcasts, doing a hillbilly show called *Songs of the West* under the name of "Pardner," announcing some shows, engineering others. His day started at 7:15 A.M. when he came in to test the needles he would use to record the fifteen-minute network news at 7:30, which would then be broadcast over WREC half an hour later from the acetate he had made. Soon he started coming in at seven, after being given the job of maintaining the hotel's PA system, which was in constant use, and in constant need of attention, because of all the conventions that took place there.

The first part of his day was over at 3:30, but then he had to be back at ten to set up for the big-band broadcast that went out on a network feed from the Skyway Ballroom on the hotel roof six nights a week from 10:30 to 11:00. All the best of the big bands (the *white* big bands, Sam was quick to note—there was no Duke Ellington, no Count Basie, "not one black person in any of the bands") played the Peabody: Tommy Dorsey, Freddy Martin, Chuck Foster, the Glenn Miller Orchestra, and twenty-three-year-old Elliot Lawrence, whose elaborate, classically influenced arrangements only added to the challenge of creating a true "live" sound. Sam had only six mikes for as many as sixteen to eighteen instruments (not to mention the announcer and the vocalist), and he took special care with the rhythm section, since the drums and upright bass in particular were always the ones to get shortchanged. But he set up differently for every band, and he took a set of lead sheets down to the control room in the basement so he could know when a trumpet or a saxophone or piano solo was coming up and then be able to mix on the fly.

"You knew in your mind exactly where everything was [by the way] you set up the mikes, and I don't say that everything was [perfect], but I wanted to make sure I got all the overtones and that nothing was wasted. I think it was probably one of the most enjoyable things that I ever did in my life. Here I was, this little upstart, I had no earthly idea I would ever even *see* a big band—and there I am, putting the biggest bands on every night. I had limited natural talent as an announcer, but I knew I had an ear for sound—and I worked my ass off."

Becky listened to all his shows at home, particularly the big-band broadcasts, which were her first love. He knew she had been worried about him, hell, he had even been worried a little about himself, but here he was on the job, loving the job, and everyone seemed to be pleased with his work. By the end of the summer, they had moved into a little upstairs garage apartment on North Waldran, closer to downtown. It had a kitchen, a bedroom, a bath, a window that opened onto a little porch with a banister around it—the baby was due before long. It was, Becky felt, so "perfect, and I was so happy with Sam that I felt kind of guilty that my family wasn't as happy as I was."

At the beginning of October, as "a comparative newcomer to Memphis," Sam shared his feelings about the city with its entire population via a kind of citizen's "opinion editorial," which the *Memphis Press-Scimitar* culled from readers' letters under the banner "This Is True Liberty, When Freeborn Men Speak Free." Longtime political boss E. H. Crump, who had run the city with an iron fist since W. C. Handy's arrival in 1909, had recently come in for a good deal of criticism from the progressive *Press-Scimitar*, and particularly from a young housewife and mother of four named Lee Richardson. Mrs. Richardson had entitled her first opinion editorial "Women Arise: Let's Run the Machine Out! Let's Have Real Government Here," and after a tut-tut reply from Crump himself ("This Is a Kindly City—Come on Our Boat Ride") had followed up with an attack on the regressive poll tax and a broad-based assault on Crump paternalism, demanding, "Why should one of our private citizens have the sole right to spend the hard-earned money we gave as taxes?"

This was a point that the black community had been making for some time now. Unlike almost every other Southern big-city boss, *Time* magazine reported in 1936, Crump had always, "cultivate[d] and deliver[ed] a solid block of Negro voters," inarguably a key element in his record over "30 years of bossdom [of] 60 electoral victories, no defeats." New Negro leaders like Brotherhood of Sleeping Car Porters president A. Philip Randolph, who had called for a March on Washington in 1941 and was its director when it was finally realized some twenty-two years later, had recently written that the black population could no longer be bought off with "gifts" like Jim Crow schools, separate parks, and segregated public housing—the next you knew, Crump would be demanding credit for "free air." "Negroes," Randolph declared with the finality of inerrant truth, "do not want to be well kept slaves."

Sam could certainly understand these arguments. They were in line with some of his deepest beliefs, and under other circumstances he might very well have been expected to address these same issues—though, as he would have been the first to concede, perhaps not as directly as Mrs. Richardson. But in this case his natural disinclination to mount an all-out assault on a seemingly impregnable position was further complicated by the fact that he actually admired E. H. Crump, seeing him as a despot, to be sure, but as a *benevolent* despot, who had rescued Memphis from the most virulent forms of racism, brokering a kind of temporary truce between the races and saving the city, in Sam's words, from becoming "a real rough, mean old river town."

And so, without in any way disparaging Mrs. Richardson's liberal slant, Sam chose to express his unabashed love for his adoptive hometown, focusing on the can-do spirit that he saw at the heart of the community and the glorious things that were still in its future.

"In every progressive community or organization," he wrote, in what could be taken as a brief for the purpose that would guide his entire life, "some one must dare and believe in a thing to the extent that he is willing to assume responsibility and obligation and thereby start the proverbial wheel to rolling." In his view, Crump was that person, the man who had rescued Memphis from gangsters like Machine Gun Kelly and Pretty Boy Floyd and frontier lawlessness, the individual who had had "the will to dare and to do something about it. . . . All I can say . . . is that it is a blessing that we have a man in our town that has political and social representatives in responsible places that can help in getting the best for us." In conclusion, he stated emphatically, "I am a native Alabamian, but I'll take good ole Memphis any day and it's all because it's a great progressive town, and just watch it: it's going to be greater."

SAMUEL KNOX PHILLIPS was born October 30, 1945. Sam had picked out the name (the middle name, that is, by which he intended his son to be known), long before the baby was born. He just liked the sound of it—he appropriated it from a local probate court judge named Knox Longshore—though if the child was a girl, he was inclined to the more conventional Carole.

He and Becky doted on the baby. They had had to sell the Dodge to pay for the delivery, but Sam walked to work with his unmistakably jaunty gait, and when they went anywhere as a family, they all just rode the bus. Even the smallest things that they did together, Becky thought, were just so *precious.* Jimmy and Erin Connolly and their little girl came

Knox's first birthday,
October 30, 1946.
*Courtesy of the Sam
Phillips Family*

to visit not long after Knox was born, and Erin was distraught to discover that the baby was sleeping in a dresser drawer with a chair under it. Becky told her sister that cribs were expensive, but that she had placed plenty of soft covers underneath and what did it matter as long as the baby was happy. Later on, she listened as the men played checkers and talked long into the night about all of their plans, about the future of radio.

Even after they moved to Birmingham at the end of the year, the Connollys visited at least once a month. Jimmy had gotten the job of general manager at WJLD, a 250-watter in Bessemer that covered the city, and he was starting up a new show called the *Atomic Boogie Hour,* a nominal hour of "race records" aimed primarily at the colored population (which, like Memphis, represented more than 40 percent of the total populace) and hosted by a personable white announcer named Bob Umbach. The logic was unassailable: there was an audience out there that wasn't being served, an audience that, however separate its retail outlets might be, was buying the same goods as its white counterpart.

It was the same logic that would soon fuel Gene Nobles' *Midnight Special* on WLAC in Nashville, and the show proved to be a success from the start, advertising "Jive, Jam, Boogie Woogie and Blues" to a listening audience that Sam was absolutely convinced was starved for something new, something different, something *fresh*. And not just a black audience either, he told Jimmy, there were white kids out there, listening, too, he felt like with the *Atomic Boogie Hour* Jimmy was on the verge of something big. Jimmy was not about to disagree, but even though the *Boogie Hour*'s time slot was rapidly expanding well beyond its original allotted time, he was more cautious about it than Sam. Jimmy was a radio man through and through—a great radio man, Sam knew, but one perhaps less devoted to the future than to the here and now, certainly one less devoted to the *cause* of human communication than to the fact of it. Sam just knew, though, that there was a new day dawning, that the race music you heard coming out on all the little labels and radio stations that were cropping up all over the country, all the records that were flooding the marketplace now that the war was finally over—records by novelty singers like Louis Jordan and boogie-woogie piano players like Cecil Gant and spiritual singers like Sister Rosetta Tharpe, not to mention the "gutbucket" blues of Arthur "Big Boy" Crudup—was more and more beginning to resemble the music that had inspired him, the music that he had first heard growing up in the cotton fields of Alabama.

J.W. AND HIS NEW WIFE, Dean, arrived in town in the fall of 1946 and stayed with Sam and Becky briefly before finding a place of their own. J.W. was "Jud" now. He had come back from service in the Pacific and married Dean Hensley, who had moved in with her family across the street from the Phillipses on North Royal when she started college in Florence in the fall of 1941. She had been waiting patiently for him ever since and, once he extricated himself from his impulsive first marriage, married him in August of 1945. J.W. had almost immediately put his gift for gab to use, advancing and announcing the John Daniel Quartet, who were still performing every morning on WSM and making appearances throughout the area, at which J.W. sold songbooks, costume jewelry, and other merchandise. It was John Daniel who christened him "Jud," because, according to tenor singer Jake Hess ("W.J." at the time), "every

Jud Phillips.
*Courtesy of Dean Phillips,
Jud Phillips Jr., and the
Sam Phillips Family*

night he had to introduce the fellows in the group [and their onstage announcer], and it was confusing. There was a W.J. Hess, there was a J.W. Phillips." So one night he simply called a meeting and assigned both men first names.

John Daniel quit the group in a quarrel with his brother Troy, and Jud became their de facto manager. When they got dropped by WSM, he brought them briefly to WLAY in Florence, but that didn't get them enough exposure to promote live dates beyond a limited radius, so Jud got in touch with Sam, and Sam spoke to WREC program director Roy Wooten, not just because Jud was his brother but because he knew the group was good. They went on the air at the beginning of October, still the Daniel Quartet, but a couple of months later they changed their name to the Jollyboys, with Jud announcing and his wife, Dean, a gospel piano prodigy from an early age and a fervent believer in anything her husband set his mind to, playing piano behind them on both the radio and at all their live dates throughout Mississippi, Arkansas, and Tennessee.

Sam and Becky saw a good deal of his brother and sister-in-law, as much as it was possible to see anyone given Sam's split sixteen-hour workday, but the two wives soon became aware of how different their husbands were, despite their closeness as brothers. Both were go-getters with a tremendous amount of ambition, both were dedicated to communication of one sort or another, with Jud's eloquence, charisma, and overall bonhomie clearly outshining his brother's, but the nature of his ambition still remained to be fathomed. As Dean and Becky knew, for all of their husbands' pride in each other and genuine dedication to each other's success, there was a tension underlying the relationship. It grated on Sam the way he felt Jud baited him, particularly about religion. It seemed to Sam that, for all of his knowledge and all of his oratorical brilliance, J.W. almost made a game of it — as often as not, seemingly, just to get his brother's goat. All the Phillips siblings, Dean had come to realize, had something about them that allowed you to pick them out in a crowd, and both Sam and Jud, the only ones whose ambition seemed to have left the world of Lovelace Community behind, got along with every one of their siblings equally, except for each other. To Becky, who had heard about J.W. ever since she first met Sam but had never really known him till now, "Jud was a terrific communicator. He was so talented. And he was very smart. They both had so many great qualities. . . ." But they were at odds with each other so much of the time — over small things for the most part, she reassured herself, the way brothers so often are. The rest of the time they were as thick as thieves.

The Jollyboys Quartet stayed on the air until March of 1947, when Jud and Dean returned to Florence, where Dean's father, Mr. Hensley, had purchased a Double Cola bottling plant in Sheffield for his son-in-law to run. Their son, Juddy ("Judson William"), was born early the following year, and in September of 1948 they moved to Petal, Mississippi, just outside Hattiesburg, where Jud ran a Double Cola and Sun Spot Orange bottling plant, once again funded by his father-in-law, and regrouped the Jollyboys, now known as the Sun Spot Quartet.

SAM AND BECKY moved into a house of their own in early 1948. Becky was pregnant again, and they were going to need more room once the baby came, so they rented the bottom floor of a two-family house on Vinton, at midtown, just around the corner from Mayor Crump's home on Peabody. Sam saw Mr. Crump from time to time, out for his daily constitutional, and he would chat with him, and Mr. Crump would address him seriously and call him Mr. Phillips, and it really tickled Sam, gave him a sense that he had really arrived. And yet for all of his enthusiasm for his adoptive hometown, he had little time to socialize, and his sense of the city's openness, friendliness, and freedom came almost entirely from work.

Mr. Wooten had by now recognized not just Sam's engineering skills but his extraordinary dedication to whatever task happened to be at hand, so he put him in charge of the record library, too, which included recordings going back to when the station first went on the air, in 1926. Sam went through it slowly, culling out records that were no longer sufficiently suitable and alphabetizing everything on three-by-five index cards, which he laboriously typed out himself, noting the filter setting that should be used (since no standardized equalization curve yet existed, and every company chose its own) on every record played. Mr. Wooten would come in sometimes after listening to one of Sam's shows on the meticulous high-fidelity system he had installed in his Whitehaven home and ask, "Sam, what [setting] are you playing this record on?" And Sam would give him a precise answer, letting him know in each instance what curve made this RCA or this Capitol or this Mercury recording sound best. Mr. Wooten never said much, Sam knew he wasn't going to waste his breath on empty words of praise — but he nodded approvingly, and *let him keep on doing it.*

At first Mr. Wooten had questions about the way Sam was recording the Skyway Ballroom bands. He wasn't sure that he agreed with Sam's theory about miking the rhythm section, his strong belief that there was something almost "anemic" about the way they were so often recorded (with everything geared to the solos and the overall blend) compared to the way they could sound. With his mike placement Sam sought to restore some of the "bottom" that was so instrumental in propelling them along — each band required something different, and you never wanted to do too much to disturb the sound of the room, "but by bringing up the bass a little and getting it to where you could hear the drummer — I mean, you had to be *really ready* because you had to meet the different schedules of volume, the rhythm patterns were arranged into their music, and the bandleaders didn't care for you [messing with their arrangements]. But they would come down to the control room the next day and listen to the transcriptions, and it got to where they really liked the contrast. And I got my boss to kind of agree!"

Mr. Wooten rewarded him with yet another show of his own, the *Saturday Afternoon Tea Dance,* which ran on Saturdays from 1:30 to 6:00,

The Skyway. *Courtesy of the Sam Phillips Family*

with just five minutes off for news, the longest record show on any of the established stations in town. It was a mix of all kinds of music, the smooth country of newcomers like Eddy Arnold, pop numbers, swing numbers like Artie Shaw's "Summit Ridge Drive" ("It reminded me of the jug bands on Beale Street, if you can believe that—with a sound like he was playing, for a [washtub] bass, with a string and a broomstick and a lard can, and it just tore me up"), and old-time parlor tunes, too—he announced in between the records, and he used Benny Goodman's "Let's Dance" as his theme song. Sam was grateful to Mr. Wooten. "He was very good to me. But he wasn't *especially* good to me. He had a commanding way about him. He was a great employer, but he wanted your undivided attention and your devotion to WREC because *he was a radio man*."

So here he was, a young man on the rise, just twenty-five years old and handsome as a movie star, modest and soft-spoken according to his fellow employees but as fanatic about sound as his hard-driving employer was. He was by now a proud father of two (his second son, Jerry Layne, was born on September 9, 1948), an attentive husband, a good son (he sent a portion of his combined $62.50 paychecks home to his mother and aunt every week) — in the little spare time he had, he would sometimes take his son Knox to watch the Double-A-league Memphis Chicks play ball at Russwood Park, where as often as not the two of them, the young father and the little boy, might shinny up a tree and watch the ballgame from outside the park, along with all the others, black and white, who either didn't have the money or, like Sam, knew that there were more important things to spend your money on. He saw himself as a self-styled man of action, with the world, if not at his feet, seemingly stretched out before him, someone who had overcome adversity — and not just adversity of material circumstance but of personal demons as well. He might have described himself in his self consciously self-deprecating way as "a little town boy" who had found his way to the big city, but he was as taken with the elegance of his surroundings as the most genuinely ingenuous little-town boy might be.

"When I first saw the Skyway in 1945," he would recall, "I thought it was the most beautiful club room I'd ever seen, just about the most beautiful room, period. The people at all the tables were all immaculately made up — you couldn't have liquor by the drink then, but you could bring your own bottle, and some of these people would have flasks that must have cost $500 or $1,000. If you went to the Skyway and heard the band and danced and enjoyed yourself, you had been baptized in the upper crust."

And yet, and yet . . . it wasn't enough. For someone so dedicated to radically egalitarian dreams, for someone who had imagined himself like Clarence Darrow righting the wrongs of society, professional success and social veneer were not nearly enough. Even the music, he was forced to acknowledge, did not come close to measuring up to the music that he had first heard from the untutored sharecroppers on his daddy's farm to whom purity of emotional communication, not perfection, was always the goal. There was none of the sense of openness and freedom that he had gotten when he first arrived on Beale Street as a wide-eyed sixteen-year-old just ten years earlier — it wasn't even the kind of reaching out to others that had been brought home to him on that same trip by the example of

George W. Truett's illustrious music director, greeting each and every one of Dr. Truett's thousands of parishioners with the most unselfish of selfish motives, because *each and every one of them belonged.* Instead, what he heard from all of the bands night after night was the turning of pages, all those dog-eared arrangements that, as great as they were, had been commissioned years and years ago and from which the imagination was no more permitted to wander than Uncle Silas would be permitted, or even choose, to join the ranks of those hidebound upholders of the "traditional values" of the Old South who thought they were excluding him even as they were themselves marching in purposeless lockstep.

It started tugging at him more and more: the original dream, however inchoate, that had brought him to Memphis, the sense that there were all these people of little education and even less social standing, both black and white, who had so much to say but were prohibited from saying it; the belief that somehow it had been given to him, in a manner that he had yet to determine, to bring it out of them, to coax out of them the inarticulate speech of the human heart. It hit him whenever he went down on Beale Street to buy records for the station library at Ruben Cherry's recently opened Home of the Blues; it hit him when he heard the down-home sounds of brand-new blues sensations like John Lee Hooker and Lightnin' Hopkins — he had never thought he would hear a gutbucket sound like that reach a broad popular audience — he knew how blacks responded to it in their own community, but this was through the medium of *radio.* And it was the revolutionizing of that medium that brought home to him most of all the change that he knew without any question now was coming.

A 250-watt Memphis radio station, WDIA, 730 on the radio dial, had in October of 1948 put the first Negro disc jockey in the Deep South on the air, and it was becoming increasingly clear that, while its programming for the moment remained mixed, the day that it would become the first all-black station in the nation was not far off. This was not altogether by design. WDIA had opened its doors in 1947 with an emphasis on hillbilly music but with the usual mix of local homemaker shows, network pickups, and block programming of shows of every sort, from soap opera to classical. Just the sixth radio station in Memphis, it was the product of a partnership between John Pepper, from a wealthy old-money family in Greenville, Mississippi, who had started a radio station in his hometown in 1939, and Bert Ferguson, an old radio hand who had joined Pepper in Greenville after a couple of years in Memphis at WHBQ. The new station was an utter failure at first, unable to find an audience until Ferguson attended a convention in Nashville, where one of the speakers brought up the idea of "targeted programming." This was based on the idea that you pitched your product — and, perhaps more important, the advertising products you were selling — at a particular audience, and the one audience that Ferguson knew was absolutely unrepresented in Memphis (with the exception of the occasional spiritual program or half an hour of "sepia blues") was the Negro audience, who comprised almost 50 percent of the population within reach of WDIA's signal.

Not long afterward Ferguson got in touch with "Professor" Nat D. Williams, a history teacher at Booker T. Washington High School and a highly respected member of the community. Williams, who was integrally involved in every aspect of black life in Memphis, from MCing shows at the Palace Theater on Beale to running the talent show for the Cotton Makers' Jubilee, the wildly successful black answer to the high-society Cotton Carnival (the Jubilee drew more than a hundred thousand, black and white, at its height), to writing a column, "Down on Beale," for the city's black weekly, the *Memphis World*, which combined informal social notes along the lines of Langston Hughes' "Simple" stories with coverage of the incipient civil rights movement. But for all of his poise and accomplishments, when Nat D. took the mike on October 25, 1948, he was completely tongue-tied. It was four o'clock in the afternoon, and he had just raced out to the station from Booker T., where his teaching duties ended at 3:15, to put "Tan Town Jamboree" on the air.

"And when they stuck the microphone out there for me to start talking," he told oral historian Ronald Anderson Walter, "I forgot everything I was supposed to say. So I broke out in a raucous laugh because I was laughing myself out of the picture. And of all things, everybody else in the place started laughing too, and that brought me back to what I was supposed to say."

That laugh, WDIA historian Louis Cantor has pointed out, became his on-air signature, and the station was on its way, gradually adding more and more black programming until, by the end of the summer of 1949, it was virtually all black. One of the first new hires, in the late fall of 1948, was a young blues singer named Riley King, new in town, who had come over from West Memphis, where he had gotten a job singing at the 16th Street Grill contingent on his landing a daily radio spot to advertise it. He walked into the station, and Nat D. spotted him and asked what he could do for him. "I want to make a record," he said. "I don't know what made me say that," King told jazz historian Stanley Dance, "because I didn't go there to make a record but to get on the air." Nat D. introduced him to Bert Ferguson, who had him sing a few songs and then offered him a job advertising Pep-ti-kon, a "blood-building" tonic that Ferguson and Pepper's new patent medicine company, Berjon, was just putting on the market. He made up a jingle to sell the tonic ("Pep-ti-kon, sure is good/You can get it anywhere in your neighbor-hood") and started out right away as "The Pep-ti-kon Boy," with just ten minutes on Nat D.'s show, for which he received no pay but during which he could advertise his own appearances every day.

Sam was totally taken with all the unforeseen, and unforeseeable, possibilities that this new station was opening up, uncertain whether it might suggest new and expanded directions for the *Atomic Boogie Hour* or possibly even provide a revolutionary new template for the radio station that he and Jimmy continued to dream of starting up on their own. He told Jimmy about it, and Jimmy came to town and holed up in a hotel room for a few days, doing little but listen to the radio for the roughly twelve daylight hours it was on. He was as knocked out as Sam on both a practical and theoretical level, but with Jimmy the emphasis was always more on the practical. For Sam, on the other hand, it was almost as if destiny had come calling.

He didn't believe in accidents, never had—but all of these things, Sam was now beginning to believe, were conspiring to push him in a direction that was becoming irrefutably clear. He had never doubted that he was meant for a higher purpose, even during his worst trials and tribulations that conviction had never wavered, and now it was finally starting to take form. He had staked out his belief from an early age, a belief not just in the possibilities but in the *necessity* of human communication, a belief in the potential of ordinary men and women to communicate, to do something—to be recognized for the *achievement* of something—truly great.

"It would have been so easy for me to have laid back with those bands I had worked so hard to get to do, but there was something not just tugging—[it was] *surging* in my soul. I didn't know just what it was, but I had a good sneaking idea.

"Because I had heard the innate rhythms of [a] people. My conviction was that the world was missing out on not having heard what I had heard as a child. Memphis was the inducement — I mean, going out and hearing a black man pick a guitar and pat his foot and put a wood box under his foot to pat as he sings. These were elements that I knew were not going away. And all of these elements resonated for, I would say, maybe a year and a half, and I wouldn't let myself think about it, as much as I wanted to — but then I said, 'I've just got to open me a little recording studio, where I can at least experiment with [some of] this overlooked humanity. I don't have any money, but I know I can build it with my own hands.' I couldn't *not* do it, not *attempt* to do it. Had I not tried, I would have been the biggest damn coward that God ever put on this earth. I was so committed in my mind, not to be a damn crusader, I guess 'explorer' is a better word. I said, I've got to have this little laboratory, I've *got* to have it, it's just absolutely, *I've gotta have it!*"

He was a beautiful young man, beautiful beyond belief. But still that country touch, you know, that country rawness, slim with incredible eyes, and very, very particular about his appearance. He always wore a gold chain, and he always used a holder for his filter cigarettes, touches of elegance — what he felt from his experience was elegance — beautifully groomed, and terrible about his hair! Beautiful, chestnut-brown hair. And he would talk about this idea that he had — I knew nothing about the music. My association, my contribution, my participation was based totally on my personal relationship with Sam.

— Marion Keisker MacInnes

MARION KEISKER MACINNES (she was married briefly but dropped the MacInnes after the marriage dissolved) was a fixture on Memphis radio. Like Becky Phillips, she had started at an early age, on a children's show called *Wynken, Blynken and Nod,* on which she had first appeared in 1929 when she was twelve. She graduated from Southwestern College in Memphis in 1938 with a degree in English and Medieval French, married, moved away, had a child, and returned to Memphis and radio in 1943. She was probably the best-known female radio personality in the city, at one point working on virtually every station in town, running from one to the other all day long to do advertising spots and popular quiz-show, dramatic, and comedy programs. In the usual manner of the day she did each of the shows under a different name (that way stations could own the name and keep the show going as a station feature, long after the role's originator had left), but she maintained a strong identity as a "personality" in her own right, and it may have been this, or just her overall dedication, talent, and versatility that prompted Hoyt Wooten to hire her full-time in 1946. She could continue to do ad agency work for other stations, but otherwise she would be exclusive to WREC.

One of the shows she did was a network feed called *Treasury Bandstand,* an outgrowth of the nightly Skyway broadcasts for which the orchestra would come in every Wednesday afternoon to sell government savings bonds. The engineer for the show, the man who cut the transcriptions that were sent to New York for later broadcast, was Sam Phillips. Sam also engineered one of her two station promotion shows, *Pleasure Hunting,* for which she wrote all the copy and then read it with a male announcer named Bill Wilds, while Sam played the "cue records" she had picked out, which were intended to remind the listener of some of the features of that evening's prime-time shows. Before long she didn't want anybody but Sam playing the records. It wasn't simply because of his engineering skills, Sam soon came to realize. "I mean, there's a lot of people around there that could have played the records just as good." It was, rather, because, "I mean, this is just the truth — she was in love with me. That was it."

Marion would have been the last to dispute that characterization. A handsome, schoolteacher-looking woman in her early thirties, with light brown hair set in a permanent wave, businesslike glasses, and a brisk professional demeanor, she was a dedicated *New Yorker* reader and devotee of the theater, considerably better educated than most of her colleagues and not hesitant about letting them know it — but with Sam her manner softened as she listened to him talk more and more about this strange dream that he had, "as I understood it, to have a facility where black people could come and play their own music, a place where they would feel free and relaxed [enough] to do it."

Marion Keisker MacInnes at WREC, May 7, 1949. *Courtesy of Preservation and Special Collections, University Libraries, University of Memphis*

Sam for his part was glad to have someone with whom he could feel free and relaxed enough to unburden himself without self-consciousness or equivocation. Soon they were driving around together looking at potential studio sites, and then in October of 1949 Sam found it, a vacant storefront in a small row building on Union, less than a mile from the Peabody, with a little restaurant with a fifty-cent plate lunch right next door. It had last been an automobile-glass and medical supplies company, and Sam spoke to the owners, Mr. Hanover and Mr. Vigland, about the extensive renovations he would need to make before ever setting foot inside the building. He had the hardest time explaining it to them. As soon as he said the words "recording studio," the two of them looked at each other in perplexity and asked what a recording studio was, and then, when he began to explain, seemed even more baffled. "But all of a sudden I knew these two old Jewish men were my friends — I didn't have the nerve to ask them about the rent, I [just] figured I had to fascinate them in such a way that they might want me in there instead of another auto-repair shop or maybe a barber shop. So I thought about it overnight, and when we met the next afternoon [in the restaurant next door], I had my story in mind."

They bought it hook, line, and sinker. When he got done describing just what his new venture would be, the bold experiment in human communication that it represented — he didn't bother mentioning that it would be primarily for the purpose of recording black people, he wasn't sure they were quite ready for that — they might not have fully understood either the purpose or the practical elements of a recording studio, but they knew that somehow or other here was someone trying to do something different, and "it sounded interesting to them." Then they opened the door to the building, all grimy and littered with junk, and Sam knew he had found his cathedral.

It was approximately eighteen feet wide by fifty-seven feet deep, with room for an eighteen-by-thirty-foot studio, a tiny reception area out front, and a control room that would be raised up a couple of feet above the studio floor so that Sam could sit at eye level with his artists and that would be just large enough to allow space for a tiny commode and a slightly larger storage area. He stepped it off with the two owners, spoke to Mr. Vigland, the contracting half of the partnership, about the structural changes that would have to be made, and agreed to pay $75 a month rent, but on a month-to-month basis — he thought this was the greatest part of the whole deal. They wanted to make sure that if it didn't work out, he wouldn't have too hard a time moving out. In other words, "they wanted to help *me* — they were thinking of me as a young man attempting to do something that they had not heard of — but at the time I don't think they thought my destiny was going to be what I hoped it would be."

So everything was set, all the details had been worked out — but he still hadn't told Mr. Wooten. And Hoyt Wooten was not the kind of person you just sprang things on. He demanded total loyalty and undivided allegiance; he would have to be convinced, Sam knew, that Sam's attention would never stray from the job at hand, his *radio* job, the one that counted, at WREC. He was more than a little fearful about actually approaching him — he didn't want to make an appointment because that would just make Mr. Wooten wonder what the appointment was about, but then he spotted him in the hotel coffee shop, having coffee, as he often did, with Mr. Plough, the owner of the pharmaceutical giant Plough, Incorporated, who lived in the hotel, and when Mr. Plough left he asked Mr. Wooten if he could sit down with him, and he told him what he wanted to do.

"I did not tell him that I had already rented the studio. I did not tell him that I was going to record black folks, because he was a good man, but he was raised up around Coldwater, Mississippi, and I just knew that that might be a little more than he could handle. But he wound up giving me some very fatherly advice."

He reminded Sam that a little studio called Royal Recording had recently opened up and then gone broke just the previous week — it had been in the paper. What guarantee was there that the same thing wasn't going to happen to Sam? Sam hastened to assure him that he had taken all that into consideration and that he had plans to develop a custom business — weddings, conventions, public events, things that people would want to keep a memory of — which would help him keep his head above water. Then Mr. Wooten said, "Well, is it going to interfere with your work here?" and when Sam asserted that it most definitely would not — he was fully prepared to continue working the same punishing schedule that he found so rewarding for as long as Mr. Wooten would have him — Mr. Wooten said, in that stern way of his, as if he suspected that you thought you had just pulled the greatest wool job in the world on him but you hadn't, "Well, Sam, I'm going to give you permission to try to open that little studio, so long as it doesn't interfere with your work."

He began going to the little storefront on the corner of Union and Marshall, sometimes listed as 706 Union, sometimes as 706 Marshall, every day after work, remaining until he had to report back for the Skyway broadcast from 10:30 to 11:00, after which he often returned for another hour or two of hard, physical labor if he could manage it. Marion was there every day, too. There was more than enough for them both to do — Sam was determined to open the studio for business on Monday, January 2, 1950, the beginning of the second half of the twentieth century, and they were already well into November.

The first thing that had to be done was to get the ornate old tin ceiling removed. Mr. Vigland took care of that. Then, although he would have liked for the height to be a little greater, "I treated the ceiling with an inverted V. The floor was hard-surfaced, anything that bounced off of it went up there and would hit the V ceiling. I put up acoustic tiles, one-foot square, all of them glued to [the] Sheetrock that I put on top when I 'firred down' the ceiling." He put horizontal Vs on the wall on the control-room end and verticals on the end between the studio and the reception area. It was all so the sound couldn't "get away and get too echoey [but] at the same time we didn't have all the deadening material that you might [ordinarily] put in a studio to where you just miss some of the overtones that you need to get." The whole aim was to capture the sound of the human voice, to provide enough artifice to allow it to come through clearly and cleanly but at the same time to keep it *natural,* in all its glorious rawness, intimacy, and individuation.

It was not so much scientifically done (though Sam could certainly talk endlessly about the science of it) as *spontaneously* done by someone who believed in sound but believed even more in feel. Over and over he paced the studio, starting in the corners, working his way toward the center, clapping his hands and listening to the reverberation until he was certain that there was enough "liveness" in every square inch of the room, "to where it [would] sound *real — R-E-A-L* — when it went into the microphone."

In all of this Marion was his altogether willing, if not always equally knowledgeable, partner. Together they constructed the floor of nine-inch linoleum squares, which they painted red. Marion painted the outer office green and white and all of the studio and control-room

706 Union. *Courtesy of Jim Cole*

woodwork white, while Sam focused primarily on carpentry and electronics, building two little cabinet speakers himself and supervising the one or two "half-ass carpenters" he was able to afford. At some point Sam and Marion had begun a physical affair, and for Marion, there was simply no looking back. She did things she had never done before, throwing caution to the wind as she put herself entirely at Sam's disposal. She risked her job, she risked her reputation. She borrowed $500 on her life insurance and gave it to Sam because there was no way to get money from a bank for this sort of venture. Eventually she made the "monumental sacrifice [of] giving up my child and sending him off to my sister.

"I was totally amazed at myself. All I wanted was to make it possible for Sam to do whatever would make him happy. I knew nothing about r&b, I knew nothing about country, and I didn't care whether I did," she said thirty years later, describing a decade of her life in which she found her own behavior "unbelievable to me now," without either rancor or regret. "I was totally enamored of Sam, I was his slave — that's the only word to use."

Sam didn't fail to appreciate her contributions ("I don't know what in the hell I would have done without Marion. She did so many fantastic things to help me — and everything she did, she did because she believed in me"), but as preoccupied, as *obsessed,* as he knew she was with him, he was equally obsessed with the studio, not just with all the details of its construction but with all the unmapped promises of its dream. Scraping together every last penny he could come up with, he acquired the equipment he would need to start the business: a Presto portable three-input mixer board, which sat at first on an old oak table that he set on the floor, where the control room would eventually go; a Presto lathe and turntable for both recording sessions and custom discs for anyone who wanted to hear the sound of their own voice; a little Bell portable recorder in a red case that he could use to record people, or events, on location; and a variety of microphones, a couple of "coke-bottle" Altecs, two or three of the old reliable RCA 77-D broadcast models, and some Shure 55s.

Some of the equipment he was able to work out a deal on with Hoyt Wooten's brother S.D., who operated the W&W Distributing Company just around the corner. All of it was decent enough, but on some he just had to scrape by on what he could afford. The one thing he was not prepared to scrimp on was the sign that would announce the presence of the Memphis Recording Service to the world — well, two identical neon signs, actually, one for each of the plate-glass windows on either side of the door. He had chosen the name, as he had chosen every other element of his brave new enterprise, with a great deal of care. "I wanted it to sound big — I was so little, and Memphis, boy, I mean, Memphis, Tennessee, was bigger than the world." The two signs, on the other hand, couldn't be too big — the cost was going to come to close to $400, but they couldn't be so big as to overshadow either the plainspoken premise of their title or the dimensions of the building. "I knew exactly how I wanted it. I wanted 'Recording' really scripted, and then 'Memphis' and 'Service' in block form." He paid close attention to each and every detail, the warm glow of the red lettering for the two framing words, the specific angle at which the scripted middle word would be set in blue — "I'll never forget going all the way across the street a number of times, all the way across Marshall and Union, and looking at that sign and thinking that was the prettiest damn thing I ever saw in my life!"

For Becky, who felt like she had scarcely seen her husband during the last two months but whose faith in him had never wavered, it was the realization of a dream that had become almost as integral to her as it was to Sam. "The one thing that amazed me about Sam more than

Sam and Becky with Dean (Mrs. Jud) Phillips, Jud Jr. (in diapers), Knox, and Jerry (in his mother's lap), 1949. *Courtesy of the Sam Phillips Family*

anything else was that he knew how to do everything, from the littlest thing to the biggest — I don't know how, but he did. He read a lot, and he learned everything he could about everything. There was nothing that he was afraid of. He was willing to try anything, because he just felt like he could do it."

She brought the boys down to see the finished studio and took a picture of Sam out front. When she pasted it into the scrapbook she was putting together for the two of them and the boys, she wrote a caption underneath that read: "A Man's Dream Fulfilled — What Next?"

I didn't open the studio to record funerals and weddings and school day revues. I knew what I opened the studio for. I was looking for a higher ground, for what I knew existed in the soul of mankind. And especially at that time the black man's spirit and his [soul].

I T WAS SLOW AT FIRST. It took him a while to even get any black people to come in, let alone come in with the idea of making a record. He didn't have a record company, he didn't have any deals lined up, he didn't even know what he would do with the recordings that he hoped to eventually make. He just knew the strength of his belief that music was not confined to the drawing room, that there was something profound in the lives of ordinary people — that there was great art to be discovered in the experience of those who had been marginalized and written off because of their race, their class, or their lack of formal education. But to find it he had to keep the doors of his little studio open until he could win their confidence, until word could get out in the community that there was a white man looking not to exploit their talent but to free up their "innate soul," to give them the opportunity to express the very things that they themselves most wanted to say. If he accomplished nothing else, he was determined at least to do that.

He went over to the Art Craft Printing Company on Union Avenue just a block or so from the Peabody and had cards made up, which constituted his only advertising. At the top of the card is the standard business information, at its center a stock image of a bow-tied, white-jacketed

Joe Hill Louis, ca. 1952. *Hooks Brothers, Memphis,* © *1993, Delta Haze Corporation* man who could very well be a radio announcer or a society bandleader at a stand-up mike, while below is emblazoned the slogan that Sam had come up with, set off with quotation marks, like a personal promise: "WE RECORD ANYTHING — ANYWHERE — ANYTIME."

In the beginning there was little opportunity to make good on that promise. For the few customers who wandered in to make a "personal" record—a song, a recitation, a special message to a loved one—it cost $2 to cut a one-sided disc, $3 for two sides, with Sam operating the Presto lathe and Marion sweeping up the acetate shavings afterward. Marion directed as much business as possible to the studio; she brought in as many of the commercial accounts that she had been recording at the station as she could, and she brought all of the prestige that she had built up over the years with her radio work to help set the Memphis Recording Service apart. Because Sam was tied up at the station every day until midafternoon, she spent much of her day riding the streetcar back and forth between the studio and the hotel, doing her banking first thing in the morning and making sure she was back at the station in time for her signature show, *Meet Kitty Kelly,* but keeping the studio open for as many hours as she could, if only to give the new business a face.

The most reliable source of income at the start came from recording Buck Turner and His Buckaroos for the fifteen-minute show that Turner, a popular western-styled performer who had had an early-morning show on WREC since the late 1930s, sent out to some fifteen stations in Arkansas. Sam had recorded his shows at the station, but, after listening to the playback in the makeshift control room of the little studio that was still under construction, Buck (christened Bodo Otto) was so pleased that he offered to put some money into the business. It was Buck who had helped buy some of the initial recording equipment and put down a deposit on a spinet piano, investing approximately $2,000 in a partnership agreement that Sam started paying off almost as soon as it began, buying out Turner completely by September of 1952. Sam, sniffed Marion, who helped with the buyout, was "not a partner person in any relationship," personal or otherwise, and Buck's wife was not happy with the arrangement either, so there was little incentive for Buck to stay on once Sam's half-hearted attempts to record him as a commercial artist rapidly came to naught.

One of the very few Negroes to come in at first, certainly the only genuine blues singer, was a dark-skinned young man who told Sam he

Buck Turner and His Buckaroos, Memphis Recording Service, 1950.
Courtesy of the Sam Phillips Family

had recently signed with Columbia Records and broadcast for fifteen minutes a day on radio station KWEM in West Memphis as Joe Hill Louis, the Be-Bop Boy. Louis, who was born Leslie (or Lester) Hill in Whitehaven, just on the outskirts of Memphis, had run away from home at fourteen and been virtually adopted by the wealthy Canale family, for whom he worked in various domestic capacities and by whom he had been given his nickname (in honor of heavyweight boxing champion Joe Louis) for his fighting prowess. He played all around town and could be seen on Beale Street almost every day, where he stood out from the other blues singers as a self-advertised one-man band (guitar, rack harmonica, and traps), but Sam had first encountered him when he stopped by on his way to a gig in Moscow, Tennessee, while the room was still under construction. He asked Sam what he was up to, and Sam replied, "I'm going to build a recording studio here once I get the building into shape." "Man, that's just what we need here in Memphis," Joe said to him and, after a brief conversation, continued on his way.

Memphis Recording Service. *Courtesy of the Sam Phillips Family*

He kept coming around, and, once Sam had the studio up and running, he invited Joe to come in and record. When he did, "he sat down at his equipment and played me everything he knew, which was quite a lot." Sam responded to the music — it was full of the crude, driving boogie sound of John Lee Hooker — but he responded to Joe even more, as "a complete individual," as someone in whom Sam recognized a kindred spirit, "a loner but not lonesome. He was his own person. I never saw him look defeated or unhappy about anything.

"Joe was a sweet guy. He was the kind of person to just drop in and say 'hi' and then keep out of the way. He was always well-dressed, sharp, a dapper man. He was well-organized and very personable. He was a treasure to me [and] I just thought, 'This is a guy that deserves to be heard, even though I realized that [because of the constraints of the one-man band arrangement] it was basically a novelty kind of thing."

But he still had no idea what to do with the acetates he had recorded, and while one or two of Joe's friends and musical associates started drifting by — veteran blues entertainers like Jack Kelly and Memphis Jug Band alumnus Charlie Burse and eighteen-year-old Phineas Newborn Jr., who held down the piano chair in his father Phineas Sr.'s big band and, with his sixteen-year-old guitar-playing brother, Calvin, was blazing a be-bop-inflected path on the Memphis blues scene — mostly it was just talk and playing in the studio so they could get used to each other and to the room.

With everyone who came in, he was the same: respectful, deferential, determined to overcome their understandable mistrust, their certainty that there must be a catch in this somewhere. If some grizzled old man came in with an oil drum and ropes, or just four strings on his guitar, "if I had had a million dollars, I wouldn't have sent out and bought a string." Because, for one thing, he wasn't going to insult a man's need, for another that man might have something completely different to say — with just four strings! On the other hand, if a seasoned professional came by with the idea that they were going to give this skinny little white man just what they thought he wanted — Cab Calloway, say, or Jimmy Rushing or Nat King Cole — Sam quickly disabused them of the notion that he was looking for anything but what resided in the deepest recesses of their own soul, he was looking for *originality*, he was looking for feeling. With all of them he listened attentively and told them honestly what he thought. Because most of all they had to believe in *him*, they had to believe in his sincerity, his commitment to *them*. Maybe nothing would come of it until their second or third visit. There was no charge, there was no rush, he assured them over and over again, in the face of their understandable suspicion that at any moment he was going to present them with the bill — they had to come to the belief on their own, they had to be comfortable with the idea that the purpose of this whole undertaking was to get them to express *themselves*.

"In a personality not really given to patience," Marion observed, "he showed patience beyond belief. Say they were to come in at three o'clock in the afternoon, and they came dragging in at 3:00 A.M. — I mean, we would usually be there painting or working on [something], but Sam would just say, 'Come on in.' He never acted like he was surprised, never said, where were you, he'd just clear the decks and listen to them." Occasionally he might suggest an "audition recording," not to give them a copy, because he was not going to let anything go out of the studio until he was fully satisfied with it, but just to let them hear what they sounded like on disc, to try to win their confidence for the day when he might have somewhere to send their audition to. Marion noted how sometimes he would sit in the little half-finished control room, acting like he was busy while the musicians started fooling around with something just to pass the time, and then all of a sudden, "Sam would come in and say, 'That's it, that's what I want.'" And the band, or the blues singer, would be totally taken aback and say, "But that's trash, Mr. Phillips." And he would say, "That's what I want." Because they had forgotten all about the *idea* of making music and were just doing it, without even seeming to give it a second thought.

It was as daunting a challenge as any he had ever faced, particularly because he had to spend so much of his time and energy on activities designed solely to stay in business, in anticipation of the day when he might finally have the opportunity to do what he had actually gone into business for. But he never wavered. He recorded weddings, church services, and conventions at the Peabody. He recorded radio spots for a faux-African herbal faith healer in his most mellifluous "announcer's voice." He persuaded the manager of Russwood Park, across from Baptist Memorial Hospital on Madison, where the Memphis Chicks played, to let him put in a PA system, and he took on the even more difficult task of persuading the owner of Memphis' most prestigious funeral home, National Funeral Home, to allow him to offer a recording of the loved one's service as a special memento for the grieving family.

It was, he was certain, one of the best ideas he had ever come up with — but selling it was another matter. He wrote down all of the positives about the experience, emphasized that he would not interfere with the intimacy of the service, promised that both he and the tape recorder, his little Crestwood or Bell, would be concealed behind a curtain, and the microphones would never be spotted — they could be hidden in wreaths, sprays, even behind the Bible on the pulpit. The recording, he insisted, would in no way intrude, but it would provide — and here was where he became an evangelist for sound — a permanent record that would STOP TIME, it would freeze things forever, just as they were, in a way that a photograph, with its necessary selectivity of detail, could barely suggest. There were, he maintained in his impassioned presentation, no negative aspects to this process — *and the man bought it.* The funeral director handed out Sam's cards to the mourners when they came in to pick out a casket — he was clear on the fact that this was merely an additional service that was being offered, it was not something the funeral home itself was trying to sell, "but I would say more than fifty percent of the people we talked to as word of mouth got around wanted [the] recording."

Overall the conventions probably brought in the most money, but the single biggest payday at the start was the School Days Revue, a talent show put on every year by Memphis' schoolchildren at Ellis Auditorium. To sell his idea, Sam first had to persuade the stage manager at Ellis, who "had been there for a hundred years and was just not a very cooperative gentleman," into allowing him to record the show. He and Sam had a prayer meeting on the subject ("I figured the knee route was better than the head route") — but then Sam had the even harder task of convincing Mr. Raymond Skinner, the head of Forest Hill Dairy, the largest dairy in Memphis, what a public relations bonanza it would be if the family of each child who performed at the School Days Revue was presented with a record of his or her performance, song, recitation, tap dance, compliments of Forest Hill Dairy. It took three or four meetings with Mr. Skinner, but in the end "I got that order for three hundred dollars. And he didn't ask me to take two ninety! I'll never forget that three-hundred-dollar order." But he would never forget Dr. Doyle Smith either, one of Memphis' first orthodontists and a lay preacher, who hired Sam to accompany and record him at some of the little country churches where he preached. "He could have done it himself really — he was a real skilled person technically — but I think he wanted to talk to me on the way out. He paid good in the early days."

All of these experiences, and many others, could well have been considered no more than annoying distractions — and Sam was beginning to grow increasingly concerned over his inability to even locate the commercial outlets he was seeking in order to disseminate his explorations of the black man's soul. With his regular duties at the station he was now working sixteen to eighteen hours a day, and the "lean and hungry look" in which he took such pride was becoming even more lean and more hungry. But somehow he never swerved in his faith, it remained fixed in his mind that this was the course he had chosen, and simply choosing it, even if it should lead to certain failure, represented a kind of success in itself. Nor was there was any doubt in his mind that he gained something valuable from every experience. Whether marshaling his arguments to persuade the head of the National Funeral Home to permit him to record a loved one's last rites, or addressing Joe Hill Louis' penchant for playing all of his songs in the same tempo and the same key, he saw it all as a study in human nature—it was no different, really, from the challenge he had faced in persuading Mr. Powell to purchase sousaphones for the Coffee High School band. What it required most of all was a belief in himself, a belief in both the justice of the cause and his own powers of persuasion.

A ND THEN ALL OF A SUDDEN, without alarums, trumpets, or premonitory signs, things started to pick up. There was a new DJ on the air, he had started with a fifteen-minute show on WHBQ (10:45 to 11:00 P.M.) the previous October, and now eight months later, in the spring of 1950, *Red Hot and Blue* had expanded to two hours a night five nights a week and three hours on Saturday. Sam had first seen him, a twenty-three-year-old loose-limbed, redheaded country boy named Dewey Phillips, playing records over a crude PA system at the W. T. Grant five-and-dime department store on Main, where over the course of the previous two years he had drawn greater and greater crowds of colored listeners as he played "race music"—blues and rhythm and blues—with an evangelical fervor that saw him shouting and singing along, to the increasing delight and the increasingly frenzied buying of the crowd.

It was the runaway success of WDIA, now claiming a good 30 to 40 percent of Memphis' daytime listening audience (WDIA, like many stations of limited means, was licensed to broadcast only from dawn to dusk), that alerted both radio and retail business alike to the purchasing power of the Negro population. And it was, not coincidentally, only a short time after Dewey took over the record department at Grant's that it became one of the top five most profitable departments in the five-hundred-store W. T. Grant chain.

Which led directly to Dewey's initial tryout at WHBQ, located at the Hotel Gayoso, just a few doors down from Grant's. The program that he took over, *Red Hot and Blue,* had been on the air for scarcely two months and was prompted entirely by program director Gordon Lawhead's recognition of the commercial model established by WDIA and the more palatable precedent set by Sam's old friend, Gene Nobles in Nashville, whose late-night r&b show, with its national exposure via WLAC's clear-channel signal, was providing a template for more and more regional "race records" shows. Lawhead's own utter lack of conviction as host doomed the program from the start. And so, against all his better instincts (Lawhead, according to Dewey Phillips biographer Louis Cantor, had initially vowed he would never put such a hapless rube as Phillips on the air), Lawhead capitulated to Dewey's relentless importuning, hedging his bets by limiting the show to fifteen minutes at first. It wasn't long, however, before he was reluctantly forced to acknowledge that the combination of Dewey's irrepressible high spirits and undeniable authenticity (including a propensity for mangling both grammar and studio equipment), along with a near-flawless ear for the kind of music — new music, fresh music, not just race music but western and spiritual music as well — that was drawing an avalanche of new fans, both blacks and an altogether unexpected number of young white listeners as well. And so Dewey's show virtually exploded on the Memphis airwaves.

That was how Sam had come to discover him, with a little bit of shock, as a kindred spirit set loose at the same time, in the same place, and in quest of the same thing. They met initially in the drugstore at the Hotel Peabody, on the corner of Second and Union, and Sam could barely contain his enthusiasm for Dewey's almost uncontainable fervor — the same kind of fervor he was looking for in his studio — but, more than that, for his sincerity. "You could not shoot a hole in his genuineness," Sam felt, assigning the highest accolade that he could assign to anyone, aside from uniqueness and individualism, which Dewey clearly possessed in equal measure. That was why he wrote to his brother-in-law, Jimmy Connolly, who was talking about expanding the *Atomic Boogie Hour* in Birmingham and who had a great daytime voice in Bob Umbach but who was looking for the kind of late-night excitement that Sam felt sure Dewey could provide.

"Jimbo Slick," he wrote in infectious "hepcat talk" after his second

meeting with Dewey, on "June-bug 8-50," at which he discovered that
Dewey was still receiving no salary from WHBQ, merely exposure for
the record department at Grant's, from which he derived a percentage
of the sales:

> Had 'nother rag chewing with "Phillips" yesterday afternoon and
> he now seems to have more interest in prop than at first indicated.
> I covered the piffle pretty thoroughly with him—JLD's follow-
> ing among the sepia set—actual negro potential etc. . . . and he
> agreed it must be a pretty good deal, [beginning] his song of $100 per
> to the tune of "Amazing _____ How Sweet the Sound".
> Seriously, Jim, he would make you a good man I am sure and an
> agreeable employee. Just a country jake like myself and will, I'm sure
> appreciate the breaks.
> I expect to run an air check tonight and will flip it to you tomor-
> row. Size it up and paste it on a pigeon. I think it would be well worth
> your time and Station's money to run back up here and let's go over
> this thing together. . . .
> That's it from the Memphis Bureau.

Two days later the general public discovered Dewey on its own.
"'Phillips Sent Me' Has Become Vital Part of City's Lexicon," read the
headline in Memphis' morning paper, defining Dewey's principal advertising ploy, no matter what the product: "Just tell 'em, Phillips sentcha."
So ubiquitous had this call become, and so popular with his Negro audience was this "lanky six-footer [with] red hair and sleepy blue eyes [and]
a Southern drawl . . . as thick as a stack of Aunt Jemima's pancakes," that
when one woman "cut up her husband somewhat in a domestic dispute,"
she dispatched the ambulance with the directions, "Carry the guy to the
hospital and tell 'em Phillips sent 'im." Less apocryphally perhaps, the
DJ's habit of "always messin' things up, including the English language,"
far from alienating his listeners, just endeared him to them all the more
and caused more than one sponsor whose name he had mangled to tell
the station, "Aw, let him mess it up."

Not to be outdone, Memphis' Negro newspaper, the *World*, ran
two articles over the next week about "Memphis' radio wonder boy . . .
that good lookin' fellow from Grant's record department," whose brash
on-air manner actually masked "a shy unassuming person with a head

A young Dewey Phillips at WHBQ. *Courtesy of the Sam Phillips Family*

full of red hair," meritorious army service, and a keen interest in "'race music' . . . as he puts it," which he acquired while attending the Memphis College of Music briefly on the GI Bill. As to the sincerity of this unlikely race hero, *World* reporter Lawrence S. Wade opined, he "strikes this writer as being an individual who thoroughly enjoys his work" and, after "'adlibbing' his way through two jovial hours, usually jumps into his shiny new car and makes a few personal appearances at the various [Colored] nightclubs about town."

By this time Sam had decided that he, and Memphis, needed Dewey Phillips more than Birmingham did, however dearly he might love Jimmy Connolly. He convinced himself that Dewey just would never fit in with the prim-and-proper Johnson family who owned Jimmy's radio station, but, really, "I started backing off because I just didn't want Dewey leaving Memphis, Tennessee." The upshot was that he and Dewey became the best of friends, not that they ever hung around too much together — Sam was never one for that, and Dewey was just constantly out in public, judging a talent contest, serving as the surprise guest MC at a record-breaking Lionel Hampton appearance at the W. C. Handy

Saul and Joe Bihari. *Courtesy of Michael Bihari*

Theatre (at which, the *World* reported, Hampton reciprocated by "playing WHBQ's most popular record on the Phillip [*sic*] program, 'Phillip Sent Me'" [*sic*]), or just showing up on Beale, where, as Sam observed, "if he went anywhere, he tore the house down. I mean, they would stop anything they were doing, including dancing, to hear Phillips get up on stage."

It was in many ways the most improbable of pairings — Dewey, the impossibly extroverted performer, always unbuttoned, always running at ninety miles an hour, whether fueled by alcohol, pills, or his own high spirits, while Sam remained solitary, driven, motivated by a goal only he could see. When Dewey stopped by the studio, though, invariably accompanied by a bottle of whiskey or a case of Falstaff beer in which he knew Sam, teetotal for reasons that completely escaped his friend, would not partake, what they shared was a total and uninhibited belief in what music could do to break down barriers, to bring people together, whatever their background, whatever their color. Whether voiced or unvoiced — and sometimes, Sam conceded, it was better to leave some things left unsaid — "we were brothers in [that] belief."

It was at the suggestion of Dewey and Buster Williams, the owner of Plastic Products, one of the few independent pressing plants in the country, that Sam first got in touch with Jules and Saul Bihari. The Bihari brothers, owners and operators, with their younger brother, Joe, of Modern Records, among the first and most successful of the indie labels, were in and out of town on a number of business-and-promotion trips in May and June, and Sam took it upon himself to write to them in early May. It was the independents who in the aftermath of World War II, when the GIs came home and money and shellac for record manufacturing once again became plentiful, focused almost exclusively on race, hillbilly, and various other forms of "ethnic" entertainment that were being almost entirely neglected by majors like Columbia and RCA. The Bihari brothers had from the start maintained one of the only self-contained independent operations in the business, but they had just sold their in-house record pressing plant for $78,000, both to provide the wherewithal for a move from their latest location in Los Angeles to Beverly Hills, and to finance the start-up of a new label, RPM, which would focus almost entirely on rhythm and blues. With the sale of their manufacturing unit, they needed to cement a deal with Buster Williams, whom Jules had advised in setting up Plastic Products just the year before.

To Sam, the Biharis seemed like the epitome of record company success. The children of Jewish immigrants, like nearly all of the other independent operators on either coast, they had come up the hard way, starting out in the jukebox and pinball business, then getting into record manufacturing in the spring of 1945 when they couldn't acquire enough records to supply their jukeboxes with material suitable for their mostly Negro clientele. Sam was impressed by almost everything he knew about them — they combined business acumen with an apparent love of the music, even if the music that they focused on represented a broader range, and often a more adulterated, pop-oriented palette, than what he and Dewey were most drawn to. In the past year alone they had had hits with big names like Jimmy Witherspoon and Pee Wee Crayton. But what impressed Sam most of all was the hits they had had with real "gutbucket" blues singers like Lightnin' Hopkins and John Lee Hooker. The success of these artists, he told Dewey, was one of the main incentives that had led him to start his own studio, to get into the business, and John Lee Hooker's "Boogie Chillen," which had astonishingly topped the r&b charts the previous year, was a model, in its savagely overamplified drive, the directness of its vocal approach, in the free-form majesty of its lyrics, for everything he wanted to do. "I just thought, Well, hey, man, these are the people, I mean, you know, to be with."

T HAT WAS WHY he wrote to them initially, and when he got a response a couple of days later suggesting that "we would be very interested in working some arrangement with you on the talent you now have and any future material," he was so excited that, without any further encouragement from them over the next few weeks, he started sending material anyway. On June 25 he mailed two sides he had cut the day before on teenage piano prodigy Phineas Newborn Jr., with his father (whose name was pronounced "Fine-us") and younger brother on drums and guitar respectively. Two weeks later he submitted samples by the Gospel Travelers, a spiritual staple on Memphis radio, and Charlie Burse, the grizzled Memphis Jug Band veteran, who, like the Newborns, had been working with Sam in the studio for some time. The number that he recorded now, "Shorty the Barber," was a novelty item offering unmistakable hints of double entendre but for the most part focusing on the life and chores of a barber. It was sung with the same raucous good humor that characterized Burse's jug band work (the Memphis Jug Band had recorded an extensive repertoire of blues with a ragtime and minstrel-show base between 1927 and 1934), and for authenticity Sam went across the street and borrowed a pair of barber shears—there was something about the exuberant spirit of the number that just tickled him. But none of the sides that he sent to the Biharis were quite what he intended—the Newborns too polished, the Gospel Travelers too professional, Charlie Burse a little too old-fashioned—and none of the material was accepted for release. It's hard to say just what his plan was. There was no question that Joe Hill Louis was his premium artist to date, not just in terms of the commercial potential that Sam believed him to possess but because he so completely embodied the aesthetic in which Sam believed: raw, untutored, following not the dictates of form or fashion but its own unpredictable kind of beauty, rough-edged and undefined. Maybe he was simply holding back his best for last—however unlike Sam that might appear to be. Maybe, just for a moment, he had lost his nerve, perhaps he was suffering from a rare spasm of self-doubt and simply submitted the music that he thought most likely to be accepted. But, he was convinced, there was no permanent harm done. Joe Hill

Louis would be the next artist he would present to Modern, and he felt as confident as it was possible to feel when you had had your studio open for nearly seven months and scarcely anything to show for it that, if they got the right song, if he could capture the man in the studio the way he knew he had the potential to come across, Joe Hill Louis just might be the one to do the trick.

In early July Jules Bihari let him know that he and his brother would be coming to Memphis in a couple of weeks to record a promising new prospect they had recently met, a young DJ on the colored station, WDIA, who called himself Bee Bee King—Sam had undoubtedly heard of him. Through the station he had put out a couple of records the previous year on the Bullet label in Nashville—the production manager, Don Kern, had given them copies, and while they weren't really anything to write home about, the boy seemed to have enough local popularity to warrant putting out another record. What they would do, Saul said, was work out a deal with Sam where they could use his studio, maybe for a small fee, or some kind of modest royalty. There was no hesitation on Sam's part. King's blues were not exactly what he had in mind to record—they were too conventional, too *predictable,* too much along the lines of what every other popular blues shouter of the day was inclined to do. But none of that meant anything. It was a door opening.

In the meantime, though, without any of the buildup or drama that should have been attendant on such a momentous event, Sam had actually had a record come out—on a Los Angeles hillbilly label with whom he had come in contact at just about the time he first wrote to the Biharis. He had met Bill McCall, the hard-driving partner in 4 Star Records, in much the same way that he had first encountered the Bihari brothers, through the good offices of Buster Williams, and McCall offered a deal that would pay him $200 for eight sides. It was a connection for which he didn't have a great deal of expectation, but McCall had not only expressed interest in some blues sides Sam had cut on a gravel-throated boogie-woogie piano player from South Memphis named Lost John Hunter, in very short order he put them out. The record was sandwiched in between 4 Star's hillbilly hits, and McCall had in fact expressed at least as much interest in Sam recording some of Memphis' local hillbilly talent. But Sam was still barely able to mask his excitement when he wrote to his old friend Gene Nobles at WLAC on June 10 with an announcement of the record's upcoming release.

"Under separate cover," he wrote, "I am sending you a '4 Star' copy of two selections by LOST JOHN HUNTER AND HIS BLIND BATS."

> "Schoolboy" is really going here in Memphis and I know you can get it rolling over that way if only you will give it the works on your race shows.
>
> Lost John is a local blind negro and will be more than grateful for any and all plugs. I sent an audition of him to 4 Star and they quickly waxed him and although I am completely out of the deal after making the masters on him, I surely would like to see him go . . . . We will appreciate any plays any time.
>
> Regards to . . . any of the rest of the gang that might happen to remember my puss.

Lost John Hunter, not surprisingly, did not bear out Sam's optimistic sales projections, and Sam went on to dutifully record not only popular hillbilly radio personality Slim Rhodes, who had long-standing early-morning and midday shows on WMC, but his business partner, Buck Turner, as well. 4 Star eventually put out four singles on Slim, but even if they had sold well, Sam still would have had little enthusiasm for the project. From his point of view, both Slim and Buck had loyal followings in the mid-South and "good solid local combos [but] I never did see anything particular about either Buck or Slim's band that stood out, as far as style." With a conventional commercial artist like Slim Rhodes, or Buck, for that matter, the nature of whose business was to remain conversant with all the latest trends, he knew he could never dig as deep as he wanted to — as much as he loved pure country music, "I had to realize that recording straight country was a buffer until I could work out what I really wanted to do."

The Bihari brothers came to town toward the end of July, and after all his long-distance communication, when he finally met them in person Sam was duly impressed. Jules, thirty-six years old, was the head of the operation, a tough customer, as Sam immediately recognized, a shrewd man who measured his words carefully but was, in Sam's judgment, most likely a fair man. Saul, thirty-two, was clearly the "outside man," the salesman, just as well-dressed as his brother but nicer-looking. "Saul seemed like one of the nicest people I'd ever met. Jules looked okay—and he probably *was* all right—but Saul, I would have believed just about anything he said."

As promised, they brought in Riley King, the personable twenty-four-year-old DJ, whose popularity on the radio, where he played music with his own combo and spun records, allowed him to find work five or six nights a week in every little cotton-patch joint and roadhouse operation within a hundred-mile radius of Memphis. He had started out as the Pep-ti-kon Boy on WDIA about a year and a half ago, going out on weekends on a flatbed truck to promote its owners' new blood-building tonic. But he had quickly become more broadly identified by a less product-oriented label, first as the Singing Black Boy, then as the Singing Blues Boy, then as the Boy from Beale Street, until, finally, he was recognized simply as Bee Bee — transmitted to the world at large on his records as "B.B."—King.

Sam liked him immediately. Motherless at nine, on his own from the age of fourteen, when his grandmother died, he was the product of a lonely, isolated childhood, mostly around Kilmichael in the hill country of Mississippi, which only served to accentuate a sensitive, insecure nature. Be kind to others, his mother had told him on her deathbed, and his kindness would never fail to be repaid — if he gave love unasked, it would come back to him many times over — and that was the credo which he continued to articulate throughout his life.

His shyness, his slight stammer set him apart from many of the other bluesmen Sam had met, but it was his wounded air that drew Sam to him most. To others this might come across simply as a pleasant, deferential manner. The *Tri-State Defender,* which would become Memphis' second black newspaper the following year, would describe him not long after its founding as "quiet-spoken" and "unassuming," with his sincerity serving as his calling card. But clearly that sincerity masked a burning ambition, a need to have not just Memphis and Mississippi but the world know of him. For Sam, who knew nothing of his background at the time, it was that hunger, that marked insecurity, which suggested his potential — it was that sense of wanting something so badly you couldn't fully express it that truly captured Sam's interest.

As a musician, though, he was distinctly limited. It was obvious that his primary influence was T-Bone Walker's cool, jazz-inflected style, with the elegant shape of his single-string guitar solos set off by

sophisticated seventh- and ninth-chord progressions. It was a style with which Sam was thoroughly familiar and one to which he was not particularly drawn, as much as anything because of its element of careful calculation—but he still saw B.B. as retaining some of that wonderful old Mississippi feel, and, as it turned out, B.B. couldn't really play in the more modern style anyway. For one thing, he couldn't always execute the pretty chords that he was aiming for. For another, his timing, which in T-Bone's case was the rock-solid basis for his blues, was erratic. But most surprising of all, he couldn't sing and play at the same time. Sam thought at first he was kidding, but B.B. assured him he was not—he had tried, and he simply could not. It had to be, Sam assumed, some kind of mental block.

It was in any case his singing at this point that was the central feature of his music. You couldn't miss the church in his voice, the influence of the sanctified tradition in which he had started out singing and playing. His uncle had married a sister of the preacher in a Pentecostal church near Kilmichael, and it was that preacher, Archie Fair, who played the first electric guitar B.B. had ever seen and who gave him his first rudimentary lessons. He strummed his own cherry-red Stella behind the gospel group he formed with his cousin Birkett Davis and then, later, after his cousin moved to the Delta with his family and he joined them there, put together another group in Indianola.

The Famous St. John Gospel Singers were modeled after the Golden Gate Quartet, whose enormous success not just on record but through regular CBS-network radio exposure inspired a generation of gospel groups to dream of pop stardom. It was only after he realized that his fellow members of the Famous St. John Gospel Singers didn't share that dream—and, not entirely coincidentally, after he wrecked his boss's tractor—that twenty-year-old Riley King set out for Memphis on his own in the spring of 1946. He had started playing some blues by then, mostly on the streets in the little towns around Indianola on market day, where he discovered that if you sang a spiritual number you got a pat on the back, but if you played a blues song, even the preacher might throw a little change in your hat. So leaving his wife of little more than a year behind, he hitched a ride on a grocery transfer truck, helping the driver unload produce all the way to Memphis, where he was determined to

Riley King. *Courtesy Delicia Davis Collection © 2008 B.B. King Museum* find his cousin, the famous blues singer Booker T. Washington ("Bukka") White.

He stayed in Memphis that first time something like ten months — his cousin got him a job and showed him the ropes, introducing him to older bluesmen like Frank Stokes and Jack Kelly, taking him out on weekends to the joints where Booker would play, even allowing Riley to second him occasionally. Booker was his mother's first cousin, and on all his visits to Kilmichael when Riley was growing up, he would show up "looking like a million bucks. Razor sharp. Big hat, clean shirt, pressed pants, shiny shoes. He smelled of the big city and glamorous times; he looked confident and talked about things outside our little life in the hills." It was a vision not just of another life but of another personality, outsized, uncontained, sure enough of himself that even when he went to prison briefly for killing a man he remained undiminished by the inequities of the world.

As B.B. later wrote, "He could have been a con man — but he wasn't." He was instead one of the great bluesmen in the Mississippi tradition, the creator of a unique body of work that told his own personal story, not just in terms of vividly portrayed external events but in relation to a state of mind that was often referenced but rarely delineated in traditional blues. ("When a man gets troubled in mind, he feels like sleeping all the time," he sang in one of his more famous songs.) He was in addition a brilliant slide guitarist, using a sawed-off bottleneck or a metal ring to slide up and down the frets and mimic the sound of the human voice. This was how B.B. himself would have liked to sound, but for some reason he was never able to master the slide (he always claimed he lacked the necessary dexterity, but perhaps it was more a matter of avoiding the inevitable comparisons). Instead he picked up on the brand-new sound of T-Bone Walker, whose "Mean Old World" and "I'm Still in Love With You" and even "T-Bone Boogie" perfectly captured the essence of what he wanted to achieve, something both technical ("he seemed to measure each pick precisely . . . [his tone] was not blurred, it was a good clean tone") and soulful, mellow, and swinging at the same time.

It was, as he came to see it, the ability "to connect my guitar to human emotions" that he most wanted to get at, and if he couldn't get it from playing slide, then an electric guitar with its ability to sustain notes ("By trilling my hand, I could achieve something that approximated a vocal vibrato") was the next best thing. With his cousin's help he got a little black F-hole Gibson, an acoustic guitar, with a DeArmond pickup and a little Gibson amp with a lot of treble, and that was the guitar he carried with him when he returned to Memphis a second time in 1948, wrapping it in newspaper to protect it against the driving rain as he made the long walk out from the bus stop to seek a job at WDIA some nineteen months before his first session with Sam.

B.B. came into the studio with his own little trio, and Sam was more than satisfied with the quality of the musicianship — it was the music itself that betrayed the singer's lack of a style of his own. The four numbers that they worked on were an inoffensive boogie, a slow paced, full-voiced version of an old Leroy Carr standard, a polite Charles Brown-styled blues with a shared piano-guitar lead, and a variation on Tampa Red's recent remake of his slide guitar classic, "It Hurts Me Too." B.B. was unquestionably sincere, he projected a kind of earnestness that was unusual in and of itself, and his vocals were strong enough, Sam realized, to fill in the spaces where the guitar dropped out — but, for all of the undeniable gospel feeling in his voice, he was almost too eager to please, unwilling at this point to extend himself into the realm of the unexpected, no matter what gentle cues Sam might give him.

The Bihari brothers seemed delighted in any case, so much so, as Sam recalled, that Jules jumped on an airplane that night and flew back to L.A. with the acetates because, he said, he wanted to rush a single out on their new label right away. Saul was supposed to bring B.B. to the studio the next day so they could all sign an agreement under which B.B. would be contracted to the Biharis' record company but Sam would have a side agreement, a kind of royalty override with some say in the artist's future disposition. But Saul showed up alone at the studio and said he had been out to B.B's house the night before and signed him to a standard union contract and Jules would be in touch from California to make a formal deal with Sam.

That was not the way they had left it, Sam protested vehemently — as he understood it, they had a firm "shake-hands" deal. But no matter how much he expostulated, Saul simply demurred in his charming way — after all, he was just the minority stockholder younger brother — and in the end Sam comforted himself with Saul's assurances that this was only the beginning of a long and profitable relationship.

WITHIN DAYS he had Joe Hill Louis in the studio to record a couple of tracks for what he was sure, with his new relationship with them, the Bihari boys would not be able to resist. As it turned out, he got just what he was looking for. "Gotta Let You Go" was straight out of John Lee Hooker, with its irresistible boogie drive but with a raucous country tone all its own. "Let's go. Hey, Caldonia," Joe shouted out with unrestrained ebullience almost before the needle hit the groove, then launched into a long, misogynistic one-chord monologue about a woman for whom he had done everything but who now just hung around beer gardens and hadn't had her hair fixed in seven years, before finally finding resolution, harmonic and otherwise, in a chorus that finally declared "I don't love you no more / I gotta let you go." "Boogie in the Park" was equally exuberant, this time in celebration of conjugal love, whether in the park or anywhere else, with the same driving overamped guitar and wheezy out-of-tune harmonica pushing the recording to the edge of distortion and sometimes beyond. The power of the music seemed to Sam irrefutable, the hypnotic combination of a singer working himself into a virtual trance and a sound — crude, raw, perfect in its very imperfection — that could not be denied. He mailed it to the Biharis on July 27 with as much certainty as he had ever felt in his life.

What happened next is almost impossible to fully decipher — but the result was crystal clear. Within days of his sending out the acetate, he heard back from Jules Bihari, but at this point, whether Jules liked the record or not was no longer the issue. What about their deal on B.B. King? was Sam's first question. They still needed to work something out. That was when Jules told him, with a cold, cutting chill in his voice, that there was no deal. They would send him the money for the studio time, they might even pay a little more. Well, wait just one damn minute, Sam cut in. That wasn't what they had agreed upon. "I mean, I was *hot*, there was some kind of cussing going on, let me tell you. I said, 'Here, here, man, wait a minute, maybe that's the way you do things in California, but that ain't the way we do business in Tennessee.' But there wasn't a damn thing I could do about it. I didn't have a signed anything with them. We had an *understanding*."

He recalled the sides from Jules and Saul on August 7. On August 8 he started writing to song publishers to clear the rights to various compositions for "my recording company, 'PHILLIPS,' which is a new label but will be one of the most publicized regional labels to hit the market."

And on August 21 he proudly sent off that imprint's first release, the two Joe Hill Louis sides that he had gotten back from Modern just two weeks earlier, with a label that declared:

IT'S THE
PHILLIPS
"HOTTEST THING IN THE COUNTRY"

As he wrote to Jimmy Connolly, getting this new venture under way was keeping him busy night and day, but he hoped to get down to Bessemer before too long "to give you the story on the deal." Just to put it in capsule form, though, he declared to Jimmy, with that same brash insouciance that he adopted both to mask insecurity and to throw up roadblocks to anyone trying to read his true feelings, "Dewey Phillips and I are partners 50-50 on our new label, and we're going to do our best to make it roll in the South. . . .

We're going to put nothing but the best race and spiritual artists obtainable on our label, and though we may not have the same number of artists that other labels have, we're going to do our durndest to have the BEST. I'd appreciate your signing on the station and signing it off with our records from time to time. In fact, I think it would make a good substitute for the STAR SPANGLED BANNER.

It was almost inconceivable — it went against all of his better instincts, against everything he ever said, whether at the time or looking back on the period: that he didn't want his own label, that he had neither the time, money, nor resources for such an enterprise, that he intended to confine himself to the creative end of the business exclusively. And to do so in such a brief space of time, with so little forethought given to the decision, contradicted virtually every impulse of his normal course of behavior. In later years he would say it was all for his friend and partner, a more freethinking and freewheeling soul ("It was to please Dewey, really. I mean I didn't . . . I didn't want it," he told me one time), but I think even Sam would have been hard-pressed to deny that it was a decision fueled almost exclusively by rage.

Dewey, it was true, had no doubt that they would succeed. And, within the few days that he allowed himself to reflect on the matter,

Sam may well have come to agree, convincing himself up to a point that with Dewey on the record, as well as Bob Umbach on Jimmy's station and Gene Nobles on WLAC, they really did stand a fighting chance. "I have the three outstanding race disc jockeys in the South behind my company," he wrote to Howie Richmond of the Cromwell Music publishing company in New York, no doubt to persuade himself as much as Richmond, "and we will see to it that no record is played any more than the 'PHILLIPS' label in this territory."

He also had the active support, both material and spiritual, of Buster Williams, whose Plastic Products pressing plant was turning out close to six thousand records a day after less than a year of operation. The forty-one-year-old Williams, the man who had introduced Sam to the Biharis, was just one more in a proud line of Memphis wildcatters and entrepreneurs. He had started out at fourteen with a roasted-peanuts operation in Enterprise, Mississippi, then bought his own drugstore at sixteen and invested the profits in what would soon become one of the largest jukebox operations in the South. After serving with the 4th Ferrying Group during the war (he trained the pilots who flew the vital Lend-Lease and matériel resupply missions), he had returned to find his jukebox business thriving. He established a distributorship, Music Sales, primarily to service his jukebox business with the latest records, and then, primarily to service *that,* had designed his own pressing machines and gone into business as only the second (by a few months) independent pressing plant in the country. Like Sam and so many other "new arrivals" in the city, Buster Williams believed in all things Memphis, but most of all he believed in the independent spirit, and he encouraged Sam from the start, extending him credit on pressing costs and then covering his risk by placing an order for three hundred copies of the record through Music Sales.

Only Marion seemed to have reservations about this new, hastily conceived enterprise. As someone who spent all of her waking hours trying to keep Sam from being upset, she never ceased to worry about his nervous temperament. And, whether for reasons of jealousy or class, or just plain personal taste, she simply did not like Dewey ("It was just something in his crude, crass upbringing—I couldn't even stand to listen to him"). Nor did she trust him—she thought Sam was putting entirely too much faith in someone whose manic energy and violent mood swings indicated an unstable nature of his own. But she recognized the depths of her own resentment (the two of them, from her point of view, went around acting like two little boys who had sworn a blood oath — "at least that's the way Sam felt about Dewey"), and she had no doubt that anything Dewey wanted from Sam he was going to get. So she kept her own counsel and said nothing about the new business. Sam wouldn't have listened to her anyway.

His ambition for the label swiftly grew. He intended to follow up the first Joe Hill Louis record with the novelty number, "Shorty the Barber," that he had recorded on Charlie Burse earlier that summer. In addition he planned to record "a negro quartet that is far superior to the Jubalaires or the Four Knights" performing "Jezebel," a Golden Gate Quartet classic, "like nobody's ever done it before!" Finally, in what I think can only be taken as either a gesture of gratitude or momentary euphoria, he announced his intention to cut a sprightly pop blues called "Your Red Wagon" (which had not too long ago been a hit for the Andrews Sisters) on his business partner, Buck Turner, who, he wrote to the performing rights society ASCAP, "has a knocked-out version of the tune [that] we feel certain . . . will sell."

And then as quickly as it started, it was over. The whole enterprise came crashing down, and Sam's mood with it. To begin with, he seems to have been forced to the realization that Joe Hill Louis, whom he had characterized just a week or two earlier to Jimmy Connolly as "an ex Columbia recording artist," was in fact still on the label, a circumstance made evident by the appearance of his second Columbia single at almost the exact moment of the launching of The Phillips.

Then, in the early morning hours of September 3, Dewey had a terrible head-on collision on Highway 70 just outside of West Memphis that killed both the driver of the other car and Dewey's companion, a nineteen-year-old girl who had moved to Memphis from Booneville, Mississippi, just six weeks earlier and was living at the Hotel Chisca with her aunt. Everyone put a brave face on it. Dewey's wife, Dot, said the girl was a friend of hers, and the station announced that though Dewey remained on the critical list, he would soon be broadcasting from his hospital bed at Baptist Hospital. Sam's faith in Dewey never faltered, but his faith in their joint enterprise may have, even as he comforted Dot, whom Becky, too, had by now befriended. It must have hit him all at once what in reality he had known all along — just how little he knew about what it took to run a record company and how much this was diverting him from his main task.

Such was the ignominious end of their record company. There was no formal conclusion, and Music Sales, and a few other independent outlets, may have continued selling the Joe Hill Louis record for another few months. But there never was a second, from Joe or anyone else, and the whole business left such an unpleasant taste that Sam rarely referred to it in later life, and when he did, he uncharacteristically (for he was a man with an almost photographic memory) seemed unable to recall any of the details.

Nor were matters helped any by the growing tension at the radio station, the increasing conflict on both Sam's and Marion's part between their dedication to the recording studio and their commitment to their salaried work. For Marion it was as much a matter of guilty conscience as anything else. At WREC "they would say to me, 'How can you even work out there? I don't know what you're doing there.' I was beginning to shortchange the station, sliding in at the last minute and doing a show that wasn't prepared properly, but they never seemed to notice, they were so overcome with wonderment that I was able to transition from what they knew of me and my background [into this environment]."

For Sam it was harder. "Everybody laughed at me. Of course, they'd try to make it tongue-in-cheek, talking about my recording niggers (and these were some of the greatest friends in the world). They'd say, 'Well, you smell okay, Sam. I guess you haven't been hanging around those niggers today.' I mean, they loved me to death. I think there was even a certain amount of admiration on [their] part that nobody really wanted to admit. Nobody can tell me that the white man wasn't a little ashamed of how he was treating the black man. There was a kind of love on the part of the Southern white person for his nigger. But at the same time it would get up to a certain point, and you as a white man didn't take your nigger any further."

It hurt. It hurt deeply. But it hurt almost as much to have had his naïveté so badly abused, to have risked his family's security and his own peace of mind for a foolish, unexamined whim, prompted mostly by the desire to vindicate himself not just in the eyes of others but in his own. Marion could see the burden of humiliation he carried around with him — at one point he broke out in a terrible case of hives — but he never wavered in his belief in the rightness of what he was doing. He never wavered in his firm conviction that the music he was seeking to record was great music, the artists whom he sought out, great artists, as great as any who had ever been heard. Where his belief momentarily wavered was in his own ability, whether he had the sheer stamina to carry on the crusade. Or the judgment.

The second Lost John Hunter single came out on 4 Star at the beginning of September and caused no more of a stir than the first. Two of the B.B. King sides appeared at the end of the month among the inaugural releases of the Biharis' new RPM label, with the legend "Singing Star of Station WDIA Memphis" printed below the newly initialed name. They didn't do much better than Lost John Hunter and His Blind Bats, with *Billboard* according one side a grade of 66, the other a 71. "High-pitched warbler does okay on jump boogie blues," the reviewer wrote of "B.B. Boogie," "in a Basie-type ork setting." The single didn't sell much anywhere outside Memphis, and the second single, released in December, didn't really do any better.

By then, though, Sam had finally decided to eat humble pie. It was with very mixed feelings that he got back in touch with the Biharis about Joe Hill Louis at the end of October, but he had nowhere else to go. Joe's one-year contract with Columbia had finally run out — Sam had seen it in writing — and he negotiated a modest new contract with Modern, signing off on it on November 24 and taking Joe into the studio three days later. He mailed off the results, including a more refined version of "Boogie in the Park" with Joe's discommodious traps weighing down the proceedings, on December 8, and sent another four sides a little later. But nothing happened. He recorded six more titles on B.B. King at the beginning of January, nothing he considered particularly outstanding, but the Biharis appeared to be satisfied, and it resulted in another release a couple of months later. The two sides chosen for the single each provided a different glimpse of the singer's potential, with the first, "My Baby's Gone," stamped by a makeshift rhumba beat that, just two years later, would become the basis for "Woke Up This Morning," one of his most enduring hits. The second, "Don't You Want a Man Like Me," offered a slow crooned vocal that never quite caught fire and, like the first, seemed in the end curiously unfinished. To Sam it was B.B.'s DJ background as much as anything else, his professional affability coupled with an almost desperate personal desire to please, that stood as the chief impediment to his breaking free of the traces of conformity and convention. But he didn't sense from their reaction that the Biharis were in any way displeased, they were, after all, just casting about for a hit — so, as a matter of pure pragmatism, he simply decided to look elsewhere, among some of the other equally gifted but less "professional" musicians who came into his studio, for that secret store of talent, that indefinable spirit that lay within the soul of every man, to which he felt that he alone could offer the unlocking key.

According to harmonica player Walter Horton (who had in fact worked with many of the other blues singers that Sam had recorded, including Joe Hill Louis, Jack Kelly, and Charlie Burse, and had recently formed a duo with B.B. King), "I was just walking around one day and decided I'd go up to his studio. Joe Hill [Louis] was playing, and so I stopped in there and played a couple of numbers, and after that [Sam Phillips] wanted me to record for him." As if to bear out this account, Sam immediately dubbed the thirty-three-year-old Horton "Mumbles" as much for his dreamy nature as his manner of speech, but the instrumental sample that he sent to Modern on January 17 is a masterpiece of sound and tone, mixing a kind of ethereal lyricism with a focused attack—and while Horton's melodies may have derived from familiar tunes, in everything else his playing represented just what Sam was looking for, a free-flowing feel that had its origins solely in the artist's imagination.

Two weeks later Sam sent the Biharis sample dubs on another artist in whom he had a strong belief, a piano player with a quirky, almost childlike sense of his own inimitability. Roscoe Gordon was twenty-two years old and had grown up on Florida Street in South Memphis, not too far from Beale, where, he liked to say, he had gotten his education. As a teenager he won the Amateur Night contest at the Palace Theater, and he picked up coaching on his piano playing from Billy "Red" Love, another young Beale Streeter, whom Roscoe, a heavy drinker himself from his teen years, described affectionately as a "winehead" but who could play virtually every style of piano, past, present, and future, with effortless ease.

From the moment he entered the studio, Sam liked him. He was a funny little guy with nothing polished about him. He had a long expressive face and an infectious enthusiasm, and he played piano with an amateurishness that belied Billy "Red" Love's teaching. His music in fact conveyed an almost fey whimsicality, driven by a distinctive rhythmic approach—a kind of lilting, loping beat built on a rudimentary boogie-woogie base.

"Roscoe was one of my favorite people. He would always come in by himself and sit down and play the piano [in this] very different way, and I thought, Well, you know, maybe we can just make a band out of this thing—we might not need any rhythm other than the way he plays this

The Roscoe Gordon Orchestra, with Billy "Red" Love on piano.
Courtesy of Richard Weize, Bear Family Records

piano." Even so, there was little question he needed a lot of work, and Sam had no idea how the Biharis would react to him — he didn't really give a damn how they reacted to him, so long as they didn't steal Roscoe from him — the main thing was, he didn't want Roscoe to change, he didn't want him to go off and try to imitate someone else, he believed in him just as he was, and he did everything in his power to convince Roscoe of that, too.

"Sam said, 'What you're playing, nobody in the world is going to play that but you.' Said, 'I don't know what it is. It's not blues, it's not pop, it's not rock. So we gonna call it "Roscoe's Rhythm."' That's what he called it. That's where that came from."

Over the course of the next month Sam worked out a deal with the Biharis for both of his new artists, and on March 1 he sent sides by both Gordon and Horton with some assurance, he felt, that the Biharis would pick out at least one single by each for release. About three weeks earlier they had finally put out the first Joe Hill Louis single, "I Feel Like a Million" and "Heartache Baby," but from Sam's point of view it hardly made up for the way they had treated him previously. From his perspective, one release over a period of six months did not exactly constitute a binding marriage. The Bihari boys might think they were the only game in town, but he'd be damned if he'd be yoked to those pissants for life. So when he met Leonard Chess, who just happened to show up in town on a Southern promotion swing the very day that Sam sent off his new sides to the Biharis, Sam listened carefully to what Chess had to say.

Leonard Chess was a tough-talking hustler from Chicago with a record company that he ran with his younger brother, Phil. Not quite thirty-four years old but looking older, with thinning hair and a gaunt, wiry body, he and his brother had arrived from Poland at eleven and seven, five years after their father had established a junk business in Bronzeville, on Chicago's teeming South Side. He had gotten into the record business in 1947 after running a tavern on the 3900 block of Cottage Grove Avenue and realizing that the live entertainment that he was presenting was in many cases as good as the records that he had on the jukebox. After buying out his original partners, at Buster Williams' suggestion he changed the name of the company from Aristocrat to Chess in June of 1950 (Buster said the new name, an Ellis Island simplification of the real family name, was short, sharp, and direct, and everyone knew the game of chess), and his first two releases were modest hits. The first, by jazz saxophonist Gene Ammons, was by far the bigger seller, but the second set the trend. "Rollin' Stone," by Mississippi-born blues singer Muddy Waters, was very much in the vanguard of the new down-home blues market, a trend that had in effect begun with the astounding success of John Lee Hooker's "Boogie Chillen" on the Modern label just one year earlier. When his tavern burned down in the fall of 1950, Leonard received a much-needed infusion of capital from the insurance, and the new label was enjoying its first big blues hit with Muddy Waters' "Louisiana Blues," which, in contrast to Hooker's improbable million-seller, was unlikely to sell more than twenty-five or thirty thousand copies. Leonard, in fact, was in town to promote that record and Muddy's upcoming release, "Long Distance Call," when Sam met him for the first time over at Dewey's show.

Sam could sense from the start that Leonard was different from the Biharis. For one thing, with a new company just struggling to get under way, he was hungrier. For another, he was less smooth, less sure of himself. But like them, he was a smart street hustler, driven, intense, and like Dewey he spoke the language of his artists informally and without affectation ("Hey, motherfucker" could be the easygoing greeting of either one, but then Leonard might lapse into Yiddish if he was in the company of a *landsman*).

"I kind of liked Leonard—he didn't really have very much money at the time, but he'd heard about my studio, and he came by, and we talked, and he said, 'Man, I'd give anything to work with you.'" And then, right on the spot, he proposed a deal—they'd split the profits 50-50 on any recording of Sam's that he released, so long as he had the right of first refusal. "And the first thing I gave him was 'Rocket 88.'"

"Rocket 88," an original number by a young group out of Clarksdale called the Kings of Rhythm, was a song that came to Sam indirectly through his association with B.B. King. B.B. had met the kid who led the group, nineteen-year-old Ike Turner, a few years earlier, when B.B. was still Riley King, still living in Indianola, Mississippi, with his wife, Martha. He was playing a little theater in Clarksdale, and this kid had a full-scale *band*, the Top Hatters, and asked if he could sit in on piano. As young as he was, he had obviously gone to school on boogie-woogie—he had both energy and imagination to burn—and at his invitation Riley stayed with him for a night or two at his mother's house. Just two years later, unbeknownst to Turner, Riley was making records, and the Top Hatters had split into two groups, the uptown Dukes of Swing, who could all read music and played the kind of swing that Sam broadcast from the Skyway, and the Kings of Rhythm, a small Louis Jordan-type of jump combo—tenor and baritone sax, plus a three-man rhythm section—that specialized in just wrecking the joint. They were coming back from a gig in Greenville when Ike saw all these cars parked by the side of the road at a big roadhouse outside Chambers, Mississippi, with a sign that announced that B.B. King was playing there tonight.

Ike had seen the posters on telegraph poles all over Mississippi, he said, with that same "peculiar name" on it, but for some reason he had never attached it to the man he knew as Riley King. When he walked into the roadhouse, "it was B.B., man, and we asked him, Could we play a song? He said, Yeah, and, boy, we tore the house down. So he said, 'Man, you guys need to be recording.' And we said, 'Well, what do you *do* to record? How do you do it?' He said, 'Well, man, this guy in Memphis has a studio, that's where I record.' He said, 'His name is Sam Phillips, and what I'm gonna do, I'm gonna tell him to give you a call, man, on Monday [for] you guys to come up and record.' I said, 'Just like that?' He said, 'Yeah.' And sure enough, Monday Sam Phillips called. He wanted to know how soon could we come up. I told him, 'Right now.' And we had no idea—*none*—what we were gonna do when we got there."

The drive to Memphis was not without incident. Everyone was in great good humor when they first set out in the pouring rain, all five crowded into a little sedan with their saxes, guitar, and drum set, and the trunk secured with a rope to accommodate the guitar amp and bass drum. Neither the weather nor the close quarters could dampen their enthusiasm, and they couldn't stop talking about what they were going to do when they got to Memphis. There was drummer Willie "Bad Boy" Sims and guitarist Willie Kizart, from Tutwiler, whose father, Lee, was a well-known local guitarist and piano player. Baritone player Jackie Brenston was the big talker in the group. He had run into Ike on the street just after getting out of the army, when Ike was putting the band together. He barely knew how to play the sax then, but Ike patiently schooled him, and he had very recently taken over most of the vocals, after Johnny O'Neal, known as "Scarface Brother" for the livid scar across his chin, left just a few weeks earlier to make records on his own. Sixteen-year-old Raymond "Bear" (for both his physique and his boxing ability) Hill, the lead tenor player, was probably the best-educated musician in the group, and certainly the most affluent—his father owned several clubs and roadhouses in the area, a café, and a service station, and his grandfather, who was Chinese (Ike alternately called Raymond "Chink" and "Hockway," which he insisted was "nigger" in Chinese), had started the Wong Grocery Store, which his mother now ran.

They were relatively unfazed when they got stopped by the highway patrol and hauled into some little country court. It was just another case of "too many little niggers in the car," they joked after they paid the fine—they were more frustrated when they subsequently had a flat tire and then went and dropped the guitar amp on the pavement in their hurry to dig out the spare. But they quickly returned to their rapid-fire banter, a combination of nervousness, anticipation, boastfulness, and verbal competition entered into freely on all sides, except when their twenty-year-old leader Ike's glowering stare stopped one of them in their tracks.

When they got to Memphis, naturally they drove down Beale, past all the clubs and pawnshops and the New Palace and the Hippodrome skating rink, which had just started to bring in all the big-name r&b acts. Then, going out Union, they couldn't find the studio — they must have driven by it three or four times at least, because they were looking for something. . . . Well, they didn't know what they were looking for. None of them had ever seen a recording studio before, but they thought it had to be something to match their dreams. Instead it turned out to be this sorry-ass storefront that looked more like a barbershop than anything else, with one of those neon signs in the window — but when they went in to ask the lady at the desk if she knew where the studio was, she told them this was it.

Sam recognized right away that the speaker cone was blown. As soon as guitarist Willie Kizart plugged in, it made a horrible sound, and everyone was crestfallen, wondering how on earth they were going to fix it or get another at short notice. But Sam pricked up his ears right away, it would sound like another sax, he told them, it would sound *different,* and he went into the restaurant next door to get some brown paper to wad up inside it. Ike didn't know quite what to make of this neatly dressed, decisive "little young white guy" who addressed them respectfully but didn't seem to have any special expertise of his own. "I just thought he was one of these smart dudes that had all this equipment. I had no expectations, man — all I could picture was B.B.'s picture being tacked up on the posters. That's the next thing I was gonna be."

Things came into sharper focus once they got to work. Sam asked them what material they had, and Ike sang a couple of originals that didn't excite him all that much, but then he asked if they had anything else, and Ike said, Yeah, they had this song, "Rocket 88," that they'd been working on — it wasn't fully rhymed up, but it got a pretty good reaction whenever they did it. They ran through it a couple of times with Ike singing, it was an almost literal take-off on Jimmy Liggins' 1948 hit "Cadillac Boogie," with the words changed a little and the beat updated, and Marion wrote down the lyrics as they played with the rocket-ship idea suggested by the new Oldsmobile model. There was something about the sound of it that Sam responded to from the first; it was different from any of the other songs they had done, but the vocal didn't have anywhere near the impact of the driving combination of horns, piano, and "fuzz-tone" guitar. Eschewing diplomacy, he asked Ike if there was anyone else in the band who could sing. He recognized that he might be on thin ice with this volatile young man who couldn't always control his temper with the other musicians ("That was just his way of getting out of them what he wanted to hear"), but he didn't really see any alternative, and, after a visible effort at self-restraint, Ike narrowed his eyes and allowed that Jackie Brenston did some vocals, too. Which was ironic, the other members of the band must have thought, because it was, after all, Jackie's song.

They could have nailed it on the first take, except that Jackie was, understandably, a little overwhelmed. The band had it from the very first notes, though, with Ike standing at the little Wurlitzer, pounding away at the keys, all the while directing everybody else in their parts — he was so full of energy and enthusiasm Sam thought he might just jump out of his skin. But it was the "rubbing" sound between the saxophone and the distorted guitar that for Sam gave the song its mark, "it was a combination I had never heard before, and it got my ear right off, even before Jackie Brenston opened his mouth." The effect was almost instantaneous, with the fuzz-tone taking the bass part, the horns riffing in unison, and Ike's storming piano cutting through the churning mix — it was like making an all-out assault on a rhythmic wall. To the end of his life Sam refused to even try to explain it. It was magic, it was alchemy, it was *modernity*. ("Rocket 88 was the hottest thing that General Motors had. It had not been on the market very long and everybody in the world, especially younger people, wanted a Rocket 88. Rocket — anything with a rocket in it — means that it's automatically moving!") Most of all, though, it was the mystery of sound, the freshness of an idea that was entering the world for the very first time.

And it was something that he believed could reach anybody, young or old, and — for all of what he chose to call its undeniable "authenticity" — both black and white. It wasn't a pop sound, but it was a pop feel, from its choice of subject to its energy and imagery. "Just listen to that record," Sam would say fifty years later with a mix of elation, wonder, and unabated pride. "I mean, it had [such] a contagious feel, it had a sound like you had not heard before."

"AS PER OUR TELEPHONE CONVERSATION," he wrote to Jimmy Connolly on March 11, just four days after making the recording, "I am enclosing herewith a copy of the letter to ['Atomic Boogie' DJ Bob] Umbach about the sensational new record, 'ROCKET 88' which is going to make my first million for me. Seriously, Jimmy, this is one of the best race records I have ever heard, and I think you'll agree with me when you hear it."

He was in the process of formalizing an "iron-clad" agreement with Leonard Chess and getting a letter of "consent and confirmation" from Jackie Brenston's mother on behalf of her not-yet-twenty-one-year-old son—he was determined this time not to be taken advantage of. When the record came out, though, it caused considerable consternation among the musicians once they saw the label credit.

They had all assumed it would say something like The Kings of Rhythm, Vocal by Jackie Brenston—Ike had never doubted it would say Ike Turner and His Kings of Rhythm, just like it should have—but, instead, the label copy read "Jackie Brenston and his Delta Cats," a name nobody had ever heard before. "I was kinda teed about it," said Ike, who saw it as a clear betrayal, but when he raised the point with Sam, the skinny, strangely intense little white guy wouldn't back down, he insisted it was because they were going to put out a release on Ike, too, and it wouldn't look right to put out two releases under the same name.

In any case, by the end of the month the record had taken off beyond anyone's expectations. "Rocket Becomes Flying Disc, Spins Toward Record Glory" was the headline in the front-page story in the *Commercial Appeal* on March 28, 1951, which not only celebrated the record's sales but trumpeted the accomplishments of the hitherto unknown and unsung Sam C. Phillips, the young "recorder behind the Rocket," a recording engineer and talent scout who had "agreements with two record companies to locate and record hillbilly and 'race' music." Sam, wrote reporter Lydel Sims, "is convinced the Rocket will move out of the race field into general popularity. He says Jackie will get 3½ percent of the retail record sales, plus whatever his contract calls for on the sheet music. Jackie, when I talked to him about it, said that if he makes enough out of it he's going to buy one of those cars."

Sam sent a copy of the story to Gene Nobles the day it came out, along with his sincere thanks to "fellows like you" and Bob Umbach and Dewey Phillips and pioneering black DJ Al Benson in Chicago, not just for playing the record but for believing in it. He also enclosed a new release "by another artist that I have scouted for Leonard." This was the single featuring Ike's two vocals (credited, as promised, to "Ike Turner and His Kings of Rhythm"). It had, in fact, been released virtually simultaneously but—despite Sam's claim to Gene that it was "going good in this territory"—with far less fanfare than "Rocket 88."

The following week, the "Delta Cats" label disappeared altogether

The Kings of Rhythm onstage, W. C. Handy Theatre, April 7 or 8, 1951. *Courtesy of the Sam Phillips Family*

when the band debuted for two nights at the W. C. Handy Theatre in Orange Mound, the neighborhood where B.B. King had first stayed with his cousin Booker White. "First Time in Memphis," the handbill announced, with the kind of staggered layout and alternating script, typeface sizes, and dramatically placed stars that the times favored.

JACKIE BRENSTON
THE TERRIFIC ROCKET "88" SENSATION
WITH
IKE TURNER
"THE KING OF THE PIANO"
AND
"HIS KING[S] OF RHYTHM"
JACKIE IS GONNA TEAR THE HOUSE DOWN

Sam invited Mike McGee, the fill-in music editor for the *Commercial Appeal,* to see the show, sitting up in the balcony with Mike and his wife in the only seating available to whites. Sam had no idea how Mike was going to like the show, but he figured it was worth a shot. "Mike was a man in his midfifties, he was anything but a music connoisseur — he had

FIRST TIME IN MEMPHIS!
W.C. HANDY THEATRE
2 DAYS ONLY - SAT. & SUN. APRIL 7 - 8
ON STAGE! ----- IN PERSON

★ JACKIE BRENSTON ★

THE TERRIFIC ~~ROCKET~~ "88" SENSATION

WITH

IKE TURNER
★ "THE KING OF THE PIANO" ★
AND
★—"HIS KING OF RHYTHM"—★
JACKIE IS GONNA TEAR THE HOUSE DOWN
ADMISSION_____ 60c Tax. Incl.

Handbill, April 1951. *Courtesy of Colin Escott*

been in real estate [at the paper], and I think he went out there with me more or less [out of] curiosity. But Ike and Jackie Brenston put on a helluva show." And so did Rufus and Bones, the comedy team who MCed the weekly amateur show at both the Handy and the Palace theaters. It was a memorable evening in every respect—the house was packed, and people were lined up around the block. But Sam still wasn't sure of Mike's reaction until his story came out the following week.

He had been a little "hazy," McGee confessed to the good people of Memphis, about "just what 'Rocket 88' might be [but] that no longer is true. It is, we must report, like two tomcats meeting on a tin roof.

> Sam Phillips of the Memphis Recording Co., who recorded the number for Chess Records, took us around to the Handy the other night to hear the recording orchestra from Greenwood, Miss., do the number. John Brochstein [more accurately, of course, Jackie Brenston] does an extremely capable job with the vocal but what was impressive was the performance of Ike Turner and His Rhythm Boys, the recording orchestra, also from Greenwood. Folks who have wondered if the Negro race would ever produce another pianist of the Fats Waller caliber can stop wondering. Ike Turner is the hottest piano player in many a day. He's not only all over the keyboard like a blanket over a baby's crib, he's one of the few who attempts it who can really play a piano and tap dance at the same time. In fact he can even get on top of the piano and play the thing upside down.

At the radio station the gibes just kept on coming—in fact, if anything, they came at an even more accelerated pace, now that Sam's secret was out. He continued to send sides to Modern: five by Roscoe Gordon on April 17 (including two cute numbers, "Ouch! Pretty Baby" and "Saddled the Cow [And Milked the Horse]") and five more by Joe Hill Louis two weeks later. It does not seem to have dawned on anyone yet, neither Sam nor the Biharis, for that matter, how the altogether unanticipated success of "Rocket 88" might imperil their relationship.

And then at the beginning of May it all seemed to catch up with Sam. He was working eighteen to twenty hours a day; he was down to 123, 124 pounds, fifteen pounds less than what he normally carried on his slender five-foot-nine-inch frame; and just like in Decatur he could feel the onset of the panic attacks that he had experienced from time to time ever since he was a boy. At what should have been his moment of greatest triumph he simply ran out of physical and emotional steam. Just as before he couldn't turn his mind off, the worries kept whirring and whirring around, and he finally told Becky he couldn't stand it anymore, he needed to be admitted to Gartly-Ramsay Hospital out on Jackson — they were the best psychiatric hospital in the city, he told her, and he thought he needed some more electroshock.

Dr. Dick McCool, director of Electroconvulsive Therapy at Gartly-Ramsay, agreed. But, he told Sam, there was no guarantee of the results. "He was a very frank man, Dr. McCool. I said, 'I really want to know if you think my judgment will be impaired after the shock treatments.' He said, 'I can't tell you, Sam, that it won't.' And he told Becky that I would be real lucky if I came out of it okay." It was a prognosis even more frightening than the one he had been given in Birmingham. To awaken from an etherized sleep and not even recognize the man he saw in the mirror. But he didn't feel like there was any alternative. He couldn't sleep, couldn't eat, as things stood he couldn't carry out his responsibilities to his job or his family. Somehow or other he had to figure out a way to beat this thing — and somehow or other his invincible faith in himself managed to convince him that he would.

He had eight electroshock treatments, one each day, with another five or six days in the hospital to recuperate. Becky would get the children off to school in the morning and then come and stay with him all day. Marion was able to keep the business going and took over some of Sam's duties at the radio station. She had been in a terrible state when Sam first went into the hospital, she had frantically besieged Becky for the initial results — but she was no more surprised than Becky, she had seen it coming all along.

When he went back to work, everybody at the station seemed to treat him like he was just going to fall apart, and Becky confided that Dr. McCool had told her in confidence he really shouldn't be pressed too much at this point, maybe ever. He pored over the therapeutic papers that Dr. McCool had given him, papers with titles like "Therapeutic Relaxation Treatment Procedures," which advocated fifteen minutes of Bibliotherapy followed by half an hour of Educated Therapy and then capped by reciting the expression "Feeling fine" twenty times each day. But it was Dr. McCool's lack of faith that in the end Sam felt was the best therapy of all. Everybody tiptoeing around him like he was some kind of damn invalid only challenged him to find that inner strength he had always possessed, "the strength that says, *Okay, I can do it.*"

The Biharis brought him a rush job almost as soon as he got out of the hospital. For the first time since January, they wanted him to record B.B. King, but this time they focused exclusively on a song that Joe Bihari, the youngest brother, had brought in. It was a brand-new Tampa Red RCA release called "She's Dynamite" that was getting quite a bit of jukebox play in the Atlanta area, but Jake Friedman, the Atlanta distributor, told Joe that RCA wasn't doing much of a job promoting it—perhaps because they had simply lost faith in the man who had been their biggest prewar blues star but, at forty-seven, could not be said to be in the forefront of the latest blues trends.

It was a pleasant enough number, charming in Tampa Red's almost unfailingly charming way, but lacking any kind of real aggressiveness, with a shouted vocal chorus from the band and a kazoo solo from Tampa. B.B.'s version, on the other hand, would mark a sea change in his recorded work. Sam got the Newborn family to come in, Phineas Sr. on drums, Jr. on piano, with sixteen-year-old Calvin playing the T-Bone–styled chords and slashing lead that had been absent from B.B.'s previous sides. There was a honking sax solo, and Phineas Jr.'s storming boogie-woogie piano sounded as if it had been ripped from Ike Turner's less well-educated book. But most of all the song revealed a degree of animation on the singer's part that Sam had never been able to get out of him before, a strident assertiveness that, if in later years "Rocket 88" had not been cited as signaling the birth of rock 'n' roll, might well have established B.B. King as one of the first avatars of the musical future. You can hear him shouting with utter abandon behind the sax solo, then driving home the lyric of the final verse with rhythmic accentuation ("You can whip it/Whop it/Hang it on the wall/Throw it out the window/She'll pitch herself a ball") before launching into the chorus one more time with a satisfied, but by no means quiescent, "Yeahhhh."

At the same time that Sam shipped the master off to California, he sent out dubs to seven DJs, so strong was his and Joe Bihari's belief in its commercial potential. Three days later, on May 30, he cut a one-song session on Joe Hill Louis, this one, too, inspired by a record that was beginning to make a little noise, though in this case the artist himself brought it to him. "'Eyesight to the Blind' [by Sonny Boy Williamson] was a song that was very popular locally, and we really wanted to get a good cut on it." Joe had learned the song from Sonny Boy, whom he knew from his broadcasting experience on both KWEM and WDIA, and Sam for the first time added drums and piano to get the best sound they could on a number that Joe himself acknowledged was a killer in its original version. With this rhythmic underpinning, Joe was able to deliver a "much more focused and upfront vocal," and this, too, was rush-released, although to even less commercial effect than the B.B. single.

Still, Sam felt good, he felt like everything was going pretty much the way it should. From his point of view he had had an illness, and now he was over it — and he didn't expect to go back there ever again. The studio was finally hitting its stride, he hadn't lost any of his outside accounts, and there was no reason to think, after the recordings he had recently delivered to both Leonard Chess and the Biharis, that business at this point shouldn't finally start to pick up. But then, not long after he returned to work at the station, Mr. Wooten called him into his office and suggested that maybe he should take it easy for a while, maybe he should take a little more time off, or slow down, or something. "Now, he didn't accuse me of being [un]stable, and of course, he had the right to call Dick McCool, and I don't think Dr. McCool gave him the greatest prognosis, because the prognosis then was so unscientific. But somehow or another that really hurt me, that this man as bright as he was, as good a man as he was, would attach some sort of a stigma to that [experience]. I was a little bit of a phony for not telling him that he was wrong, I was back on the job doing fine — and I kind of understood, because everybody else back then felt that way. But it really hurt."

It gnawed at him. It gnawed at him for a little more than two weeks, until he couldn't stand it anymore: the looks, the suspicion, the sense that he was just being pitied. He went home and told Becky that he couldn't go on this way, that as hard as he had worked to get where he was, and as much as he loved the work that he did at the station, this wasn't what he wanted to do anymore. Becky told him just to do what he thought was right, they'd be all right. So he quit his job in June of 1951. He was twenty-eight years old, he had a five-year-old and a two-year-old at home, one hit record on the charts, a serious misunderstanding in his first real business relationship, with the Biharis, and an uncertain alliance with his new associates, the Chess brothers. It was hard to say how events would unfold, but he knew one thing: he was not going to fear the future anymore.

"ROCKET 88" hit number 1 on the *Billboard* rhythm and blues charts on June 9 and stayed there well into July. By the end of August it would sell over one hundred thousand copies. In the ads that Chess Records took out in the trade magazines the sky was clearly the limit. "Climbing to the TOP," proclaimed the girl in the bathing suit, who sat astride a crudely drawn version of the same rocket on which a fully clothed, giddily excited young married couple was perched in the original Oldsmobile ad for "a driver's dream come true." But for all of the promise that the "Hottest Little Label in the Country" held out for their sensational new act, the seeds for the band's dissolution were already planted and well under way.

Basically, what it came down to in the view of everyone except the principal figure himself was that Jackie Brenston had gotten the big head. Ike Turner was still seething that Jackie's name had gone on the record when everyone knew it was Ike's band. But it wasn't just Ike, who might have been volatile under the best of circumstances. Raymond Hill, the sixteen-year-old lead saxophonist, was sufficiently irked that he commandeered the band and played gigs around the Delta as Raymond Hill and His Delta Cats, on occasion featuring "Jackie Brimson," while the real Jackie Brenston was out on his own. According to Ike's admittedly imperfect recollection, the only date the original band played together following the record's release was the triumphant Handy Theatre performance in April, and while that may not have been the literal truth, it didn't miss the mark by much. In fact, when Leonard Chess pressed Sam for a follow-up by the band, it proved so impossible to get

The Wolf at radio station KWEM, 1951. *Courtesy of Bill Greensmith*, Blues Unlimited

Jackie and the Kings of Rhythm back in the studio at the same time that, with Leonard's permission, Sam picked out a "Rocket"-styled number written by versatile pianist Billy Love and recorded Billy playing and singing it with an all-star Memphis contingent behind him. He then purchased both song ("Juiced") and performance from its author and gave it to the record company to put out under Jackie's name.

For the first time, Sam felt like his star was truly in the ascendancy. Chess rush-released two more of his recordings in this new hard-driving "swing boogie" style, including a gruff-voiced novelty item by Rufus Thomas, the WDIA DJ who had hosted the Handy Theatre show. The Biharis, too, suddenly seemed more receptive, as he completed an animated B.B. King session, this time showcasing B.B.'s own lead guitar, delivered another unclassifiable number by Roscoe Gordon and sent in sides by eccentric blues drummer Willie Nix and harmonica wizard Walter Horton in the gutbucket blues style that he himself personally favored. Perhaps almost as significant, a western swing outfit from Chester, Pennsylvania, called Bill Haley and the Saddlemen put out a cover version of "Rocket 88," and while Sam didn't think much of Haley's version—it didn't come close in his view to matching the intensity or drive of the original—the very fact of its popularity with a white audience went a long way toward proving a point that he found himself returning to again and again in conversations with Leonard Chess and the Bihari brothers: this music didn't have to be limited to an audience of a certain complexion, this music wasn't restricted to any one segment of the population, this was a music that, by its very nature, potentially had universal appeal.

To protect his business interests, on June 28 he signed both Ike and Jackie to what amounted to personal service contracts and, for the $910 he had advanced Jackie already, obtained ownership of Jackie's hit song. Just how little either Sam or Leonard Chess understood of the music business at this point can be gleaned from the fact that neither one had a publishing company, and Sam never gained anything from his ownership of the song. In fact, unbeknownst to him (and without, so far as I know, any subsequent recognition or complaint on his part), Chess had already given the publishing to its lawyer in exchange for services rendered, and he in turn had sold it to Hill and Range, among the most prominent of the upstart young BMI song publishers who had taken advantage of the boom in "race" and "hillbilly" recordings after the war. The personal services contracts with Ike and Jackie (as well as with the pianist Phineas Newborn Jr. and most likely others, too) were couched in identically optimistic language and painted a rosy future in which Sam would receive 5 percent of each artist's gross income ("including any and all remuneration for personal appearances, stage engagements, recording contracts, etc.") in return for his exclusive guidance, advice, and recording services. Marion witnessed the agreements, and Sam breathed a quiet sigh of relief at having finally figured out how to make an honest living without having to start a record company of his own—which he was determined not to do—in what he had long since found to be a very "dirty" business.

But if this plan could ever have had a chance of working, by now it was too late. The runaway success of "Rocket 88" had finally touched a nerve with the Biharis. At first they seem to have treated Sam's giving the record to Chess as just another harmless eccentricity by this undoubtedly eccentric, and no less naive, maverick studio owner in Memphis. They had continued to do business with Sam well past the time that the record hit number 1. They had accepted the Roscoe Gordon and raw blues sides that Sam had sent them for future release. But then at the end of July, the extent of his financial betrayal seems finally to have hit them, as they announced in the trades, in the cold, unemotional language of commercial enterprise, just what they intended to do about it.

"Modern Inks Seven Artists to Pacts," was the headline in *Billboard,* with Ike Turner, Jackie Brenston, Phineas Newborn, and Walter Horton included, and the stipulation that Jackie, and presumably all the others from Memphis, had now joined the American Federation of Musicians in Atlanta (something unavailable to them in the more strictly segregated climate of their hometown). "Tho 'Rocket 88' has been a top seller, Chess [has] no pact with Brenston," the press release unhesitatingly declared, essentially positing union membership as the only basis for a legitimate contractual relationship.

"I had a deal with Phillips to pick up all the stuff he made," Jules Bihari declared in an interview nearly twenty years later. When "Rocket 88" hit, he said, "that sure blew the deal." Which as far as Sam was concerned didn't match the facts in any way, shape, or form. There was no way in hell it was an exclusive deal. And if it was, the Bihari boys hadn't lived up to it from the start. Of all the recordings he had sent them in the eight months between the time they had first met and Leonard Chess' arrival in Memphis, the only record they had actually put out was the Joe Hill Louis single that they had sat on forever. From Sam's point of view, it was all just a bunch of bullshit—to the Bihari boys it was all about the money, pure and simple, they would just as soon ruin him as look at him. But he was not about to acquiesce. And besides, by now he had seen it, he had heard it, he had found what he had been seeking all along, that magical meeting of flesh and spirit, where, as he would later say, "the soul of man never dies." He had over the past month met and recorded the music of the man he would consider the greatest talent, the most profound artist he ever encountered, the Howlin' Wolf.

HOWLIN' WOLF, born Chester Arthur Burnett in White Station, Mississippi, near Tupelo, in 1910, had an early-morning broadcast every Saturday on KWEM in West Memphis, selling farm implements and dry goods and advertising his appearances in the area. He had acquired his name as a young boy because of his fear of the wolves that had once prowled the Mississippi hill country ("My grandfather was one of them away-back guys, whiskers way down to there, [and] he used to tell me stories about the wolves before they cleaned up . . . that part of the country"), and in the '30s, when he took up music full-time, he cemented the identification by adopting J. T. "Funny Papa" Smith's "Howling Wolf Blues" as his signature tune.

An announcer at the station told Sam about the Wolf and said he ought to listen in, and when he did, it seemed his life was forever changed. "I mean, I tuned him in, and it was the worst pickup you ever heard, and as I recall, I heard one number, and I instantly, I *instantly* said, 'THIS IS WHAT I'M LOOKING FOR.'"

He called the station and invited Wolf to come in and talk, anytime, day or night, whatever suited him best. The man he met was imposing— six three, well over two hundred and twenty pounds, with a broad, handsome face, smooth, dark skin, and a manner that indicated wariness, suspicion, and a residue of deep hurt. He was someone, Sam knew, would have been easy to dismiss, he volunteered scarcely anything personal in that gruff, scoured voice unlike any Sam had ever heard, and yet, Sam felt, he possessed "a certain element of confidence, he knew he had something to say," and as they talked, Sam could sense that as much as he might be reading the Wolf, Wolf was reading him, too. "He was highly, highly intelligent, in many ways the sweetest man you'll ever know, and the strangest man in many ways, too."

Sam was so struck by his differentness, he was so drawn to the par-

ticularity of his demeanor, but he didn't want to "overpromise" anything. He simply suggested that maybe Wolf could come in with his
band sometime — they could try a few things, just see what they could
get. Wolf showed up several days later with a guitarist and drummer in
tow, plus an assortment of harmonicas, and before long the trio was just
blowing as if Sam wasn't even in the room, encouraging one another with
unrestrained shouts while he switched the mikes around and adjusted
the levels to get the absolute maximum out of each individual sound.
Most of all, though, he was just stunned by the uniqueness, the overwhelming thrust, subtlety, and power of the Wolf's voice, as riveting an
instrument as he had ever encountered in all his life.

The guitarist Willie Johnson's playing very nearly matched its inspiration as Johnson, a small, dark-skinned man of twenty-eight with a
cherubic face and haunted eyes, created the effect almost of playing
two guitars at once, a role imposed upon him perhaps by the trio format
but one that he would very likely have carried out in any context by
the sheer inventiveness of his playing. He combined not just lead and
rhythm in the conventional sense, putting together a combination of
thick, clotted chords and deftly distorted single-string runs, but then
he threw in bebop inflections, along with echoes of T-Bone Walker's
delicate phrasing and the dirtiest sound you could ever imagine being
drawn from an electric guitar. Drummer Willie Steele meanwhile socked
away with undiminished good cheer, while Wolf's harp playing filled the
air with a broad pneumatic vibrato, as guitar and harmonica fused to
create a single impenetrable line of attack.

But it was Wolf, Wolf's *voice*, that unwaveringly compelled attention. It was a voice that mixed the roughest elements of the Delta blues
styles on which he had been weaned with its most graceful modulations, cutting through the studio atmosphere with a sandpaper rasp, an
almost overwhelming ferocity, but retaining at the same time a curious
lyricism, a knowing combination of fury and fragility, which set it off
from any other blues singer in that rich tradition. It was at one and the
same time, Sam would always say in later years with his ingrained love
of paradox, both the worst voice he had ever heard in his life and, in
its own inimitable way, the most beautiful. There was no other way of
saying it — he sang "with his damn soul."

They concentrated on two songs that changed with every take, a
throbbing mid-tempo blues called "How Many More Years," which

seemed to be Wolf's calling card, and a more conventional up-tempo number, "Baby Ride With Me," that served as a showcase for Wolf's pulsating rhythmic drive and Willie Johnson's unrelenting attack. For one of the few times in his life, Sam couldn't think of a thing to do. "I was totally blinded by the sound of his voice. I'm not sure that I heard anything in the way of instrumentation. I mean, I was sure enough that I knew I didn't have everything quite right. But his distinctiveness was so overwhelming to me that I couldn't find a way to make a suggestion. Wolf and Willie alone — I knew it wasn't going to wind up with that, it would wind up with [more] structure on the piano — but I didn't want anything much but Wolf, I mean, the minute I opened the microphones and that look came over his face, like, 'I'm getting ready, I'm getting ready, everybody else better be ready, too.'"

But he knew he could do better, once the initial spell began to wear off. He knew the Wolf had even more to offer than just the elemental energy that poured out of him, he knew he could do more to bring it out, not by complicating things but by simplifying them, by helping to frame all the contradictory ingredients that constituted the uncategorizable whole.

He did add a piano in subsequent sessions, if only to fill out the bare bones of the sound, and they continued to work on the same two songs, always subtly changing, and sometimes not so subtly. Sam continued to be overwhelmed by the sheer force of the music and by the intensity of its presentation. He was fascinated by the Wolf, mesmerized each time the man sat down at the mike with his harps spread out all around him.

> He would set in the middle of the studio and he would stretch those long legs and his feet out in front of him — his feet had to be a number sixteen shoe. And when he opened up his mouth to sing, this guy hypnotized himself along with you. To see him on a session, it was just the greatest show — the fervor in that man's face, his eyes roll[ing] up into his head, sweat popping out all over, setting up on the front of his chair and locked into telling you individually about his trials and tribulations. He's the only artist I ever recorded that I wish I could have had a camera on — the vitality of that man was something else.

But there was something else, too. As their acquaintance grew, Sam sensed a reserve even deeper than the simple aversion to boastfulness he had intuited from the start. Wolf never spoke of it, but the loneliness came out in his music, not so much in his lyrics as in the acute feelings of rejection he communicated ("The Wolf didn't look for things that rhymed—he looked for a choice of words that let you know [what] he had experienced"), the sense of estrangement and mistrust he conveyed. He had grown up a solitary child. His mother had abandoned him when he was very small to take up the life of a traveling evangelist. He had scarcely seen her over the years, and when he did she made no secret of her disapproval of his life and music. Reunited with his father at the age of fifteen, he had found a place for himself until he was drafted into the army in 1941, at the age of thirty-one. Stationed in Tacoma, Washington, he showed the kind of dedication to self-improvement that he would display all his life, as he learned to read and write so that he could write letters home. Then in the summer of 1943 he had a full-blown nervous breakdown.

"Pt. is a mental defective," was the initial diagnosis. Several weeks later the "nervous spells" that he was experiencing were described more precisely as periods "during which he becomes extremely tense, cries freely & shows tendency to destroy furniture—on one occasion started kicking at steel gate (with size 17 feet); again, lifted a bed up into the air. During his agitated episodes he is fearful & begs to be allowed to go home to his father. Denies delusional ideas and hallucinations. . . . States he has always had 'nervous spells.'" By the end of September, as he awaited a Certificate of Disability Discharge, the doctor overseeing his care noted, "Can't be troubled except cautiously—doesn't like anyone to put their hands on him." And just before his discharge: "Shows essentially no change in behavior. Causes no trouble unless he has a 'nervous spell'—still can't be interested—hard to handle—must be careful not to make him angry."

It was something of which he was deeply ashamed and almost never spoke. He was deeply patriotic and unwavering in his physical courage throughout his life. "The serviceman was anxious to be inducted and many times said he wished the draft board would hurry up and call him," wrote the volunteer Red Cross worker in Arkansas who interviewed his father, Dock, to research his case. "He writes that he likes the Army and is getting along fine, that he wants the family to pray for him and help the war effort in every way possible. All members of the family write

regularly to him and try to encourage him and assure him that they are doing their best back home." And in fact when he returned to civilian life, he went back to his father's farm, where he continued to help out at plowing and planting time, even after he had moved to West Memphis and taken up a full-time life in music.

There was no way Sam could have known any of this at the time — in fact, he never learned anything of this part of Wolf's history — but there was no question that he felt a kinship, and a closeness, with the man that went far beyond music. It was something of which he nearly always spoke, even when a latter-day interviewer simply wanted to hear about Elvis Presley. He never took Wolf's gruff manner to express in any way the full complement of the man. And indeed there was something about Wolf that compelled attention beyond the ordinary, even if he kept his own counsel and never said a word.

The great blues singer Johnny Shines first met Wolf in Hughes, Arkansas, in the early 1930s when Johnny was still in his teens. "I didn't know it at the time," Johnny wrote in a draft for his uncompleted memoir, *Success Was My Downfall*, "but Wolf did farm work during the week. I usually saw him only on Saturday and Sunday nights. As far as I knew he could have crawled out of a cave, a place of solitude, after a full week's rest, to serenade us. I thought he was a magic man." "I was kind of afraid of him," Johnny said another time. "I mean, just to walk up and put your hand on him. Well, it wasn't his size, I mean, what he was doing, the way he was doing, the sound that he was giving off. *That's how great I thought Wolf was.*"

Sam could just as easily have spoken those words. That was why he was so unwilling to accept a result that he would have proudly pronounced a success with anyone else. They kept fooling around in the studio, working not so much to refine the music, really, as to bore down into its molten core. He could experiment with mike placement, he could improve the engineering — and he did. He switched to an omnidirectional mike because of the way Wolf constantly moved his head from side to side, and he kept cranking up the sound to the point where it was just on the edge of distortion, sometimes past it, so that the

"Pvt. Chester Arthur Burnett, Picket line Troop G, 9th Cavalry (colored) from Aberdine [*sic*], Mississippi, cleaning frog of horse, while Staff Sgt. Columbus Rudisal, Goffney, S.C., looks on, Sept. 12, 1941." *U.S. Army archives*

music could jump right out of the jukebox but the needle would still stay in the groove—if only barely. He tried to give the piano player more confidence—the piano part may at this point have been merely filling out the sound, but it still didn't have the muscularity that the music called for. He tried to get the band to forget his presence in the studio, hanging back behind the glass as they just jammed, coming out only to indicate approval or make a slight mike adjustment that might be accompanied by an equally unobtrusive suggestion. But most of all, he knew he needed to get the Wolf so comfortable in the studio that he could just kick off his shoes, both figuratively and literally, and reach down for that part of him that was buried somewhere deep within.

He sent auditions to both Modern and Chess, even as he continued to work with the band. He had no intention of stopping before he reached a point that declared, This is the core of what you are looking for. This is the *pure essence*. For the first time he felt as if he had in Marion a full partner in his enthusiasm for the music. Despite the indifference she had always shown toward not just the music but its practitioners (they were for the most part, in her view, an ill-behaved lot who trucked in mud on the linoleum floor without the slightest regard for all the effort she put in to keep things clean), she was utterly charmed by Wolf, by the spontaneity of his style and the gentleness of his demeanor. Marion put it down initially to the single-mindedness of Sam's focus. "Sam played Wolf over and over. I have some marvelous old discs of Howlin' Wolf that have maybe fourteen sets of lyrics to 'How Many More Years.' You couldn't be in the presence of Sam's intense motivation and drive and hear him making all these comments about [the music] without picking something up. But Sam's favorite Wolf story was my Wolf story. I was over at the studio [one night] either painting the floor or woodwork, totally absorbed in what I was doing, and all of a sudden I heard this voice, sounding like it was coming down from the sky. 'Miss Marion, what you doing down there on the floor?'" She was scared to death at first, of course, but then she realized Wolf had been passing by and, when he saw the lights on in the studio, had come in out of concern for her. And she retained her fondness for both him and his music all her life.

IT WAS ONLY after the Biharis had indicated a final and irrevocable break with their *Billboard* announcement that they had signed all of Sam's discoveries to exclusive contracts at the end of July that Sam at last turned in a record to Leonard Chess that he felt did full justice to Wolf's talents. This time he got Roscoe Gordon's mentor, Billy "Red" Love, for the piano chair. Fair-skinned, freckle-faced, and barely twenty-one, Billy was comfortable in every style (as witnessed by his impersonation of Ike Turner on the latest Jackie Brenston and His Delta Cats release), and it was his distinctive piano figure that served as the intro to "How Many More Years" before Willie Johnson's thunderous guitar chords and Wolf's inexorable vocal took over the play. The other side, oddly enough, was not "Baby Ride With Me," the track they had been working on all these weeks, but an entirely different number, which dispensed with piano altogether and led off with a feature not present in either of the other songs: Wolf's howl. In this case it took the form of an almost unearthly moan, starting low and gathering force over the first eight bars of the song, until it coalesced in a single focused blast that seemed capable of ripping the innards out of Sam's prized omnidirectional mike.

"Moanin' at Midnight" was the very embodiment of all the loneliness and all the ferocity implicit in Wolf's music. The howl came from the "blue yodel" of Jimmie Rodgers, the so-called Father of Country Music, whom Wolf always acknowledged as a direct influence, and Crystal Springs, Mississippi, bluesman Tommy Johnson, whose delicate filigreed style, punctuated with wordless falsetto ululations, was the point of origin for much of the subtle lyricism underlying Wolf's otherwise extroverted approach. But the performance itself was inimitable, with the same hypnotic power that Sam himself had experienced from the very first time he had heard the Wolf but imbedded now in the grooves of a record in a way that the world itself could fully apprehend it. There may never have been a more powerful example of blues committed in the pure Mississippi style, not by Wolf's mentor, Charley Patton, widely acknowledged as the progenitor of Delta blues, nor by anyone else who has arrived on the scene before or since. "I can take one damn record like 'Moanin at Midnight,'" Sam told Wolf co-biographer James Segrest, "and forget every damn thing else that the man ever cut." Not that he ever would. As far as Sam was concerned, there was no question at that moment that he was going to go on recording Wolf until the day that one of them died. But there was equally little question that they had achieved something together that would be around for the ages. No less than if it had been carved in marble, in granite. It would be there, Sam was convinced. It would be there. As big as life itself.

Gene Nobles.
Courtesy of
Nikki Nobles

The record came out on Chess at the end of August and hit almost immediately on the regional charts. "Under separate cover I am sending you the number by THE HOWLIN' WOLF that I told you about," he wrote to his old colleague WLAC DJ Gene Nobles on September 3. "It was released in Memphis last Friday and is already the biggest number in town . . . no bulls — it is, according to [Buster Williams-owned distributor] Music Sales. 'MOANIN' AT MIDNIGHT' is the side — I know I'm partial but it is the most different record I ever heard." Sam didn't doubt for a moment that both sides were masterpieces, and both made the national r&b charts, with "How Many More Years" reaching number 4. But it was "Moanin' at Midnight" on which Sam bestowed his ultimate accolade: *"the most different record I ever heard."* Of all the superlatives that he could — and often did — bestow, this was the greatest in his multifarious vocabulary. To Sam if you weren't doing something different, you simply weren't doing anything at all.

E VEN AS ALL THIS was going on, he had become embroiled in yet another business misunderstanding, this time with Leonard Chess. On August 15, just before Wolf's epochal single came out, Sam put down $1,000 for a bus for Jackie Brenston. He had argued long and loud against it. He kept telling Leonard that Jackie didn't need a bus, Jackie couldn't afford a bus, Jackie didn't even have a band to carry around in a bus at this point. But Leonard was under constant pressure from his biggest star. Sam could understand: Jackie *wanted* a bus. And Leonard just said, "Find him a damn bus. I'll pay."

Sam found a guy named Perry Little, who piddled around on the edges of show business and drove for the black county schools. He had an old Flxible passenger bus for sale, it looked pretty sharp, but when Sam asked him about it, Mr. Little said, "Well, I have to tell you, Mr. Phillips, the reason I'm getting rid of it is that it don't get any mileage on it." So Sam got back to Leonard, and by this time Leonard was so committed he couldn't have backed out even if he had wanted to. Sam took Jackie out to see the bus, "and, boy, you would've thought it was a Rolls-Royce or something," Jackie was so excited. Leonard told him to go ahead and make the deal, Leonard would send a cashier's check the next day. As Sam recalled, he put the money down, but then the check didn't arrive, "and so here I was with Perry Little, I had promised him he had a deal. And I'm trying to think where [to get] the money. I got some of it from [Hoyt Wooten's brother] S.D. I rounded up the rest some way or the other. But do you know, I never got the money out of Leonard Chess for the bus."

It remained a thorn in his side all through the fall, as he continued to make payments on a bus that, as Sam had predicted, was never really fit to be on the road. Each time it broke down Sam was out a little more money, and the last time, it had to be towed back to Memphis, where it sat on the street just off Hernando until Sam finally had it towed to his own driveway.

There was very little new business to be transacted with Chess at this point, because all of Leonard's money appeared to be tied up in the records he already had out. Sam couldn't really blame him for that. Hell, that was just business. But there were other, larger issues as well, mostly centering on what he perceived to be Leonard's lack of any real belief in the music's ultimate potential: a potential to change things, a potential to break down barriers, a potential to reach an audience of previously unimagined breadth and proportion. In the end, though, what it all came down to was that Sam just didn't trust him anymore. And meanwhile, the bus sat in mute reproach, mocking his continuing naïveté, in the driveway at 1928 Vinton.

For the kids, on the other hand, for six-year-old Knox and even three-year-old Jerry, the bus was a symbol of another sort, a never-ending reminder of the pride they felt in a father who was different from anybody else's father that they knew, a father who, in the little time they got to spend with him, emphasized over and over, to their own occasional bewilderment, the importance of being yourself, the imperative to be a rebel without becoming an outcast, to always choose individualism over conformity. They listened gravely to their father's lessons—he never treated them like they were *children,* that was another way in which he was different—but then there was the bus, which in and of itself summed up so much of the differentness of their whole family. There was the rolled-up sign in front that announced "Jackie Brenston's Rocket 88," and they had cap gun fights with neighborhood friends in the aisle and in between the seats. But none of their friends had heard of Jackie Brenston. Jackie Brenston was a colored man, a Negro. When they went down to the studio with their mother, the room was always full of Negroes, with their daddy right in the middle in his coat and tie, introducing them to the musicians with pride—to Roscoe Gordon, who was always fun to be around, or Howlin' Wolf, or Joe Hill Louis, or "Mumbles" Horton.

They were taught always to address colored people as Mr. and Mrs., whether it was the minister or the yardman or one of the musicians, to treat everyone with respect—they were all God's creatures. They were going to hear the word *nigger* quite a bit, their mother told them, she imagined they already had, but they must never use it. It was a sign of ignorance and false pride. Often when they went downtown, they stopped by Goldsmith's department store first. It had a wonderful toy department, and Knox, the older one, loved the Lionel trains. But he was perplexed when he saw the two water fountains, one for white, one for colored—there was no such distinction at the studio. Their father taught them that that was *wrong.*

Their daddy was the handsomest man they knew and their mother the prettiest woman. When Daddy punished them for something they had done, they didn't say a word in protest, they knew he was right. But once he was done scolding them, he was finished. And Mother always comforted them afterward. Everything he did he did with his own particular style. He dressed differently, he combed his hair differently, and when he surprised them and drove up in a stylish 1948 Hudson, it didn't look like any of the drab used cars that any of their neighbors had, it was as sharp and shiny as a brand-new Cadillac. Even if he was just playing catch with them, he had his own distinctive way of winding up or holding the ball across the seams or bouncing the baseball off the back of his wrist into his hand.

Becky watched her husband with unabashed admiration. She saw the way he way he was with his artists. She saw the way he was with their boys. For all of the doubt and fear that she had witnessed, he seemed absolutely fearless and doubtless. No matter what the situation, he was always in control, always certain that he was right — and, she thought, he almost always was. But she never knew exactly what he was thinking, he was so taken up with another world, which existed as much in his own thoughts as in the physical universe, that she no longer felt he shared his innermost feelings with her.

They went to church every Sunday, Idlewild Presbyterian over on Union, a great Gothic structure modeled on Lincoln Cathedral in England, and she knew he was a believer in his own way, but he never voiced his beliefs to her. His mind always seemed to be elsewhere, if not on work — well, she *knew* what he was doing, but she was not going to confront him on his behavior. She found fault with herself. She felt she must be wanting in some way. And she thought somehow if she could just play her assigned role to greater perfection, her duties as wife, helpmeet, mother, maybe she could overcome some of the ways in which she knew she had failed Sam in some way or another.

As for Sam, it's hard to say. He always spoke his mind, as Becky observed, even if it hurt. In difficult or tragic situations he was always the first to lend a helping hand. He never mistreated her or lied to her directly — and he made no great attempt to conceal his actions. From the time he was a young man, hard work and excellence had been his goal. He was determined to be the best announcer, the best radio engineer, the best record man, the best father, the best son — and in many respects he was. But he was, clearly, not the best husband — and it was one of the few subjects he skirted with me in all of our conversations and interviews over the years. Occasionally there might be glimmers, allusions to the perfection of the work, the imperfection of the life. But he never made excuses or boasted. To the end of his life he was simply determined to go his own way. He loved Becky. From my perspective, he appreciated, but didn't really love, Marion. But he had needs. And he was not going to apologize or make excuses.

W HEN HE FIRST OPENED THE STUDIO, Sam would always recall, "there were times when it didn't look like anybody was going to show up. This was a raw desert out there, no water, no oasis by any manner of means. Not a camel in sight." It was almost like that now, in the fall of 1951, and he was thrown back once again on his original resources: funerals, conventions, personal records, ingenious ploys, like helping a lawyer get his client out of a charge of violating Memphis' anti-noise law by inventing a device to measure the decibels emitted by his car's exhaust. After the flurry of records that Chess had released in the wake of "Rocket 88"'s groundbreaking success, there was a virtual shutdown of new Memphis Recording Service releases over the next three months, and Sam was left with little but a stinging sense of pride as he watched "Moanin' at Midnight" enter the Juke Box Top 10 at the beginning of October.

Sam could understand it. Leonard Chess was clearly preoccupied with building his own label, not with feathering Sam Phillips' nest. The Biharis meanwhile had flung down yet another gauntlet, coming into Memphis just two weeks before Wolf's Chess sides began to chart and recording first Wolf, then B.B. King with a portable Magnecord tape recorder. Their first release on Wolf, cut at the radio station in West Memphis where he worked, was "Baby Ride With Me," one of the two songs Sam had been working on with him from the start. It was retitled "Riding in the Moonlight" and had been effectively realized in the studio, as Wolf brought all of his energy to the performance, overriding any sonic defects in the recording. The other side was far less effective, a copy of Wolf's crashing masterpiece labeled "Morning [as opposed to "Moanin'"] at Midnight," with the introductory moan barely audible and, despite Wolf, the overall sound not even close to matching the magisterial effect of the original. In keeping with Modern's continuing appeal to the union over the legitimacy of Chess' signing of Jackie Brenston, the label announced through the agency of its owners, the Bihari brothers, that it had "inked a term disk contract with Howlin' Wolf, Memphis blues warbler," on exactly the same grounds.

They recorded the first B.B. sides at the colored YMCA on Lauderdale and Linden in Memphis. "I called B.B., and I said, 'I'm coming in,'" said the youngest brother, Joe, twenty-six years old and now in charge of the new "field recording" division. "We rented a room in the black YMCA, big room, and had to put up blankets over the windows so you wouldn't

Joe Bihari, B.B. King, and DJ Hunter Hancock, 1954. *Courtesy of Ace Records*

hear the noise from the cars outside." According to Bihari, "it just was not working, and I told everybody, I said, 'B.B., come on, everybody, take a break.'" He had been using Phineas Newborn Jr. on piano, as he recalled, "but he played jazzy—he wasn't good at blues, or he didn't want to play blues, and that's why nothing was really happening." During the break another piano player "wandered in," he had just been listening and now sat down at the upright Joe had rented for the session and started playing exactly what Joe had been looking for. So after the break, he paid off Phineas Newborn Jr. and hired the new piano player. "That piano player," said Joe, "was Ike Turner."

Whether or not this is exactly the way it happened, and there are, certainly, numerous (though not unrelated) variations, the session proved to be momentous in two fundamental respects. The first was that B.B. King had his first national hit with Modern, "Three O'Clock Blues," an old tune of Lowell Fulson's that B.B. had often played as a DJ, which hit number 1 on the r&b charts in early February 1952. The song was close to the kind of thing Sam had been groping for in his last sessions with B.B., with a pair of saxophones providing a churchy background to the gospel overtones of B.B.'s voice. Here, though, for the first time voice and guitar were fused, the approach was more muscular, more compressed — the record was stamped once and for all as B.B. King's and nobody else's. Ike's contributions to this sound, whatever the tangled truths of everyone's memories, were not all that significant, but his place in Joe Bihari's esteem could not have been higher. There was something about Ike, sharp, in charge, always on the hustle, that really captured Joe's attention.

"I hired Ike. I bought him a car. I bought him a Buick Roadmaster. I gave him some of my suits — we wore the same size. I gave him an expense account and a weekly salary. I said, 'You go scout talent all through Mississippi, Texas, Arkansas, Louisiana, and when you have talent, you call me. I'll come in.'"

They took a first tentative trip together in November, almost certainly pre-Roadmaster, where they recorded two members of a down-home trio with drums (they would record the second guitarist on their return in February), with the harmonica player performing in the explicit style and repertoire of the first Sonny Boy (John Lee) Williamson, an enormously popular prewar figure, while guitar player Junior Brooks directly evoked one of Muddy Waters' recent hits. It was just a rehearsal for a series of wild and woolly trips that they would set off on, beginning in January, in the course of which they would seek out both greater- and lesser-known talent, confront and evade various representatives of the law, and cement a partnership in which they would frequently use Ike's mother Beatrice's house in Clarksdale, in the Mississippi Delta, as their home base.

Sam viewed these activities with a certain amount of asperity. He had nothing against Joe — his quarrel was with Jules and Saul. And he left it to the Chess boys to protect their territory. As for himself, he was disgusted with the raiding, the double-dealing, the whole business, but what could he do about it? He had no interest in going out in the field and recording people who might or might not have something of their own to say, just like you would record a funeral, off the cuff with a portable tape recorder. He had no interest in stealing somebody else's artists; he was determined to develop his own. Like the Wolf. Though there was never going to be anybody else like the Wolf.

So he put his faith in his own resources, redoubling his efforts to attract business, redoubling his efforts to find *original* talent. He continued to work to make the studio a reflection of his vision of "natural sound." He built his own cabinet speakers and a "fast-peak limiter" so that he could cut his own masters with confidence. Nobody loved distortion more than he did, Sam said, but even that could get out of hand — you wanted to encourage people to express themselves, to allow them to maybe get a little overexcited, but still have the electronic ability "to catch them just before they would get out of proportion" and not have to tell them to back up and do it all over again. Mostly, though, he continued to rely just on setting the mikes.

He was proud of his RCA 77-D microphones, and his Shure 55s, and the sleek new Altec black pencil omnidirectional that he used almost exclusively for the Wolf. Every piece of equipment in the studio bore his stamp — he knew exactly what he wanted to use each one for. He would say to Marion, "I really want this piece of equipment. Do you think we can afford it?" But she knew she didn't get a vote. If he wanted it, he was going to get it — somehow. "He had a passion for the best equipment, by his standards — whatever he got was the best [that he could afford], one piece at a time." He wanted to get Marion an air conditioner for the outer office, but they couldn't afford that yet. Instead he got a little air conditioner for the studio — a Philco home unit from Lowenstein's department store downtown that could barely cool the studio while the control room remained a sweltering box.

At the end of September he sent off the master of a new Rufus Thomas song for a Christmas release on Chess, and at just about the same time, he cut a session on Roscoe Gordon. He had found a song he thought would be perfect for Roscoe and brought it to him. It was called "Booted" and, with its cheerful celebration of the pleasures of alcohol, seemed just right for Roscoe's breezy, boozy style. Sam told him to put himself in the spirit of the song, which Roscoe conceded, "by me being already halfway raunchy," he had no trouble doing, and they got a take that everybody was pleased with in no time. Roscoe volunteered that his chauffeur's cousin, Robert Bland, himself a singer, whose mother had a popular restaurant on Third just off Beale, had recently driven him to a gig in Arkansas, and when Roscoe got caught up in a dice game in the back room, had filled in very effectively with a set of his own, featuring Roscoe's "Love You Till the Day I Die." Sam recorded the young man, Bobby Bland, doing that song, and, although all of Roscoe's records to date had been released on Modern, sent off both Roscoe's and Bobby's acetates to Leonard Chess. It was one of the last sessions that he cut on acetate, as he prepared to convert to tape, a process he had held off on until they were able to eliminate some of the high-frequency hiss endemic to the size of the magnetic particles used to make the tape. But now at a time when he had no idea if he was even going to survive, let alone succeed in this difficult business, he went out and bought a top-of-the-line 900-P Presto tape recorder. He never wavered in his belief that if he failed, he would at least know that he had given it his all. "And I would have been a much happier person than I would have been had I not done it. Period."

When he went home to Florence, he could always hold his head high. He wanted his boys to know the values he had grown up with. He wanted them to know not just his mother and Aunt Emma but his brothers and sisters, too, who lived such different lives from the ones his children would enjoy. Uncle Silas would always come by, he was living with Bessie Foster now, a black lady who worked on people's feet and took good care of him—he never failed to amaze Knox and Jerry by telling them exactly how many chickens there were in the chicken house and what all their names were. He would take Knox up on his knee just like he had little Sammy. He would tell him tales of Africa, that beautiful land with the battercake trees and the Molasses River, on the porch of his grandmother Phillips' house. Sam's mother didn't worry about him as much anymore. She had been so worried when he had gone off to that hospital in Birmingham—that was something she had witnessed firsthand. But even with this brief recent relapse (which she had learned about only after the fact in a letter from Becky), she was confident that things had straightened out for him, he was always so well-dressed and *confident,* and she knew how prudent he was about money. And she adored the children, even if she didn't get to see anywhere near enough of them. But sometimes, she wrote to Sam in a tone that was disturbingly familiar, she got so blue she didn't know what to do with herself. Occasionally his mother and Aunt Emma would make

Jud (in uniform) and Dean Phillips with the Sun Spot Quartet (C. M. Lingle, Gerald Howell, George West, and Bill Wilson), Hattiesburg, Mississippi, 1951. *Courtesy of Dean Phillips, Jud Phillips Jr., and the Sam Phillips Family*

the journey to Memphis, but they would always hurry home again before they had much of a chance to visit.

It would have been almost impossible for anyone at home to fully understand the life he led, or the life to which he aspired, with the possible exception of his brother Jud (J.W.), who had been living in Petal, Mississippi, just outside of Hattiesburg, for the past five years, managing the bottling plant that his father-in-law had set up for him and working for the Petal Water and Sewer Company. Jud's ambitions, though, Sam knew were of a different order. He was a born leader with the kind of gifts, for salesmanship, for motivation, for charismatic inspiration, that demanded a larger stage. He was still managing and announcing his little gospel quartet, renamed the Sun Spot Quartet to advertise the drink he was bottling, but Sam knew he had greater plans both for them and for himself — his mother thought someday he and J.W. might even be able to work together, and Sam just hoped they could both live up to the dreams their mother had for them.

Business started picking up a little in December. Sometime around the beginning of the month he recorded Harmonica Frank, a grizzled white medicine-show veteran in his forties who sang and played the harmonica without making use of either his hands or a harmonica rack, simply rolling the harmonica around in his mouth and then rolling it back to the side again as he declaimed the lyrics of his blues and humorous entertainments in a parched, self-amused voice. He had been captivated by Frank when they met, and first recorded him in July, signing him immediately to a management contract. He was not by any stretch of the imagination a great artist, but he was a compelling one, a true original, of the sort that Sam had always been drawn to. "Frank Floyd was a beautiful hobo. He was short, fat, very abstract—and you looked at him and you really didn't know what he was thinking, what he was going to say or sing next. He had the greatest mind of his own—I think hobos by nature have to have that—and that fascinated me from the beginning. And then he had some of these old rhymes and tales and stuff that he had embellished, and some of them were so old, God, I guess they were old when my father was a kid."

He recorded "Howlin' Tomcat" and "She's Done Moved" this time, two blues staples, for which there would be no reason to have any commercial expectation. Harmonica Frank just tickled him. He was difficult to market, Sam realized, not just because of the peculiarity of his sound but because he was primarily a visual act. With that harmonica in his mouth as he sang, he was more of a novelty act than any of the other singers Sam had recorded, but Sam was convinced there was a place for him, if you could just find the right kind of setting to present him in. He was "a very fascinating character." And, as Sam was always quick to point out, "[You] don't throw away any good characters!"

Chess had found a place for Frank in any case in their new hillbilly series, inaugurated the previous summer with fanciful claims for Frank's first single (it was "just as great if not greater" in its field, Leonard announced to the trades, than "Rocket 88," and the label took out an ad for its "Folk Smash!!"). Sam recorded Bob Price, too, a more conventional country crooner along the lines of an adenoidal Eddy Arnold, for the new Chess series. Price had grown up in Tishomingo, Mississippi, with a musician acquaintance of Sam's from WLAY, Quinton Claunch, and Quinton, who had moved to Memphis three years earlier to take a job selling building and hardware supplies, brought him into the studio along with a little band from the Tishomingo-Muscle Shoals area. For Quinton it was an opportunity to reconnect with music, but for Sam it was more in the nature of a favor for an old friend—Price was simply not quirky enough, not even for this readymade new hillbilly market, and Sam doubted that there was a bluesy bone in his body. The results in any case were satisfying to no one, including Leonard Chess, who suspended his brief country music experiment shortly thereafter.

Sam recorded the Southern Jubilees and the Gospel Tones, but as much as he loved the old-time black gospel sound, he couldn't sell it to anyone. He was no less enthusiastic about "Doctor" Isaiah Ross, a self-proclaimed healer of the more profane soul and a considerably more marketable commodity, whose romping "Doctor Ross Boogie" marked not only the start of Sam's wholehearted embrace of magnetic-tape recording but served as yet another tribute to the ecstatic electric boogie of John Lee Hooker. Doctor Ross, a twenty-six year-old native of Tunica, Mississippi, who had acquired his nickname in the army and generally alluded to himself in the third person without reference to his given name, was a disciple of Joe Hill Louis and was studying to become a one-man band along the lines of his friend. For the time being, though, he was accompanied in the studio by his Jump and Jive Boys, who in this instance consisted of one guitarist, his friend Wiley Gatlin, and another friend on broom, along with his own foot-stomping and enthusiastic Sonny Boy (John Lee) Williamson-styled harmonica playing. Sam got an enormous kick out of the raw gusto of his performance. ("Doctor Ross want all y'all / Let's get together and boogie a while," he proclaimed in a half-chanted, half-sung invitation.) But it was his mid-December session with Howlin' Wolf, as blistering, if not as cataclysmic, as the first, that once again established the high ground for all of his recording ventures.

Once again, there was something almost unearthly, or at the very least altogether unpredictable, about the music. Wolf cut four or five titles with any number of different variations. There was a boogie and a blues, each with the theme of moving to California—Beverly Hills in particular—to "prepare for myself in my older days." There was a slow blues in which for the first time on record (but by no means the last) Wolf explicitly expanded upon his larger-than-life persona ("They call me the Howlin' Wolf, darling, you found me howling at your door"), while "Look-A-Here Baby" told an extemporized tale of thwarted courtship ("'So sweet to meet a girl like you, Darlin', what might be your name?' / She said, 'None of your business, you don't understand' / 'Well, okay'"). There was a variety of themes and musical approaches, but each number, with the sole exception of "House Rockin' Boogie" (released as "Howlin' Wolf Boogie"), suggested underlying themes of abandonment, betrayal, and a desperate desire for some form of security.

Wolf by now felt thoroughly at ease in the studio. He would just sit there, his feet stretched out in front of him, massive, inscrutable, rocking in his chair. "He gave the appearance of being totally unconcerned, but his surroundings meant so much to him. Once he felt at home, there was no way for Wolf to be anything other than himself. Once you broke that barrier, you had all he had to offer. I knew even at that time it went beyond the point of black and white. I just didn't know where to go with what I had."

B UT HE WAS CONVINCED that there was going to be a future to figure it out in. Almost in spite of themselves, the Biharis and Leonard Chess — not to mention the breathtaking artistry of the Wolf and its indisputable popular success — had shown him the way. The acceptance of the records (Wolf's, Muddy Waters', B.B. King's rapidly rising national hit), the growing commercial impact of the raw gutbucket blues, along with Hank Williams' almost equally raw expression of undisguised emotion in the country field, told the story of the public's hunger for something unaccommodated, something real.

The Biharis in particular provided a blueprint not so much for a method as for a market. Around the first of the year, twenty-six-year-old Joe and Ike Turner set out on their field-recording adventure in earnest, with Jules occasionally joining them. At the beginning of February, Jules and Joe announced the formation of a new label, Blues and Rhythm, "which will concentrate on blues waxings [from] the Deep South," with eighteen new artists already signed and a "talent rep" hired.

They were, clearly, seizing upon a whole new trend. "For the first time in many months," Hal Webman wrote in his February 9 column in *Billboard*, "Rhythm & Blues Notes":

> the down-home, Southern-style blues appears to have taken a solid hold. . . . The Southern market appears to have opened up to its widest extent in some time . . . [as] such artists as B.B. King, Howling Wolf, Roscoe Gordon, Fats Domino, Sonny Boy Williamson, Light-

nin' Hopkins, John Lee Hooker, Lowell Fulson, Billy Wright, Muddy Waters, etc., have taken a fast hold in such market areas as New Orleans, Dallas, Atlanta, Los Angeles, etc. Even the sophisticated big towns, like New York and Chicago, have felt the Southern blues influence in wax tastes.

Joe and Ike hit Memphis, Helena, Greenville, Texarkana, Monroe, Louisiana, and the Greyhound bus station in Ike's hometown of Clarksdale, which Joe converted into a serviceable studio. They recorded new talent and old, attempted to poach Elmore James and Sonny Boy Williamson (the second Sonny Boy—"Rice" Miller—who had assumed the name several years earlier in the wake of the first Sonny Boy's death) from the redoubtable Lillian McMurry, proprietor of Trumpet Records in Jackson, Mississippi. Mrs. McMurry hit the Biharis with a $1.001 million lawsuit (one million for damages, a thousand for costs)—she was not about to surrender her top artists (Elmore's "Dust My Broom," one of the great unreconstructed landmarks of the downhome movement, had hit the r&b Top 10 earlier in the year) to a bunch of Yankee carpetbaggers. Two years later Mrs. McMurry would receive a token settlement, and she would lose Elmore James to the Biharis before that, when his contract ran out. But for the time being Modern Records and its subsidiaries were enjoined from releasing any of the sides Joe had cut on Trumpet-signed artists.

Sam didn't like any of the funny business—he had great respect for Mrs. McMurry, and he had nearly equal respect for the legitimacy of contract law. He believed in finding his own talent, untried, unproven, untested, and giving it a chance to flourish. And he didn't think much of Jules' attitude toward the blues in any case, which had been evident from the day they first met. All you had to do, Jules was fond of saying, was "stick a microphone out there and let them play," and all too often from Sam's point of view the Biharis' recordings reflected just that attitude, even when it was the youngest brother, Joe, who was in charge.

But there was no point in dwelling on the negative. Joe Bihari was a likable enough fellow. In fact, when six months later Joe asked Sam if he could re-edit John Lee Hooker's "Boogie Chillen," a recording Sam had by now come to realize they hadn't made but licensed from a Detroit record distributor named Bernie Besman, he jumped at the chance. John Lee, it seemed, was between engagements; his original contract with

Besman had run out, and he wasn't quite ready to sign with the Biharis, who thought — correctly, as it turned out — all he needed was a little shove. So in the fall of 1952 Joe brought Sam the master, and he took it on as a kind of sacred trust — this, after all, was the record that, more than any other, had influenced his approach to recording. The result to contemporary ears does not appear to have been particularly successful, but Sam was proud of it. He had, he felt, maintained the "total intrigue" of the original, while reordering it to lead off with the singer's excited exhortation, "Boogie, chillen!," then rearranging the verses to tell a more "sequential" version of the story while interspersing repeated splices of that same insistent shout. It was for him a first-and-last experiment of this kind, but Joe was pleased with it, and Modern put the record out in November as "New Boogie Chillen," just before signing Hooker to a direct contract with the label.

At the moment, though, in the early months of 1952, Sam was as much inspired by all this recording activity in his own backyard as he was challenged by it. And almost inevitably he began to think about the one subject he had sedulously avoided from the start: starting his own label. He still didn't want to do it. It was too risky. It involved him too much in the sales and accounting, not the creative, end of the business. And he didn't know if he could succeed. But more and more, events were conspiring to push him in that direction if he wanted to stay in the record business. He was beginning to be afraid if he didn't join the battle, he would no longer be able to keep faith with his artists or himself.

His mother died in January, and the whole family gathered for the ceremony at the North Wood Methodist Church. Jimmy Connolly, Judge Longshore (the man for whom Knox was named), and Jud's father-in-law, Mr. Hensley, were among the pallbearers, and Aunt Emma, almost inconsolable, signed sadly with her favorite nephew. With Mother and Daddy both gone, she and Uncle Silas were the only ones left to take care of at home. "Son, you are so thoughtful about me," his mother had written to him recently with the kind of intense sincerity that they shared, "you are like most girls are about their mother. I think you are wonderful, Son." Everyone talked about Madgie Phillips' kindness and generosity, her gift for making each one welcome in a special way, whether or not she knew you were coming, her beautiful flower garden, and the chimes

Sam and his mother. *Courtesy of the Sam Phillips Family*

that would always ring out from the old round face clock on the mantel. "I wish I could be there with you," Marion wrote to Sam in Florence. "I feel I knew your mother so well and loved her very much . . . through your loving thoughts and words. . . . I know that nothing can ease your loneliness and loss, but perhaps just to know that those who love you share your sorrow may give you some small solace." And she signed it "With all my love."

C HESS AND THE BIHARIS settled their ongoing squabble on February 15, with an item in *Billboard* announcing, "The Biharis turned over exclusive pact to Howlin' Wolf to the Chess Fraters, while Chess brothers gave four Roscoe Gordon masters [and any claim to his contract] to Modern." It seemed as if the Biharis might have gotten the better end of the deal, as Roscoe's Chess recording of "Booted" (the Biharis had their own version out) was rapidly climbing the charts, on its way to becoming Roscoe's first number 1 hit. For Sam that just may have been the trigger. He had had two number 1 r&b hits now, and one number 4, in less than a year; he had discovered the Howlin' Wolf; and he had a wealth of talent still to record—but what did he have in the way of material reward to show for it?

He started off with a flurry of recording activity at the end of February. He cut a seventeen-year-old DJ from Forrest City, Arkansas, Walter Bradford, with more of a gift for self-promotion than for singing, then on the same day scheduled another Joe Hill Louis session, but this one — marked "SCP"—for himself. Veteran blues singer Jack Kelly "came with 'Mumbles' Horton for session," Marion noted in the logbook, and in due course Sam sent the dubs off to Chess, along with dubs from the Walter Bradford session. Then on March 1 he recorded a fifteen-year-old sophomore from Melrose High School, one of Memphis' three colored institutions, each with its own distinguished music program, who had been coming by with his little r&b combo, the Rockets, for the past few weeks.

Johnny London had found his way to the studio almost by accident. "We saw the studio and wanted to record," he told music historian Rob Bowman, "so we went over and talked to Sam Phillips." Sam was intrigued by the four high school musicians, all of whom had come under the influence of Melrose music director Tuff Green, a veteran Memphis musician and band leader who had played bass with B.B., Roscoe, and the Newborns, among others. They did some demo sessions, and then,

DANCE

AT THE

HIPPODROME

The Nation's Finest Night Spot

500 BEALE AVENUE

The HOWLING WOLF In Person And His House Rockers

FOR YOUR DANCING AND LISTENING PLEASURE
ONE OF THE NATION'S NEWEST SENSATIONS
BLUES SINGERS — TUNES SUCH AS
HOW MANY MORE YEARS
PASSING BY BLUES
RIDING IN THE MOONLIGHT
AND OTHER HIT TUNES

ONE NIGHT ONLY!!

SAT. NIGHT, JAN. 26

9:00 P. M. TILL 1:00 A. M.

ADMISSION IN ADVANCE, $1.00   AT DOOR, $1.25
Reservations Call 37-2232
Advance Tickets At
PAUL'S TAILORING CO., 184 Beale Ave.
PANTAZE DRUG STORE, Beale & Hernando
HIPPODROME, 500 Beale Ave.

Tri-State Defender, January 26, 1952. *Courtesy of Preservation and Special Collections, University Libraries, University of Memphis*

according to London, "[Sam] fell in love with what we were doing, and he decided that he'd 'hire' us."

They cut two sides on March 1, an instrumental and a blues number called "When I Lost My Baby," with Becky Phillips on vocals. ("Sam just knew I liked to sing," Becky recalled years later. "I can't remember the song exactly but I remember the beat of it.") Sam gave dubs of the record to Dewey Phillips, who played it on the air that night, and he sent acetates to Chess by Air Express four days later. Evidently he had second thoughts, though, because on March 8 he called Johnny back into the studio to recut the instrumental, "Drivin' Slow," along with a second, thematically named instrumental, "Flat Tire." That night he sent off the new dubs to two r&b DJs, along with acetates from the Walter

Bradford and Jack Kelly sessions, to be "aired," as Marion noted, as an introduction "to [the] new SUN label."

In later years Sam would always speak of the decision coming about only after long and hard deliberation—and undoubtedly it did. But when it came, it came fast. The name "Sun" seems to have been percolating for some time—or perhaps it was just that no other name seemed right. To Sam, "Sun" represented a new day, opportunity, the dawning of hope. "I wanted something short, simple, [with] a common denominator that was hard to forget. And I think the sun was fairly common: wish for it in the wintertime, too damn much of it in the summer!"

The next step was to come up with a design for the record label, and there Sam encountered one of those happy coincidences that he felt always marked his life and were more in the nature of fate than coincidence. He went down to the Memphis Engraving Company, diagonally across from the Peabody, with his heart in his hand—he didn't know if he'd be able to afford it, he didn't even know if they'd take the job. He had drawn up a couple of rough sketches and was told to go to room 3 upstairs, where who should he run into but an old schoolmate, Jay Parker, Coffee High School, class of '44, who had played sousaphone in the marching band. They had a good laugh over that, and Sam explained to him just what he wanted to convey with the name and the label. It had to be real, and it had to be simple, and it had to reflect the sun, with a rooster crowing for a new day.

When he came back the next day, Parker "had almost exactly what I had in mind," using a single color (for economy and simplicity) against the bright golden paper he had chosen to announce the label's name. There were eleven shaded sun rays surrounded by a staff of musical notes encircling all but the bottom part of the label's outer edge. The notes were in the same burnt umber as all the lettering except SUN (at the top) RECORD COMPANY (across the spindle hole), and MEMPHIS, TENNESSEE (on the bottom crescent of the circle), with each yellow letter set off by that same "rusty brown" shadowing (S-U-N) or backdrop. The only thing missing was the rooster.

"I said, 'I got to have room for this'—I wanted that rooster in the center—'but I don't want it too crowded.' So he drew my rooster for me and realigned some notes and the staff around it, and that label never changed—except I did not anticipate 45s—we were dealing with 78s, with the little hole in the middle—so in the end I had to drop my little rooster!"

On March 27, the first Johnny London records were pressed by Plastic Products, one thousand at a cost of $135. It's hard to know what became of the other two releases — most likely they were never pressed, let alone issued — but Johnny's was given Sun catalogue number 175, with Jack Kelly and Walter Horton's collaboration (as Jackie Boy and Little Walter) assigned the arbitrary starting position of 174, and Walter Bradford and the Big City Four following as Sun 176. Of the four missing tracks, just one minute of the A-side of the Jack Kelly single has survived, a rollicking but somewhat nondescript jug band number called "Sellin' My Stuff." From the evidence of a later recording session, the Walter Bradford record was probably no more distinctive, and one can only surmise that after test-marketing the acetates on various local radio programs, including Walter Bradford's own radio show in Forrest City, Sam simply — and altogether uncharacteristically — lost his nerve.

Even if that is the case, however, the one single that he did issue, made up of Johnny London's two instrumentals, is no less problematic. The B-side, "Flat Tire," is little more than a cute, conventional blues tricked up with a very odd sound in which London's alto lead sounds as if it's coming from an echoey cave far, far away. On "Drivin' Slow" the sound is no less odd, but much closer at hand, as Johnny plays a harsh, almost sonically distorted lead while the tenor plays a bluesy riff over and over in the background and the piano supplies steady support. From what Johnny has said, there seems little question that Sam knew what he was looking for. He made them do it over and over until "he found the sound that he wanted," a "hollow sound" that, Johnny was certain, he had never tried before. "He created a chamber that he didn't have, something similar to a telephone booth. It was a home-made thing, 8' by 4', something like that."

The real question is why. It's a pleasant enough blues, and according to London it got a lot of airplay in Memphis as well as booking dates for the band. But even by Sam's standards it was weird — not so much unique as just plain weird — and more to the point it was far from the straightahead blues with which one might have thought Sam Phillips would want to inaugurate his new label. I never heard Sam speak about this; in all the years I knew him, and all our far-ranging conversations, I never heard him bring up this record, or any of the first three scheduled releases on the Sun label. The most I ever heard him say, when I asked about "Drivin' Slow" directly, was that he knew that "as an instrumental number it would be more difficult to sell." Nor am I aware of any other interviews in which he explained his reasoning.

It's hard to say what might have happened if he had put out records he believed in more — or why he didn't — but it was in any case a moot point. The label didn't last much longer than "It's The Phillips" had a year and a half earlier, and it made no more of a mark, as Sam came face-to-face with the very problems he had been so apprehensive about all along — cash outflow without commensurate inflow, the distractions of trying to sell as well as create your own product, most of all the lack of a distribution network to get the records any farther than the Memphis city limits. So in the end he was left with little more than the wisps of a dream, a name for his record company if he could ever manage to get it off the ground, and a label design that he felt neatly encapsulated everything he wanted to say about the new day dawning. But the records clearly didn't, and though he said in later years, "I don't think [there] was anything that indicated that we had thought about giving up," I always felt this was more in the nature of whistling past the historical grave-yard. It wasn't in Sam's character to "give up," certainly, but no matter how discouraged he may have been, at the very least he recognized the need to retrench and rethink, in characteristically analytic fashion, just how he might go about reaching his goal.

By April he was sending out dubs to Chess once again. But with their differences out in the open once and for all (Sam's declaration of independence, however short-lived, did not go unnoticed), things were not about to be put back together again. On every issue, it seemed, Sam and Leonard vehemently disagreed, from the whole business of the bus, which continued to fester, to the proper way to record the Howlin' Wolf. He had another session with Wolf in the middle of the month, but of the eight sides he sent the label, Chess put out only one, and between April and December, out of all the other material Sam sent them, they released just four singles by any of his other artists.

As a result he was forced to find other outlets. In July he recorded Roscoe for a new Memphis label, Duke, which precipitated yet another lawsuit from the Biharis. By the end of the summer, Duke, which had been started by WDIA's white program director, David James Mattis, had been taken over by Don Robey, the light-skinned owner of Peacock Records in Houston and reputedly the city's black numbers boss, who was said to have put a gun on his desk and declared, whether by word or gesture, "We have a deal." Sam had tried Robey in May with some of his rawest cottonpatch blues to date, by Sleepy John Estes, a fifty-three year-old native of Brownsville, Tennessee, midway between Jackson and Memphis, who, like so many others, just showed up at the studio one day with his battered guitar and new store-bought teeth. Sam was knocked out by his music — Sleepy John, who had first recorded for Victor in the '20s, was a brilliant songwriter with a unique "crying" style of singing — but evidently his teeth didn't fit, and at one point they went flying across the room as he put his heart and soul into the performance. Sam persuaded him to put them in his pocket ("I said, 'Don't break them, save them, you might have a girlfriend that you want to see'"), and Estes, who had gone blind a couple of years earlier, even returned for a second session with a harmonica and washboard-playing friend — but Sam was never able to sell any of the sides, which he considered priceless and which remained unissued until they came out in England some thirty years later.

He did some recording for Trumpet Records' Lillian McMurry, the lady who had given the Biharis such a hard time when they tried to steal her artists. And he sold a couple of hard blues sides that he had recorded on Joe Hill Louis earlier in the year to 4 Star proprietor Bill McCall, who had put out the very first records ever to come out of the Memphis Recording Service. But clearly he no longer had enough of a ready market to sustain his recording activities. There was a brief flicker of hope when Leonard Chess announced the formation of a new sister label, Checker, in the spring, but then just a couple of months later Checker had an entirely unexpected instrumental hit by Muddy Waters' virtuosic harmonica player, Little Walter. "Juke," which topped the r&b charts for five weeks in the fall, not only smashed all previous Chess sales records, it pretty much put paid to any hopes Sam might have had of promoting his own harmonica virtuoso, Walter Horton, as brilliant in his way as his younger namesake, in whom both Leonard and the Biharis had shown some interest in the past.

What hurt most about this final break with Chess was losing Howlin' Wolf once and for all. He had had one last session with Wolf in October — from Sam's perspective it was the least satisfying session yet, with Chess insisting on a fuller horn section and Sam complying by putting together an off-kilter trombone-saxophone combination, probably not the "commercial" direction that the label had in mind. From Sam's point of view

Leonard Chess, like the Biharis, was more interested in "excitement" than in "feel." And while to the casual observer, or even to the passionate Wolf fanatic, the difference may have seemed slight, Sam clearly felt pressured ("I don't think they wanted to take the time to say, 'Hey man we're proud of this damn music'"), and, in any case, there were to be no more sessions. For the next year and a half Leonard Chess did his best to get the Wolf to quit Memphis, and Wolf, who could be as obstinately principled as the next person—in fact, sometimes considerably more so—staunchly resisted. There were no more Wolf singles until January 1953, when two sides were culled from the last session, and then, as if to say to Wolf, 'If you don't move to Chicago, you're through,' nothing for the last eleven months of the year. Wolf got so fed up that he appears to have recorded some sides on his own, probably at the radio station, and then gone to Les Bihari, the oldest of the Bihari brothers, who by 1953 had moved to Memphis and, with his brothers' active participation, started a studio and a label, Meteor, of his own. According to this Bihari, neither the most stable personality nor the most reliable of sources, "Howlin' Wolf came to me, and he says he's supposed to have a record released. I called Leonard and I told him I had Howlin' Wolf in the office, and if he wasn't going to record him and put it out, I was." After being assured that Chess had no intention of letting Wolf go, Bihari evidently sent the tapes to the label, and just two or three months later, finally satisfied that the time was right, Wolf set out for Chicago, where he would remain until his death in 1976, an unrivaled exponent of the raw, wrenched-from-real-life feel that for Wolf (and for Sam, too) was at the heart of the blues. "I turned my farming business over to my brother-in-law, my grandfather's farm that he left me. I moved to Chicago in [1954]. I had a four-thousand-dollar car and $3,900 in my pocket. I'm the onliest one that drove out of the South like a gentleman."

It was a bitter pill to swallow. According to Sam it was the greatest disappointment he would ever experience in the business. There was not another artist "that I would have had out here to entertain anybody from the President of the United States to the poorest person, black or white, that I might run across." And if he had had the opportunity to do so, he always said in later years, Wolf would have provided an "entirely different approach to rock 'n' roll." He could have been "the counterpart of Elvis—this guy would have been huge with white youngsters, along with black. You will always take something to your grave that you regret. I'm not going to take many things because I've been too blessed. But I guess I'll take to my grave not having the Wolf around. This seems crazy, but it's a fact. I don't know that anybody else ever got the joy out of Wolf I got."

But there was, he knew, nothing he could do about it. And more and more he was turning his attention once again to his earliest ambition. He didn't know whether or not he could ever launch a record company with the kind of broad national scope that alone would satisfy him, but by God he could see no reason that he and Jimmy Connolly didn't have the know-how to start up a radio station of their own.

FIVE | Perfect Imperfection

H E AND JIMMY had been talking about the subject almost constantly since the beginning of the year. Hell, they had been talking about it, in one way or another, ever since the day they met. But in June they formalized their plans with a provisional partnership in which they split nine-tenths of the ownership and gave one-tenth to L. A. Alburty, an old Memphis radio hand who had been part owner and general manager of WHBQ, in exchange for the expertise and advice he could provide.

The aim was exactly what Sam's goal for the studio had been all along: to provide a forum for Negro talent and self-expression, to serve both the black community and the community at large by drawing attention to the rich, generous, and diverse culture that had been so ignored by history and ill served by prejudice. It was "the intent and purpose of the applicant," Sam wrote in their first FCC application eight months later, in February of 1953, "to allot a definite part of each broadcast day for the sole purpose of improving Southern Negro-white relations." Furthermore, unlike WDIA, where almost all the behind-the-scenes figures, from executives to engineers, were white, their proposed station would be staffed by Negro engineers, copywriters — "as much of the employed personnel as possible" — and the daily schedule, outlined in precise detail, would be tailored specifically to the needs of the community, from "It's Your Turn Now," a "round table and panel discussion of current issues that particularly involve or affect Negroes," to "Letters Home" and "For the Boys," programming for "Negro boys and

The Prisonaires on the air. Johnny Bragg is third from left, next to the mike.
Courtesy of Colin Escott and Dave Booth, Showtime Music Archives (Toronto)

girls in service" and their loved ones, to a range of sacred and secular recorded music and talent shows "devoted to local, and regional live talent for the purpose of encouraging more community participation in the station's operations." By the time they submitted their application, Alburty would be gone and the partnership name changed from the Memphis Broadcasting Service to the Tri-State Broadcasting Service. Alburty's replacement, Clarence Camp, was one of the biggest jukebox operators in the mid-South, an early partner in (and an early departure from) Buster Williams' Music Sales record distributorship, and while he would remain an almost entirely silent partner, his qualifications for one-third ownership were just as compelling as his predecessor's, in this case the value of both his business connections and his money. Financial practicalities aside, however, it didn't much matter to Sam and Jimmy. This was their dream.

They plotted and planned it all through the summer and fall of 1952. Jimmy brought to the enterprise not just his own long experience at WJLD, where he had introduced the *Atomic Boogie Hour* and then as general manager presided over the conversion of the station to a predominantly black market, but his wife Erin's sales expertise, which, everyone in the family (including her sister Becky) agreed, was probably equal to anyone's in the business. Sam, of course, brought his unquestionable love of the music, and his fierce belief in it, along with his equal belief in the potential of what radio as a pure vehicle could achieve. He saw it every day with Dewey, who by now was such a gloriously yawping fixture on the Memphis airwaves that it seemed sometimes as if the music was being defined by the exhortatory enthusiasm of the man who was playing it.

"Dewey could convince you that if you missed what he did, you were going to miss the best. And the next record coming up was [going to be] even better!" They were closer than brothers, Sam always liked to say, based on a shared passion and what Sam took to be a secret complicity. But outside of that passion Dewey was a hard person to get close to, for reasons that had as much to do with Sam's single-minded dedication to his work — and both men's fundamentally solitary natures — as with Dewey's self-destructive impulses when he was off the air. (He had had his second disastrous car crash earlier in the year, from which he would

Sam and Jimmy Connolly. *Courtesy of the Sam Phillips Family* suffer debilitating pain for the rest of his life.) As someone who neither drank nor felt comfortable indulging his own extroverted impulses, Sam sometimes enjoyed observing Dewey more than actually being with him when they were in each other's company, in public or in private.

Jimmy on the other hand was the most down-to-earth, straightforward, easygoing person in the world. He had his own indulgences — he probably drank more than he should — but there was no one that Sam respected or relished spending time with more. They could still enjoy a game of checkers, and they went fishing together whenever they got a chance. In the summer they would meet back home in Sheffield, Alabama, and, while their wives were visiting with their parents, go out on the Tennessee River in Jimmy's boat. No two families could have been closer. When they visited Jimmy and Erin and their daughter, Dot, in Birmingham, Knox would go around with his aunt Erin on her advertising rounds, where she was greeted by everybody in the black neighborhoods with easy familiarity. When the two of them went into the Krispy Kreme together, the man would always give her a dozen donuts fresh out of the fryer and make sure that the little boy ate one or two while they were still piping hot. Jimmy and Erin had a pegboard up on the wall, and sometimes as the whole family would watch the wrestling matches on Saturday night on TV, Uncle Jimmy would sit back in his chair and blow smoke rings that started out small and then just got bigger and bigger as they floated up over the pegs. He was, said Knox, the world's champion smoke ring blower, and as the adults talked excitedly about the radio station they would someday all operate together, the little boy would sit entranced. To Knox, his mother and father, his uncle Jimmy and his aunt Erin — "all four of them were Radio Land!"

It was a result for which in many ways Becky devoutly might have wished. As excited as she was by the recording studio, as persuaded as she was of her husband's vision, she longed for the stability of radio — and secretly she hoped that this might bring Sam back to the way it was when they met, to how it had been when they first set out upon their life together. For Marion, too, there existed, at least in part, the same desire. There would be a role for her, she was certain, at any station that Sam was involved in, and it would bring him the kind of recognition and reward that he so richly deserved. Although each approved separately and wholeheartedly of anything that Sam set his mind on doing, neither was altogether persuaded of the certainty of his present course. Either of them, Sam thought, would be perfectly happy if he just happened to wake up some day and started recording the big bands again at the Hotel Peabody.

But that was not, and never could be, the limit of his ambition. Dare to be different, dare to be great, dare to take on the challenges that life hands you without flinching had been the mantra he had embraced since his teens. He was not about to give up his little laboratory, no matter what else might come along. He was not about to abandon his almost inexpressible dream.

He maintained his connection with Lillian McMurry's Trumpet Records. He continued to cut tracks on performers who just happened to wander in. ("He'd just listen to anything they wanted to play," said Marion with a mixture of amazement and admiration.) At the beginning of November he recorded some sides on a hillbilly piano player from Covington, Tennessee, named Red Hadley, who had a little band that Sam thought might have some potential. He brought in black drummer Houston Stokes, who played on many of his blues sessions, to add a little oomph to the sound, cutting two instrumentals on Red and a Lefty Frizzell "answer song" with a hard Hank Williams edge. He cut some nice sides on Joe Hill Louis and Walter Horton and even talked with Leonard Chess about the possibility of establishing a new basis for a business relationship. And on the recommendation of Buster Williams he sent out dubs to Jim Bulleit, the legendary record man whom Sam had first met at WSM when he was looking for a job at the Opry, who had only recently returned to Nashville and started up a new label of his own.

JIM BULLEIT WAS A MAN of grandiloquent speech and amplitudinous gestures. Like so many others in the record business, he had started off in radio. A college-educated, well-spoken, elegant, almost professorial figure, he was born in Indiana in 1908 and got a degree in music education from Illinois Wesleyan but discovered almost immediately that he had no aptitude or interest in teaching — so he put the voice training he had gotten in college to use as a radio announcer. After the usual small-market apprenticeship, he had migrated to San Francisco for CBS in 1943 and, when he found that he didn't like the West Coast,

Jim Bulleit, right, with Birmingham distributor Danny Cassella on left, and fellow salesman Jack Howard, Birmingham, 1949. *Courtesy of Martin Hawkins*

relocated to Nashville, where he took a job as an announcer with WSM, home of the Grand Ole Opry.

He was soon promoted to run WSM's Artist Service Bureau, the Opry's booking agency, which he turned into a financial windfall, both for himself and for the Opry. He also met Francis Craig, a member of the family that owned National Life, owner of WSM ("We Shield Millions") and the Grand Ole Opry. Craig, in his midforties, was a well-known society bandleader, a pianist with a subdued ragtime flavor who had formed his first band in 1921 while still a student at Vanderbilt. He began his broadcasts from the Hermitage Hotel on the night that WSM first went on the air, in November of 1925, and made records over the years with a succession of vocalists, including Kitty Kallen, Dinah Shore, and future *Hit Parade* singer Snooky Lanson. In 1946 Craig was offered the job of music librarian and announcer at WSM, but before retiring as a bandleader he wanted to rerecord his theme song, "Red Rose," which he had written for his wife some twenty years earlier.

He approached Jim Bulleit, who had recently left the station under

somewhat clouded circumstances (it had been suggested in some quarters that he might have been taking personal kickbacks for his booking
activities), to record the song for the record label he had just formed
with the backing of local jukebox operators Eugene Cashion and C. V.
Hitchcock. Bulleit was reluctant initially. In less than a full year of operation his biggest hits had come, surprisingly, in the r&b field, but he
allowed himself to be persuaded and in January of 1947 went into WSM's
Studio C to record "Red Rose" and three other songs of Craig's choosing.
He picked one of the songs, "Near You," as the B-side, an odd, almost
unfinished mix introduced by more than a minute of Craig's own somewhat aloof version of stride piano, then followed by an orchestra backed
vocal that seemed almost to have been interpolated as an afterthought.
In April of 1947 he put the single out, doing everything he could think
of to promote Craig's signature song, even dropping roses from an airplane on the day of its release. Still, the record wasn't selling until a DJ
in Griffin, Georgia, turned it over and played the B-side. Within weeks
"Near You" had sold 80,000 copies, by July 185,000, and in October of
1947, it passed the million mark. It was number 1 on the pop charts for
seventeen weeks, one of the longest-selling pop successes of all time,
hit number 1 in England, Sweden, and throughout much of Europe,
and became radio and television comedian Milton Berle's theme
song. Jim Bulleit had a new house, Francis Craig had a new career.

Within eighteen months Bulleit had been forced out of the company
and, in his ever-resourceful but not always provident way, had embarked
on a headlong hegira of sales and promotion that saw him starting up a
number of record companies and song publishers without notable success, supervising national radio promotion for Hadacol patent medicine,
signing and almost immediately losing the song publishing of country
music's latest superstar Lefty Frizzell, and running the Louisiana Hayride's booking agency in Shreveport for much of 1951. He returned to
Nashville in January of 1952, briefly entered the insurance and securi-
ties business, and launched his new label, J-B Records. In October he
started up an r&b division and had just released Eddie "Guitar Slim"
Jones' "Feelin' Sad" (in the same vein as Jones' explosive number 1 hit
for Specialty, "The Things That I Used to Do," little more than a year
later) when Sam got in touch with him at the end of that month.

Sam sent him some mellow T-Bone Walkerish sides that he had just
cut on Walter "Tang" Smith, the trombonist who had played on Howlin'

Wolf's recent "big band" session. When Bulleit bought the sides for $250, Sam sent him some more, including a couple of raw "cottonpatch" blues by Charles Thomas, whom Sam touted as possessing a style "a lot like Johnnie Lee Hooker's but I actually think he does a better vocal than Hooker."

Bulleit deferred a decision on the Charles Thomas sides, even after Sam lowered his price, but he scheduled the "Tang" Smith for release and at the same time brought up the idea of a potential partnership. The partnership would necessarily depend upon the participation of Sam's wealthy radio patron, Clarence Camp, and, on the basis of Sam's notable success with "Rocket 88" and "Booted" in particular, would put Sam in charge of recording, Bulleit in charge of sales and promotion. As they went back and forth on the matter, it soon became evident that Bulleit saw Camp as providing him with a way to cut some of his debts, with the new partnership reimbursing him at least in part for the investment he had already made in his company and the back catalogue he would bring to the new label. Once Sam made it clear that he was not in full agreement with this plan, Bulleit's demands came down to no more than a couple of thousand dollars, and then when it turned out Clarence Camp would not be returning to Memphis from his Florida vacation until late spring and had indicated to Sam that he would be unable to consider the matter until then, for some inexplicable reason—perhaps because as an instinctive venture capitalist all he needed to get in was the sense that he already *was* in—Jim Bulleit proposed that they go full speed ahead. So long as it was understood that he would continue with his own label, J-B Records, and his own little distribution business.

It would have been entirely understandable if Sam had felt more than a small degree of hesitation. Anyone who carefully considered the matter might have noticed the glaring holes in Jim Bulleit's résumé, the wildly unpredictable trajectory of his career. But most people did not. Like Jud, to whom Sam was occasionally inclined to compare him, Bulleit possessed that innate magnetism that made it difficult to see that he could fail as spectacularly as he succeeded. As Bulleit himself said, looking back on it all ruefully some twenty years later, his timing was never quite right. But to Sam, Jim Bulleit was the man who had recorded "Near You," a gifted radio announcer who had only to open his mouth for the words to flow out, a record man who, even if he was down on his luck, knew everything there was to know about distribution and the trials and tribulations of the independent operator. Best of all, as he repeatedly told Sam, he cared nothing about the creative end of the business — that was Sam's department. If Sam could just deliver the goods, he knew he could sell them. And so, without any further preamble or hesitation, Sun Records was reborn.

B Y MID-JANUARY they were in business. There was a moment when Sam was prepared to defer to Bulleit's more established name in the industry and wondered if they should call their new venture Bullet Records, but when he found out that the "Bullet" name was tied up by Bulleit's original partners, he wrote that after thinking it over, he believed "Sun" "to be as good as any other Label name we could conjure up and I, of course, have had the art work done and have got three electro-plates that we can use [and] then we can save $50.00 or 60.00 and too can get labels immediately."

The initial release that Sam had in mind was going to be three solid gutbucket blues efforts, the John Lee Hooker styled sides by Charles Thomas, a vocal and an instrumental by West Memphis blues personality Willie Nix, and two sides from Joe Hill Louis sessions with pianist Albert Williams and Nix on drums. At the last minute, though, Sam changed his mind. "You will note that I have changed the flip side of Nix's number," he wrote to Jim on January 15, "and put another vocal instead of the instrumental." Also, instead of the Charles Thomas, he had decided to release "a number by [a] boy I do not know," Handy Jackson's "Trouble Will Bring You Down," a slow "crying" blues with a blurry overamplified sound that seemingly had little to recommend it other than Sam's instant and instinctive feeling for it. "I really believe in this number," he wrote to Bulleit immediately after recording it in the midst of a session that featured pianist and vocalist Gay Garth, following up several days later by stressing that Jackson, a singer with whom prior to the session Garth himself was altogether unfamiliar, was the one he was "banking on."

Jim in any case did not object. To Jim, in fact, it was in many ways all the same. He owned 50 percent of a new record company without any investment, or any exclusivity, on his part — he was not "banking on" anyone. As far as his personal views were concerned, they were, like much of his view of human nature, curiously abstract. He found in Sam a not particularly compelling mix of fervor and naïveté — he was a nice enough guy, but Jim found him "reserved, [almost] stand-offish." And he thought too well of himself, too, when it was clear that "he was [just] lucky, like me. These guys would just walk in the studio, and he would record them."

It was all the luck of the draw anyway. Sam's recordings had hit before, and they could hit again. Jim's time was taken up with practical considerations, like running a list of his distributors by Sam, presenting Sam with a sample invoice, and submitting a draft of the letter he proposed to send out to introduce his customers to the Sun label, in which he touted other record companies he represented as well and characterized Sun as a new account "I have just taken on [that is] owned by Mr. Sam Phillips who has given so many hits to Leonard Chess." He stressed to Sam the need to establish credit with at least three pressing plants across the country so that, should a record take off in a particular region, they could cut down on the prohibitive cost of long-distance shipping.

The next few weeks were a whirlwind of activity and practical advice. Jim advised Sam to make sure he numbered his invoices consecutively, to be aware that while 78s remained the dominant format in the Southern r&b singles market, 45s were making rapid inroads and Sam should be prepared to start their manufacture in significant numbers at some point soon. Jim offered to put Charles Thomas out on his own label if Sam liked, almost as if Sun and J-B Records were two branches of the same business. He educated Sam about the federal excise tax, a 10 percent surcharge on manufacturing costs that was a holdover from the war years and that added 4.2 cents to the cost of every record you pressed, regardless of how many you sold. Since Jim was going to own the publishing on all of the songs they recorded, Sam should get a co-write on as many of them as possible. He and Sam needed to squeeze every penny that they could out of every record that they released if they wanted to survive. Jim could speak from experience, it was going to be a very tight squeeze.

Sam took it all in and simply applied it to a business methodology that, with Marion's help, had been meticulous from the first. He established credit with Nate Duroff's Monarch pressing plant out on the Coast and with Shaw Record Processing Company in Cincinnati. Even more significantly, through the personal advocacy of Kemmons Wilson, he established a relationship of fiduciary trust with Buster Williams, whose Plastic Products right there in Memphis would be his

The first Holiday Inn, with Kemmons Wilson and his mother, Doll, standing under "The Great Sign." *Courtesy of Kemmons Wilson Companies*

most important pressing plant and whose distribution arm, Music Sales, would be just as important in all his sales throughout the mid-South.

He had always liked Buster, from the goodwill he had shown not just toward Sam but toward all the independents, helping Leonard Chess in particular to get a solid foothold in the business. He admired Buster, too, for his fiercely independent spirit, as he peered out myopically through his little dirty glasses on a world that he saw as a gold mine of opportunity. But it took Kemmons Wilson, another Memphis free spirit, to reinforce the relationship to the point that Buster felt comfortable — out of both faith and hometown pride — in virtually bankrolling the new label.

Kemmons was a local home builder and World War II flying ace, who on a family driving trip with his wife and five children to Washington, D.C., in the summer of 1950 had had the revelation that what the country needed was a good family hotel. He had opened his first Holiday Inn in Memphis two years later, with a commitment to provide comfortable, dependable accommodations, cheerful decor, and, above all, affordable prices — $4 for a single, $6 for a double, children, however many, free. Within months he opened his second motel, on Third Street downtown, and had just announced his plans (with prominent local builder Wallace Johnson) to open two more, covering all four corners of the city, with a blueprint for a national franchising campaign by the time the fourth Memphis Holiday Inn was built in 1953. Like Sam, he came from humble circumstances, and had been forced to quit school in his teens to help eke out a living for himself and his widowed mother, Doll (his first entrepreneurial venture was to borrow $50 for a popcorn machine that he set up in a local movie theater lobby). Sam met him just after he opened his first Holiday Inn, and they hit it off right away. Once Kemmons vouched for him with Buster Williams, Sam said, it was not so much a matter of credit as belief. To Sam, both Kemmons and Buster, too, with their faith in democratic possibilities, in imagination and the common man, were "the essence of what America has always been about." Having people like Kemmons and Buster put their trust in him, seeing "a guy like Kemmons come along and start with nothing to speak of but an idea — very little financing, but a desire and a belief that he could make a difference — [it] gave a guy much younger than him, ten years to the day, a lot of encouragement not to give up that easily."

THE FIRST THREE RECORDS were released on January 30, 1953, just two weeks after the partnership with Jim Bulleit had informally commenced. Despite Sam's strong "feeling" about it, the Handy Jackson passed almost unnoticed, by both the marketplace and posterity. The two that accompanied it, however, Joe Hill Louis' "She May Be Yours (But She Comes to See Me Sometimes)" and Willie Nix, The Memphis Blues Boy's "Seems Like a Million Years" were everything that Sam Phillips had ever promised himself he would deliver.

The Joe Hill Louis record was not dissimilar to other Joe Hill Louis sides, reflecting both his singular strengths and his endearing weaknesses. It was the product of two sessions in which Louis' guitar and harmonica took the lead, but Willie Nix's drums on "She May Be Yours," and Albert Williams' piano on both sides, provided a rhythmic solidarity that Joe could not always summon in his more commonplace one-man-band setting. Both sides showcased the unique joie de vivre of Sam's first discovery (actually, as Sam himself would have pointed out, Joe Hill Louis was a clear case of the artist discovering *him*), but it was the A-side, "She May Be Yours," a medium-tempo boogie with a heavy beat, squalling harmonica solos, and the rough vocal bleeding purposefully

Willie Nix's wife, Patty, and her cousin Nevada (in white dress) in a cotton field, ca. 1951. *Courtesy of Delta Haze photo archive*

through the harmonica mike, that revealed the way in which even when much of what Joe sang was taken from traditional sources, it reflected, Sam said, something "very personal to him."

The Willie Nix numbers were even more distinctive, as befitted a proud free spirit referred to by one fellow bluesman as "a little aviatic." Nix had come to Sam's attention originally through his radio show on KWEM at just about the same time he had first heard the Howlin' Wolf, but he appeared to be as drawn to the life of the open road as to any form of professional advancement. Just the manner in which he conveyed the simplest facts of his life showed an imaginative flair that suggested not so much that he was "fantasizing about things that could never be," in the elegant formulation of blues historian Jim O'Neal, as that "in his mind he was simply stating what ought to be." The single was the product of an October session which Sam had originally submitted to Chess and presented the same quartet format as the Joe Hill Louis, only this time requiring two musicians (Nix's versatile guitarist, Joe Willie Wilkins, and seventeen-year-old harmonica player James Cotton, another West Memphis regular, who had already recorded for Sam with Howlin' Wolf) to fill in for Louis' guitar-harmonica combination.

"Baker Shop Boogie" was a rollicking romp with all the usual double entendres about jelly roll, baking bread, and rolling dough, a head-shaking solo by Cotton that came straight out of his mentor Sonny Boy

Williamson's book, flawlessly modulated guitar interpolations, and a burbling enthusiasm that carried it right out into the uncharted waters that Sam was always looking to explore. It was the other side, though, "Seems Like a Million Years," that was the real gem. Even at a slow-drag tempo, it kicked hard ("Willie was not the subtlest of drummers," Sam commented, "but he drove a session along"), and, with the beautifully articulated rumblings of Albert Williams' piano and Joe Willie Wilkins' unerring instinct for the right touch at the right moment, it dug deep. "Some drinks to keep from worrying," Nix declared, "Some just ride from town to town / No need for me to drink to keep from worrying / 'Cause it's slowly carrying me down." As striking as the mood was the sound that Sam drew from the little combo, with each part distinctly separated but all coming together to create the feel that Sam knew Willie was capable of, if he was just given a little encouragement.

It was the revived Sun label's fourth release, though, number 180 in a series that had begun so inauspiciously the year before with Jackie Boy and Little Walter's unissued Sun 174, that represented the pinnacle of Sam's work to date. Once again it featured Walter Horton, this time as half of a duo billed as Jimmy and Walter and made up of himself and guitarist Jimmy DeBerry, with Houston Stokes helping out sparingly on drums. The A-side, "Easy," was a harmonica instrumental that in anyone else's hands might have seemed little more than a harmonic restatement of Ivory Joe Hunter's 1950 blues standard, "I Almost Lost My Mind." With Walter's genius for tonal variation, however, it embraced a shimmering new palette, as verse follows lyrical verse, sounding at first, with its full rounded vibrato-laden tone, as if the harmonica is coming from inside a bottle, then gradually taking on additional force and meaning until, with a mix of reverb, angry squalls, and sheer volume, the lyrical gives way for a moment to a mood almost of aggression, then subsides once again — though not altogether — to the pure beauty of its original inspiration. There is no bridge, just a compact turnaround at the end of each verse, and Jimmy DeBerry's unamplified guitar could not play more uncomplicated blues changes throughout — but the effect is riveting, seeking, in Sam's uncompromising terms, to capture no more and no less than unfettered self-expression.

The other side, "Before Long," opens with the same unamplified guitar and in some ways offers much the same affect — except this time there is no Walter, with Jimmy DeBerry's delicate, somewhat wobbly vocal substituting for the harmonica. Once again the presentation could not be simpler, the message could not be more intimate. "I worked all the summer / And all the fall / Gonna spend Christmas / In my overalls

But I'll get a break
Somewhere
Before long

It was, said Marion, quoting the lyrics from memory, "a perfect example of the twelve-bar blues." But she recognized, too, that its utter simplicity, its sound of unforced intimacy, was not in any way a matter of chance. It was a product of Sam trying to make every record as perfect as it could possibly be. Not perfect in the usual conventional terms, perfect *in its own terms*. What Sam was after, as he told her over and over, as he told anyone who would listen, was perfection of feeling, not perfection of technique. A few months later Jimmy would be back in the studio with a pianist and drummer backing him, this time without Walter. He was singing a stop-time blues that he called "Time Has Made a Change," with a completely different feel (in this song even the little babies were "bopping") and a completely different sound from the earlier session. Here Jimmy played crude electric guitar, and Sam recorded the piano so that it sounded like the kind of honky-tonk upright you might hear if you wandered into your local barroom. Just as they completed the second chorus and were about to launch into a tinny piano solo, there was the shrill sound of the telephone ringing in the outer office. Far from taking this as a deterrent — well, who knows exactly what went on in Sam's mind, whether he somehow or other made a thematic connection between the interruption of the telephone and the song's message, or to Sam's ears the phone's ring was simply in tune with the band. You know, I think I'll just let Sam tell it. But remember: that phone remained a part of the record for all eternity.

"I love perfect imperfection, I really do, and that's not just some cute saying, that's a fact. Perfect? That's the devil. Who in this world would want to be perfect? They should strike the damn thing out of the language of the human race. You think I was going to throw that cut away for one of them good ones that didn't have a telephone ringing in the middle of it? Hell, no, that's what [was] happening. That was *real*. You know how much it would cost to make a noise like that [as] a sound effect — by pushing a button? And that ain't the real thing. People want the real thing. There's too much powder and rouge around. You know, I'm a crazy guy when it comes to sound."

Well, I'm not going to argue with that, and I don't know too many people who did if they were given the opportunity — whether because they were intimidated by the profundity of Sam's thought or the fanaticism of his belief. But that was Sam's aesthetic, that was the intensity that he applied to every session — and I should be clear here. There was nothing intense about the way in which he dealt with any of his artists. Putting pressure on *them* was the furthest thing from his mind. The intensity came solely from the unremitting faith he put in the process. As he said one time, amplifying further on his mistrust of a safe result: "I like the marker in the road that makes you keep walking. And when you get to that marker, you think you're not going to move on? Sure you are. You think you are not going to enjoy doing that? Sure you are. You think you're not going to stub your toe? Sure you are. You think you're not going to get tired? If you don't, you're cheating yourself — you're not getting the most out of what's available to you, *right then.*"

Sam was not going to cheat himself — or any of the other equally idiosyncratic individualists with whom he had cast his lot. There was no question now that he was going on to the next marker, and the one beyond that, and the one that at this point he could barely see out on the far edge of the horizon. He felt a renewed sense of purpose, a renewed belief in the music in all of its glorious individuation. Some sessions were going to reflect no more than high-spirited exuberance, others the bottomless profundity of the Howlin' Wolf. Some he would record with a delicacy of touch, others with the same kind of over-amped drive that he had discovered with "Rocket 88." But all would reflect to the fullest extent that he was capable of the unmodified fulfillment of their inspiration, all would reflect the circumstances of the moment that gave them birth. And all that was required of him was the quality of "transference" that enabled him to put himself in the place of each person who stood in front of the microphone. That was how, he said, he was able to give each and every person who came into his studio a sense of self-worth. "Put it another way, give them confidence in their ability." He knew without a doubt — don't ask him how he knew, he just *knew* — "that I could discern things that were different." That was the one characteristic on which he prided himself most.

"A NEW INDIE RHYTHM AND BLUES label was launched here [in Memphis]," *Cash Box* announced in its March 21, 1953, issue, echoing the PR release that Sam had written and Marion polished and sent out. It cited Sam's work with "such outstanding artists as Jackie Brenston, B.B. King, Howlin' Wolf, Joe Hill Louis, Roscoe Gordon [and] Willie Nix"—a stellar roster, to be sure, but more striking, if less readily convincing to the everyday businessman, was his unwavering commitment "to give every opportunity to untried artists to prove their talents, whether they play a broom stick or the finest jazz sax in the world."

But this was no time to worry about nuance. He cleared up the matter of the Sun name—there was another Sun label in Albuquerque that had started up the previous year, not to mention a Yiddish-language Sun in New York ("The Brightest Thing on Records") going back to 1946, though at this point it seemed to have lapsed. Sam dealt with the Albuquerque label—they had had a regional hit with a western number the previous summer, but they relinquished the name without a fight.

He had by now acquired an old RCA 76-D radio board with six inputs from a station in South Carolina for $500—"of course that was a lot of money, [and when] I got that damn thing down here, all the electrolytic capacitors . . . were just cooked." But he had it up and running in a week's time and operating with a greater flexibility and precision of sound than he had been able to get out of his portable Presto. He plunged an additional $700 into studio improvements and hired an accountant with a law degree, Roy Scott Jr., whose father was Kemmons' accountant. Like Kemmons Wilson and Buster Williams, Roy was another flying buff, and Sam was won over by both his easygoing manner and his unquestionable expertise. He helped Marion, a meticulous record keeper, set up the books on a somewhat more formal basis, and he complimented her on the efficiency with which she was already running the business. Sam had by now come to realize that he would never be able to pay the onerous federal excise tax right off the bat, but Roy advised him that even if he couldn't pay, he needed to submit a precise account of what he owed—the IRS wasn't likely to shut him down for his failure to make the payments until he had the assets to collect them from.

Sometimes it seemed as if there weren't enough hours in the day to do all the things that he needed to do, but his spirits never flagged. As he would later tell an old friend, WLAC DJ Hoss Allen, it was the greatest time of his life—not in any damn nostalgia sense ("I'm not one who likes to look back on the 'great old days'") but more for the challenges it presented that would be forever imprinted on his memory, as big, as real, as full of force, fun, and fury as life could be. His new partner, Jim Bulleit, was an unwitting source of some of the fun. Sam and Marion pored over his letters from the road, full of boastful grandiloquence and flowery eloquence that failed to disguise his innately nervous nature. Not a letter arrived, laughed Marion, generally speaking an admirer, that did not include some version of the phrase "Cold words on paper cannot fully explain or express this." As if he needed somehow to convey his regret that time and space should have intruded between them in any way. "That," said Marion, "got to be a byword between us." The upshot more often than not was a request for money. But as Marion was fully aware, "Jim had the expertise. He had the contacts, he had the distributorships, he was a very eloquent, elegant, knowledgeable person."

SAM HAD BARELY HAD TIME to settle into the new house at 1028 McEvers Circle. It was the first house he had ever owned, purchased for a little more than $10,000 on January 21, 1953, with $2,000 he had been able to set aside from his Chess Records hits serving as the down payment. It was a modest gabled bungalow with a small front porch and an attached garage in a postwar Levittown-like development out by Kennedy veterans' hospital, the same neighborhood in which he and Becky and the baby had lived when they first moved to Memphis and boarded briefly in that nice lady from Sheffield's home. There were just two bedrooms and a single bathroom at the end of the hall, and it sat on a corner lot, giving them a nice yard — but for Becky it would not have mattered if it had been more modest by far. It was their first real home.

They started going to church at Ascension Lutheran, just down the street on Getwell, where they fell in love with the young minister, Pastor Armin Barnick, and his wife, Carol. It was a small church, with folding chairs for the congregation, and more suited to Sam's taste than Idlewild Presbyterian's formal gloom. Pastor Barnick was a fine speaker, and Knox became an active participant in Sunday school classes.

Most of all, from Becky's point of view, it was a real neighborhood, with lots of other kids around and young families in the same situation as they were, getting their feet on the ground. Sam wasn't home much of the time, but when he rounded the corner in his sleek 1948 Hudson, the boys would come running up with their little terrier, Penny, and it

Our new home at 1028 McEvers Circle

Early 1953. *Courtesy of the Sam Phillips Family*

almost seemed like everything was just as it should be. Knox was a grave little boy who observed his father closely—he had a genuine curiosity about what his father did, not just how things were done but why, and Sam was always glad to explain to him in straightforward adult terms. One time he accompanied his father to the studio and, losing his balance, fell against the Memphis Recording Service sign in the window and broke it. Knox was terrified. He knew exactly how much that sign meant to his father ("It was his *life*"), but Sam didn't say anything—he didn't have to. They both knew it would never happen again.

Jerry was different. Even at four and one-half he was more like his father in his bristling independence and determination to speak his own mind. Almost reflexively he learned to withhold himself in small ways, and he was much more inclined to get into trouble than Knox, but it only took a word from Sam to set either of the boys straight. Becky wished it was easier for Sam to show his affection. He was never as demonstrative of his feelings as she would have—as he would have liked, she often thought—though he always welcomed the boys' guileless demonstrations of their love. But a lot of men were like that, she knew, and she never doubted his love and loyalty to them all — it was just that in this, as in everything else, he was bound and determined to go his own way. He was, she wrote, in an admiring portrait she presented to him many years later, an individual "who always follows his own lead, even if it is not the popular thing to do, [someone who] holds back emotion, [is] always in control, never minces words, [but] gives encouragement when he feels it is deserved." She knew how much Sam believed in his new record label, and for that reason she believed in it, too. When she and Sam and the boys all attended church together on Sunday, it made her proud. She was glad he liked Pastor Barnick, because that meant that he was more conscientious in his church attendance than he had been at any other time in their marriage. And if he wasn't faithful to her in the conventional sense of the word, it just made her more determined to try a little bit harder. Because she knew, no matter what anyone else might think, his true fidelity to her, to his little family, was never in doubt, just as their faith in him remained unchallenged.

S AM WAS KNOCKED OUT by Big Mama Thornton's "Hound Dog" the first time he heard it. Performed with ripsaw gusto by the singer, an Amazonian twenty-six-year-old blues shouter from Montgomery, Alabama, and modified by a delicate Latin-flavored "rhumba-boogie" beat, the record struck a communal chord somewhere between low comedy and bedrock truth. It totally tickled Sam on both levels. "I said, my God, it's so true. You ain't nothing but a hound dog. You ain't met your responsibilities. You didn't go to work like you [should]." And it gave him an immediate idea for a follow-up — from the *man's* point of view.

He had been looking for a song for part-time WDIA disc jockey Rufus Thomas (Rufus supported his family working five days a week in a textile mill from 6:30 in the morning until 2:30 in the afternoon) ever since his last session almost a year ago. Chess had released three singles on Rufus from the recordings Sam had submitted, but none of them had clicked, and Sam was convinced it was simply because he hadn't yet found Rufus the right material. Rufus was more of an entertainer along the lines of a Louis Jordan than a straight blues singer, something brought home to Sam when he saw him perform his comedy routine as the opening act for the "Rocket 88" show at the Handy Theatre two years before. With his gruff Louis Armstrong–influenced voice, quick wit, and eye-popping antics, he was the perfect candidate to reply to the harsh accusations Big

Mama Thornton had thrown out in her song, this time leveling them at a "bossy woman"—but Rufus balked at the idea at first. For one thing, he had never heard the expression Sam had found to give the song both its theme and title. Just what, he asked, was a "bear cat" when it came to male-female relations? Sam said he wasn't sure about Memphis, but this was a common phrase in the part of Alabama where he had grown up. "I said, 'Rufus, hell, you don't know what a damn bear cat is? That's the meanest goddamn woman in the world.'"

Rufus agreed in the end to do the song that Sam sketched out for him, which, in the time-honored tradition of answer songs, was a virtual carbon copy of "Hound Dog," with lyrics, chord progressions, and rhythmic structure all patterned directly on the original. Sam scheduled the session for March 8, just one day after Peacock Records placed an ad in *Billboard* announcing that "Hound Dog" was going to be a "HIT, HIT, HIT"—but then Rufus took umbrage at the band Sam had put together. Rather than the Louis Jordan-oriented sax-led combo they had used on his previous sessions, this was the "country" rhythm section that Sam generally employed on his downhome blues sessions, with Joe Hill Louis' guitar taking the lead. Louis wasn't playing "right," protested Rufus, an astute communicator who prided himself on his "pleasing" personality but for all of his clowning had a stubborn streak when it came to his own sense of self-determination. Nonetheless, he threw himself into the song with the same brash charm that he brought to all of his performances, complete with yowls, growls, and fervent imprecations to "Git it, git it, git it, aw listen to that old cat, Aw, kick it, Miss Kitty."

The result was peppier than Big Mama's version, with a more straight-ahead beat, but Sam was under no illusions about surpassing the original. "Hell, we didn't come close to being as good as Big Mama. She could have done that song a cappella and convinced me that, by God, you ain't nothing but a damned hound dog!" Still, it was a thoroughly entertaining novelty number, and Rufus carried off his performance with genuine conviction—the one unvarying test Sam applied to any material he let out of the studio. He released the record just two weeks later, labeling it unequivocally as it was "'Bear Cat' (The Answer to Hound Dog)," and it got the lead rhythm and blues review in the same March 28, 1953, issue of *Billboard* in which "Hound Dog," destined to be number one on the r&b charts for seven weeks later that spring, first charted. True to *Billboard*'s prediction, it hit almost immediately. Sam could hardly believe it when the first orders came in. Gwen Kesler of Southland Distributors in Atlanta called just days after the record was released and said, "Sam, this thing is fantastic." He said, "Well, Gwen, how many are you gonna order?' and when she said five thousand, he was floored. None of his other releases had sold five thousand records total. Buster Williams followed suit, and then he phoned Alta Hayes at Big State in Dallas, to let her know that he didn't think she would want to get left behind. It kept on selling, and by the middle of April, it, too, had charted nationally.

But there was a problem. Don Robey, the owner of Duke/Peacock Records, who held the publishing on the song through his Lion Musical Publishing Company, objected almost instantly that, since the song was so obviously a copy, Sun Records should have applied to Lion for a mechanical license (this is a statutory payment to the song publisher of two cents per record — customarily divided with the songwriter — for the right to mechanically reproduce a copyrighted composition). When Robey, a notoriously tough man in all of his affairs, didn't hear back from Sam right away, he followed up with a letter on April 4 giving Sun four days to indicate compliance or face a penalty rate of five to eight cents per record "for the intrusion upon the rights of others."

It was a strange situation, as *Billboard* noted in a series of contemporaneous stories about the newly developing trend to challenge copyright ownership of answer songs. Common practice up till now, *Billboard* pointed out in its April 4 issue, had been "to regard the answer as an 'original.'" Rhythm and blues in particular had seen virtually no challenges to this assumption until just four months earlier, when, "with the r&b field becoming of such importance to pop publishers," a number of lawsuits had been filed. Perhaps, *Billboard* had suggested the previous week in its "Rhythm and Blues Notes," the practice had gotten a little out of hand with the release of "a wild thing called 'Bear Cat'" and a number of other recent releases so soon after the appearance of the original, leading some in the industry to speculate that "the diskeries soon may be bringing out the answers before the original records are released."

Sam's partner, Jim Bulleit, was thrown into something of a panic. He commissioned a formal comparison study — which only went to prove what Sam had known all along. The two songs were identical. He questioned whether Sam fully understood the business of publishing. He pleaded with Sam to release more product, since "releasing is the life of this business. . . . Don't let the distributors forget us." And he constantly asked for money, stressing in one letter, "I wouldn't nor haven't asked for money unless I needed it. Please understand and let me have the money, PLEASE."

In the end Sam settled. He knew he was in the wrong, given the new copyright climate, and he had neither the resources nor the inclination to drag out what seemed certain to be a losing battle. On May 18 he wrote a check to Lion Musical Publishing Company for $1,580.80 and gave up all claims to the publishing. It was unquestionably a disappointment, and, maybe just because he never liked to have his nose rubbed in it, it left him with something of a lingering bad feeling about Don Robey. But that was just business. The record itself was an unqualified triumph. Sales kept climbing, and it eventually reached number 3 on the r&b charts, not dropping off again till the middle of June. Sam had already had big hits with other labels, but this was the first he had ever had on his own. And even if in the end, for all of the spirit that Rufus brought to it, there was no denying that it was a "copy" tune, and in spite of all the legal and financial trouble it had caused him — nothing could diminish the satisfaction he took, the pride that came with Sun Records' first real breakthrough success.

It caused him to redouble his efforts in the studio, to redouble his efforts to get to know the DJs, the distributors, all the people he would need to make a go of it in the business. He was disturbed by what he was beginning to see as Jim's lack of good judgment when it came to sizing up people — many of Jim's distributors seemed poor prospects for Sun's type of material, and when they did place orders, it was almost impossible to get some of them to pay — but Sam wasn't sure how much of that could be attributed to Jim's almost permanent state of impecuniousness. In any case he was not to be deterred. He had always thought of the studio as his "cathedral." Now he saw it more as a kind of living presence. "What we had," he said, "was a church of the spirit that fed on itself," a house of worship in which he could express his faith in his own unequivocally private terms.

IT WAS JIM BULLEIT who brought him the Prisonaires, and if Jim did nothing else (besides inspiring him to finally leap with both feet into the record business), Sam considered that this alone might be enough. The Prisonaires were a quintet confined to the Tennessee State

Penitentiary in Nashville who owed a combined total of about 850 years to the state. Convicted of crimes ranging from murder to larceny to six counts of rape (that was Johnny Bragg, their lead singer, who, with six consecutive life sentences, accounted for 594 of their aggregate years), they would unquestionably never have had the chance to perform outside the prison walls had it not been for the election of thirty-two-year-old Governor Frank Clement, a new-fashioned evangelical politician with a strong liberal bent and an oratorical flair. Clement took office in January of 1953 and immediately installed his boyhood friend, James Edwards, as warden. Edwards, a six foot two strapping World War II veteran, had served in a Marine Corps military battalion for twenty months after the war, assigned for most of that time to the Fort Meade prisoner stockade. That experience, and Frank Clement's belief in him, were his only qualifications for the job. And when Edwards expressed some reservations about moving into the warden's quarters on the prison grounds with his wife and two daughters, Clement invoked their shared faith, stressing how integral the social reforms he intended to implement were both to the welfare of the state and the simple Christian values which they both espoused.

Together they embarked upon an ambitious humanitarian program at a prison that had up until then been known as "Swafford's Graveyard" for the warden that Edwards replaced. Among the numerous fruits of Edwards' progressive approach, which came accompanied by the inevitable accusations of "mollycoddling" and soft-on-crime and communistic tendencies from the press, was a new furlough policy, which began with the Prisonaires appearing without charge (a key feature, since there was no state budget for "entertainment") at gubernatorial receptions and social functions. They sang spirituals mostly and were an unquestionable hit with the governor's guests, but even more so with the governor, who had staked his faith on the promise of rehabilitation, or, as he put it, "the hopes of tomorrow rather than the mistakes of yesterday." Soon they were appearing at church events and Rotary and Exchange Club meetings, with the warden or his diminutive wife, "Red," driving them to their engagements, and within a matter of weeks they started singing on the radio, first on WSIX, a white station that featured hillbilly music and black gospel quartets, then on the black station, WSOK, as well.

That was how music publisher, record man, and sometime label owner Red Wortham, a longtime associate of Jim Bulleit's, first became aware of them. WSIX announcer Joe Calloway kept urging him to come out to the prison with him sometime and meet the boys in person. "He came round three or four times," Wortham told music historian Martin Hawkins, "and said, 'Red, you really need to go out and listen to those boys because they're GOOD!'" Eventually Wortham agreed, and he was sufficiently impressed to return a second time to record them.

He pitched the tape first to Dee Kilpatrick at Mercury and Paul Cohen at Decca, but when he didn't hear back right away from either one, he brought it to Jim Bulleit, who worked out of Wortham's office downtown at Fourth and Union. Bulleit listened to the tape, which contained four songs — a spirited version of Louis Jordan's "That Chick's Too Young to Fry," a dreamy pop song, a 5 Royales-type r&b number, and an ethereal ballad that could have been an Ink Spots original, written by lead singer Johnny Bragg and another convict, Robert Riley. Bulleit, whom Red Wortham judged to be "a bit of a finagler," said that it sounded fine to him but that he would have to get it to his partner, Sam Phillips, in Memphis, and Wortham had to be satisfied with that, even though, as the owner of the publishing on at least two of the songs, he was anxious to get things moving.

Sam got the tape at the end of April. He was predisposed to the project simply because it was "tied in so intellectually with what I was trying to do," but then when he heard the lead singer's pure tenor voice, so similar to that of the Ink Spots' great innovator, Bill Kenny, with its soaring falsetto, controlled vibrato, and aching vulnerability (but in a way even more vulnerable, perhaps simply due to the singer's plight) — "Well, I mean, then the devastation came over me." He knew he couldn't miss out on this opportunity — he just had to do it. "For something like this to come along, for all of the circumstances to be [right] — you can imagine how I thought I was dreaming!"

THE NEXT HURDLE was to persuade the governor to let him record the group in Memphis. Because if he was going to do it, he wanted to do it right. He got Jim Bulleit to set up an appointment.

Sam had no doubt that Frank Clement would be favorably disposed toward the project. He had heard the governor speak in Memphis at the Overton Park Shell in his election campaign the previous fall, and he had been bowled over by his combination of evangelical rhetoric and social idealism. To Sam, "Frank Clement was the greatest governor we ever had. He was the most far-reaching and, at the same time, both incisive and reflective person that has ever run our state. If we needed new taxes, if we needed prison reform, if we needed mental health reform — which we did — well, then that's what he called for." Sam also suspected from his oratorical flights that he was a frustrated preacher, and from that he devised a plan.

He had recently recorded a young man just about his own age with one of the clearest and most beautiful voices he had ever heard. Howard Seratt was the twelfth of seventeen children, born and raised on a farm outside Manila, Arkansas, who had contracted polio before the age of two. Though he remained on crutches for the rest of his life, he never let his handicap limit him. He taught himself harmonica and guitar at an early age, sang in a hillbilly band during the war, and then, after a religious conversion, turned to spiritual music exclusively. Which was how a Forrest City disc jockey named Larry Parker discovered him, singing and accompanying himself in a church in Mariana, and was so struck by his talent that he got the idea of starting a record label just to put out records by Howard Seratt. So he brought him in to Sam to record him, and they cut two titles, "Make Room in the Life Boat for Me" and "Jesus Means All to Me," which Parker put out on his newly formed St. Francis label. Sam had tried halfheartedly at that time to persuade Seratt to record some secular songs ("Oh, that man! I never heard a person, no matter what category of music, could sing as beautifully"), but it was clear Howard was not going to deviate from his beliefs, and Sam was the last person in the world to try to impose his vision on another. But now, he thought, the very unwaveringness of Howard Seratt's commitment might prove an asset in his quest to persuade the governor. What if he brought Seratt, and his record, with him when he went to meet Frank Clement? Might that not be a way of killing two birds with one stone?

That is exactly what happened. He brought Howard Seratt and an evangelist preacher from North Dakota with whom Seratt had been traveling, the Reverend C. O. Ray, to meet the governor, and Clement didn't have a lot of time for them, but then "Howard unpacked his guitar and harmonica and proceeded to sing." It worked just as Sam had hoped. The governor was captivated, not just by the music but by Sam, and every objection he raised about how his critics would crucify him if every "i" wasn't dotted, every "t" crossed Sam seemed to have anticipated and was prepared to sweep aside. Subsequently he met both Warden

Rev. C. O. Ray
Bismarck, North Dakota

Honorable
Frank G. Clement
Governor Of Tennessee

Howard Seratt

Sam C. Phillips, P
Sun Records,

Visiting Governor Clement with Howard Seratt and the Rev. C. O. Ray,
spring 1953. *Courtesy of the Sam Phillips Family*

Edwards, whom he liked immediately for his good heart (though he
wasn't any "bleeding heart" either), and his wife, too, who was as tough
as the warden in her own way and insisted that you call her "Red" — and
together he and Edwards ironed out all the practical details. Sam would
pay for the mileage between Nashville and Memphis, he would pay for
the armed guard and trusty who would accompany the group as well
("It wasn't right for the taxpayers to pay for my fucking experience"),
and they would take a percentage of any royalties from the records and
set up a fund that the prison population at large could draw from so the
other prisoners wouldn't get jealous.

The session was set for Monday, June 1, and the Nashville party
showed up at the studio in a specially modified elongated Chevrolet, with
Jim Bulleit driving, a little after 10 A.M. Sam bought coffee for the guards
at Miz Taylor's next door and brought in food and coffee for the prisoners, who, like all of his artists, were not permitted to eat in the restaurant. They were visibly nervous, and visibly excited, too, particularly

by the thrill of driving down Beale Street at Bulleit's behest on the way to the studio. Sam realized from the start that it wasn't going to be an easy session. He had brought in Joe Hill Louis once again to play guitar, and that worked out on their r&b number, "Baby Please," on which John Drue, one of the short-timers (he was scheduled to be paroled in October but planned to continue with the group even after his release), sang lead. Not only the tempo but the energy of the slow-paced demo was stepped up with the insertion of Joe Hill Louis' crudely strummed electric guitar, which Sam recorded both through Joe's little amp and with the naked sound of the strings bleeding faintly into the vocal mike. When it came to the number that was their centerpiece, though, Joe Hill Louis never entered the picture. It was the five Prisonaires on their own, with William Stewart artfully keeping time on acoustic.

"Just Walkin' in the Rain" was a song Johnny Bragg had written just months earlier with the help of Robert Riley, a more musically organized fellow inmate but not a member of the group. "Well, I called myself a singer," said Johnny in later years, in his characteristically soft, self-effacing, and ultimately deflective way. "I'm not going to say I *was* a singer. I tried to sing. One day it was raining heavy, and me and Robert Riley was walking to the laundry, and Bob said, 'Johnny, I wonder what the little girls are doing now.' And I said, 'I don't know what the little girls are doing, but we better hurry and get out of this rain.' And I started singing that song. Now Bob Riley was a smart man—I wasn't too smart myself, just had a little talent—and he put some [more] lyrics to it. In fact, we had a lot of lyrics. I couldn't write mine down—I ain't had no education, see? I just had that talent. Ain't that strange?"

The song they wrote was romantic, wistful, and transcendent in a way that would be difficult to define but managed to define itself in the delivery of the opening lines: "Just walkin' in the rain / Getting soaking wet / Torturin' my heart / By trying to forget." It was a classic Ink Spots derivative, with its conventional pop melody and formal diction and expression—all that was missing was the rumbling Hoppy Jones bass monologue that accompanied so many of the Ink Spots' big crossover hits. (Like the Golden Gate Quartet in the religious field, the Ink Spots presented themselves in the most "acceptable" fashion, and between 1939 and 1947 had had an astonishing fourteen Top 5 pop—that is, white, mainstream—hits, including seven number 1s.) "Just Walkin' in the Rain" clearly had the Ink Spots' style in mind. And yet it had something undeniably original about it, too. Maybe it was the situation of the singers. Maybe it was the song's emergence from what Sam called Johnny Bragg's "tongue-tied," lisped-tongued speech. Maybe it was simply their dedication to their craft under circumstances almost unimaginable to those who had had a taste of the good life.

"We used to practice, practice, practice," Johnny said. "We didn't have no microphones, so we used an echo with buckets. Everybody would get a bucket, and you could put that bucket up to your ears and, you know, a sound would come out. I wanted to be the Ink Spots — and I thought I *could* be the Ink Spots. I was young, crazy, I didn't know. I used to sing sitting in the cell. People be hollering and clapping their hands — this was the black wing at that time. 'Listen to the nigger.' 'Listen at him.' 'Well, let the nigger sing a little bit.' 'He can sing, can't he?'"

To Sam the demo possessed a delicate, quavering beauty, admirably seconded by William Stewart's classically spare guitar — but he thought it could achieve a greater intensity. And that's what they spent all day and well into the night looking for. They worked and worked on it. "Sam Phillips wanted everything to be perfect," Johnny said many years after the fact. "Ain't nothing wrong with that. We started early in the morning — and now it's four o'clock, five o'clock, six o'clock. Mr. Sam was something else."

And in the end they got what they were looking for. When the session was finally over at 8:30 P.M., and they all poured back into the prison transport for the four-hour return drive to Nashville, the final version had the intensity that Sam had been seeking all along — a quiet intensity but an altogether focused one, too. As with "Baby Please," he had gotten them to slightly advance the tempo, but with no diminution of control and fewer side effects, as Johnny's spectacular falsetto was less frequently displayed and eliminated altogether at the end. The sound was more closely miked and, as a result, more intimate, the almost reverential conclusion both statelier and more spiritual. But overall the feel was so close to the original, it would be hard to say what any of the exhausted participants might have thought. Except for Sam. To Sam they had done justice to an idea as well as a sound. And whether or not the record was a hit, they had accomplished just what they had set out to do.

WITHIN TWO WEEKS pictures had been taken, label information submitted, a four-page publicity folder assembled, and an ambitious promotional push planned, mostly by Jim, with Sam retaining final approval. There was a story in the *Nashville Banner* on June 17 which reported on Warden Edwards' talk to the Nashville Exchange Club on the subject of prison reform in general, its aim and effectiveness, with its effectiveness demonstrated "by the prisoner quintet [which entertained] Exchange Club members. This group of Negro singers, which has already recorded several songs," the paper reported approvingly, "was loudly applauded by the civic club."

The record was officially released on July 8, and a week later the *Press-Scimitar* ran a third of a page feature at the top of page 32 headlined "Prison Singers May Find Fame with Record They Made in Memphis." It recounted anecdotally just how the record had come about, scrupulously assigning roles to everyone from Governor Clement and Warden Edwards to Johnny Bragg and the other Prisonaires, Joe Hill Louis, Red Wortham, Jim Bulleit, and, of course, the "painstaking Mr. Phillips," who had insisted that they work "until the records were cut just right." Phillips, the story pointedly made clear, "has established a reputation as an expert in recording negro talent." There were tentative plans, the *Press-Scimitar* suggested, "to take them to New York to appear on big t-v shows" but these were all predicated, the reporter pointed out, on "Just Walkin' in the Rain" being as big a hit as Sam Phillips firmly believed that it would be.

It was. At least it was right off the bat, selling close to thirty thousand copies in its first two months on the market and garnering a tremendous amount of publicity, both local and national. Not only that, for the first time all of Memphis was aware of Sam and the studio, which, as *Press-Scimitar* reporter Clark Porteous pointed out, had been around since 1950. For the first time, too, Sam felt, he was getting an all-out endorsement from Dewey. Not that Dewey had been anything but positive about any of Sam's efforts — but Sam understood he wasn't going to play Sun records out of friendship, any more than he was going to play anybody else's records for love or money, on a show that he considered his temple as much as Sam considered the studio his. "I wasn't getting through to Dewey somehow. I guess maybe he wanted to see me prove that I could do it, or else I could fall off the damn cliff and break my damn neck and it would be all over. But this Prisonaires thing fascinated the hell out of him." And when it began to fascinate other people, too, when Sam found out-of-town DJs "who believed in what I was doing as much as Dewey did" — well, then quite naturally, that had to have some influence on Dewey. Because, as Sam could certainly understand, he wouldn't want to be left out.

Not only that, Sam had another record in the works that he just knew Dewey was going to love — and that he was pretty well convinced the world was going to be knocked out by, too. On June 18, while they were still gearing up to put out the Prisonaires, the Wolf's piano player, Bill Johnson, known to all the musicians as "'Struction," had brought in a young harmonica player and vocalist named Little Junior Parker, who had come up in West Memphis, singing and playing with Wolf and Sonny Boy Williamson and his friend and contemporary Bobby Bland, and Junior Wells and James Cotton as well. Through Ike Turner Little Junior had cut a single for the Bihari brothers a year and a half earlier, with one side in the sophisticated blues-crooning style of T-Bone Walker and Charles Brown, the other featuring him shouting the blues in the equally sophisticated deep-throated "crying" style of Roy Brown. He called his band the Blue Flames, and by the time they arrived at the Sun studio, 'Struction had replaced Ike on the piano bench, and the guitarist's place had been handed down by Memphis virtuoso Matt Murphy (later to become famous for his role in Dan Aykroyd and John Belushi's Blues Brothers band) to his little brother Floyd, eighteen years old and possessed of a technique that, while perhaps not as forceful as his brother's, was even more fluid.

Sam was intrigued by their potential. They came in with a few songs that didn't much interest him, songs clearly in line with what Sam took to be Little Junior's conventional jukebox-oriented "uptown" taste — but the combination of 'Struction's piano, Floyd Murphy's guitar ("He was so young, but the way he played, it sounded like two guitars"), and something in Little Junior's voice, not so much its distinctiveness as its *pliability*, just drew him in. They had one song, "Fussin' and Fightin,'" a takeoff on Eddie Boyd's big hit of six months earlier, "Five Long Years," and very much in keeping with Little Junior's previous efforts, but Sam kept pushing them to produce something with more of a gutbucket feel, something more along the lines of John Lee Hooker's "Boogie Chillen" — he wanted, as Floyd later remembered, "that raw stuff." So they obliged.

They came up with a number that Junior called "Feelin' Good," with exactly the same moral as the John Lee Hooker classic (no matter what anybody else might say, "we gonna boogie anyway"), the same seemingly extemporized spoken passages, and the same rhythm—but with an ensemble drive (Hooker's record was solo) and a playful melodic approach that were strikingly new. Sam kept encouraging them to intensify the feeling, to fuse their efforts together more tightly, and in the end they got it, with the pianist's left hand providing the structure and Floyd's guitar providing blazing rhythm riffs all the way to a natural fade at the end. "Once we got that rhythm going, all I did was get Junior, when he said, 'Well'—I just had him hold that [note]. I mean, he held it a little while, but that wasn't enough. I wanted to hear 'Welllllll' as long as he could hold it—and just boogie behind."

That note was the key to the song's success. When Junior came into the first chorus after a breezy spoken intro taken directly from Hooker ("You know, the other day I was walking down the street / I met an old friend of mine"), that first, single-syllable word took on almost all the properties of a chorus in itself. Stretching it out for a full four bars, Little Junior turned "Well" into a breathlessly elongated "Whoaaaaa" until, finally, he hit the release button and broke into the lyric ("Feel so good / Gonna boogie till the break of day") that was the message of the song. When the record came out three weeks later, following right behind the Prisonaires', Sam felt like Sun Records was finally, really on the map. It took about a month for the song to achieve anything more than local status, but by October it had reached number 5 nationally, Sun's third significant hit in just eight months and sure proof in Sam's mind that he was not just pursuing some quixotic vision of his own.

He put the Blue Flames together with Rufus Thomas, too, on a song of Joe Hill Louis', "Tiger Man," as a follow-up to his hit record. He got a great performance out of Rufus, complete with Tarzan jungle calls, and the band was even better, with Floyd Murphy's slashing guitar providing a complete blueprint for the crossover market that Sam was convinced was just waiting around the corner, but he held back the song's release over Jim's vehement protests (and to Rufus' expressed displeasure), because "Bear Cat" was still doing business.

IN MANY WAYS, things couldn't have been going better. The record company was making more and more of a name for itself. Sam finally owned his own home, and at the end of June he put $1,050 into the radio station in order to shore up their application for an FCC hearing. They had a $75,000 letter of credit from the First National Bank of Memphis, and, in an impressive feat of creative bookkeeping, Sam was able to declare a net worth of $12,600, which included $8,200 for equipment and $1,500 (minus $300 still owed) for Jackie Brenston's bus. Jimmy, who proposed calling the station WBEE ("Before you say no," he wrote to Sam on May 13, "listen to some of the ideas for promotion and publicity"), had a little harder time coming up with a comparable net worth (he included $3,000 of household furniture to reach a figure of $10,500) and, at Sam's prompting, put together a résumé that underscored his extensive experience in radio as well as whatever "civic affiliations that you can point to with pride, with emphasis on the sympathetic understanding of the problems of the Negro."

Everything seemed to be clicking. The one exception was the partnership with Jim Bulleit. For one thing, Jim was getting more and more jumpy. The nervousness that had first manifested itself with the "Bear Cat" lawsuit showed no sign of abating, and, perhaps not coincidentally, he seemed to be increasingly desperate for money. From Sam's point of view, Jim's principal failing was that he always took the short-term view, whether with respect to people or finances. His approach to marketing, for example, amounted to little more than throwing as much product out there as you could, then seeing what stuck. Which might make sense if your primary commitment was to churning up activity for your distribution business. But it was the exact opposite of Sam's commitment — what he was firmly convinced was the only course you could take if you truly believed in what you were doing — to put everything you had behind every record you released and not give up until the market proved you wrong. Sam allowed himself to be thrown off course one time when he put out a "cocktail-hour" record by Dusty Brooks and His Tones that Jim had picked up somewhere or other — but he was not going to do it again. And he was tired of getting letters and phone calls every other day pleading for new releases in the most dire and doom-filled terms. "This trip wasn't too successful," Jim wrote on June 15, even as he was getting good orders for the upcoming Prisonaires release. Many of the distributors, he declared with a straight face, "thought we were out of business" because of an absence of the kind of release schedule he was calling for. Sam's response was not recorded but can easily be imagined. This was just not the way he intended to do business.

Still, Jim Bulleit was a highly recognizable name; on the strength of

"Near You" alone he would have retained a reputation in the business, and Sam could certainly see his ongoing value to Sun Records. It was simply that, stuck as he was in the studio in Memphis, he couldn't figure out a way to control Jim's heedless excesses of spending or behavior on the road. Then, suddenly, a solution presented itself.

Jud Phillips had been coming into the studio to record the gospel group, the Sun Spot Quartet, that he was managing while running the Sun Spot Orange and Double Cola bottling plant down in Hattiesburg. He had been selling the records at their shows for the last couple of years, and he wondered if Sam might now be interested in putting out one or two Sun Spot releases on his new Sun label — it certainly made sense, with the coincidence of their names. Sam was happy to oblige his brother with session time, and he cut a number of new sides on the group — they had the kind of good old-fashioned gospel harmonies that he and Jud had grown up on, with Jud's wife, Dean, providing sturdy piano accompaniment — but he knew Jud would understand when he said he couldn't see any way of selling their records on the label.

Jud did not demur. He was a salesman, but he could be a realist, too. But, he confided, the bottling plant wasn't really working out, he was tired of Hattiesburg, it was simply time to move on. Sam wasn't surprised. He knew Jud had made quite a splash in town — he knew everybody from the volunteer firemen to the high muck-a-mucks who directed the Kiwanis and Chamber of Commerce — but things always ran down for Jud. And he knew how Jud must be languishing there. Running a bottling plant could hardly accommodate either Jud's ambition or his breadth of vision. So Sam proposed the idea that had been lurking in the back of his mind for some time but that, up till now, he had never been able to find expression for.

Why didn't Jud come to work for him? He could start out as a kind of "vice president" in charge of promotion, a minister without portfolio — but if things really clicked, well, who knew where it might end up? Jud responded to the opportunity with both enthusiasm and sensitivity ("We have wanted to get together for so long [but] if you later decide we can't do it I'll be glad to step out") as Sam explained to him all about Jim. How Jim had many good points but that the distribution network he had cobbled together was a disaster, the costs had to be controlled and the accounts receivable collected, the whole system, in fact, needed to be restructured and reevaluated. Which was a challenge, but one that Sam was confident could be met if Jud were simply to accompany Jim on all his sales trips and put the fear of God into him not with overt threats but in that disingenuously charming way that Jud could always call upon, letting him know you can't bullshit a bullshitter.

Sam knew his brother. He knew his good points and his bad points, and he was well aware that Jud, no less than Jim, had a propensity for extravagant statements and extravagant spending. But he knew, too, that Jud was a shrewd judge of character, and he knew how much Jud wanted this opportunity. "Should you need me before Saturday," Jud wrote at the outset of their informal arrangement, "call me at home. If you want me to help you with the shipping of records or anything just call me, I'll be glad to do it." And if the radio station deal came through, Jud wrote in the same letter, "I might be of [even] more help to you." Signing off jauntily "Your bud, Jud."

Sam was genuinely touched by Jud's enthusiasm and his evident willingness to put himself at the service of his brother in whatever way Sam might require. He couldn't think of any alternative anyway And, for all of Marion's unexpressed but impossible-to-miss skepticism that he could work with *any* partner, least of all this eager-beaver, fast-talking brother of his, Sam was confident that, with the proper controls, this combination might really succeed.

It did, to begin with. Jim liked Jud, in fact he liked Jud a helluva lot better than he did Sam. Where Sam could be chilly and removed, Jud was warm, charismatic, extroverted, and full of life. Despite their physical resemblance, Jim noted, "You wouldn't even know they were brothers, really" — their personalities were just that different.

B
UT THE PROMISE of a tripartite arrangement, if that was what it was intended to be, barely survived the first sales-and-promotion trip Jud and Jim took together at the end of July. "I got back to Nashville this am," Jud wrote to Sam on July 28 after a five-day visit to Washington and New York. "Had a long talk with Jim. I put the fear in him regarding the business." In fact, Jud, with no apparent authority to do so (he was at this point no more than a minister without portfolio on a salary of roughly $75 a week), had suggested to Jim that perhaps he should just leave the business. To which Jim, with that indefatigable good cheer that had so endeared him to Sam at the start, simply responded that he thought he would stick it out, that, as Jud reported, he continued to believe "the three of us can make some good money out of the operation." He didn't even seem to take it amiss when Jud made it crystal clear—with that same combination of brash confidence and disarming charm that he brought to all of his enterprises—that if this new arrangement were to be realized, Jim would be under the authority not just of Sam but of Jud, too. He would be in charge of sales, to be sure, but with certain very explicitly defined restrictions. It might all work out, Jud concluded his report to Sam, because now Jim knew "where he would stand in this matter, and he knows, too, that I know why he acts like he does."

That same day, Jim had also taken Jud out to the Tennessee State Penitentiary to visit with the Prisonaires, who, Jud wrote to his brother, "are getting from 10 to 25 letters every day from all over the country. They plan to bring all of them to you when they come over [to record

Elvis at the Eagle's Nest, ca. September 1954. Courtesy of Elvis Presley Enterprises

again the following week]. They make me think of a bunch of baby birds. They are fine boys — all of them. I get a great joy out of helping people that I think really appreciate it, and I know you do too."

It was in the immediate aftermath of that recording session that it all fell apart on a trip to the Fort Pillow State Penal Farm, just outside Dyersburg. Governor Clement had asked Sam if he could accompany the Prisonaires to an informal concert Warden Edwards had set up at the prison — maybe Sam or Jim could say a few words to inspire hope in some of the inmates. Jud drove up from Hattiesburg, and the three of them set out from the studio, but whether it was because the force of Jud's admonitions had finally registered with Jim, or he was simply feeling ganged up on in a business deal that had seemed so foolproof at the start, he and Jud started arguing before they had even left the city limits. And despite all of Sam's efforts to get his brother to quit, Jud wouldn't stop egging the other man on.

Sam finally stopped the car. He didn't know what was going on, he said, but he was tired of all this bullshit, and if Jud thought he didn't mean it, he'd whip Jud's ass, even if he weighed 125 pounds soaking wet to Jud's 180. Things quietened down a little after that, but inside, Sam was seething. From his point of view, there couldn't be one ounce of dissension in this enterprise, what he was trying to accomplish was just too important for them all not to speak with one voice. But if it came down to choosing one or the other — well, for all of his shortcomings, Jud was, after all was said and done, still his *brother.*

It took a month to get Jim out. He twisted and squirmed, went through a "siege" of changing his mind, sensibly refused a proposal to get out of the company while retaining half his stock as deferred recompense ("I have nothing personal against Jud. I think he is a terrificly fine business man . . . but it is unwise for anyone to give away [half] their stock and lose any chance to have a voice in the operation"), and then, with the assurance that Sam would personally guarantee a full buyout, and with the stipulation that, since he had initially secured their services, he would receive a 1 percent royalty override on all releases by the Prisonaires, agreed to a price of $1,600, with $400 down and $1,200 payable in three predated bank checks written over the next three months. At the end of a frantic week of negotiations, Sam must have breathed a sigh of relief, but at the same time when he wrote to Jud, back in Florence now, to let him know that the contracts had been

The Prisonaires on WSOK, 1953. Left to right (by my somewhat tentative identification): Ed Thurman, Johnny Bragg, Marcel Sanders, unknown, John Drue, and guitarist William Stewart, with songwriter Robert Riley kneeling. *Courtesy of Richard Weize, Bear Family Records*

sent out from his attorney Roy Scott's office, he was forced to acknowledge just how desperate the financial situation was. "Jud, I am sorry," he wrote in response to his brother's request for money, "but we were unable to send but $100.00 to the bank due to the fact that they have got us down to a balance of $50.00. Maybe by the time you get this letter if you absolutely have to have more we will have received something from the distributors."

For all of the label's success, sometimes he just didn't know how he was going to keep going. The excise tax was hanging over his head like a Damoclean sword. The IRS had yet to determine exactly how much he owed, and there was no money to pay it anyway — the government, Sam realized, could close him down at any moment, what it all came down to was their belief in *his* belief. At the same time, he was still paying off the money he had had to borrow from Leonard Chess after the "Bear Cat" debacle just to keep his head above water. And, with the exception of Little Junior and the Blue Flames' "Feelin' Good," which was finally beginning to nibble at the bottom of the national r&b charts, none of the new singles were doing anything at all. Not Rufus' irrepressibly buoyant follow-up to "Bear Cat," "Tiger Man." Not any of the cotton-patch blues he had coaxed so lovingly out of artists like Jimmy DeBerry and Walter Horton and D. A. Hunt. Even the Prisonaires had stopped selling, with sales of "Just Walkin' in the Rain" stalled at thirty thousand copies and their spiritual follow-up, "My God Is Real" (credited to the "Prisonaires, Confined to Tennessee State Prison, Nashville, Tenn."), barely causing a ripple.

That was probably what galled Jim most. Not just that they had missed out on a golden opportunity, but Red Wortham, who had held on to the Prisonaires publishing, was making more money than the two of them combined and stood to make even more with "Walkin' in the Rain" cover versions in future. In the greater scheme of things, Sam knew, it didn't really matter. He was no less proud of the record, he was no less proud of what it stood for. And it continued to generate both publicity and goodwill, long after it had fallen off the charts. *Life* magazine assigned a photographer to go out to the prison for a planned feature, and the national Negro weekly *Jet* ran a short piece that would be the basis for a full story in its sister publication, *Ebony,* an oversize glossy with extensive pictorials (much like *Life,* on which it was modeled). But however gratifying all this recognition and affirmation might be, it didn't put food on the table.

And then, when Jud went back out on the road, it suddenly became plain to Sam that things were even worse than he had thought. As Jud sent back extensive reports from a different city every day (sometimes two a day), Sam was forced to recognize that not only had Jim Bulleit continued to show an almost unerring instinct for putting his faith in the wrong people, he had set up a distribution system that incorporated all the worst elements of the record business in terms of both fecklessness and bad faith. He had also put the loose network of independent labels that he had assembled in a jerry-built distribution company of his own ahead of his representation of Sun, forcing local distributors in Shreveport, Dallas, New Orleans to take a whole bunch of records on other labels that they could never sell if they wanted "Bear Cat" or "Just Walkin' in the Rain" or any other Sun record in which Sam had invested all his faith and time and credibility. People didn't trust Jim, people didn't like Jim, he had made promises to the distributors that he couldn't keep ("Jim promised [the Richmond distributor] free Sun records," Jud wrote, "to compensate for all the bad stock they were caught with on his other labels"), and for all of his grand gestures and eloquent speech, he seemed to understand neither the problems nor the financial needs of the black DJs who for the most part lived on a system of record company welfare to supplement the barest minimum (if that) of radio station salaries. Quite simply, the whole system would have to be rebuilt.

And that is exactly what Jud set out to do. He was as good at it as Sam had known he would be. Bluff, quick on his feet, and with a gift for communication that Sam had always envied, he achieved success from the start. Against his own inclinations, and not infrequently against the distributor's optimistic expectations, Jud limited record orders to a realistic level in order to restore the label's much-damaged credibility. With the very same instinct on which Sam had always prided himself, the ability to "read" people ("You know how I can ask questions and lead people on into almost telling me the whole story," Jud wrote to Sam at one point), Jud found trustworthy new distributors and, always at Sam's direction, made better arrangements with some of the old ones. He reassured Sam on this point again and again, writing in one letter: "Hope I've made it clear. I did not tell him you would do that. I told him I would talk to you about it and if you did decide to work out some deal, all of the details would have to be agreed to in writing." Signing off, as per custom, "Your bud, Jud." He took black DJs out for drinks and dinner and made new friendships and financial arrangements with them. "Met Hot Rod [Hulbert]," he wrote from Baltimore at three in the morning, "and we all went out for dinner at 12. First time I've ever been in a negro night club, and I met all the high up negroes. They treated me nice and said they would do all in their power to help us. Really got in. Hot Rod said he knows you. He used to be at DIA. I think they are really on our side."

IN MID-SEPTEMBER, following Sam's instructions, Jud was able to straighten out their account and extract a check from one of their poorest-performing distributors, Everett DeGolyer, who, as Jud pointed out with typical generosity, was not a bad guy, just someone who "has been taken for a ride," very much like a couple of fellows they both knew from home. "Enclosed please find check in the amount of $1795.73," Jud wrote with scarcely disguised jubilation in his second letter of the day from Dallas on September 17, 1953, explaining that he had given the company "$500 off for returned merchandise and $500 discount to get the money. I have spent one day with them and the attorneys, and I am really proud to get this much out of them. Trying to get out to Oklahoma City in the morning at 5:15 AM so I can get that lined up." Then he was off to Houston. "I have worked night and day," he concluded, "to get this thing cleared up. Sure didn't want to leave until we got most of our money."

But if he was hoping for a warm letter of congratulation and approbation in reply, he was, as always, disappointed. What he got instead were instructions about how to deal with the Atlanta account, in a formal businesslike letter dictated to Marion and signed "Yours sincerely," with "Sam C. Phillips," typed underneath the signature. Anyone reading the exchange would have quickly concluded how much Jud craved approval — perhaps significantly, he had changed his sign-off by now to "See you" — but it would have been equally evident that, whatever the reason, this was something that was not in Sam's nature to give.

Maybe it was, as Marion said, that Sam was simply not a partner-type person. But I would say from my own observation — and from hearing Sam talk at length about his brother over the years — that it came down less to a mistrust of his brother's business sense and reliability (for which he had more than sufficient reason) than to his own aversion to being indebted to anyone, least of all his brother. There was always that sense of uncertainty hiding behind the confident, magisterial manner, and while Sam was unfailingly magnanimous in awarding praise (and remained so throughout his life), he was not willing to allow himself or, more important, the integrity of his *work,* to be held hostage to the playing out of any polite collaborative process. Money was certainly part of the problem ("It may look like I'm spending too much," Jud wrote tellingly on November 22, "but I'm not wasting a penny"), and with the FCC hearing on the radio station hovering on the horizon, Sam was doing all that he could to keep two enterprises afloat while remaining fiercely dedicated to the welfare of his little family and his deaf-mute aunt in Alabama.

I can hear Sam's voice in my ear, I can hear him protesting, as he sometimes did, "I'd be the first to give Jud any goddamn credit he deserved. I just wish he had done half the things he claims the credit for. I always had the greatest admiration for his abilities. But he was a person of extreme jealousy of me. And that's just the fucking truth." And maybe in the greater scheme of things he's right, unquestionably in hindsight he has all the objective evidence on his side — Jud was in some respects the furthest thing from the truth teller that Sam always prided himself on being. All I can say is that as I read over the letters, both for substance and for style, this is the way it struck me. Everything about Jud's nature cried out for approval. Sam might have said, "That's not the fucking point." And maybe it's not. But Sam was no more capable of changing his nature than Jud was.

He was in any case faced with a host of impending financial calamities. And worst of all, he wasn't putting out any records. Not because he had slowed down or shrunk in any way from recording the music in which he so strongly believed. Ike Turner had surprisingly turned up in the middle of the summer, with Little Milton (Campbell), an eighteen-year-old blues singer from Greenville, Mississippi, who could play convincingly in just about any style, in tow. Sam signed Ike to a one-year contract as a "talent scout" and recorded both Little Milton and various members of Ike's band. He continued to log any number of other sparkling blues sessions, from dates with guitar virtuoso Earl Hooker and teenage harmonica player James Cotton to new recordings by the uniquely spirited one-man-band "Doctor" Isaiah Ross and harp player Walter Horton, not to mention a follow-up session on Little Junior's Blue Flames, whom he recorded on August 5 in expectation of releasing a new single as soon as "Feelin' Good" had run its course. But with the exception of the second Prisonaires release, "Tiger Man," and a charmingly old-fashioned country record (as the first of its kind on the Sun label, it was marked "Hillbilly" on promo copies) by a family band called the Ripley Cotton Choppers, who came to him initially through his old WREC boss, Hoyt Wooten, he put out no new recordings from the beginning of July to the beginning of November, a period of four months. He simply didn't have the money.

The *Ebony* article on the Prisonaires came out in November, a four-page spread extolling the manner in which the group was acting "as goodwill ambassadors for [a] revolutionary and sometimes condemned prison rehabilitation program." After the failure of "Tiger Man," Rufus Thomas evidently announced to Sam his intention to go to Starmaker, a short-lived WDIA label venture, when his contract with Sun ran out in March. Starmaker had collapsed by then, but whether it was a matter of Sam's hurt feelings or Rufus' injured pride, Rufus never returned to Sun. Joe Hill Louis appeared on the Meteor label under a pseudonym, though his defection didn't affect his relationship with Sam in the way that Rufus' did, and he continued to supply songs for other artists to record, and continued to record for Sam himself, though he never had another Sun release. If Buster Williams hadn't continued to carry him, Sam often said, allowing him to continue to press records on credit until such time as he could pay, he didn't know what he would have done.

The Little Junior Parker record that he had been sitting on since the beginning of August was the one for which he had the highest hopes. Both sides were equally arresting. The first, "Love My Baby," had a churning rhythmic structure, built as much on the overamped drive of Blue Flame Floyd Murphy's chording as on the singularity of his blazing lead, while the second, which Sam poetically named "Mystery Train," was the familiar tale, as Sam put it, of a loved one leaving home. It was a traditional song with traditional lyrics — from Sam's point of view it derived its power from the immensity, the *mystery,* of leave-taking ("It's like a funeral — I mean, it was a big deal, to take a loved one and put them on a train, maybe they will not get back") — and his one contribution, aside from messing around a little with the rhythmic structure, getting the musicians to take it at half speed first before letting them pick it up so a normal tempo felt like a whoosh of release, was to insist that the train the singer was taking be sixteen coaches long, not eighteen or twenty-eight or fifty, as Sam said Junior himself wanted it to be. To Sam sixteen sounded just about right. It was a feel song, like "Love My Baby," dependent not on pyrotechnics but on the gathering rhythms of the train — but "Love My Baby" was the one of which he was most proud, "Love My Baby" was the breakthrough. It had a pulsating rhythm that he believed could very well set a whole new trend, something that could help knock down the wall between black and white musicians and markets. One time struggling to explain its appeal to me, he found himself utterly, and altogether uncharacteristically, at a loss for words. "I mean you tell me a better record that you've ever heard," he challenged me. And when I couldn't, he said, "You just should have been there, Peter."

He finally put the record out on November 1, along with a third Prisonaires single, this one with accompaniment on one side by Ike Turner on guitar — but despite the continued allure of Johnny Bragg's voice, it did no better than the last. The Blue Flames' single, on the other hand, while it didn't get the immediate reaction that "Feelin' Good" had, got some solid regional play, and Jud was out for over a month promoting it. Jud's letters continue to show a steady pattern of success both in collecting money owed and reorganizing the distribution system, most of all in helping to restore Sun's good name. "I don't plan to leave a stone unturned," Jud wrote on November 15, describing the pervasive sense of mistrust "of an[y] organization that Jim was connected to." It might look to Sam like he was "taking a lot of time in each location," he continued, "but I'm taking no more than I feel is absolutely required." But there is no sign of any emotional reciprocity on Sam's part.

In Washington, D.C., Jud met with three IRS agents who said that Sam's claims for tax relief with respect to the excise tax were going to be disallowed, it looked as if he was going to have to pay the full assessment of up to $8,000 (on which he had paid not a single penny with the required quarterly filings), but since the commission had yet to rule officially, he should see the IRS director in Nashville to avoid having to pay a 25 percent penalty for late filing. Jud also saw the lawyer Sam had retained in Washington to look after his FCC application, which, Jud reassured his brother, Sam could be confident was in capable hands. In New York he met with a representative of BMI, the performing rights society, which represented both songwriters and publishers, about licensing the publishing company that Sam had been planning to set up ever since Jim (who had handled all the publishing during their brief partnership) exited the company. He visited *Billboard*, too, the trade bible, which was vital to the acceptance of any small independent label. He was so busy, he didn't even have time to come home for the funeral of his and Sam's nephew Jack Darby, their sister Mary's younger son, a promising baseball player who had been killed at eighteen in a tragic automobile accident. He got sick in Cleveland, was forced to share a $15 hotel room with a fellow traveler in Cincinnati because of a convention of automobile dealers, and ran into a real SOB in Pittsburgh ("I knew everybody couldn't be that nice without there being a SOB somewhere. . . . He can kiss my a—"). It could be rough at times, he was inclined to remind Sam not infrequently, but he was determined to make this trip worthwhile, and he was proud of everything that he had accomplished to date.

By January Jud was gone. There is no record of what led to the final breakup, Sam never addressed the precipitating incident if there was one (he and Jud, he told one interviewer, "had difficulties with going ahead at the same speed"), but by the end of the month, Jud was dividing his time between Hattiesburg and Florence, where he had gone to work for radio station WJOI, and they were talking about how best to proceed with the dissolution of their partnership.

There was no money in the till. Marion had gone back to supplementing petty cash with money from her salary as assistant program director at WREC. When Jud's wife, Dean, wrote to Sam on February 5 requesting $300 to settle what was owed, Sam replied to his brother: "Right now we do not have that much in the bank, but . . . I'm sure we will have a check from somebody before the week is gone." Leonard Chess had come in, he wrote, "and I paid that off . . . and a lot of other things have hit us pretty hard, but I will send [the money] the minute we get it."

He lost Little Junior Parker to Don Robey at Duke Records in December. Junior had been out on tour with Duke artists Johnny Ace and Big Mama Thornton since the beginning of September — which Sam had originally thought could be a big boost to Little Junior's career. But then it was reported in *Cash Box* on November 7, just as "Mystery Train" was beginning to break, that the "terrific little blues belter [was] currently being groomed by Peacock & Duke prexy Don Robey for mighty big things." Sam immediately made a person-to-person call to Robey, his nemesis in the "Bear Cat" lawsuit, but Robey was not one to be easily deterred, and Sam heard that he had Little Junior in the Duke studio in December. At this point Sam had his lawyer, Roy Scott, fly to Houston to confront Robey directly, and when that, too, failed and there was a subsequent announcement in *Cash Box* in December that Robey had signed Little Junior and the Blue Flames to an exclusive recording contract, Sam informed *Cash Box* that "such a contract could not legally exist and that Sun Record Co., Inc. would take whatever action was necessary to protect our rights." Which he followed up on with a $100,000 lawsuit.

Jim Bulleit was still causing him problems as well. In February he informed Sam that some five months earlier Jud had promised him the Sun publishing that he and Sam held in common — in Jim's publishing company — as an inducement to sell his shares, an important point of information now that he was thinking of selling his publishing company. Jud adamantly denied having said any such thing, and there was a brief, angry flurry of correspondence in which Sam set the uncompromising tone. ("Now if you want to . . . call in your lawyer [if you can get one to take the case] then I'm ready. Or if you want to live up to your obligation and not try to railroad another one of your stunts over on somebody then we will sit down and settle up. But get this, buddy . . . I'll stake my reputation with yours any day of the week and will be glad at any time to do it.") That seemed to do the trick, as Jim swiftly capitulated and transferred all of the Sun material, as they had originally agreed, to Sam's newly licensed BMI publishing company, Hi-Lo.

He cast about for any and every way that he could think of to improve his situation. He came up with the idea of a management company that would provide representation for each of the artists he had under contract, calling for a 5 percent commission on gross earnings. It was to be called the Exclusive Booking Agency, and he signed all of his new artists to it. But in the end, like all the other moneymaking schemes he had come up with in the past for which he seemed to have little heart, he never put the plan into practice.

He was on the road for almost the entire month of February, putting over five thousand miles on the black 1951 Cadillac four-door he had bought a few months earlier with a down payment of $750 for just this purpose. If Jud had continued to be involved, he might have been better able to focus on what really mattered most, making records (he was unable to schedule a session for the next two weeks, he wrote to Jud on February 15, because of the constant travel), and some of Knox and Jerry's most vivid early memories of their father they were now eight and five respectively — were of going to the pressing plant with him on the weekend and helping him load up the trunk of his car with records. Sometimes that was the most they got to see of him, as he set out on his latest sales and promotion trip through Louisiana, Texas, and up into Oklahoma, before he could turn around, come back home, and start all over again.

He finally put out the first new Sun releases of 1954 at the end of February, four records in all, after canceling as many more. He led off with another Ike Turner discovery, a newcomer named Billy "The Kid" Emerson, a singer and pianist from Florida with a flair for highly crafted, quirky, and idiosyncratic songwriting in the blues vein. Next was a single by a hard-blowing local harmonica player and sign painter named Coy "Hot Shot" Love (he advertised both his sign painting and his distinctive philosophy on the back of his bicycle as he rode all around the streets of South Memphis), whose "Wolf Call Boogie," for all of its heavy amplification, would hardly have been out of place in a 1920s "race" recording catalogue.

The two other new releases were a different matter altogether. The first was the inaugural contemporary country single on Sun. It was by Earl Peterson, a twenty-six-year-old country DJ from Michigan, who showed up at the studio for an audition with his mother and billed himself as "Michigan's Singing Cowboy." The B-side was a smoothly sung ballad referencing Hank Williams and put across with a good deal of warmth. The featured number, "Boogie Blues," with which Peterson had auditioned, was a cheerful hillbilly boogie update along the lines of Hawkshaw Hawkins, but with allusions to some of Bill Monroe's more extravagant bluegrass yodeling numbers.

The second was deep-seated country gospel, by Howard Seratt, the Arkansas singer he had carried over to Nashville to help persuade Governor Clement to let him sign the Prisonaires. Seratt, whom Sam considered to be one of the most beautiful singers he had ever heard, accompanied himself on guitar and harmonica. When he had first come to the studio the previous year to cut some sides for his manager's custom label, Sam was well aware that his music didn't have a chance in the pop market, but he couldn't restrain himself from recording Seratt again and this time putting the record out on his own label. Maybe in the back of his mind he was still hoping to convert Seratt to a more secular approach — but he knew that was a pipe dream. Seratt had made himself very clear, and in the end Sam wouldn't have wanted to change his mind anyway. But there was something haunting about the music, something about the pure spirituality and honesty of the singer's voice that failed to lead anywhere except to reinforce Sam's conviction that music like this needed to be preserved, that someday music like this, presented properly, could reach an audience that, even if it didn't know it, might just be hungering for something more.

For the first time, there was a strange lack of direction in his thinking. When he opened the studio he knew exactly what he was doing, however much it might go against all the odds: offering an opportunity, as he said again and again, to "some of those great Negro artists in the South [who] just had no place to go." He had hewed to that belief without hesitation or equivocation for the last four years. But now, it seemed, he was no longer as certain of his path. Not because the music was any less compelling, or his purpose any less clear. But he had run up against the outer limits of what he felt he could accomplish in this particular way — like the other independent record company owners, he had come to the realization that, no matter how big a hit he had in the r&b field, he was never going to sell more than sixty thousand copies, one hundred thousand at the outside—and for the most part he was going to sell considerably less. And yet he was aware there was an audience out there that was just *waiting* to be inspired by this music.

"Teen-Agers Demand Music with a Beat, Spur Rhythm-Blues" was the page one headline of the April 24 issue of *Billboard,* only the latest in a long line of Delphic pronouncements, keenly observed but subject to a wide variety of interpretations, dating back over the last couple of years. "The teen-age tide has swept down the old barriers which kept this music restricted to a segment of the population," wrote Bob Rolontz and Joel Friedman, in a long front-page article that was borne out by Atlantic Records' virtually simultaneous launch of a new label, Cat Records, made up of r&b artists and intended to appeal directly to this trend. "Southern bobbysoxers began to call the r&b records that move them 'cat music,'" wrote Atlantic executives Jerry Wexler and Ahmet Ertegun only a little disingenuously a couple of months later in *Cash Box.* "And what kind moves them? Well, it's the up-to-date blues with a beat."

Sam saw the same trend—hell, *everybody* saw it, you couldn't miss the fact that something was going on—but he saw it in a somewhat different light. With Little Junior's "Love My Baby," he felt like he had stumbled onto something, even if he couldn't sell it. It was the same kind of thing he had hit on with "Rocket 88," the same kind of concentrated big-band riffs, this time in a guitar-driven format but with a sense of almost uncontainable energy, owing less to electricity than to youthful high spirits. It was the kind of music that could appeal to all types, black and white, it was the kind of music that kids, *teen-agers,* could call their own, if only he could somehow find the right mode of expression for it. He saw the opportunity, but he didn't know what to do with it. And he saw the resistance to it in his visits to some of his distributors and jukebox operators. "They'd tell me, 'These people are ruining our white children. These little kids are falling in love with the niggers.'"

He was not about to argue with them—he was not about to get up and start preaching to them. He couldn't have afforded to expose himself in that manner, even if he had been so inclined. And he couldn't logically see his way to a solution. In the end, conditions simply had to be right. He didn't believe in luck necessarily, but the moon had to be in the right place, the wind had to be blowing in the right direction. Sometimes you just had to bide your time. But a day was coming, of that he had no doubt — and he was convinced that it wasn't going to be long. He just hoped he would still be in business when that day finally arrived.

H E FOOLED AROUND with as many recording dates as he could. He recorded another Little Milton session with Ike Turner, this time taking advantage of Milton's remarkable facility for different blues styles to cut a ballad that approached one of B.B. King's most murmurous pleadings and a ripping up-tempo number that echoed Elmore James' "Dust My Broom." Two weeks later Ike brought in his longtime saxophonist, nineteen-year-old Raymond Hill, who had played on "Rocket 88" three years earlier, and Billy "The Kid" Emerson, who was still playing with his band. Sam continued to record youthful harmonica player James Cotton, who had first recorded with Howlin' Wolf — but in a configuration that eliminated the harmonica and focused on the overamplified, distorted, manic guitar playing of sometime Blue Flame Pat Hare, who was working up a session of his own that would feature "I'm Gonna Murder My Baby."

His brother-in-law, mentor, and radio partner Jimmy Connolly tipped him to a sometime WJLD employee, Sidney "Hardrock" Gunter, who had acquired his felicitous nickname not from the music that he played but from an incident that occurred when he was a teenager loading up the car for his first musical gig and the trunk lid fell on his head. Amid cries of consternation from his fellow band members, he just said, "Give me the banjo," and his friends, concluding that his head must be hard as a rock, gave him the nickname. Gunter, who despite a long apprenticeship in country music had always been drawn to boogie-woogie, from the irrepressible drive of Pinetop Smith's "Pinetop's Boogie Woogie" to Erskine Hawkins' more sophisticated "Tuxedo Junction," had had a huge regional hit in 1950. "Birmingham Bounce," on Bama Records, was a genial variation on "Pine Top's Boogie Woogie." ("Bounce" was the operative word, with respect to both tempo and mood.) It might very well have gone on to become a major national hit, except that the owner of Bama Records, a tiny local label, had obstinately refused to lease the sides to Decca, when the major label, recognizing the song's commercial potential, persistently pursued a deal. The result was that Decca cut the song on Red Foley, their biggest country star, and he went on to have a number 1 country (and a number 14 pop) hit with it, with r&b sales covered by Lionel Hampton and Amos Milburn, and a total of twenty-one covers in all. Not long afterward, Gunter was called back into the army and, following his discharge, spent about six months with the Wheeling (West Virginia) Jamboree, returning to Birmingham and going to work at WJLD in July of 1953.

Hardrock had another song, Jimmy told Sam, one that was just as good, with just as much crossover potential as "Birmingham Bounce"—in fact, it was very much the same, with Hardrock introducing each instrument and talking through the verses in a typically upbeat manner. The song, according to Hardrock, was supposed to have been called "We're Gonna Rock 'n' Roll, We're Gonna Dance All Night," but when it was originally issued on Bama four years earlier as the follow-up to "Birmingham Bounce," all but the last four words were dropped. Jimmy was convinced that the time was right for "Gonna Dance All Night," particularly with the success that Bill Haley had recently had with a similar sound. So Sam went to see Hardrock perform at the American Legion Hall in Birmingham and tried to get him to come back to Memphis to rerecord the song. But Hardrock had entrepreneurial ideas of his own and set up a session in Birmingham, shipping the finished sides to Sam. And while it didn't measure up to what Sam felt he could have captured in his own studio, it did convey much of the uninhibited spirit of the music.

It wasn't that he was looking for something in particular. He was looking for something *different*. The idea—always—was the same: to find that unique quality, "to find that spiritual elixir to bond this thing together." He was like "a chemist in a lab," Sam frequently said, "who just knows he's close to something." But just like that chemist, he wasn't going to know what it was until he finally stumbled upon the happy marriage of all the elements that he couldn't quite put his finger on. When Malcolm Yelvington, a thirty-five-year-old country singer first started coming into the studio that winter on a tip from the Ripley Cotton Choppers, Sam told Malcolm that he really wasn't interested in straight country. "I said, 'Well, what *are* you interested in?' And he said, 'I don't know. I won't know till I hear it.'" Malcolm had a friend with him named Charlie Yoakum, "and Charlie said, 'Well, Mr. Phillips, you should listen to everybody who comes through the door then.'" He did, Sam said. Which was exactly how Malcolm got an audition for his group, the Star Rhythm Boys, and how eventually, almost a year later, he got a release on Sun when he hit on the idea of recording a song for which he himself had no great love but which Sam pronounced "different."

S AM HAD TO GO TO HOUSTON at the beginning of April for a hearing requesting a preliminary injunction to prohibit Duke from putting out any more records by Little Junior Parker. He had thought he had the thing worked out. Little Junior had assured him that it was all a misunderstanding and they had even scheduled a recording session for the beginning of March. But then Don Robey had somehow gotten in the middle again, or maybe Little Junior was just bullshitting him, which he found difficult to believe—but in any case he drove to Houston on April 6 to put his case before a judge. The hearing was scheduled for federal district court, under the jurisdiction of Judge Ben C. Connally, but Connally, the son of Texas' recently retired senior senator Tom Connally, was on vacation, and the judge who was brought in, an octogenarian who seemed altogether unacquainted with the recording business, refused to issue a temporary stay, especially after Little Junior testified for the defense. Meaning that for all practical purposes Robey had won, even if Sam continued to pursue justice, as he vowed he would do until hell froze over.

On May 1 he finally released the Hardrock Gunter record, which he had had for nearly three months now, along with Billy "The Kid" Emerson and Raymond Hill's new singles and a recording by a local hillbilly singer named Doug Poindexter, who made his living as a baker and sounded like a phlegmatic Hank Williams. His group, the Starlite Wranglers, had a kind of spark, though, and there was definitely something different about the B-side, "My Kind of Carrying On," a blithely up-tempo and slightly off-color number written by the guitar player and manager, Scotty Moore. What distinguished it most to Sam's ears was the interaction between Moore and bass player Bill Black, the bright, rhythmic energy of the guitar as it opened with a jaunty takeoff on Nashville guitar virtuoso Chet Atkins' popular thumb-picking style. The other element that made the record different was its *sound*. Along with the two other singles released that day, it introduced for the first time Sam's own version of the "artificial" echo that had become a common recording technique, following the experiments of studio engineer Bill Putnam and recording pioneer and guitarist Les Paul six or seven years earlier. Sam put his special stamp on it, applying the name "slapback."

Sam had long been fascinated with echo. For his first Sun release, on sixteen-year-old "Alto Wizard" Johnny London, in 1952, he had constructed a special "echo chamber," a telephone-booth-like box, and he had experimented with the technique off and on over the last couple of years. But he had never achieved the result he wanted—to his ears, placing the vocalist or lead instrumentalist in a box, or placing a speaker in a resonant hallway or bathroom, as many engineers did, created too cavernous an effect. He knew, of course, that it was *all* "artificial." But what he was looking for was the richness and fullness and *naturalness* with which the human ear could be tricked into thinking it was actually hearing sound without artifice. People were used to listening to music in honky-tonks and bars. He didn't want to stun them with too clean an overall impression, he wanted it to sound more familiar but different at the same time. What he was really aiming for was "just a little bit of beautiful clutter." What he came up with was a technique for creating a slightly less controlled version of the delayed, or repeat, echo that had become a hallmark of Les Paul's work.

It was an idea, obviously, that was in the air. A self-taught electronics tinkerer, accordion player, and home inventor named Ray Butts in Cairo, Illinois, had already come up with a similar concept for electric guitar when he put together an amp that he called the EchoSonic, with a "3rd Dimension Tone," in 1952. To get the "multiple-sound echo effects" that, he advertised, "you have always wanted," he placed a tape inside the amplifier that operated in a continuous loop, as it chased after the live sound with just enough of a delay to suggest the depth and richness that Bill Putnam and Les Paul had created with their studio recordings. Chet Atkins, a great admirer of Les Paul and open to all sorts of musical experimentation himself, bought one of the first EchoSonics, and the sound was heavily featured in his playing on the Davis Sisters' "Rock-A-Bye-Boogie," which was popular in the fall of 1953. But the first inkling that Sam had of just how he might achieve the same effect in his own tiny studio occurred when he got his first Ampex 350 tape recorder at the beginning of 1954.

This came in the midst of a general upgrading of equipment that flew in the face of every financial exigency screaming out at him for attention every day. As Marion observed, Sam might scrimp on everything else, in fact, he could even make a virtue out of it (Sam was always sure to tell her how nice she looked "with my pretty little cotton dresses sticking to me because we [still] couldn't afford an air conditioner out front"), but he would never skimp on the recording equipment. And while he was more than happy with his fifteen-year-old converted RCA radio console,

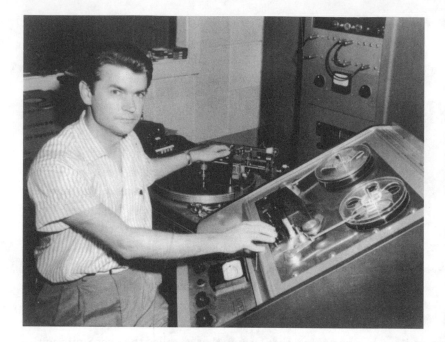

Sam at the board with new Ampex 350, fall 1954.
Courtesy of the Sam Phillips Family

from the time the Ampex 350 came on the market the previous summer, with its state-of-the-art technology, he just knew it was something he had to have.

It was while playing around with the Ampex that he first got the idea for "slapback." It suddenly occurred to him that in the time it took the tape to move across the three heads of the machine, from record to erase to playback, "that would give me a [very] slight delay, [and if] I turned it on playback and fed it back into the board, I would have a controllable sound." The trouble was, he would be slathering that sound—whether it was close together at fifteen inches per second or more spread out at seven and one-half—on every element of the recording, thereby restricting the dramatic effect he wanted to achieve. The only solution was to acquire a second Ampex, which he did with supreme financial disregard. He mounted the second tape recorder on a rack behind him to his right and designated it as his "slap" machine, applying it to Billy "The Kid" Emerson's and Doug Poindexter's vocals, and Raymond Hill's saxophone, on the three records he recorded between April 12 and April 15.

Nothing happened. None of the records sold. The Doug Poindexter single, with Scotty Moore's bright lead guitar, barely shipped three hundred copies, though Scotty himself wasn't easily discouraged. He was an ambitious young man, twenty-two years old, with four years in the Navy behind him — he worked as a hatter at his brothers' dry cleaning establishment, but he had every intention of making his living as a professional musician. He knew the Starlite Wranglers were not going to be the way he was going to do it. For one thing, Doug Poindexter didn't have the forward-looking musical attitude that you needed to make it in the competitive, forward-looking music business; for another, no one in the band was prepared to give up their steady jobs to travel, with the exception of his friend, bass player Bill Black. So he got in the habit of coming down to the studio several days a week after he got off work to talk to Sam about the future. They would go next door to Taylor's restaurant for a cup of coffee if Sam had the time — Scotty just liked to listen to him talk, mostly about the changes that he saw on the horizon. "He knew there was a crossover coming. He foresaw it. I think that recording all those black artists had to give him an insight; he just didn't know where that insight would lead."

On May 8 Sam drove over to the Tennessee State Prison in Nashville with his portable Presto 900-P tape recorder. Governor Clement was running for reelection, and his political opponents, not to mention the newspapers, had been jumping all over him for his irresponsible ideas on prison reform ever since the Prisonaires had started making outside appearances the previous July. Sam entered the prison gates not without a certain amount of trepidation — it was a maximum-security prison designed to hold twelve hundred with a population of a thousand more. But he knew that if he were to show fear, he would only be drawing further attention to himself. So, with the warden accompanying him, he ate in the prison chow line. ("Man, I can tell you, I didn't eat a whole lot. Because I tried to speak with as many of the men as I could.") And he put forty or fifty prisoners to work hanging canvas with him to deaden the sound in the prison's concrete-block movie theater. He didn't want any extra guards. He just wanted as many prisoners as possible to participate in the process. And he left the prison at 2:30 the following morning with two songs for the Prisonaires' next and, as it would turn out, last single release.

He also left the prison with an acetate that had been set aside for him by Red Wortham, the song publisher who had steered the Prisonaires to Sun. He listened to it when he got back to Memphis. It was a plaintive ballad called "Without You," sung in a quavering voice that sounded like a cross between the Ink Spots and a sentimental Irish tenor—he could never remember, he may never have known, whether it came from a prisoner, and it was not really an accomplished performance, but the song stayed with him. He thought it might have some potential, but he didn't really know what to do with it any more than he knew what to do about the Prisonaires or the Starlite Wranglers or the vast potential audience that he was more and more convinced was out there somewhere.

He was at a crossroads. It seemed that for all of the fervor of his belief, for all of the success he had enjoyed, with the Wolf, with "Rocket 88," and with Little Junior's Blue Flames, he just couldn't get himself situated on a solid foundation. Not for the first time it occurred to him that he just might have to quit. He had certainly given it a good run. He had always believed that life was a process to which you devoted yourself at every stage without ever knowing how it was going to come out. "If the best comes, fine. If it doesn't, don't be disappointed. Just make sure, wherever you get with your mission—make sure that up to that point, step by step, you were satisfied."

That was exactly what he had tried to do. That was what he could honestly say that he had done. He had always been prepared to take other roads if need be. He was closer than ever to achieving his earliest dream—his own radio station. If that were to come about, maybe he should simply be satisfied—it might even be better for Becky and the boys. And if it didn't, well, he knew he could always get a decent job as a radio engineer—he could even work for Jimmy's station in Birmingham. He wasn't worried about being able to just make a living.

But he didn't want to just make a living either. Lately he had been thinking more and more that the key lay in the *connection* between the races, in what they had in common far more than what kept them apart. There were always going to be "some bastard white people," he knew, but far more to the point was the spiritual connection that he had always known to exist between black and white, the cultural heritage that they all shared "to bond this thing together. Not to copy each other but to just—hey, this is all we've got and we're going to give it to you. This is our Broadway play. This is our Tin Pan Alley. This is what it is. This is

Fishing with Knox. *Courtesy of the Sam Phillips Family*

for real. We hope you like it." To Marion he had begun to talk more and
more about finding someone — and it had to be a white man, because the
wall that he had run into with his recordings practically *proved* that in
the present racial climate it couldn't be a black — who might be able to
bridge the gap. "Over and over I heard Sam say, 'If I could find a white
man who had the Negro sound and the Negro feel, I could make a billion
dollars!'" And he would always laugh, Marion said, as if to underscore
that money was never the point — it was the *vision*, it was what would
come afterward.

THE SONG that he brought back from his Nashville trip continued
to haunt him. There was something about it — for all of its sentimentality, there was a quality of vulnerability about it, and he thought
more and more that he'd like to have someone come in and give it a
try. The only one who came to mind was a kid who had stopped by the
previous summer and for $4 cut a "personal" record for his mother.
Like the singer on the demo, like the Prisonaires' Johnny Bragg, he was

unmistakably influenced by the Ink Spots' lead singer, Bill Kenny, and in fact, one side of the two-sided acetate was the Ink Spots standard "That's When Your Heartaches Begin." The boy had come in to cut another "personal" in January or February — Sam couldn't imagine that he was more than a year or so out of high school — and evidently he stopped by from time to time to talk with Marion, Sam was well aware of that fact because Marion was going on about him. He didn't really know, but when Marion brought up his name for what seemed like the thousandth time, he thought, Why not? The boy had the same yearning quality in his voice that Sam heard in the Nashville number, attached to the kind of purity and fervor that you might be more inclined to assign to religious music. Sam had no idea of his full potential, but there was no question, he was certainly *different.*

So he had Marion call him.

Elvis Presley came into the studio on Saturday, June 26. He arrived, he would say in later years, almost before Miss Keisker hung up the phone, and for the first time Sam really had the opportunity to take his measure. He was nineteen years old, a good-looking boy with acne on his neck, long sideburns, and long, greasy hair combed in a ducktail that he had to keep patting down, but what struck Sam most was his quality of genuine humility, humility mixed with intense determination. He was, innately, Sam thought, one of the most introverted people who had ever come into the studio, but for that reason one of the bravest, too. He reminded Sam of many of the great early blues singers who had come into his studio, "his insecurity was so *markedly* like that of a black person."

They worked on the number all afternoon, with Elvis accompanying himself inexpertly on his own beat-up little guitar. When it became obvious that for whatever reason the boy was not going to get it right — maybe "Without You" wasn't the right song for him, maybe he was just intimidated by the damn studio — Sam had him run down just about every song he knew. He didn't need much of an invitation, and he didn't finish every song, but what Sam sensed was a breadth of knowledge, a *passion* for the music that didn't come along every day.

"I guess I must have sat there at least three hours," Elvis told *Memphis Press-Scimitar* reporter Bob Johnson in 1956. "I sang everything I knew — pop stuff, spirituals, just a few words of [anything] I remembered." Sam watched intently through the glass of the control room window — he was no longer taping, and in almost every respect this

Elvis Presley, outside 462 Alabama, with 1941 family Lincoln, ca. 1953-54.
Courtesy of Elvis Presley Enterprises

session had to be accounted a dismal failure, but still there was *something....* Every so often the boy looked up at him, as if for approval: was he doing all right? Sam just nodded and spoke in that smooth, reassuring voice. "You're doing just fine. Now just relax. Let me hear something that really means something to you now." Soothing, crooning, his gaze locked into the boy's through the plate-glass window that he had built so that his eyes would be level with the performer's when he was sitting at the control room console. He didn't really know if they were getting anywhere or not, it was just so damned hard to tell, especially when you were dealing with someone who was obviously unaccustomed to performing in public. But then again, it was only from just such a person, pure, unspoiled, as raw, as untutored as anyone who had ever set foot in this studio, that he felt he could get the results he was looking for. He *knew* this boy, he knew where he came from, he could intuit all the things they had in common in background and sensibility — what you could never tell was whether it would ever add up to anything.

He sent the boy on his way, exhausted. There was something about him — Marion kept after him all week about how the session had gone. One day they were sitting at Mrs. Taylor's with Scotty, and Marion brought up the boy again. "This particular day," Scotty said, "it was about five in the afternoon — Marion was having coffee with us, and Sam said, 'Get his name and phone number out of the file.' Then he turned to me and said, 'Why don't you give him a call and get him to come over to your house and see what you think of him?' [Bass player] Bill Black lived just three doors down from me on Belz that ran into Firestone [where Bill worked] — I had actually moved just to be near Bill — and Sam said, 'You and Bill can just give him a listen, kind of feel him out.'"

Scotty called Sam at home the following evening. They had had their audition and it had gone much like the one Sam had conducted the previous Saturday. Bill had been none too impressed, and Scotty's wife had just about bolted out the back door when the kid arrived wearing a black shirt, pink pants with a black stripe, white shoes, and that long greasy ducktail. They ran through the same assortment of songs — hillbilly, pop, Billy Eckstine's "I Apologize," the Ink Spots' "If I Didn't Care," Hank Snow's and Eddy Arnold's latest hits, and, if Sam could believe it, a Dean Martin-styled version of "You Belong to Me." They were all ballads, all sung in a yearning quavery tenor that didn't seem ready to settle anywhere anytime soon and accompanied by the most rudimentary strummed guitar. Well, Sam said, what did he think? It was in a sense Scotty's decision — this might be the vocalist he had been looking for to sing with his band. "Well, you know, he didn't really knock me out," said Scotty, never less than completely honest. "But the boy's got a good voice." "You know, I think I'll just call him," Sam said, "get him to come down to the studio tomorrow — we'll set up an audition and see what he sounds like coming back off of tape." Should he bring the whole band? Scotty asked. The Starlite Wranglers? No, Sam said, he didn't think so. "Just you and Bill, just something for a little rhythm. No use making a big deal about it."

The three of them showed up the next night around seven. There was some desultory small talk, Bill and Scotty joked nervously between themselves, and Sam tried to make the boy feel at ease, carefully observing the way in which he continued to both withhold himself and thrust himself into the conversation at the same time. At last, after a few minutes of aimless conversation and letting them all get a little bit used to being in the studio, Sam turned to the boy and said, "Well, what do you want to sing?" This occasioned even more self-conscious confusion as the three musicians all tried to come up with something they knew and could play — *all the way through* — but after a number of false starts they finally settled on "Harbor Lights," which had been a big hit for Bing Crosby in 1950, and worked it through to the end, then tried Leon Payne's "I Love You Because," a beautiful country ballad that had been a number-one country hit for its author in 1949, and a number-two hit for Ernest Tubb, also on the hillbilly charts, the same year. They tried each song again and again — each take was slightly different, but each time the boy flung himself into the performance, clearly trying to make it new. Sometimes he simply blurted out the words, sometimes his singing voice shifted to a thin, pinched, almost nasal tone before returning to the high, keening tenor in which he sang the rest of the song — it was as if, Sam thought, he wanted to put everything he had ever known or heard into one song. Scotty's guitar part was almost invariably too damn complicated, he was trying too hard to sound like Chet Atkins — but then there was that strange sense of inconsolable desire in the voice, there was the unmistakable thrill of hearing free, unfettered emotion being conveyed without disguise or restraint.

Sam sat in the control room, trying to look fully engaged but unconcerned at the same time. Every so often he would come out and change a mike placement slightly, talk with the boy a little, not just to bullshit with him but to try to make him feel more at home. He was happy enough with the interaction between the musicians. There was a reason he had chosen them to accompany the boy. Scotty was the best-natured person in the world — he never made any demands and he didn't take himself too damn seriously. Bill on the other hand was a cutup. He was a natural mixer who could get a laugh out of a perfect stranger. And while he was no more a virtuoso on his instrument than Scotty, he could slap that bass to create the kind of driving, propulsive effect that Sam felt this little trio was going to need if it was ever going to be able to get across. But still, they hadn't gotten anything usable — and he wasn't sure exactly what to do. You never wanted to quit a session like this too early — you might just kill any chance of confidence developing over time. But it was a real question as to how long you wanted to keep things going, too. Staying with it too long could create a kind of mind-numbing quality of its own, it could smooth over all the rough edges you were trying to bring out and banish the very element of spontaneity you were trying to achieve.

Finally they decided to take a break — it was late, the boy was clearly discouraged, and everybody had to work the next day. Maybe, Sam thought, they ought to just give it up for the night, come back on Tuesday and try again. Scotty and Bill were sipping Cokes, not saying much of anything. Sam was doing something in the control room, and, as Elvis explained it afterward, "this song popped into my mind that I had heard years ago, and I started kidding around with [it]." It was an up-tempo song called "That's All Right, Mama," an old blues number by Arthur "Big Boy" Crudup. "All of a sudden," said Scotty, "Elvis just started singing this song, jumping around and acting the fool, and then Bill picked up his bass, and he started acting the fool, too, and I started playing with them. Sam, I think had the door to the control booth open — I don't know, he was either editing tape or doing something — and he stuck his head out and said, 'What are you doing?' And we said, 'We don't know.' 'Well, back up,' he said, 'try to find a place to start, and do it again.'"

The rest of the session went as if suddenly they had all been caught up in the same fever dream. They worked on the song. They worked hard on it, but without any of the laboriousness that had gone into the session up to this point. Sam worked to get them to see the song in more of a flow — he got Scotty to cut out the conventional turnaround and cut down on all the stylistic flourishes that were mucking it up. "Simplify, simplify!" was the watchword. Bill's bass became more of an unadulterated rhythm instrument — it provided both a slap beat and a tonal beat at the same time — all the more important in the absence of drums. They continued to work on it, refining the song — but the center never changed. It always opened with the ringing sound of Elvis' rhythm guitar, up till this moment almost a handicap to be gotten over. Then there was Elvis' vocal, loose and free and full of confidence, "sounding so fresh," Sam said, "because it *was* fresh to him." With Scotty and Bill finally falling in with an easy swinging gait that was the very *essence* of

With Knox and Jerry and their friend Tommy Tidwell (at left), fall 1954.
Courtesy of the Sam Phillips Family

everything Sam had dreamt of but had never been able to fully imagine. It was almost like recording the Wolf. There were no studio tricks employed. He didn't even use his new discovery of slapback, which he had applied primarily to guitar on at least one of the other completed selections. There was just the purity of the music.

The first time Sam played it back for them, "we couldn't believe it was us," said Bill. "It just sounded sort of raw and ragged," said Scotty. "We thought it was exciting, but what was it? It was just so completely different. But it just really flipped Sam." And the boy? By the end of the evening there is a different singer in the studio than the one who started out the night. For Elvis, clearly, everything has changed.

Sam sat in the studio after the session was over and everyone had gone home. He was bone-weary, but he just wanted to savor the moment. When he got home, he woke up Becky, and, as she would always remember it, "he was excited, he was happy, and he announced that he had just cut a record [that was] going to change our lives. I didn't understand at the time what he meant, but it did. He felt that nothing would ever be quite the same again."

DEWEY PLAYED IT on the air the next night and had Elvis on his show. Dewey had gotten so excited when Sam played the acetate for him that he requested two copies to play both simultaneously and sequentially, and when he played them, the response was instantaneous. Forty-seven phone calls, it was said, came in right away, along with fourteen telegrams (or was it 114 phone calls and forty-seven telegrams?)—the numbers took on a mythic significance almost instantly. He played the song seven times in a row, eleven times, seven times over the course of the rest of the program—it doesn't really matter. It seemed as if all of Memphis was listening. And they were all listening when Dewey called the boy's home, and his parents dragged him out of a movie theater on North Main and sent him down to the radio station on the mezzanine floor of the Hotel Chisca to be interviewed. "I was scared to death," Elvis said. "I was shaking all over. I just couldn't believe it." After several minutes of idle chatter, including the name of the high school, Humes, from which he had recently graduated ("I wanted to get that out," Dewey said, "because a lot of people listening thought he was colored"), Dewey said, "All right, Elvis, thank you very much." "Aren't you going to interview me?" Elvis asked. "I already have," said Dewey, leaving Elvis to ponder all the things he might have said.

But there was, Sam immediately recognized, a real problem with such instant fame. There was no record. There was no other side. They went back into the studio the following night and, in Scotty's recollection, ran through one song after another, trying to recapitulate the spontaneity of "That's All Right." "Then Bill jumped up and started clowning, beating on his bass and singing 'Blue Moon of Kentucky' in a high falsetto voice, more or less mimicking Bill Monroe [this was Bill Monroe's classic bluegrass tune, which was, in Monroe's version, a *waltz*], and Elvis started banging on the guitar, playing rhythm and singing, and I joined in and it just gelled."

Once again the song just seemed to spring up like Topsy, as they pursued several different approaches, including a slowed-down blues, but all in driving 4/4 time. It may not have been quite the natural event that the first song was—the fact that it was not, in Sam's view, is evidenced by the slapback echo with which he surrounded the vocal, so that it almost doubled back on itself. But it achieved the desired effect. "That's fine," you can hear Sam say, at the end of one early take. He speaks once again in that soothing, almost crooning voice, the voice of reason, the voice of confident imperturbability. "Hell, that's different," he says to the three musicians anxiously awaiting his verdict. "That's a *pop song* now, nearly 'bout." And Elvis, Scotty, and Bill all burst out in nervous, self-reassuring laughter.

THE RECORD CAME OUT officially less than two weeks after the first session and from the start sold like nothing else Sam had ever released. Like nothing else, in fact, that Memphis had ever experienced. "May we please call your attention to [our new Sun release] 209—'That's All Right' and 'Blue Moon of Kentucky' by Elvis Presley," Sam wrote to *Billboard* writer Bob Rolontz, who penned the rhythm and blues column. "This record was put on the air here in Memphis last Friday, July 16, and sales have been phenomenal. . . . According to our local distributor, it is being bought by practically every operator with all types of locations . . . and retail purchasers range from teenage white kids to dyed-in-the-wool Negro blues enthusiasts on the 'THAT'S ALL RIGHT' side, while the Hillbilly set young and old are setting the pace on the 'BLUE MOON' side. Ruben Cherry, owner of 'Home of the Blues' [record store], says: 'The potential of this record is unlimited because of its apparently universal appeal. I've never seen anything like it!'" He followed up with a press release on August 2, after the *Memphis Press-Scimitar* had run a story in which Marion, who had accompanied Elvis to the newspaper offices, had more to say than the young phenomenon ("He was very hard to interview," said reporter Edwin Howard. "About all I could get out of him was yes and no"), and Sam had gotten him placed on an all-star country show hosted by Memphis DJ Bob Neal at the Overton Park Shell.

"Presley's first release on Sun has just hit the market," read the two-page typed sheet, which called attention to the earlier discovery of B.B. King, Roscoe Gordon, Little Junior, the Prisonaires, and the Howling Wolf by the company's "youthful president," and cited "reports from key cities indicat[ing] that it is slated to be one of the biggest records of the year. Music Sales Company, Memphis distributor for SUN, sold over 4,000 of the disc in the first week—something that no record has done since [Patti Page's across-the-board, 1950 number-one pop hit] TENNESSEE WALTZ." It went on to call attention to the "three-way" appeal of the record (pop, hillbilly, and r&b), declare that with this new signing the label was poised to "move strongly into the C&W field," and to point out that the nineteen-year-old artist had "never done any professional work before his recording stint for SUN." At his "big-show" debut, however, at Overton Park Shell, "with such established artists as Slim Whitman, Billy Walker, and the Louvin Brothers, his reception was overwhelming, with autograph seekers refusing to go home until he gave an impromptu performance of the two top-riding numbers backstage."

However accurate the release may have been—and Sam's written expression was always a pretty accurate distillation of reality—it failed to summon up the drama of the Overton Park performance. For one thing, Elvis was nervous almost beyond measure. "Man, I'm so glad to see you, Mr. Phillips," he blurted out when Sam arrived a few minutes late. "I just didn't know what I was going to do."

Sam responded as he always had, with both his artists and his children, with tempered but quietly evangelical enthusiasm. "It's like when somebody's mother is real sick and you tell them everything is all right, and yet you know there's the possibility that his mother might die. I said, 'Look, Elvis, we'll find out whether they like you or not.' And then I said, *'They're gonna love you.'* Now I didn't know that, and if you want to call me a liar or a fake or saying something that I didn't know to be the truth—but I believed that once he started to sing, once they heard that voice and the beautiful simplicity of what those three musicians were putting down. . . . You see, Elvis had confidence in me, he knew I wasn't going to throw him to the lions. So I gave him my best clubhouse pitch, not too many curves, 'cause I knew even if he struck out four times and left three people on base each time, after the ballgame was over that could be overcome, too."

The one thing he hadn't calculated was what Elvis would put into the actual performance, whether intentionally or not. When Elvis went onstage, Scotty said, his knees were knocking so loud you could almost hear them. Master of ceremonies Bob Neal made the introduction, and then the three musicians, none of whom had ever appeared in a setting even remotely resembling this one, were on their own. "We were all scared to death," said Scotty, and Elvis, instead of just standing flat-footed and tapping his foot, raised up on the balls of his feet and leaned into the microphone as his legs began to quiver. "I was scared stiff," Elvis explained, but "with those old loose britches that we wore," Scotty said, "it made it look like all hell was going on under there. During the instrumental parts he would back off from the mike and be playing and shaking, and the crowd would just go wild, but he thought they were actually making fun of him."

Cash Box ran Sam's press release virtually unchanged as a brief feature on August 14, along with a "B⁺ ("Excellent") review near the top of their "Rhythm 'N' Blues Reviews," that cited "a feelingful vocal with more than just a backer-upper bass and guitar support. . . . Listening and re-listening convinces one that the deck could make a great deal of noise." The following week Sam splurged what little money he could put together on a half-page ad in the same weekly trade.

POP —
HILLBILLY —
R&B
A HIT !
ALL THREE WAYS
ELVIS PRESLEY'S
"THAT'S ALL RIGHT"
AND
"BLUE MOON OF KENTUCKY"

read the headline in a slanted cross between cursive and block lettering, with a cash register ringing up crudely rendered dollar signs. "Not in history," Sam wrote with the same blunt directness that typified all of his promotional efforts, "has a record sold as many records in less than two weeks [in the Memphis territory] as the new and different release just out by ELVIS PRESLEY. . . .

> Operators have placed it on nearly all locations (white and colored) and are reporting plays seldom encountered on a record in recent years.
>
> According to local sales analysis, the apparent reason for its tremendous sales is because of its *appeal to all classes of record buyers.* In fact, the owner of one large local retail store says: "I BELIEVE PEOPLE WHO NEVER BOUGHT A RECORD ARE BUYING IT. I NEVER SAW ANYTHING LIKE IT!"

L ONGTIME VETERANS of the record business had never seen anything quite like it either. From the start, there was a certain element of controversy over race mixing as well as the boy's natural sexuality, but in the view of Malcolm Yelvington, a steadfast hillbilly singer and father of two teen- and near-teenage daughters who had become instant fans, such matters paled in the face not only of the good feeling but of the inherent *spirituality* of the music. It wasn't just that this young kid had grown up in a religious environment, like so many of the rest of them. It was how he mixed the sound, and exuberance, of spiritual music with blues and country in a way that no one else had before. So that it sounded to Malcolm both deeply familiar and dramatically new at the same time. It was, Yelvington realized, what Sam had been looking for when he told Malcolm he was waiting for a sound he hadn't heard before. It was different enough to elicit a call from Paul Ackerman, the erudite forty-six-year-old music editor of *Billboard,* whom Sam had never actually spoken to before but for whom he had conceived a great admiration for his consistent championing of rhythm and blues, country music, and all such "unadulterated," idiomatic, and purely *American* sounds. "You've either got to be crazy or a genius," declared Ackerman, a soft-spoken man with an unmistakable New Yorker's accent. "There isn't any in-between." And Sam, for whom this was to be the beginning of an enduring, lifelong friendship, was inclined to agree.

I T WAS AS IF he had been caught up in a whirlwind. He put every penny, every ounce of energy he had into the record, ignoring the naysayers, turning a blind eye to the financial perils, trying to overcome the doubts of critics and silence his own. He launched a volley of correspondence intended to persuade but not strong-arm some of his more reluctant distributors. ("I had to keep from being impatient with people who hadn't heard anything like this before. I never said, 'Well, you wait and see, because, hell, I didn't know myself.'") But, with Jud back in Florence, he had no other choice but to be on the road. He drove to Nashville to try to persuade the top WLAC jocks, like Gene Nobles and John R. (Richbourg), not to mention Randy Wood and Ernie Young and Louis Buckley, who owned the record stores and one-stops that sponsored their r&b shows, to get on the record. He traveled to New Orleans and Atlanta and all the little towns in Mississippi and Arkansas. But mostly he stuck to the "Dust Bowl" circuit, cross the river at Greenville, head for Monroe, then Shreveport, Gladewater, Houston, Dallas, and all points in between, and back in Memphis dog-tired at the end of the week.

It was on one of the very first trips, in early August, that he learned a lesson that would stick with him the rest of his life and become such a staple of Phillips family lore that in later years his sons, Knox and Jerry, could practically recite it by heart. He arrived in Shreveport, where he immediately went to see T. Tommy Cutrer, the top country jock at KCIJ, with whom he had worked at WREC when he first arrived in Memphis. They hadn't really stayed in touch, but Sam had always thought highly of Tommy, who in turn considered Sam a fine fellow, if somewhat reserved, someone whose expertise lay in the sound and engineering field. But when Sam played him the record, T. Tommy, still laid up from a bad automobile accident in which he had lost a leg, practically recoiled. He told Sam he'd really like to be able to help him out, but "Blue Moon of Kentucky" was a bluegrass anthem, and if he played the record, they'd run him out of town.

Next he stopped by KENT, just a few blocks away, where he got together with Fats Washington, a paraplegic black man with a popular rhythm and blues show, who had played all of his big records, from Little Junior and the Wolf to "Rocket 88." Fats, the most personable guy in the world and a part-time songwriter, too, who would soon give Johnny Ace the lyrics to his blockbuster hit, "Pledging My Love," put "That's All Right" on the air but was careful to explain to his listeners that he was doing this strictly as a personal favor. "I got this man, Sam Phillips, in the studio with me here," he announced, "and he thinks this is gonna be a hit. And I'm telling him that this man should not be played after the sun comes up in the morning, it's so country." He was unable to sell Stan Lewis, the young proprietor of Stan's Record Shop, on the record either, and he left town depressed and disappointed but aware of two things. That he had to be sure he wasn't fooling himself. And that he couldn't tell men who were his friends, men whose living was dependent on their ability to assess the tastes of their listening audience, what they could and couldn't play.

He didn't do any better in Houston, where after visting his distributor, Steve Poncio at United, he went to see twenty-three-year-old Paul Berlin, Houston's top pop jock and a native Memphian, whom Sam had taught to run the board when he was a youngster, performing on Lowenstein's Junior Theater on Saturdays on WREC. Berlin, whose stock-in-trade was the big pop records by Patti Page and Jo Stafford and Les Paul and Mary Ford, did all but wrinkle up his nose at his onetime mentor. He said, "Mr. Phillips, I wish I could play your record, but that music is so ragged I just can't handle it." Maybe later on, he suggested, perhaps implying that the music might somehow improve.

So I left and checked out of my hotel, the Sam Houston, this old flea-bag hotel — I was going to drive into Dallas and try to catch the jukebox operators, Mondays and Wednesdays were their days. But I started out and got about sixty, seventy miles out from Houston and I ran into a dust storm, the dust got so bad I could not breathe. So I turned around and went back to Houston to keep from smothering to death, slept in the lobby of the Rice Hotel till I could leave the next morning for Dallas. And I walked into my distributor — that was Bill Emerson, Big State — and Alta Hayes was working the counter, and she looked at me and said, "Sam you look like hell." I said, "Okay, by God, you look the same to me." And Alta was a good-looking woman, and a great person, and she had a great ear, too. But I'll never forget, she said, "Well, you know why I look like hell to you is because you look like hell to me."

Which was, as Sam later recognized, "a classic fucking statement." But not one he was in any mood to understand at the time. "Alta was filling orders, but she said, 'Let's go up to the corner and have a cup of coffee.' Well, I didn't want a fucking cup of coffee. I didn't want *anything*. I just wanted to be let alone. But I didn't want to be let alone, really. And I went in with Alta, and she ordered a cup of coffee for me and she said, 'You're going to drink it.' And she ordered a cup of coffee for herself and a chocolate éclair — I'll never forget that chocolate éclair."

And then she just stared at him, and she said, "Don't you have any sense at all, Sam? You have got a hit." He said, "Alta, how can you be so damn cruel," he told her he didn't want any of her damn *sympathy*, and he launched into his tale of woe, how he had been turned down by Fats and T. Tommy and Stan and Paul Berlin, and she just sat there, a good-looking, full-figured woman with a phenomenal ear, and she repeated, "Sam, you got a hit. Not only that, you got a hit with both sides!" And she didn't oversell him either. She was the same with him as he would be with one of his artists. She told him what the jocks and the retail owners and the record operators were all saying — *in Dallas* — she told him she'd place the record in Stan Lewis' record store and get him to sponsor it on the air, she told him that T. Tommy was going to rue the day he had failed to get on board. But most of all, she *read* him, just like he read his artists, and when he left Dallas, "I can tell you, I was feeling a helluva lot better."

On August 28 "Blue Moon of Kentucky" entered *Billboard*'s territorial country-and-western chart for Memphis at number 3, and the following week "That's All Right" joined it at number 4. By September 11 "Blue Moon of Kentucky" had topped the same chart, and within a couple of weeks "That's All Right" was charting as a "C&W Territorial Best Seller" in Nashville, too—but that still didn't stop the doubters. When his Miami distributor wrote to him on September 24 that certain jukebox operators in the northern part of the state wouldn't touch the record because it was "too racy," Sam responded with equal diplomacy. "We can understand," he wrote, "that [it] might pose a problem for you by being so different and hard to catalogue. There is quite a big movement going on, which has come to our attention, to 'keep country music country' (whatever that is) and some DJ's, like the operators you mention, are reluctant to play the sides because they don't want to set a precedent. This we know, however, when they do play the record and let the public decide, it takes off." What's more, he wrote, offering yet another palliative, he had just arranged for Elvis to appear on the Grand Ole Opry (which should do a lot, Sam wrote, "to boost his popularity"), and a Louisiana Hayride appearance, too, was in the offing.

The Opry, to all intents and purposes, was pretty much for show, just so they could say that they had performed at the shrine of country music. Sam called in every favor he could from his time in Nashville and finally got Opry manager Jim Denny to agree: if it was worth it to Sam and the boys to drive over, he would give them a one-time-only spot — and just one song, too, "Blue Moon of Kentucky" — on Hank Snow's Royal Crown Cola segment from 10:15 to 10:30. That was more than fair, Sam thought, and would certainly help with some of the skeptics, but Shreveport's Louisiana Hayride was another matter altogether. Like the Grand Ole Opry, the Hayride was a weekly show that went out on Saturday night over a 50,000-watt clear-channel station (in both cases that meant reaching much of North America if the atmosphere was right) with, in addition, a network feed that enabled it to reach 198 stations for an hour the third Saturday of every month. The Hayride, which Jim Denny referred to derisively as the Opry's farm club because so many of its big acts eventually defected to Nashville, had launched the careers of Hank Williams, Slim Whitman, Webb Pierce, Kitty Wells, and Faron Young, and, Sam thought, could very well make Elvis Presley a star.

He accompanied Elvis to the Opry on October 2. "He made a tremendous showing," he wrote to Bill Sachs, who wrote the "Folk Talent & Tunes" column for *Billboard*, "and the crowd really warmed to him. You never would have dreamed that here was a lad who less than two months ago had never made any professional appearances of any kind. . . . But what really overwhelmed Elvis was the wonderful treatment given him by all the Opry stars, [who] went out of their way to meet him, and shake his hand, and congratulate him on his record." Which, while it never really departed from the facts, served to disguise Elvis' own disappointment that, against all the odds and against everything that Sam had prepared him for, Jim Denny (someone Sam saw as one of the flintiest but overall one of the fairest men of his acquaintance) was not sufficiently bowled over to burst out of the wings and offer Elvis a lifetime contract on the spot.

The trip to Shreveport two weeks later for the Hayride was a different story. They missed the turnoff at Greenville because Bill had them all laughing so hard at one of his jokes that no one was paying any attention to the road, and then Scotty almost hit a team of mules as he struggled to make up the time. Sam and Elvis went to see T. Tommy, who, as Alta had predicted, was singing a different tune (and playing the record) by now—but T. was clearly taken aback by the boy's appearance ("My wife commented, 'That boy needs to wash his neck'"), and the boy hardly opened his mouth during the whole visit. Record store owner and local entrepreneur Stan Lewis, at twenty-seven a seasoned veteran of the music business, was considerably more enthusiastic. But it was the audience at the Municipal Auditorium, a thirty-eight-hundred-seat hall with perfect acoustics just around the corner from Stan's record shop, that came as the real surprise. That audience, Sam reported to Bill Sachs on October 19, with perhaps a little bit of hyperbole but not much, "demanded five encores and was still crying for more when time ran out," and the Hayride made good on its promise to offer Elvis a contract as a regular on the occasion of his next appearance.

Sam's report, though, did not fully register the impact that the experience had had on him. He had sat in the audience himself, initially with the idea of providing support, and he noticed there were some young people up from a college in Texarkana, where Elvis' record was getting some play. They were on their feet when Elvis finished "That's All Right," the first of his two numbers — which was not altogether surprising — but then to Sam's amazement *everyone* was up on their feet. "I mean, all types. Old people, fat people, skinny people, listen, it was just one of those things that just comes up, and you say, Man, I'm not believing this. Some big fat lady — I mean, it took an effort for her to get up, and she got up and didn't stop talking, right in the middle of the next number, she didn't know who I was, she just said, 'Man, *have you ever heard anything that good?'"*

It was as if for the first time he was seeing the picture whole. "I mean, Elvis had this factor of communication. The audience saw in him the desire to please — and yet he had something about him that was almost impudent in a way. That was his crutch. He certainly didn't mean to be impudent. But he had enough of that along with what he could convey that was just beautiful and lovely — and I'm not talking about physical beauty, because he [wasn't] that good-looking then by conventional standards. I calculated that stuff in my mind: are they going to resent him with his long sideburns — that could be a plus or a minus. But when he came through like he did, it was neither. *He stood on his own.*"

I T DIDN'T MAKE HIS SITUATION any less perilous, though. "Business has been stinking," Sam wrote to Jim Bulleit in mid-August, and at this point both Buster Williams and Nate Duroff, his West Coast record manufacturer, had been carrying him for nearly a year now. Without a follow-up to his hit, he was still having trouble collecting from his distributors, his debts were mounting by the day — and for all of the unprecedented success of Sun 209, he was still teetering on the edge of bankruptcy.

But he didn't have time to think about any of that, as he stayed out on the road, trying to make sure that success did not kill his little company. If he had only had Jud to go out for him — but he didn't have Jud, and Jud would have just been spending money that they didn't have. Their next oldest brother, Tom, older than Jud by five years and a full-time employee at Scott Paper Company in Mobile, took the record around the Gulf area of Mississippi and Alabama on weekends — but he wasn't having much luck ("Mostly they threw out the record, and me out behind it"), and Sam was left in the same position that he had put himself in at the beginning: a one-man operation entirely dependent on his own energy and resources, with Marion as his invaluable sounding board and amanuensis.

He tried not to let on to Elvis — he knew that he could never let any doubt intrude into the boy's world. He couldn't let Elvis know, realistically, the adversities that they faced, "because Elvis would have thought he had let me down." But most of all, Sam was aware, Elvis had to believe in *him* if he was going to believe in himself. He didn't come from the same kind of world that Sam and his brothers and sisters had — Elvis' parents were good souls, good country souls, but it was clear that their son was the source of their strength, not the other way around. And yet as he got to know the boy, he continued to discover surprising inner reserves. He had, certainly, recognized his extraordinary feeling for music from the first, his extraordinary sensitivity in fact to everything that was going on around him. But he hadn't necessarily picked up on an intellect that was equally extraordinary in its own way.

There was, to begin with, his photographic memory — the boy only had to hear a song once, he never failed to take in anything that was said to him, he possessed the born mimic's ability to reproduce and transmute virtually anything that he observed. But more than that — *much* more than that — he possessed a thirst for knowledge, he possessed a voraciousness for a world of experience and imagination that went far beyond his limited exposure to it. Sam felt a kinship with him that allowed him, sometimes, to finish Elvis' thought without ever embarrassing him. Marion said Elvis was like a mirror, with everyone seeing in him what they wanted to see, but Sam saw in him the very person that he himself was but rarely showed. Where Elvis appeared unsure, tongue-tied, incapable of expressing himself, Sam saw in him the same kind of burning ambition that had driven Sam from the start, he was only lacking the ability to *verbalize* it.

In the studio they worked and worked — they worked every chance they got, whenever Sam was in town, whenever Elvis and Scotty and Bill, who were booked one or two nights a week now at the Eagle's Nest on Lamar, were available. They were searching desperately for a follow-up, doing their best to recapture that elusive sense of freedom, that unplanned carelessness that had caught them all up the first time. The sessions would go on and on, said Marion, "everyone was trying very hard, but everyone was trying to hang very loose through the whole thing." In a sense Sam had a clear picture of exactly what he wanted to hear, "certainly not note for note, but I knew the essence of what we were trying to do. But I also knew that the worst thing I could do was to be impatient, to try to force the issue — sometimes you can make a suggestion just [to change] one bar and you kill the whole song. And sometimes you can be too cocky around people who are insecure and just intimidate them. I mean, as far as actually saying, 'Hey, man, don't be scared,' I never told anybody in my life not to be scared . . . don't go calling attention to [what] you already know they are scared of. I was never a real forward person, because I didn't give a damn about jumping out in front to be seen, but I tried to envelop them in my feelings of security."

There was one session after another, ballads mostly (the slow numbers, Sam said, could "hang you out to dry") — but, in his judgment, the world wasn't waiting for another pop ballad singer just now. Scotty and Bill could occasionally be musical stumbling blocks, but it was their very ordinariness that had most recommended them in the first place, it was their down-to-earth quality that permitted Elvis to feel that he himself was not on trial.

Sam's one organizing principle was that it had to be fun. "I could tolerate anything, we could have tensions as long as I knew that we all had confidence in what we were trying to do, and I could get everybody relaxed to the point where they could hear and react to something without that threshold of apprehension where you almost get to a point where you can't do anything right. Every time we did a number, I wanted to make sure to the best of my ability that everybody *enjoyed* it."

To Marion it was like a puzzle to which only Sam held the key. "I still remember the times when everyone would be so tired, and then some little funny thing would set us off — I'd see Elvis literally rolling around on the floor, and Bill Black just stretched out with his old broken-down bass fiddle, just laughing and goofing off."

That didn't stop Sam from pushing them to deliver something they weren't always certain that they had. It was all about that feeling of camaraderie. It might have been easier to use a drummer, but he never wanted to intrude on their sense of shared experience. So he had Bill slapping sometimes till his fingers got raw, and if Scotty got a little too flowery, he was not above telling him that what they were looking for was "biting bullshit—everything had to be a stinger." Elvis' voice he treated like another instrument—miking it just so, with a Shure 55 or an RCA 77-D, was the key to that sense of intimacy and anticipation. He wanted simplicity to the point "where we could look at what we were hearing mentally and say, 'Man, this guy has just got it.'"

"Sam would push us in the studio," Scotty said. "Once you got a direction, he'd work you so hard you'd work your butt off, but he wouldn't let go until he got that little something extra sometimes you didn't even know you had." Once in a while he might call for a key change that he knew they weren't going to like, just to shake things up a little, sometimes when they were in a situation where they weren't getting anywhere he might call for a tempo so slow they were all ready to scream, but then, Sam said, "we would come back and find a tempo, and it felt so good, you know. It was like hit[ting] a home run."

H E FINALLY put out a second single in October, with a Memphis pre-release at the beginning of the month, the general release some four weeks later. He didn't do so without a certain amount of trepidation. He had held off this long not just out of his commitment to let the first record have a chance to really breathe but out of his refusal to put out another just for the sake of having a new release—he was resolute in his determination not to put out anything that didn't measure up to the startling clarity and directness of the first. When they ultimately got it, it was in its own way as fresh as the original pairing: an exuberantly melodic, irrepressibly triumphant version of "Good Rockin' Tonight," a number-one 1948 r&b hit by leather-lunged blues shouter Wynonie Harris, and a casually delivered, Dean Martin–styled version of "I Don't Care If the Sun Don't Shine," a number originally written for the 1950 Disney animated feature *Cinderella*. Sam took it as a measure of Elvis' sense of almost impish rebellion—"that's what he heard in Dean, that little bit of mischievousness that he had in his soul when he cut up a little bit"—and the playful way in which he employed slapback to support it seemed to reflect a similar attitude on his own part.

Sam had no misgivings about the record itself—both sides genuinely tickled him. The one thing that continued to give him pause was that sales for the first single still showed no signs of diminishing, as Elvis' popularity just continued to grow and grow. But he knew they needed a second single at this point, if only to get the distributors to pay for the first (it was common practice then, as now, to see little compelling reason to keep your accounts straight with a little record company that, more likely than not, was just going to go away). When the new single didn't sell as well as the first, they went right back into the studio as soon, and as often, as they could. It was even harder now, with Sam still on the road four or five days a week, and the boys, who had all quit their day jobs by now, playing the Hayride every weekend and as many dates as they could pick up during the week both in the Memphis area and, in conjunction with their newfound Hayride celebrity, around Louisiana and Texas as well. Scotty had been managing the group up till now, but he didn't have the time or the connections to get them a lot of bookings, so Sam enlisted Bob Neal, the prominent Memphis DJ who had hosted the Overton Park show in July, to try to set up some tours, with an eye toward taking over management at the end of the year.

On November 10, after canceling what would have been one final release by the Prisonaires, Sam put out the first two Sun singles in four months by anyone other than Elvis Presley. They were both more than creditable. Sun 211 was Malcolm Yelvington's much-delayed debut with a hillbilly version of Stick McGhee's rollicking novelty blues smash from 1949, "Drinkin' Wine Spodee-O-Dee." Sun 212, on the other hand, was a new single by sometime one-man band "Doctor" Isaiah Ross, whose "Boogie Disease" captured all the qualities of uninhibited good times, emphasized even more by the slapback effect, as applied to an already overamplified guitar, that characterized so much of the early catalogue.

Neither record did a thing — Sam simply didn't have the resources or maybe, if he were to be completely honest about it, the will, to focus on anything but Elvis right now. He didn't like it, he refused, in fact, to admit it even to himself — he'd be damned if he let himself become known as a one-artist label. But the reality was, he had no choice. Not only was the Elvis market growing, evidenced as much by personal appearances as by record sales, the boy's artistry and ambition were growing almost by the day. He was like a sponge, soaking up every influence with which he came in contact — Sam couldn't have held him back if he had tried. He was able to come up with a third single fairly quickly, a bright country novelty original Sam had picked up from a theater manager in Covington, Tennessee, and an old blues number, "Milkcow Blues," to which Sam appended the word "Boogie" and got Elvis to add a spoken introduction to the speeded-up, boogie part. "Hold it, fellas, that don't move me," he announced, with just the faintest hint of amusement in his voice. "Let's get real, real gone for a change."

ONE DAY THAT FALL a lanky, raw-boned country boy named Carl Perkins showed up at Sun's door. He was originally from Lake County, Tennessee, in the northwest corner of the state, on the Mississippi, but his family had moved to the Jackson area after the war, where he and his brothers, Jay and Clayton, formed a band. He was twenty-two years old and had been working as a baker in Jackson before he quit to play the honky-tonks full-time. Then one day his wife, Valda, heard "That's All Right" on the radio. "That sounds a lot like you, Carl," she said. And that was what had given him the idea.

He arrived with his brothers in a 1941 Plymouth, with the bass tied on top covered by a nine-foot cotton sack. Sam wasn't there when he arrived, but Marion showed no interest whatsoever, according to Carl's recollection, in either his talent or his potential. "We've got this new boy, Elvis Presley," she told him, and they weren't listening to anybody else. When Carl told her he sounded something like Elvis, she said that wasn't going to do him any good—they didn't need anyone else that sounded like Elvis Presley just now.

It was at this point in Carl's account that Sam showed up. Bear in mind that Sam was still driving the same black 1951 Cadillac that he had purchased just one year earlier, but Carl's version lends all the more piquancy to the story of someone who had grown up even poorer than Elvis and would always be certain that Marion looked down upon him because of his need.

"I took my hat and started out the front door," he said.

> As I did, there was a 1954 Coupe de Ville Cadillac almost took the front bumper off my old Plymouth. A man got out dressed just like the car. He had on a light blue pair of trousers and a dark blue coat. I thought to myself, That's either that Presley boy, or that's the man that owns this place. I said, "Are you Mr. Phillips?" He said, "Yes." I said, "My name's Carl Perkins, and that's my brothers sitting there in the car, and we come down to pick for you." He said, "I ain't got time." I said, "Mr. Phillips, please. Just one song. Will you?" I guess I said it just that hurt. He said, "Okay, get set up. But I can't listen long." We was set up and picking before he could get back to the

control room. Afterwards he told me, "I couldn't say no. Never have I [seen] a pitifuller-looking fellow as you looked when I said, 'I'm too busy to listen to you.' You overpowered me." I said, "I didn't mean to, but I'm glad I did." That was the beginning right there.

S AM HEARD SOMETHING right away in Carl's voice. Once the oldest Perkins brother, Jay, had finished with his Ernest Tubb imitations (Sam didn't mask his lack of interest, and Carl thought Jay was going to take a swing at him), Carl sang a song he had first started fooling with when he was fourteen. It was a song about taking a girl named Maggie to the movies on Saturday night on his old mule ("Just climb up on old Becky's back, and let's ride to the picture show") — the boy didn't even have a good title for it, but Sam was *tickled*. There was a real push to the way this old lantern-jawed farm boy played and sang — he sounded like a hopped-up Hank Williams the way he just jumped on the vocals. But it was his guitar playing that really struck Sam, the dancing little fills he played behind his singing, the way he interwove voice and guitar with a naturalness that Sam had never heard from any other hillbilly singer ("That thing was going to move somewhere that it didn't normally move with a good guitar picker"), almost like some old blues singer. That was just fine, he told Carl, it was *original* — but he needed to hear something else. If he didn't have anything right now, why didn't he go home and write himself a pretty ballad? Two weeks later the boy called up and sang it to him over the phone. It was indeed a beautiful ballad — Carl called it "I'll Be Following You," but Sam changed the title immediately in his head to "Turn Around" and told Carl to come back into the studio.

But as much as he would have liked to work with him to the extent that the boy's talent deserved, he simply didn't have the time. So he turned him over to two fellows he had known from Florence, who had been in to see him just a few months before.

He had worked with Quinton Claunch, a thirty-two-year-old native of Tishomingo, Mississippi, on a hillbilly release for Chess Records a couple of years earlier — but he had known Quinton ever since Quinton had moved to the Muscle Shoals area with his family in the early 1940s and helped put together a group that became known as the Blue Seal Pals when Blue Seal Flour started sponsoring their broadcasts (which Sam occasionally announced) on WLAY. Bill Cantrell, a country fiddler from Hackleburg, Alabama, had joined the band not long afterward.

A very young Carl Perkins.
*Courtesy of Stan Perkins
and Colin Escott*

Then Quinton moved to Memphis after the war and took a job as a traveling salesman, and Bill, who had a gift for electronics, moved to Chicago before returning to Memphis himself in the early '50s. There he went to work for the streetcar company first, then for Memphis Light, Gas and Water, Memphis' three-service municipal utility — but both he and Quinton retained their passion for music, and their intention to do something about it.

They wrote a song called "Daydreamin'," which they gave to a hillbilly singer from Arkansas named Bud Deckelman. Bill had originally met him in Chicago, but he was living in Memphis now and working occasionally with Scotty Moore. Bud did a helluva job with the song, so they demoed it and took the acetate to Sam. Neither Bill nor Quinton had had much contact with Sam over the years, and Quinton hadn't really kept up with the label after the failure of the one hillbilly artist he had brought to Sam — but both he and Bill were well aware of the stir this Presley boy was making. Sam said he liked their song, and he liked the singer, but when he offered his carefully considered but not particularly helpful critique (this should be changed, that should be changed, he wasn't sure exactly what it was, but he felt like there was something missing), they got pissed off and took it to Jules, Saul, and Joe Bihari's eccentric older brother, Les, whom the family had set up with his own label in Memphis, Meteor Records, in early 1953, just to get him out of their hair. He had had one big hit at the label's inception, Elmore James' "I Believe," which Joe had recorded and the brothers had given to Les in case Lillian McMurry was moved to sue Elmore again for breach of contract, but since then, Meteor Records might just as well have been out of business. Les was crazy about their demo — but then because Meteor had such minimal working facilities of its own, Quinton and Bill brought Sam the record to master. By November "Daydreamin'" was a big regional hit, topping the country charts in Cleveland, Memphis, and New Orleans, and as Quinton saw it, Sam couldn't stand to have missed out on the record's success, particularly given that this was the vein he now so clearly wanted to explore. So he called them in and asked if they'd like to work with some of Sun's hillbilly singers. Their first assignment was the Perkins Brothers Band.

Mostly they worked with Carl on polishing his new ballad — Carl was such a raw talent that he needed to be taught simply to stay on mike or to deliver his lyrics with the appropriate emphasis and in the right order. They saw Carl in much the same way that they imagined Sam did, as having the potential to be one of the most authentic country singers out there — but there is a moment that serves to underscore the limitations of their vision. Bill is coaching Carl on where to place the emphasis in the lyrics when someone says, "What do you boys think about Elvis Presley?" "Man!" comes Carl's unabashed response. "Good artist," Cantrell says, while acknowledging, "I don't like that kind of stuff, I don't go for it, but it's great stuff." "Boy, it's something, isn't it?" Carl chimes in. To which Bill may very well have assented with a nod but can only be heard to repeat, "It isn't my kind of stuff."

S AM ENGINEERED the one actual session that they did in the studio, as Carl laid down two beautifully realized versions of "Turn Around," featuring Quinton on electric rhythm guitar, Bill Cantrell's astringent fiddle, and a hint of steel guitar by a local musician named Stan Kesler. With "Movie Magg" (the title that Sam had conferred upon Carl's audition number), Sam had a perfect candidate for a brand-new Sun single by a promising new artist in just the direction that he was looking to pursue. But he didn't put out the record, nor did he call another session, for another three or four months.

It was ironic that his moment of greatest triumph should have generated his mood of greatest doubt. He never wavered in his vision. But now that the means to achieve it was at hand—and not through any overt declaration of purpose either but in the same celebratory spirit that was at the heart of all the music that he had ever recorded—he seemed strangely unsettled, confident that the future lay in the same vast reservoir of untried, untested, untapped talent that he had always known to exist and that he was just now getting a fresh opportunity to explore, but uncertain just how to explore it, how to find the new world that he had so long prophesied was just waiting to be discovered.

The music was vitally important, *Billboard* editor Paul Ackerman reassured him in the phone calls that had by now become a highlight of his week. Ackerman was starting to get pressure from some of the high mucky-mucks in Nashville to leave "that nigger music" alone, he told Sam in that quiet way he had of expressing erudition without a trace of condescension—but he'd quit before he gave in to that kind of pressure. It only went to show, he said, voicing thoughts that Sam had not dared to articulate even to Dewey, had scarcely spoken aloud to anyone but Marion and Becky, and then only in the most roundabout terms, that the music was waking people up, that the music was making a difference, that this music was going to change the world.

But Sam wasn't sure if he could hang on till then. "I have just received your letter," he wrote to Jud, on January 28, 1955, "and it apparently is not clear to you yet that Sun's liabilities are three times the assets and that I have been making every effort possible to keep it out of bankruptcy. As you well know, we have had only Presley, and with his Union contract of 3% of the 89¢ price, plus the fact that the songs cost 4¢ per record, it has been virtually impossible to make anything." What he didn't tell Jud was that he continued to be in deep trouble with the IRS over the excise tax. The more than $8,000 he had been forced to pay in January of 1954 on his overdue 1953 tax had left him in a hole he didn't know if he would ever be able to dig himself out of. What he did tell his brother now was that he had been forced to issue "merchandise credits"—in other words to write off as uncollectable debt—more than $7,000 since July, while paying full royalties and pressing costs on all those records he had reluctantly given away for free. Surely, he wrote to his brother, to whom he still owed $800 for his share of the business, Jud could "see the precarious position of the company. . . . Anybody less interested in saving face would have given it up long ago, but I intend to pay every dollar the company owes including you, even while I know that there is no possible way to even get out with a dollar."

Just nine days earlier he had brought Elvis to Sheffield, just across the river from Florence, under the aegis of a two-week series of shows that Elvis' new manager, Bob Neal, had booked. He urged family and friends, brothers and sisters, to come out and hear this fresh new talent, but mostly they did not. "I got a singer that you all need to hear," he told his seventeen-year-old niece Dot (Jimmy and Erin Connolly's daughter), but she knew what her Uncle Sam was like, and she wasn't going to get caught up in another one of his enthusiasms. "I'll never forget," she said, "I told him, 'I'm not going to go hear some country singer.' And he said 'Y'all are going to be sorry, 'cause this guy's gonna make it.' [But] I didn't go."

A lot of other people did, though, and the show was an unqualified success. And Elvis went on the radio to promote the show, and the girls all went crazy when, as the unsigned story in the *Tri-Cities Daily* predicted, "the rhythmic beat of 'That's All Right Mama,' '[Blue] Moon of Kentucky,' and other Elvis Presley favorites fills the air" And undoubtedly many folks who had not previously heard the just-turned-twenty "fastest rising 'country music' star in the nation" left the show, as the story was confident they would, "as full-fledged fans."

THRU THE PATIENCE OF SAM PHILLIPS —
SUDDENLY SINGING ELVIS PRESLEY
ZOOMS INTO RECORDING STARDOM

read the headline on the nearly half-page story in the *Memphis Press-Scimitar* on February 5, 1955. It marked Elvis' first show at Memphis' showcase Ellis Auditorium, his first appearance in Memphis as a recognized "star" (while listed at the bottom of the bill, he was presented in a featured spot introducing "Memphis' Own" in type as big as the headliners'), and it was written by Robert Johnson, the *Press-Scimitar*'s top entertainment writer and a near-contemporary of Marion's at Southwestern College in Memphis. It recounted for the first time the full story of Elvis' spectacular rise, but it devoted almost as much space to

Sam Phillips, who, Johnson pointed out, had earlier been "responsible for a new trend in the field which the trade publications call R&B and country (or hillbilly) music" and was now creating "a good-sized ripple in the frenzied circles of record business." "I've never made a record with an established star yet," Sam was quoted, and, it was strongly implied, he never would. What he was interested in from the start, Johnson wrote, was "genuine, untutored negro jazz [made by] negroes with field mud on their boots and patches in their overalls," but what he had found with Presley was just as fresh and original as the free-wheeling expressions of B.B. King, Joe Hill Louis, and the Howling Wolf. "Sam doesn't know how to catalog Elvis exactly. He has a white voice, sings with a negro rhythm which borrows in mood and emphasis from country style. Marion Keisker, who is WREC's Kitty Kelly and Sam's office staff, calls Elvis 'a hillbilly cat.'

"While he appears with so-called hillbilly shows," Johnson concluded, "Elvis' clothes are strictly sharp. His eyes are darkly slumberous, his hair sleekly long, his sideburns low, and there is a lazy, sexy, tough, good-looking manner which bobby soxers like. Not all record stars go over as well on stage as they do on records. Elvis sells."

Which Sam could only fervently hope would continue to be true.

Elvis and Dewey onstage, Ellis Auditorium, February 6, 1955.
Courtesy of Elvis Presley Enterprises

SEVEN | Spiritual Awakenings

S AM HAD HOPED AGAINST HOPE that the new Presley single would sell well enough to finally put him on a solid financial footing. He was desperate to pay off Jud, who had assigned his shares in the business to the First National Bank of Florence as security against a loan and was now talking about taking even more drastic measures if Sam didn't come up with the cash. But "Milkcow Blues Boogie" didn't sell any better than the second single, and for all intents and purposes Sam found himself right back where he started, begging his creditors for patience, chasing accounts receivable, fending off the IRS, and doing all that he could to defuse his brother's wild-eyed schemes. In Jud's current state of mind, there was no telling what he might do — but, whatever else fate might have in store, Sam was determined not to let his brother sell the company out from under him.

Elvis' management deal with Bob Neal was off to a good start anyway. Sam didn't think much of Neal — in his view the man was possessed of neither vision nor imagination. But he was well known as both a radio personality and entertainer (he not only MCed but did comic routines and played the ukulele on shows that he promoted), and he was well placed to get Elvis bookings in Arkansas and Mississippi, anywhere, in fact, within the two-hundred-mile radius of the strong WMPS signal on which his show went out. There was an announcement about the new arrangement in the *Press-Scimitar* on December 29, and Bill Sachs ran a squib in *Billboard* on January 8 citing a five-date regional tour. But in the meantime something altogether unexpected happened.

Through the success of some of his Louisiana Hayride bookings in

December 4, 1956. *Courtesy of Elvis Presley Enterprises*

East Texas, the boy had come to the attention of Colonel Tom Parker, the self-styled impresario who had until recently guided the career of Eddy Arnold. Arnold was probably the biggest all-around pop star ever to emerge from the country music field, with movies, his own television show, representation by the prestigious William Morris Agency, and a sophisticated uptown singing style that lent itself to broad popular acceptance. Since his break with Arnold, Parker had taken over the management of Hank Snow, one of the best-selling artists on the current hillbilly charts, and formed a booking and management company, Hank Snow Enterprises–Jamboree Attractions, with him.

Sam knew nothing about Parker personally, other than that he took an immediate dislike to him when they met between shows at the Ellis Auditorium appearance in February. Bob Neal had arranged the meeting and didn't have to say anything to convince Sam that Parker, in combination with his star, Hank Snow, could break the boy in territories that neither he nor Sam had entrée to. Parker, a purposefully crude, heavyset man who spoke in a guttural drawl and insisted that all his underlings call him Colonel, following an honorary appointment he had received from Louisiana governor and country music singer Jimmie Davis, almost immediately offended Sam, suggesting that, as much as he might like to help this talented young man, there wasn't a whole lot he could do so long as he remained on a little label like Sun — had Sam ever thought of selling the boy to RCA, which was doing such a wonderful job for Eddy Arnold and Hank Snow? It was all Sam could do to keep from taking a swing at him. Still, he told Elvis afterward that there was no better promoter in the business than Tom Parker, and, not surprisingly, it turned out that Parker was able to do a great deal: by May Elvis had toured with Hank Snow throughout the South and Southwest, opening up new territory in New Mexico and West Texas, Florida and North Carolina, and adding substantially to both his record sales and his personal-appearance income.

But it wasn't enough to make much of a difference to Sun and the Memphis Recording Service. Sam was still chasing distributors for what they owed him ("We don't want you to feel that we are overly solicitous about the account," he wrote to one distributor, who also had a label of his own, "[but] being in the record business yourself, you realize, I'm sure, that it is absolutely necessary that we stay on a current basis") and still trying to soothe their concerns about the exact nature of Presley's appeal. It was particularly galling when someone like Nate Duroff, who had always so generously extended credit to him for his West Coast pressing costs, reported that a local distributor was "of the opinion that the Elvis Presley records [will] not sell in Los Angeles. . . . He suggests that a Rock and Roll in western or hillbilly, such as Bill Haley records would move good out here."

He didn't give a damn about Bill Haley, who had covered "Rocket 88" in what Sam considered laughably inoffensive fashion and had made a career out of bouncy, if uninspired, versions of up-tempo r&b and boogie-woogie flavored with a western style. His latest, a rerelease of his 1954 recording, "Rock Around the Clock," which had been picked to play over the titles of *Blackboard Jungle,* the up-to-the-minute Hollywood picture about today's rebellious youth, seemed almost certain to be his biggest seller yet, and Sam could well understand the appeal of the music — actually, he thought Haley's records were pretty damn good, if you didn't require even an atom of originality. But goddamnit, *the man had nothing new to say.* It was the same damn beat you could hear on a Bob Wills record — this was not music that was going to shake up the world. And if this was what he needed to do with Elvis Presley to get a hit, if he needed to kill the spirit of something as fresh and daring and alive as Elvis' music, hell, that would be like committing a capital crime, he'd rather leave the business altogether.

The business in any case seemed to be leaving him — he felt like he was losing ground every day. He hadn't put out a single new Sun record since January 8, Elvis' twentieth birthday, when he released both "Milkcow Blues Boogie" and an intricately constructed new blues by Billy "The Kid" Emerson, "When It Rains It Pours." But with neither the means nor the manpower to market a new release effectively, and with none of the back catalogue selling except for Elvis' first record (which continued to enjoy exceptional success), he came up with a stopgap solution. Rather than continue to press records with uncertain prospects of commercial success and try to distribute them on a national scale, he returned to an idea that had first occurred to him the previous year, an "audition" label called Flip, on which he could release the various hillbilly artists that Quinton Claunch and Bill Cantrell were working with, but strictly to a local market. This would mean, according to his own interpretation, that he would not have to pay union rates, shipping, or anything but local pressing costs because he would simply be test-marketing the records in Memphis.

Cutting country in the studio, 1955. Back, left to right: Sam, Quinton Claunch, former Blue Seal Pal Dexter Johnson, and unknown. Front, left to right: Snearly Ranch Boy Stan Kesler, Bill Cantrell, and Sam's cousin (and Jerry Lee Lewis' forty years–plus accompanist) nineteen-year-old Kenny Lovelace.
Courtesy of Maggie Sue Wimberly (Sue Richards)

The first release, in February, included the Carl Perkins single that he had been holding for some time, and a novelty item called "Split Personality" featuring a gravel-voiced piano player named Smokey Joe Baugh whose vocals alternated with crooner Bill Taylor's in a tangled tale of conflicted desire. (As Marion Keisker put it, it was a comic treatment of the story of Dr. Jekyll and Mr. Hyde in hillbilly time.) Sam was crazy about the Carl Perkins record—to him "Turn Around" was as deeply felt as anything that Hank Williams had ever done—and "Split Personality" just tickled him, with the smooth-voiced singer murmuring "I love you," while the other, the dark side of the split personality, is snarling "I hate you," in that deep, guttural voice. He was intrigued by the possibilities of exploiting that voice, which seemed to have been influenced by the singer's exposure to Howlin' Wolf, whom Smokey Joe Baugh, along with the rest of the band, had met in the course of their broadcasts on KWEM in West Memphis. But neither record did a thing without the benefit of any real distribution or promotion.

He put out two more singles on Flip, in April, before a combination of union opposition and a renewal of faith — or maybe it was just hope on Sam's part — led him to virtually abandon the label. One was a well-crafted harmony vocal by the Miller Sisters, sisters-in-law, actually, from Tupelo, Mississippi, whom Sam compared favorably to the very popular Davis Sisters, and who sang a wonderful, almost Cajun-flavored original set off by Bill Cantrell's "corn-stalk" fiddle and the spoons-playing of Claunch and Cantrell's other tutee, Charlie Feathers.

Charlie Feathers was, conceivably, the cream of the crop. A masterly vocalist and incandescent spirit from Slayden, Mississippi, near Holly Springs, he had grown up on Bill Monroe bluegrass and cotton-patch blues, with a rambunctious personality whose nature could barely be contained within the confines of either. Sam saw him as possessing almost unlimited potential, with all of the blues feeling he could put into a hillbilly song. What they got in the studio — complete with yelps, hiccoughs, and the propensity to stretch out his syllables like a damned gospel singer — was only a tenth of what Sam was convinced he had to offer. But Charlie, as Sam was equally well aware, could certainly test your patience. Or as Quinton, a great champion of Charlie's talent, put it, "He was his own worst enemy. He didn't trust anybody. [It was like] he'd wake up in a new world every morning." A world in which Quinton, ordinarily easygoing to a fault, just didn't want to pick up the phone sometimes, he got so sick of listening to Charlie's bullshit.

It didn't really matter anyway. Neither Sun nor Flip could do anything for Charlie at this point, any more than the label could do anything for the Miller Sisters — even though Sam was determined to keep trying. Just as he was determined to keep trying with the few blues acts he still had left on his roster. He continued to believe there was room in the commercial marketplace for a striking talent like Billy "The Kid" Emerson. Or for the gutbucket blues that had first gripped his imagination. At the end of March Ike Turner brought in a harmonica player named Sammy Lewis, along with the Wolf's old guitarist, Willie Johnson, and together they created a sound so explosive that when Willie called out, "Blow the backs off it, Sammy," you felt like he really would. Sam continued to record blues pianist Eddie Snow with onetime Blue Flame Floyd Murphy, and Roscoe Gordon, one of his first, favorite, and most eccentric blues artists, was talking about coming back to him — they already had plans for a June session as soon as his Duke contract was up — but Sam was more and more aware there was little he could do at this point for any of these artists. Maybe if he had stayed in the rhythm-and-blues field, he could have continued to have hits that sold fifty- to seventy-five thousand copies, he could have kept on making the same old rounds, he could have continued to eke out a living by plowing the same damn row. But now he knew, somehow or another, without compass or map, he had stumbled upon the future, he was certain that the world was just waiting to explode—and he wasn't going to, he just *couldn't* step back and watch from the sidelines.

And it wasn't just Presley either—it was the limitless prospects that Elvis Presley's music had unleashed. It wasn't about cutting a hit record, it had *nothing to do with* cutting a hit record—it was, rather, about that "spiritual elixir" that he had discovered, that mutuality of experience and self-expression, that shared sense of exclusion, dispossession, and, yet, still, *possibility*—he knew many would see him as deserting the black man, and that haunted him. But as Sam saw it (and he saw it as clearly as he had ever seen anything in his mind's eye), what he was doing was to help open doors through which black artists and white artists alike—poor people deprived of education and opportunity but possessed of innate wisdom, talent, and imagination—might someday pass.

A TALL, LANKY BOY named J. R. Cash (that was his given name, and the name by which he had always gone until he joined the service) was one of those poor country boys with a different mind-set. He had first started coming around the studio in February or March, some eight months after getting out of the Air Force. Twenty-two years old, from a little town in Arkansas called Dyess, he had headed straight for Memphis with the idea of somehow getting involved in the music business, arriving on virtually the same day that Elvis cut his first record, at the beginning of July. After a brief side trip to Texas to marry the girl he had met just before being posted to Germany three years earlier, he returned to Memphis, where he secured both a new car and a job as a door-to-door salesman for the Home Equipment Company through his older brother, Roy, an automobile mechanic. He also enrolled at Keegan's School of Broadcasting on the GI Bill, because he knew by the example of all the country stars who had pursued that path that radio was as good an avenue as any to a musical career. Through Roy, too, a sometime musician himself and proud of his brother's musical inclination, he met three other mechanics at the big Chrysler dealership on Union, where Roy worked, who had formed a little "practice" band of their own. Soon the four of them were playing late into the night, fooling around with Hank Williams tunes and popular numbers by Ernest Tubb and Hank Snow, with J.R. doing most of the singing and occasionally contributing a gospel original he had written. One of the men, Red Kernodle, played steel guitar, though with a good deal of tentativeness, as he had only recently acquired an instrument of his own. The other two strummed rhythm, much like J.R. — but they decided they were hardly going to be able to present themselves to the public with three acoustic guitars playing virtually the same part, so Marshall Grant bought a bass and Luther Perkins bought an electric guitar, and they all learned to play together.

John Cash (he was at this point alternately John and J.R.) was by his own account the worst salesman in the world, the kind of salesman who would follow up his initial pitch to a customer, as often as not poor and black, with the advice that they really didn't need to buy this washing machine from him on the installment plan. One day he saw an old black man sitting on his porch in Orange Mound playing the banjo. Cash, whose passion for music ran the gamut from Roy Acuff singing "The Great Speckled Bird" to black gospel singer Sister Rosetta Tharpe's inspirited version of "Strange Things Happening," started talking to the man, who turned out to be a Memphis blues legend, Gus Cannon, founder of Cannon's Jug Stompers, a popular recording group in the late '20s and early '30s, whose signature tune was the jaunty, vaudeville-flavored "Walk Right In." From then on Gus Cannon's porch became a regular stop on his rounds; no matter what else might be pressing on his mind, including how he was going to be able to support his family on a meager salesman's salary, with a baby now on the way, he would always swing by — to talk, once in a while to play or mix in his own distinctive bass voice, but most of all to listen not just to the music but to the unique perspective and experience of the man.

Cash started going by the Memphis Recording Service, he often said, because it was on his way to Keegan's School of Broadcasting — but it was also just down the street from the Chrysler dealership where his brother and three fellow band members all worked. Elvis Presley's success certainly impressed him, too. He had seen Elvis perform on a flatbed truck in front of Katz Drugstore at the opening of the brand-new Lamar-Airways Shopping Center, and he was knocked out not just by the music but by the galvanizing force that could come from a simple trio format—he even got to meet Elvis afterward and was impressed by his enthusiasm, conviction, and polite demeanor. But what motivated him most of all, as it happened, was rejection, as he stopped by again and again and was rebuffed each time without getting so much as a perfunctory audition.

He introduced himself to Mr. Phillips initially as a gospel singer, and Sam said he loved gospel music himself but he didn't have any way to sell it. He told Marion all he wanted was a chance, and Marion said Sam didn't have the time for him. Finally he just sat down on the curb one day and waited until Sam showed up "and I stood up and I said, 'I'm John Cash, and I've got my guitar and I want you to hear me play,' and [this time] he said, 'Well, come on in.' I sang for two or three hours, everything I knew. Hank Snow, Ernest Tubb, Bill Monroe, I remember singing 'I'm Going to Sleep With One Eye Open (From Now On)' by Flatt and Scruggs—I even sang an [old] Irish song I'd been singing all my life, 'I'll Take You Home Again, Kathleen,' just to give him an idea of what I liked. He said, 'You've really got a range of material you understand and have a feel for.' He said, 'You say you got a group? Come back and bring those guys and let's put something down.'"

When they came back, they were all nervous, Red Kernodle most of all. "He was so nervous he couldn't play," Cash recalled. "We did about three [numbers] with the steel guitar, and he [just] packed up and left. He said, 'This music business is not for me.' And I thought the songs sounded terrible, so I didn't argue." Sam didn't really want steel guitar anyway—that, plus the fiddles and the choruses, was just the kind of thing that made every record coming out of Nashville sound exactly the same. But there was something absolutely intriguing about this little group. Just the difficulty they had putting something together, the very tentativeness that they exhibited in attempting to master their instruments—it was the damnedest thing, it was an *original sound.* Luther painstakingly picking one note at a time, Marshall slapping away at his recently acquired bass ("Marshall, when you play," was Sam's only piece of advice, "slap the hell out of it") and doing his best to stay in tune. It was nothing but rhythm, a funny, awkward kind of rhythm—boom-chick-a-boom, boom-chick-a-boom—it was, Sam was quick to realize, *the only way they could play.* But at the heart of it was this Cash boy's voice, its sincerity, its conviction, its very *believability.* Sam wasn't sure just how to characterize it—it reminded him a little of Southern gospel progenitor V. O. Stamps in its depth and certitude, you could hear the influence of Ernest Tubb, or even Bill Monroe—but at the same time it didn't sound like anything else he had ever heard. For all of the boy's evident sincerity, there was an exploratory quality to the music—maybe it was the slight quaver in his voice, maybe it was the uncertainty of his pitch, maybe it was the band's struggle just to get through a single song that made it so compelling in all its painful honesty.

There was one song in particular that Sam liked. "Hey Porter" had started out as a poem that John wrote on the eve of his return from Germany and now offered as both a warmly nostalgic salute to his Southern heritage and a sharply tuned interchange of humor, wordplay, and observation. It was almost, Sam thought, like a traditional folk song as sung by Burl Ives, but with more bite to it and a hard-won musical arrangement that had been agonizingly put together note by note. There was something reassuringly familiar about it—it was a train song ("Hey, porter"), a homecoming song ("How much longer till we cross that Mason-Dixon line?"), and yet it was at the same time charmingly original, too. But he didn't hear anything else that he could release.

John did have a prison song he had written—it seemed a little morbid, though, and he sang it in a high, strangely affected, almost plummy voice, as if he were imitating Marty Robbins. It started out "I hear that train a-comin'/A-comin' round the bend"—but Sam didn't think they needed any more train imagery either. So he told him to go home and see what else he could come up with. "Go home and write me an up-tempo weeper love song," Sam said—and *then* he would put out a record.

That was exactly what J. R. Cash did. It took all of two weeks for him to come up with a fully formed song—it came to him from listening to Smilin' Eddie Hill on WSM, the Opry flagship station. Every night he would announce, "Stay tuned, we're gonna bawl, squall, and climb the wall." The idea first struck him as the basis for a novelty song, and he wrote it originally as "You're Gonna Bawl, Bawl, Bawl." But then he reconfigured it as a real country weeper, a brashly *up-tempo* weeper with an almost cocky tone that he called "Cry! Cry! Cry!" and when he brought it in to Sam after working out an arrangement with Luther and Marshall, Sam heard it right away. He recorded it with the same raw panache that Cash imparted to his delivery—the slapback only served to add to the overwhelming sense of presence that three faltering instruments and one booming voice, served up unadorned, could create.

To Sam these two songs only began to suggest what this surprisingly self-possessed young man might be capable of. For all of his polite, self-effacing manner, J. R. Cash seemed to maintain an unshakable center, with a deep faith, a sly, tongue-in-cheek sense of humor, and a broader experience of the world than Sam had seen in most of his artists. He was a voracious reader whose songwriting stemmed as much from imagination as experience, and his upbringing in the "cooperative community" of Dyess, a socialist settlement, really, created by the Roosevelt administration as an experiment in rural reclamation, could only add to his breadth of perspective.

There was some talk initially of crediting the record to "The Tennessee Three," the group's loose title before Roy Cash's brother had joined — but Sam said, No, John was front and center on the record, and, furthermore, he thought "Johnny" Cash sounded better than "John," if you were looking to appeal to young people. John objected at first — he had *never* been a "Johnny," he remonstrated, it seemed too insubstantial somehow, it seemed almost too juvenile (the only time he had ever called himself "Johnny" was in the love letters he sent home from Germany to his teenage fiancée) — but he wasn't going to argue the point too strenuously with Mr. Phillips. He knew this was his big break, and besides, it seemed like Mr. Phillips had been right about nearly everything else up till now. He was beginning to feel like Mr. Phillips could "see something happening that nobody else could," could see something not just in him but in Elvis, too, and all the others, that they could not necessarily see in themselves. So he agreed to the name change. When the record came out, it would be by Johnny Cash and the Tennessee Two, but with artist royalties split 40-30-30.

He went to his boss at the Home Equipment Company, George Bates, to see if he would sponsor a fifteen-minute show on KWEM to help promote his new career. Mr. Bates had been very good to him in the eight or nine months he had worked for the company; he had advanced John money nearly every payday, and he had told him frankly that he didn't think he'd ever make much of a salesman, but he allowed him to keep trying. Whatever his opinion of John's musical talent — if he had one at all — he never hesitated about sponsoring the show. The only question he had was whether John thought he would ever be able to pay back the money that he owed — over $1,000 at this point — "and I said, 'One of these days I'm going to walk in here and give you a check for that full amount,' and he said, 'Well, I hope you'll be able to, but I've taken care of you because I believed in you, and I believe you will do *something*.'"

Johnny Cash and the Tennessee Two debuted on the air on May 21, just a few days after the "Cry! Cry! Cry!" session, and three days before his little girl, Rosanne, was born. Surprisingly, he didn't play either of the songs on his scheduled Sun release, and even more surprisingly, for all of his self-disparagement and Mr. Bates' assessment of his selling capabilities, he was a very convincing salesman, cool and confident and focusing on Cool-Glo Awnings as a plausible alternative to the more expensive option of air-conditioning. He sang "Wide Open Road," an original number that he had written in Germany, and a jaunty version of the Sons of the Pioneers' "One More Ride," both of which he had already auditioned for Mr. Phillips, and solicited listener requests for future broadcasts — if he didn't know the song already, he and Luther and Marshall would endeavor to learn it. Then, after highlighting Luther's guitar playing ("Luther, step up and show all the little children how to play a big boogie"), he concluded with "a good sacred song, one of my own, I wrote it a while back," and sang the song he had first tried to interest Sam Phillips in, the one he considered his best composition, "Belshazzar."

The record came out a month later. It was one of the biggest thrills of his life, Cash often said, to hear his record played on the radio for the first time. For the first time, too, he was beginning to think, "I might can make a living at it, and I won't have to do all those other things I don't want to do, like be a policeman or work as a disc jockey or a [salesman] — maybe, you know, by the end of the year I might make enough to pay the rent." But when he took a promotional copy to Elvis' manager, WMPS DJ Bob Neal, and Neal dropped it and broke it, "I thought my world had ended. I didn't think they'd make another one!"

SAM ALWAYS got a kick out of the story — and the comically woebegone way that John would always tell it — but in a sense it summed up (comically? tragically?) how he himself was apt to feel on occasion. Because for all of his artists' faith in him, for all of the confidence he exuded and the certainty that one way or another they were on the right path (as Johnny Cash gratefully acknowledged, "Mr. Phillips would listen to anything I wanted to sing or talk about, [but] he had no reservations about telling you what he thought"), he just really didn't know if his ship was ever going to come in — or, maybe more to the point, if he was going to be there when it did. He put out three r&b records on the same day as "Cry! Cry! Cry!" (One of them, Billy "The Kid" Emerson's "Red Hot," he wrote to West Coast pressing plant operator Nate Duroff, was "taking off big and going white [even though] other Emerson releases have been strictly for the Negro trade.") The Cash single attracted a good deal of DJ attention, and both Bob Neal and KWEM jock Dick Stuart indicated their interest in working with the boy. But none of the records were selling worth a damn, and he was still concentrating on the new single by Elvis that he had put out at the end of April.

I T HADN'T COME EASY — none of the sessions had, there were just so many damn ideas floating around — but Sam thought it was the best they had done so far. Sometime in February or early March Elvis had come in with a rhythm-and-blues tune, "Baby Let's Play House," that had recently been a halfway hit on Ernie Young's Excello label. It really wasn't much of a song, it probably wouldn't have even made the charts if John R., the increasingly popular late-night DJ who had by now attracted a broad biracial national base, hadn't flogged it so much on the show that Ernie's Record Mart sponsored on WLAC. But Elvis heard something in it, and Sam did, too, once Elvis injected that characteristic note of bubbling irrepressibility, which was never even hinted at in the original. "Oh, baby, baby, baby, baby, baby," Elvis opened with a hic-coughing stutter that just knocked Sam out every time, with its utterly uninhibited, unpredictable, insensate declaration of joy. This was only borne out by the alteration of attitude that Elvis brought to the lyric when he changed the traditional "You may have religion" to the playfully self-referential "You may have a pink Cadillac" as prelude to the song's one finger-wagging piece of advice, "But don't you be nobody's fool." It was, Sam thought, as perfectly spontaneous a moment as anything any of his artists had ever created on record.

For the B-side he had picked an original country number written by two members of the Snearly Ranch Boys, the hillbilly backing band who had come in with Quinton Claunch and Bill Cantrell and were named for the proprietor (Mrs. Snearly) of the rooming house (the "ranch") in which they all resided. Stan Kesler had played steel on most of the Flip sides; Bill Taylor was the loving Dr. Jekyll on "Split Personality"; and the song, "I'm Left, You're Right, She's Gone," was a simple, catchy tune based on a Campbell's Soup ad, with the kind of corny wordplay that gave it a commercial country feel. The only trouble was, Elvis didn't like it — he didn't like the song at all — when they got together for the session in early April. Sam wasn't sure just what the trouble was, whether it was the "cute" lyrics or the simple little melody, but he was clearly resistant to the idea. Sam had brought in a drummer for the first time, but they fooled around for a while with a drumless, slowed-down, bluesy approach until Sam was able to get Elvis back to the point of the song and, with the drums providing a solid, jangling background, take some of the weight off the vocals and achieve the pretty, almost delicate tone that Sam had envisioned for the tune all along. Sam knew he hadn't sold Elvis on the song completely, but it was the kind of thing they could use to help diversify his appeal. With Elvis breaking his voice somewhere between traditional hillbilly style and his newly patented hiccough, it wasn't exactly Nashville, but it had enough of an air of commercial familiarity, Sam thought ("I wanted the simplicity of [that] melody line"), to do the trick. "We just had to do a little bit of crawling around to see where we were before we got into the race."

Sam went out with Elvis for a few days at the end of April to help promote the new record. It was the first time he had ever done anything like this, and while it was necessarily tied in with visits to DJs, distributors, and jukebox operators, it represented a rare kind of self-indulgence for Sam, it was almost like a busman's holiday.

The first show was a traveling Hayride broadcast from the Heart O' Texas Coliseum in Waco, with Slim Whitman, the star of Elvis' debut performance at the Overton Park Shell the previous July, headlining. Slim drove up in his brand-new Chrysler New Yorker, with its one-foot-tall "twin-tower" taillights, and he told the folks about his first exposure to Elvis, when he had no idea who this kid with his name misspelled in the ads could possibly be. He couldn't believe it at first, he told Sam backstage, but he saw right away why Elvis appealed to so many people. It wasn't the way he looked, it wasn't the twitches or the moves. It was the way he *communicated,* the way he spoke to people through his music.

Sam could scarcely believe it himself. It was as if Elvis were drawing inspiration not just from the other performers but from the audience as well — as good as he had been in front of a hometown crowd at Ellis Auditorium just three months earlier, he was that much better now, every aspect of his demeanor and manner reflecting an unwavering faith in the future, it seemed, as much as in himself.

In Houston they went to see the great songwriter, thirty-eight-year-old Leon Payne, whose beautiful ballad "I Love You Because" Elvis had sung at his very first session. Payne was blind, living in a trailer out near Magnolia Gardens by the San Jacinto River, where Elvis was scheduled to play that afternoon, and it was a big thrill for Sam to meet the composer of so many indelible standards, including "Lost Highway."

But that was just an interlude. The new record started selling well even before it was officially released in mid-May — Sam had indications from everyone from Alta Hayes in Dallas to Jake Friedman in Atlanta that this could be Elvis' biggest seller yet, and national coverage in fan magazines like *Country Song Roundup, Country & Western Jamboree,* and *Cowboy Songs* was picking up almost every day, even as *Cash Box* named Elvis the "Most Promising Country Male Vocalist of 1955" in their July 2 issue. But in the meantime, offers for his contract had started coming in.

Mitch Miller at Columbia Records was the first. He got in touch with Bob Neal when Neal was out in West Texas with Elvis, and Neal called Sam. Sam didn't say no outright, but he named a price upward of $20,000, and Miller told Neal, "Oh, forget it, nobody's worth that much." Frank Walker, president of MGM Records, telegrammed Sam on June 8, after having heard from Jud that Elvis' contract was available, but Sam turned him down summarily along with a succession of suitors that included Capitol, Dot, and Mercury. And although he acted as if selling Elvis' contract was the furthest thing from his mind, part of him — the part that was so cash-strapped that he couldn't even keep up with the money he owed Elvis for record royalties — was sorely tempted. On the other hand, he had no intention of putting his fate in the hands of strangers. And whatever his eventual decision might be, he was keenly aware of the dangers of having everyone think that Elvis' contract was for sale when it wasn't — and having his own brother, with whom at this point he could barely bring himself to speak, actively fueling the rumors. As difficult as it was now to get his money from distributors, it would be next to impossible if they thought no more Elvis Presley records would be coming. But there was little he could do about it other than turn down the offers as fast as they came in. No matter what he said to Bob Neal, he knew how much it was in Neal's interest, not to mention his new partner Tom Parker's, to place their act with a major label. So he quietly seethed, recognizing that he had little other alternative given the position he was in.

THE BUSINESS with the radio station was finally coming to a head. It had seemed sometimes as if the licensing process was never going to end — the FCC had issued, then rescinded, then reissued a permit to proceed the previous December, and just in the last month or two, the Tri-State Broadcasting Service had actually gotten approval for a transmitter site around the corner from the studio on land owned by Clarence Camp, the money man Sam had originally found to fund his and Jimmy Connolly's dream. But for all of his feelings of relief, there was still something fundamentally missing. Sam and Jimmy's intention from the start had been to operate a Negro station both for the benefit of the community and for the "purpose of improving Southern Negro-white relations." But when, in June of 1954, WDIA, a dawn-to-dusk operation for its first seven years, got a 50,000-watt signal and a license to operate twenty-four hours a day, enabling them to reach what they estimated as 10 percent of the total black population of the country, and when shortly thereafter another Memphis station, WCBR (later to become known as WLOK), began to serve the same constituency, Sam wrote to the FCC in October that his station's emphasis would necessarily have to change "to an extent which cannot at this time be specified."

The trouble was, eight months later he was still unable to specify just what those changes were going to be, and even though he and Jimmy stayed up late into the night talking on the phone, Sam had yet to come up with an idea that was going to make their station as *different* as, in his mind, it needed to be.

He got the boy from Jackson, Carl Perkins, back in the studio in early July, and this time he took another approach. Carl had been rehearsing his deep country sound diligently with Quinton Claunch and Bill Cantrell, and the first of the two finished songs that they got reflected it, with Quinton setting a tic-tac rhythm on the bass strings of his electric guitar and Bill playing a mournful country fiddle. But with "Gone, Gone, Gone," a carefree original freely based on traditional lyrics, Sam for the first time took a fresh tack. It began the way they had rehearsed it, as a full-band performance, with Bill's fiddle clearly audible, but then Sam turned down the fiddle mike until all you heard was a faint echo, more like a "ghost" blues harmonica, as Carl's sprightly guitar took over both rhythm and lead.

"That must be my gal, yours don't look like that," he sang with unrestrained delight and then, after repeating the line, concluded with a not-so-innocent wink: "I know my baby, she's so round and fat." It was what Carl had been saying all along, it was what he had told Sam when he first showed up on the Sun doorstep and declared that he sounded something like this new boy, Elvis Presley. Sam hadn't wanted to hear it then, but it struck him forcibly now. It was just like Carl said. This was the kind of music that he had said all along he wanted to record, this was the kind of music that he played every night in the honky-tonks, *feel-good music*, the music he had learned from working beside black people in the cotton fields when he was growing up. When the music got going right, it had a little "click" to it, it was the same thing from Carl's perspective that made the gospel guitar of Sister Rosetta Tharpe "dance" — and the more he got into it at this session, the more he let loose, breaking his voice and pushing the rhythm, scatting and interjecting his name into the lyrics, exhorting himself and his fellow musicians, "Let's go, cats," as the song lifted off. Sam was determined to put out the record right away, but at the same time, he knew he didn't have the resources to make it a hit. He understood now how when "Carl's voice moved up in tempo, it took on a different cast." If the public ever got to hear what this boy was capable of, Sam thought with a mix of euphoria and regret, there was no limit to what he might achieve.

IT WAS JOHNNY CASH, though, on whom he pinned his highest hopes for an immediate hit. He worked "Cry! Cry! Cry!" hard with the DJs and distributors, and even though he had little success at first, he continued to believe in the record. He told John exactly what to do when he was out on the road. Be sure to have a supply of records in the trunk, whenever he heard country music on the radio, follow the sound to the station itself — the signal would get stronger as he got closer. Then just go in there and shake some hands. Don't go worrying the disc jockeys to death — "they're busy, they can't talk to you all the time. Right after you say hello, let your second line be, 'Man, I sure appreciate you playing my records.' Don't go in there cocky. Don't be no smart aleck. That's not what this is about. You're just passing through and stopping to thank them."

Cash was an apt pupil in this, as he was in all things. When he played the Overton Park Shell with Elvis on August 5, as an Extra Added Attraction on Bob Neal's Eighth Annual Country Music Jamboree, far from being intimidated or overselling himself, he saw it as a chance to stand out on his own. "Johnny Cash . . . was simply great," the *Tri-Cities Daily* reported of his appearance with Elvis in Sheffield three nights earlier, pronouncing him "a coming star [with] a couple of tunes that sounded like the best of Presley's bops, but his voice was different — deeper." The *Memphis Press-Scimitar* meanwhile ran a headline "Country Rhythm Fills a City Park," with his and Elvis' pictures superimposed above a photograph of the turn-away crowd at Overton Park. Within a month the record was number 1 on *Billboard*'s Memphis country chart, showing up on other regional lists around the country until, finally, it hit *Billboard*'s national country charts at the end of November.

But it was in the studio, in the preparation and cerebration that he put into every rehearsal and every session, that Johnny Cash impressed Sam most. Despite the shortcomings of his band, he was as quick a learner as Sam had ever seen, and his songs, which in many cases had started out as little more than sentimental little poems, were growing rapidly in both scope and ambition. With many artists, Sam was well aware, words could easily become mechanical, especially familiar words, but John always put his words together however reassuringly commonplace they might be — in ways that made them fresh and original. He had that rare gift of allowing each listener to imagine the things he was singing about from their own point of view — it didn't matter whether a song was conjuring up darkness or light, there was always someplace you could go.

For some reason Sam's thoughts continued to linger on the prison song John had sung on one of the earliest sessions, "Folsom Prison Blues" — Johnny believed in it so strongly that Sam was beginning to think he had misjudged it, had simply failed to recognize its potential. What if John were to take it a little faster and sing it more in his natural range. Then, Sam thought, it might actually have some pop potential.

John was fiercely resistant to the idea at first. He had conceived of "Folsom" in a completely different way — as a slow twelve-bar blues, a kind of lonesome love song from behind bars. But even if he hadn't been so resistant, the process of transforming it into a more up-tempo number, with a less melancholy mood, would still have posed a real problem. Because of their acute awareness of their own musical limitations, the trio always rehearsed meticulously before going into the studio. They would spend weeks sometimes preparing the songs they planned to record. "We just weren't versatile enough as musicians," said bass player Marshall Grant, "to make changes in the studio." But now that they were being called upon to radically revise their approach to one of John's signature songs, those limitations were glaringly revealed in a way that tested everyone's patience and, in Sam's seriocomic telling, very nearly broke up the group.

Luther, Sam had long since come to realize, could barely pick one string at a time, and then with very little sense of certainty. It almost defied belief to watch him try to find his way to the simplest statement of melody, while Johnny Cash, whom Sam otherwise considered as patient and even-tempered a man as he had ever met, would grow increasingly choleric at Luther's seeming inability to stumble through a single phrase. Sam took Luther aside. "I had him pick to me, you know, just by himself, we'd go through it and get that take, that feel, that essence [till] everybody knew, 'This is it.'" Then they would try another take, and at just about the point that it seemed they might actually get through it, Luther would hit a note that had never been heard before. "I mean, you would utter a little prayer," Sam said, "sometimes even close your eyes and not move a meter, and you'd want to stuff cotton in your ears and say, 'Let [him] get through it, let me just wake up [and find out] that he made it.'" But he never did. And yet when Johnny expressed his embarrassment and displeasure—to Sam, not to Luther—and even suggested replacing his "lead guitarist" just so they could get the cut, Sam held firm and said, "Look, John, you can take your ass out the front door, but leave me Luther." Because Luther was one of the key elements to the absolute distinctiveness of their sound.

He tried to get John to reimagine the song. John might *think* he had written a song about a prisoner behind bars dreaming of the outside world, but actually he had written something more universal in its appeal. Think of it like we're all in prison in a way, Sam said, maybe John should just start thinking about it like that—and then add a beat to it! To accentuate the beat, Sam thought he would mike the session a little differently and bring out the sound of the acoustic guitar, through which he had had John thread a little piece of paper at the neck like some of his blues singers had done, to create a kind of snare drum effect. But the trick was to get John to hear it, too, which in the end he did, only after he was convinced that Sam had penetrated to the heart of the song. "That was a part of Sam Phillips' brilliance. If the song was there, if he *knew* the song was there, then he felt at liberty to play with it and doctor it until he had it in that groove that he was hearing in his head. And [then] I started hearing it in my head, [too]."

He heard everything that Sam was saying, it seemed, right down to his vision of the new age that his and Elvis Presley's and this new boy Carl Perkins' music was ushering in. By the time he had finally succeeded in recording not just "Folsom Prison Blues" but its B-side, "So Doggone Lonesome," at the end of September, he had fully absorbed the lesson. "So Doggone Lonesome" from his point of view was "the best song" he had ever written, but, he noted with self-conscious sarcasm to an Air Force buddy just days after the session, it probably wouldn't sell more than three or four copies, "because I don't have a steel guitar in the band. Heck, people don't want anything different. . . . Shoot, those teenage girls don't care about catchy rhythm. They want to hear a pretty steel guitar. 'Cause *everybody* has a steel guitar. Guess I'm just wasting my time. My music is so shallow and simple."

Sarcasm aside, it was exactly the kind of thing that Sam might have said. How many times had he heard Mr. Phillips declare that Nashville was locked into fiddles and steel guitars, that what country music needed was a fresh new sound, a return to plain unvarnished emotion — or else it was just going to wither on the vine and die? Well, he for one was convinced. He was no more going to be bound by category than Elvis Presley. And when he finally succeeded in recording "Folsom Prison," no longer dour but with a new, bright message of existential unconcern, he had fully absorbed the lesson. "Don't listen to the music on the record," he wrote to his friend at the end of November, just as the new release was about to come out. "Listen to the rhythm."

CERTAINLY THE LESSON had not been lost on Elvis. He had gone into the studio in mid-July during a brief lull in his increasingly frenetic personal-appearance schedule, cutting a new record just as "Baby Let's Play House" hit number 15 on *Billboard*'s Country & Western Best Sellers chart. It was the first time an Elvis Presley record had shown up on any of the national charts, and Sam had no intention of putting out a new record anytime soon, but with the growing difficulty of finding any open time, he jumped at the opportunity to get Elvis into the studio. Just a week before the session, Scotty Moore traded his Gibson ES-295 for a blond Gibson L-5, to go with the EchoSonic amplifier he had bought from electronics wizard Ray Butts at the end of May. With the EchoSonic, which created a repetitive-echo effect of its own, Sam had the opportunity, simply by miking Scotty's new amp, to apply the "slapback" technique to more than one source at a time.

The song that he wanted to concentrate on, Little Junior Parker's "Mystery Train," was a natural for Elvis, who had always said that "Mystery Train" was one of the songs that first drew him to the Sun studio. To Sam, Little Junior's version was an unimprovable classic—but he had a different approach to the song in mind for Elvis. He played Scotty "Love My Baby," the B-side of the Little Junior single, with its churning riff by Floyd Murphy. He knew Scotty couldn't play as well, but that wouldn't matter if he could just get Scotty to open up and play a little more on the "uncautious" side. What he wanted was "a not too perfectly scheduled anticipation," and that is exactly what he got. The only take that has survived is the issued take—which sounds very much as if it may actually have been the first take as well. Because the feel is so loose, so exuberant, so much like the first time they finally got untracked on "That's All Right," once again with scarcely any vocal slapback, but this time with so much more awareness of both the risks and the rewards. "Mystery Train" was the greatest thing he had ever done on Elvis, Sam knew, with Elvis' acoustic guitar just ringing out and driving the rhythm and a sense of spontaneity so unforced that at the end you can hear Elvis laughing, "a little yodel-type laugh," as Sam described it, "because he didn't think it was a take." It was, in Sam's mind, the very essence of perfect imperfection.

The other side didn't come anywhere near as easy—in fact, it didn't come easy at all. It was much the same problem as the last time, when they had gone in and cut "I'm Left, You're Right, She's Gone." Once again Sam had gotten a cute country number from Stan Kesler, once again Sam had a drummer in the studio (though not the same drummer). And once again Elvis balked at the idea of going in a direction that just didn't appeal to him at first—he didn't dig Charlie Feathers' tormented demo, the chord progression was nothing but country, and it was a slow song, too. But Sam loved the hook, and he was convinced that, with all the airplay that "I'm Left, You're Right, She's Gone" had gotten, it was just the thing they needed to underscore the breadth of Elvis' talent for distributors and record buyers alike. "So we got it going, and [drummer Johnny Bernero] was doing four-four on the beat, and I said, 'That don't help us worth a shit, Johnny.' I told him, 'What I want you to do is do your rim shot snare on the offbeat, but keep it four-four until we go into the chorus. Then you go in and go with the bass beat at two-four.' And by doing that, it sounds like 'I Forgot to Remember to Forget' is twice as fast as it really is. And Elvis really loved it then."

But there was another element that gave the song its different appeal. Once he had overcome his initial aversion, a new note seemed to enter Elvis' voice. Each of the songs that Sam had released on him so far had been sung in a high tenor, despite Sam's awareness from the many ballads they had left on the shelf, from the very first day he had entered the studio and paid $4 to record the Ink Spots' "That's When Your Heartaches Begin," of his considerably wider range. On "I Forgot to Remember to Forget" he flirted for the first time with adult sensuality, dropping his voice slightly on the last line of each verse before reentering the next verse in his more conventional keening style.

They tried one more song that day, an obscure r&b number that Dewey had been playing on the radio called "Trying to Get to You." Once again, Sam recognized with a mix of admiration and surprise, Elvis brought something altogether new to it, in this case the kind of gospel fervor that you heard underlying all of his work but that Sam had never heard him express all-out before. They weren't quite there yet, Sam felt like if they had time to try another take, maybe slowed it down a little and retarded the beat, they could get something as good as anything Elvis had ever done. But that could wait, and Sam had every reason to be satisfied. This had been a banner session, maybe the most productive one yet, and with "Baby Let's Play House" holding steady on the national charts and gaining airplay all over the country (by August 13 it was number 5 on *Billboard*'s "Most Played by Jockeys" c&w list), there was no hurry about selecting a new single.

Except, contrary to all of his prior practices, he did. On August 1 he put out "Mystery Train" and "I Forgot to Remember to Forget," Elvis' fifth Sun release, along with an indiscriminate trio of hillbilly and r&b records and "Gone, Gone, Gone," Carl Perkins' official Sun debut.

It's hard to say why he did. You could argue that it was Elvis' ever-increasing popularity (in Jacksonville, Florida, they had practically torn the clothes off him), perhaps he felt he had missed out on other opportunities by being too cautious, as Jim Bulleit was always accusing him of being—but to me it seems more likely that it was his gut belief in the record, not so much its commercial potential as its artistic worth. "It was," Sam said, speaking of "Mystery Train," as he frequently did in later years, "the greatest thing I ever did on Elvis. I'm sorry. It was a fucking masterpiece."

Within days of the session he had shipped the tape off to be mastered by Bill Putnam at Universal Recording in Chicago with the words, "Give me 'hot' level on both 78 and 45's and as much presence peak and bass as possible!" written boldly on the Scotch Magnetic Tape box. There were two noteworthy aspects to this transaction. One was that up until now he had done all of his mastering himself, on his own Presto lathe. The other was that he should be willing to trust *anyone* to bring out the sound in what he recorded, given how much he knew you could lose in the mastering process. But this was Bill Putnam, universally acknowledged as the progenitor of modern studio recording and one of Sam's true heroes in the business. Bill Putnam not only had the kind of equipment that was needed to get the levels that Sam wanted for this record, Bill Putnam had the kind of "feel" necessary to bring out the excitement he felt.

Milton Tasker "Bill" Putnam had built his first studio at the age of twenty-six in 1946 in Evanston, just outside Chicago. He was from a well-to-do family in Danville, Illinois, and his father, a well-known businessman, was nearly as interested in ham radio transmission and commercial radio (he had a popular country music show) as his son was. Putnam developed the first commercial use of repetitive, or artificial, echo in 1947, along with a technique for creating multitracked vocals (actually multilayered, with the singer stacking his vocal one on top of another) that predated his friend and fellow inventor Les Paul's more widely embraced tape technique by several months. He engineered almost all of the Mercury label's recordings, cut rhythm and blues for Chess and Vee-Jay and just about every other independent operation in town, and even produced some country sessions for the primarily "highbrow" London label. Everything about Putnam's approach appealed to Sam, from the Scully lathes that he used, which could cut so much deeper than the one deep cutting head Sam had on the Presto, to his approach to building a studio, which harnessed state-of-the-art technology and seat-of-the-pants feel—but what impressed him most was Putnam's unmistakable appreciation of sound, not as something to which you applied one all-purpose technique, but as a living, breathing organism.

He had met Putnam when he was in Chicago with Dewey Phillips a couple of months earlier for Leonard Chess' son Marshall's bar mitzvah. He had gone by the studio and talked with Putnam and his wife, Belinda, who as it happened was a talented engineer and tape editor herself. He told Bill exactly what he was looking for, he wasn't going to spend days and nights on a record and then just "send it off somewhere and have them kill the impact by setting up a standard that they put on everything that came in." Each one of his records had its own individual character, each had a different indicator for where the voice should be, what the pre-emphasis curve should be — if he was going to entrust his records to anyone, what he expected was an *individualized approach* to every one. Bill nodded as he drank his beer and taped the conversation so his wife, who had gone off to do work of her own, could listen to it later. That was fine, he said, "Just send me up what you want mastered. Make a notation [of what you want] and let me send a master dub back and you play it and see if we're screwing it up." Elvis' record was the first one that he sent to Putnam, and it came back sounding exactly the way it was supposed to sound.

"This [disk] is certain to get strong initial exposure," *Billboard* wrote of "I Forgot to Remember to Forget" in an August 20 Spotlight Review. "Presley is currently on the best selling charts with 'Baby Let's Play House,' and the wide acceptance of this side should ease the way for the new disk. Flip, 'Mystery Train,' is a splendid coupling, with the guitar outstanding." A judgment that would only be underscored when in a Best Buys Review a few weeks later, *Billboard* pronounced, "With each release, Presley has been coming more and more quickly to the forefront." And cited the corresponding sales.

For Sam it was everything he could ever have hoped for, and yet, not surprisingly, he continued to feel pressure mounting from all sides. New offers for Elvis' contract were coming in all the time, as it became increasingly obvious not only that Tom Parker was actively soliciting them but that Parker had somehow wrested control of Elvis' management from Bob Neal. Sam could see that Neal was in way over his head — that Parker just had the poor guy bamboozled. But there was a change in Elvis, too, not so much in his own relationship with Sam as in his father's. Mr. Presley was a man of few words. Sam had always liked him even if Marion didn't — he knew lots of people just like Vernon Presley out in the countryside around Florence, in his own family, for that matter. But now Mr. Presley's silences were beginning to seem more resentful than reserved, almost surly at times, as if he suspected

Sam of cheating his boy somehow of the kind of opportunity that Tom Parker was saying he could provide — if he could just get Elvis signed to a major label. The worst thing was, Sam could understand the logic of the argument — he hated it, and he despised Parker for playing not so much on hopes as on fears — but he knew, too, that he owed Mr. Presley's boy more money than he could presently hope to repay. With the growing success of the records, with this sudden explosion of sales — they had probably sold a hundred thousand copies of Elvis Presley records on Sun since the beginning of the year — he already owed Elvis close to $3,000 in back royalties, and if the new record kept selling, it would come to even more. Sam was determined to pay him every penny — he had yet to welsh on a debt, and he would liquidate every asset he had before he did — but the question was when. And how long before Tom Parker poisoned the well irrevocably so it would make little difference if he did?

"You don't have to be an outcast to be a rebel," Sam always told his boys. That had been his lifelong credo. But lately he had begun to feel more and more like an outcast, sometimes he felt like he might even be sacrificing his own family — not just their future but their present — to a vision that might only bring ruin. He tried to give the boys the benefit of his wisdom. Instead of reading to them or indulging them, the way most fathers did, he treated them like equals. But lately he had become more and more worried about Knox. The little boy who was so attentive to every aspect of his business, who patterned himself so gravely after his father, almost reminded Sam *too* much of himself. In third grade he had started becoming frightened of storms. He would before long grow so disturbed by the "duck-and-cover" tornado alerts that boomed out over his new school's public address system that sometimes his mother would have to borrow a neighbor's car and come pick him up at school. On days that the weather was really bad, he wouldn't go to school at all. It just broke Becky's heart to see her big boy suffer so, and it worried Sam that he might have somehow passed this gene on to his oldest son. But he never questioned Knox's need. "He didn't [tell me], 'Knox, don't be afraid of storms anymore.' He would just grab my hand and say, 'Stay home, Knox. You know, it's frightening — but we'll get through this.'" He found a woman psychiatrist who was particularly good working with children, and he told Knox that this was the way you addressed your fears — it wasn't anything to be ashamed of, it wasn't any different than going to the doctor for a cold. And just like with any common physical

Sam's siblings and family, late 1955. Front, left to right: Irene, Aunt Emma, Knox, Jerry, and Becky. Back, left to right: Turner, Sam, unknown, Turner's wife Verna, Bill Phillips (Turner's son), and Mary. *Courtesy of the Sam Phillips Family*

ailment, you could be sure if you searched for it diligently enough, there was always going to be a cure.

That was the belief Sam always tried to stick to. But it was a belief that was sorely tested at times. He could always convey confidence to others, but sometimes his own confidence couldn't help but waver. Even though she would never say so, he felt like he was letting Becky down. He knew he could never live up to the idyllic vision she had of their lives together. He felt bad that he hardly ever went to church with his family anymore, that there was no time for fishing or checkers or any of the innocent, commonplace pursuits that he and Becky had once so enjoyed with Jimmy Connolly and his family. He no longer had any time for Marion, who sensed his growing distance but didn't know what to do about it. There was no time for anything but business — and it seemed like all of a sudden there was no margin for error, it felt sometimes in the spring and summer of 1955 like everything was just closing in.

The radio station needed to be up and operational by the fall, and Sam knew for sure now that Jimmy was pulling out. He didn't blame him. They still talked about it all the time, but with their "Negro station" no longer possible and Jimmy's adored only child, Dot, about to get married and settle down close to home (Sam would record the wedding ceremony in June), it was clear that Jimmy was not going to leave Birmingham or the security of his position as general manager of WJLD. So Sam was faced with the necessity of finding a new partner fast or, after all this work, losing the station altogether. And even after he had finally scraped together the last $800 that he owed Jud for his partnership in the label, Jud, who was working at a Ford dealership in the Florence area now, refused to cash the checks and suggested that it would take another $1,200 to satisfy his financial needs.

When his doctor, Henry Moskowitz, suggested that it might be beneficial to take a drink or two on occasion just to ease the tension, Sam at first demurred. He had up to this point never taken a drink in his life. He didn't like what it did to Jud, he didn't like the prospect of losing control. But on reflection he decided it was probably a good suggestion and, even though he never really got used to the taste of liquor, found that a Scotch and milk after work now and then relaxed him, just as Dr. Moskowitz had said it would. It led, in fact, to a new sense of openness that he found genuinely pleasurable. Sam had never been a "sociable" person; both as boy and man he had simply considered himself to be too busy. But now for the first time, at the end of a long day he might go down to WHBQ, to the mezzanine floor of the Hotel Chisca on South Main — the "magazine" floor, as Dewey Phillips always referred to it on the air, whether making an intentional or unwitting joke, you could never be sure — where Dewey was finishing up his nine P.M.-to-midnight shift. "Get yourself a wheelbarrow full of goober dust," Dewey was very likely announcing when Sam walked in the door, "and roll it in the door [of whatever sponsor Dewey happened to be representing], and tell 'em Phillips sent you. And" — with a wink to his visitor — "CALL SAM!"

Sam loved to watch Dewey operate, there was such a manifest sense of self-belief in the way Dewey threw himself into his broadcast, there was such a sense of sheer glory-bound joyousness — the same spirit that

Sam tried to inject into every one of his sessions. Now, afterward, they might occasionally have a drink or two together (or, in Dewey's case, probably quite a few more — though Dewey would no more take a drink on the air than Sam would dream of drinking on a session). Or they might just go to the Gridiron for the best bacon and eggs with grits you could get in Memphis after midnight. For the first time Sam was able to fully abandon himself to an unplanned moment. And when he came home in the early-morning hours, different somehow than he had ever been before, Becky never said a word — she was just glad to see Sam forget about his troubles for a little while. Marion, on the other hand, hated it: she hated the idea of the drinking, she hated what she judged to be its coarsening effect, most of all she hated his new intimacy with Dewey, whom she considered to be a crude, crass, uncultured little man. She had never been able to listen to his show. But now, she felt, rightly or wrongly, he had become "a very potent threat to my personal relationship with Sam."

Then it seemed as if gradually the clouds began to lift. Somehow Sam was able to forestall a showdown with Jud, persuading him to hold off for the time being at least on turning over his shares to the bank. And the new Presley single, whose impulsive release had appeared to be such a worrisomely risky venture, was selling briskly without any indication of dislodging "Baby Let's Play House" from the national Top 10. Best of all, he rapidly resolved the radio station crisis in ways better than he could ever have imagined.

At his lawyer Roy Scott's suggestion, he had called Kemmons Wilson, the maverick Memphis entrepreneur whose Holiday Inn motels were by now located in eleven states. It was actually Roy, whose father, Roy Scott Sr., was Kemmons' longtime accountant, who initiated the contact, and when Kemmons, who could never resist a "different" approach to business (a temporary setback was for Kemmons never a mistake but a learning experience), indicated his interest, they worked out a deal. Kemmons would put up $25,000 as a stake and in exchange receive a 32 percent share, equal to Sam's and Mr. Camp's (the original "silent partner" on whose land they were about to build their transmitter), with Roy Scott getting 4 percent in lieu of legal and accounting fees. But Kemmons, who had been so instrumental in helping Sam out when he needed to establish a line of credit with Buster Williams' pressing plant, had another idea. Why couldn't he serve not just as an investor and silent partner but, in a mutually beneficial arrangement, as a rent-free landlord besides?

Kemmons had a storefront space available that he thought might be suitable just across the entryway from the coffee shop and check-in desk of the Holiday Inn on South Third Street downtown. Sam took one look, "and I said, 'God, I want that!'" And not just because there would be so many people coming and going. It was the modernistic premise of the whole Holiday Inn approach, with its distinctive green-and-yellow color scheme, free ice, free parking, free television, air-conditioning and a pool, and clean comfortable accommodations as fresh and brand-new as the radio station itself. "It was," he was certain, "just the right place to be." And for Kemmons, there couldn't be a better way to draw attention to his business. It fulfilled his lifelong belief that free advertising was the best advertising.

It was mid-August before he decided on the format he wanted to establish for the new radio station—but then it was an idea as revolutionary as the original concept for the studio had been, as defiant in its own way of established tradition and something in which he believed just as strongly. He was going to establish the first All-Girl radio station in the nation.

He could advance any number of good reasons for pursuing this course, and he continued to go over them with his brother-in-law, even though Jimmy at this point had no formal role in the new venture. Number one, women, like Negroes, were an underutilized resource, a vast pool of unappreciated talent in a highly competitive world. He had no question about the talent. Becky, for one—he had never known a better announcer than Becky, from the time he first met her when she was just a seventeen-year-old high school student. Desire, for another—that could play both ways. Oh, I know what you're thinking, he said to Jimmy, and it was true, the idea had natural sex appeal. And certainly there would be some "sexiness" on his station—radio, after all, was a product of the imagination. But the other aspect of desire was the desire these women would have to prove themselves, a determination no less intense, if more femininely expressed, than all his untrained, untried musicians. Plus, the music that they would play would have nothing to do with the music he was recording—it would be "beautiful music," "easy-listening" music, programming with "glamour, sparkle [and] spice," for the housewife at home and the girls at the office, Doris Day and Percy Faith and the

The first location of WHER, in the third Holiday Inn.
Courtesy of the Sam Phillips Family

Glenn Miller Orchestra, the kind of music in many instances that Sam had broadcast from the Skyway Ballroom at the Hotel Peabody and that Becky had always presented with such incandescent charm.

Becky took it as a tribute. It was just what they had always talked about, it would serve as a true partnership, it represented a mutual love for the very thing that had first drawn them together. She immediately started making plans for the kind of shows that she would do, for the way she would have to train the other girls (because nearly all of them would come in without any prior experience)—she even knew the motto she would use: "A smile on your face puts a smile in your voice." She was positive it would be a big success, she was sure it would bring them closer together.

Marion was just as excited. She took it almost as much as a tribute to her. She would quit her job as assistant program director at WREC, she told Sam, as soon as he was ready to go on the air. Don't do that, he tried to tell her—he needed her at the recording studio, and besides, it would be a mistake to put all her eggs in one basket before the station proved itself. But she was not to be gainsaid. She didn't think she'd ever been as excited about anything in her life, even if it meant giving up a

guaranteed salary. And besides — she didn't tell Sam this, she was barely able to admit it to herself — *she was not going to be left behind.*

Sam applied to the FCC for the station's new call letters at the end of August. To match its new identity he had come up with the acronym WHER. At the same time he placed a classified ad in *Broadcasting-Telecasting* magazine:

> Wanted: Fresh, friendly, female voice for metropolitan station. Must be versatile, experienced, good looking. Unparalleled opportunity for girl who can qualify.

The underlying pretext was that there was a single position open, and all responses were to be referred to Radio Station WSLC (the station's most recent designation), Tri-State Broadcasting Service, at 706 Union Avenue in Memphis.

One of the first responses came from a woman named Margie Abbott, a former Memphian with an extensive background in radio, music, and theater who was presently assistant station manager at KONI in Phoenix, Arizona. "Dear Margie," Sam wrote back on September 8:

> I received your audition tape and letter this morning. I have given all the material close attention and am very, very well pleased with your qualifications. I believe we have a job here that you would enjoy tremendously and which you could handle capably.
>
> We mean to have a facility that we — and the community — will be proud of. We are going to handpich our personnel, being as sure as is humanly possible that each person is suited to the job and is extremely versatile and flexible. The job we have in mind for you will be one of responsibility and importance, and you will be called on to do a variety of things, all of which you are apparently well trained and qualified to do. It will also mean that you will have to work hard. As we all intend to do, but believe me, the work will pay off.

The salary would only be $80 a week to start off with, Sam wrote, nothing like what she was worth, but they were a new operation, who

Becky at WHER, ca. 1956. *Courtesy of the Sam Phillips Family* "must of necessity proceed with caution insofar as salaries and all expenses are concerned." But he was confident both of her success and the success of the operation, and once they all had their feet on the ground, she could certainly expect more. "I realize that all the information I am giving you about the new station is somewhat clouded," he continued, "and I am sorry that this is necessary, but we are keeping our plans a closely guarded secret, as the immediate success of the station will depend to an unusually large degree on the surprise element."

In fact, only Becky and Marion (and his partners) were in on the secret. And it wasn't until Margie wrote back to accept the job, appending the news that she was going to go back to being "Dottie" when she returned to Memphis (that was fine, Sam replied, he liked the new name, "maybe I'll just change mine. Ha"), that she was let in on the secret, too.

Construction on the new station began almost immediately. Sam hired a woman named Denise Howard who was just out of college and had opened her own advertising and interior design firm in an office downtown not two weeks earlier. Her mother, who was very much involved in Memphis cultural affairs, knew Marion from her connection to the symphony and suggested that Denise call her about this little radio station that her boss, Sam Phillips, was planning to put on the air. Marion asked if she might be able to stop by the recording studio that Saturday, and Denise waited around for hours, finally getting to see Sam after his "rock 'n' roll session" concluded (she presumed it was a rock 'n' roll session — she knew nothing whatsoever about that kind of music). He told her he was sorry, he didn't have time to speak to her now, but could she come out to the house in a few days? That way she'd get to meet his wife, Becky, who was a radio gal herself, and they'd have a chance for some uninterrupted conversation.

When she did, she was *inspired.*

> He said, "I've just got this idea. I've been working on it for some time, and Mr. Wilson and I are partners, and we're opening the station on South Third." (I'd never been to the building in my life, of course.) But the more he talked about it — I mean, he's a man, when you start talking to him, you don't know what he's going to cover, he's got so many avenues and interests your mouth's just hanging open, and the more he talked, [the more] my mind was spinning like a top, and I went home and had two notebooks filled in a week.

This was before she even saw the space. When she went down there with Sam, she was utterly taken aback.

I walked into the place, and, of course, from the front you never know till you open the door what you're going to see — but this room was roughly twenty or twenty-two feet wide by fifty-feet long — it looked like a big long hall! He was saying, "I've got to have this, and don't forget, I've got to have a room for the sales girls to write copy, and I have to have an office for our program director, and then I have to have our studio facilities and our lobby," and I'm looking at him, you know, I hadn't been out of school that long, but my forte was space planning, and I told my parents when I went home, This was the biggest challenge — I said, "I don't know where I'm going to put everything!"

She made the most minute calculations — she created a sales room that was nine feet long and forty-two inches wide, and then where the right-hand side of the wall faced the street, she left one foot of display space for the station's letters. At one point she had an elderly carpenter building seventeen-inch shelving for the room, and he said, "Lady, I don't know what you're trying to do, but you'll never be able to do it." Whenever he was working on something in the room, she would have to crawl out of it and hand him a hammer, because "you couldn't get two derrieres in that room at one time."

And all the while Sam kept volleying ideas at her, not in a way that was annoying but, quite the opposite, that she found genuinely stimulating. "We'd start, and I'd say, 'Sam, we're both going to have a headache from this.' Sam never knew hours — [we] could be down at the studio, and it would be four o'clock, and before we knew it, it would be seven or eight o'clock" — and all thoughts of dinner would be long forgotten.

The only obstacle was Kemmons Wilson's mother, Doll, who, with his wife, was the light of his life, and who had free rein at all of his hotels. She showed up one day and told Sam that she was in charge of decorating for Holiday Inns and she was going to decorate the radio station in chartreuse. Sam didn't confront her exactly — he just sidestepped her. And he sang to her occasionally, too, leaving her utterly charmed. But he'd be damned if he'd decorate any radio station of his in *chartreuse*.

Sam, Elvis, and Marion in front of 706, September 23, 1956.
Courtesy of Tom Salva

"MYSTERY TRAIN" hit the national charts in mid-September, the week after "Baby Let's Play House" had its highest combined showing (number 7, Most Played by Jockeys; number 15, Best Sellers in Stores). But even as the earlier single continued to hold its respectable position as a store best seller, "Mystery Train" forged ahead of it by one place in the first week, while "I Forgot to Remember to Forget" was number 10 on the radio airplay list. From that point on, the new single continued to rise precipitously, while "Baby Let's Play House" effectively dropped off the charts.

On October 24, with all the hiring done but work at the new station still continuing at a frenetic pace (they had been scheduled to go on the air four days earlier), he got a not altogether unexpected telegram from Tom Parker from the Warwick Hotel in New York. "Dear Sam," it read:

Elvis Presley and his parents Mr. and Mrs. Presley have requested and authorized me to handle all negotiations on an exclusive basis towards affecting [sic] a settlement of the Elvis Presley recording contract with you and the Sun Record Company. . . . Please advise me your best flat price for a complete dissolution and release free and clear.

This was, finally, too much for Sam. Up until now it had all been something of a dance whose consummation, if preordained, had not yet needed to be squarely faced. Now, with a real, honest-to-God national hit on his hands, he felt as if he was being undercut by the very process he had allowed to be set in motion. "I was pissed off, I got so goddamn mad, I called up Bob Neal and I said, 'Bob, you know, what the hell you doing to me?' He said, 'Aw, Sam, I ain't doing nothing,' and I said, 'Goddamnit, you're associated with Tom Parker and he's putting out this bullshit, after all of what I've been through to get this guy going, he's putting the word out to my distributors that I'm gonna sell Elvis' contract.' I said, 'Man, this is killing me, you're not just messing with an artist contract here, you messing with my life. You just don't deal with these people [the distributors] unfairly. They're in this damn thing, too.' I said, 'This could cost me the company.' I said, 'This has got to stop.'

"So I called Tom Parker at the Warwick Hotel in New York, and he said, 'Sa-a-am, how you doin'?' And I said, 'Well, I ain't doing worth a damn. Why is it that every distributor I got says that this man is on the block?' I said, 'Look, Tom, this has been going on now basically for three or four months, but I thought nothing of it, 'cause I couldn't get confirmation from Bob Neal that you good friends of mine would be trying to do me in — advertently or inadvertently.' He said, 'Oh, noooo, Sam, no, I don't understand thaaaat.' And then he said, 'But would you be interested in selling Elvis' contract?' So I said, 'I hadn't really thought about it, Tom. But I'll let you know.' So he said, 'Well, look, think about it, and let me know.'"

He had, of course, thought about it — he just hadn't focused on it. But now he did. As unpalatable a solution as it might be, as much as he hated being forced by any man, let alone Tom Parker, to follow a course he had not set for himself, this might be his only way out. He desperately needed capital — not just for his record company but to get this new idea in radio up and running, too. He had artists he couldn't promote, records he couldn't release, all because of an absence of cash. He had in the end been able to persuade Jud to accept a final payment of $1,300 ($500 beyond the $800 contractually owed) in exchange for any and all interest in the company, past, present, or future. It had been all he could do to scrape the money together just ten days earlier—and now, for all he knew, Parker might very well find some legal loophole to persuade the boy to leave, with or without his consent. He carefully considered his options, took stock of his situation, and called Tom Parker back almost immediately.

The price that he named was $35,000, plus $5,000 for Elvis for back royalties, more than anyone had ever paid for a popular recording artist before (by comparison Columbia had paid $25,000 for the contract of Frankie Laine, an established star, in 1951). The Colonel did little more than clear his throat. He would, he said, look into it.

They met on Saturday, October 29, at the Holiday Inn coffee shop, just hours after WHER had finally gone on the air. Although the *Press-Scimitar* ascribed the more than one-week delay to "ladylike tardiness," Sam had been up at this point for three days straight, installing the electrical ground system and personally running all the line checks. Evidently by coincidence, Hill and Range song publishing attorney Ben Starr had arrived on the same day to work out a deal tied in with a forthcoming Elvis Presley songbook. Under the proposed agreement not only would Hill and Range, probably the biggest and most aggressive force in country music song publishing in the country, publish the folio, they would also be licensed for the next year to represent the Sun publishing catalogue in Europe as well as promote motion picture tie-ins and domestic cover versions of Sun catalogue songs for 25 percent off the top. After listening to Starr's proposal, Sam left him in the WHER studio and joined the others in the coffee shop across the entryway, squeezing into a booth next to Bob Neal, and opposite Parker and his assistant, Tom Diskin. Parker brought up the money once again, as if to make sure he had heard correctly over what might have been a bad telephone line. Thirty-five thousand? he said. Well, you know that's a lot of money. I don't know if I can raise that kind of money on an unproven talent. He went over great in Jacksonville, but you talking about $35,000. That's right, chimed in Tom Diskin. That's a helluva lot of money. How much money you made on that boy anyway?

That was simply too much for Sam. He had kept his mouth shut when Parker had talked like that at their first meeting, but he'd be damned if he'd let that sorry-ass, fat sonofabitch ride roughshod over him again, with his flunky doing the talking.

"I said [to Diskin], 'It's none of your goddamn business. In addition to that, I didn't invite you down here. I invited Tom Parker.' Tom elbowed Diskin on the outside seat of this booth and said, 'Shut your mouth.' 'Cause, man, I was ready to get up and whip his ass. Or get whipped. Parker said, 'Look, I don't know where we can go.' He said, 'Sam, there's not a lot of people believe in this thing. But how can we work this deal?' I said, 'Well, first thing, you just keep Tom Diskin's mouth shut.'"

They finally worked out an option deal. The option would take effect on Monday, October 31, and allow Parker until midnight November 15 to raise $5,000 as a down payment. Sam never budged on the purchase price, and the entire sum had to be raised, and the contract executed, within one month, by December 1, 1955. The $5,000 would not be refundable, and the deadline for both its arrival and execution of the contract would not be extended. Sam had no idea how likely it was that Parker would find a buyer or how likely it was that he would get stuck for the money. Personally, Sam didn't much care — certainly the $5,000 would come in handy even if the deal didn't go through. But he did have an uncharacteristic moment of self-doubt. Back at the radio studio, after taking care of the Hill and Range business, Sam ran into Kemmons Wilson, and, suddenly fearful of what he had done, asked Kemmons, whose opinion he respected enormously both as a friend and a businessman, what he thought about the deal. "He said, 'Jesus Christ, thirty-five thousand dollars? Hell, he can't even sing, man. Take the money!' I said, 'Well, I just done it, and I don't know if they will come through or not.' He said, 'You better hope they do.'" It was not the answer he had expected, but it made him feel a little better, if only for the casual spontaneity of Kemmons' response. But he remained torn.

The following day, Knox's tenth birthday, he and Marion set out early for Houston, a six-hundred-mile drive, in order to be in U.S. District Court the next morning for his long-awaited hearing (it had been more than eighteen months now) on the Little Junior Parker theft-of-personal-services case. For all practical purposes, of course, the outcome had been long since established — Little Junior was at this point a recognized star on Don Robey's Duke label. But even though many might have, and *had,* been deterred by Robey's reputation and associations (as one of his short-term associates put it, "he wasn't scared of the forked-tongued devil himself"), Sam was not going to be deflected or scared off. He was determined to have his day in court.

They practically got killed on the way. Sam was driving — Marion didn't know how to drive — and somewhere outside Shreveport he fell asleep and woke up just in time to get the car back on the road. He pulled into a pasture and told Marion he needed to sleep for a little while, but she had to stay awake — Marion was subject to narcolepsy — and to be sure to wake him up after an hour or two so they wouldn't miss their court date in Houston.

The regular judge, Ben C. Connally, was clearly more sympathetic to the case than his superannuated substitute back in April of 1954 and, after several days of court testimony by Sam, Marion, Robey, and others, awarded unspecified damages to Sun Records for what he found to be a clear case of contractual interference. Eventually cumulative damages, including punitive, were set at $17,500, and after lengthy appeals, which wound their way all the way to the Supreme Court in what was deemed an historic case, Sam finally got his $17,500, plus interest.

Tom Parker still hadn't made his deal by the time Sam and Marion got back to Memphis. Sam had not in fact heard a word from Parker, who was doing everything in his power to make the case to RCA, with whom he was firmly entrenched as a result of his long-term management of Eddy Arnold and his more recent association with Hank Snow. But for all of his initial efforts, and all of his company connections, he simply could not get the label to budge from a high bid of $25,000, which he knew Phillips would never agree to accept.

Sam meanwhile was increasingly certain that he had made the right decision. It was more than just a matter of economics. Sam had from the very start of Elvis' success been determined that Sun Records was not going to become known as a one-artist label. More to the point, he was equally determined to prove that Elvis Presley was not a fluke, that the idea that Sam had espoused from the start, the vision that he had first glimpsed on an Alabama farm — that there was a wealth of talent out there just waiting to be discovered (and a world just waiting to embrace it, even if that world had no idea what it was waiting for) — was not some damn ivory-tower *theory*, it was the goddamn truth. But without the capital to support his vision, he knew, he would never get the chance to realize it. All of these artists that he had sitting out there in the bullpen would never even get into the game. As Kemmons had told him, trying to explain not only why it was necessary for him to sell Elvis' contract but the basis for his own risk-embracing business philosophy, "You've got to get new money coming in to do anything." Whatever Kemmons' opinion of Elvis' talent, no one could have stated the case more succinctly. And no one could have better understood how much — against all the dictates of his heart, against all that he knew he and Elvis could still accomplish — Sam was now hoping that Tom Parker would come up with the money.

Elvis was named Most Promising C&W Artist in *Billboard*'s annual Disc Jockey Poll announced at the Country Music Disc Jockey Convention in Nashville on November 10 as well as in the November 12 issue of the magazine, in which "I Forgot to Remember to Forget" reached number 3 on the best-seller list. On November 15, the last day of the option, Sam got a midmorning call from Tom Parker notifying him that RCA had come up with the money. Parker asked Sam if he wanted the money wired to him, in order to conform strictly to the terms of the deal, but Sam said no, just send it special delivery for arrival by midnight the following night, and sent a telegram to that effect. They would have to get together in the next week or so to finalize all the arrangements, and that would, naturally, take place in Memphis.

On November 18, with the $5,000 in hand, Sam put in a rush order at all three of his pressing plants for the new Johnny Cash and Billy "The Kid" Emerson singles. He also planned Sun releases for Charlie Feathers and Maggie Sue Wimberly, a fourteen-year-old from Florence, Alabama, whom Quinton Claunch and Bill Cantrell had discovered (through fellow former Blue Seal Pal Dexter Johnson) singing with a family group in church. At the same time, he scheduled another session with Carl Perkins, his first in six months, but this time, with Elvis no longer in the picture, with an eye toward finally capturing Carl's contagiously upbeat, shimmering "bop" style.

The formal execution of the contract took place at the Sun studio, as agreed, on November 21. Various RCA executives, Bob Neal, Hank Snow, Tom Diskin, and Tom Parker all attended, as well as Elvis and his parents. The photographs mostly show various configurations of smiling middle-aged men with their prize. The exceptions are one that includes Elvis' mother and father, Vernon and Gladys, with Gladys kissing her son's cheek and the Colonel's steadying arm on her shoulder. The other

Bob Neal, Sam, RCA attorney Coleman Tily, Elvis, and Colonel Tom Parker
on the occasion of RCA's purchase of Elvis' contract, November 21, 1955.
Courtesy of the Sam Phillips Family

shows Sam and Elvis shaking hands across RCA attorney Coleman Tily,
each with an expression of what appears to be nothing but genuine goodwill and an eagerness for the future to begin (Bob Neal and Tom Parker
are beaming on either side).

Marion missed the signing ceremony. She was working her shift
over at WHER, but she had hired a new girl to take her place. This
was eighteen-year-old Sally Wilbourn's first day of work. A brand-new
high school graduate from Coffeeville, Mississippi, a town of less than
a thousand, out in the country between Water Valley and Grenada, she
had been sent over from Miller-Hawkins Business School, where she was
learning typing and shorthand. She had never heard of Sun Records, had
no idea who Elvis Presley was, and Marion had left her with instructions
to answer the phone—but with no idea of what to say when she did.

Colonel Parker, Hank Snow, and Elvis all came over to the radio station after the signing. For the first and only time in its existence WHER
played an Elvis Presley record, "Mystery Train," and Marion introduced

Hank Snow, whom she considered a vainglorious little popinjay, and put him on the air, almost wincing when Snow claimed credit for discovering Elvis Presley, when, as she recalled, he couldn't even remember Elvis' name when he introduced him on his segment of the Opry little more than a year earlier.

Marion, on the payroll at the recording studio now for the first time, at $60 a week, in addition to her WHER salary, quickly schooled the new girl. She had been hired to work afternoons while Marion was at the radio station, but frequently she worked long into the night, helping Marion catch up with the increasing flow of business, which included filling orders for "Mystery Train"/"I Forgot to Remember to Forget" until the end of the year, by which time both sides of the record would have reached as high as number 4 on the *Billboard* country best-seller list. Sally didn't say much — Marion wasn't sure how bright she was, but she was a sweet little thing from the country all decked out in petticoats, and she clearly kept her ears open and possessed the rare gift of being able to take criticism. To Sally, Marion was "a very educated person — I was not — but she had no common sense. You always knew Marion's feelings about anything. You could tell if she was in a bad mood the minute she walked in the door. I would sit there and listen to her [talk about] her son, her mother, and everything that ever happened to her. She told me right away that she was in love with Sam. That was one of the first things she told me."

As for Sam, Sally had a very different kind of reaction.

"My first impression of him was [of] a nice-looking man, he was extremely polite to everybody that came in that studio, never rude to anybody. It didn't matter what they wanted or how they talked or what they said, he was just always nice to them, and that just had to register with you, and it did. But yet you could hear him on the phone talking business with somebody — there was nowhere to go, really, to hide from anybody, we all were right there together, you know — and he made a great impression with everybody that met him."

Sam meanwhile had little interest in doing anything but moving forward full steam ahead. This was his moment, if there ever was to be one. For the first time, he had the money to back up his beliefs, and his "last words of sage advice" to Elvis as he left the studio might just as well have applied to himself. Don't ever stop believing in yourself, he told Elvis. Don't ever let anyone make you doubt what you know to be true.

They'll throw all this shit at you, but you let them know what you feel and what you want to do. Just be prepared to "go down trying, and if you do, I'll guarantee you're going to change some things. And if it doesn't work," he said, "you ain't lost a goddamn thing."

For all of his outward diffidence Sam had no doubt that Elvis understood. He wasn't so sure about RCA. He didn't know if RCA's head of specialty singles, Steve Sholes, who had been instrumental in persuading the company to buy Elvis' contract, had the backbone to keep all those damn *bureaucrats* out of the creative process. He fervently hoped that he did. Elvis' success was almost as important to Sam as his own — in so many ways it reflected the sum total of all of his judgments.

All these years he had had to keep his nose clean. The jocks and distributors that he dealt with every day "could have said, 'This goddamn rebel down here is gonna turn his back on us. Why should we give this nigger-loving son of a bitch a break?' It took some subtle thinking on my part, and it took some withstanding of things that would be said about you all over. But I had the ability to be patient. I was able to hold on almost with a religious fervor. But definitely subdued. I wasn't looking for no tall stumps to preach from."

He had sensed in Elvis a kindred spirit almost from the start. "I don't think he was aware of my motivation for doing what I was trying to do — not consciously anyway — but *intuitively* he felt it. I never discussed it [with him]; I don't think it would have been very wise to talk about. For me to say, 'Hey, man, we're going against [this],' 'we're trying to revolutionize that.' Or, 'We're trying to put pop music down [and] bring in black —' The lack of prejudice on the part of Elvis Presley had to be one of the biggest things that ever could have happened to us."

It was almost subversive what they had done, sneaking around through the music. They had gone out into this no man's land, "where the earth meets the sky," as Sam always liked to put it, without so much as a map or a compass, with nothing more than their own belief in the innate spirituality of the music. "But we hit things a little bit, don't you think?" Together they had "knocked the shit out of the color line."

Billboard editor Paul Ackerman, whom Sam had finally met at the Dee Jay Convention in November, continued to offer nothing but unqualified admiration. Sam hit it off with him even more in person than they had over the phone — it was as if he had found not just a sophisticated New York voice to articulate his vision but a blood brother as close to him as

Dewey Phillips or Jimmy Connolly, whatever the differences in background and education. Every week their telephone conversations only reinforced Sam's belief in himself and Paul's belief in the redemptive properties of the music. A *Billboard* feature by executive news editor Bill Simon the very week that Tom Parker was finally able to put together his RCA deal led with the statement: "There are few boundary lines left in music," and then went on to point out that "Southern audiences, who once craved an exclusive diet of hillbilly platters, [no longer] practice segregation in their platter preferences." This was due, Simon wrote, as much as anything else to "the spectacular rise of Elvis Presley in the field. Presley gets spins on r&b, as well as country shows, and as prominent a pop deejay as Bill Randle [at the top of the pop firmament at the time] insists that Presley is a potentially top pop entity."

Still, Sam knew as well as any man: "Anytime you think you know what the public is going to want, that's when you know you're looking at a damn fool in the mirror." And he was determined, insofar as it was within his power, not to find himself staring back at a fool.

THE WORLD TURNED UPSIDE DOWN

CARL PERKINS called him at the studio on the morning of Saturday, December 17. He told Sam he had just written a song called "Blue Suede Shoes." Was it anything like the old spiritual "O Dem Golden Slippers?" Sam said jokingly, but then Carl sang him the song, and he knew right away. It was somewhere between a novelty number and a lighthearted declaration of independence, with the lyrics suggesting in nursery-song rhymes that the unnamed object of desire, the *world*, in fact, could inflict any humiliation that it wanted on the singer ("You can burn my house / Steal my car / Drink my liquor from an old fruit jar") just so long as you, singular or plural (and this was the exuberant refrain of the song), "Don't step on my blue suede shoes." Sam didn't hesitate for even a second. If the boy could put it across with that much flair on the telephone, they needed to set up a session right away.

The song had a curious history. It stemmed from a conversation between Carl and Johnny Cash, whose second single, "Folsom Prison Blues," Sam had just released, after giving "Cry! Cry! Cry!" a full five months before it finally reached number 14 on *Billboard*'s national country best-seller list at the end of November. Carl and John were playing a date with Elvis in Amory, Mississippi, on December 13, and Cash, who had been urging Carl to record a real "bop" song now that Elvis was out of the Sun Records picture, told Carl a story about a black serviceman named C. V. White, a cool operator with whom he had served in Germany. He and his buddies were all standing in the chow line one night when somebody stepped on C.V.'s toes. "Hey, man," said C.V. drily, who like everyone else was wearing regulation black Air Force–issue shoes, "I don't care what you do with my fräulein, [just] don't step on my blue suede shoes." Just a few nights later, after getting home late from a hometown gig, the song came to Carl. His wife and two little babies were asleep, so he sat out on the steps of the public housing project where he lived and sang the lyrics softly to himself, attaching a nursery rhyme introduction he remembered from playing hide and seek as a kid ("One for the money, two for the show . . .") and then writing it all out on a brown paper bag that hc had to first empty of potatoes.

Sam arrived for the session in the light-blue, four-door 1954 Cadillac with the dark-blue top with which he had rewarded himself after selling Elvis' contract, the very one from which Carl would always imagine him to be emerging at their first meeting. He had all the jauntiness of a ship's captain and all the optimism of a man embarking on a voyage he had planned for all his life. Carl and his brothers and the drummer, "Fluke" Holland, had rehearsed the song over and over in the two days since he had written it. His older brother, Jay, was still having a little trouble holding up for the full two-beat stop-time, but Sam kept the tempo so slow at first that soon everyone got it. It was, as Sam recognized, a very simple, rolling vamp, but "you say a vamp is a vamp is a vamp. That's not true. Sure, you can change the tempo and all [that] stuff, but there's a certain feel on a vamp — once you get that thing going, it's kind of like the Hallelujah Chorus in a black church."

That was his job — to keep them on the rhythm — and that was what he stuck to for the most part. But his principal contribution, as both Sam and Carl remembered it, came about as the result of a mistake Carl made on the second take. He had just got done singing his little windup introduction when, in the same spirit of carefree celebration with which the rest of the song was invested, he inadvertently shouted out, "Go, cat, go," as the cue for the first iteration of his theme.

"I said, 'Mr. Phillips, that's wrong. That's supposed to be "Go, *man,* go." We got to do it again.' He said, 'No, that's right—let's leave it like that.' I said, 'Besides that, Mr. Phillips, I made a bad mistake on my guitar.' He said, 'Yeah, but you covered it up real quick.'" Then he played it for Carl in the control room. "'You see,' he said, 'that one's got the excitement.'" And he repeated to Carl what he had told so many of his other artists, "No one's ever going to hear the mistake but you." And while they did do a third take at Carl's insistence, there was never any question as to which was going to be released.

Sam was so excited about the session that rather than ship them off to Chicago to have them mastered by Bill Putnam, he cut the masters in the studio himself and by the end of the workday had sent them off by air express to have stampers made, the first step in the manufacturing process. This was a "RUSH job," he wrote to Jack Rosen, who was making the stampers. "We are waiting to run this number NOW." In the meantime, he cut dubs for the local DJs, and Dewey played the *hell* out of the song over the next two weeks, before it was officially released on January 5, 1956.

You could tell it was going to be different from the start. On the very first day, Music Sales, Sam's Memphis distributor, put in an initial order for four hundred, then ordered six hundred more by the end of the day. In Dallas, Alta Hayes of Big State, who had been the first to give Sam hope that his experiment might actually catch on, moved twenty-five hundred copies out the door. By the end of the month it had passed one hundred thousand sales, and Sam was advertising it as a bona fide "three-way smash" (pop, country, and r&b). After gross sales of $45,000 in the last quarter of 1955, a new high for Sun, the label suddenly rocketed to nearly six times that amount in the first quarter of 1956, and then to an almost unimaginable $350,000 in the second quarter, representing sales of something like 865,000 records.

The impact on Sun's tiny three-person storefront operation was almost impossible to imagine. For Sally Wilbourn, who had gone to work at the end of November and just turned nineteen the week that "Blue Suede Shoes" came out, it was as if her whole world had turned upside down.

> It just seemed like everything burst wide open. You have to remember what [we] didn't have. You didn't have electric typewriters. You didn't have photostat machines. You didn't have calculators.

Everything was carbon copy. Every sample that went to a radio station had to be packaged individually [with] a label typed and put on
them, and then you had to weigh them and put postage on them.
Records wore out. Juke boxes would just wear them out. I was packaging records, going to radio stations every day, you know—and
answering the phone. I didn't know a lot but I was capable of learning. It got to the point where Marion and I were working every night.
Then I started working Sundays, doing invoices, because there was
nobody else to do it except her and me. Just doing the billing was the
biggest job. We would have to get in the studio on Sunday afternoon
and spread all of those invoices from every distributor out in the
middle of the floor. We had no [other] place to do it, and some of
them were so thick because we were selling so many records. The
phone was ringing all the time—[we were still answering] "Memphis
Recording Service." But then every time we answered, somebody
would say, "Is this Sun Record Company?" And everybody had the
same question. "How do you make a record?" That was the question every time. So finally, okay, we answered the phone "Memphis
Recording Service and Sun Record Company." But that took too long
to say. So that's how it just got down to "Sun Record Company"—but
Sam really had a problem giving up "Memphis Recording Service."

Elvis, meanwhile, seemed to be foundering at RCA. The company
held off releasing his first single, a sixteen-bar blues called "Heartbreak
Hotel," until the end of January, and to Sam's ears, with its somber lyrics
and plodding pace (it was just too goddamn slow for a "rhythm man," he
said), it was little more than "a morbid mess." Perhaps even more revealing, they had tried to duplicate Sun's unique "slapback" sound without
any idea of how it was achieved and in the process created a clattery kind
of echo effect (achieved by putting a mike and an amp at opposite ends
of a long hallway and then feeding the sound back into the studio), at
stark odds with the warmth and intimacy that Sam had sought to create.
There didn't even appear to be much enthusiasm at RCA for the
single. At least, that was what Steve Sholes, the specialty singles division
head, who had pushed for Elvis' signing and now found his job in jeop-
ardy, told Sam when he called to see if it would be all right for RCA to

Sally Wilbourn. *Courtesy of the Sam Phillips Family*

put out the cover version of "Blue Suede Shoes" he had cut on Elvis just three days after "Heartbreak Hotel" was released. With the Carl Perkins original breaking in all markets, this was not a question Sam wanted to hear, but he couldn't help but be sympathetic to the way Steve described the difficulties he was having getting anything out of Elvis in the studio. And he was even more taken aback when Sholes asked plaintively, "Did I buy the wrong guy?"

No, he had not signed the wrong guy, Sam told him unequivocally. But, he declared equally unequivocally, Sholes and RCA were going about things all wrong. "I told him what I told him when he bought the contract in the first place—just don't try to make Elvis what he's not instinctively. The worst mistake you can make is to try to shape him into some damn country artist, or anything else, if it just doesn't naturally flow that way. I told him, 'Just keep it as simple as possible.'" As far as releasing a cover version of the Carl Perkins single, "I told him, 'Well, Steve, I can't keep you from covering it. But that would really hurt me, I mean it really would.'" And Sholes, whom Sam saw as a man of great decency if not imagination, agreed to hold off on the release, and then to put it out only on an EP (an extended-play 45, with two songs on each side), which theoretically would not compete on the singles chart. "I said, 'Well, Steve, if you will do that, that will help immensely.'"

By the time Elvis' version came out almost two months later, it didn't matter anyway. "Heartbreak Hotel" had finally broken into the pop charts (as of March 24 it stood at number 11, with Carl's "Blue Suede Shoes" at number 9), and the two records were chasing each other up the charts—*all* the charts—in a manner that had never been seen before. In a series of editorials in *Billboard,* some written by Paul Ackerman, all informed by his fiercely democratic views, the "growing trend for the country and western, pop and rhythm and blues fields to merge into one big 'Mongrel music' category" was duly noted with reference to "two heretofore strictly c&w artists—Elvis Presley and Carl Perkins. . . . It's interesting to note," an unsigned article reported in the March 10 issue, "that Perkins records for Sun, the label which gave Presley his start. Even more interesting is the fact that Perkins is on seven r&b territorial charts this week and is moving up strongly toward the national top r&b retail chart. If he makes it, it will be the first time a c&w artist has ever appeared on the national r&b list." The following week Carl Perkins' "Blue Suede Shoes" did just that, placing number 9 on the r&b Best Sellers and Disc Jockey lists, 10 on the Juke Box plays, and making history (along with black artists like Chuck Berry and Little Richard crossing over in the opposite direction) in almost exactly the way that Sam had for so long predicted.

At the same time, Paul Ackerman's unconditional embrace of this new "'Mongrel music' category" seems to have excited an equally unconditional xenophobic response from Nashville's country culture. "It has already been suggested," Ackerman wrote in the March 17 issue of *Billboard*, "that country artists with r&b-styled material, or r&b-styled delivery, be excluded from the best-selling country chart." Such exclusion, Ackerman suggested slyly, would not only be wrong, it would be un-American, striking at the very foundation of the free enterprise system in which "competition is the soul of business.

"*The Billboard* cannot disregard trends as reflected in its charts. . . . An Elvis Presley or Carl Perkins or an Eddy Arnold who sells in various fields must be reported as such. They cannot be arbitrarily dropped out of any one chart. They will be dropped when the kid with the 89 cents feels it is time for a change."

WHER, MEANWHILE, was doing better than even Sam could have expected in a climate of free enterprise all its own. With a signal of just 1,000 watts, even if it *was* "1000 Beautiful Watts," it could barely reach beyond the city limits, but it was the talk of the town. It seemed like just about everyone in Memphis was intrigued not just by the sultry voices but by the concept itself, not to mention the design of its miniature offices and studio in the spick-and-span new showcase Holiday Inn downtown. The whole idea intrigued the public, just as Sam had hoped it would: the idea of women operating a business on their own, the dollhouse decor with its pretty pink-and-purple pastels, the women's hose and undergarments hanging good-naturedly on a clothesline outside the powder room, the provocative names assigned at Sam's direction to each of the tiny divisions, with the studio known as the Doll's Den, the two control rooms marked Playroom A and B, the newsroom designated as Propaganda, and the powder room itself Hedda Hopper. It was all in good fun, and travelers and native Memphians alike always stopped to gawk.

"It was easy to sell," from Becky's point of view, "because it was so different. The listeners really didn't know what to expect. They used their imagination—they would hear the girls and just kind of picture them in their own minds, [whether they were] blond or brunette."

She had never realized how much she had missed it—the excitement of radio, the thrill of being needed and of helping Sam once more in the workplace. "I'm having the time of my life," she wrote to her sisters, even if she had to get the boys up early and be out of the house by 8 A.M. to get to work in time for her 9:30 show. "It is so wonderful being on the air again. I didn't know I like[d] it so much. And the station is a darling. It is so beautifully decorated." But, she said, one assumes with tongue in cheek, "this station better be a success. If not I may be begging at your door!"

She and Sam worked out the programming together. It was, said Becky, a type of programming "that wasn't offered by any other Memphis radio station at the time, lilting music beginning at six in the morning and playing until the sun went down. We tried to make a balance, fast, slow, female vocalist, instrumental, male vocalist—and certain type shows were [distinctive]—like my show, 'Listen While You Work,' was an upbeat kind of thing, because people were working. But our music was all wonderful, easy listening—Sam wouldn't play anything from the things he recorded, [because] he wanted it to fit the WHER format, he wanted it to be beautiful and match the feminine voices."

Some of the girls took more adventurous directions of their own. They might, for instance, program a series of songs that could serve as a code for the status of their current love life. Certain songs were proscribed for one reason or another, some of Dinah Washington's more suggestive numbers or Billie Holiday's "Love For Sale." If on occasion some rebellious soul took it into her head to play one of those songs, she would get a call immediately from Doug Cousar, the station engineer, who seemed to have ears in the back of his head—but he was as easily won over as the casual listener by the disingenuous protestation, "Oh, Doug, oh, Doug I forgot." And, of course, everyone got a kick out of it when they went to the foreign news by announcing, "And now the news from abroad." It was rumored that the first time they ran that announcement, one of their listeners ran into a telephone pole in his car. Which, as even the girls at WHER would have been forced to admit, was most likely the stuff of urban legend. But the point was, it was all good, clean fun.

From Sam's point of view, though, it was something more. It wouldn't have been worth doing without the fun, but it was also about "the power of communication, [the opportunity for] women to step out and let people know how capable they were." These women were determined as much as any of his artists to be not just the best in town but the best they could be, and he was determined to give them all the tools he could to achieve that goal.

From the women's point of view, what really won them over was the trust he put in them. He was a good-looking man, and not above a little flirtation, but they felt, almost to a woman, he didn't condescend to them. What impressed her most, said Bettye Maddox, who joined the station later that year, was the laid-back, infinitely patient way he had of explaining things to her. "And, also, he *listened*. He listened very carefully — to me and my ideas." He treated them all with respect, even if he might call up after hours after a drink or two to see if they might like him to come over. But he was always easily diverted.

Some of the businessmen they called on, soliciting ads for the station, didn't like it one bit. One time, Bettye said, she walked into the offices of a department-store chain on Main Street, "and the man said, 'Oh, are you one of them? What do you all do out there all day?' Like we were some kind of aliens." Sometimes she was the only woman pitching her wares in a room full of ad salesmen shooting her looks, and the female receptionist would wave her in first, giving her a nod of complicity. Unquestionably, that sense of complicity spread, as WHER, the home of "beautiful music," gradually infiltrated doctors' and dentists' offices, car-dealership showrooms, supermarkets, and even the operating room at Baptist Memorial Hospital. They did remotes from locations all over Memphis. One of their most successful, in March of that year, was an all-day Sadie Hawkins Day broadcast from Hull-Dobbs Ford Agency downtown, right behind the Peabody, with Sam dressed up as the *Li'l Abner* character Marryin' Sam in tails and a stovepipe hat and the girls all in off-the-shoulder Daisy Mae blouses and short fringed skirts. The agency, which billed itself as the largest Ford agency in the world, announced that they sold a record number of cars that day, and Hoyt Wooten's brother Roy, the program director at WREC, came up to Sam in his silly outfit and, with his ubiquitous cigar clamped firmly between his teeth, confessed, "Man, you know I've been listening to this all morning." Then he regarded Sam balefully, with a look of contriteness that didn't often come over Roy Wooten's face. "You know," he said, "I thought you were stupid as hell when you started that all-girl station."

Sam ended up buying Becky a little Ford convertible that day, splash-ily painted white and orange — it was the last thing in the world she would ever have picked out for herself. But she accepted it happily. She loved it, she told Sam. It was really cute.

B Y THIS TIME Sally and Sam were "involved." It had started almost at once. For Sally, who had had little experience of men or life ("I really didn't have an education. I was from Coffeeville, Mississippi, and I didn't know much"), Sam, in his crisp white shirt and blazer, his pants creased just so, was like the man of her dreams. "He was the most confi-dent person I ever met. When Sam [told] you something, you just kind of believed it, but he would never lie to anybody, and he never talked out of his head. He always told people the truth — if you want[ed] to know his opinion, just ask him. And that was true about any audition that he did. But he never [told] anybody to give up and go home. He would never make a statement like that to anybody. It was always work hard, [believe in yourself] — people enjoyed talking to Sam, even if it wasn't what they wanted to hear, and Sam enjoyed people, too. You always knew where you stood with Sam. You were in his life, because he wanted you there. He would always let you in as far as he wanted you to go, and that was about it, you know."

She listened, she observed, she spent every afternoon in the studio with Sam by herself — and she fell in love with a married man, something that went very much against both her upbringing and her inclination. But she couldn't help it — she sensed a hunger in Sam, she knew he wanted her, and, for all the confidence he possessed, sensed a need in him that was unfulfilled. She didn't excuse herself, she had always been a practical, level-headed girl, and she wasn't going to seek refuge in the idea that she had been taken advantage of. All that she knew was that she wanted what he wanted, and she was not about to calculate the consequences.

She was at the studio day and night, she spent every waking hour that she could with Sam — she knew that he didn't want to be alone, and she made herself useful to him in every way she could. There was nothing to hold her back. "I had no baggage — absolutely no baggage at all. I had nothing."

They would go down to the Chisca almost every night toward the end of Dewey's show. "That was something he just had to do because Dewey would get his feelings hurt [if] Sam wasn't down there just about every night." Sally was well aware of Marion's feelings about Dewey—he was just *common,* she told Sally over and over again—but she enjoyed Dewey, and she could see how much Sam and Dewey enjoyed each other. Most of all she could see how Sam enjoyed letting his hair down with Dewey in a way he did with no one else, the way they razzed each other and would get in arguments and fuss and still just take pleasure in each other's company, even though at this point Sam scarcely drank with Dewey at all.

After the show, they might go to the Gridiron, or the Pig 'N' Whistle out Union—it got to be such a regular thing, and Dewey would always make such a fuss about the fact that Sam Phillips was right there in the studio with him ("Dee-gaw. Call Sam!") that after a while Marion started listening to the program just to keep tabs on Sam. And on those rare nights when Dewey didn't announce his presence in the studio, Marion would call Becky looking for him on the pretext that she had something to ask him about work. She was beginning to suspect Sam was having an affair, she confided to Sally, there were nights he was neither with Dewey nor with Becky, and it was driving her crazy trying to figure out what was going on.

Then she persuaded Sam to get her a little aqua-blue Nash Metropolitan, a push-button automatic, so she could go back and forth between the station and the studio and save on cabs. The first day she had the car, in mid-June, she followed Sam to Shreveport, frantic with suspicion, but she turned around and came back the next morning, telling Sally that maybe it was all a false alarm, he hadn't taken any woman with him and he didn't seem to have a mistress down there.

SAM SURPRISED CARL PERKINS onstage at the Dallas Sportatorium in mid-February, while "Blue Suede Shoes" was still on the rise. Carl was playing the Big D Jamboree, where, in a traveling version of the show, he had had sell-out crowds in a blizzard in West Texas two weeks earlier, performing seven encores of his hit. Sam was in Houston, promoting the record, and he got the idea to just show up in Dallas and surprise Carl with something special. He called up Carl's wife, Valda, to get Carl's shoe size and then consulted with Steve Poncio, his Houston distributor, about where he might purchase a pair of blue suede shoes. This turned out to be not as easy as he had imagined—blue suede shoes were not exactly a fashionable item before the song was released—but Steve was a resourceful fellow and managed to locate a pair in the right

size. Then Sam got some glitter and glued it on the shoes and worked it out with the show's producer, Ed McLemore, that he would train his spotlight on the shoes all during Carl's act so they would really sparkle.

Carl was as touched as a man could be. "I was just about to go out on the stage when he said, 'Wait a minute, cat'—he always called me 'cat'—he had this box under his arm, and he took out a pair of blue suede shoes [with] blue sparkles all over them. They kind of had that flip-down feeling—good-looking shoes. Man, when the lights hit them things on the Big D Jamboree, that house went wild. And Sam flew from Memphis to Dallas to put them shoes on my feet."

From Carl's point of view, nobody could have looked out for his interests more than Mr. Phillips. Sam was the one who had bought him his first stage clothes at Lansky's on Beale Street, where Elvis shopped, "them old loud, silk, puffed-sleeve shirts that nobody else would wear—well, the whites didn't want to. Lansky's at that time catered to blacks. You got to remember that Elvis, Cash, none of us, had anything. We were very poor. And it was Sam who did for me."

The *Memphis Press-Scimitar* ran an article on Carl's newfound success on February 27, two weeks after the Big D appearance. "Blue Suede Shoes" had already sold 250,000 copies, Elton Whisenhunt reported, with 75,000 more on order—which represented twice as many sales as Elvis Presley's biggest seller on Sun, "Blue Moon of Kentucky." Perkins had recently signed a one-year contract for weekly appearances on the Big D Jamboree at $350 a week. There was more about Carl's and Sun's success ("Sun records are the hottest thing in the c&w business now," said Sam, "the first time anything like this has [ever] happened in Memphis")—but the unexpected upshot was that Carl got thrown out of the $32-a-month public housing apartment in Parkview Courts in Jackson, where he lived. He had received no royalty payments to date because the record was so new, but as he told the paper some months later, he never had any doubt that Mr. Phillips would advance him whatever he needed.

He was back in the studio by mid-March with a new song, "Boppin' the Blues," a rocking boogie that Sam was convinced would be the perfect follow-up single, once "Blue Suede Shoes" stopped selling. He came in with a number of other promising songs that he had written, but the one

Carl Perkins showing Johnny Cash his blue suede shoes, spring 1956.
Courtesy of Colin Escott

Sam picked out for the flip side was a collaboration with Johnny Cash, "All Mama's Children," inspired once again by an old nursery rhyme ("There was an old woman that lived in a shoe," it began—but in this case all the old woman's children were destined not only to rock but to bop till they popped). Everything was just as loose as at the previous session, and just as much fun, with Sam's peculiar insistence that you had to be both completely relaxed and at the same time mean *everything*, put your whole soul into the music, until it was no longer just another session but, as Carl described it, an exhilarating life experience.

It was just the greatest way in the world to cut raw music—there was no rush, no clock on the wall, we didn't work it that hard, we really didn't take it that serious. It was just an easy carefree feeling—that was the beauty of it.

He knew [when] I made a mistake. He'd say, "I know what you're talking about, I'll show you when we listen back to it. But, Carl, that's not bad, it's got too many good things [in it]." I'd say, "But, Mr. Phillips, it's full of mistakes," and he'd say, "Okay, do it again." But then he'd say, "Listen, see, the excitement's gone. The mistakes are not there, but it don't have the feeling the other one did." And he'd always keep the one he liked.

He just seemed to know. He'd step out from behind that little old glass window, and he'd say, "All right, boys, we just about on it now—do it again. Do it one time for Sam." Oh yeah, he did me that way all the time. It was just that type of thing—you just forgot about making a record and tried to show him. It was things like that that'd cause me—I'd walk out on a limb, I'd try things I knew I couldn't do, and I'd get in a corner trying to do it and then have to work my way out. I'd say, "Mr. Phillips, that's terrible." He said, "That's original." I said, "But it's just a big original mistake." He said, "That's what Sun Records is. That's what we are."

As record sales for "Blue Suede Shoes" neared a million, Sam asked Carl if he didn't think he should be upgrading his mode of transportation, especially now that he would be making his prime-time national television debut on *The Perry Como Show* on March 24, the same night that Elvis would be making his final appearance on the considerably lower-rated *Stage Show*.

Carl wasn't sure just what Sam was getting at, he said he didn't really have the money to be thinking about things like that, and besides, he had just bought Valda her first washing machine, but Sam said that he had arranged things with his friend Joe Canepari at the Southern Motors Cadillac dealership down the street, and Carl should just go in and pick out whatever model he wanted.

Carl was touched beyond measure — he confided to Johnny Cash that Sam said he had made a vow to buy a brand-new Cadillac for the first Sun artist to sell a million records — and he went into Southern Motors and picked out his car, a dark blue, four-door Sixty Special with a white top which with options would come to around $5,000. Unfortunately it wasn't going to be ready in time for his departure from Memphis on March 20, so Mr. Canepari offered him a loaner, an eight-seater 1953 Chrysler Imperial "built like a railroad car."

It was the loaner, the *Memphis Press-Scimitar* reported, that saved his life. The driver, Dick Stuart, a longtime KWEM DJ and Charlie Feathers' brother-in-law, who had only recently become Carl's manager, fell asleep at the wheel and plowed into the back of a pickup truck just around dawn on the morning of March 22 outside Dover, Delaware. The driver of the truck, a local farmer, was killed. The Chrysler rolled over four times and plunged off a bridge, landing upright beside a stream. Carl's older brother, Jay, broke his neck and had severe internal injuries, while Carl suffered a broken collarbone and concussion. So it was that, instead of performing "Blue Suede Shoes" on *The Perry Como Show* on Saturday night, he found himself watching from a hospital bed as Perry extended his best wishes for a speedy recovery. Elvis, meanwhile, refrained from performing his version of "Blue Suede Shoes" on *Stage Show* that night and sent Carl a telegram offering to help in any way he could.

He didn't get back on the road for another month, and then it was without Jay, who continued to suffer excruciating headaches from the accident. He didn't get to appear on *The Perry Como Show* until May 26, two months after his originally scheduled appearance, and sometime after "Blue Suede Shoes" had lost much of its momentum, though it remained high on most of the best-seller lists. He had gotten his Cadillac by then — there was a story in the *Press-Scimitar* by Bob Johnson that pictured both the car he had wrecked and the car he was receiving "as a gift from Sam Phillips, owner of Sun Record Co.," with Sam handing over the keys to Carl. It was a moment he would always treasure — or at least treasure until years later when he realized that the cost of the Cadillac had been deducted from his royalties. For Sam this was something of a painful subject in later years—he was certain he had never spoken to Carl in the terms that Carl, with his natural generosity of spirit, had understood him to use. According to his own recollection, he had told Carl quite plainly that he wanted Carl to have a new car and that he would happily advance the money and get it for him at dealer's cost, which came to something like $1,500 below the sticker price. But he never corrected the newspaper caption, and from the perspective of Johnny Cash, who like Carl remained unaware of the accounting issue for many years, that simply raised the question *Where's my Cadillac?* when his new single, "I Walk the Line," had accumulated sales of nearly a million some six months later.

J OHNNY CASH brought the song to Sam just days after Carl's accident. His current single, "Folsom Prison Blues," had been on the national country charts for over two months and sold close to fifty thousand copies (it currently stood at number 6 nationally)—but it was clearly not going to break out of the country field. It would, in fact, be doing well to sell twenty-five thousand copies more. John had his own views on the subject. Six months earlier an Air Force buddy had asked him why his first record hadn't done better. "Reason #1," Cash replied sensibly, "New artist. Reason #2—Small label. Reason #3—No financial backing." But now, with the infusion of money from Elvis' sale and the runaway success of "Blue Suede Shoes," things had changed dramatically. Perhaps most dramatic of all was Sam's reaction to the new song. Despite all the things Johnny Cash had going against him as a pop star (voice, instrumentation, and subject matter that, as Sam would write in a publicity biography several months later, expressed itself most frequently in "somber, melancholy ballads that seem to tell a story of deep loss and sadness"), with this song he was convinced that Johnny Cash was his next big crossover artist.

The new song was as unique in its provenance as it was in its appeal. The decidedly peculiar chord progressions (which, as Sun and country music historian Colin Escott wrote, "reverse the usual country progression—starting on the unstable dominant chord instead of the rock-solid tonic that begins just about every country song [and] begin[ning] each verse with the pair of chords that normally ends a song") stemmed from a misunderstanding—or maybe it was just a joke. While Cash was stationed in Germany, he bought a Wilcox-Gay tape recorder at the PX, and one night while he was working his five-to-eleven shift as a radio operator, somebody must have come in and fooled around with the recorder, leaving the tape halfway unwound. When he played it back from the beginning, he heard a sound so haunting, and so defying of rational explanation (at the end there emerged an unearthly voice that seemed to be saying "Father"), that he played it over and over for close to six months, trying to decipher the weird sound. Then one day he respooled the tape and discovered that it had been on backwards and upside down all that time. When you played the tape the way it was supposed to be played, it was just someone strumming chords on the guitar and saying at the end, "Turn it off." But he continued to try to recapture that original sound.

The lyrics seemed to stem from the pervasive sense of guilt he had felt in various ways all his life, a reactive sentiment that had found vivid expression in the anguished letters he wrote to his seventeen-year-old fiancée, Vivian Liberto, from Germany. He had met, courted, and to all intents and purposes become engaged to her, all in a whirlwind six weeks, while he was stationed in her hometown of San Antonio in the summer of 1951, and they would remain apart until his discharge three years later. He had tried and tried, he confessed in one letter in December of 1953, but he just didn't have the willpower to stay in his room alone, so he had gone to the Airmen's Club and got drunk. There was a floor show at the club—a strip show—and he hadn't done anything wrong, but "there was two women in it and honey they took everything off of their breasts. Honey they didn't have a thing on from their waist on up. Please don't be angry with me Viv. . . . You know I was true to you. I'm always true to you honey. . . . I won't ever have any girl but you."

Clearly the road offered even greater temptations, and a performer's life, Cash quickly learned, was likely to be even more guilt-ridden. One night, playing a show in Texas with Carl, as the guys exchanged boastful stories and indulged in loose talk, the way men often do, John declared, a little wishfully perhaps but thinking of Vivian and their little girl at home, "Not me, buddy, I'm walking the line." And Carl sat up straight and said that was it, "I Walk the Line" was the title of Johnny's next big hit.

It was a song idea that had been on his mind for some time. He had been fooling around with different ways of saying it, different ways of conveying the underlying sentiment—being true to himself, being true to Vivian, being true to God (at first he was simply going to call it "I'm Still Being True")—but now he quickly settled on Carl's suggestion, and within twenty minutes "I Walk the Line" was done.

When he sang the song for Sam, he sang it as a slow love song in the same kind of plaintive voice with which he had first sung "Folsom Prison." The lyric was predictable enough save for its striking opening image ("I keep a close watch on this heart of mine / I keep my eyes wide open all the time / I keep the ends out for the tie that binds / Because you're mine / I walk the line"), but it was no less striking in its sincerity, and the characteristic quiver in his voice carried a note of conviction absent from all but the most directly communicative of singers. The melody was pretty much as he had developed it, an adaptation of the misheard tape, except that each verse modulated downward and, as though to cue the modulation or maybe just to maintain pitch, he provided a wavery hum to introduce each verse. He had been concerned at first that Sam might not like it—there was no real precedent in country music for either the chords or the humming—but Sam liked it fine, he embraced it without reservation, *aside from the tempo.* Couldn't John do it a little more up-tempo, he demanded, couldn't he give it a little more of a beat?

John fought him on it tooth and nail. Speeding it up would ruin the sentiment of the song, he protested. And besides, the flip side, "Get Rhythm," was a pure rhythm number, a song he had written initially with Elvis in mind, about an old black man who had been shining shoes at the Memphis bus station when he got back from Germany. The old man "was taking it real slow and easy, [and] I said, 'You don't do a lot of poppin' with that rag like most shoe shine men do.' He said, 'That's the trouble with the world now. There's too much poppin' and not enough shinin'.'"

Which was the whole inspiration for the song, and the underlying message, even though he was never able to work it directly into the lyrics. Sam loved it anyway, and he wouldn't let John give it to Elvis. But it didn't serve as a countervailing argument for maintaining the subdued tone of "I Walk the Line" either. In the end Sam was finally able to persuade him just to *try it,* the same way he had persuaded Carl to keep "cat" in his song. More to the point, the same way he had gotten John to take "Folsom Prison Blues" out of the gloom into the sunlight of a distant but beckoning freedom.

So John did it the way Sam wanted him to, even though he still didn't like it — and he left the studio that day convinced that Sam would never be able to bring himself to like it either, that they had an understanding that it was the slow version that would be released. "The first time I heard it on the radio, I called him and said, 'I hate that sound. Please don't release any more records. I hate that sound.'" But the more he heard it, the more he learned to like it. And once the record was an assured pop success, "Sam said, 'That's what music is all about. It should be universal.' And I said, 'Well, Mr. Phillips, that's what I've always believed too.'"

With "I Walk the Line" he achieved an apotheosis of both self-expression and sales — Johnny Cash for the first time became the artist Sam had envisioned, not "just another good singer" but a singular one. The record was released on May 2, when "Folsom Prison Blues" was still among the top country sellers. By the end of the month "I Walk the Line" had sold more than half of what the previous single had achieved in total sales in five months, and less than two weeks later had passed "Folsom Prison" in the Top 10 Country Best Sellers. By the third week in June, it stood at number 4 on the national charts and was number 1 on the Memphis best-seller list, with both "Blue Suede Shoes" and Carl's new single, "Boppin' the Blues," right behind it, followed by "Heartbreak Hotel" and records by two Sun newcomers, Roy Orbison and Warren Smith (singing a Johnny Cash composition), at 5 and 6. To take care of this burgeoning roster, Sam set up Bob Neal in business. Neal, who in Sam's view had been dealt a dirty hand by Tom Parker in the takeover of Elvis' management, was more than open to a change and, with Sam's financial backing, established his booking and management office, Stars Inc., confined almost entirely to Sun artists ("the biggest drawing cards in the rock and roll business"), in the Sterick Building downtown.

Everyone wanted to know the secret of Sun. Jerry Wexler of Atlantic Records, which was just beginning to enter this new rock 'n' roll field but had created an r&b crossover of its own with Ray Charles, was constantly teasing Sam about the key to his sound: how exactly did he get that discreet slapback effect that could lend rawness to some of his records while at the same time adding intimacy and depth to the barebones instrumentation of Johnny Cash and the Tennessee Two? Sam shook his head reprovingly — he wasn't going to just give away his secrets. But the joke, of course, was that there was no secret. Or at least

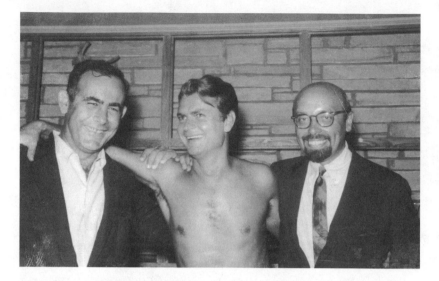

Sam, at home with Atlantic Records vice president Jerry Wexler (left) and president Ahmet Ertegun. *Courtesy of the Sam Phillips Family*

that the "secret" had nothing to do with recording technique. *The secret was simply patience and belief.*

"The most outstanding record label operation, currently owned by an indie broadcaster, is Sun Records, the Sam Phillips firm," *Billboard* declared in an article which, citing diversification as the key to the music business's future, linked his two enterprises, and his two great loves. "Phillips, who owns WHER, Memphis," the story went on, "negotiated a plum $40,000 deal for himself with RCA Victor on Elvis Presley last winter, and hit the charts barely a month later with two new artists, Carl Perkins and Johnny Cash." From every point of view, and against all the odds, Sun Records, in the words of the old song, was sitting on top of the world.

O NE AFTER ANOTHER THEY CAME. They had been arriving in a steady stream since the beginning of January — poor country boys (though few as poor as his "Blue Suede Shoes" man, Carl Perkins) who had read about Elvis, or in many cases actually encountered him, and now, emboldened by the phenomenal success of Carl Perkins and Johnny Cash as well, found their way to the Sun Records door.

Every day the postman would bring a sackful of tapes. Whenever

Sally picked up the phone, there was somebody wanting to sing to her. Or they would just show up in person for an audition. To Sally it was a source of wonderment and, not infrequently, exasperation: the patience Sam would show to each and every one of them when there weren't, really, enough hours in the day. "Sam listened to so many auditions, so many of them. Any and everybody. They [might] have a guitar, or they could play the piano, some had no instruments at all. But if he was there and had the time to do it, he did. He was always honest, [always] truthful, but no matter if he turned them down (and most of the time he did), they always seemed to feel better when they left."

For Sam it was all about aspiration — it was all about respect. "I found out that these poor white boys were just [as scared as] the black. These people unfortunately did not have an ego — they had a *desire*. But to deal with a person that had dreamed and dreamed and dreamed, and to deal with them under conditions where they were so afraid of being denied again —[my job] was to get an arrogance out of them they did not even know they had. I was always in charge, but I had to [let] them know that they were going to be the one that did it. Because no way did they need anybody else looking down their nose at them."

There was no question that this was the future. None of his other records were selling — not the hillbilly, not the r&b, just this revolutionary new music that combined raw gutbucket feel with an almost apostolic sense of exuberance and joy. It represented, it *embodied* in its very essence, the same faith in progress, the same willingness to dare all that had propelled Sam from childhood on. It was the same feeling that Sam had gotten from the black church and from the singing that he had heard in the cotton fields as a boy. He felt an acute sense of guilt about forsaking the music that had first inspired him, that had led him to open his studio, and on which his entire faith was based — but he was, after all, only a one-man operation. And he rationalized that what he was doing was not so much deserting the black man as continuing to broaden the base for the *acceptance* of black music, providing the market with what it needed *right now* through the almost unstoppable momentum of rock 'n' roll.

Sam certainly turned out to be right in his historical overview. The triumph of African-American music as the common coin of American popular culture was already well under way. But one wonders — as Sam could never allow himself to wonder — if in some part of his being he wasn't more comfortable, more at ease with these ragamuffin white boys whose experience so closely mirrored his own. With the great blues singers — with Howlin' Wolf, for example — he found himself in a state closer to awestruck wonder than the cool sense of control he was now able to adopt in his mentoring role. Even with younger, less spellbinding counterparts like Little Junior Parker or Joe Hill Louis or Rosco Gordon (the last of his original artists on the Sun roster, who had come back to him the previous year and even had a minor hit in the spring of 1956 with a novelty song called "The Chicken"), it would seem that for all of his great gifts of insight and empathy — and they *were* great — he could never be as fully at ease as he was with the artists he was working with today. Maybe in the end it simply came down to the little boy in Alabama who, with his acute sense of racial injustice, wished he had been born black, sensed in the black community a spirit of pride, "presentness," and perseverance, that he could only aspire to himself. Whatever the case, with Elvis Presley, Carl Perkins, and Johnny Cash, and with the whole parade of young farm boys who followed, there was nothing enigmatic to Sam either about what they had experienced or how they chose to express themselves. They were, simply, Sam C. Phillips, removed by ten years from his own direct experience of the Depression but no less marked by it, part of a larger family circle that he had not known since leaving Alabama and that he was not about to abandon now.

Warren Smith was one of the first to arrive, and one of the most talented. Twenty-four-years old, raised in rural Mississippi, and just out of the Air Force, he had shown up at the Cotton Club one night and sat in with the Snearly Ranch Boys. Their steel player, Stan Kesler, who had written "I'm Left, You're Right, She's Gone" and "I Forgot to Remember to Forget" for Elvis, brought him to Sam, who was impressed with his brooding good looks and pure country voice. All he needed, said Sam, was a good song. So Stan wrote him one, a good country song called "I'd Rather Be Safe Than Sorry," but then Sam phoned and said he had a rhythm song, "Rock 'n' Roll Ruby," for the new guy that Johnny Cash had written when he was down in Shreveport playing the Louisiana Hayride. Stan played steel on the session, Snearly Ranch Boys Johnny Bernero and Smokey Joe Baugh were the drummer and piano player, and the idea was that this was going to be a joint enterprise in which the whole band shared equally, since the group leader, Clyde Leoppard, had been paying room and board for Smith at Mrs. Snearly's boardinghouse. But when the single came out, Smith reneged on the deal, and the royalties for the record's remarkable sale of seventy thousand copies in the first three months all went to him. Which was one reason that Warren Smith, an intense, not infrequently moody young man who Sam thought had unlimited potential in the country field, was not particularly popular with his fellow musicians.

"He was the kind of character that needed to be loved a lot," Sam said. "But a lot of people didn't like him, he perceived that they didn't, and it was his fault in most cases." He didn't much like the song Sam had given him either — everyone agreed it was not one of Johnny Cash's most distinguished compositions nor did he like the direction its popularity portended for him. But it was a helluva performance, and if, as Sam said, "Warren had a lot of emotional problems," he could declare with equal honesty, "[he was] just interesting enough that I liked him a whole lot." And he had no doubt that he could persuade him to lean a little bit in the direction of this vibrant new music, at least for a while. So long as they didn't abandon hillbilly altogether.

"Rock 'n' Roll Ruby" was released on the same day as Jack Earls' "Slow Down." Earls was an eccentric figure who had run off briefly with the carnival in his early teens and was exhibited in a cage as "The Wild Boy." He arrived in Memphis in 1949, at the age of seventeen, and went to work driving a delivery truck for a bakery. Elvis turned his mind around. He had heard that Elvis had been discovered by just walking in and cutting a demo at Sun, so, sometime in early 1955, he got together the guys he had been playing with — "about six or eight guitars" — paid his money, and cut a record himself. One of the guys in the band said, "You know, when we get this demo made, they're gonna be hammering on your door." Nobody ever hammered, said Earls, but "Sam called me back. He liked my voice, and he told me, 'We're gonna have a hit record. But you gotta get a band. Your band ain't worth a shit.'" So he helped Jack put together a band and told him, "When you get something going, come back and we'll have an audition."

It took over six months, with Earls and his group coming back into the studio time and time again, but finally they came up with two songs that Sam liked. The single had already been scheduled when Earls played Sam a song he had just written called "Slow Down," "and Sam had a fit! He came out of [the control room] jumping up and down, and he never changed nothing." He even went so far as to drop one of the songs he was going to release, "Hey! Jim," which was the whole reason he had given the group its new name, the Jimbos, and when he put out the record at the beginning of April, it rewarded his faith by selling briskly enough in certain markets to make Jack Earls a little money and earn him a place on the Stars Inc. roster of performers. He had many more sessions with Sam, but "Slow Down" was his first and last issued Sun record, not because Sam didn't recognize what Sun historian Colin Escott calls the "agonized intensity" of his voice and the irrepressible enthusiasm of his performance, but because, quite simply, he was happy playing the Palms Club in Memphis every weekend, and he could never be induced to leave his job at the bakery.

Sonny Burgess was a different story. He showed up at 706 for the first time at the beginning of the year, having played a couple of gigs with Elvis, as well as attending several others, in and around his native Newport, Arkansas. He had his heart set on a career in baseball until he went in the army, where his baseball skills kept him from getting shipped off to Korea with the rest of his company, 80 percent of whom he was told were killed in combat. When he got out in 1953, he felt like his future in baseball was over, and he went back to cotton farming with his father, focusing in his spare time on music. The band that he formed with some friends, the Rocky Road Ramblers, started out playing hill-billy but before long changed its name to the Moonlighters and branched out to become an all-around dance band, featuring numbers like "Stardust," "Moonglow," and "Harlem Nocturne," as well as the Jimmy Reed / Big Joe Turner kind of rhythm and blues that Sonny in particular loved.

Elvis changed everything. The first time Sonny saw him, in March of 1955, "he was just the best we had ever seen." It wasn't a matter of the recognition he was getting — there was no thought that what he was doing was just something they had been doing all along. "It was different — felt different. [And] after that, we just wanted to be on Sun Records, man. That's all we could think about, to get that little yellow record in our hands."

They finally screwed up the courage to make the ninety-mile drive to Memphis in early January. "We just went up there and said, 'We want to see Mr. Phillips.'" He listened to everything, played them a copy of Little Junior Parker's "Feelin' Good" (they might, he said, think about recording that someday), and told them to go home and practice some more and come back when they thought they really had something. That is precisely what they did. They picked up a couple of additional guys (they wanted to add a saxophone, but a friend of theirs, Jack Nance, who was a music major in college, had a trumpet, so they settled for that), and they came back at the beginning of May with one of the oddest sounds, and one of the oddest approaches to musical mayhem, that Sam had ever encountered.

They had worked up two songs in particular, "We Wanna Boogie," which was loosely inspired by the Little Junior Parker original (*very* loosely), and "Red Headed Woman," which in its equally raucous, chaotically out-of-tune messiness, seemed a category unto itself—and Sam flipped. When Sam played it back for them, Sonny and the rest of the band cringed and begged Sam to let them redo it. Sonny didn't like the distortion on the guitar, he didn't like the tone of the trumpet—he knew they could do better. But Sam said none of that mattered, it was the feel that counted. "What he wanted [us] to do in that studio was to play like [we] were doing a show. He wanted that enthusiasm, he thought folks could hear that on the tape. So that's how we did it. We played for Sam. He was our audience, and we tried to impress him the same way we did an audience." To Sam, Sonny and his group's whole delivery (the band was now called the Pacers) exemplified great spirit, great confidence, and great nerve. "They were a working band [who] knew what they were doing, and they had a sound like I've never heard. Maybe Sonny's sound was too raw, I don't know—but I tell you this. They were pure rock and roll."

When the single came out three months later, *Billboard* deemed it a "jumping, pounding boogie . . . shouted and orked with plenty of spirit [that] should get plenty of Southern action, r&b-wise," and while it never charted, Sonny was soon out on the road with an all-star Stars Inc. package. There his true genius manifested itself, as he and the Pacers perfected an act that, as Sam suggested, reflected the very essence of rock 'n' roll.

For if the records that Sonny Burgess made never sold in the numbers that Sam might have hoped, his and the Pacers' acrobatic, noholds-barred, physically and emotionally uninhibited stage performance rapidly became legend. They took their steps from rhythm and blues groups like the Red Caps, with whom they frequently crossed paths in Mississippi, they did splits and back flips, jumped into the audience from the stage, no matter how high, even from the balcony on occasion. They formed a human pyramid on top of the bass, climbed up on the edge of the audience's seats, and developed a dance called The Bug, where Sonny would throw a "bug" at one of the guys, "he'd start itching and going crazy, then he'd throw it on somebody else, and we'd throw it all around the audience," and general madness would break loose. They were all young, they were all athletic, and it was all in good fun. Just in case there was any doubt as to who the spotlight was supposed to be on, Sonny took to wearing the most extravagant outfits, going down to Lansky's to get his clothes, favoring red and yellow tux jackets at first, then a bright red suit to go with his red Stratocaster. One time he got the idea of dying his hair white, like Shell Scott, the private eye in the detective-book series, but when his wife applied the peroxide, it came out an orangey red, and with his orange hair, red suit, red shoes, and red Fender guitar he could even refer to himself sardonically as the Red Clown. It was, said Sonny, something like a three-ring circus. "The music just made you feel good. You'd get in that groove, and, man, it made you want to dance if you could[n't] dance a lick, you know, you'd get high just with the music. That was it. Man, you just felt so good it was like you wanted to jump out of your skin."

Ray Harris came to the music with less natural aptitude perhaps but in almost exactly the same way. Closer to Sam's age (he was nearly thirty) than any of the others, he grew up in a family of sharecroppers in Mantachie, Mississippi, a tiny hamlet fifteen miles outside of Tupelo. He moved to Memphis in his early twenties and was working with Bill Black at the Firestone Tire & Rubber plant when Bill invited him to a session with a kid that he and Scotty Moore were working with at Sun. Ray's recollection of just what song they were cutting varied in the telling, but his reaction never did. A hard-core hillbilly fan with strong opinions on most matters, he watched this guy, Sam Phillips, working with this funny-looking kid. Harris had grown up on a steady diet of the Opry, Hank Williams, Bill Monroe, and Monroe's sometime fiddle player Merle "Red" Taylor, who was kin to his wife. Now as he sat in the control room with Sam, watching the little trio of musicians struggling with the same tune over and over again, he just didn't hear what they were going for. But then "Sam would listen to the playbacks and say, 'This is it! Yeah, man, this is it!' And here I am, not understanding [it], but even before the end of the session it was starting to hit me. I'd played a little back around Tupelo, and I listened to Presley and thought, 'Hell, that boy ain't doing anything I can't do.'"

So he set about trying to prove that he could. Lacking nothing but real musical talent, he put together a band and practiced night after night. As sometime Sun talent scout Bill Cantrell (who two years later would be one of the principal founders of Hi Records along with his partner, Quinton Claunch, and Ray) told Sun historian Colin Escott: "He couldn't sing, and he wasn't good to look at, but he didn't care. You could hear him practicing from two blocks away. He would open the door wearing nothing but his overalls, dripping with sweat. He had an old portable recorder, and he'd go back to singing and sweating." The neighbors got so agitated that he had to promise them free copies of the record when it came out, which, however dubious they may have been of the outcome, at least assuaged them for the time being.

Eventually he came up with something that Sam liked, a song called "Come On Little Mama" that Colin Escott dubbed a pure distillation of "maniacal energy," with limited musicianship, virtually indecipherable lyrics, and a delivery that Sam found irresistible. "I'll never forget it," Sam told Escott, "he was so intense he looked like he was going to have a heart attack every time he played. 'Rack 'em up, boy[s], let's go!'" was his exit line for a session that wasn't going well, and while the record itself could not by any standard have been accounted a hit, it did sell four hundred copies in Memphis on the day of its release, perhaps in part to relatives of some of the very neighbors to whom Ray had promised free samples.

Probably the most talented of this new wave of "second generation" rockers was Roy Orbison, a twenty-year-old college student from Wink, Texas, who had grown up with a deep love of country music, which his father, an oil rigger, had passed on to him. He was an odd duck in high school, short, jug-eared, and awkward-looking, with thick unflattering glasses that only emphasized a pasty, moon-faced complexion — he wrote poetry, drew cartoons, and at some point early on, perhaps to defuse the common perception that, with his poor eyesight and pale coloration, he was an albino, dyed his hair black. He put together his first band, the Wink Westerners, in 1949, when he was thirteen, sticking to staples by Ernest Tubb, Hank Williams, and then Lefty Frizzell, who became his passion, and declaring in his 1954 high school yearbook: "To lead a western band is his after school wish / And of course to marry a beautiful dish." Then Elvis came along.

Roy first saw him in the spring of 1955 while attending college at North Texas State in Denton, where he was studying geology freshman year, before later switching to English and history with the idea of going into teaching. His father had written to say that he had just seen this terrible new act on a package show—this boy was just plain amateurish—and Roy decided to go check it out for himself. It was a life-changing experience—for both Roy and the Wink Westerners. The band switched over almost instantly to rhythm and blues and rock 'n' roll, and when Roy transferred to Odessa Junior College his sophomore year, he changed the name of the band as well, to the Teen Kings, and got his own television show for the twin cities of Odessa and Midland, Texas. The band's featured song was one he had picked up in Denton from a North Texas State English major named Dick Penner. Penner, who would go on to become an English professor at the University of Tennessee, always claimed that he and his musical partner, Wade Moore, had written the song, a novelty dance number called "Ooby Dooby" ("Hey, baby, jump over here / when you do the Ooby Dooby / I just gotta be near"), in just fifteen minutes on the roof of their frat house, which was where Roy first heard them singing it.

It was a catchy tune—there was something utterly charming in its very simplicity—and Roy and the Teen Kings demoed it at Jim Beck's studio in Dallas, where Lefty Frizzell had cut all of his early hits. When nothing happened with that version, they rerecorded it at Norman Petty's studio in Clovis, New Mexico, in March of 1956 (Petty was just months away from his historic first recordings with Buddy Holly, yet another Elvis disciple), for release on the newly formed Je-Wel label. Roy had met Johnny Cash just a month earlier when he passed through Midland and Odessa and appeared on Roy's television show. Did Johnny have any suggestions for how he could get on Sun Records? Roy asked, and Cash gave him the studio phone number. "I told Sam that Johnny had said that I might be able to get on his label. He said, 'Johnny Cash doesn't run my record company' and hung up on me."

Now, with a record out of his own, he was enjoying even greater local attention. One of the first people he took it to was Cecil Holifield, the proprietor of the Record Shops in Midland and Odessa and one of Elvis' earliest boosters in the area. Within days of the record's release he called up Sam and played the record for him over the phone. Sam's first reaction was positive. It sounded to him like "some of the novelty hits from the thirties and forties" that he and his band had played back in Florence, but he couldn't really hear it on the phone. So Holifield sent it express delivery, and Sam called him back, and after learning that Roy was not yet twenty-one (he was not yet even twenty) and that neither parent nor guardian had signed the recording contract for him, he told Cecil to tell the boy to be in Memphis in three days with his band. With Holifield's help, he got a court order that stopped distribution of the Je-Wel recording, and three days later, Roy and the Teen Kings, consisting of a standard rhythm section of bass, drums, and acoustic guitar, with electric mandolin and Roy himself on driving lead, were in the studio.

One of the things that most impressed Sam from the start, apart from the singer's soaring, full-throated vocal range, was his *seriousness,* even in his approach to a fundamentally silly novelty number like "Ooby Dooby." The Je-Wel recording was fine — someone else might have been tempted simply to purchase the master — but Sam was convinced they could do better. He liked the band, he liked the unusual "overtones" that the electric mandolin gave to the music. But most of all he prized the single-minded dedication that this not-quite-twenty-year-old gave to the project at hand.

They recorded take after take, but unlike almost any of the other artists Sam had worked with, black or white, Roy approached every take virtually the same. "Roy was a perfectionist in the best sense. I don't think people generally know how good a guitar player Roy was. His timing would amaze me, with him playing lead and filling in . . . he would do a lot of combination string stuff, but it was all *pushing* real good." According to musicologist Dave Sax, who listened minutely to each take to pick out the master for a definitive 1994 reissue, Sam had the band do the song over and over, with the variation restricted sometimes to no more than a single vocal inflection or bringing up the sound of the rhythm guitar ever so slightly, until in the end "it was so tight that it [almost] jumped out of the grooves."

That was the version Sam put out at the beginning of May, along with a second song, a rocker called "Go Go Go," cowritten with drummer Billy Pat Ellis, that was almost as good. It came out on the same day as Carl Perkins' "Boppin' the Blues," the follow-up to "Blue Suede Shoes," but it far outsold Carl's record, for which Sam had had such high expectations. It went on, in fact, to sell some two hundred thousand copies, entering the *Billboard* pop charts in the middle of June, spurred on by a spiffy half-page ad that Sam had crudely drafted, then marked up, as he did all of his ads. In this one, the title was block-printed in red nine times at an angle, once horizontally, with "OOBY DOOBY HAS CAUGHT FIRE" at the center in black, as grayish flames threatened to smother the letters.

Roy Orbison was the new star on the horizon, unquestionably. But there were others for whom Sam had great hope as well. One was "sultry feline redhead" Barbara Pittman, the new Snearly Ranch Boys vocalist, applauded by *Billboard* for "the back shack sound, female style" of her Sun debut. Pittman had run away with cowboy star and bullwhip performer Lash LaRue's traveling show in her mid-teens and was told by Sam "to go out and learn how to sing" the first time she presented herself at the studio.

Then there was Harold Jenkins, whose father was a Mississippi riverboat pilot, and who gave up a promising professional baseball career, and a deep dedication to country music, when he returned from serving in the army in Yokohama for two years and encountered the entirely unexpected sound and popularity of Elvis. Right away he named his new band the Rockhousers and wrote them a signature song, "Rock House," which he played for Sam in one of his many lengthy (and unsuccessful) auditions for the label. ("We were trying to create in the studio," he told Colin Escott. "We'd play for four or five hours without a break, we were so wrapped up in it.") Sam liked the song well enough to appropriate it for Roy Orbison's next single.

Hayden Thompson, on the other hand, was an eighteen-year-old from Booneville, Mississippi, where he had experienced his own life-changing experience when he first heard and met Elvis in January 1955. Following high school graduation in the spring of 1956, he traveled around with his band, the Dixie Jazzliners, and a print of the Bill Haley "rocksploitation" feature *Rock Around the Clock,* performing at movie theaters with a showing of the movie sandwiched in between. They played West Memphis for several nights that summer, which led to an audition at Sun, which led in turn to a second audition in October, where Sam finally found someone ready to attempt Little Junior's rhythmic masterpiece "Love My Baby." The record itself wasn't actually cut for another two months, and then it remained unissued until the following September, the only single to be released from Thompson's numerous Sun sessions, but the foundation for a legendary reputation among latter-day rockabilly fanatics.

It was no wonder, in a way, that Sam's erstwhile partner, Jim Bulleit, should have seen Sam as little more than a lucky so-and-so, as he watched with asperity from the sidelines. "These guys would come in there by droves," he told Sun historian Martin Hawkins. "I'm not taking a thing away from Sam, but they give him all the credit for discovering these people. Well, it wasn't so. [They] discovered Sam."

But what Bulleit missed, what many people could easily miss, was the patience and effort it took, the almost unshakable self-belief that was required in what had remained for so long a fundamentally one-man operation — and the effect that this projection of unwavering calm and confidence could have on all the "untried, unproven, untested" musicians who came into his studio. There was no more escaping the intensity of his belief than the intensity of his gaze. "I told them there was no such thing as failure when they left here, whether they ever got a record out of here [or not]. I wasn't trying to make them feel good. I was trying to tell them *the odds* were good — they were better for them than they were for me. And I had been down that path just like they were going down it now." He was just trying to tell them, as he had so often told himself, not to be afraid.

It seemed like every one of them took that lesson to heart, even those who in later years might have had their differences with him. "Sam Phillips' contribution was to get us to sing with soul," said Roy Orbison, who came to feel strongly that his talents were never fully appreciated, or exploited, at Sun. To Johnny Cash, Sam quite simply "encouraged me always to do it my own way, [to] use the influences of other people but not to ever copy. He made me believe in myself." To another singer, who came along a little later and had nothing but harsh words for Sam's failure to properly promote him, there was never any question about what he derived from his studio experience. "He made you comfortable," said Billy Riley, "he would make you so comfortable in the studio you could go in there and just turn loose. He [made] you feel like you *were* somebody, whether you were or not." As Harold Jenkins, who later became the rock 'n' roll star, and country *superstar,* Conway Twitty, said of his own unsuccessful stint at Sun: "The studio was like a hole in the wall, but it looked like Radio City in New York to us. You used your own band, and you played. You had to create." And even if he never did get the Sun single he so desperately wanted, he at least got the *opportunity.* Years later he ran into Sam. "I know you were disappointed that we didn't release a song on you," Sam said and invited him to come by the studio some time and listen to the tapes. Twitty did, Colin Escott wrote, and he was amazed at how bad they were. But that didn't take away from the value of the education.

Perhaps the most striking example of this commitment to process more than merely measurable result came early on in Sally Wilbourn's employment at Sun. "One day," she said, "this young man walks in. He has on overalls, which you never saw at that time anymore — only on my daddy did you see them. He had no instrument. He walked in and he wanted an audition, and Sam said, 'Okay, okay. Let's hear what you got.'

"Do you know this man sang 'Old MacDonald Had a Farm'? And he made those animals sound so real. I got so tickled, I had to practically crawl under my desk [to keep from laughing], but Sam never cracked a smile. He could sit there like that, you know — but the strangeness of it as that man sang his song. And when he got through, he turned around and walked right out the door. Sam came out and said, 'Where did he go?' and I said, 'I don't know.' He said, 'You know, I would like to have something like this. We could probably use this in commercials. I mean, this guy is so great with all these animals.' But he was gone. We never saw him again."

To Sally it was an occasion never to be forgotten — not just the strangeness of the man's appearance and disappearance but the impenetrability of Sam's response as well. "I couldn't talk for two hours. I had never witnessed anything like that. I mean, he could bark like a dog, he could grunt like a pig—[but] *what were you thinking?* Sam just wanted to talk to the guy. It was so good. It was one of the most amazing things I've ever heard, and yet it was so funny. I couldn't stop laughing."

O NE DAY IN JUNE another young man showed up at the studio. Square-jawed, puckish, genially handsome in a Hollywood-second-lead kind of way, at twenty-five Jack Clement was a Marine veteran, Arthur Murray dance instructor, professional musician, sometime English student at Memphis State University, and would-be record man. He had been born into a respectable middle-class family of dentists and businessmen in Whitehaven, on the outskirts of Memphis, and enlisted in the Marines at seventeen. This came after he persuaded his father to let him visit New Orleans with a friend when school got out junior year — and then, after spotting the recruiting office on Canal Street one

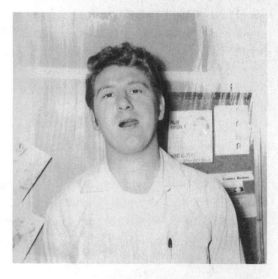

Jack Clement agape in
the Sun studio, 1956.
*Courtesy of the Sam
Phillips Family*

day ("Here's this Marine Corps sign [with] this guy in his beautiful dress
blues and everything") deciding that a life of derring-do was preferable
to senior year and, after informing his parents of his decision, just not
bothering to come home for a while. He had always fancied himself a
nonconformist, a free spirit in search of adventure. "I just hated high
school. I just didn't want to be there. I was kind of wild and woolly. I
wanted to be out traveling around, hanging out in pool halls and camping
out in hobo camps and all that, take my guitar, go out and charm people.
I wanted to spend the night, sing for my supper. *[Sly comic pause.]* Well,
shortly after breakfast. 'I'm too full to sing now. I'll sing for you right
after breakfast.'"

Joining the Marines was clearly the next best thing.

He was stationed for the last twenty-six months of his duty in Washington, D.C., where he was assigned to the drill team and the Drill and
Bugle Corps, which specialized in ceremonial details, like attending the
arrivals of visiting dignitaries, like Winston Churchill, Charles DeGaulle,
and Princess Elizabeth, and escorting them around town. He also met
country and bluegrass royalty, like the Stoneman family, and started
playing bluegrass in all the little joints up and down Eighth Street.
On leaving the Corps after four years of service, on June 15, 1952, he
embarked upon the life of a professional musician.

Eventually he found his way back to Memphis and was playing steel
in Sleepy Eyed John Lepley's western swing band out at the Eagle's Nest

when Elvis, Scotty, and Bill started playing as an intermission act in the summer of 1954. He was also attending school on the GI Bill (he thought he might like to be a writer) and supplementing his income as a dance instructor, a field of endeavor in which he had no previous expertise but about which he had no hesitancy, given his openness to every kind of musical experience.

Then in 1955 he met a truck driver named Ronald "Slim" Wallace, who played bass in his own little band, the Dixie Ramblers, and had a club out Highway 51 pretty much solely to indulge his own musical passion. Jack started working with him on weekends, and then when Slim sold the club and bought another one in his hometown of Paragould, Arkansas, about ninety miles away, Jack played with him there every Friday and Saturday night. They were driving back to Memphis together one night when he persuaded Slim that they should start a label together. "Jack was riding in the backseat, and he said, 'Big Slim, let's go in the recording business.' I said, 'Jack, how do we do that?' He said, 'We'll build your garage into a studio, and we'll record there.' He said, 'I'll do the work.' I said, 'What will we use for money?' He said, 'We'll use your truck-driving money.' So the next day Jack was at my house and went to work." In short order he got Sleepy Eyed John to sell them an old Magnecord recorder and a four-channel mixer that John had acquired from WHHM, where he worked, and in two or three months they were practically in business.

Before the work was complete, though, they had a roadside encounter with the man who was destined to be their first artist and forever change Jack's fortune. This was how it happened, according to Jack, in a story that Slim would tell with only a little less embellishment, and perhaps a slightly greater degree of chivalry.

One night, it was Christmas Eve, 1955, we were driving back from Paragould. It was me and Slim and Slim's wife and this girlfriend of hers that had come along that night and got really drunk and we stopped at this coffee shop in Jonesboro. I hadn't been eating much all evening, so I said, "I'll stay out here and look after her." Well, I'm sitting there, and she got out of the car and starts walking around and along come the cops. I get out of the car to see if I could help or something. They locked us both up. I wasn't even drunk. I'm not sure I'd even had a beer that night.

Anyway, Slim stayed over to get me out of jail the next morning—
his wife [took] the car and went on back to Memphis. I got out kind
of early, it's Christmas Day, now, and I'm married, I can't get word
home or nothing. So anyway we went down to the bus station to see
if we could get a bus, [but] there wasn't going to be a bus out until
late that afternoon so we decided we'd hitchhike. So we're out on the
highway and along comes Billy Lee Riley, and he recognized Slim.
I had never met Billy, but he picked us up and took us about thirty
miles. We talked about—

Well, why not let Billy Riley take up the story here?
"I was living in Memphis doing whatever I could," he told Memphis
music writer John Floyd.

My brother in-law was a meat-cutter, so he got me some jobs doing
that. But I was in Jonesboro visiting my wife's folks—my folks lived
in Nettleton, about three or four miles away, and I was going to go to
my mother's house. Along the way I saw two guys on the road hitch-
hiking, so I picked them up and said, "I'm only going three or four
miles, but I'll take you up to the highway, where you'll have a better
chance of catching a ride." Come to find out, it was Jack Clement
and Slim Wallace—that was the first time I'd ever met those guys.
[And] we got to talking about music, and I told them I was a singer,
a country singer, and before we had quit talking, I had brought them
all the way to Memphis—I didn't even go to my mother's house! Slim
Wallace lived on Fernwood, and they were building a studio in the
garage. So they took me out there and showed me what they were
doing and asked if I'd like to maybe work some in their band. I said,
"Yeah"—it paid about ten, twelve bucks for a Saturday night. After
they got the studio finished, I was supposedly going to be the first
artist on Fernwood Records.

I suppose at this point it would make sense to give Billy Riley a proper
introduction. Born in Pocahontas, Arkansas, he grew up in a poor, share-
cropping family (he quit school at the age of ten) that moved from one
plantation to another in northeast Arkansas. He went into the service
at fifteen, and when he got out four years later, in 1953, he formed a
country band, singing Hank Williams mostly at little clubs and on the

Billy Riley in action. Note Roland James [*sic*] amp, J. M. Van Eaton on drums.
Courtesy of Richard Weize, Bear Family Records

radio. He had a feeling for the blues that he always attributed to working next to black sharecroppers in the fields, but, as with just about everybody else in that part of the country, it was Elvis who changed his musical outlook. "At first I was like a lot of other people, 'Man, this guy's crazy,' you know. [But] then when I saw him onstage, it just tore me up, I thought 'Man, hey,' you know, 'I can do that.' And I did."

Not right away, though. Jack and Slim worked with Billy for months, both at the club and in the emerging garage studio, where they taped and studied everything they did. There was no question in Jack's mind that Billy could be the one. Strikingly good-looking with chiseled features and high Indian cheekbones, Billy possessed a musical adaptability, almost a chameleon-like ability to evoke a variety of different styles, as well as a charismatic unpredictability that made him both exciting and difficult to deal with. Finally, in May, after months of experimentation, Jack thought they had something ready — but the studio still was not finished, and Jack didn't think Big Slim possessed the requisite skills to play bass on the record. So he booked time at radio station WMPS, and he hired a second bass player, persuading Slim that two slapping basses were better than one and would give their record a unique sound. They had a guitarist in the band, and Jack arranged with local drummer Johnny Bernero, who worked at Memphis Light, Gas and Water, the municipal utility, and had cut several sides with Elvis at Sun, to play on the session.

In addition, he invited a guitarist he had just met through Doc McQueen, a bank accountant with songwriting ambitions, whose home was a gathering place for musicians he had gotten to know from demoing his songs. ("His wife was very liberal-minded [that way]," said one.) Roland Janes had met Doc originally because the diesel mechanics school he was attending on the GI Bill was next door to Doc's house. But that wasn't the reason Roland was in Memphis. Twenty two years old, born in rural Arkansas but raised by his mother in St. Louis after his parents split up, he had come to Memphis purely for the music. A thoughtful, quick-witted man who had not quite completed high school but possessed a penchant for observation and wordplay, he had first visited Memphis just before enlisting in the Marines and returned upon his discharge in the summer of 1955 because there "just seemed to be something pulling me, I don't know what it was—I didn't know anyone, I think the spirit had something to do with it." He was not in any sense a full-fledged professional musician, but he had played in a hillbilly band with his Arkansas cousins from the time he was twelve and was open to all kinds of music. Perhaps it was his temperament as much as his playing that convinced Jack that he was the right man for the job.

They had already cut one conventional hillbilly number and were preparing to cut "Rock With Me Baby," a kind of steady-rocking cross between Elvis and Carl Perkins that Billy had worked up, when Roland came into the picture. It was the first time Billy had met Roland, and they really hit it off. "We just got into the studio," said Billy, "and we cut it. It was exciting and new. It was enjoyable."

Once they had a good track on the new number, the next step was to get the record mastered. Memphis Recording Service was the one place in town where you could be sure of getting a solid professional job done—despite all the other pulls on his time, Sam was reluctant to abandon either this or the personal recording service that had first brought Elvis to his door. Jack had by this time given up on school and was working at a building supplies company out on Poplar. He had one afternoon a week off, so he brought in the tape and came back the following week to pick it up. It was June 15, Jack said, he would never forget the date, because it was the anniversary of the day he had gotten out of the Marines.

> Sam was sitting out in the front office by himself and he said, "Come on back here. I want to talk to you." So we went back in the control room, and he said, "I really like that record you brought me. It's the only rock and roll anybody's brought me around here. That's the only real rock and roll anybody's brought me."
>
> He asked me if I'd be interested in it being on Sun. He'd pay us a penny a record. I said, "Well I'll talk to my partner, Slim, and let you know." He said, "Well what are you doing?" I said, "I'm working out at Clark and Fay. I don't like it very much." He said, "Well maybe you ought to come to work for me." So I said, "Maybe I should." Two weeks later I went to work at Sun. All that never would have happened if I hadn't got stuck in jail that night, got picked up by Billy Riley the next day. So the Lord does work in mysterious ways his wonders to perform. Especially when it comes to rock and roll.

It turned out Sam didn't much like the hillbilly side, so they quickly cut another original as a replacement, a haunting blues called "Trouble Bound" that was unmistakably (and not coincidentally) reminiscent of "Heartbreak Hotel." Sam was just as knocked out by it as he had been by "Rock With Me Baby," and he had the record out on Sun within a month, on August 3.

Sally looked somewhat askance at the new employee, Marion even more so, while Jack assessed Marion as "kind of like an old-maid schoolteacher, very firm and very business-like — she was madly in love with Sam." Both women might have viewed Jack with a certain amount of misgiving, because he was more than a little mischievous, determinedly eccentric, and not at all what either might have thought was the perfect match for Sam. But both recognized that Sam needed *someone*, if only to listen to all the tapes that were coming in over the transom and audition some of the desperate-looking hillbillies who kept showing up at the door. In addition to which, with his own musical skills he was perfectly suited to rehearsing whatever Sun acts needed rehearsing. Sam just needed someone other than Sally and Marion to be in the studio all the time. That was what made sense.

For Jack it was a heaven-sent opportunity. He was prepared to do anything that was asked of him (his first day on the job was spent helping Sally and Marion pack records), but his real reason for being there was that he was fascinated by the whole process of making records. And he was fascinated by Sam.

"I'd never met anyone like Sam before. With Sam, there were no in-betweens, it was all absolutes — it was either great or forget about it, it was either Shakespeare or it ain't worth a shit. But if he liked something, he couldn't contain himself. He'd have you play it again and again, while he says, 'Listen to that part! Ain't that great? Play that part again.'"

Sam's intensity was something that Jack had never experienced before. He was such a great salesman, Jack quickly realized, he believed so completely in his own product that he was "almost fearsome at times." But at the same time he had the power to "make you want to perform for him. Because if he liked something, you believed him. I think the center-piece of Sam's genius was his ability to make people want to please him."

It was nothing like the way Jack himself, by nature a meticulous craftsman, would have acted. Weaned on bluegrass, Jack prized virtuosic performance and the ironic reserve of a good novelty song. "I wanted a bunch of ringing guitars, I played bluegrass and Hawaiian music, a lot of the stuff I wanted to do was kind of cute." With Sam, on the other hand, it was all about passion, naked and undisguised.

Sophistication in any case was not an option. "The musicians we were working with just weren't that quick and polished. They were [mostly] learning. They were basically gifted amateurs." And the sessions themselves at first seemed scarcely organized. The mission was always to find something different regardless of how many blind alleys you went up, regardless of the number of missteps, irrespective of how long it took. "The clock didn't mean anything. Everybody was having fun. Sam never really told me a lot about what to do and what not to do. 'Just get in there and have fun, do whatever you want to do, let the guy do the thing, and you capture it. And if it ain't perfect, okay.' He didn't mind certain little mistakes. I did. And it kind of threw me for a loop at first. But he was right!"

And yet for all the informality of the sessions, Jack couldn't miss the formal distance that Sam deliberately cultivated between himself and his artists. For all of their closeness, there was never any surrender of authority, outside the studio there was scarcely any "fraternization," and every one of them called him "Mr. Phillips," even Johnny Cash. Jack himself had trouble at first knowing how to address his employer. Sam never broached the subject directly, and Jack was disinclined to call someone not much older than himself, with whom he was working so closely, by a prenominal title — but on the other hand, he couldn't quite bring himself to call him Sam either. So for a while he just avoided any direct form of address. He wondered about it at first, the deliberate detachment that Sam created, but then after a while it made a kind of sense. Jack himself, with his disarmingly ambiguous Cheshire cat's grin, always sought to encourage at least the appearance of nonchalance. But for Sam, clearly, maintaining his distance was his way of establishing just who was in charge, of sustaining the illusion of democracy without ever giving up the reins. It was as if they were all very much a family, as Sam would later articulate it, but he needed to preserve his "authoritarian demeanor" to inspire belief. "I wanted them to know at all times that I knew what I was doing, even [if] I maybe didn't." And in the studio he needed them to know that however much he loved them, however much he was committed to doing his best to always take care of them, they were going to have to work not so much to earn his respect as their own.

Jack studied the way Sam conducted business, too — his refusal to expand beyond his capacity or put out more records at a time than he could effectively promote, his unwillingness to extend more credit to his distributors than he was sure they could handle or press more records than he thought he could sell. These were lessons of restraint and parsimony that, after a long and illustrious (but more often than not financially imprudent) career as record producer, songwriter, and label owner himself, Jack would readily admit he had never been able to incorporate into his own business practices. But even if they clearly limited the growth of Sun Records and sometimes hurt less successful artists who were unable to command sufficient attention on their own, these principles were all that stood between him, Sam insisted, and financial ruin. They represented the hard-earned lessons of deprivation.

Most of all, though, what Jack remarked upon was Sam's own sense of ease — the way he carried himself, not just metaphorically but *physically*, too. "There's no way to describe Sam," Jack would declare in later years at the drop of a hat — and from the perspective of someone about whom one could very easily have said the same thing. "You [had] to see him. You've got to see the way he moves, the way he — he's the most *dynamic* person I've ever seen. I never met anybody like Sam. There's nobody like Sam. He scares the shit out of some people. But I got a big kick out of him. Most of the time. I mean, [here was] this wonderful nut that was going to teach me everything he knew about making records. I was in hog heaven!"

S AM FOR HIS PART couldn't have been more tickled. He was won over by Jack, he was *intrigued* by him from the start. Here was a gifted musician and incipient producer, blessed with a keen wit and intellectual curiosity — but most of all he was an independent spirit after Sam's own heart. After six and one-half years of working alone, he welcomed Jack as a free thinker and eager acolyte, and even if, as Jack suggested, they might have their occasional tiffs, he never for one moment regretted his decision.

Jack was an avid student. It only took him a few days before he started badgering Sam for the secret of his sound — and even though Sam generally tended to be coy about the details of a technique that any good sound engineer could have figured out for himself, he didn't hesitate for a moment in revealing it to his new employee. He showed Jack all about the equipment, he showed him how to mike everything for maximum impact, too. He took Jack down to Marked Tree, Arkansas, where he was putting in a second little radio station, and he confided to Jack on their forty-mile drive down and back that it was radio that was his first love.

The first artist he let Jack work with on his own was Roy Orbison, doing the song that Harold Jenkins had brought in to perform with his band, "Rockhouse." Jack put plenty of slapback on it ("It was really a sound effect — it was the only effect we had"), but Sam seemed satisfied with it. Jack took a somewhat dim view of Roy Orbison at the time. "I thought he and his band were kind of pissy," he told Memphis music writer John Floyd with wry amusement at his own shortsightedness. "Roy always had these crazy ideas. He wanted production numbers like he ultimately wound up doing. I told Roy he'd never make it as a ballad singer. He never let me forget that either. . . . But me and Roy got to be big buddies [later]."

He cut some other sessions, too. He would have liked to have cut Johnny Cash. But Sam kept Cash and Carl Perkins to himself. Cash at this point was selling so many records that Steve Sholes, riding high now on Elvis' unprecedented popularity, even tried to buy his contract. The negotiations never really went anywhere ("Johnny could be bought," Sam wrote back to Sholes somewhat disingenuously on July 11, "but he'll come high. Of course any deal would be subject to Johnny's consent"), but not long afterward he told John he wanted to talk to him, as he had once talked to Elvis, about the perils of success.

He called me into his office and turned around and faced me and punched me in the chest with his finger and said, "Let me give you some advice." I said, "Well, okay." He accented every word with a point of his finger in the middle of my chest. I thought he was going to take me in and really eat me out about something. I thought maybe a doomsday had come, and I would have to quit recording or something. But the important thing he had to tell me was, "Don't ever get fat." And, there's not been a week in my life that has gone by since that day that I haven't thought about the advice that Sam Phillips gave me.

In August Sam finally acted on a conclusion that he had come to some time earlier, in fact almost from the moment that "Blue Suede Shoes" first hit the charts: that the publishing deal he had made with Hill and Range when he sold Elvis' contract was fundamentally inequitable to his own self-interest. He had given Hill and Range something he should never have given away, namely 25 percent of the revenue from every domestic cover version or motion-picture use of any Hi-Lo song published up until mid-November of the current year—which he had by now come to realize he could sell just as easily himself. It was an unbreakable contract with a company with whom he wanted to continue to work, with respect to foreign rights, anyway—but, as he saw it, there was nothing in the contract that said he had to publish all his songs in the Hi-Lo catalogue. So he formed a new publishing company, Knox Music, and put all of the songs that he acquired from that point on into it, negotiating a separate deal with Hill and Range for the new company, limited strictly to foreign rights, under a more mutually beneficial arrangement.

On September 10 he completed the purchase of a new house in a leafy area of Memphis "out east" that had barely been developed. The whole family had been driving around every Sunday for what seemed like weeks to ten-year-old Knox, looking at various other houses in the area. There had been one on Perkins just around the corner that they kind of liked — it was redbrick and kind of modern — but it wasn't sufficiently distinctive for Sam. Sam was just about to give up, if he couldn't find a house he liked, he'd build a damn house on his own, when on this particular Sunday they turned onto Mendenhall, a pretty little curving street between Poplar Pike and Walnut Grove, "and we got to 79 South Mendenhall," Knox recalled, "and, man, that was it, all in turquoise and a beautiful sort of pink. It was the most beautiful house I'd ever seen in my life."

Everyone in the family reacted the same way, Sam most of all. It had been designed by the builder, Chester A. Camp, who specialized in "houses of the future," in a U shape, with an interior courtyard, a pale adobe exterior with red mortar to accentuate its delicate highlights and an overhanging turquoise-colored roof, a spacious den with a back wall and fireplace made from the same Arkansas cut stone that carried over onto the patio, and a latticed carport that looked like it had been made for Sam's two-tone, air-conditioned Cadillac. The interior design, executed with flair by an enterprising forty-two-year old decorator named George Golden and already about 75 percent complete, was if anything even more futuristic. Golden, a former Lipton tea salesman with a taste for the eclectic and a flair for self-promotion, had several flatbed trucks cruising around Memphis day and night, decked out with illuminated "three-foot-wide miniature rooms, built to scale, complete with carpet, wallpaper, and a two-foot sofa, upholstered in chartreuse satin. That sofa," said Golden, reminiscing forty years later, "caught everyone's eye."

That whole bold approach didn't just catch Sam's eye — it captured his heart. "It was," he said, "a home I'd never expected to own" — as if, he said, someone else had built the house he had envisioned in his dreams — and he didn't hesitate in putting down $26,000 of the $56,500 purchase price (the equivalent of approximately $491,000 in 2014 dollars), with Mr. Camp holding the mortgage on the rest. It was almost eerie how closely it conformed to his imagination, there was nothing "great or fancy" about it at all, "but it was as *original* as anything I had ever seen." He loved the horseshoe shape, too, "you [could] go all the way from the den into the master bedroom without bothering a soul — and so far as people's comfort [goes], if they're tired of what you're doing they can change localities." But when Knox first saw the U-shaped hallway, "I mean, I wasn't used to anything like that, and I said, 'Dad, who lives over there?' He said, 'I'll walk you over there.' So we just walked around the hall and—*we* lived there!"

I T MIGHT HAVE SEEMED like an idyllic picture—and it was, in every respect but one.

Marion had finally found out about Sam and Sally. And it wasn't by following Sam around in the car he had bought for her. Nor did she pick up any lingering looks between them. It came about, in fact, by accident.

Sally had moved out of her aunt's house in South Memphis in June and moved in with her sister Shirley, who had just graduated from nursing school and found a tiny two-room apartment within walking distance of Baptist Hospital. Then they met another girl, a relative of a relative, and together the three of them got a much nicer place in a duplex on Harbert, off Lamar. That was where she was when she was talking with Sam on the phone late one night—he was in the control room, and Marion was out front, and Marion, wondering who he could be speaking to for so long so late at night, picked up the phone.

She was devastated. She couldn't believe it at first—she had confided to Sally all of her feelings about Sam. But she didn't blame Sally. Sally was just a poor, silly little girl. She blamed Sam, and she lit into him right away. What was he thinking of? Didn't he have any sense? He was going to ruin this poor girl's life. When he offered nothing more than that it was none of her business, those were not his intentions, and he didn't see why things couldn't just continue in the same way, she told Becky. She told her where Sally lived. She told her she thought Sam was there now. And Becky got in the car, practically blind with grief, and went over there to confront—she wasn't sure just what.

She found Sam there. She begged him, she pleaded with him, she brought up the vital interests of their children—but Sam was impervious. And Sally evidently had no shame. Becky looked at her with growing dismay. This girl was not going to get out of the way. She looked at her husband, and she realized with a sinking feeling that nothing she said was making any impression. He didn't apologize, he didn't deny—and she knew that this girl, this *young girl,* played a part in his life that he was not going to disown. To Becky, "Sam was a good person, he loved doing good—[but] he always knew exactly what he wanted, and no matter what he did, he never lied about it," no matter how much it might hurt. She was utterly crushed, she felt a total sense of betrayal, and she was furious at Sally, but she clung to the idea — even though her keen intelligence told her it wasn't so — that if Sally were somehow simply to disappear from the picture, things could just go back to the way they had been.

Sally for her part observed the scene not so much with disenchantment as with a disconnection from it. She had known all along that this was not just a casual affair — but now she knew for certain that this was the man with whom she was going to cast her lot. She was seeing a whole different side of him now in a way — and yet it was exactly the same. It didn't matter what you said to Sam, "it didn't matter that you were married to him, it didn't matter that you had his children. If that's not what he wanted to do, he wasn't going to do it. He just never acted that way."

Becky left the apartment. That was the end of the confrontation — no more was ever said. This was just the way it was going to be. Sally knew her role — and she thought she understood Becky's, too. "He wasn't looking for a wife. It would have never [worked] if I had wanted to get married and have children. He would have just been somewhere else. He wanted somebody with him — *all the time*. I was that person. Sam [might] not be talking, he may not be doing anything — I could be sitting in the front office and him back in the studio, but he wanted somebody there. He just never wanted to be by himself. I knew that I was never going to leave."

S AM WAS OUT OF TOWN when a young man from Louisiana showed up at the studio with his father one day in October. It has often been said — not infrequently by Sam himself — that he was in Florida with Becky and the boys, but the only family vacation that anyone else can remember is a trip to Chicago with their enterprising interior designer, George Golden, to pick out furniture for their new home at the city's fabled American Furniture Mart. ("It was," Knox recalled, "like the furniture mall of the world!")

In any case he was out of town when Jerry Lee Lewis and his father, Elmo, arrived from Ferriday, Louisiana, having sold all the eggs from their little farm to make the trip. Lewis, his long blond hair swept back to show a smooth, open face framed by big ears and a scraggly goatee, was just twenty-one but seemed younger, with the almost manic energy and willed self-belief of a speeded-up cartoon character. He had read a magazine story about Elvis that cited Sam Phillips as the guiding light behind all these rising stars — Elvis, Johnny Cash, Carl Perkins, even B.B. King — and he said to his father, "This is the man we need to go see."

Sally wasn't sure quite what to make of this brash young man, but she went back to the control room to tell Jack that there was a man out there who said he could play piano just like Chet Atkins played the guitar. According to Jack: "I said, 'I want to listen to *that*,' and she brought him back, and he played 'Wildwood Flower,' and he really *did* sound like Chet Atkins playing the piano. Well, that intrigued me. So I went back in the control room and put on a tape."

When Sam heard the tape, it was as if, he said, Jerry Lee Lewis had stepped out of a dream he was fixing to have. "They put that tape on, and I said, 'Where in *hell* did this man come from?' I mean, he played that piano with *abandon*." But that wasn't all; others might do that just as well. "Between the stuff he played and didn't play," Sam said, "I could hear that spiritual thing, too. I told Jack, 'Just get him in here as fast as you can.'"

Jack had every intention of calling him but, ironically, Sam was out of town again when Jerry Lee showed up at the studio on Friday, November 9, arriving once again unannounced. This time he was with his cousin J. W. Brown, a sometime musician who worked at Memphis Light, Gas and Water, and with whom he was staying out on Coro Lake. Sam had just left for the fifth annual Country Music Disc Jockey Convention in Nashville, a gathering of the country music community at which Johnny Cash would get much the same recognition this year that Elvis had the year before. He had taken Sally with him for their first out-of-town trip, and they were not going to be back, he told Becky, until late Sunday night. Jack was not going to wait that long — after Sam's reaction, he wasn't going to risk letting the boy get away a second time, so he set up an audition session for the next day, getting in touch with Billy Riley's guitarist, Roland Janes, and leaving it to Roland to contact Billy's new eighteen-year-old drummer, J. M. Van Eaton, a recent high school graduate who had been drafted for the band after they heard him in the studio with his own band, the Echoes.

Roland and J.M. had worked a couple of sessions for Jack at this point and kept busy playing local dates with Billy around Memphis and northeast Arkansas — but they certainly didn't consider themselves seasoned "professionals," and Jack didn't lead them to believe this was anything more than an audition session with a piano player from Louisiana who might or might not prove to have the stuff. When he showed up, they were a little disconcerted by their first glimpse of him. "We came in," said Roland, "and Jerry was there with Jay Brown. Jerry had a little pointed goatee, which was unusual back then, and he was very — I don't want to use the word *arrogant*, I don't mean that, but *boisterous*, really into what he was doing." Jay had a broken arm, but he was carrying a Silvertone guitar, and Jerry said he could still play rhythm. Which, said J.M. with ironic self-deprecation, "was pretty weird. And I'm thinking, 'Man, why did they drag us down here? You know, we're starting to be record stars now, we don't need this!'"

But then Jerry Lee started to play, and all doubt was erased. Roland and Jimmy Van Eaton could only compete in wonder-struck admiration. "I'd never seen anything like it," said Jimmy. "I've never seen anybody play a piano like that." It was, said Roland, "like hearing a whole different music that you'd never heard before. He played equally well with either hand. He could do full ons with his left hand as good as most people do with their right hand, [and] he had this rhythm, this fantastic bass rhythm — I mean, the music never stopped."

They must have cut thirty songs, one after another, just like that. He sang blues, hillbilly, spirituals with equal ease. He cut Gene Autry's "You're the Only Star in My Blue Heaven," Jimmie Rodgers' "Waiting for a Train," the old Stephen Foster-inflected spiritual "Hand Me Down My Walking Cane," and "Little Green Valley" (originally written and recorded by Carson Robison, the "Granddaddy of the Hillbillies," in 1928) — and succeeded in reshaping each and every one of them with an infusion of swing, attitude, and transformational genius. He had brought a single rollicking original with him, "End of the Road," which was itself a reworking of a 1929 Irving Berlin composition (as sung originally by Bing Crosby and, more recently, Frankie Laine) — but so radical a reworking as to be virtually unrecognizable. And to all of his offerings, whether altogether spontaneous or frequently performed, he brought an ineluctable spark that caused them to defy the confines of any studio setting, dancing out into the ether on an impetus all their own. He kicked every song off on piano and set such a solid beat, such an *infectious* beat, Roland said, that it was almost like they were locked into a telepathic groove. "I mean, we knew what he was going to do before he did it, and he knew what we were going to do. I think he and J.M. [could] cut records by themselves, and it'd sound like a whole orchestra!"

Toward the end of the session, when it seemed like things were finally beginning to taper off, Roland went to the bathroom, and J.M. and Jerry Lee kicked off a version of Ray Price's "Crazy Arms," which had been number 1 for six months at this point and had just been cited by *Billboard* as the country music disc jockeys' "favorite" record of the year. Jerry Lee and J.M. were still playing the song when Roland came out of the bathroom. It sounded like they were just messing around, so he picked up the upright bass that was lying on its side and plucked a couple of notes — he didn't really know how to play the bass, but it wasn't going to matter because he wasn't on mike anyway. Then Billy Riley, who had stopped by to see what was going on, picked up Roland's guitar and hit a bad chord just as they wound up the song — and everyone got a good laugh out of that.

Jack played the tape for Sam when he got back from Nashville, and he practically jumped out of his skin. He didn't have to hear any more than the trilling, rock-solid boogie-woogie of the opening notes on piano before he reached over and stopped the tape. "Now I can *sell* that," he said to Jack. Then he listened to the vocal, full of fun, confidence, and irrepressible self-delight, and he was even more convinced. "Crazy Arms," the last number they had done on the session and currently at the top of the country charts, was, Sam announced, a *certifiable hit!*

At first he thought maybe they should get the band back in and recut it. But in the event, Roland and Jimmy were out of town playing some dates with Billy Riley. And the more he listened, the more he liked it, bad guitar chord and all.

So he cut an acetate and took it down to Dewey, who just about wore it out, playing it simultaneously (more or less) on both his turntables. He had the record out three weeks later, on December 1, with the label boldly proclaiming "Jerry Lee Lewis With His Pumping Piano." He didn't know how many it would sell, but he knew if he missed out on talent like this, he might just as well cut his ears off. "'Cause they ain't no good — get in my way, get in my way, you don't need them anymore." And to Jerry Lee he simply declared, "You are a rich man." And he sensed that this boy, with all his talent and all his confidence, knew exactly what he meant.

E VERYBODY DID THEIR BEST to keep Jerry Lee in town — nobody wanted to see the wild boy from Louisiana disappear again. Jack got him a job playing with the Snearly Ranch Boys at the Cotton Club in West Memphis — sometimes he would play drums and piano at the same time, alternating on vocals with Barbara Pittman. Roland and J.M. enlisted him in the Billy Riley band and took him over to Arkansas for some of their gigs in Truman and Blytheville and Osceola. Sam introduced him to Bob Neal, who promptly booked him into a Stars Inc. show at the Community Center in Sheffield with Carl Perkins and Warren Smith. And Sam hired him to play piano on the upcoming Carl Perkins session on December 4. He thought it could give Carl's sound a lift, and it might even give his next release a commercial boost.

Carl was dubious about this new cat at first, with his arrogance and the kind of ungovernable self-regard that no one had a right to show in Mr. Phillips' studio. But then as they began to play and feel each other out musically, he thought it was turning into maybe his best session yet. "I mean, Jerry Lee played the piano like he wanted to play it, and you didn't tell him — if he didn't want to play it the way you wanted to, he'd say, 'Well, there it sits. You play it.'" But there was no question he could deliver. He may have been cocky, Carl thought, but he was ready to fulfill every musical promise that he made.

As it happened, Carl's daddy, Buck, was in the studio that day — the only time, Carl would sometimes ruefully recall, his father ever attended a session — and "my daddy said, 'Carl, do you know the old "Matchbox Blues"?' And I said, 'No sir, I've heard some of it but I don't know it.' And he told me some of the words, and I kind of scratched them out on a piece of paper." But he knew he had to come up with something different, and he started fooling with a little boogie lick on guitar, and then Jerry Lee joined in with some rumbling boogie-woogie bass notes — that's when they really knew they had something. Jerry Lee was firing fusillades at him, and he was just shooting back with triple-string runs of his own. "Pickers — no one has to tell them. Everybody feels it. You can't keep from smiling when it's right. And when it's [really] clicking, it's hard to get it unclicked. I mean it's just gonna stay there."

That was when Elvis walked in. Naturally everything came to a halt as the musicians all gathered around Elvis and his girlfriend, a dancer from Las Vegas, and Sam, who was accustomed to Elvis' unannounced drop-ins, welcomed him warmly but in a way that was not going to draw attention away from his present-day musicians. He no longer had any worries about Elvis finding his voice at RCA. When "Don't Be Cruel" had come out that summer, it had finally set his mind at ease. He didn't give a damn about "Hound Dog," the A-side — as far as he was concerned, it couldn't touch Big Mama's original — but when he first heard "Don't Be Cruel," driving back from Daytona Beach, Florida, with Becky and the boys, "I practically drove off the road. When I heard that vamp, I said, 'Glory Hallelujah, now *there* is a groove.'"

It was "a sad story with a happy beat," but more than that, for the first time, it seemed like Elvis himself was really in charge. "It was the total spontaneity. And the rhythm was moving along just right — it [was] pushing him, [but] he still had command." But that was what differentiated Elvis from so many of these other boys, Sam felt: Elvis could learn from his mistakes, where they were just destined to repeat them.

They started off just fooling around, singing snatches of various remembered songs in between excited conversation as they gathered around the piano. Sam immediately recognized the potential, if only for a publicity photo, and he called Johnny Cash, who said he had to do some Christmas shopping with his wife but he could come down to the studio for a few minutes. Then he called Bob Johnson at the *Press-Scimitar* and the bureau chief of the local UPI wire service, Leo Soroka, and by the time they arrived John was already there, and he and his two fellow Sun stars, Carl and Jerry Lee, grouped around Elvis at the piano. There they all are, poised to burst into song, with Jerry Lee unsurprisingly leaning in, Carl with a tight-lipped look of serious concentration, John in a striped, collegiate-style windbreaker, and Elvis looking expectantly over his shoulder at his musical colleagues, as his house guest, Marilyn Evans, sits on top of the piano in what could have been a cheesecake shot were it not for her very modest informal attire.

This was his "Million Dollar Quartet," Sam proudly announced, with the 1956 equivalent of air quotes, as Elvis, Bob Johnson reported in his "TV News and Views" column, "started to Fats Domino it on 'Blueberry Hill,' [and] that very unrehearsed but talented bunch got to cutting up on [that] and a lot of other songs." It was, as Johnson astutely described, "an old-fashioned barrelhouse session with barbershop harmony."

Soon the reporters left, and so did Johnny Cash, but the music went on. Sam had Jack turn on the tape recorder — or perhaps Jack just took the initiative ("I thought all that carrying on ought to be recorded") — but no one bothered to position the mikes or balance the sound, Sam and Jack were out on the floor as much as they were in the control room, it was all strictly unplanned.

The Million Dollar Quartet: Jerry Lee Lewis, Carl Perkins, Elvis Presley, and Johnny Cash, December 4, 1956. *Courtesy of Colin Escott*

They sang just about every type of song they knew — blues, bluegrass, spirituals, pop, and r&b — with Elvis taking the lead, accompanied at first by Carl and his brothers, with Smokey Joe Baugh, the gravel-voiced half of "Split Personality," on piano. Elvis introduced a number of songs, but perhaps the most fascinating was his own "Don't Be Cruel," which he said he had heard performed by "this guy in Las Vegas [with] Billy Ward and His Dominoes that was doing a take-off on me. He tried so hard till he got much better, boy, much better than that record of mine." There are polite but vehement murmurs of demurral. "No, wait now, I mean, he was real slender, he was a colored guy, he got up there and he'd say —" And here Elvis began to perform the song in imitation of the singer imitating him. "He had it a little slower than me. . . . He got the backing, the whole quartet, they got the feeling on it, he was hitting it, boy. Grabbed that microphone, and on the last note he went all the way down to the floor, man, looking straight up at the ceiling. Man, he was cutting out. I was under the table when he got through singing. . . . And all the time he was singing, them feet was going in and out, both ways, sliding like this. . . . He's a Yankee, you know," said Elvis, remarking with bemusement upon the singer's pronunciation of "tellyphone," and then singing the song, with that pronunciation, and in the singer's style, over and over again. "All he needed was a building or something to jump off," says someone, won over by the sheer enthusiasm of Elvis' description. "That's all he needed," agrees the unknown singer's foremost admirer. "Man, that would've made a big ending."

Not too long afterward Elvis jumps into Chuck Berry's "Brown Eyed Handsome Man," and that sets off an almost adulatory discussion of Berry's singing and songwriting abilities. "I just come back from a five-week tour with him," says Carl as they tease out the lyrics, laughing out loud at all the clever twists and turns the song takes. "You ought to hear some of his stuff, setting around," says Carl. "Man, he set down behind the stage, and just —" Everyone expresses their unqualified admiration, including Sam. "That's a rolling stone," says someone, borrowing one of Sam's favorite expressions of approbation, as Elvis comes back to the song again and again.

They all contribute to the music and the mood — Carl sings a beautiful version of Wynn Stewart's recently released country classic, "Keeper of the Keys," and there are ragged harmonies galore. But at the heart of the session, inevitably, are the spirituals on which they all grew up, with Jerry Lee flinging himself into the high harmonies with unrestrained, if occasionally unfocused, abandon, and even though Sally has told me that Sam didn't do any singing, I like to think I can hear that bass voice of which he was so inordinately proud joining in.

"Softly and Tenderly," "Just a Little Talk With Jesus," "I Shall Not Be Moved," "I Just Can't Make It By Myself" ("Me and Elvis knew the words to every song, because we were raised up in the same church," said Jerry Lee. "People wouldn't know that, but that's the way it was") — there is no mistaking the fervor in the voices. "Boy, this is fun!" Jerry Lee exclaims at one point, as Smokey Joe Baugh says, "You oughta get up a quartet."

It is a moment of perfect innocence. It is also, in many ways, a moment of pure vindication, the proof for Sam that somehow this music — the music of poor blacks and poor whites that had been overlooked for so long — *was not going to be forgotten.* At the end Jerry Lee Lewis, who has been not so patiently biding his time, finally gets his chance in the spotlight, as he tears through one song after another to everyone's indulgent appreciation. "That boy can go," Elvis has already informed Bob Johnson. "The way he plays piano just gets inside me." And now he proves it. Conversations are continued, everyone makes plans to get back together again sometime soon. "That's why I hate to start these jam sessions," says Elvis. "I'm always the last one to leave." You can hear doors slamming, and conversations trailing off. And then it's over.

It meant so much, said Sam, almost *because* it was so totally unplanned. "It was totally extemporaneous. Everything was off mike—if it was on mike it was by accident. [But] I think this little chance meeting meant an awful lot to all those people not because one was bigger than another [but because] we all started out at this place, every person in that room was electrified by the fact that we were together." It was in many ways, Sam told British journalist Roy Carr in 1980, like an old-time revival meeting, with each person in the room "motivated by the same common denominator. . . . The only way I can best describe exactly what happened that day is to liken it to a spiritual awakening through music."

Sam used the story that ran in the paper the next day as an ad in the form of a letter to DJs, with the picture front and center and a handwritten message appended at the bottom. "Our only regret!" it began. "That each and everyone of you wonderful D.J.s who are responsible for these boys being among the best known and liked in show business could not be here too!"

Some of the writers at *Billboard* had taken to referring to the new music as "Rock-A-Billy," but Sam hated the term. To him it was no more than a cute saying made up by people determined to dismiss the real impact of the music. Rock 'n' roll, he genuinely believed, had changed the world. It was the daring, the emotional freedom, the *spiritual essence* of it.

He was steadfast "in the faith of reason," but he was messianic in his belief in the music. "For so long we were ashamed of our heritage, we were afraid of ourselves—you were scared to confess the things that you really liked." It was the music, not politics or organized religion or anything else, that had set people free. "I mean, I really feel that way. To me the entertainment of people—the ability to entertain with the spiritual qualifications of these people—is just almost *boundless*. You know, there was a deep-seated feeling for God with probably every artist that came in my studio—whether they knew how to express it, or amplified it, or showed it in any way. *But they showed it to me in the way that they did what they did.*"

J OHNNY CASH'S "I Walk the Line" had sold 750,000 copies to date, the *Memphis Press-Scimitar* reported in a half-page story on January 7, 1957, as "the magic door swings open for still another young Memphis singer." Cash seemed poised for the same kind of mass crossover success that Elvis had achieved over the past twelve months, wrote Bob Johnson, Elvis' most astute early chronicler, and Sam was in no position to disagree. Johnny Cash had already set the world of country music on its ear, and now he was selling the real, unvarnished thing not just to hillbillies but to a teenage audience that seemed hungry for the honesty and authenticity of his music. There was no one who appreciated that honesty, or the decided *peculiarity* of John's music, more than Sam. There was no one who valued more the fundamental seriousness, the unabashed ambition of the artist and the man. And if he had had to be absolutely honest about it, Sam would have been forced to admit that he was drawn more to Cash's personal perspective and philosophical point of view ("With Johnny Cash you hear things that life is so precious about and yet life is so unfair about, and yet he'll always turn it around [so] that there is a place that I can go") than to that of any artist he had ever worked with. But if he were to be equally honest, the artist for whom he currently had the highest expectations, both commercial and artistic, was Jerry Lee Lewis.

Lewis, he thought, just might be the most naturally talented person he had ever worked with. Not the most charismatic (that would be Elvis), not the most commanding (that would probably be Cash), not the most profound (that would unquestionably be the Wolf), but the most

Jerry Lee Lewis in full flight. *Courtesy of the Sam Phillips Family* versatile, the most innately musical, the one who took the most pure pleasure and delight in his music. All that he needed to really take off was the right material. And Sam didn't have any doubt that he'd come up with it. Because even if he didn't write his own songs, he could create them on the spot—just like he had come up with a whole new take on Ray Price's "Crazy Arms" after the damn record had been playing on the radio for over six months. Jerry Lee's version of the song was a classic—hell, it was a complete *original*—even if up to this point it had attracted more notice than sales. Jerry Lee Lewis, Sam told a reporter, was "as deft as a concert pianist," but unlike a concert pianist he had a wealth of improvisational motifs to draw from in every song.

Sam had never seen anything like it—not even Elvis could approach the full scope of knowledge that this boy brought not just to the music but to every song that he sang. Jerry Lee Lewis, Sam recognized from the start, was like a walking encyclopedia—with a phonographic memory for everything he heard but the transformative talent to turn it into something utterly distinctive of his own. He had seen the great blues piano players of the South—Sunnyland Slim, Memphis Slim, Champion Jack Dupree—at the colored juke joint in his hometown of Ferriday, Louisiana, that he persisted in hanging around despite the active discouragement of the proprietor, Will Haney, "a great big man, big as a door [who] could just pick you up and sail you like a football if he wanted to." Jerry Lee could talk to you with equal enthusiasm and authority about Sister Rosetta Tharpe and B.B. King (as a youngster, he liked to say, he followed B.B. King's music "quite desperately. . . . Man, if I could play guitar like B.B. King, I'd be president"), but he could discourse with equal authority on the music of Gene Autry, Bing Crosby, Frank Sinatra, Al Jolson, and Fats Waller, too, and throw in a convincing rendition of Tommy Dorsey's "Boogie Woogie" for good measure.

It was the damnedest thing—in the absence of the first element of discipline or common sense in his private life, he applied the most extraordinary discipline to his playing, starting with when his father mortgaged the family home to buy him a Starck piano and he devoted six, seven, eight hours a day just to practicing. According to family legend, his mother brought him meals at the piano sometimes, and when his younger sisters complained, or failed to grasp why he should get such special treatment when they were forced to work in the fields or do ordinary household chores, he simply announced to them, "I am the great

I AM." Which was not so far from the high self-regard he customarily showed in both his bearing and his music, with his inclination to refer to himself with almost comic grandiloquence (but without a trace of irony) in so many of the songs that he sang. And yet he was so irrepressibly full of fun—there was an impish quality to every aspect of his behavior, from his brash demand for attention to his relentlessly upbeat piano playing—that somehow or another, almost despite himself at times, he couldn't help but engage you.

Sam sometimes just had to scratch his head. He had never encountered such unequivocal self-belief. The way the boy talked about himself. The way he just put himself forward. The way he would argue the Bible at the drop of a hat. And there was no question he knew his Bible. He had attended the Southwestern Bible Institute in Waxahachie, Texas — briefly, he said—until he introduced a boogie-woogie treatment of "My God Is Real" in chapel. He was in short the ultimate original in an atmosphere that sought out, that *prized* originals. He was an original, Sam concluded approvingly, in the absolute meaning of the term. But as proud and self-proclaiming as he might be, Sam knew that this newcomer needed to be carefully nurtured to bring out not just the arrogance but the sensitivity that lay not far beneath the surface. He was a complex person, Sam recognized, yet in many ways one of the most straightforward people you could ever meet. He was, as Sam told Sun historian Martin Hawkins, "an informal person [but] the conditions had to be right. You had to have a good song, of course, but atmosphere is nearly everything else. Jerry had to know that the people around him . . . understood him."

For the time being Sam was committed to simply putting him to work as often as he could in the studio, with Carl Perkins, with this new boy Jack had brought in, Hayden Thompson, with Billy Riley, while Bob Neal started adding him on to Saturday-night bills starring Carl Perkins or Warren Smith in all the little towns nearby. He even played a few club dates in Arkansas with Billy Riley and the guitarist and drummer who had accompanied him on his first record, Roland Janes and Jimmy Van Eaton, after a studio matchup with Riley one week after the "Million Dollar Quartet" session that was just as explosive, and just as disciplined, as the recordings he had made with Carl.

It was Roland, the somewhat reserved, self-reflective guitarist, who brought in the number that they concentrated on at the Riley session.

Roland had a friend named Ray Scott who gave him a demo of a song called "Flyin' Saucers Rock & Roll," and Billy was really tickled by it, so the band worked it up and played it for Sam. Sam liked it just fine—but it needed something more, he said. They needed to sound like they really came from outer space. So Roland kicked it off with the whammy bar and played his solo breaks with lots of string bending, and Jerry Lee contributed a steady-rolling undercurrent, and the sax player, Marvin Pepper, at Sam's prompting screamed loud vocal encouragement. When Sam heard it, Billy said, "he just jumped straight up and said 'Man that's it. You sound like a bunch of little green men from Mars!' He said, 'That'd be a good name for this band, the Little Green Men. That's what we'll put on the record.'" So that's what they called themselves once the record came out at the end of January, and at Sam's direction, they went right out and bought themselves a matching set of green suits at Lansky's in order to be able to better play the part.

Billy's stage act was just as wild as Sonny Burgess'—he rolled on the ground, jumped in the air, one time, in Jonesboro, Arkansas, at Arkansas State, even hung from the rafters by one arm after climbing up on top of the piano, which then fell off the stage, leaving him dangling there. Unfortunately the suits turned out to be made of a worsted material something like pool-table cloth and after a song or two became so heavy with sweat that they felt like they weighed a hundred pounds. Which, when the whole band lay down on their backs on the floor, could cause a little bit of a problem just getting up.

Roland and Jimmy Van Eaton, the drummer, had fully intended to stick with Riley—but he was temperamental and difficult to work for, especially when he was drinking, and despite all of Sam's exhortations and personal assurances that it couldn't miss, the record just didn't look like it was going to be a hit. So when things started picking up for Jerry Lee and he got booked to play Dallas' Big D Jamboree at the end of February, they jumped ship and became the Jerry Lee Lewis band.

They played a little club in Blytheville called the Twin Gables on Friday night, February 22, on the way down. It was just Jerry, his cousin Jay Brown, who had accompanied him to the studio when they cut "Crazy Arms" in November and had by now acquired an electric bass, Roland, and J.M., and the club was barely big enough to accommodate a group of even that size. In fact there was just room for Jerry and J.M. on the bandstand, Jay and Roland had to stand on the floor, and every time J.M.

socked the drums, dust sifted down from the heavy draperies tacked up on the ceiling to deaden the sound, coating the new jackets they had bought to play the Jamboree.

It was a four-hour job, so you really had to throw just about every song you might be able to play together as a band into each set — and then some. Not long into the evening Jerry played a boogie-woogie figure to introduce a song he said he used to sing when he was down in Ferriday, and the band fell in behind him. Before he had even gotten halfway through, Roland said, the people just started going crazy, "bopping all over the floor, you know how they do in Arkansas." And as soon as they finished, the audience wanted to hear it again. "Play that 'Shakin'' song," they kept calling out. "They just loved it, man, they insisted on hearing it over and over." And the same thing happened when they played the Big D the next night and then an upstairs club nearby after the show. "So we all agreed," Roland said, "as soon as we get back to Memphis we need to go and see if Sam will let us cut that. That's a dandy."

The song was "Whole Lot of Shakin' Going On." It had first been recorded in 1955 without any real chart success — or anything like the boogie-woogie approach that Jerry Lee brought to it — by r&b belter Big Maybelle. Jerry had first heard it performed by a Natchez disc jockey named Johnny Littlejohn at the little club across the river from Ferriday where he ordinarily performed, "and he was playing drums and singing, and I stood there and listened, and I said, 'Man, that is fantastic.' I said, 'That's a hit.' And I [started doing] it pretty close to exactly the way he done it. Word for word. The way he [would] say, 'Easy. Let's get down real low. Stand it in one spot, and wiggle it around a little bit.' I picked it up from — I didn't *steal* it. I just kind of took it!"

When they played it for Sam, he didn't hesitate for a minute. Memories differ, but if they didn't cut it on the spot, they went back into the studio the next day, and after four or five takes they had it.

There has never been a more breathtakingly iconic moment. Jerry kicked the rhythm off, just the way he always did — it was at heart a boogie-woogie number after all — with J. M. Van Eaton's drums and Roland's muted guitar coming in close behind. But where in the early takes the vocal is mannered, almost as if the singer is not fully committed to a consistency of approach, with tempo flirting with the frenetic, and the piano wavering in its attack, the final take exudes a sense of pure command and rumbling authority that, as brilliant as all of his previous studio extemporizations may have been, had never been altogether realized before.

This sense of authority is unmistakably aided by the liberal application of slapback not just to the vocal but to the piano as well—and by the almost total eradication of J. W. Brown's electric bass, which had been disconcertingly present in earlier takes. Most of all, there is a sense of sheer uninhibited fun, underscored by a selective use of glissando and the controlled variations of tone achieved in both the recording and performing process. When Jerry swings into his first solo with an "Aww, let's go," the record takes off, though nothing physically changes, and then when he calls out "Ro, boy," to invite Roland's string-bending solo, there is simply no turning back.

The record concludes with the Johnny Littlejohn spoken passage that may well take its original inspiration from Clarence "Pine Top" Smith's 1929 classic, "Pine Top's Boogie Woogie," in which the singer is directing similar double entendres at an unseen audience, who are bidden to dance to the music at his direction. ("Now when I say, 'Hold yourself,'" says Pine Top. "I want you to get ready to stop/And when I say, 'Git it,' I want you to shake that thing.") In this case Jerry, after directing the band to "get real low one time now," turns his attention to one particular, imagined girl, whom he exhorts to "kind of stand in one spot, wiggle around just a little bit," before concluding, "That's when you *got* something." At which point he turns his attention back to the band, delivering a single irrefutable command ("Now let's go one time") before capping the exuberantly throbbing finale with yet another glissando.

Neither J.M. nor Roland had any point of comparison in their musical experience. They were, unquestionably, participants in the process, they were undeniably contributors—but there was no doubt in either of their minds that, without in any way underestimating their own contributions, they had never encountered such genius before, and they doubted that they ever would again. To Sam, what it all came down to was that Jerry had found his voice, that, for all of the insecurity that Sam suspected lay just beneath the swagger, "he had that basic sureness about what he was doing. And he believed that what he was doing was good." For Jack, whose recollection of the moment was as poetically true as it was factually fogged, "We'd been working and working on a song I wrote called 'It'll Be Me,' and it was getting a little stale, and the bass player spoke up and said, 'Hey, Jerry, let's do that song we've been doing on the road that everybody likes so much. So I said, 'Okay, well, let me go turn on the machine.' So I walk in the control room and sit down [just as] they're playing the chord, and we did it. No dry run, no nothing, just BLAP, there's 'Whole Lot of Shakin'.' One take. Now *that* was fun."

Maybe that's the best description of how it actually happened, even if there were in fact at least three or four alternate takes, because that's what it sounds like. For all the discipline that was required, for all the careful attention to feel and sound, it came out as pure and unself-conscious as if it *were* a first take, as if it could never have been anything but what it was. It was the perfect definition of everything that Sam strove for in his "little laboratory of sound": a thoroughly professional recording that sounded as if it had been put together with a minimum of polish and a maximum of spontaneity.

B UT EVEN THAT was not enough to keep the band together. Jerry's thirty-year-old cousin Jay, whom Jerry was still staying with in a household that included Jay's wife and two kids, was clearly going to stick it out. But for Roland and J.M., the trip to Dallas had tested the limits of their patience — at least for the time being. They didn't hold it against Jerry — neither one of them thought there was a malicious bone in his body, but he was just too difficult to deal with sometimes, he was as jumpy as a hyperactive child. He didn't really mean anything by it, said Roland, always an appreciative student of human nature, "but he would argue with a signboard, just for the sake of arguing. I don't think he cared one way or the other, he just liked to argue. So we got in a big argument on the way back from the Big D Jamboree. We were talking about picking cotton, and I said, 'Yeah I can pick three hundred pounds of cotton a day'—which I could when I was a kid. Jerry said nobody could pick three hundred pounds of cotton a day. I said, 'Hell, they can. I did.' I was pretty serious-minded [in those days], and I didn't like nobody telling me what I just said wasn't true. I wouldn't have said it if it wasn't true. So we quit," Roland concludes, still amused at the memory "and stayed with Riley."

But those were the hazards of the road. Roy Orbison had had his whole band quit on the spot just two months earlier over the question of money and credits. (The drummer, Billy Pat Ellis, had not been listed as cowriter on the B-side of the first single, "Go Go Go," and the record label, and all the publicity, focused on "Roy Orbison," not "The Teen

Kings," as the rest of the band felt had been agreed from the start.) The money, of course, went with the credits, and while the band had all believed that any income derived from their recordings would be split equally five ways, that was not the way it worked out.

They were playing a session in mid-December when the band, the same boys Roy had come up with from Texas, just walked out, loading up the Cadillac that was the symbol of their success with all their instruments and heading home to form a new band. The session was salvaged when Sam called J.M. to come in and play drums ("Mr. Phillips called me *personally* — usually Jack would call — and I thought, 'Boy, this is the real do!'") and got Roland and Stan Kesler to play guitar and bass — but Roy was devastated. After the session Roy came back to the house with Sam, and he stayed there for about a month with his fifteen-year-old girlfriend, Claudette.

None of Sam's artists had ever stayed with him before — it was clearly against his principles. But this was a special case. Roy was so brokenhearted that Sam knew "the one thing for me to do was to stay as close to him [as I could], and I'd either drive him crazy or make him forget about the fact and that it was not going to be a fatal shot. Roy liked to cry real easy, he felt he had been [so] let down — and I told him I hated that they left, but we couldn't overcome that. I said, 'Roy, those fellows just don't know how much fun they're missing. You know, we're going to have some fun. Hey, the fun has just *started!* Maybe they don't know that — so we shouldn't be too mad at them.'"

For Knox, eleven at the time and, like his eight-year-old brother, a devoted follower of rock 'n' roll, it was a real-life education of a different order from his visits to the studio or Elvis' late-night swoops upon the family. "It was the first time I actually could see Sam giving someone he really cared about like Roy some hard advice — I mean, I was real young, but I thought, 'You know what? It's a different way he's saying it but it's the same advice he's been giving me. It's the same thing.'"

For Knox there was something genuinely comforting, even inspiring, in seeing the broader lesson that his father was trying to impart — and to understand that the gulf of expectations that he feared all those lofty moral precepts could create, the perceived distance that he felt he might never be able to bridge with a father he wished so much he could have had more to himself, did not really exist. "That was the first time I actually knew that Sam was just trying to make people better. I mean, he wasn't in the studio trying to inspire [anyone] or record them. He could say the same thing that would teach you the same lesson if you were talking to him about charcoal or motorcycles. It was the same lesson. So after that — it was the first time I ever felt like [one of] his artists. I felt no different than Roy Orbison. I saw no difference in Jerry Lee Lewis and me. I mean, they were his story, and his fundamental, foundational message" — and as he recollects the moment some fifty years later, Knox, like any son who has lost his father, starts to cry — "his fundamental, foundational message was through music, and it worked with life, and it seemed like it always would."

For Marion Keisker, though, there could be no such comfort. She still loved Sam, she always would, desperately, in her own ironically self-lacerating fashion, but they had at last come to a bitter parting of the ways. In language almost shocking both in its coarseness and lack of circumspection, Marion told me in our first conversation in 1981, "He just put boot to butt and set me out on Union Avenue." In that same conversation she stressed that she was "just his slave — there's no other way to put it" but made clear that it was by no other choice than her own. Sally was still trying to maintain a careful neutrality around Marion, who continued to see her as little more than "a sweet little girl in petticoats up out of Mississippi," who was being taken advantage of by Sam. But from Sally's point of view, "it just got to the point where Sam and Marion could not work together under any circumstances, and Marion just didn't know what to do." She came into the studio less and less frequently, and when she did, she was short-tempered with the artists, and her mood with Sam alternated between tears and rage. "She was just so devastated and upset," Sally observed, "and they were fighting all the time, and Sam finally said, 'I can't do it anymore,' so it happened, and it was [for the] best, I guess."

Marion left both the studio and the radio station in February of 1957, at the end of the month, with no more idea of what do next than she had had when she and Sam first entered the storefront location some seven and one-half years earlier. Without the cause of Sam to dedicate herself to she drifted around for the next six months. She got another job in radio, but her heart wasn't in it. But then, as Bob Johnson reported in his August 21 column in the newspaper, she joined the Air Force to see the world. "She was driving around about 3 one morning," Johnson wrote, "in a blue and pensive mood . . . when this public service announcement about the glorious life the Air Force offered came on. 'All at once I realized that it was me they were talking about,' she said." So she took her comprehensive tests and went in with a captain's commission. Her son, she told Johnson, would live with her sister in Cuyahoga Falls, Ohio, and she was soon dispatched to Germany, where she served as information officer in charge of the Armed Forces television station at the Ramstein base, where she was stationed. It would be another twelve years before she returned to Memphis, with a renewed commitment to feminism and acting (she was a founding member of the Memphis chapter of the National Organization for Women and one of the leading lights in Memphis professional theater), as well as a concern for the first time for her own place in history.

S AM PUT OUT Jerry Lee's new record at the end of April while Jerry was in the midst of a "broken" two-month tour with Carl Perkins and Johnny Cash. There was considerable feeling, both within the company and without, that "Whole Lot of Shakin'" might just be too "vulgar" for the market (Johnny Cash always liked to recall how he begged Sam to push the other side, Jack's composition "It'll Be Me," as if to mock his own lack of commercial astuteness), but Sam never wavered, and the record sold strongly from the start.

Carl for his part never hazarded an opinion about the record. He was increasingly mired in a state of angry self-pity, as his records stopped selling, his older brother Jay's headaches, seemingly the result of their terrible automobile accident on the way to *The Perry Como Show* just one year earlier, were getting worse and worse, and he himself, as he would freely admit in later years, fell into what seemed like an inescapable pattern of drinking and denial that left him ashamed and dissatisfied with both himself and his work. But more than anything he just felt sorry for himself, as he watched brash newcomers like Billy Riley and Jerry Lee Lewis going past him, and he felt more and more personal resentment at Mr. Phillips welling up within. After all, wasn't he the one on whose hit record the success of this company had been built, he was the one Sam had given the Cadillac to—and he was the one Sam had called right after he sold Elvis' contract and told, with no hint of a closing date, "You're my rocker now."

If he could have been objective about it, as he was more than willing to admit in later years, he might have conceded that the company was

Sally Wilbourn. *Courtesy of the Sam Phillips Family*

probably doing all it could. His latest single, "Matchbox" backed with "Your True Love," a cheerful easy-rocking ballad that Sam had speeded up on tape so that he and his brothers (who provided an echoing chorus) sounded like a bunch of teenagers, had gotten a lead "Spotlight" review in Billboard, and Sam had followed up with a half-page ad two weeks later headlined "That Sensational Carl Perkins Boy Has Done the Impossible Again." Nor had Sam given up on the record, continuing to take out ads and pitch distributors long after it was evident that the single was never really going to break through.

The tour took them on great jumps through the South, Midwest, Texas, and Canada, as they wore out a late-model Lincoln (Johnny Cash and the Tennessee Two), Buick (Jerry Lee, his cousin Jay, and their new drummer, Sonny Burgess' old drummer Russ Smith), and Cadillac (the Perkins boys) on roads that in Canada were sometimes not even paved. Most of the dates went well, there were good paydays for Cash and Perkins, but at $100 a day for the trio, Jerry Lee was doing his best to break even. Carl continued to be irritated at Lewis' smug self-confidence, at what he took to be an almost insufferable compulsion to show off his own arrogance — but he was a helluva showman, even Carl had to admit, whether or not he rubbed everyone else the same way.

One of the early stops on the tour, almost needless to say, was the Community Center in Sheffield, just across the river from Florence, where Sam had started every one of his artists, beginning with Elvis. Cash, Perkins, and Jerry Lee played there on April 2, with Carl's record at number 82 on the pop charts and Jerry's still waiting to be released. Some of Sam's family showed up, including his brother Jud, who was operating a used-car lot in Sheffield. Carl and John both knew Jud and were struck like everyone else by his irrepressible high spirits, but Jerry, with irrepressible high spirits of his own, didn't know a thing about him and might not have even noticed if Jud had not put himself directly in his line of vision. "I was walking offstage, and I looked, and I saw this man standing there — and it was just like looking at Sam Phillips. I knew they had to be relatives. And he told me, 'I'm Jud Phillips, Sam's brother,' and he walked me on down to the dressing room." There he told Jerry that he thought he was the most talented young man he had ever seen in all his years in show business, and he was going to tell Sam just that, and then, after calling his wife, Dean, who remonstrated that they had nothing in the house to eat but sardines, he asked Jerry and the rest of the troupe back to his house.

When they arrived, Jerry made a beeline for the piano, sat down, and simply started playing—touching on everything in his repertoire from Gershwin to Muddy Waters. As the rest of the crew sipped on their drinks and ate sardines and onions on crackers, Jud was mesmerized. If he had been impressed before, now he was truly sold. "I saw something in Jerry Lee Lewis," he told Sun historian Martin Hawkins, "that I had never seen in any [other] artist. When he went to the piano in my little living room and started playing and I heard him play tunes like [Artie Shaw's] 'Summit Ridge Drive,' tunes that you wouldn't believe that this guy had in his repertoire, I thought in my mind, 'Now this cat is not a cat that's just well rehearsed, that's picked up on one or two tunes and [has them] down to perfection. This guy has got depth. It's just a matter of bringing this into focus. And attempting to merchandise and get a reaction.'"

"He told me," said Jerry Lee, "just where we could go and how we could go and what we could do." Then he told Sam. And that was how, a couple of months later, in the middle of June, Jud came back into the company.

Sam might have needed to be sold — but he didn't need to be over-sold. He knew what his brother could do. He knew his brother's flair and creativity, his sheer likability. And he knew Jud was right about the new Jerry Lee Lewis record. He had never believed in anything more. And with Marion gone, and things looking as if they were finally starting to pick up again after the lull that had followed Carl Perkins' "three-way" hit, he knew he could use help now more than ever. He might have gravitated initially toward Bob Neal — Bob was a solid, sober-minded family man, with a hardworking wife and a brood of seven — but maybe that was just the trouble. Bob, as Sam had by now concluded, lacked both imagination and common sense. Sam had set him up in a business that should have been a gold mine, but to Sam's utter consternation the damn cat was losing money. Dewey might have been more to Sam's liking, but clearly Dewey, for all of his frenetic inventiveness, fueled all the more now by his dependence on alcohol and pills, was not the kind of person you could go to for everyday chores. So as of June 19 he announced that he had hired a National Sales and Promotion Director and, with understandable misgiving — and the same tincture of love and irritation that Jud always seemed to bring out in him — gave his brother the credit cards that he needed for the job.

By then Jerry's record was poised to enter the national pop charts, selling up to thirteen hundred copies a week in Memphis alone before hitting number 1 on *Billboard*'s Territorial Best Seller list on June 3 ("The platter is taking off like wildfire," *Billboard* reported in a C&W Best Buys review, "Tho in release only a short while, all areas list it as a top seller"), when Jud came up with his idea. They both knew, Jud said, that Jerry was tearing up the stage night after night on tour — in Billings and Beaumont and Des Moines and Duluth. That was all very well, but at this rate it might take them two years to break a star that, as Sam hardly had to be reminded, was as bright as any in the firmament. What if, Jud said, he took the boy to New York and pitched him to Ed Sullivan, pitched him to Steve Allen (these were the hosts of the two top-rated Sunday-night variety shows), not on the basis of a runaway hit record but on the basis of talent alone. It was, clearly, an unconventional strategy — everyone else waited for national sales to light the way — but this was an unconventional talent, unconventional, he might have added if he thought he needed anything further to convince his brother, *in the extreme*.

Sam didn't need any further convincing. He could see Jud's point just as surely as he could see the expense account mounting up, and, with his usual admonishments to Jud about keeping the spending down, even as he recognized their utter futility, he gave his brother the go-ahead. So Jud put out some feelers, and he and Jerry flew to New York, where Jud had booked a luxury suite at the Hotel Delmonico on Park Avenue.

After a few calls, Jud got a fifteen-minute appointment with Steve Allen's manager, Jules Green, and Henry Frankel, NBC's talent coordinator, on a Friday afternoon. He and Jerry walked in, and Frankel's first question was, "Well, Jud, what can you let me have? Have you got any pictures or records?" Jud told him no, and Frankel turned to Green and said, "How do you like that? That's the first time we've had a salesman come in here without anything to sell."

Jerry by his own account was just sitting there chewing bubblegum and reading a Superman comic book, while Jud told the two men he had brought them "the most dynamic new thing in the music business" and that they had to watch him perform because "this is an action artist!"

"The man," recalled Jerry, "looked at Jud like he was crazy. I just sat there blowing bubblegum. This guy looked at me, and I looked at him. Finally he said, 'Okay, kid, let's see you play piano and sing.' I walked over to the piano, and this guy sat down and put his feet up on his desk like he was going to get a big laugh. The minute I started in on 'Whole Lot of Shakin'', this guy came up out of his chair and got down behind me and just crouched down looking over my shoulder the whole time I was playing. When I finished, he said to Jud, 'I'll give you $500 if you don't show him to anyone else. And bring him back first thing Monday morning. I want Steve to hear him.'"

They stuck around for the weekend — Jerry got to ride the Coney

Island roller coaster—and after meeting with Allen and solidifying a booking for the end of July, they went home. With the record at number 30 on the pop charts, Sam placed a half-page ad in the July 15 issue of *Billboard,* announcing that there was "gonna be a whole lot of shaking going on on the STEVE ALLEN TV Program on July 28," and three days before that date, he and Jerry took the train to New York.

They argued about the Bible the entire way. It was, said Sam, all in good fun—Jerry knew more about the Bible than he did anyway. Once there, they went right over to NBC's midtown rehearsal studio, and Steve was busy, so Jerry marched over to the little spinet at the back of the hall and sat down and began playing. But not just playing, Sam noted with a little bit of shock, he just started pounding that piano, as if he were determined to convert everybody in the room before he even got on the show. "I didn't expect him to whack down on that piano [like that], I mean Steve was talking to someone just five paces [away]." Sam was a little alarmed—"I mean, this was the great Steve Allen, I mean this cat was hot"—and when Allen turned around and cut off the conversation, "I thought he was fixing to holler at Jerry Lee, or [both of] us—I mean, Steve had a way of sometimes being a little abrupt—but he just said he had never heard anything like that, and he could not wait till Jerry Lee got on the show."

Jerry Lee's appearance surpassed all expectations. Sitting at a white grand piano whose turned up key-cover had a mirror to reflect Jerry's acrobatic pianistics, he gave what can only be called an all-out performance, if all-out suggests starting at a hundred miles an hour and accelerating from there. Dressed in black pants, white belt and white shoes and a striped short-sleeve shirt with rolled up sleeves, his blond hair was cut short in back but piled up on top in long curly locks that cascaded forward in waves as he threw himself into the performance. With the drummer set up in back, and Jay swaying from side to side as he played an almost entirely unnecessary electric bass, Jerry Lee Lewis was the whole show, eyes rolling, feet flying, mouth constantly agape while his hands madly raked the keyboard and his expression suggested a casual cruelty that was only belied by the mischievous inventiveness of his playing. It was, a visitor from outer space, or just an everyday adult, might have thought, an occasion somewhere between a cheerfully satanic cult gathering and a religious revival conducted in a kind of self-possessed trance. And when at the end he sent the piano stool (actually a chair) flying offstage as he stood up and flung himself into the final verse, perhaps the comedic high point of a characteristically comedic show was reached when the chair came flying back, and Steve Allen, presumably the propeller of the chair, came ambling on with a grin on his face to congratulate the nation's newest star.

He signed Jerry to an immediate second appearance on August 11, with a third scheduled for the fall. The record exploded, just as Jud had predicted it would, almost immediately bringing the label's overall record sales back to its previous peak of close to a million singles a quarter, a level Sun had not come close to achieving since "Blue Suede Shoes" had dominated the charts more than a year earlier. By September 9 it had reached number 1 on the country and r&b charts, falling just short in the pop field, where in one of the great miscarriages of musical justice it was eclipsed by Canadian teenager Paul Anka's saccharine "Diana" and film actress Debbie Reynolds' even more saccharine "Tammy."

While they were still in New York, Jerry was signed to an appearance in the upcoming rock 'n' roll film *Jamboree* (it would "star" Fats Domino along with various other lesser luminaries, while cannily inserting spot announcements from at least fifteen well-known DJs to promote their own shows and locales), and Jud took him to Jack Dempsey's restaurant on Broadway, where Jerry met the former heavyweight champ. He was also signed to a number of appearances on Alan Freed's blockbuster "Big Beat" rock 'n' roll revues as well as a booking at Harlem's famed Apollo Theater in September, which might have proved a challenge to any other white rock 'n' roller but according to his own testimony did not faze Jerry Lee in the least.

Meanwhile Sam took advantage of being in New York by grabbing the opportunity to announce to the world at large the formation of a brand-new label, Phillips International. It would be very different from Sun, Sam declared, "more general in its repertoire [and] scope," and it would undoubtedly take "three or four years to build [the] international sales web" it would need to reach its intended goal of worldwide success. It would in a sense be analogous to WHER in its emphasis on variety and breadth, and in its conscious courtship of a more diverse, grown-up audience.

"Announcing a New World of Entertainment," the brochure that was being put together to accompany the launch would soon proclaim. The "Sam C. Phillips International Label" was but "the latest outgrowth of [the] idea" that its founder had originally had: "(1) to develop new [and] unknown talent…and (2) to bring universal acceptance to the country and race music which a majority of people either shunned or furtively enjoyed when there was no one around to take note."

The new venture would be "devoted also to the development of new talent" but, although many of the first releases might be rock and roll, "future plans call for a wide variety of music, including standard pop and jazz," with every artist possessing his own "individual 'sound'— a production element which Sam Phillips personally and constantly looks for, produces, and insists upon in any record." Music, everyone who worked at Phillips International firmly believed, "is the international language — can make friends, bridge the geographical and cultural barriers, and perhaps promote a bit of international understanding." And while Sam was unquestionably the catalyst, there were others involved, including Jack Clement, Sally Wilbourn, and "brother Jud Phillips, Sales and Promotion Director of Sun and Phillips International, a man behind the scenes, but a powerful factor nonetheless."

With respect to its founder, in a biographical sketch that appeared to lean heavily on the autobiographical, Sam was described as "his own best press agent — personable and friendly.... 'Dynamic' is the key word in the thirty-four-year life-to-date of Sam C. Phillips. For Sam life has been an adventure — marked by change, change, change." After detailing his history, background ("like so many intellectually inclined persons, Sam took an intense interest in religion in his early years"), and appearance ("like his manner informal and relaxed"), the account focused on a description of the man himself. "Sam says, 'You don't have to figure me out. I'm the simplest man you ever met.'" Which might have been evident on casual acquaintance, the anonymous author was willing to concede, but "spend some time with him, and you'll observe that he has a mind that gathers, sorts, and assimilates facts like an IBM machine; a powerful will that pushes right through to its goal looking neither to the left nor to the right; tenacity like a snapping turtle; and a strong, strong self-confiden[ce] that likes challenge above all things."

All true enough. And there were, certainly, high hurdles ahead. A number of industry eyebrows were raised by the scope and ambition of what clearly remained if not a one-man operation an operation firmly under the control of one man, and some even questioned the very name of the new label not just for its grandiosity but for its challenge to the international Philips Electronics, a Dutch company that was the foremost electronics and appliance manufacturer in the world and had since the early 1950s developed one of the leading record companies in Europe, with American distribution through Columbia. Sam didn't see the problem. If Philips wanted to come into the American market under its own name, as he had heard that they might, well, Phillips International (with a double "l") was there first.

ONE OF THE FIVE ARTISTS to be featured in the new label's initial release, scheduled for the fall, was Bill Justis, the Memphis Recording Service's newest employee. Justis, the son of a well-known Memphis roofing contractor, a university graduate, tennis player, and onetime member of the country-club set, was a thirty-year-old jive-talking jazz aficionado who, after playing the trumpet for many years, had taken up saxophone and formed one of Memphis' leading society bands. Until recently he had expressed nothing but hipster scorn for rock 'n' roll, which he dismissed as the new barbarism ("Strictly squaresville, girls," he might have said to the trained musicians in his band), but he had been converted by a simple awakening to the opportunity that democracy and capitalism provided to even the unwashed and unskilled. He read an article about Buck Ram, the accomplished composer, arranger, and big-band veteran, who guided, managed, and virtually owned the r&b harmony group the Platters (the Platters had over the last few years enjoyed chart-topping crossover success with songs he had written, like "Only You" and "The Great Pretender"). Although the records possessed the kind of sophisticated arranging skills that he might well have valued, it's unclear just what Bill Justis thought of the Platters' sweepingly romantic music. But there was one thing, he said, that struck him in his perusal of the story: how much money Buck Ram was making. That was when he went out and bought $80 worth of rock 'n' roll records for analysis and study and promptly discovered how "simple, yet basic and savage" the music was and, at the same time, how "difficult to perform."

"Since May," Bob Johnson wrote in his much-read *Press-Scimitar* column, "Bill's orchestra has been playing a lot of rock 'n' roll for teen dances." It was sometime in this period that he was hired, whether by Sam or Jack Clement, to arrange a session at Sun, and after hearing it, Sam complimented him on his work "and asked me to come see him sometime." Not long afterward he did, and Sam offered him a job at

$90 a week as "Musical Director," which meant, Justis explained to writer Martin Hawkins, that mostly he did arrangements, and, since few of the musicians could read, "I did a lot of arranging." And, soon, overdubbing as well, both voices and instruments, which suited Jack's inclination toward novelty numbers and his ambition to expand the Sun sound.

Jack, who was still getting only $65 a week, may have been the primary vehicle for his introduction, and was certainly his most frequent musical collaborator, not to mention partner in pranks — but it was, oddly enough, Sam who provided the inspiration. Sam, said Justis, a man clearly not inclined to encomiums or, for that matter, open displays of emotion, "created enthusiasm in everything he did. When he talked, you *had* to listen. He could get you charged up to knock your brains out for Sun Records." He possessed a gift for persuasion, of which Justis would ordinarily have been highly suspicious — but in this case he admitted he was as swayed as the inexperienced young artists and writers with whom he now found himself working.

The other musicians looked more than slightly askance as this bald-headed beanie-wearing self-styled and venerable outsider, who called them by nicknames of his own devising, addressed them collectively as "kiddies" or "little girls," and gave them sometimes indecipherable directions like "stop bugging the mike." But they soon grew used to him, as he invited them to collaborate with schooled members of his "orchestra," like guitarist Sid Manker, an accomplished jazz musician who gave lessons to half the up-and-coming young players in Memphis.

One night in early summer, events were taking their own increasingly familiar, semi-anarchic course. With Sam gone, according to Jack Clement's recollection, he and Justis had been working on some material with little success for much of the night: "It was about three o'clock in the morning, everybody was stewed, and we were about to quit." Then Bill said, "We got this thing we've been doing in the clubs" — it wasn't much more than a riff that he and his guitarist, Sid Manker, had cooked up — but Sid took the lead, and Roland Janes, the one musician in the room who was decidedly not "stewed," mostly played rhythm, and because the saxophone player who Bill had wanted to play the part was sick, Justis himself played sax. That was the reason, Justis said, whether by way of explanation or as an excuse, for the "off-tone. I was [so] out-of-shape on the sax, but I think that was what helped to sell it."

Sam was knocked out when he came in and heard the song for the first time. It probably had little to do with the five different melodies that Bill claimed existed in counterpoint within the song, or with the horn overdubs that Bill and Jack would later add. "My God," Sam said, "it just blew me away. [Just] three chords in it, like most of my stuff. That's all I wanted. That's enough." What was it called? he asked Justis. Its working title was "Raunchy," Justis said, explaining that when they had got done playing it, he had said to the fellows, "sort of kiddingly, 'Well, that sounded real raunchy.'" So that was what he thought he'd call it. Sam didn't bat an eye over a title that he knew would invite a lot of criticism over a word with explicit (and somewhat seamy) sexual connotations. In fact, he got kind of a kick out of it. That's it, he said emphatically. Bad connotations or not, "that's exactly what that record is!" He wanted to put it out yesterday, if possible — but his cooler head prevailed, and he decided to save it for the debut release of his new label in the fall.

THERE WAS ANOTHER NEW EMPLOYEE at Sun that summer in another, newly created position. Barbara Barnes, a twenty-four-year-old University of Alabama graduate from Corinth, Mississippi, who had been working in telephone sales at WMCT TV, after interviewing with the newswire service UPI for a job. Leo Soroka, the head of Memphis' UPI bureau, whom Sam had called along with Bob Johnson to witness the Million Dollar Quartet session, hadn't had a position for her at the time, but he remembered her when Sam mentioned that he was looking for someone to handle the ever-increasing volume of copy writing and publicity generated by the label. Sam was immediately impressed by this accomplished and ambitious young woman, who would go on to become a college English professor, and offered her a full-time job on the spot. Barnes for her part was not so sure. Although she found Sam himself to be "the most interesting person, full of energy, [with that] intense stare that he had," she felt that she didn't know enough about either him or the record business to cast her lot with Sun for life — even though, in his low-key but decidedly evangelical way, that was exactly what he seemed to want her to do. But she could, certainly, commit herself to working for him in a temporary position, writing liner notes for the long-playing albums he was planning to release on Johnny Cash and Carl Perkins in the fall, the company's first, and, under his direction, putting together the text for the brochure that he was assembling for his new Phillips International label, which would provide an introduction both to the label and to him.

It was she who was the nominal author of the unsigned biographical profile that introduced the booklet. ("Now," she wrote, after Sam himself had told the Sun story so many times, "someone else is getting a chance to tell the story. This account is biased only in that—I like Sam and I believe in Sam, almost as much as Sam believes in Sam.") And if some might have suggested that all this self-belief might be bordering on megalomania, what Barbara found most refreshing about her interaction with her new boss was his willingness to *listen*. As a radio-television journalism major with scarcely any professional prospects, she was well aware of the limited opportunities available to women, not to mention all the patronizing slights that so many men could throw out without even recognizing the offense that they were causing. But Sam, for all of his jaunty self-confidence, was, in Barbara's view, "really sort of a humble person. Not like what I saw on TV in later years [when] he had lost that quality that I remember most. But then he had a humility that to me was very, very appealing and touching (not always—he *did* like oratory!) but he treated his employees so well in so many ways, in ways that other people might not have. In a lot of cases he would defer to me, ask me what I was going to do, or what I thought, or what I had decided. And it was a very strange phenomenon in the work world."

In other ways Sam and Sun looked a little bit like something out of the Wild West to her when she first went to work there. It was, she wrote in amazement, like so many visitors before and since, "like a shotgun hole-in-the-wall wedged between a greasy spoon and a used-car lot, and was completely surrounded by Cadillacs. There was a pale neon sign in front of the dusty and dilapidated blinds. . . . Inside the door was a reception area with two desks, where the secretary, Sally Wilbourn, and the stenographer, Regina Reese [another recent hire], worked. When Sam came in, he usually stood up or sat on the short sofa between the two desks." That was yet another reason she turned down the full-time job at first: the sorry state of the physical plant. There was no place for her to even contemplate running a full-scale promotion office. But Sun was in the process of rapid transformation, she quickly realized, even as she stuck to her original resolve.

Marion, too, had noted that the surest way to find the Memphis

Recording Service location was to look for "the chicken coop nested in Cadillacs." Barbara saw Marion only once, just before she joined the military, when she came into the office "in a state"—but Barbara never found out the reason for her state, in fact she was never introduced, and Sam wasn't inclined to gossip. She heard plenty about Marion from Jud, though, who called in from the road every morning just about the time she got in, and was quick to tell her how dependent Sam had been on Marion to begin with, financially and otherwise. The owners of the building, Mr. Hanover and Mr. Vigland, would come in from time to time, seemingly to assess the state of things and, as Sun's fortunes improved, to raise the rent a little—but the rent was still only $150 a month, and, with the exception of Jud's promotion expenses, there was no excessive spending in any area of the business. The reception area, it was true, was finally air-conditioned—but the air conditioner leaked on almost everyone who came in. And Sam's attitude simply seemed to be that if he had simple needs, everyone else could content themselves with simple satisfactions as well. He didn't need a fancy office. He didn't need to impress anyone with *appearances*. He was aware that the major record companies up till now had shown nothing but contempt for everything he believed in. He was aware that they had all just laughed at him and all the other independent record companies. But while they laughed, "while their eyes were closed to us who were hungry [but] knew what we were doing and weren't shackled by corporate routines, we grew beyond [anything that] they expected."

He wasn't going to change his way of doing business. He wasn't going to saturate the market, he wasn't going to do like his good friend, Randy Wood, of Dot Records in Gallatin, Tennessee, and press up more records than he was certain he could sell. He made it plain to his distributors that he would stick with the records he put out. He wasn't going to put out a bunch of records he didn't believe in. "We could have probably sold twice what we did, but the returns would have been up, and we would have started getting careless." No matter what Jud or anybody else said, he simply wasn't going to operate that way.

He was meticulous, as Barbara quickly became aware, in everything he did. He paid his bills scrupulously and knew and accounted for every record sold. He had no interest in raiding other labels for talent. And he treated her the same in salary and responsibility—and the degree of autonomy he was willing to give her in dealing with distributors and vendors — as he did any man: it was all about who could do the job. She had never met anyone quite like Sam before, every day was like a new adventure that she couldn't wait to tell her roommate about when she got home from work. She couldn't believe that one person could operate so effectively, so *motivationally*, in so many different spheres at once. She thought sometimes he was like a spring so tightly wound he must surely snap, "wiry," in the sense that the term must first have originated. It seemed to her sometimes like "he almost had too much energy for one body."

S OME OF THAT ENERGY was dissipated that summer in rare moments of relaxation around the twenty-by-forty-foot pool that he had just had built to his own very exacting specifications in the spacious back-yard. With an eight-and-one-half-foot deep end, it was two and one-half feet deeper than any built in Memphis up till that time, and he had a new stone wall built with the same difficult-to-obtain red mortar that set off the adobe bricks of the rest of the house. He still made a point of telling interviewers that he worked sixteen hours a day — and on many days he may well have. But with Jack and Bill Justis running many of the sessions, and a capable staff to take care of everyday correspondence and distributor and pressing-plant orders, some days he might not come in till midafternoon, though there was never any question of his authority when he did. The boys practically lived in the pool that summer ("No matter who came over," Knox said, "Jerry could outdive them and I could outswim them"), and Sam took great pleasure in the pool, and great pride, too. On Sam's recommendation Elvis employed the same company, Paddock of California, to build his pool on the fourteen-acre country estate he had just purchased for over $100,000 out on Highway 51 South, near the Mississippi state line. He was also using the same decorator, George Golden, who he knew had done such a great job for Sam at the house on Mendenhall.

Elvis was home in Memphis for most of the summer and came by the house frequently to play pinball, shoot bumper pool, listen to music on the sophisticated hi-fi system that Sam had built in the den, or just generally shoot the shit. It didn't matter what time of night Elvis arrived, Becky would always wake the boys. He'd show up at midnight as often as not, usually with a bunch of his friends, and, Knox fondly recalled,

Elvis and the boys. *Courtesy of the Sam Phillips Family*

"Mother would come back to our bedroom and say, 'Boys, Elvis is here. Do you want to get up?'" Then he and his eight-year-old brother would get dressed and find their way into the den, where Elvis would be "slinking around the pool table like a cat, and we would just try to imitate his coolness by osmosis — I mean we both had ducktails, and we bought our clothes at Lansky's and had black velvet added to the top of our sports coat lapels to look like him. But the most extraordinary thing about him, I realize now, had nothing to do with externals. It was the way he made everyone around him feel like they belonged, the way he might squeeze your shoulder when you were playing pinball with him or look at you like you really had something to say." One time, Knox would never forget, "Elvis leaned over and hugged me and he just said, 'Stay with me, Knox, stay with me.'

"Elvis loved my mother's scrambled eggs, he really did love them — he loved my *mother* is what it was." The thing that Becky always liked to remember most was serving breakfast with the sun coming up over the patio, and Elvis giving her a kiss on the cheek, "and the smell of fresh coffee was in the air, and all the people around were so sleepy and ready to call it a night, and we always hated to see them go." Sam certainly shared all of those feelings, but the story you were most likely to hear from him in later years, especially in the presence of the legions of idolatrous Elvis fans whom he seemed to take particular pleasure in dismaying, was the time that Elvis came out to the house one night and he just didn't seem like himself. He was sitting in one of the little swivel rocking chairs by the stone fireplace in the den, and he motioned to Sam to follow him into the living room, where they could have some privacy. There, with Sam's permission, he pulled down his pants and showed him a swelling just above his penis. He was scared to death, he confessed, he thought maybe he had syphilis or something, and he didn't know what to do.

"Well, being an old country boy, I looked at it, and I knew it was a damn carbuncle — we called them an old-fashioned risin'. I said, 'Well, Elvis, how long you had it?' He said, 'Mr. Phillips, it's been there about a month.' I said, 'Elvis, man, with the size that it is and the core that it has in it, it looks like you must have been worrying about this thing for three or four months.'" So he called his doctor, Henry Moskowitz, thinking he might come over and take a look, but Dr. Moskowitz told him to take Elvis down to Baptist Hospital, he'd call ahead and see if they couldn't just take care of it. "As soon as they opened that thing up, boy, that thing popped about two feet in the air!" And on their way back to the house, "Man, you just couldn't shut him up. It was as if he'd been freed from prison after ninety-nine years!"

To friends and family he was the same old Sam, delighting in saying and doing just as he pleased, or maybe simply incapable of acting any other way. To Jimmy Connolly's twenty-year-old daughter, Dot, two years married to a young Birmingham baseball executive of whom her uncle thoroughly approved: "I just never really heard anybody talk like that when I was young." He could express his passion for baseball, civil rights, or the white bathing suit she had with a gold top ("He was always saying, 'That's the prettiest thing I've ever seen. I'm going to hire you to stay in my pool'") with equal enthusiasm and at equal length. "He never took anything bad about anything anybody did. If they worked toward overcoming it and being a better person, that was just a part of their lives no matter what. He was a very accepting person, a very understanding person." Dot's father, Jimmy, Sam's original radio boss and first partner in his radio venture, still visited all the time and remained his closest friend, and they talked all the time about reviving their partnership and getting a radio station of their own in the near future in the Birmingham area, where Jimmy remained general manager at WJLD, an almost entirely black station now.

Friends and relatives back home in Florence were only just beginning to realize how successful he had become, but when he heard from them, he was prepared to drop everything—at least for the moment—and return to an arcadian dream. He summed up his feelings to a Florence newspaper reporter writing the first hometown profile of this "Local Man Who Made Good." "I love Florence like nothing else in the world," he declared, pointing out that it was "one of the cleanest towns morally and physically" that he had ever seen—viewing its future, wrote reporter Lorene Frederick, as "unlimited. 'It has a good balance in farming and industry,' he said, adding almost wistfully, 'you can get off work at 4:30 and be at the dam fishing by 5 o'clock.'"

He was even more specific in his expression of recognition and obligation in a letter he wrote to one of the prominent Florentines named in the story, Dr. Thomas Cloyd, his childhood physician, who was looking for a musical audition for the son of an old friend. ("I don't claim to be any kind of a critic," wrote Dr. Cloyd. "All I can say is this young man is trustworthy, energetic, sober . . .")

"I am delighted to have your nice note," Sam wrote in reply. "I know of no other person that I had rather hear from.

> *I just want to say how many times I've looked back over the many things you did for me — undoubtedly you were one of the biggest influences in my life. In fact I don't know what I would have done without your stable hand and wisdom and your [un]usual professional ability.*

And, of course, it could almost go without saying that "we shall be delighted to show Charles [the young man in question] every courtesy and give him a thorough audition." And should the opportunity arise, "Becky (my wife) and I want you and Mrs. Cloyd to come to Memphis and spend at least the weekend with us. Any time you will your plane or train ticket will be waiting on you." And he signed his heartfelt letter, "Your boy, Sam."

It was perhaps not quite as easy for Knox and Jerry, who observed their father's central role in everybody else's life but sometimes missed

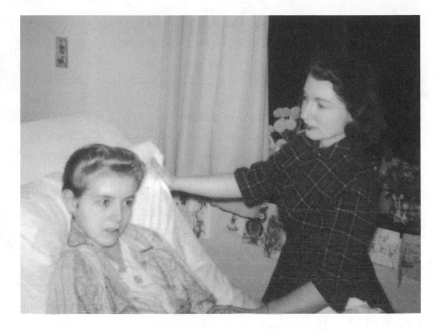

At Baptist Hospital, where Knox was hospitalized for several weeks in February 1958 with acute nephritis. *Courtesy of the Sam Phillips Family*

it in their own. For Knox it appeared to be easier to swallow — he had taken his lesson from observation and absorbed it. For Jerry, more like Sam in both his stubbornness and his reserve, it was undoubtedly harder. Even at eight or nine, with a decided sense of style of his own, he was somewhat wary, even critical of his father's. It wasn't so much that he wanted Sam to be like everyone else's dad (though occasionally there was that) — he wanted his attention. And he was well aware, even resentful to a surprising degree, of how much of that attention seemed to have turned away from his mother.

"My mother — there's no sweeter, more angelic person in the world than my mother, [so] there was no lack of love. I didn't have any wish-my-daddy-was-home-playing-ball-with-me kind of thing. I mean, we come from an era where, you know, the mother stays home and the dad works. So there's nothing unusual — he was an absentee father in a way, but at the same time he was always very much there, in your psyche. I don't ever remember him ruling with any kind of iron fist. But he expected honesty and integrity. He expected fairness. He expected, I won't say he expected excellence, because I don't think he ever was looking for excellence in anybody. He was looking for the unfinished, raw product. And I think he just wanted [Knox and me] to be honorable people that were able to think for themselves and make decisions."

Which, as Jerry recognized even then, was a very tall order.

And yet for Knox and him it was in so many ways an idyllic life. They were, consciously, the children of rock 'n' roll, the products of a freedom that every day was proudly proclaimed at home as well as in the world at large. They had a little tape recorder and would record productions of their own in their shared bedroom, with their mother assisting at the controls and their cousin Dot their intended audience. They each pursued rock 'n' roll fashion in their own way, with their biggest point of contention at this stage as much a matter of internal as fraternal debate over which of Elvis' records they liked best. Or whether, as Jerry Lee Lewis continued his meteoric rise that summer, they were not perhaps equally drawn to Sun's newest star, who would come out to the house sometimes and just dive in the pool, his long blond hair fanning out behind him like a mermaid's.

Becky for her part was just happy to see Sam a little more relaxed. She didn't think about the situation at work — she forced herself to put that out of her mind. Part of her felt that if she could just be the perfect wife and mother, if she could provide Sam with everything he needed and be the person that Sam would always turn to when things didn't go exactly as they should, then somehow or other it would all turn around and everything would go back to the way it was supposed to be. Her religious faith sustained her. It bothered her that Sam no longer went to church as often as he once had — but that was just Sam. He was a good man, she knew. She believed in him no less now than she had on the day they met, his hair full of raindrops and a smile on his face unlike any she had ever seen before.

She still went to work at WHER for her three-hour shift every day Monday through Friday. She still enjoyed working with the girls, and she never stinted in the meticulous preparation of her own shows, but with the station so firmly established (despite only a 1,000-watt signal, it was well on its way to carrying more financial advertising — banks, real estate, and insurance firms — than any other station in town), and with the girls so well trained she didn't need to spend so much of her free time at work anymore, and she treasured the extra time she got to spend at home with her boys. In July *Billboard* reported on a con-

Jerry Lee Lewis, with Knox, Jerry, their cousin Thomas Jefferson Phillips Jr. (at left), and stuffed animals. *Courtesy of the Sam Phillips Family*

tinuing source of wonderment to the industry: "No Sun record will ever be set on a WHER turntable." It was, *Billboard* suggested in a follow-up story, a policy "dictated not by personal taste but by business opportunity." But the reporter did not fail to note the "iconoclastic" tendencies of its owner, who made his claim of musical purity with "puzzling pride [for] a cat to whom many bow as the patron saint of rock and roll."

A recent hire at the station, Bettye Maddox (she would become better known as Bettye Berger after her marriage to Louis Jack Berger, a prominent Memphis businessman, whom she later divorced) was one of the "girls" most likely to flirt with trouble by playing some of the "suggestive" album tracks marked with a big red "X," but she got away with it by either feigning ignorance or falling back on flustered, fluttering confusion. Bettye was beautiful, blond-haired, buxom, a twenty-six-year-old mother of three with a notably breathy voice who had recently gotten divorced. She had been modeling for a number of local businesses, but there wasn't enough steady work, so in November of 1956 she and her roommate had come up with the idea of opening a men's accessory shop at the Peabody, with the sales force drawn exclusively from their model friends, who would serve the men martinis in evening dress. Bettye had read about Sam, about his spirit of freewheeling enterprise — she knew all about WHER — and she and her roommate put on their best modeling outfits, hose, and hats to meet him for an appointment at Taylor's Restaurant next to the recording studio.

He listened carefully to their proposition and said he would get back to her in a day or two. When he did, he asked her to meet him at the studio. He had thought about her idea, he said, and as interesting and different as it was, the plain fact was he just didn't know enough about the retail business to invest in it. But would she be interested in a job in radio?

They rode over to the station in Sam's iridescent-blue El Dorado convertible — "the prettiest car I've ever seen" — and, after introducing her to the other girls and showing her around this miniature pink-and-purple fantasy, he offered her a job in sales, starting Monday.

Sam, she would quickly come to realize, truly loved women — "he was flirtatious, he liked to come into the [WHER] studio and build us up — maybe in his fantasy world we were his little harem. But I don't think he had affairs." He told her straight out when she first went to work that he never called any of the girls at home. "He said, '[You can] put your mind at rest, that's one thing I never do. I never make passes.' I thought, That's wonderful. Even though he was a good-looking man. I mean, I knew he was married. But that night, he called me. And wanted to come by!"

But nothing ever came of it — or his flirtations with any of the other girls, so far as she knew. And she would have known, she was almost certain, because they all liked Sam, they all gossiped about him, and they all talked about their personal affairs. One time early in their acquaintance, Sam and Bettye were in a steak-house bar on Madison, and Sam got real close to her and took out his cigarette lighter to illuminate her face and said to everyone within viewing distance, "Look at that mouth. Aren't those the prettiest teeth?" Another time, just after she had met him, he asked her what she was up to as she was walking out the door. "And I said, 'I'm in this beauty contest and I'm going to borrow a dress,' and he looked at me for a minute and said, 'I think you're too fat.' And I *wasn't* fat. But it tickled me that he did it — that he had the nerve to do it." Because men generally tended to treat her with a greater degree of flattery — and circumspection — for what she considered to be the most obvious reasons.

She continued to be confounded — and more often than not intrigued — over the next forty-five years in the course of a relationship that seemed to always hover somewhere between an unspoken competition and an intimate flirtation. Sam, she said, for all of his "laid-back, very self-confident [demeanor], was the most insecure man about love I've ever met in my life." And the most consumed by it.

THAT MAY WELL have been the case. But whatever the truth of Bettye's assessment, as everyone from his sons to his recording artists to Bettye herself fully recognized, Sam was not about to be deterred from his goals. Which were focused on radio at this point almost as much as on the record company. The little radio station that he had acquired in Marked Tree, Arkansas, the previous year hadn't turned out to be worth much, and he soon sold it to the mayor. But now he and Earl Daly, his partner and engineer in the Marked Tree venture, were getting involved in another one out by the naval base in Millington. And he was continually thinking of additional radio projects: the station in Birmingham with Jimmy Connolly, maybe even another all-girl station in a different Southern market.

He was finally beginning to feel that his financial future was assured. In August Kemmons Wilson tipped him off that Holiday Inn was soon going to be making a public offer, and on August 20, the first day that the stock went on the market, he bought 200 shares, about all that he felt he could comfortably afford, at $9.75 a share. Other people might have bought more, others might have gambled on the stock by mortgaging home and business, but even with Kemmons involved, and for all his faith that the investment would pay off handsomely, Sam was not about to abandon hard-won caution. Nor did he have any regrets when, some thirty years later, he finally sold his stock, which had grown to 4,000 shares through stock splits at approximately $70 a share.

HE SEEMED HAPPY to let Jack take over more and more of the producing chores. From Jack's point of view it was a welcome expansion of his duties — and he had lots of new ideas. Early on, once he got a handle on Sam's unique approach to echo, he had suggested extending it even further, increasing the number of inputs so that you could have multiple slapback sources instead of the single one, usually the vocal, that they had been limited to up till now. Sam listened carefully and agreed that it made sense, and he got Doug Cousar, in his capacity as studio "sweeper," to build a little outboard splitter with five inputs, and one output to the "slapback" machine, which then fed back to the "master" tape recorder with a variable delay. That way they could create individualized effects for up to five different sources at once, and whether it was Sam or Jack at the board they made full use of this expanded potential, particularly with Jerry Lee Lewis, for whom the "slapback" sound virtually became another susurrating, sibilant instrument.

He listened to Jack, too, when Jack made the case for the studio band getting paid a basic hourly rate — $2.00 at first, then $3.00 — rather than the $15.00 a side they had been getting, no matter how long it took to complete.

The band certainly deserved the raise. As Sam would have been the first to acknowledge, it was both peerless and indispensable. The nucleus was the same as it had been since the previous fall, Billy Riley's (and then Jerry Lee Lewis', and then Billy's again) band, with Stan Kesler added on bass, Jimmy Wilson if they needed a piano (Wilson had recently come to town and lived above Taylor's with his pet raccoon), and Billy himself as utility man. But it was Roland Janes' stinging guitar and Jimmy Van Eaton's unique combination of swing, marching band, and shuffle rhythms on drums that anchored them — that and the atmosphere that Sam generated in the studio. Sam encouraged them to experiment, Roland and J.M. both said, he encouraged them to find their own way. Sometimes they'd just be wandering around in the wilderness, it seemed, but when he heard something he liked, he'd come charging out of the control room, all stoked up, declaring, "That's it! That's what I want — *there*." And they'd keep on cutting it until they got the feel just right.

Sometimes Jack ran the session and Sam ran the board — to the musicians in many ways they were virtually interchangeable, though on the whole they probably had more confidence in Sam. Jack was brilliant and closer to their own age, and everyone enjoyed his company, but at times it seemed like he was almost too clever for his — or their — own good. With Sam, on the other hand, even someone like Billy Riley, who viewed the world through a veil of suspicion and regarded Sam as a "charmer," not really a term of endearment in his vocabulary, could see the difference Sam made. "He could make you feel like you were somebody, whether you were or not. He never criticized. He would always come up, 'Man, you are doing great. I want you to just do it this way.' [And] he would make you so comfortable you could just go in there and turn loose."

From Roland's point of view, there was no doubt that Sam in fact saw you as a better person than you saw yourself. He put no more stock in appearances than he did in formal education or social graces — when he believed in you, he believed in you wholeheartedly, and he made you believe in yourself. There was no real pattern to what they did, there was rarely any formal preparation for a session, whether it was Billy Riley or Jerry Lee Lewis, teenage big-band leader and future TWA pilot Jimmy Williams, or someone who just happened to walk in the door. Occasionally they might know what song they were going to be recording ahead of time. But more often, Roland said, Sam would simply say, "Let me hear what you've got," and if he liked it, he'd say, "Well, let's take a cut on that." And if he didn't, he would just ask to hear some more. The rehearsals were part of the session if the session took off, and if not, they were just auditions

They were more like a family than a record label, said J. M. Van Eaton. Nobody ever wanted to go home — and if you didn't have a session, you were likely to find yourself at the studio anyway, if only to check out what was going on. "Everybody just wanted to come and hang out. We would sit in the booth next door at Taylor's. 'Man, heard y'all played last night. How'd it go? Draw a big crowd?' That kind of stuff. Just having a good time with friends." It was, everyone agreed, Big Fun. To the point that, as J.M. said, "I would have probably paid them to let me come down there!"

As with most families, though, one person remained firmly in charge. Even Jack recognized that. Whether or not Sam was present for the recording itself, he was always the one to pick the take for release — in fact, some were inclined to say that even when he was *not* in the studio, given the extent to which it was so completely imbued with both his spirit and his philosophy, he could very well be credited with the success of the session himself. Jack was not entirely inclined to disagree. "He was the boss, and everybody said, 'If Sam likes it, it must be good.' If he *really* liked something, he'll let you know. He either liked it or he didn't. That's one thing I learned from Sam — it's either entertaining or it ain't. You know, it's *still* fun for me when Sam likes something I do," Jack said thirty years later, long after he had established a legend of his own.

Sam for his part took as much pride in Jack's inventiveness and creativity as he did in the musical accomplishments of any of his artists. Even if he had a point of vociferous disagreement, he nearly always gave Jack his head, just as he did all the others, so long as he was convinced that Jack was pursuing his own individual path. That summer, Sam put him in charge of a Johnny Cash session for the first time. "John was the last one Sam let me work with. He was kind of Sam's fair-haired boy. Sam took a lot of pride—he loved Johnny Cash. He really respected [him]—he used to tell me what a great guy Johnny was and how easy he was to work with. He'd go out on the road and write songs and work them up with his band, come in and record them every few weeks. Sam just thought the world of Johnny Cash."

It surprised Jack in a way that Sam would be willing to finally let John go—but then again it didn't. In some ways he took it as an endorsement of Sam's faith in him, in others as a sign of Sam's growing desire to disentangle himself a little from the day-to-day affairs of the business. It was only natural, after all, that he might have reached a point where he simply wanted to do something else once in a while, after all this time running the show by himself.

As far as Johnny Cash went, Jack shared all of Sam's feelings of affection and admiration. He had liked John from the day they first met—he had appreciated as much as anything what the public might often miss, his sense of humor. "Let's go to Taylor's," he'd say, "I think I got a little too much blood in my coffee system." And John always got a big kick out of it "when we'd go to Taylor's Restaurant next door to Sun, they had all the Sun records on the jukebox, and we'd play 'I Walk the Line' [that] started with that hum," and everybody in the room would just fall into line, imitating John with a unison hum. He was also the first person Jack had ever seen who could never be parted from his ubiquitous nasal inhaler. He'd keep it on the speaker in front of the control room window, and sometimes, Jack said, after he took a sniff, it looked like he got another foot taller.

They concentrated on two songs at the initial session. In "Home of the Blues," a cowrite with a little of the same country blues flavor as his first effort, "Hey, Porter," Cash was striving in his own words for some of the purity that he found in folklorist Alan Lomax's blues field recordings (the song was named for the record shop on Beale Street, perhaps equally folkloric). "Give My Love to Rose," on the other hand, was a beautiful ballad patterned loosely after a popular western folk song from the 1920s, "Give My Love to Nell." Jack overdubbed Jimmy Wilson's piano and muted background voices on "Home of the Blues," and the ensemble sound came off a little muddy in places because of the overdubs, but both songs lived up to the by now classic Cash standard, and neither did anything to radically change the Johnny Cash sound.

They worked on a number of other songs that summer as well, songs meant for John's first album. Among these were a couple more originals, and in the manner in which nearly every pop album at this time was put together, familiar songs from other sources, presumably intended to broaden the artist's appeal. In this case, true to John's own inclinations, they drew on folk song–like material like "The Wreck of the Old 97" and Leadbelly's "Rock Island Line," as well as mournful country standards by Hank Williams and Jimmie Skinner, and, at long last, a beautifully articulated gospel number, with the Tennessee Two joining in on approximate harmony vocals.

THE FIRST PHILLIPS INTERNATIONAL release finally came out in the middle of October. The release consisted of five different, relatively unknown artists, from Barbara Pittman, described in the catalogue as "sweet and sultry" and answering to the name of "Tiger" (she was the first female singer to really get a push from Sam since Big Memphis Ma Rainey in 1953), to "tender tenor" Buddy Blake, a balding father of two teenage sons (probably the source of his "hep . . . feel for youthful music"), to nineteen-year-old Hayden Thompson, whose tightly wrought version of Little Junior Parker's "Love My Baby," with "Billy Riley's band [and] Jerry Lee Lewis' 'pumping piano'" as the advertised backup, finally received its long-awaited release.

The Bill Justis instrumental, "Raunchy," was clearly the pick of the litter, despite the reluctance of certain disc jockeys and distributors to go anywhere near a record with such a suggestive title. In the face of their open concern (even Dewey Phillips expressed his misgivings) Sam looked the word up in the dictionary and made the discovery that while its primary meaning might well be "obscene, lewd, or sexually explicit," it could also simply mean "unkempt." Which he reported back via telephone and telegram, his articulation presumably unaffected by the tongue lodged firmly in his cheek. None of which would have made any difference if the record hadn't sold so well right out of the box,

though perhaps an even greater measure of its success was the prolifer-
ation of strong pop, rock, and r&b covers that it inspired within a week
or two of its first release.

Sam seemed to relish not just the controversy but the competition.
"IS 'RAUNCHY' A HIT!?" Phillips International Records demanded in
a red-and-black half-page ad in the October 28 edition of *Billboard,* just
as the pop version by Billy Vaughn and the r&b one by Ernie Freeman
were beginning to get attention. The question, Sam seemed to sniff as he
raised other equally obvious questions ("Will Ike Play Golf Tomorrow!!
"Is New York Big!! Has a Cat Got a Tail!!!"), barely deserved a response.
But the answer was in the upside-down text underneath. "There are covers galore already," Sam wrote, "and no doubt more to come," but "the
original" was on Phillips International. "It's fresh — It's Different" — and
"already a sure hit" in five major markets.

Two weeks later he underscored the point with a full-page ad, bordered by multiple prints of a single bow-tied head-shot of Bill Justis,
with a bold headline in red. "PLEASE TAKE JUST A MINUTE: IT
WILL PAY BIG DIVIDENDS!!!" "We at Phillips International and Sun
Records," Sam patiently explained, "have always tried to create, never
copy," and while "some uncouth and very unrealistic claims are being
made as to 'who has the hit'— Our answer to this is, we are willing to
have you compare. . . . But, more than that, we are happy to just wait till
the verdict of the record-buying public is in!" Reports from distributors
and disc jockeys all across the country, Sam reported, were in near-
unanimous agreement that Justis' record could be the biggest instrumental hit since Tommy Dorsey's "Boogie Woogie." A matter of real pride
to Sam on any number of fronts but also, in a very real sense, "because
we know [this] can be a tremendous 'shot in the arm' for instrumental
music in months to come. This will add more of a balance and variety to
the music business which has been so good to us all. Let us never become
stereotyped and parasitic. The best in commercial music has yet to be
discovered. Let's create — so as to continually find it." And he signed the
missive, "Appreciatively, Sam C. Phillips."

In the end Sam's faith was amply rewarded. He shipped two million
copies of "Raunchy" in the first two months of its release, but no matter
the sales outcome, he would have won the competition hands down
because he held the publishing on a song that went to number 2 pop in
Bill Justis' version, number 4 in Ernie Freeman's, reached number 6 on

the country charts (Justis), number 1 on the r&b (both), and got at least another million sales as the B-side of Billy Vaughn's pop hit "Sail On Silvery Moon," which itself went to number 5, while "Raunchy" got to number 10 in his version.

S AM HAD LITTLE TIME in any case to analyze all the niceties of the situation. He was at this point operating on at least half a dozen different fronts, but the most important by far was the marketing of the follow-up single to Jerry Lee Lewis' "Whole Lot of Shakin'," which had finally begun to slow down after nearly four months on the charts. The song that Sam had picked both as the next single and as the number that Jerry would perform in *Jamboree*, the rock 'n' roll "exploitation" film he had signed for when he was in New York the previous summer, had come in through Sam's publishing partner, Hill and Range, and was written by Otis Blackwell, a rhythm and blues singer and songwriter who had already given Elvis Presley two of his biggest hits to date, "Don't Be Cruel" and "All Shook Up." The new Blackwell song, "Great Balls of Fire," was just perfect for Jerry, it was exactly the "high, hard, fast one" that Sam felt he needed to deliver — but there was a catch. The demo, by Otis Blackwell, was so damn good. "I said to myself, how in the world are we going to even approach this demo?" But on the other hand he knew if anyone could do it, Jerry Lee could — and Jerry certainly agreed.

They had gone into the studio at the beginning of October under pressure to deliver a master for the movie and quickly polished off a frenetic, somewhat unfocused take that might be good enough for a movie but scarcely did justice to the song. "It come off good," said Jerry, who might have been hard-pressed to point to a performance of his that didn't, "but I knew it wasn't right. I had to do that record some more." So they kept working on it, not just on the stop-time intro, which required precision and discipline on everyone's part. ("'Great Balls of Fire' was the toughest song to start that I ever tried to record," said Sam. "We worked our ass off, because those breaks had to be exactly synched with his voice.")

Jerry threw himself unstintingly into the effort — at least fifteen false starts and takes have survived — but there was something either in what he took to be the hidden message of the song or in his mood of the moment that seemed to keep catching him up. Clearly it was not the lyrics themselves, just another explicit take on the utter shock of love — and it seems evident that if the exclamation used to convey that shock had been "Jumpin' Jehosophat" (as it would be in another, later song), Jerry Lee would have had no problem. But at some point the biblical overtones of "Great Balls of Fire" brought the session to a grinding halt.

"H-E-L-L," was the loud start of Jerry's passionate protestation. "It says, Make merry with the joy of God *only*, but when it comes to *worldly* music, rock 'n' roll, anything like that—you have done brought yourself into the world, and you're in the world, and you haven't come on out of the world, you're still a sinner. And I mean you're a sinner, and unless you be saved and born again and be made as a little child and walk before God and be holy—and brother, I mean, you got to be *so* pure. No sin shall enter there—*NO SIN!* For it says, 'no sin.' It don't say, 'Just a little bit.' It says, *No sin shall enter there.* Brother, not one little bit. You got to *walk* and *talk* with God to go to heaven. You got to be *so* good that it's pitiful. I'm just tellin' you what I know," he declares, his voice full of phlegm and the incantatory fervor of the Pentecostal preacher.

"Now, look, Jerry," says Sam, who has been biding his time, as others in the room have either been mocking Jerry's apocalyptic language or urging him to get on with the session. "Now look, Jerry," says Sam in his most mellow and reasonable-sounding voice, "religious conviction doesn't mean anything resembling extremism. All right. Do you mean to tell me that you're going to take the Bible, that you gonna take God's word, and that you gonna revolutionize the whole universe? Now, listen. Jesus Christ was sent here by God Almighty."

"Right!"

"Did he convince—did he *save* all of the people in the world?"

"Naw, but he *tried* to."

"He sure did. Now, wait just a minute. Jesus Christ came into this world. He tolerated man. He didn't preach from one pulpit. He went around and did good."

"That's right! He preached EVERYWHERE."

It went on with increasing passion, and increasing disagreement, touching on matters of practice, interpretation, and Manichean belief. ("You're so right," Jerry threw back at Sam at one point, "you don't know what you're saying.")

"Now, look, now, listen," said Sam, "I'm telling you out of my heart, and I have studied the Bible a little bit—"

"Well, I have, too. I've studied it through and through and through and through, and I know what I'm talking about."

"Listen, if you think that you can't do good if you're a rock 'n' roll exponent—"

"You can do *good,* Mr. Phillips, don't get me wrong—"

"Let me finish now, wait a minute now, listen, when I say *do good*—"

"You can have a *kind heart*—"

"I don't mean, I don't mean just—"

"You can help people."

"You can SAVE SOULS," said Sam.

"NO! NO! NO!—How can the DEVIL save souls? What are you *talkin'* about? Man, I got the DEVIL in me. If I didn't have, I'd be a Christian."

Which was the nub of it, really. As Jerry said years later, "We were discussing religion—who was right, who was wrong, we done everything but fist-fight, so to speak. And come to find out, he was wrong, and I was, too, because there is no such thing as religion. The word 'religion' is not even in the Bible. It's *salvation.* Sanctification. Are you sanctified? Then you're Christian."

To Sam, on the other hand, these were merely philosophical stumbling blocks along the road. They were the struggles that everyone had to face, particularly anyone of a creative or philosophical temperament whose station in life might have changed, causing them to question whether they were living by the ideals with which they had been raised. Being as strong in the faith in reason as he was himself, he felt that it was up to each individual person to work out his own solution, "it is up to you to decide that, man, if I'm doing something wrong, do something about it and not get in a tug-of-war with yourself." That is what he had always tried to communicate to his artists, not just to Jerry Lee but to all of his boys. To Sam "the gifts that these people [possessed] were almost boundless"—but it was always up to them to decide.

The next night, or maybe it was the night after, the crisis seemed to be past, as Jerry launched into a very different sort of sermon on the pleasures of oral sex. "Eat a while, gag a while, I do like to eat (hope you ain't putting this on tape)," he declared as his cohorts bided their time and he launched into yet another assault on "Great Balls of Fire." In the end his performance was a masterpiece, a song that in anyone else's hands would have been little more than an exuberant novelty number but through the controlled application of energy and belief became a triumph of technique, an exquisitely etched miniature of epic proportions. Perhaps most surprising of all, through Sam's sure sculpting of the raw material, it became virtually a drums-and-piano duet, with guitar and bass lost in the mix (the result solely of deft microphone placement), and voice and piano alone, augmented by lavish use of slapback, carrying all the excitement.

Sam put out the single at the beginning of November, just as "Raunchy" was beginning to really pick up sales. He designed a one-sheet and an ad to go with it announcing: "SUN *has its' own* SATELLITE

THE BALL OF FIRE
JERRY LEE LEWIS
SINGING HIS FABULOUS NEW
SUN RELEASE
"GREAT BALLS OF FIRE"
|||||||||||||
INTRODUCED TO THE NATION
SUNDAY, NOV. 3 ON THE
STEVE ALLEN SHOW

The single was released with a picture sleeve, along with an Extended Play 45 entitled "Jerry Lee Lewis The Great Ball of Fire," and earned a glowing lead review in *Billboard*, followed by a full-page ad replete with crude outer-space imagery and saluting the sensational success of Sun's very own Satellite on his rocketlike rise up the charts.

It was a moment of pure triumph for the company, but, not surprisingly, not everyone was in a celebratory mood. Carl Perkins for one was thoroughly disillusioned. Mr. Phillips, he believed, had promised him the sun, the moon, and the stars—but nothing had gone right for him, really, since the automobile accident. His drinking was only getting worse, to the point that without acknowledging the fault he could recognize the shame. And it certainly didn't help to watch this strutting peacock, Lewis, that Mr. Phillips was always going on about just sail right by him without so much as a backward glance. ("I tried to make him feel welcome and comfortable," Carl later wrote of their first encounters, when it was Carl who was the star, "but he opened all them smart-aleck doors to start.")

He had been cast in *Jamboree*, too, Carl told himself. In later years he would even say that he had been offered "Great Balls of Fire" first but chose a nondescript song called "Glad All Over" instead ("I thought both of them was junk!") — though, given both Sam's and Jerry Lee's independent testimony, this seems doubtful. Most of all, though, he was deeply resentful that he was getting neither the attention nor the respect that he deserved — he didn't even get his own distinctive Sun moniker. In his somewhat revisionist version he confronted Sam straight out about it. "Mr. Phillips," he said, "you got Jerry Lee Lewis of the brain. Every time I come in here, you want to play me something he's done. I'm sure he's making you a lot of money. I know he's got hit records. But you even put on his records 'Jerry Lee Lewis and His Pumping Piano.' You ain't never said nothing about me and my guitar." Well, said Sam, they would have to do something about that. Carl would be his "Rockin' Guitar Man" from now on.

But it was too late. The die was already cast.

Carl and Johnny Cash had a meeting with Columbia country music head Don Law when they were out in California at the end of August. It had been set up by Bob Neal through California booking agent Stew Carnall when the two of them played the Town Hall Party, Los Angeles' equivalent of the Louisiana Hayride (with a three-hour live television broadcast every Saturday night), on August 31. They met with Law later that night at the home of Town Hall stars Lorrie and Larry Collins, the seventeen- and fourteen-year-old sister-and-brother act billed as the Collins Kids. Stew Carnall, who had become a half partner with Neal in Johnny Cash's management contract and would marry Lorrie Collins at the beginning of the new year, seems to have been the catalyst — though there is little question that Neal saw this as an opportunity to move up in the world of television and movie entertainment with his principal client, Johnny Cash, leaving Memphis and a meddlesome partnership with Sam Phillips far behind.

It didn't take much to persuade Carl that he would be better off with a new deal. Nashville power broker Jim Denny had told him that he wasn't getting his full share of writer's royalties when he was laid up in the hospital after the accident and Denny was trying to sign him to his own publishing company. And even though Sam had allayed Carl's concerns at the time, and both he and John were about to register as BMI songwriters under the new direct-payment system (previously BMI had for the most part paid performance royalties to the song publisher, with the understanding that they would be passed on to the writer), when it came right down to it, he just didn't trust Mr. Phillips anymore.

John had concerns of his own, entirely apart from business. He thought maybe Carl was going a little overboard about that—although there was no question in his mind that even if Sam was, strictly speaking, *honest* with them, at the same time there was information that was being withheld, whether because he thought they wouldn't understand it or because he thought they would. But there was one thing he was certain Carl was right about: Sam had Jerry Lee Lewis on the brain. And he was tired of being treated like a child. And not just financially either. He had projects of his own that he wanted to embark on—the long-delayed gospel album, for one, other ideas he had for pursuing ambitious thematic concepts, like an album of western songs, or another with the historical impact and scope of Merle Travis' *Folk Songs of the Hills*. But Mr. Phillips was adamant in focusing on the singles market, in sticking with the tried-and-true.

Don Law listened to their articulated concerns, and intuited others. Columbia Records would not be able to pay any advance, he said—the figures simply didn't justify that—but they would pay a full 5 percent artist's royalty on every record sold. Which added up to a lot more, Carl was quick to point out, than Sun's measly three—and with Columbia Records you didn't have to worry about whether they were good for it. As for John's ambitions, Columbia Records was ready to support anything he wanted to do. What about a gospel album? John said. Absolutely, Law agreed. And if John had any concerns about the company being behind him on that, or anything else, why didn't he meet with Goddard Lieberson, Columbia's erudite new forty-six-year-old president (he was a producer, classical pianist, and composer and had pioneered in the introduction of the long-playing record) anytime he was in New York.

So two months later, on November 1, after pondering the matter at length and talking it over in excruciating detail with each other and with Bob Neal, they both signed confidential letters of intent, with the agreements to be executed when each of their present contracts ran out.

John went into the Sun studio on November 12 to record his new single, a pop song written by Jack Clement in the bland, inoffensive manner of recent hits like "A White Sport Coat (And a Pink Carnation)" by Marty Robbins and "Young Love" by Sonny James, and deliberately aimed at the "teen" market. It was even called, probably not without irony, "Ballad of a Teenage Queen," and John had attempted it without success a month earlier. He really didn't care much for the song, but this time they were able to get it without too much trouble, with Jack producing and Sam running the board as Jack provided ringing rhythm accompaniment on his big J-200 Gibson guitar.

The song that John really cared about was one he had written recently while he was on tour, which he believed to be his finest composition yet. He had been reading an article about himself in a magazine, "Johnny Cash Has the Big River Blues in His Voice," but he barely got past the title when he was inspired to write the song. "Big River" incorporated all the elements that had distinguished his songwriting from the first — wit, conviction, and striking lyrical originality, with a strong suggestion of his deep-seated rooting in the "folk" tradition — but it possessed as well the kind of illimitable impact (was all the clever wordplay merely entertaining, or did it intensify feelings of loss and alienation, as it would one day in the songs of one of Cash's keenest students, Bob Dylan?) that few other artists could suggest. Jack played guitar and bass drum at the same time on this one, with the Tennessee Two, and Luther in particular, reduced to a more complementary role — but at the end of the day, there was no question in anyone's mind that they had created another great Johnny Cash record.

The same could not be said about anyone's feelings about the other song. Jack had to wait two or three days before he could take advantage of John's absence at the annual Country Music Disc Jockey Convention in Nashville to overdub voices on "Ballad of a Teenage Queen." Bill Justis arranged the voices ("I brought in a barbershop quartet and a church soprano, and they had no blend at all — but they did sound commercial"). Sam had never liked the song, but after he heard the overdub, he told Jack years later in a spirit of pure collegiality, "I went home and prayed about it: 'Lord, is it coming to this?'" He never changed his mind about the song, Jack said with amusement, but on the other hand he never showed any hesitation about putting it out.

Johnny Cash in any case was the man of the hour at the DJ Convention in Nashville. "Attention, DJ's," read the only ad on the awards page: "JOHNNY CASH says . . . 'Thanks a million!' Johnny's first LP is now ready — just in time for Christmas Sales!" And Sam had shipped in several hundred copies of the album for John to give out to the DJs, which he did with characteristic aplomb. But inside he couldn't help but have a queasy feeling. He had never dissembled to anyone before in quite this way. He didn't know how he was ever going to be able to tell Mr. Phillips the truth.

BILLY RILEY had already made his own dissatisfaction abundantly clear. He had what he felt to be more than sufficient cause. He had never gotten the hit that he and Sam both knew he deserved. When "Flyin' Saucers Rock & Roll" came out earlier in the year and failed to register on the charts, he was disappointed, but he had been easily assuaged. These things happen, Mr. Phillips explained to him. Everywhere that people heard the record, it had *exploded*, it just never caught on with the general public. Besides, he had another record in the can that he was sure was going to be his big hit. Just around the time that "Flyin' Saucers" came out at the beginning of February, Sam had played him an old Sun rhythm and blues recording by Billy "The Kid" Emerson, a raw, high-spirited extended double entendre called "Red Hot" that he wasn't even sure he could match. But they jammed on it and somehow or other came up with a beat of their own, with Jerry Lee Lewis once again providing the driving boogie-woogie piano fills, "and we just made a real wild, Little Richard–type thing out of it," it was definitely *different*, and in the end everyone agreed they had something that was at least as good as "Saucers," if not better.

Sam held the record for six months, until, finally, he decided the moment was right, releasing it on August 13, 1957, as Jerry Lee Lewis' "Whole Lot of Shakin'" was still climbing the charts. Maybe that was the mistake, maybe it just wasn't meant to be, but the new record didn't sell any better than "Flyin' Saucers," with a couple of thousand sales in Memphis in its first month of release and no orders coming in after October. To Billy it seemed clear: Sam had simply sold him out. His record *could* have been a hit, Mr. Phillips even conceded it *should* have been a hit — it *would* have been a hit, Billy was certain, if Sam hadn't transferred all of his allegiance to the very man Billy had given a break to (he was playing piano on the damn record!), who in Billy's considered opinion had no more talent in his whole body than Billy Riley did in his little finger.

He just got madder and madder, until one night he got drunk and came storming into the studio, and, when he discovered that Sam wasn't there, in a story that would grow and expand in his account over the years, he started yelling at Sally and kicked a hole in the bass fiddle.

Sally called Sam, and Sam told her to lock the door and not to let Billy leave under any circumstances. When he arrived at the studio, he sat and listened to Billy as the recriminations came pouring out. Sam had deliberately *lost* the record, Billy yelled at him, he had let the record die. He had colluded with distributors — Billy had heard that he had even canceled orders for Billy's record, telling the distributors that he was backing a *hit* now. He had probably even called up the DJs and told them not to play Billy's record. All to curry favor with his current favorite.

Sam just waited him out. Now, Billy, he finally said in his calmest, most reasonable voice, that doesn't make any sense. Not even the worst businessman in the world would do something like that — and he was not the worst businessman in the world. Think about it, said Sam, you'd have to be a crazy man to kill a record you had a chance to make some money on, even if it was a record by your own worst enemy. And Sam was confident that Billy knew that, far from being Billy's enemy, there was no one in the whole world, with the exception of Billy himself, more invested in Billy Riley's success than Sam Phillips. And Sam didn't think he had to tell Billy, he was not just talking about money now, he was talking about plain old unvarnished faith in another human being.

"Sam got there," Billy recalled to music historian Robert Palmer, "and we went back in his little cubby hole and talked all night till sunup. Sam told me, '"Red Hot" ain't got it. We're saving you for something good.'" When he left, Riley said, he felt like he was walking on air. "I felt like I was the biggest star on Sun Records!"

T HE WHOLE FAMILY visited New York over the Christmas holidays. Sam had business to take care of, and Jerry Lee Lewis was opening at the Paramount Theater on Broadway on Christmas Day, with only Fats Domino above him and Buddy Holly and the Everly Brothers just down on the star-studded bill. Sam and Becky and the boys rode the train up from Memphis, switching from a diesel to a steam locomotive in North Carolina, which still mandated the use of coal — Knox and Jerry were mesmerized by both the journey and by the city. With Becky they visited all the tourist sites, from the Empire State Building to the Statue of Liberty, and the whole family went to former heavyweight champion Jack Dempsey's restaurant and the hillbilly comic-strip musical, "Li'l Abner," while Sam and the boys let off steam by doing one-arm push-ups in their hotel room whenever they could.

Knox and Jerry on the Statue of Liberty ferry, New York City, Christmas, 1956.
Courtesy of the Sam Phillips Family

The show at the Paramount, Alan Freed's latest seasonal Big Beat celebration, was, it went without saying, the highlight of the trip. Sam bumped into his old friend Paul Ackerman, the erudite *Billboard* editor, running around backstage so excited he could barely contain himself. He was just so tickled he almost hugged Sam, it was for both men the perfect realization of a long-held dream. When he was approached by reporters, Sam declared that Jerry Lee Lewis was "the most sensational performer I've ever watched, bar none." And this, wrote Ren Grevatt in his "On the Beat" column, "from the man who also developed Elvis Presley and Carl Perkins." Sam also told anyone who would listen that what they were seeing onstage from *all* of the performers represented the kind of spirituality that, if used in the right way, could change the whole way — hell, it already *had* changed the whole way that people of every stripe, black and white, young and old, rich and poor, treated one another. But that didn't make its way into anyone's column.

For Knox and Jerry, there could have been no greater thrill. The balcony was shaking, people were screaming — it was probably the greatest experience they had ever had in their lives. A magazine reporter, spotting their ducktails and their sharpest Lansky's outfits, even solicited their views on the Elvis-Jerry Lee controversy, asking if they were going to keep their hair like Elvis' or change their hairstyle now "to copy Jerry Lee's crisper style." They weren't certain, they said, but they were thinking about writing a song on the subject, which would be dedicated to Jerry Lee.

But then Becky found out about Sally, who had been at the hotel since the beginning of the trip, staying on another floor. Sally wasn't sure how she found out — she had barely gone out of her room the whole time. She thought maybe Sam just told her. Becky in any case never said a word to the boys. She just gathered them up and took them to the train station. "She never let on," said Knox, "but it was palpable. I mean, I didn't understand what was going on, I didn't know about Sally, but you could feel something was wrong. We're in New York, we've never been here, we're having a good time — and then we're leaving early." She was determined to shield them, Knox later recognized, no matter how badly hurt she may have been, and in the end, "it was a good experience basically because of what she did. All that rock 'n' roll stuff was cool," said Knox, but it was the strength of his mother's love, her determination to keep them all safe and together, whatever the cost, that in retrospect became the lasting impression he took from the trip.

By the time the new Johnny Cash single, "Ballad of a Teenage Queen," came out at the beginning of January, Carl Perkins was already gone. That was all right — Sam had been well aware that Carl was unhappy, and Carl had reason to be unhappy. He was regretful that he hadn't been able to do more for Carl. He wished there was more time in the day, he wished he could delegate better, he wished that Carl could have gotten all the success that he deserved — but more than anything he wished him well as he focused on promoting Johnny Cash's new single to a whole new market.

But then he ran into a very disturbing rumor. At first he dismissed it out of hand, but it kept coming up again and again from one distributor after another. Johnny Cash, they said, was leaving him, too.

He simply refused to believe it. If John were leaving, Sam was convinced, he would have told him. Sam could certainly understand the blandishments and sweeteners, financial and otherwise, that might tempt him, but if there were any real problems, wouldn't he come to Sam first? There had been ongoing talks with Bob Neal about raising John's royalty rate, with Neal arguing for 5 percent and Sam fully prepared to go to 4, as he just had with Jerry Lee Lewis, even if he wasn't prepared to concede the point until they clarified the whole picture a little better. But still the rumors kept flying—John was going to sign with Capitol, someone said, which Sam *knew* wasn't true. John had already made his deal—though with whom was never specified. Finally, he just confronted Neal directly. He called him up, and Neal said he didn't know a thing about it. But something about the way he said it didn't sound right, and the distributors' questions kept on nagging.

He called Neal again and demanded a meeting with John as soon as he got off tour. He never heard back from Neal, but in the meantime he conducted his own investigation. When he heard that John was back in town, "I called Bob and said, 'Where's Cash?' He said, 'Oh, I meant to call you. He's at home.' I said, 'I'll be down to pick you up. Meet me in five minutes downstairs. You call Cash and tell him we're coming out now.'" By now, he knew, the outcome was a foregone conclusion, but he wanted to give John a chance to at least look him in the eye and tell him the truth.

So they went out there, and Sam just said it straight out. He said he knew John had signed an option to go with another company, even though Bob Neal denied it. Now, which was the truth? And John squirmed uncomfortably—he couldn't even look at him—and said, "No, Mr. Phillips, I have not." Sam almost couldn't believe it—the man was lying to him to his face—and, almost reluctantly, he brought forward the evidence he had uncovered. He had gone to the American Federation of Musicians in New York, he knew that if John had signed an option agreement, it had to be on record with the union, and they confirmed that they had the contract on file. But John still denied it.

"It was the only time that Johnny Cash ever lied to me in his life," Sam always said in later years, with which Johnny Cash shamefacedly agreed. It was, he would even go so far as to admit, the only time he could think of that he had ever lied to anyone about something of substance—and he had no excuse, other than that he wanted to avoid a scene. He could think of all the rationalizations—he was underpaid, Sam expected too much and gave too little, Sam had lied to *him* by not educating him to the business of music—but none of them justified the basic betrayal.

It taught him a lesson, Johnny Cash said toward the end of his life. "I've apologized to him many times [over the years]," and in fact it only took a year or two for their relationship to be back on a firm footing — but none of that could erase the disappointment he felt in himself not for the decision he had made but for lying to someone who had every reason to expect him to tell the truth.

As for Sam, who had always prided himself on his ability to communicate — on his ability to "read" people — he couldn't understand how he had missed it. If John was so dissatisfied, why hadn't he come to Sam with his complaints? Why hadn't Sam sensed it? He didn't give a shit about Neal. Neal had his own narrow interests. But John was a person of an altogether different stripe. Sam could rationalize that it was the big record companies, that someday, inevitably, there would no longer be any room for the independent. He could rationalize that it was jealousy pure and simple — these boys had simply forgotten how much he had invested in them. "They saw it as if we were petting Jerry Lee. They had forgotten that we had brought them along the same way." He continued to pursue the matter halfheartedly for another month or so until, finally, on March 14, Bob Neal sent him a telegram: "Regret to inform you Johnny has made decision to continue with plans to go with Columbia at expiration of contract. We will issue no announcement of change before July first." He felt heartsick at the finality of it all. But maybe what bothered him most, something he could barely even acknowledge to himself, was the sense that, for the first time, he might no longer have the stomach for the fight. But that was something easily suppressed in the whirlwind of activity that had become his life, in the immediate demands that were pressing down upon him from all directions.

"Ballad of a Teenage Queen" proved to be every bit as big a hit as Sam had jokingly feared it might become. By January 27 it stood at number 8 on the country charts; three weeks later it was number 1, where it remained for the next ten weeks, while cresting at number 16 pop (number 14 on the most-played-by-DJs list), Johnny Cash's best showing to date, and substantially higher than anything he would achieve on the Columbia label for the next eleven years.

In the meantime, Sam or Jack recorded Jerry Lee Lewis every chance they got. It was as if they were folklorists, like Alan Lomax, taking down every variation of every song that their subject knew so that future generations might know the full cultural diversity of their heritage. Category did not exist. Jerry had such a wild, untamable musical range, his fertile imagination leaping from hillbilly to blues to spiritual numbers, big-band instrumentals, folk standards, affectingly sentimental songs of the South, and the Marine Hymn seemingly without the slightest doubt that he could match or surpass any performer at his own game. He took on Elvis ("Good Rockin' Tonight," "Hound Dog," "Don't Be Cruel," and "Jailhouse Rock" at a single sitting), Hank Williams, Jimmie Rodgers, and originals that he might only be hearing for the first time, all with equal verve and conviction. One of Sam's favorites was an old gutbucket blues called "Big Legged Woman" that kicked off with a traditional verse, "Big-legged woman / Keep your dresses down / You got something baby / That'd make a bulldog hug a hound," and went on from there. Jerry just flung himself into it, improvising freely both lyrically and instrumentally, and throwing in the patented purr that he had been working on ever since he was a kid (this was a kind of lascivious gargle that he had developed originally not for a song, but for "whenever I'd see a cute girl walking by — I'd purr at her"). At the conclusion of the song, after throwing in one last unexpected twist ("Well, let me tell you something / What I'm talkin' about / Bet my bottom dollar / There ain't a cherry in this house"), he let out a self-scandalized whoop, while declaring exuberantly, "It's a HIT!" And it was, everyone would have been perfectly willing to agree — even if it wasn't released for another decade, and then certainly not in any form that would qualify as a commercial hit — in its own singular and inimitable way.

There were always new refinements but never less than 100 percent investment in the performance (the old Sister Rosetta Tharpe gospel number "99½ Won't Do" might have been invented to describe Jerry), and Sam was overcome again and again by this incomparable talent.

After the great success of "Great Balls of Fire" (it went to number 2 pop and number 1 country and would remain on the charts for five months), the song that they settled on for his next single was yet another offering from the pen of Otis Blackwell, and yet another novelty song whose main point of release was the whoosh of breath at the end of every verse: "You leave me, ahhhhhh, breathless — uh!" Once again there were many days spent in the studio and many approaches taken, from the frenetic to the just plain silly, but in the end the record was a triumph of artistry and imagination applied to achieve an effect that was at once both unabashedly lewd and unabashedly innocent — in which, in other words, the material was once again elevated by the sheer inspiration of the performance.

Jerry's private life, Sam sometimes felt, reflected another side of that ungovernable gift of imagination and self-belief. Faith, as Sam well knew, could sometimes lead to hardheadedness, and there was no one stronger in his faith than Jerry, whether in his religion or himself. He was, to all intents and purposes, completely ungovernable when it came to matters of taking advice. His first real royalty check, at the end of the previous year, reflecting much of the success of both "Whole Lot of Shakin'" and "Great Balls of Fire," had come to well over $40,000, with at least an equal amount due in the royalty statement that would account for sales through June. Put some away, Sam tried to advise him. Even the squirrels do that. But Jerry was impervious to any such suggestion. In fact, his only contribution to the financial conversation was a request at the end of March that Sam loan him $17,000 to buy some cows. Sam was momentarily stymied. What would be the point of that — and where had he come up with such an idea? Undeterred, Jerry said a fellow he knew had come up with the idea as a way to minimize his tax burden with the government; if the cows all died, this fellow told him, he could write it all off, and then he would owe the IRS scarcely anything at all. Sam tried to remonstrate that this wasn't the way things worked, but in the end he wrote the check, and he never did find out what became of the cows.

Far more significant was the perilous state of Jerry's marital affairs. Jerry had been married twice already, once at sixteen to the daughter of a traveling evangelist for whom he played the piano, then a couple of years later, while he was still married to her, to a woman named Jane Mitcham, from whom he had yet to be divorced. But then, just before leaving for New York at Christmastime to play the Alan Freed show at the Paramount, Jerry had married his thirteen-year-old cousin Myra, the daughter of his bass player, Jay Brown, with whom he had been staying since his arrival in Memphis. At first Jay wanted to kill him. Then he went to the district attorney. But in the end he reconciled himself to the idea of having a talented son-in-law with whom he could travel the world, and, rather than take out his anger on Jerry, "he came home and did the next best thing," Myra said. "He gave his daughter a whipping."

Jerry's most recent marriage was one of the principal reasons Sam had gone to New York with his lawyer, Grover McCormick, in the first place. Judge McCormick was an old-timer and a very smart man, and Sam had hoped he might be able to extricate Jerry from this latest mess while at the same time persuading him to say nothing about his marriage for the time being. Which had worked up to a point, because although they had not yet been able to straighten out Jerry's domestic affairs and secure a divorce from his second wife, no one outside his immediate circle of family, friends, and fellow musicians seemed to have heard a word about it.

"Breathless" hit the market with fully as much impact as the first two singles. Jerry debuted it on the brand-new Saturday-night *Dick Clark Show* on the ABC network on February 15. It was a full-scale premiere, featuring a number of favored guests from Clark's five-afternoons-a-week *American Bandstand* dance party, but none was more favored than Jerry Lee, who had appeared three times in little more than two months on *Bandstand* the previous fall. Perhaps because the clean-cut, twenty-eight-year-old Clark, whose unthreatening good looks would allow him to claim the title of "World's Oldest Teenager" well into middle age, was so taken with him, or maybe just because he insisted on it, Jerry Lee Lewis was the only artist permitted to perform his song live, which he did with great élan in an ocelot-trimmed dinner jacket, with his hair looking like it was peroxided, and his hands moving seemingly at the speed of light.

That was when Jud came up with one of his greatest sales pitches. Dick Clark was in negotiations with the Beech-Nut chewing gum company to sponsor his show. He had been forced to go on the air without a sponsor, he confided to Jud, because of the prevailing skepticism in corporate circles that rock 'n' roll could ever attract a prime-time audience. Once the initial ratings were in, though, Beech-Nut announced that it was picking up full sponsorship to promote its brand-new "flavorific" Spearmint gum from the third show on. Why not, Jud then suggested to Clark, leaping into previously uncharted territory with the same élan that his client exhibited at the keyboard, tie in a promotion of Jerry Lee's new record with the gum? It was, he said, a perfect fit. Jerry even chewed Beech-Nut gum. Clark could simply bring him back for a command return performance, and they could offer signed copies of the record "free" for just five Beech-Nut gum wrappers and fifty cents postage and handling.

Jud presented the idea to Sam — and, subsequently, to history — as the salvation of a good friend (in this version Dick Clark was on the verge of losing both his sponsor and his show) and the making of the record. He may even have presented it this way to Clark, who seemed to have almost as much of a soft spot for Jud as he did for Jerry Lee. Sam took it all with a grain of salt. The record was doing fine on its own—it was just about to hit number 15 on the Top 100—and he barely knew Dick Clark. But he thought it was a cute gimmick that wouldn't cost all that much and would certainly gain them some publicity. So he got Jerry Lee to forgo artist royalties on all Beech-Nut sales, and he signed off on his own publishing royalties for the B-side. Then, as a precautionary measure, he had Barbara Barnes, who had just come back to work in the newly created position of publicity director (he had let Jack build her a little office in the back after convincing Sam that he could do it for less than $100), go out and buy an autograph stamp, while informing the entire staff—consisting at this point of Sally, Regina, Barbara, and Marion's teenage niece Connie Keisker, who was the official "sample-record packager"—that they had better be ready for the flood of orders that was likely to come in.

Not even Jud could have anticipated the dimensions of that flood— and even if he had, no one would have believed him. It completely overwhelmed the four women, Sally said, "it just hit us right in the face, and we had to go out and hire six or seven people, set up a packaging line in the back of the building, and teach them how to do it." Soon every square inch of studio space was taken over by the task just as long as there wasn't a session scheduled, and anyone who wasn't doing something else was recruited for the effort. In the end thirty-eight thousand copies of the record were shipped at a cost of $10,636.61, and some additional money was held back, with Sun and Dick Clark splitting the roughly $6,500 that was left. But it went on and on, Sally said, long after they had been forced to let their extra help go, because the demand was so great that Beech-Nut ran out of gum in certain markets and was forced to extend its offer.

Roland Janes rejoined Jerry for the new Alan Freed package show he was headlining that featured sixteen acts, including Chuck Berry and Buddy Holly. The tour opened with a two-day engagement at the Brooklyn Paramount at the end of March and was scheduled to stay out for the next forty-two days. Roland had been won over when he went out on a brief western tour with Bill Justis earlier in the month that included

Jerry Lee, and he started sitting in with Jerry, who was only carrying a trio, with Jay on bass and Russ Smith on drums. The guitar really filled out the sound, but more than that, the music was so alive and exciting he just couldn't resist. So he set out with Jerry again some ten days later.

Every night on the Big Beat tour was like a newly minted musical experience. You never knew what Jerry was going to play, you never knew what Jerry going to do—"he did whatever he wanted to do," said Roland, "and did it very well." Some nights he might dance on the piano, others he might be a little more sedate, he pulled a lot of strings out of bad pianos—and Roland didn't blame him. The piano was his *instrument*—it was the one thing in life he was dead serious about. "A lot of the antics just depended on the mood he was in at the time—[they] probably helped set the mood. But Jerry Lee was [always] more or less the same." Because, however often he might run a comb through his hair at every show, the music was always the red-hot center of the performance.

The same could not always be said for his father, Elmo, who was out on the road with them for much of the tour. Elmo, a volatile man who had gone to prison for bootlegging when Jerry was a little boy, always maintained a deep-seated love of family as well as a real musical talent of his own—but he could make his son seem positively shy. "Mr. Elmo," said Roland, "always said what he thought and backed up what he said. He was a fine guy, strictly Louisiana all the way—but he kept on getting us in trouble." One time he pulled a knife on some members of Sam "The Man" Taylor's r&b orchestra, after a dispute in which racial slurs were undoubtedly exchanged. Another time he got into a shouting match with Larry Williams, with whom a good number of the other performers had a beef because of his habit of trying to outdo them with their own hits. But most dramatic of all was a confrontation with Chuck Berry in which racial epithets were once more bandied about. The way Roland remembered it, the dispute arose over a parking space—or, more precisely, Berry's angry complaints that his car had been blocked in by Jerry Lee's in the alley adjacent to the stage entrance of the theater they were playing. Jerry Lee could never recall the time or place, but he did recollect that "Chuck and my daddy kept mumbling and looking for a fight. I don't know exactly what was said, but [Daddy] run after Chuck for two or three blocks, saying, 'You know what we do with cats like you down in Ferriday? We chop the heads off them and throw it in a Blue Hole [Lake].' I believe he would have done it if he'd caught him. [But] we came downstairs next morning, and there sat Chuck and Daddy having breakfast, no problem at all."

Every night Jerry and Chuck would get into it onstage. Jerry Lee was the undisputed headliner, but there was a persistent argument from Chuck, to Jerry's mind the Hank Williams of rock 'n' roll (which was about as high a compliment as he could bestow), over who was going to close the show. The ferocity of the competition was such that on the few occasions when Chuck did get to close, Jerry did everything in his power to prevent him from even getting a chance to go on. One night, according to an oft-repeated legend, he took out a Coke bottle full of gasoline and burned the piano to the ground, declaring, "I'd like to see any sonofabitch follow that." Did he really do it? If he did, neither Roland nor anyone else on the tour actually witnessed it. But *could* he have done it? Well, that's another story.

Irrespective of the question of literal or figurative truth, the one thing that Jerry Lee and his father were certain of was that no word of any disputatious behavior should get back to his mother, Mamie. Chuck Berry was in a class by himself as far as Jerry was concerned. But if he was ever inclined to forget it, his mother was right there to straighten him out. "My mama," he said, "thought Chuck Berry was the king of rock 'n' roll." When he asked her, "What about me, Mama?" she gave him a loving but skeptical look. He was good, she said, "You and Elvis are good, son — but you're no Chuck Berry. Chuck Berry is rock 'n' roll from his head to his toes."

It was, as Roland said, all in good fun — or at least most of it. In Cleveland they had to leave the stage in a hurry when a black girl flung her arms around Jerry, planted a kiss on him, and wouldn't let go — and a minor race riot ensued. In Boston the police stopped the show, inciting a riot that should probably have been attributed to police panic but that led to serious charges against Freed, on an antiquated anti-anarchy Massachusetts statute, for "inciting the unlawful destruction of property." There seems no doubt that this was part of a concerted effort not just to bring the tour to a halt (which, after a number of subsequent cancellations — and Freed's almost instantaneous dismissal by New York flagship station WINS for a violation of the "moral clause" of his contract — it effectively did), but, in conjunction with other similar efforts across the country, including the congressional "payola" hearings at which Sam had just testified, to kill rock 'n' roll outright.

It was the combination of race and commerce, as Sam fully realized, that was fueling this national movement, and it was aimed not merely against the "mongrel" music that had excited opposition from the start but against the very people who were making money off it. The congressional payola hearings, for all of their piety in decrying the mere thought of "pay for play" (the practice of record companies paying the DJs, in cash, goods, or services, for playing their records), had, in fact, been instigated by the attempts of the long-established performing rights society, ASCAP (the American Society of Composers, Authors and Publishers), which for many years had held a virtual monopoly on collecting songwriting royalties, to put its upstart rival, BMI, out of business. With its embrace of rock 'n' roll (scorned by ASCAP like "race" and hillbilly music before it), BMI had surpassed ASCAP in all but catalogue sales, and its demise could do nothing but undermine the independent record companies and song publishers who were its primary beneficiaries.

Very little of this touched them out on the road. It was not about high-minded ideas, as Roland never failed to point out, it was about *music,* and while it would have been impossible to be blind to all the explosive social and racial injustices that were playing out just offstage, the music helped bring everyone together, irrespective of political differences. Roland roomed with Jerry — Jay and Russ liked to go out and have a big time, but Jerry was for the most part a homebody, reading his comic books, going to a horror movie double bill whenever there was an opportunity — sometimes if there was a quiet Sunday morning, they might even go to church. Roland, a preacher's son, had no doubt whatsoever of his roommate's sincerity in any respect. His judgment might occasionally be suspect — well, more than occasionally — but the spirituality that he invested in his music was something that virtually no one who came to know him even a little at this time could miss. Almost every night, Roland said, after the show was over and the audience was gone, Jerry Lee would go back out on the stage, sit down at the piano, and start playing. Soon others would begin to drift in from backstage, "and the next thing you know you got a jam session going on with all these big stars and Jerry Lee at the piano, leading the chorus. He just had this charisma in his music and his personality that he'd draw them all around. I don't think I've ever known anyone who loved music more than Jerry Lee," Roland said. But there were many nights when he wished Jerry could just hurry up and get done. They needed to get back to their hotel room. They needed to get on to the next town.

S AM WAS BUSY getting Jerry's first album ready for release. He wasn't going to put his three biggest hits on it (this was a common strategy at the time — the idea was that if you included hits on an album, it might diminish the sale of singles) but instead a wide assortment of Jerry's music, from "Crazy Arms," his first record, to a new, rollicking version of "Matchbox Blues" to "Goodnight, Irene."

"Jerry Lee's version of 'When the Saints Go Marching In' will probably strike you as something quite out of the ordinary," wrote Sam, who conceded that "it probably seems a little unusual for a record manufacturer to write his own liner notes" but put it down to unabashed admiration for his artist. "Only a southerner who has attended camp meetings or other revival-type gatherings," he pointed out in his encomium to both performer and performance, "can fully appreciate the quality of fervor and abandonment that Jerry Lee gives to this selection." He planned to release the album at the end of June, soon after Jerry got back from a six-week English tour, and he was optimistic enough to order a hundred thousand slicks of the cover printed up.

The English tour was the first real sign of the entrepreneurial legerdemain of Oscar Davis, whom Sam had installed as Jerry's manager the previous October in a kind of byzantine partnership that had Becky as Sam's stand-in in the operation. Davis, whom Sam had always been fond of, was an impresario of the old school, with his jaunty boutonniere, elegant cigarette holder, and drawling Boston accent — he had in fact introduced Elvis' manager, Tom Parker, to his prospective client while doing advance work for the Colonel during a period of temporary financial impecuniosity. This English tour from Oscar's point of view was only the start of what he was certain would be his crowning achievement. They had at least thirty-seven dates booked and could reasonably anticipate grossing close to $100,000. From Sam's point of view the tour would unquestionably sell, but, much more important, it would serve to cement Jerry Lee's growing worldwide reputation. With Elvis in the army, Little Richard recently enrolled in Bible college, and no direct pipeline to Mamie Lewis' opinions, news reports were increasingly prone to anoint Jerry Lee Lewis as the uncrowned "king of rock 'n' roll." Sam didn't give a damn about titles — you could characterize him any way you liked, but you couldn't *categorize* him. As Sam saw it, Jerry Lee Lewis had not even begun to realize his full artistic or commercial potential. There was no question that he stood on the brink of a limitless future.

His feelings about Johnny Cash and Bob Neal were hardly as sanguine. In fact, they just continued to simmer. He had severed his business relationship with Neal; he closed down Stars Inc., their mutual booking agency, as Neal prepared to move his site of operations from the office Sam had rented downtown to his suburban home. As far as Cash was concerned, Sam continued to feel angry and hurt — but not so angry, and not so hurt, that he could not turn his attention to a follow-up single, after the unprecedented success of "Ballad of a Teenage Queen."

Jack had written a new song, once again pop-oriented but in nearly every respect, including both subtlety of philosophical message and understated charm, several notches above its predecessor. They went in to cut "Guess Things Happen That Way" on April 9, once again with a slightly augmented band, an overdubbed chorus, Jack running the session, and Sam engineering. Sam had no doubt that the record was going to be a hit (it turned out to be an even bigger hit than "Queen," reaching number 11 on the pop charts), and it was at this point that the idea seemed to take hold: he was not going to let Johnny Cash go without ensuring that he left a backlog of material behind. He wrote John a letter reminding him of his contractual obligations and suggesting that if he didn't fulfill those obligations by recording the roughly two dozen songs that a casual reading of his Sun contract would confirm that he owed, Sun Records was prepared to sue Cash and his new record label, too, for "tortious interference." Then he told Jack that it was up to him to run the sessions and get the songs out of Cash.

Jack didn't altogether welcome the assignment. He was uncomfortable with the rift that had grown up between the two men, and disappointed, too. He could see how hurt John was, he could see how hurt they both were — but for the first time, he had a sense of the limits of his mentor's vision. Sam had just *forsaken* John at his moment of greatest triumph. What Billy Riley said was true in a way: with the rise of Sun's newest, piano-playing star, Sam never seemed to have time for anyone else. Jack could almost pinpoint the exact moment it had happened with Cash. John had come in excited about something — he wanted to have lunch with Sam next door at Taylor's, "and Sam just told him that he was all tied up with this Jerry Lee Lewis hit." It was almost like Sam had blinders on, and things that should have been clear to him, that would have been clear to him if he could just have turned his gaze for a moment, escaped his attention, and then his control.

It wasn't easy getting John into the studio at first. John's immediate impulse was to resist — he didn't give a fuck what the contract said. No one was going treat him as anything less than a man, least of all Mr. Phillips. But eventually he was won over by a combination of guilt, fear, common sense, and Jack's promise that whatever they did, they were going to have fun, and they weren't going to record any bad songs either. In the end, they had something like seven or eight sessions on four separate dates between mid-May and mid-July, recording a few songs by Hank Williams, some new ones written by either Jack or a new piano player named Charlie Rich, and, surprisingly, half a dozen originals by John, either self-written or cowritten with Jack. Sam calculated that he had two years' worth of material by the time they were done.

He released both "Guess Things Happen That Way" and Jerry Lee's new single, the title track of the new MGM feature *High School Confidential*, on May 19, with each getting a *Billboard* "Spotlight Review" predicting widespread, instantaneous success. Within two weeks both had fulfilled that prediction — but in the meantime a great deal else had happened.

Sam had spent much of the early part of the month trying to straighten out Jerry Lee's tangled legal affairs. He was scheduled to leave for England on May 21, and at this point he was planning to take his entire family with him. In the end, his parents declined to go, but his fourteen-year-old sister, Frankie Jean, would be accompanying him, along with the entire Brown clan (Jay, his wife, their three-year-old son, Rusty, and against virtually everyone's advice, Rusty's thirteen-year-old sister, Myra — who was, as Jerry proclaimed to one and all, his damn wife, and he wasn't going without her). Whether she actually was or was not his wife remained somewhat open to question, since the formal divorce decree from his previous wife, Jane Mitcham, had still not come through, but Sam and his lawyer, Judge McCormick, kept working on it, and the papers were finally signed on May 13, eight days before his scheduled departure. Both Sam and Jud remonstrated with Jerry that he'd better keep Myra under wraps, if he didn't, the press was going to eat him alive. Sam was by no means certain that the message was getting through—he didn't think he'd ever met anyone with a more obstinate streak than Mr. Jerry Lee Lewis—but on the other hand her family would act as camouflage, and at least Oscar Davis would be there to take care of things.

IT TURNED OUT that Oscar wasn't up to the task. For reasons best known to himself he appears to have confined his role to that of jovial host, and even at the airport was unable to keep a reporter from the *Daily Mail* away from Myra long enough to prevent her from telling him that she was Jerry's wife. And lest there be any mistake about it, when they got to their Mayfair hotel, Jerry proudly proclaimed to the same reporter that certainly she was his wife, she was fifteen (an exaggeration that he seemed to feel was appropriate to the occasion), and at the prodding of the reporter that yes, he had been married before, she was in fact his *third* wife, but now, he said, "I've found the right one." And went on to detail all the problems he had had in his two earlier marriages.

The reaction was instantaneous—not just from the press but from the fans as well. "Baby snatcher," "Disgusting," and chants of "We hate Jerry," were just some of the milder expressions of dismay to be heard on the first two nights, and when Oscar called a press conference on the third day, he conceded, "There is every possibility of the tour ending abruptly. I don't want to cancel [it], but I may have to."

He did—the next day. At the airport another *Daily Mail* reporter caught up with a disconsolate Jerry Lee sitting with "his 13-year-old bride. He was so keen to get away," the reporter wrote, that he and his wife and sister and the Browns had all arrived at the airport eight hours before their flight was scheduled to depart. He perked up a little when he was asked for his autograph, and some of the old bravado returned. Despite the cancellation he was confident that he would be paid in full, the fans were great, and he'd like to come back someday. Money didn't bother him anyway, he said. He had a new $600 lawn mower at home, and he was looking forward to just riding around on it. "I didn't need this tour," he said. "I earn $20,000 a week back home."

As he talked, Myra nervously clutched his hand, snuggled up to him, and laid her head on his chest. Her pale face had no make-up or lipstick [and] she bit her unpolished nails as Lewis went on. . . .

"Look, we love each other, and we want it to stay that way. Other people should mind their own business."

"They're just jealous," said Myra, as Oscar Davis arrived just before the plane took off to report on his ongoing negotiations for a fair financial settlement.

It was hard to discern whether Jerry Lee felt remorse — or even regret. As he would say years later, "I told Jud [Phillips] Myra was my wife, and I was going to introduce her as my wife. And I did. I never did have the business sense to deal with lawyers or managers. I didn't think that was right, because I had to do my own thing, my own way. If I got someone telling me how to spend my money, how to make my money, what I can drink, what I can take, what I can't, where I can go . . . that's bullshit. I can't work that way."

Or, as he told another English reporter just the day before his unceremonious departure, after detailing once again, without apology or excuse, his bigamous behavior: "Everybody thinks I am a ladies' man and a bad boy — but I am not." In his own eyes he was neither victim nor villain. He and his wife were very happy together, he said. "I am a good boy, and I want everyone to know that," he declared, without a trace of irony, no doubt confounding both his intended audience and his own expectations of himself alike.

IN A SPIN

SAM'S PLAN FOR JERRY consisted of equal parts Penitence, Rehabilitation, and Barely Suppressed Indignation. There was no question in his mind that this was, if not a plot, an opportunity for all the naysayers, all the industry critics, and outright opposition who had been there from the start to jump on the bandwagon and "point the finger of scorn" not just at Jerry, not just at him — but *at the music*. Distributors dropped their orders for the new single, "High School Confidential," returning any stock they were sitting on. DJs simply stopped playing the record. "So many people," Sam said, "wanted to do in rhythm and blues [and] rock 'n' roll, and this was just what they were looking for."

But there was still no doubt in his mind that he could win the day. Everything in which he believed was being challenged, his very livelihood was in danger of being taken away — but he had overcome greater odds than this before. He was damned if he would just give up and walk away.

Under Jerry's signature he composed "An Open Letter to the Industry from Jerry Lee Lewis," a curious form of apology couched in language that seemed to reflect Sam's own sense of disabused innocence as much as its putative author's. It went out to every one of his distributors and all the DJs, who at this point from Sam's point of view were just spouting moral outrage out their ass, and it ran in part in *Billboard* on June 9.

"Dear Friends," it began (and remember: this is Jerry Lee speaking), "I have in recent weeks been the apparent center of a fantastic amount of publicity and of which none has been good. But there must be a little good even in the worst people, and according to the press releases originating in London, I am the worst. . . .

> *Now this whole thing started because I tried and did tell the truth. I told the story of my past life, as I thought it had been straightened out and that I would not hurt anybody in being man enough to tell the truth.*
>
> *I confess that my life has been stormy. I confess further that since I have become a public figure I sincerely wanted to be worthy of the decent admiration of all the people, young and old, that admired or liked what talent (if any) I have. That is, after all, all that I have in a professional way to offer.*

The letter briefly addressed the specifics of his divorce from his second wife, Jane Mitcham ("Jane and I parted from the courtroom as friends") in terms with which Sam was necessarily familiar, since he and his lawyer had negotiated them. And it concluded, on a note of self-pity strikingly uncharacteristic of either its putative author or ghostwriter: "I hope that if I am washed up as an entertainer, it won't be because of this bad publicity, because I can cry and wish all I want to, but I can't control the press or the sensationalism that these people will go to to get a scandal started. If you don't believe me, ask any of the other people that have been victims of the same."

But appealing to the public's sense of compassion and fair play over a bigamous marriage to a thirteen-year-old first cousin once removed didn't work any better here than it had in Great Britain. Nor did the booking that Oscar Davis arranged on short notice at the plush new supper club that Lou Walters (until very recently proprietor of the world-famous Latin Quarter) nightclub had just opened in New York City. "From the very start it didn't look like a good match," reported *Billboard*, "and from the time Jerry Lee Lewis stepped out to his piano on the stage of Lou Walters' grandiose new Café de Paris, the mismatch became more obvious. It was like putting the Boston Symphony in Birdland." The six-day engagement was terminated "by mutual consent," Ren Grevatt reported, on opening night, with the club itself filing for bankruptcy one week later. And, after two spectacular fiascos in a row, Oscar Davis was to all intents and purposes out of the picture, despite continuing for several more months as Jerry's nominal manager.

This might have been an opportune moment for strategic reappraisal. Everyone else at Sun seemed to recognize the gravity of the situation. To Barbara Barnes, "All of us realized it was a disaster, it was just a disaster," while for Sally it was all those records coming back that provided the proof. "I mean it happened overnight. In one day Jerry Lee Lewis went from what he was to nothing. You couldn't sell a record. You couldn't get one played on the air. And that was the truth."

But Sam was unwilling to accept that truth. Far from taking public reaction as a warning sign, he seemed almost to be galvanized into an ever more rash course of action. Just for a laugh, Jack Clement and his girlfriend, singer Barbara Pittman, had thrown together a novelty item called "The Return of Jerry Lee." It was modeled on the recent series of "Flying Saucer" records that had achieved widespread popular success, in which a variety of hits were sampled to answer some of the questions that might be posed by newly arrived visitors from outer space. Jack took the same formula and applied it equally irreverently to the circumstances of Jerry Lee's hasty departure from England, with Elvis' friend, Memphis DJ George Klein, posing a seemingly innocuous question in his gravest announcer's voice, only to be answered by a throwaway line from a Jerry Lee Lewis record. Perhaps its most trenchant exchange came when Klein, in the guise of reporter "Edward R. Edwards," asked his ostensible interview subject how he had proposed to his wife. "Open up, honey, it's your lover boy, me, that's a-knockin'," came the opening line of "High School Confidential." There were professions of regret ("I'm feelin' sorry") and brash proclamations of pride ("I ain't braggin'/It's understood")—and Queen Elizabeth's response to the whole situation wasn't bad either: "Goodness gracious, great balls of fire."

They got it done in no time and took it to Sam, expecting it to provide a momentary distraction from all the gloom hanging over Jerry Lee Lewis' career, just a good in-house joke. When Sam heard it, though, he flipped and, to everybody's surprise, had it pressed up right away as a one-sided single for radio play.

"We think it's a cute record," Sam told *Billboard*, after mailing out the sample to DJs. "It makes light of the British episode, which is the way we think the whole thing should be treated anyway." In fact, Sam said, if the response continued to be as good as initial radio reaction, he might even put out the record commercially, with Jerry Lee's own self-composed "Lewis Boogie" on the flip side. Which he did less than a week later.

But for once, it seemed, Sam's sure instinct for decisive action, the same instinct that had served him so well in his unswerving commitment to the music, utterly failed him here. No one else (leaving aside recalcitrant teenagers like myself) found the record funny. No one else was prepared to laugh the incident off. There was no airplay for the new record, whose fine boogie-woogie B-side, cut more than a year earlier, merely reinforced the brash tone ("My name is Jerry Lee Lewis, I'm from Louisiana," it began with typical panache, "I'm gonna doya a little boogie on this here piana") of the "George and Louis Narration," as it was billed. There was no uptick in sales, no diminishment of returns—nothing changed, except possibly for the worse. Even Dick Clark, long one of Jerry's greatest champions, had deserted him, not only dropping "High School Confidential" from his *American Bandstand* playlist but making it abundantly clear that he was not going to have Jerry Lee Lewis on his show again anytime soon. (It was "a very cowardly act," Clark would later declare.)

Sam did everything in his power to buck Jerry up. He let Jerry know there was no question whatsoever in his mind that this was going to blow over—he couldn't say when, exactly, it might be a while and he'd be lying if he tried to sugarcoat the pill. But he and Jerry were both in it for the long haul, and he knew for a fact that this was *not* going to be the end of Jerry Lee Lewis' career. He believed it, too—Jerry simply possessed too much damn talent for the hypocrites and pharisees to keep it hidden from the public for long. But he couldn't make any headway with his distributors, no matter how hard he tried—he called every one of them personally, some over and over again. "I told them the truth, absolutely the truth of the whole thing, and I told them I had some fantastic things that were going to be contained in this album" that was due to come out any day. But in the end almost no one bought the self-titled album, as remarkable a showcase as it was for the breadth of this remarkable performer's talents, and he was stuck with almost a hundred thousand album covers—which, as Sam was always quick to point out, did not come cheap.

It was discouraging, no doubt about it. But for the moment he just didn't know what else he could do. To Sam, Jerry was as much a victim of his own innocence as his obstinacy. Things like this had been happening to men and women since the beginning of time—"it was a story you could write [a book] about, the psychology of how something like this could happen." But from Sam's perspective "it could only happen to Jerry Lee Lewis right on the springboard of way over the rainbow." And factoring in the defection of Johnny Cash and Carl Perkins to the siren call of the big record companies, it said something to Sam that he found almost impossible to put out of his mind. He wasn't going to feel sorry for himself, but he wasn't going to struggle against fate either. And he wasn't going to lose his own sure sense of self, no matter what the world might have in store for him.

As for Jerry, he acted as if it didn't bother him in the least. He and Myra were in love—he knew that much, and that was *all* he needed to know. And those who were closest to him believed him. "I don't think he ever realized," said Roland Janes, who would continue working with him for the next few years. "He didn't think he did anything wrong. He was very sincere. I know that he truly, dearly loved Myra. I mean, he still wanted to have his good times. But he was like a kid genius in a way, and over the years Myra kind of grew up, and I don't think he ever did. But he was actually a genius at the same time."

He never complained, Roland said, speaking in terms that might equally well have applied to Sam. But even so, there was an observable difference in him after he returned from England. "Jerry's a very, very proud man," Roland said, "and I really and truly think he didn't understand what all the uproar was about. But it did get to him—there was a certain sadness [and] he probably became a little more arrogant as a self-defense mechanism."

He had gone, as he famously said, if not necessarily with mathematical precision, from $10,000 a night to $250 a night, but he was not going to beg any man for anything. "What could I do?" he said. "Holler and scream?" He was still Jerry Lee Lewis—the only one.

NONE OF THIS IMPINGED in any case on the ambitious plans that Sam had formulated for a brand-new, forward-looking, and up-to-the-minute recording studio, with all the latest technology and ultramodern, space-age design. In fact, if anything, this latest debacle only solidified those plans all the more. The future clearly did not lie in carefully nurturing and developing a roster if the big record companies, or fate, or some damn character flaw or event that no one could ever have predicted, was simply going to come along and snatch it away. And there was no question that the marketplace was rapidly changing. It was no longer a singles market, stereo and the long-playing album were here to stay, and with the demise of "personality radio" it was becoming more and more evident that rock 'n' roll was losing its lock on the buying public, whether by accident or design.

A little company, a makeshift studio, couldn't possibly compete under these conditions — *unless* it provided a service that the big record companies needed. That was where the studio came in. Everybody needed some place to record, a sleek modern studio that could provide quality, service, and *guaranteed hits* for reasonable rental fees. And having a full-scale studio at his disposal would allow Sam to diversify his own recording activities — whatever new trends might transpire, the beat, he was confident, was never going to go away. The new climate, Sam suggested to *Billboard* some months later, might very well provide a resurgent demand for "authentic rhythm and blues." Furthermore, there was likely to be a market for modernized versions of the standards, not to mention the potential for a revival of some of the best aspects of the swinging big-band sound.

He threw himself into the new venture with a fervor that had been largely missing from his studio involvement since Jack and Bill Justis had taken over so many of the producing chores. He had found the perfect location in early June, a former Midas Muffler shop just around the corner from 706 Union that could easily be gutted and designed by its new owner in a way that would instantly stamp it as the home of Sam C. Phillips International Recording. It had room for two studios, including one which at forty-five feet by forty-five feet would be nearly four times the size of his current location, and Sam planned to equip it with all the latest audio features, including (for variable acoustics) custom-built reversible wall panels reflective on one side, absorptive on the other, three live echo chambers to update Sun's patented slapback sound, and two German-made Neumann lathes, one mono, one stereo, which at a cost of more than $30,000 apiece would permit him to match the mastering standard that Bill Putnam, the pioneering designer and developer of Universal Recording in Chicago, had long provided for the industry. Sam signed the contract for a distinctive broken quarry-tile roof with an elevated dance floor and bandstand on June 24 and engaged contractors, carpenters, and engineers to begin work on the building immediately. "Woodshed recordings" had had it, he told the world as the new studio began to take shape—from now on, he said, almost as if he were trying to persuade himself, he would be *"concentrating everything on sound."*

As for the label, it was, necessarily, a time of retrenchment. Jud was the first to go. He collected his last paycheck on July 11 and moved back to Florence, taking with him the customized Greyhound bus that had been such a nagging bone of contention between him and his brother. The bus was a dream that Jud had long had, a kind of rolling hospitality center on which he could freely dispense drinks and favors in all the cities he visited on his never-ending round of promotion tours. So far it had cost Sam close to $8,000 in its two-month life span—which included the installation of velvet-red draperies and carpeting, a lounge equipped with a full-sized television set, an elaborate sound system, two big captain's chairs upfront, a fully stocked bar, and various other sundries and amenities that continued to be added even as the bus continued to undergo one costly repair after another. It barely made it to New York on its inaugural trip in the middle of May, and when Jud orchestrated a grand arrival in Sheffield a month later for Jerry Lee Lewis' return to the tiny community center where he and an unknown Jerry Lee had first met, they had to back up again and again to get up the hill to the Wilson Dam, with Jud exhorting the bus, the driver, and the assembled multitudes, "She'll make it. She'll make it." It was, said Knox, a wide-eyed passenger on the trip and even at twelve a keen but never unkind observer, "a total, first-class bad bus."

It wasn't just the money, Sam was always quick to point out. It was the differences that had existed between them since childhood. Jud simply didn't seem to have any common sense. He was not a businessman in any way, shape, or form—and as charismatic as he might be (and Sam would be the first to admit he was charismatic), he was as likely to go out and captivate the first drunk he met on the street as someone who might actually be useful to them in business—and then tell that drunk,

Jerry Lee and Jud on the bus (a later bus, but still . . .). *Courtesy of Colin Escott*

or that businessman, all the things that Sam and the company were doing wrong, and all the ways that Jud would do them better.

For now, in any case, Jud made it perfectly clear that he was not abandoning either the entertainment industry or Jerry Lee Lewis, even as he retreated to selling used cars in his hometown. After all, he was the one primarily responsible for the success of both Sun and its most recent number-one artist, and, without any need for a title, he became in effect Jerry's manager while making plans for a triumphant reentry into the music business that would eclipse in the boldness and sweep of its vision anything his brother had ever done.

Johnny Cash finished up his last recordings for Sam on July 17 and, at the urging of Bob Neal, who had little doubt that his only client was on the threshold of a bright new future in the movies, moved to California with his family about a month later. For all of his anger and disappointment over the dissolution of their relationship, Sam wished him well — and he wished himself well, too, in a letter to the industry that appeared in both *Billboard* and *Cash Box* in September.

"Sun Records has patiently recorded Johnny Cash with always

potent material," he pointedly wrote, "first in the country category and gradually manipulating his material and approach to songs to gain him a fantastic following in the pop field. . . .

Through the help of our Sun distributors and our ever faithful D.J. friends we have built another artist into a solid commercial performer who sells records one after the other. Sun has always believed in building artists, not just selling a single record. This has been our aim since the beginning and will remain so.

It was also Sun's aim, Sam stressed with no less sincerity than self-interest, to continue selling Johnny Cash records. To that end, ever since learning of Cash's intention to sign with Columbia, Sun had spent the last five months "producing some of the finest sides for future Sun releases on Cash that we have ever had the pleasure of cutting.

Please believe us when we say you are in for some tremendous releases on Cash on SUN for at least the next two years.

Our thanks to Johnny for being a wonderful person to work with during our association. We are going to miss him no end around 706 Union, but our aim is to keep him "hot" on Sun "If the Good Lord's Willing and The Creek Don't Rise."

> *Appreciatively,*
> *Sam C. Phillips, President*
> *Sun Record Co.*

For all of those reasons, and others unspoken, he put everything he had behind "The Ways of a Woman in Love," the first departure-anticipatory Cash release, which rose to the top of the country charts in October and even reached number 24 pop, while Columbia's initial release languished in its wake.

Roy Orbison, too, left that summer. He had grown increasingly unhappy with Sam over his neglect by the company and the direction of his career. For whatever reason, Sam just never had time for him anymore, and Jack continued to make light of his aspirations as a ballad singer, even as Roy insisted with greater and greater vehemence that this was precisely what he wanted to do. The result was that he barely got to record at all, and when he did he was palmed off on Jack and Bill Justis, who fed him novelty songs and novelty productions for which he had neither love nor affinity, as he watched the company slowly drift apart with a mixture of relish and regret.

Early in the year he wrote a mid-tempo song, "Claudette," as a tribute to his wife, and he gave it to the Everly Brothers, who had had two number 1 pop hits in a row the previous year, at a show in Hammond, Indiana. They recorded it within a matter of weeks and put it out as the B-side of their next single. By May, the A-side, "All I Have to Do Is Dream," stood at the top of the charts, and through the Everly Brothers Roy met the song publisher Wesley Rose (also the publisher of Hank Williams), who signed him to a songwriting and management contract and encouraged him to move to Nashville. By the end of September, Roy had cut a single for RCA. Which led in turn to a lawsuit by Sam challenging his right to sign any of these new contracts. In the end he agreed to sign over the rights to all of the songs he had written and recorded at Sun to Sam, finding even further support for the bitterness he would continue to feel for the rest of his life at the way he had been treated by Sam.

Sam for his part sensed some form of collusion — he didn't think it was accidental that Roy should jump ship in the wake of all these other desertions, and he was pissed off and hurt that they should all be rejecting him in this way. He was at a strange point of paralysis in his thinking. On the one hand, he blamed himself for the departures — they stemmed as much as anything else from his own distraction. At the same time, he knew — or he thought he knew — there was nothing he could do about it. Eventually they would all leave him for "a bunch of bullshitters talking big money." But it preyed on him that he had never gotten the most out of some of his artists, that because of limitations of time or attention he had failed them, he had failed to deliver on the promise that he had originally seen in them. Roy perhaps most of all because of the meticulous craftsmanship that he brought to his work. Sam wasn't sure that he would ever have taken the big-ballad orchestral route that would soon provide the perfect vehicle for that craftsmanship with one enduring pop standard after another (probably not, he was perfectly willing to admit — "perfectionism" scared him), but he knew that he could have, he *should have,* done better by Roy.

The business, it seemed, was changing in every way. Dewey Phillips, who, as much as any man, could be credited with sharing the vision that had propelled Sam from the start, was out of a job. Growing demands for uniformity of presentation, along with an ever-increasing reliance on pain pills, had doomed Dewey, and at the end of July he did his last show on WHBQ, the station that his maniacal exercise in inspired anarchy, *Red Hot and Blue,* had helped to build. Just before he was scheduled to leave for his new job in Little Rock, just 135 miles from Memphis (though for Dewey, as his biographer Louis Cantor wrote, it might as well have been on the moon), Elvis' mother, Gladys, died, at the age of forty-six, and Sam and Dewey drove out to Graceland together.

They found Elvis inconsolable in his grief, alone in a crowd of friends and family who were unable to persuade him to leave his mother's body. Drawing on his own experience at the funeral home in Florence, when as a very young man he had been thrust into the position of reassuring a bereft mother that she could entrust her dead child to his care, Sam got Elvis to go out to the pool with him, away from everyone else. He would never forget, he said, the dead leaves by the pool. Slowly they started talking—about death, about mortality, about what it is like to lose someone you can never replace, and how death comes to us all. Sam explained to him "exactly what the mortician's field of work was. Elvis kept talking about the body and how he didn't want to give it up to anyone else. [But] he knew I wasn't going to give him any damn bullshit or try to make him artificially feel good about it. [And] eventually . . . I was able to convince him to let his mother go."

Dewey left for Little Rock the day after the funeral, but within weeks he was on the phone, begging Sam to help him get back home. Sam was able to get him a job at WHEY, the little station in Millington, about twenty miles outside of Memphis, that he had gotten involved in after selling his station in Marked Tree, Arkansas, and Dewey was back on the air by the end of the year. Even that distance proved too much for Dewey ("I was so hungry to get back in Memphis," he told *Press-Scimitar* columnist Bob Johnson, "I was ready to change my name to Maybellene and go with [Sam's all-girl station] WHER"), and by the following August Sam had helped get him a spot at a revamped WHHM, at one time one of Memphis' premier stations. There he would remain for nearly three years—but, sadly, he never regained his equilibrium, his popularity, or his confidence. At this point it was hard to see Dewey, even from Sam's wholly forgiving point of view, as anything but a lost soul.

Jud soon found believers in Florence, three prominent doctors, in particular, willing to put up what Jud said was something like a million dollars for him to start his own record company. So he did. It was supposed to be called "Jud," but then there was a printing error with the labels, so it became "Judd" when the first record, "Back to School" and "Sweet and Innocent," the very song that Roy Orbison would cover within a matter of weeks in his RCA debut, came out in August. It was a local effort through and through (written, performed, played, published, and produced — albeit in Nashville — by Shoals-area songwriters and musicians), and Jud almost immediately got the singer, Bobby Denton, a recent high school graduate from Cherokee, just outside Florence, booked on the September 6 Saturday-night *Dick Clark Show.*

"We Made It!" wrote Bill Jay, the *Florence Times* reporter Jud had invited along for the twenty-three-hour ride to New York on his "special customized bus outfitted for future Denton and Judd Records tours." Jud had in fact just taken official possession of the bus for a nominal sum of $6,500, which the purchase agreement seemed to recognize might very well never be paid but which specifically exempted its previous owner from any future liabilities or creditors' claims. They rolled into New York at about six o'clock Friday morning, Bill Jay reported, with Dr. Al McClendon, one of the label's principal investors, the driver, a porter, and the barely twenty-year-old singer and his wife in tow. As impressed as he was with the bus's "plush and swanky" accommodations ("Man, what comfort!" Jay wrote), the reporter was even more impressed by Jud's appetite for the business. While everyone else was planning a leisurely day off, focused mainly on taking in the sights, Jud was off to the races, "touring the Tin Pan Alley offices, the record and agency marts and the network officers." As Jay observed, Jud was certainly well known here, and "he really gets around." There was no question that he had big plans for his new company — and they didn't stop with Judd Records' first "hit" single. The "energetic brother of Sun Records executive Sam Phillips," fired up as he was with all that evangelical faith and zeal, was clearly going to put his hometown of Florence, Alabama, on the map.

Sam had no such faith at this point in any aspect of the business as it was currently constituted. He and a number of other record manufacturers had gotten together to air their views at the big NAMM (National Association of Music Merchants, an umbrella organization going back to 1901) Convention, in July. With Sam and Vee-Jay Records General Manager Ewart Abner as co-organizers, they had determined "with a spontaneity born of necessity" to create an organization of their own, made up exclusively of independent record manufacturers and distributors, in hopes of ensuring their survival. Sam and his lawyer, Roy Scott, went to the initial meeting in Chicago at the end of September with about forty other like-minded attendees, including Atlantic, Imperial, Duke, Vee-Jay, Specialty, and Keen Records executives. ("We huddled together like sheep," said Atlantic vice president Jerry Wexler, "for protection from the storm.") There was lots of bullshit, as Sam saw it, and lots of lively discussion, much of it instigated by Sam. There had been a time, not so long ago, when he might have refrained from voicing his opinions quite so directly, but more and more he had come to be guided by the philosophy "Make your prints known. You better leave a footprint, man, so they can find your ass." This was a matter of life and death, goddamnit, and they had better all be prepared to have their ass found.

In the end it was agreed to hold a full-scale convention in Chicago the following June. Ewart Abner, a longtime veteran in the r&b business and one of the few blacks in a position of such executive prominence, was elected provisional president, Sam vice president, and Roy Scott was appointed legal counsel, with Sam paying all legal expenses until the organization was fully vested in June. The name they decided upon was ARMADA (American Record Manufacturers and Distributors' Asssociation), suggested by Keen Records' Andy Litschi, which Sam thought was perfect with its evocation of a great historical era—he just hoped they wouldn't meet the same fate that the Spanish navy had some 375 years earlier at the hands of Sir Francis Drake.

He visited Chess Records' new headquarters at 2120 South Michigan Avenue while he was in town. Leonard Chess showed him the in-house studio that this twenty-three-year-old whiz kid, Jack Wiener, a protégé of Bill Putnam's, had built for him. Wiener had been doing all of Sam's mastering for the last year or so, ever since Putnam had decamped for the West Coast, and Sam got together with him to talk about the new studio he was building in Memphis, for which he wanted Wiener to design a custom board. He watched Leonard's brother, Phil, produce a session on Chuck Berry, too, and was not particularly impressed. He had never thought Phil, or Leonard for that matter, had much of a feel for the music—they were *businessmen* first and foremost—but there was nothing you could do to keep Chuck Berry's spirit down. It was that same irrepressible spirit that Sam had always sought in the music that he recorded—"he had that *abandon*. You listen to the lyrics, man, [and] you want to do a little bit of everything that he talks about in his songs." It almost didn't matter what you did at the board, it didn't matter what was the subject of his song, it was the *vitality* of the man and the music—there was simply no way you could keep that from coming out.

He and Leonard talked about old times. Leonard kidded him that if he hadn't screwed Sam on that Jackie Brenston bus deal, Sam would probably have sold Elvis' contract to Chess. Sam chuckled and said maybe so, but he was no longer interested in ingratiating himself. He believed at this point he had *proved* himself—and he wished to hell, as he had wished more times than he could count over the years, that he had somehow or another been able to block the Howlin' Wolf from going to Chicago and casting his lot forever with Leonard and Phil Chess. There was so much that he and the Wolf could have done together—but, so far as he knew, the Wolf had never looked back.

It was, all in all, time well spent: the weekend meeting, getting together with Leonard, getting a chance to see Chuck Berry in action. Leonard might very well be a cutthroat businessman—they were *all* cutthroats as far as he was concerned, but, hell, they were all just men in business for themselves, there was no point in dwelling on any of that. Sam had always been a firm believer in the power of positive thinking, he had struggled so hard to beat back the black tide of despair, and he was not about to give in to it now.

This new ARMADA enterprise, he told Barbara Barnes when he got back from Chicago, could be the salvation of the industry. What was the alternative? If the majors regained their hold on the record business, like they were trying to do now, that would be the death of the music. Only if the independent labels banded together—*and* were able to resolve their differences with their distributors, who seemed to be looking for a deal that eliminated all risk by permitting them a policy of unlimited returns—could they survive. Self-interest alone should dictate the result. These record company owners and distributors were intelligent people, he insisted, *business*people of some acumen—they were not going to all march like lemmings into the sea.

As if to demonstrate his renewed faith, and perhaps also to safeguard his investment, Sam re-signed Jerry Lee Lewis to a new five-year contract at the beginning of September, with a 5 percent artist royalty rate (up from the 4 to which he had agreed just nine months earlier) and recognition of a yet-to-be established publishing company in Jerry Lee's name. Although Oscar Davis was still technically his manager, Jerry asked Jud whether he should sign the new contract, and, surprisingly, Jud for once seemed to defer to his younger brother. So on Jud's advice he signed, he told journalist Chet Flippo in 1989, for "no guarantee, no nothing" at a time when, he declared, "I could've been on Columbia Records [and] never . . . had no downfall at all." But evidently not even Jud joined him in this thinking at the time.

Sam put out two more releases on Jerry in rapid succession, one in August, one in November — but neither did anything. The second, "I'll Sail My Ship Alone," a wonderful rollicking tribute to one of the few piano players Jerry ever acknowledged as an influence, "hillbilly boogie" pioneer Moon Mullican, was attached to an imaginative promotion Jud had come up with for the artist he was now at last officially managing. To encourage renewed sales interest, Sam wrote to his distributors, Sun Records was making available a special edition of the new single, on which the artist had forgone all royalties, at a cost of only sixteen cents per record. There would be just one hundred thousand copies made available at this price, and each regular Sun distributor would have "an option on a percentage of the 100,000 records identical to the percentage of records you sold of the total volume of 'Great Balls of Fire' . . . Jerry Lee Lewis' greatest-selling record to date." All orders were to be sent to Jud Phillips at 1154 Hermitage Drive, Florence, Alabama, with billing to come from the Sun office. "Thanks," Sam signed off, "and Good Luck!"

Jud meanwhile was building up his business from his home on Hermitage Drive, just as he had said he would. Jerry Lee Lewis was only a stepping-stone to greater things. He signed Cookie and the Cupcakes, an r&b act out of Louisiana, and leased a record by them called "Mathilda" that he proudly put out as Judd Records' second release. His faith proved justified as the record eventually rose to number 47 on the pop charts and came to be recognized, as music historian John Broven has written, as the "quintessential anthem" of South Louisiana "swamp pop." But Jud's plans envisioned a broad sweep of sales and promotional activities, which he incorporated under the banner of "Promotions Unlimited" and which would rapidly come to include touring buses for both Jerry Lee and Cookie and the Cupcakes (Jerry Lee's would advertise "The Great Ball of Fire" and display red, licking flames) and concert dates on which his two stars would appear as co-headliners. So convinced was he of the limitless possibilities, and so convincing in his personal salesmanship, that he got Sam's and his next-older brother, Tom, who had been working for the Scott Paper Company in Mobile for more than ten years, to quit his job, mortgage his home, and even cash in his life insurance to get in on the ground floor of the business. "Dad was easily swayed," said Tom's son Johnny. "And if you're easily swayed, the worst person you could be around was Uncle Jud, because, I mean, he had a gift. Uncle Jud said, 'This is how much I need,' and Dad did his best to raise as much as he could — anything that had any value he sold and he put it into working with Uncle Jud on Jerry Lee Lewis."

For Tom, a mild-mannered man who had always not so secretly wanted to be in the record business himself (he had taken it upon himself to go out to Gulf Coast radio stations for Sam with Elvis' earliest records), it was like a heaven-sent opportunity. He trusted Jud, just as he trusted Sam, and his faith never wavered as he went out first as Jerry Lee's road manager (he knew buses from his early experience working in his wife Lucille's family bus business in Sheffield — Lucille was Sam's wife Becky's cousin) and then, as Jud's ambitions expanded, as something like a full-fledged partner. He even brought in another investor, a well-to-do Mobile businessman who was his neighbor, and put his oldest son, Tom Jr., out on the road with Jerry.

Sam viewed all of these developments with more than a little skepticism. The record manufacturing business was hardly anything to put your faith in at this point — and he didn't think Jud had any more idea of what he was doing than he ever had. Nor could he shake the suspicion that Jud was like a serpent whispering in Jerry's ear about how Sam didn't really love him, he had *never* loved him, it was Jud who had championed Jerry — and he had little doubt that if that *was* what Jud was doing, Jerry would believe him. But he could never catch him at it, and there was nobody working harder for Jerry right now than Jud — even if it seemed sometimes like a hopeless task.

There was very little else in the current crop of Sun releases to excite Sam, other than to try to stick it to Columbia once again with another Johnny Cash release (this one, "It's Just about Time," barely scratched the country Top 30, but the next, "Luther Played the Boogie," drawn from a 1955 session, hit number 8 the following May). He was spending less and less time in the studio in any case, leaving almost all the work to Jack and Bill Justis and Cecil Scaife, a veteran radio and record promotion man Sam had met early on at KFFA in Helena, Arkansas, whom he had hired in November to more or less replace Jud.

From Sam's point of view one of the few rays of sunshine on an otherwise bleak horizon was Charlie Rich, an extraordinarily gifted twenty-five-year-old piano player who was crazy about jazz and had not only written a number of songs for Johnny Cash's pre-departure sessions but three of Jerry Lee's last four sides, including "It Hurt Me So" and "I'll Make It All Up to You," on which he had even played piano. Rich, who had been a star football player at Forrest City, Arkansas' Consolidated High School, and studied music briefly at the University of Arkansas, had been set up on a five-hundred-acre farm in West Memphis by his wealthy uncle Jack, after four years in the Air Force — but after a couple of years of farming, he was rapidly going broke both in spirit and in pocketbook. "As a farmer, he made a pretty good piano player," said his wife, Margaret Ann, an equally ardent jazz buff (in high school Charlie was known as Charlie Kenton for his dedication to jazz pianist and arranger Stan Kenton, while Margaret Ann modeled herself on Kenton's singer, June Christy, and they were the lone subscribers to *Down Beat* in their hometown). "I just knew," said Margaret Ann, "at least I thought I knew, Charlie was never going to be happy farming. It was always the music [he] cared about."

Charlie had been playing little gigs around town for the last year or two, solo and sitting in with jazz combos, and he and Margaret Ann had recently met Bill Justis at a Musicians Union party they had attended. There was some conversation about Sun Records, the label Bill worked for, but Margaret Ann had little expectation that Charlie would follow up on the opportunity with which he had been presented ("Charlie just didn't think a record company would be interested"), so one day she left the kids with a sitter, took some of the tapes they had made on the little Webcor tape recorder that was their first household possession, and went in to see Justis herself. He listened politely, responded in his usual deflective, hipsterish fashion (What was she coming to see him for, was his first verbal sally, if she was already Rich?), and then gave her some good advice: if Charlie could learn to simplify his style, if he could just cut it down to the basics and see how *bad* he could get, then Bill thought he might be able to really get somewhere. Why didn't she have Charlie come into the studio sometime, and they could talk about it?

It took her about a week to persuade Charlie to go in, but Justis made good on his promise. He gave Charlie a bunch of Jerry Lee Lewis and other records from the returns out back, Charlie said, "and he told me I'd have to learn to play the piano as technically bad as some of the other artists on Sun. . . . Only then could I make a good recording." It wasn't that Justis failed to recognize his potential. "I thought from the start he was a real good talent." The problem was his versatility, the fact that "he was such an exceptional musician," and that with his penchant for everything from Oscar Peterson and Miles Davis to B.B. King, he had not yet even come close to settling on a style.

Charlie took the records home and studied them carefully. At first he was a little taken aback by the primitive nature of the music — he was well aware of Elvis, in fact vocally he bore more than a passing resemblance to Elvis, with Frank Sinatra, Nat King Cole, the Four Freshmen, and maybe even a little bit of Eddie "Cleanhead" Vinson thrown in for good measure. But this was a whole different approach to music, discarding not just ninth chords and diminished sevenths but any pretense of sophistication, and after he got over his initial shock, he gradually came to recognize the bedrock of feeling that was at the heart of this music. It didn't hurt that like almost every other artist on the Sun label, he had grown up on gospel music and one of his first tutors on piano was a black sharecropper on a big plantation outside Crawfordsville that his father farmed, named C. J. Allen. It was C.J. who had helped mold his feeling for the blues. There were something like two hundred black families on the plantation that his father rented, "and you could hear the music in the cotton fields just riding your horse down a path" — but C.J. would frequently come by the house to sing and play the blues while Charlie's father, who had a wonderful voice (he was, said Charlie, "the Original Hippie, he was 290 pounds and beautiful, man"), would join in singing and playing the guitar.

Charlie formed a fast friendship with Bill Justis — he started playing with Bill's big band at the Peabody and the Hotel Claridge, and with a five-piece jazz combo, too, and by March of 1958 he was playing sessions and getting some of his songs cut. They were, in fact, his and Margaret Ann's songs for the most part (she helped with the words), but they both felt it was probably better at this point not to muddy the waters with a co-credit. He was working in the studio with Justis and Jack Clement almost exclusively, but his talent as a songwriter and a session player did not escape Sam's notice. He had some initial reservations about signing Charlie as an artist because of his value in the studio, but he didn't hesitate for long, signing him to a three-year recording contract on April 25, followed by a formal songwriter's contract on June 1 that carried with it an advance of $550.

It was not simply Charlie's talent that drew Sam to him. There was no question of his potential as an artist. And he was a handsome man, too. Big (six foot two, with a football player's build), with wavy, graying hair that only lent distinction to a sensitive, slightly fleshy face, he brought a different kind of sex appeal to Sun. The girls in the office all drooled over him, said publicity director Barbara Barnes. He was, said singer Barbara Pittman, "one of the best-looking men I'd ever seen. Elvis was pretty, but Charlie was handsome." And to Sally his very sensitivity, his almost painful shyness and reluctance to put himself forward in any way, let alone become a star, was part of the intrinsic appeal. To Sam, though, it was as if he had found another brother under the skin, like Dewey in a way, even more, though, like the Howlin' Wolf, improbable as that comparison might seem to anyone but Sam.

For Sam recognized in Charlie someone who felt every sling and arrow of outrageous fortune just as keenly as the Wolf or, for that matter, as Sam himself. Despite the self-styled triviality of his pop compositions, he was, as Sam saw it, a blues singer of a different order. And for all of the fact that he came from a decidedly more affluent background than any of Sam's other artists except for Jack and Bill Justis, he gave evidence in the way he sang and played his music, particularly the unaccompanied demos he kept churning out in the studio, of a range of emotions he could not otherwise even begin to express. Like Wolf, like Elvis, like all of the artists to whom Sam was most drawn, he poured out all of his feelings in his music—he possessed, in a term Sam reserved as his greatest compliment, the ability "to see all around his head, to hear all around his head," as if his very nerve endings were exposed.

"No one could get more out of a song than Charlie," Sam said. "He just didn't throw words away." There was no time for emotional embroidery with Charlie—he was able, quite simply—or Sam might have amended that to *compelled*—to put his naked feelings into his music.

Sam started going out to see Charlie when he played the Sharecropper on weekends. It was the one time Sally could remember their ever going to listen to an artist perform—Sam just didn't have time for that—and Charlie was singing jazz standards almost exclusively, not ordinarily

Sam's favorites. He was almost always drinking heavily, though it never seemed to affect his music, just took the edge off his pain — and Sam was able to unwind, too, drinking companionably with his attorney, Roy Scott, who loved Charlie's music nearly as much as Sam, in a way he rarely did in public. They were long, leisurely nights. "Charlie got lost in the music," said Barbara Barnes, who would show up frequently with a boyfriend. "I loved to hear Charlie play and sing in this atmosphere. He wasn't [just] playing to entertain." Part of Sam regretted that he was not able to re-create that same atmosphere in the studio. But somehow, for all the looseness of the studio sessions, Charlie was not able to let go in the same way, even if he was drinking — which, under the supervision of Jack and Bill, he frequently was. At the Sharecropper the alcohol seemed to fuel something else for both singer and listener — Sam couldn't imagine Charlie any happier. It was the one time that he seemed sure of himself and his ground.

Sam finally okayed a release on Charlie in October — it was on the Phillips International label, and it wasn't a very good record, a song Margaret Ann had helped shape with the explicit aim of getting him on Dick Clark's Philadelphia-based *American Bandstand* (it was called "Philadelphia Baby"), with an equally undistinguished pop artifact on the other side. Both songs were marked by un-Sun-like modulations, adept piano playing, and a throbbing voice that would have been more suited to more throbbing material. The record did get Charlie booked on *American Bandstand,* but then the appearance was canceled at the last minute. The record didn't really sell, and, Sam had to admit, it didn't deserve to sell. But he blamed himself. Even though he had had nothing to do with it other than to approve its release, he felt more than a twinge of guilt that for the first time he had left something about which he so passionately cared entirely up to his lieutenants.

In the meantime he responded to Charlie's wife Margaret Ann's plea for help with their household bills. If they could just get out of debt, she told Bill Justis, she felt like they could make a fresh start. So Sam told Charlie to have her come by the studio, and he had Sally make out checks to the doctor, the dentist, the drugstore, the oil company, the grocery store, and clothing and farming supplies stores, thirteen checks in all, adding up to something like $1,000 on top of Charlie's regular writer's draw. Maybe, he consoled himself, it just wasn't Charlie's time yet. When it was, he felt certain, he would be ready to give himself over

Under construction, April 1959. *Courtesy of Colin Escott*

to Charlie's music body and soul, with the same single-mindedness of purpose that he had devoted to every other one of his major artists.

Right now, though, construction work on the new studio was occupying more and more of his time. What had started out as an opportunity to expand the horizons of the Sam Phillips Recording Service, Inc. was consuming almost all of his attention and drawing him away for days at a time from anything to do with making records. "Every decision, every inch in that building," said Sally, "there was a decision that had to be made, and Sam made every one. Then Denise Howard [who had designed the WHER studios in the Holiday Inn] came in to do the decorating on the colors and the carpets and all of the furniture and Sam's office" — and Sam, as Denise would have been the first to attest, oversaw all that, too. It was Denise who came up with the overall Piet Mondrian design, but it was Sam who insisted on and refined all the futuristic accoutrements and art deco refinements, the flourishes of geometric patterns and bold blocks of color, along with individual touches like the pyramidal shapes on the front of the building, the built-in jukebox on his irregularly shaped custom desk, and the opening notes of "Raunchy" painted gaily on the transom above the door. "He loved it," said Sally. "It was his first project, from the ground up, and he saw what he had created . . . and he loved it!"

Barbara Barnes watched all of these developments with a certain degree of concern. In some ways she saw the company standing at the dawn of a new era, with Charlie Rich its next big star, Bill Justis, with all of his musical cleverness and nose for trends, a sure bet for another smash, and Jerry Lee Lewis almost certain to be returned to his rightful place in the musical firmament. As for Sam, she did not detect any lessening of energy, determination, self-confidence, or vision—it was just that his focus had so radically shifted. It was no longer just the construction project that consumed his attention, there were FCC applications and site permits to be filled out for the new radio station in Lake Worth, Florida, just outside West Palm Beach, a second all-girls station to be modeled on WHER, which he hoped to have on the air by the following spring. And then there was, of all things, a zinc mine in a tiny hamlet in a remote north-central area of Arkansas called Yellville.

The zinc mine came about when Sam saw a chance to buy out his original radio partner, Clarence Camp, the wealthy jukebox operator who had financed the operation when he and Jimmy Connolly first filed for a radio station back in 1952 and who had remained a 32 percent partner in WHER ever since. Camp, who had no interest in radio and more shares in the zinc mine than he cared to hold on to, came out to the house with his partner, Parker Henderson, to tell Sam what a bright future zinc mining had, despite the prevailing opinion that zinc had reached its peak demand during World War I. This was a mine that was not played out, Parker Henderson exhorted Sam enthusiastically, there was all kinds of ore just waiting in the ground to be unearthed—the challenge was to figure out how to mine it and then, in the absence of good roads and regular trains, how to get it out of Yellville.

Sam was intrigued by the challenge, but he was even more intrigued by the opportunity to become undisputed majority owner of WHER. (Kemmons Wilson, of course, would retain his 32 percent share.) So after a protracted discussion about the mechanics of ore extraction and a careful examination of the pictures of the mine that Parker Henderson had brought with him, he proposed the idea of a swap. For $42,500 Sam would purchase two hundred thousand of Mr. Camp's shares in the mine, along with all of his interest in the radio station and a five-year extension of the station's lease on Mr. Camp's land as a transmitter site. In the end it was a deal that was clearly to everyone's benefit, and everyone's satisfaction, but perhaps to his own surprise as much as anyone else's, Sam's interest in the technical challenge of zinc mining had been piqued, and the mine would soon become more than just a footnote in his financial portfolio.

"Well, boys, I'm a millionaire," he announced to Bill Justis and Jack Clement, in an expansive mood very likely fueled by drink, and indeed his 1958 income tax filing shows a net worth of over $700,000, taking in all of his various holdings (including Arkansas Zinc and Lead, a $25,000 partnership in some oil wells that he had gone into with Buster Williams, and Gold Coast Broadcasting, the umbrella organization for the new radio station), not to mention the substantial amount of money he had in the bank. There was no question, said Sally, that he was proud of having achieved such a quintessential American marker — "but after that, you know, it never really muttered, he never knew how much money he had." This just showed how far he had come.

H E FIRED JACK AND BILL at the beginning of February. It was all due to a misunderstanding. It was late at night, and they had been running a session, and everyone was drinking — and then Sam came in, and he had been drinking, too. The way Jack told it, "Sam was out there setting in the bass drum case, just being silly. Then him and Justis got to arguing, and Justis was kind of snotty. I was living out in Frayser, across the Wolf River, and it was starting to snow. So I said, "I've got to go" — I didn't say why, just I had to go. Somehow or another, Sam took that to mean, 'Well, don't hang out with this idiot,' or something like that. So the next day I came in, and there was these two big yellow [Sun Records] envelopes. One for me and one for Bill Justis that he had composed the night before." The letters were dated February 5 and appeared to have been typed by Sam. They were identical except for the salutation. "Mr. Jack Clement," Jack's began:

> Your services have been terminated with this company.
> Your services have been appreciated.
> I sincerely hope that you feel that they have. You must realize that
> much responsibility rests on my shoulders and that I have never tried

to encoumber any encoumberance on any situation or circumstance
that has ever occurred. Therefore, I feel that you two people have not
entirely had the best interest of this company in mind.

Please believe me when I say I'm sorry to loose you, but when we
feel that we must know more than the man that's paying the bills, we
must all prove it.

> My best,
> Appreciatively,
> Sam C. Phillips

The next day, Sam offered to help Jack and Bill set up their own labels and to distribute them, if that's what they wanted—but that didn't change the fact of their firing. For all the ambiguity of the spelling and language that Sam used in the letters ("There was some kind of strange use of the English language in there," Jack noted), Jack never doubted that the root cause of their banishment was that Sam's feelings were hurt. But Sally suspected there might be more to it than that. Sam had given Jack and Bill an interest in publishing companies of their own the previous summer (the split was 75-25 for Sam), and before long it began to appear as if their own songs, or songs that were being funneled into their companies, were being pushed harder at the sessions that they produced. It didn't come to very much money, but with their salaries seemingly topped out at $90 a week, Sally wondered if that wasn't the real reason for their banishment. Whatever the case, while their departure may have marked a watershed for the company, it never changed the nature of the relationships. After a suitably brief period of separation, Sam and Jack renewed their friendship and continued to be the best of friends to the end of Sam's life (Bill remained close as well, until his own early death at fifty-five), and whatever else Sam may have felt on the subject, he never said another word about it.

He didn't have that luxury with Jud. Less than two weeks after firing Jack and Bill, he became aware that Jud was trying to peddle Jerry Lee Lewis' recording contract in New York, representing himself as Jerry's legally constituted agent to at least two independent record companies, and probably more. Sam remonstrated with him on the phone to no avail and then wrote to him at the Manhattan Hotel, where Jud was staying with their older brother Tom on what Tom took to be an ordinary promotion trip, if anything associated with Jud could be construed as ordinary.

"Dear Sir," Sam wrote on February 18:

> *This is to formally notify you in writing as we have numerous times on the telephone and in person of the damages you are causing in trying to "peddle" or sell Jerry Lee Lewis' services as a recording artist to another record manufacturer, when you are fully aware of his existing exclusive recording contract with this company.*
>
> *This company has had to go to considerable expense in sending our attorney to New York to try to get you to cease your contractual interfering. Your utter disregard for our rights under our contract has caused this company great harm in the trade by causing the various people in the trade to believe that this artist is a free agent.*

"We have this very day," Sam went on to write, "notified all major independent record manufacturers and all major record manufacturers," and he had written to American Federation of Musicians officer Henry Zaccardi as well, stating to one and all his plain intention to "prosecute to the fullest extent of the law any and all parties concerned with such a contractual interference," including his brother.

Which should have been the end of the matter.

Jerry Lee Lewis would clearly remain an exclusive Sun recording artist, and Jud would continue to be his personal manager. Judd Records was at this point enjoying its first national hit, as Cookie and the Cupcakes inched their way into the pop Top 50 while touring the country in their newly outfitted bus. As for Jud—everyone, as Sam ruefully observed, loved Jud. They saw him, it seemed, as an invincibly likable, perpetually raffish figure, a "colorful character" of great charisma and charm ("Jud was a juggernaut," said Atlantic vice president Jerry Wexler, "he had that great Southern charisma, and if you knew what was good for you—I mean there was no threat there, just that . . . gift of persuasion—you'd find yourself in agreement in a hurry") who clearly had gotten his brother's goat in a misunderstanding that reflected not one bit on his freewheeling reputation.

But in retrospect, this was where everything started to unravel.

It's hard to know what Jud could have been thinking. Perhaps he had a premonition of disaster, though this would hardly have been like Jud, who possessed a Micawberish faith that something was always bound to turn up. Perhaps it was simply having a hit, which has been the ruin of many an independent label without a follow-up hit to sustain it — which was certainly the case here. For without that follow-up, Judd Records couldn't get paid by its distributors even as pressing and manufacturing bills were mounting up and the buses continued to break down, and cash became an increasingly scarce commodity. Jud's doctor investors had long since disappeared, and with no money of his own Jud was forced to persuade Tom and their Mobile partner to go even further out on a financial limb, until in the end they lost everything. In September of 1959, Bill Lowery's NRC Records of Atlanta took over the label, with the announcement that Jud would be "joining NRC's offices here [in Atlanta] and will work on promotion for both the Judd and NRC labels." This, in fact, never happened. Instead, Jud remained in Florence, where he went back to the used-car business, while his wife, Dean, continued to work at her job at the Florence Implement Company and her long-suffering father, Mr. Hensley, continued to foot the bills, almost bankrupting himself in the process.

"I got a letter today from [your attorney] Roy Scott telling me to pay back the next 2 payments on Jud's note," Mr. Hensley wrote desperately to Sam on September 11, appealing to his son-in-law's one other sure source of support. "To save me I cannot make those payments."

He thought that he and Sam had an agreement that Sam would cover the note, while he himself took care of the $30,000 floor plan for Jud's used-car lot (essentially a credit line with the bank for car purchases), which he would be paying for the next year or more.

> *I have mortgaged my home, cashed my insurance policies and still owe a lot of money — that I am trying to pay each month. . . . As soon as I get this other paid then I will try to get you paid. But right at this time I never had less in my life. And can hardly meet my obligations first of each month and my wife and I both working.*

And so Sam once again accepted his responsibility. He wasn't going to leave Mr. Hensley in the lurch. Much less his brother.

As for Tom, he tried to go back to Scott Paper Company, but the job was no longer open. The power had been shut off at the house, which Tom had spent all his off-hours building by hand while the entire family, five kids at home, his wife, his mother-in-law, and himself, stayed in a little two-bedroom shack — but the house was no longer theirs anyway, he told the children. "Dad called Uncle Sam," recalled his sons Johnny and Skip (Samuel), twelve and eight at the time, "and [said], 'You know, I don't have anything. Do you have anything I can do?' Uncle Sam goes, 'The only thing I have is this old warehouse [at the back of the studio], where all the returns come back to. If you want to come up here, you can work there.'"

Sam sent the family money to live on while Tom got himself situated in Memphis. Then, finally, "Our mom drove us all up from Mobile in an old Plymouth — we didn't have enough room for the spare tire, so it was in the backseat and the little kids [sat] on top of it. Mom didn't even have a driver's license — she never drove after that trip, not one time — but Dad couldn't come get us, so she just said, 'Okay we're driving up,' and [as soon as] we got here, Dad put us to work in the warehouse." Eventually that became the family business — serving as a retail record store, one-stop distributor, and recording studio (under the umbrella names of Select-O-Hits and Select-O Sound), a succession of small independent labels, and eventually, after Tom bought out his brother's interest in 1978, the key distributor for rap and hip-hop (from the Sugar Hill Gang's "Rapper's Delight" to all of Three 6 Mafia's early hits) in Memphis.

That was the happy ending. The third partner, the Mobile businessman, as Johnny and Skip recalled, killed himself, and when they went to pay their respects at his house, one of his kids said, "My dad killed himself because of your dad." And there was nothing they could say, even though they knew it wasn't their dad at all. It was their Uncle Jud — and what he had done had affected their lives in a similar way, if not nearly as much.

Yet somehow they could never hold it against him. Uncle Sam and Uncle Jud were so similar, and so different at the same time. Once the family had moved up and settled in Memphis, Johnny and Skip said, "Uncle Jud and Uncle Sam would come by sometimes with Aunt Becky and Aunt Dean on Sunday afternoons when we weren't working, and they'd sit up [very straight] on this broke-down old sofa that Dad had, with the springs all broke on one side, and the three of them always ended up talking about Silas Payne and the music, you know, and the influence [of] what happened to them back in northern Alabama."

Tom was teetotal at the time. He had been a bad drunk as a younger man but had vowed not to touch a drop again until the youngest of his seven children, Kathy, who was then five, graduated from high school. Sam and Jud, on the other hand, were a very different story. To Johnny and Skip it was both comical and educational. "Uncle Jud was always drinking. I mean Uncle Jud you just never saw [sober] — he went to bed drinking and woke up drinking, and he was so flamboyant you really couldn't tell when he was drunk or not. Uncle Sam got more like Dad did when he would drink. He was a little bit over-affectionate. I mean Uncle Sam had never been a real affectionate person, at least to me. He was always outgoing, he was always extremely nice to us, he basically took care of [anyone] in the family who needed help without ever saying anything about it. But if he had a few drinks, he was a different person. [Whereas] Uncle Jud was *always* outgoing, every one of his nieces and nephews were like his children."

It went without saying which one the kids were rooting for when the two of them got into it, as Jud goaded Sam over one long-standing issue or another, and Sam, in his inflamed state, was unable to refrain from joining in, and Tom, who remained imperturbably calm throughout it all, was forced to step in as referee.

"Uncle Jud," said Sam's younger son, Jerry, who with his brother witnessed some epic battles on his own, "was always my favorite uncle — I think he was Knox's, too. I mean, you couldn't help but love him. He was just a great guy, you know, handsome guy, personality plus — he'd take you fishing, let you smoke, and all that stuff. But when they started drinking together, you could be sure things were fixing to start happening. And one of Uncle Jud's flaws, I thought, was he preached bad stuff to me and Knox about Sam, he'd tell us stuff that he shouldn't have been telling us. You know, sometimes I even agreed with him, but I just thought, this is kind of weird, some of the things he'd say to us about our daddy. I'm not sure at what point all that started, I just think when they disagreed on something Jud would make it a point to make sure everyone knew Sam's faults. But Sam, you know, I really give it to him, he never defended himself to us, he never said, 'Well, you know, your Uncle Jud —'" As much as he might be seething inside (and Jerry knew by his own nature how much *he* would be seething), "he never, ever came back with any rebuttal."

THERE WAS LITTLE to capture Sam's interest among the spate of new Sun and Phillips International releases, with the exception of a radical rock 'n' roll reworking of Nat King Cole's "Mona Lisa" by a sixteen-year-old singer from Jackson, Tennessee, named Carl Mann. Carl Perkins' original drummer, W. S. "Fluke" Holland, who, with Perkins no longer able to support a touring band, was on the verge of quitting the music business (he would instead join Johnny Cash and stay with him for the next forty-five years), brought the boy into the studio with the band he had been working with around town, and Sam was tickled enough by the irreverence and originality of his approach to sign him. "Mona Lisa" was unquestionably different, "an old tune with a new lift" as Sam would describe it in a publicity release, that Carl delivered "in his own highly individualistic manner." Whether you liked it or not, you were going to notice it, Sam said, and no doubt the controversy it engendered (ASCAP, according to Sally, in its role as self-appointed guardian of the music, tried to block Mann's similarly revamped version of Rodgers and Hammerstein's "Some Enchanted Evening" some nine months later) appealed to Sam, too — but what it was that appealed to him about eleven-year-old Sherry Crane's "Winnie the Parakeet," released during the same time period, may remain forever indecipherable.

Aside from the new recording studio, much of his time and attention at this point was focused on the new radio station in Lake Worth. He had located the frequency through an old friend from Florence, Garland Burt, with whom he had originally worked at WLAY and who had continued his radio career as announcer, then news director and program director at WLAK in Lakeland, Florida, after the war.

In February they found a suitable five-acre property for both the studio and the radio tower, and Sam sent Roy Scott and Earl Daly, the radio engineer with whom he had been involved in Marked Tree and Millington and who, like Roy, was a licensed pilot, down to Lake Worth in the little Cessna C-172 Sam had recently bought. He still didn't fly himself — he had sworn off flying following his rocky flight back from Chicago after Leonard Chess' son Marshall's bar mitzvah four years earlier. But the plane got a lot of use for business purposes, proving a good substitute for Jud's bus on short promotion trips as well as a quick commute to Lake Worth for Roy and Earl.

Sam himself made the fourteen-hour drive a number of times over the next few months, taking the family on vacation to Daytona Beach in April (he loved the sun and sand, observed his son Jerry, eleven at the time, "but he thought beaches make people lazy"), but whether he was in Florida or Memphis, he was never far removed from the challenge of putting the new station on the air. The whole family drove the two hundred miles from Daytona Beach to Lake Worth to see the new studio, and Sam stayed on there after the family went home. Dottie Abbott, Sam's first hire at WHER and still its program director, was screening job applicants while helping to establish the same format in Florida that had proved so successful in Memphis. The call letters for the new station were WLIZ, in tribute, Sam said, to film star Elizabeth Taylor, a glamorous symbol of female success, and the station's slogan when it went on the air at the end of May was "You'll love LIZ, LIZ loves you."

"It's an axiom in radio, based on painful experience, that lady announcers don't have what it takes," was the lead for *Billboard*'s June 1 story on LIZ's debut. "Last week, a certain rule-buster . . . Sam Phillips by name, opened a new station in Lake Worth, Fla., . . . with the promise that no live man's voice would ever be heard on it. . . . He made the move with serene confidence because three years ago in his home town of Memphis, Phillips opened a 1,000-watter, named it WHER, staffed it entirely with 'femsees,' and sent quivers thru the town that have still not let up." He also made clear, *Billboard* reported, that no Sun or Phillips International record had ever been played on WHER and never would be. *Billboard* puzzled over this, but, really, there was no mystery about it. For Sam, diversification alone offered any hope of success in the music business as it was currently constituted. The way Sam saw it, much of the point of the "payola" hearings that were still going on in Washington was to put the little man out of business — with one easy way being to charge collusion on the part of any independent record manufacturer who had the temerity to acquire his own radio stations and then left himself open to the accusation of "self-dealing" by playing music in which he had a financial interest.

But, as Sam had pointed out in his voluntary testimony to Congress the previous April, while nearly all of the songs in Sam's publishing catalogues were registered with BMI, not only had his radio station played none of his own songs but nearly 80 percent of the songs that it played were registered with ASCAP.

In addition, he offered a ringing defense of capitalism and creative diversity ("I am sure that this Committee is aware of the fact that 'creative talent' is not limited to a group or class, but rather to the genius of the individual," which had been greatly encouraged by BMI's "broad and divergent mode of operation") while stressing the punitive nature of forcing the independent entrepreneur to divest himself of assets that the big corporations could retain. "I respectfully submit," he concluded, "that the passage of this proposed legislation would . . . be an unnecessary and discriminatory barrier to the freedom of individuals, such as myself, to engage in lawful competitive enterprise" — and he was clearly determined to hold on to that same freedom now.

"I BELIEVE THE RECORD BUSINESS is still in its embryonic stages," Sam declared to the *Memphis Press-Scimitar* in an April 29, 1959, story headlined "He's Made $2 Million on Disks — Without a Desk." Rock 'n' roll wasn't dead, he went on. "The kids got tired of some of the 'typical' Rock and Roll, but I think they've shown they don't want any big change." Sam Phillips, on the other hand, the story pointed out, was prepared for change. "One day within the next two months," reporter Edwin Howard wrote, "Sun and Phillips International and related firms will be moving to swanky new studios nearby. 'Because we ran out of corners for corporations,'" Sam joked, while insisting that the luxurious trappings had nothing to do with the spirit of the music. There had always been doubters, he said at the conclusion of the article.

> A lot of people thought we were thru after Elvis. We came up with Carl Perkins. They thought we were finished when he had some bad luck and began to fade. We came up with Jerry Lee Lewis. Then Bill Justis. And altho Johnny Cash is no longer with us, we're still bringing out new singles by him and we have two LP albums and three EPs that are consistent top sellers. If people don't realize it now, let me say it one more time: We're in this business to stay.

And yet, for all of his brave declarations and repetitions of faith (the fact that "we are moving into a period of greater variety in taste," Sam told *Billboard* around the same time, represented "a healthy trend that will help stabilize the singles business"), it seemed sometimes like he was whistling in the dark. Rock 'n' roll — *real* rock 'n' roll — was invoked now more and more as if it were some dazzling, ephemeral moment forever frozen in the past; for all of Sam's talk of material success, his own records were no longer selling; and as his proud presentation of accomplishments might indicate, he seemed preoccupied in a way he never had been before not so much with the task in front of him as with all the skittering activities of yet another corporate CEO, however diverse and eccentric, by the standards of any ordinary corporate officer, those activities might be.

The new studio, in fact, was not even close to finished — Sam was too taken up with everything from the plantings to the rooftop dance floor and the furniture in his office, and he remained dissatisfied with the customized four-channel mixing board that Jack Wiener had built for him, to the point that Wiener kept coming down from Chicago to try to correct the problems. He was on his way to spending well over half a million dollars on the building, but, for all of his well-deserved reputation for thrift, he didn't care about that. He had the money to spend, and this was what he wanted to spend it on — he was just determined to get every detail right.

The first official ARMADA Convention gathered in Chicago on June 8 and 9, and Sam attended with high hopes, seeing it as perhaps the last opportunity for the independent distributors and record manufacturers, who had been cast in adversarial roles both by custom and legislation, to take a stand against a complete takeover by the majors. Something like 180 distributors and manufacturers attended, with panels specifically addressing such far from abstract technical issues as rack jobbing, transshipping, one-stops, record clubs, returns policies, bootlegging, discounts, and free goods, although "legal ramifications" prevented the organization from establishing any across-the-board official policy. It was all the more encouraging, *Billboard* reported, because, unlike most such conventions "it did not have the air of carnival or bacchanal, [instead] the distributors and manufacturers present spent their time in serious business discussions and behaved in an orderly and no-monkey-business manner."

But the highlight of the convention, according to nearly every participant, was the address of their newly elected vice president, Sam Phillips, who seemed to have taken it upon himself, to the delight and displeasure of equal numbers, to be the conscience of the industry.

Sam had given a great deal of thought to his address — he had always had grave misgivings about openly showing your hand to those you were seeking to convert. But the times were too desperate to hold back now, and the record men too imperiled. They stood, he felt, at an irrevoca-

ARMADA, Chicago, June 1959. Left to right: D.C. distributor Harry "Pop" Schwartz, unknown, Ewart Abner, Sam, and Roy Scott. *Courtesy of the Sam Phillips Family*

ble moment of crisis. Their very livelihood was threatened. And so he simply let fly.

"I got up and looked every one of these people, some of them double my age, in the eye. I said, 'There is no place in the independent record industry for anybody that's timid.' I said, 'You know, I love the inertia of the big companies. I mean that. I love that. But they can't create shit. They can shove an Eddie Fisher down our throat and put it on [a] network they own. But we can beat them.' I ripped every Jew, every Gentile, every black you can think of. I said, 'When in the hell are we going to grow up?' Man, I didn't hold back anything. I said, 'If you want to be little boys and act like goddamn thugs, then our records, abilities, talent, work, and everything is going to wind up — we're all going to be working for the big theater. We've got the chance of a lifetime here — we've been so innovative, and yet we don't do the right thing about our artists. We steal from each other. And we steal from the total principle that we have got to have to stay in business. We're going to [have to] act like something other than crooks.'"

He beat the cuff links off his shirt. It was, said flamboyant Mercury promo man Shelby Singleton, "a fist-pounding, fire-and-brimstone" speech in which Sam called them all "a sorry bunch of bastards." And in the end got a standing ovation. But they didn't like it, Shelby said, they didn't like it one bit.

Sam was well aware that he was not going to win any popularity contests, but he relied on Roy Scott, now officially elected as counsel to the new organization, to pave the way for him. "I always took Roy with me, 'cause where I was deficient in being somebody to talk to, Roy was just one of those people that could get acquainted with anybody and they all loved him." He came back from Chicago still of the belief that ARMADA could be the salvation of the industry—but just as convinced that time (and the herd instinct that had gotten them into this fix in the first place) was clearly not on their side.

Over the next six months nothing much happened, although Sam remained fully involved in both policy planning and strategic thinking. From his point of view ARMADA was becoming sidetracked trying to form an alliance with the RIAA (Recording Industry Association of America), which had been dominated by the majors since its founding in 1952 and was unlikely to have any interest in helping the independents now. But he remained in constant contact with ARMADA president Ewart Abner and other members of the board and was not about to give up on the organization yet, even though his faith was wavering.

What he became more and more involved in, though, improbably enough, was the zinc mine. He and Sally began taking long weekend trips to Yellville, Arkansas, fording streams in his blue '58 Cadillac, with his all-purpose foreman, O. T. Alexander, driving them occasionally (O.T. was construction foreman for the studio, too) and Mr. Camp's partner, Parker Henderson, a frequent presence. Roy Scott flew in from time to time in the little Cessna, and Sam even went up in it one time—but their flight came to a quick end when, after barely clearing some power lines, they flew over a cemetery and Sam just told Parker Henderson, who was piloting it, "Parker, turn this plane around." And, Sally said, he did. "He just made a loop and came back." And that was the last time Sam went up in the air for a very long time.

There was only one decent place to eat in the area, a little restaurant called Spring Lake between Yellville and Harrison, and they stayed at a motel right on the river a little way out from Yellville. For lunch every

Arkansas Zinc and
Lead Corporation.
*Courtesy of the Sam
Phillips Family*

day they had Vienna sausages from the general store in Maumee, the
little settlement at the head of the rugged trail to the mine.

But it was not just a pastoral idyll. "Sam really got into it," Sally said.
He got into every aspect of the operation—but it was the mining issue,
she said, to which he addressed himself first.

"They had this bucket that carried the miners down, and they would
fill it up with all this rock and dump it in the crusher, and then you
had to have water to carry it down to where it becomes ore. Sam said,
'The bucket is too slow. You can't get enough ore up here to do anything
with.' So he designed a motor that shot that bucket out of the ground.
Then he built a dam on this little stream so we would have all the water
that the creek was furnishing because, you know, it takes a lot of water
in mining to wash all of this stuff down. And, oh, goodness, here comes
a flood and just washes the dam all the way down! So then he builds
the dam again, and do you know that the beavers took it apart piece by
piece!"

What amazed her was that, no matter what happened, Sam never
got upset, he never lost his temper, just addressed himself (sometimes

literally) to the problem of getting back up the hill. It must have seemed sometimes almost like therapy. One thing after another could go wrong, Sally said, but in this rural retreat he never lost his appearance of calm equilibrium.

In the fall Sam took Becky and the boys to see the mine. He had a brand-new 1960 purple El Dorado with air suspension, a white vinyl top, and solid white interior. He had a setup with Southern Motors, the Cadillac dealership just down the street from the studio, to trade in his two Cadillacs every year or so at optimal value and get two new models, generally a convertible and a hardtop, that were always distinctive in color and design — there were probably no more than five others in the world made just like the purple El Dorado, he told Knox.

It was a real family outing. They got bologna sandwiches — "the best bologna sandwiches in the world," as Knox recalled – but when they got near Yellville, it seemed like they would have to turn back, as water from the swollen mountain streams covered the road and rose up above the rims of the wheels. But, to Knox's surprise, "Sam thought, 'Hell, I'll just drive through [it],' and the car lifted up — it was the weirdest thing, driving through the mountains in Yellville, Arkansas, in a brand-new El Dorado Cadillac with air suspension that looked like one of those cars with the giant tires that are raised up real high these days as trucks. Then when we got there, Sam went down in the mine. All the way down. He was talking to all the guys, and they wanted him to go down, and he didn't really want to go. But he did. I thought, now wait a minute, he wouldn't even get in his own airplane, but he went down in this mine. All the way down. I have no idea why he did it, but he did — and he came out looking okay. But he never went down again."

The last time Sam and Sally visited Yellville, in the early spring of 1960, they drove on to Lake Worth to see about the radio station. That was where Sam got the call from O. T. Alexander informing him that the ore had "flipped over." Which meant, Sam had to explain to her, that the vein they were mining was no longer there, and there was nothing to be done about it. "And do you know," said Sally, "we never went back. We never [even] went back to that place to see." All of the books and business records for the enterprise were in the little motel room that O.T. had been staying in, and that was where they remained. Sally always wanted to go back at some point, if only to revisit a place where they had

had such good times. But, she concluded, it was just something that Sam had wanted to do and was involved in for a while—and then he wasn't.

THE NEW STUDIO had been inaugurated, appropriately enough, by a Charlie Rich session at the end of October 1959. It wasn't officially open yet—the work would not be completed for another month, Sam told *Billboard* optimistically just after the session—and it wasn't a real session but an overdub of a track recorded two weeks earlier at 706 Union, adding vocal backup and percussion and beefing up both the echo and handclapping in one of the new studio's three discrete echo chambers.

The record had sprung out of Charlie's dissatisfaction with his second Phillips International single. It had been eighteen months at this point since Charlie had first come into the Sun studio—he had gotten a lot of cuts on his songs by other artists, and he had played on a lot of sessions, but his first single had deservedly bombed, and the second, released in June, hadn't done any better. This would have been fine with Charlie—he would have been perfectly happy to stay in the background, it seemed—but Sam saw not just commercial potential but an unexpressed desire that Charlie simply was unable to give voice to. It was Sam who had insisted that Charlie record "Big Man," the B-side of the second single, a song that had been kicked around some in the studio by its writer, Dale Fox, and that with its overt gospel feel, Sam felt, might be the trigger to unleash some of Charlie's intensely held emotional reserve. ("Modesty, modesty," Sam joked, looking back on the experience. "I wanted to slap him sometimes, but he was a big, handsome man, and I was afraid I might get my butt kicked!") But Charlie didn't like the song for the very reason that Sam did. The "Big Man" of the title was referring directly to God, and Charlie felt that was sacrilegious. Sam was able to overcome his initial reluctance at the session but not his underlying objection—so he suggested to Charlie, Why not write a new song of his own with the same feel, the same musical spirituality but with an altogether different message?

The song that Charlie came up with was "Lonely Weekends," an up-tempo number that, in the manner of many Sam Cooke songs (a singer and songwriter that Charlie much admired), hid a melancholy message beneath a bright exterior. "Oh, I make it all right / From Monday morning till Friday night / But oh those lonely weekends" was its equivocal — but unquestionably universal — opening, and often in later years Charlie underlined the solitary message with a slow, repeated coda.

Despite Sam's explicit encouragement to write something for himself, Charlie evidently remained convinced that he had simply written another good number for Jerry Lee Lewis to cut in his own explosive fashion. Or maybe this was just more of the reflexive modesty that Sam was so determined to overcome. In any case, Charlie said, when Sam heard the demo, "I think he liked the sound of it, and he said, 'Well, why don't Charlie just cut it?' I didn't know whether that was just a put-down [of the song], but I come to find out that he actually did want me to cut it, and it was the first thing that we cut at Sun [for the Phillips label] that we actually had a good reception on." Which didn't occur until six months later, in the spring of 1960, when "Lonely Weekends" peaked at number 22 pop, and he finally got to appear on Dick Clark's *American Bandstand* and was invited to go out on Clark's next national tour — but for Charlie the most exciting thing to come out of this brief encounter with fame was when he flew to New York to talk to Clark about the tour and wandered into a little jazz club in the Village. "We just walked in off the street, and there was [legendary but little-known British expatriate and Frank Sinatra inspiration] Mabel Mercer. I can't really describe it, just her and a piano player — it was one of the grooviest things in the world, just so cool, outasight. No, we didn't do [the tour]. God, she was outasight."

THE OFFICIAL OPENING of the Sam C. Phillips Recording Studio came almost one year after the "Lonely Weekends" session, with a lavish party on Saturday, September 17, 1960, attended by close to two hundred people, including fifty out-of-town industry guests, who were treated to dinner at the Holiday Inn on South Third and a moonlight dance on the Mississippi riverboat, the *Memphis Queen,* with a Sunday-afternoon open house for the public to follow. Sam had spent three-quarters of a million dollars on the "plush" new quarters that he deemed with true American-century pride "a little Cape Canaveral of the recording business," the *Memphis Press-Scimitar* reported, as "his eye [took] in the two floors of studios, control rooms, mastering rooms, mailing rooms and offices which lie beneath the penthouse executive offices."

He had, for the occasion, dyed his hair blond — Sally didn't know

Sam Phillips Recording Service. *Courtesy of the Sam Phillips Family*

why, he just decided to do it, and he loved the new look until it started turning a yellow orange, and then it took a while to grow out. The party was a great success, except when it came time to go to dinner and Sam's two black Chicago distributors, George and Ernie Leaner, who had been in business since 1950 and would go on to found the "Chicago hard soul" label, One-derful, were refused admittance. He just couldn't do it, Kemmons Wilsons said, he just couldn't flout Memphis' segregation laws, no matter how passionately Sam argued against the inequity of the situation — and in the end Buster Williams took them both home to dinner, and they rejoined the party on the *Memphis Queen*.

It was, said Sally, "one of the happiest days of our lives" — but at the same time, as she well knew, "by the time that we were [finally] able to move into the new studio, Sam felt that the phonograph record business was not something that he wanted to continue in himself." The studio business maybe. The construction business. Song publishing. Radio. Selling and repackaging the Sun catalogue in LP form. But as far as "spending [his] time and money to take an artist and build them up and get a hit, and the next thing you know, there's a major record label talking about they're going to sign them and guarantee them $60,000 a year, Sam wasn't going to do it. He just wasn't going to do it. He just no longer had any faith in the phonograph record business as an independent label."

You have to consider that maybe this is after-the-fact rationalization. After all, how could Sam have known at this point how it was all going to turn out? And he was certainly in the process of expansion. But there was no question his heart was not in it anymore. I suppose one could theorize that it all stemmed from what he still viewed at this point as Johnny Cash's betrayal or, in the case of Jerry Lee Lewis, fate's intervention, but he could no longer see a clear path to the future. And whether it was self-protectiveness or an understandable element of self-deception that caused him to pull back (radio, he told himself, was his first love, and it offered just as creative an outlet as record producing, and a more dependable source of income), pull back he did — even as he expanded the recording options and manpower of the Sam C. Phillips corporate operation.

At the new Sun, Bill Fitzgerald, formerly head of Buster Williams' Music Sales distributorship, was general manager; Cecil Scaife was doing promotion and a little a&r (artist and repertoire); Sam had recently hired Elvis' old guitarist Scotty Moore to be production manager and engineer; and longtime songwriter Charles Underwood ("Ubangi Stomp") was assigned the title of "a&r manager." It was as if over the past year Sam had set out to create a skeletal structure, in the form of the kind of elaborate hierarchy he had always eschewed, to convince the world, and himself, that he was still in business.

To any objective observer it might have seemed like a hollow claim. And yet at the same time, there was a curious, contradictory, and almost wholly inexplicable note at the end of the *Press-Scimitar* story on the studio opening. "Phillips," Amusements Editor Edwin Howard reported, "will also soon open a large new recording studio in the Cumberland Lodge Building in downtown Nashville."

I N MANY WAYS no one could have been more surprised by this development than Sam Phillips. About a year earlier, almost as a favor, Sam had set up an old acquaintance from Florence, Kelso Herston, as Sun's song publishing representative in Nashville, with the aim of both pitching and acquiring songs. Kelso, twenty-eight years old and a real

go-getter, had been in on the start of the sputtering new Muscle Shoals–
area music movement. Along with James Joiner, he had helped found
Tune Records two years earlier, whose first and only hit, "A Fallen Star,"
was recorded by high school senior Bobby Denton, soon to become Judd
Records' first recording artist. Not much was happening in the Shoals
area at this point, though (Joiner had gone back to his family's bus company), and Kelso was desperate to get to Nashville anyway, where fellow
Florentine Buddy Killen was making a splash in song publishing after
acquiring Elvis' first big hit, "Heartbreak Hotel," for the publishing company he worked for, Tree, in 1956.

Kelso called Sam, whom he knew more by reputation than from the
one or two brief encounters he had had with him on Sam's occasional
visits home ("When we started doing records down there, Sam inspired
us — we [all] wanted to *be* Sam Phillips") and, without telling him his
idea, made an appointment to see him in Memphis the next day. He
waited and waited at the studio, he arrived at midmorning, "and Sam
didn't get there until the sun was almost down. I remember he came
around the corner in that Cadillac convertible. And, man, I thought, God
here he is, he looked so great in that Cadillac, you know, with his hair
blowing in the wind and a little yachting cap on his head. And he said,
'Well what do you have in mind?' and I said, 'Well, you know, I've been
going up to Nashville a lot, my friend Buddy Killen is there, and I've been
trying to work into the business. I just think that maybe since Nashville
is becoming a bigger center every day that maybe you'd be interested in
having your publishing representative up there."

Sam didn't even pause to think about it. "He said, 'That's a pretty
good idea.' He said, 'Let's get Roy Scott over here. But first I'm going
to take you over and show you the new studio.' So we went over and
looked at it, and then we came back to 706 Union, and Roy was there,
and he said, 'Tell Roy what you told me.' Then Sam said, 'What do you
think, Roy?' And he said, 'I think it's a damn good idea.' And Sam said,
'Okay, how much money would you have to have,' and I told him, and he
said, 'That's no problem.' He says, 'Go to Nashville and rent some space
and we're in business.' That's how it happened."

At Buddy Killen's suggestion Kelso rented an office on the ground
floor of the Cumberland (Masonic) Lodge Building. Down the hall on
the other side was Buddy's company, Tree Music. Directly across the
hall was country music star Marty Robbins' company; Bill Lowery, who

had just bought Judd Records, and was the powerhouse of publishing in Atlanta, was next-door on the right; and the Wilburn Brothers, with seven Top 10 country hits in the last three years, were on the left. The Masons meanwhile maintained their offices on the second floor.

Kelso never did much business for Sun on the publishing end. It took him a long time to get any sound equipment from Sam, and the catalogue had been pretty well worked, at least the hits had, though Kelso did eventually get an album cut by Patti Page on "I Walk the Line." He never really signed too many writers either — it was hard to get writers, even unknown ones, without offering them some kind of cost-of-living draw, or weekly salary, something Sam was adamantly opposed to until the writer had proved his worth. In fact, Sam seemed to take no great interest in this new enterprise, which surprised Kelso a little, he wasn't even sure why Sam had gone into this in the first place unless it was simply to give a hometown boy a break. But he didn't waste too much time trying to figure it out. Because, really, his new situation was a golden opportunity for someone looking to get a foothold in the music business. The Cumberland Lodge Building was ideally situated, with WSM located half a block away and the old Clarkston Hotel, where many of the musicians stayed, right next door.

Soon Kelso began playing on the Friday night Opry, which was broadcast from the WSM studios, and then he began getting more and more session work as one of the two resident Danelectro specialists in town. (The Danelectro was a six-string electric bass that provided the "tic-tac" rhythm popular on so many Nashville recordings of that time.) But what really engaged Kelso's interest was the studio on the third floor of the Cumberland Lodge Building, an old theater that the Masons must have used to hold meetings and put on shows. Just recently, though, Billy Sherrill, the quick-witted twenty-three-year-old son of an itinerant Alabama preacher and alumnus of Tune Records (Billy had cowritten "Sweet and Innocent," Roy Orbison's first RCA recording and Bobby Denton's debut on Judd), had followed the familiar path of migration from Florence and virtually moved into the room after a friend of his, Billy Ray Cooner, had rented it from the Lodge and set it up as a "dub studio" with a few rudimentary pieces of equipment.

Billy Sherrill wasn't doing much — anything he could, really, jingles, one-man copy records that degraded with every overdub — but Kelso, who had originally pitched Billy's song to both Bobby Denton and Roy

Orbison, couldn't get over the potential of the room. It was, he told Sam, just a beautiful space going to waste, forty by sixty-two with a twenty-foot-high ceiling and almost perfect acoustics. Set up your control room on the stage, and you could record live without even using baffles to contain leakage—you could stand anyplace in the room, and the sound was virtually discrete. It was obvious Billy Ray Cooner didn't have the money to sustain the operation, but Billy Sherrill would be the perfect person to look after the room, Kelso told Sam—and Kelso was convinced Sam could get it cheap.

Sam wasn't interested. He was having enough problems getting his own studio off the ground in Memphis—they were at this point, in the spring of 1960, well over a year overdue. And Nashville was locked up anyway. Nashville, as Sam well knew, had its own little cliques, and they were unlikely to welcome any outsider who came in, particularly (and this was something Sam didn't say to Kelso) if that outsider was Sam Phillips. No matter what Kelso said, he couldn't get Sam to even go upstairs and take a look at the room. But then, one night in the middle of June, coming back from the second ARMADA convention, in Atlantic City, Sam and Sally encountered a driving electrical storm and decided to stop off in Nashville rather than continue on. The convention had been deeply discouraging—*Billboard* described it as "chaotic [and] confusing," and, in a decidedly more boosterish account, even *Cash Box*'s story concluded, "Many people who attended were disappointed at the lack of results, [as] after a variety of opinions and inability to get all manufacturers to agree on 'methods' of doing business it was officially announced that 'the policy of an individual company is its own decisions.'" That inability to come together—on *anything*—had borne out all of Sam's worst fears. He and Ewart Abner had been replaced as president and vice president, and from Sam's point of view it had come not a moment too soon.

According to Kelso, he and Billy Sherrill were in the studio cutting a Jerry Lee Lewis sound-alike session when the storm hit and sent sparks flying all around the studio.

> I said, "Let's get out of here, man, we're going to get killed." So we went downstairs to the office, and right in the middle of this storm here comes Sam, Sam and Sally, they'd been to a convention in Atlantic City, and the weather got so bad they couldn't even see to drive.

So I started telling Sam about the studio [again], and he goes, "Ahhh, I don't want to talk about another damn studio." And I said, "Well, you know I just wish you'd go up and look at it. It's a great room, and we're getting a great sound." He said, "No, no, I don't even want to consider that." So I [tried] one more time, and he said, "Okay, let's go up there and look."

And he went *crazy*.

You know, he started clapping his hands, and [saying], "Yeah, we'll put a sound booth over here. We'll do this over there." And then he said, "Who in the hell owns this?" I said, "A guy by the name of Billy Ray Cooner." He said, "Where is he?" I said, "He went home to Haleyville, Alabama, for the weekend." He said, "Well, get that son of a bitch on the phone now. I want him to come back up here tonight!"

So I finally reached him, and he said, "What's going on?" And I said, "Sam Phillips wants to talk to you about that studio. He wants you to come back tonight." He said, "Tonight?" He said, "Man, there was a bad thunderstorm [driving] all the way down here. I don't know if I want to get out tonight." I said, "Well, if I were you and wanted to unload that studio, I would head back tonight while he's [still] in the mood." And he did. I can't remember if we stayed up all night waiting for him, but he came in and Sam made the deal with him that night, and in the next couple of days Sam had contractors up there tearing that place apart.

Whether or not this is the precise chronological sequence—papers were officially passed on June 28, some two weeks after their unplanned stopover, and surely construction could not have begun for at least another week or two—it's close enough. Sam threw himself into the project with an enthusiasm, and an *abandon,* that had long since deserted him on the Memphis project. Over the next seven months he labored night and day to create the studio he had envisioned ever since embarking on construction at 639 Madison in Memphis. He would come over to Nashville for two or three days at a time, sometimes with Sally, sometimes not, supervising every aspect of the work, right down to the smallest detail. He covered the ceiling with black burlap and put in soft, colored lights. "He had all these guys gluing big rolls of soundproofing fiberglass to the ceiling," said Billy Sherrill, who Sam had working on the project around the clock. "Once they glued that to the ceiling and Sam [attached] the burlap, it was like being outside [with a] dark night sky. But he said, 'Now listen to me. Sound, Billy boy, dissipates upward. And once it gets to that ceiling, by God it's going to stay there.'

"Sam designed the whole thing. I remember the first order of the day, the day he started working on it, here came about four guys with a barrel full of twenty-penny nails. Sam hated to walk on a floor [that] squeaked. He said, 'That's one thing that just drives me crazy.' And he had those guys nail all the planks — I'll bet [no more] than two inches apart, so the entire studio, there'll never be a squeak."

He built louvers for the walls, so you could, in effect, "tune the studio like a guitar. He put in all these ten-, fifteen-, twenty-foot-long one-by-twelves and then covered them with real thick fiberglass and made louvers out of them, so you could turn them and make the wall live, or you could put them back and [it would] be dead. And there were no parallels. No parallels. If there was a glass or a wooden wall, anything glass or wood in the studio couldn't be parallel to that wall, 'cause it would set up little echoey things that bugged his ears.

"He was completely different from anybody I'd ever met. He knew what he wanted, and you couldn't really talk him out of it. [But] he was never overbearing or mean. I guess the big thing he taught me was not to worry about the little things. If a mike had a little buzz to it, you just sort of turn it down and work [around it] — don't try to get everything perfect. He said, 'Nothing's perfect. Everything should have a flaw in it.' He would preach and preach [that lesson]. Then he'd send me down to the Krystal, and I'd get a whole bunch of Krystal burgers — back then they were eleven cents apiece. And I'd bring a whole big sack of Krystal burgers back, hoping that he'd forgotten [what he was talking about] and get on something else. And he'd pick right up where he left off!"

Sam worked on the engineering with a couple of guys he knew from WSM, Jim Lockhart and Tom Sparkman, to help with the setup. And he brought over Denise Howard, the young woman whose first job had been to miniaturize WHER in a Holiday Inn entryway, to help execute his vision for the studio's design. "It was the greatest room," said Sally, who had been astonished that Sam would even entertain the idea of embarking on another such venture after all the frustrations of the last. "It was the most amazing room that you have ever been in. You could sit in that room and just feel the sound of it."

It opened in early February 1961, just seven months after Sam had

bought the studio from Billy Ray Cooner. For all of Kelso's imprecations, he held off on hiring Billy Sherrill as his chief engineer (he said he needed somebody "with a little gray hair" to instill confidence in the kind of big corporate clients he hoped to attract), but he did hire Billy essentially as studio manager, utility engineer, and chief cook and bottle washer at a salary of $40 a week — and he gave him the run of the place.

Nashville regarded the new studio with a good deal of suspicion — there were any number of disparaging remarks, not to mention outright threats of union intercession (if Sam Phillips thought he could run a studio in Nashville the way he ran his little fly-by-night operation in Memphis, he had another think coming), but Kelso had no doubt of the operation's eventual success. Nashville had only two major studios at this point, Owen Bradley's Quonset Hut and RCA's Studio B, and the big labels were having to stack up their sessions (and their hand-picked session musicians) to get time in one or the other. "We needed another studio," said Kelso. "That was the turning point for Nashville right there."

"The lights dim and a soft blue hue dips the room into a reflective mood," wrote Nashville insider Charlie Lamb in early June in the trade publication that he published, *The Music Reporter.* "Broadway? Movie set? No. It's the beginning of a recording session at the spanking new Sam C. Phillips Recording studios in Nashville." By then the studio, as Lamb remarked, was doing a land-office business. In April Johnny Cash had been in with Don Law for a marathon three-day session; in May, Carla Thomas cut the follow-up to her Top 10 pop hit, "Gee Whiz," for the new Memphis r&b label, Stax; and all the major labels as well as independents like Chess were making use of what Lamb called "the largest platter palace in town," with two offices thoughtfully "left open for [out-of-town] A&R men to use." And in what amounted to an unofficial proclamation of welcome from one of the city's biggest boosters, Lamb declared that the location of the Phillips studio in Nashville "is another vote of confidence for Music City from another of the high-ranking potentates of today's musicdom.... One more notch in the city's musical six-gun that is making the biggest recording noise in the nation today."

Sam couldn't help but be quietly pleased not just to see his vision borne out but to be embraced by the very clique that had done everything

Jerry Lee Lewis, Boots Randolph, and Sam at the Nashville studio, September 11, 1962. *Courtesy of the* Nashville Tennessean in its power to knock him down from the start. There continued to be pockets of resistance, not only from Nashville diehards but from musicians as well ("That's the craziest thing I ever heard of," said one "A-team" player, who was constantly busy already. "How can I be everywhere at once?"), but the success and sound of the new studio gradually overcame even its fiercest critics. Not to mention the opportunities that it opened up both for the record companies and new session players, who had up till then been frozen out. But unquestionably Sam's proudest moment came with the first two sessions at the new studio.

The first, on February 9, marked what would almost instantly become Jerry Lee Lewis' first hit in almost three years. Jerry had cut Ray Charles' "What'd I Say" at the new studio in Memphis twice already, addressing the song at the second session in a wild, unfettered version that certainly reflected the untamable spirit of the artist—but it was shrill and out of control in a way that Sam doubted he could sell. Now, with the original Memphis rhythm section all gone (Roland Janes and Billy Riley had started their own label, Rita, while J. M. Van Eaton, discouraged by the lackadaisical attitude that seemed to have overtaken Sun, had gone into the vending machine business), Sam was impelled to call for a change in venue as well as tone.

For the Nashville date, he assembled the same all-star team that had played on all of Elvis' recent sessions (and those of every other country or pop star who recorded in Nashville), along with Kelso on tic-tac guitar. And Jerry took a much more modulated approach this time—the raw, almost out-of-control vocals were replaced by a calm air of bacchanalian assurance, and the record was more compact in sound as well as spirit, with its length reduced by nearly a minute and the new room producing a deeper, more natural resonance. But most of all it was Jerry's playing that set the tone—on the Memphis version, his piano alternated with Martin Willis' stuttering sax, with glissandos and stutter in uneasy competition, but here, with no other instrument competing for the lead, Jerry Lee offered a masterly lesson in controlled, con brio pianistics. The record in fact was marred only by a cooing chorus, almost obligatory for anything coming out of Nashville at the time, a poor substitute for the writhing, orgiastic exchange between Ray Charles and his Raelettes on the original.

Sam was so excited about the record's prospects that he put it out just three weeks later, and it entered *Billboard*'s Hot 100 on April 3,

Sam and Charlie Rich at the Nashville studio, February 11, 1961.
Courtesy of the Sam Phillips Family

reaching number 30 by the beginning of May. It was a genuine pop hit, with some country, r&b, and even British chart success thrown in for good measure, a vindication of sorts for both talent and persistence, as Jerry Lee's show dates started picking up as well (in the fall he would embark on a thirty-day tour with the incendiary r&b star Jackie Wilson in what was billed without exaggeration as "The Battle of the Century").

As proud as he was of Jerry's success, though, Sam may have taken even greater satisfaction in the outcome of Charlie Rich's session on February 11, two days after Jerry's. It continued to frustrate Sam, it *distressed* him that he had never been able to get out of Charlie the feeling that he knew was inside him. "It was my fault, it damn sure wasn't his," he would always say—he never gave Charlie the attention he deserved, the same attention he had given to all of his earlier artists, and even this one session would do little to assuage the guilt. Charlie had simply come along at a time when he was too preoccupied with other concerns—and for all of his unbounded love for Charlie's music, he was always the first to admit he would prove no more able to focus on it in the final two years of Charlie's Sun contract than he had for the first four. But this one time, with this one song, in the inaugural week of his magnificent new studio, he could feel justifiably that he had touched some of the unfathomable wellsprings of guilt, pain, and emotion that he would never fail to hear in Charlie Rich's music.

Charlie had tried the song "Who Will the Next Fool Be," in Memphis a couple of months earlier. Like all of his best compositions, it combined heart, head, and quietly smoldering intensity ("Charlie wasn't a demonstrative type of guy in the studio," Sam said), but here it achieved an emotional spaciousness as well, as Sam set it off with almost the same rhythm section and chorus (plus sax and strings) that he had used for the Jerry Lee Lewis session.

It was a song of almost desperate bitterness and despair modulated with the ironic edge that Charlie always brought to a self-consciously created hip sensibility. "After you get rid of me / Who will the next fool be?" Charlie sang, as always lagging just a little behind the beat and then, as the song progressed, showing off those little curlicues of style, breaking meter, throwing in swoops of unexpected emphasis, reaching for the high vaulting end of his range to reveal deep measures of hurt. What differentiated it in one respect from so many of his earlier recordings for Sun was that, for all of its built-in commerciality (like all of Charlie's songs it had a well-defined hook), it recalled no other hit or genre — it was what Sam would have called *Charlie Rich music*, because, without departing from its carefully mapped-out form, it was at its heart both inimitable and undefinable. Like Jerry Lee's, Charlie's piano not only established the lead but provided all of the cues necessary to fill in the accompaniment, though, of course, in decidedly less spectacular fashion. But what cemented the success of the performance, and left it forever open to interpretation and reinterpretation, was the profound fluidity at its core, the achievement of, as Sam said of Charlie's music at its peak, "the whole contouracle" of human emotion, presented in two minutes and twenty seconds by a master painter.

Sam didn't produce a lot more sessions at his new studio, but he came to really appreciate Nashville — though in a different way than he might have expected. He didn't comport himself there in the same way that he did in Memphis — he had no more reason to trust the Nashville music establishment than he ever had, and, as Sally noted, "he walked with a little lighter tread" when he was around them. But in his own studio, in his own domain, he was utterly at ease, with Kelso reluctantly taking on the formal role of studio manager (it cut into his session work), Jimmy Lockhart and Billy, too, handling the engineering chores, and Sam for once just enjoying the luxury of his surroundings — enjoying his removal from the day-to-day worries, duties, and responsibilities that had consumed him for so long and soaking up the sounds, the experience, the *moment*, in this beautiful, airy, high-vaulted temple that he had built.

He would mainly show up at night, Kelso said. "He used to stay up most of the night — he drank most every night, but he never had any cigarettes. He'd say, 'Kelso, you got any cigarettes?' and I'd give him a cigarette. Then later on, he'd say, 'You got any money on you?' He'd start fooling around and say, 'I don't have a damn dime.' I'd say, 'What do you need?' and he'd say, 'I'd like to have a half pint of Cutty Sark.' And there was a liquor store almost next door, and I'd go over and get him a half pint, and it wouldn't be an hour and he'd say, 'Kelso I need another half pint.' 'Well, why don't I just get a pint?' 'No, no. Just a half pint, just one more, that's all I'm gonna need.' And then he'd send me for another one. But, of course he didn't necessarily drink all of it himself."

It surprised Sally in a way — but then it didn't. Sam had never really drunk all that much, and then mostly when he was around Jud — he had never had the time, and he didn't really like the taste of liquor either. But here in Nashville, here in the studio, it was as if they had entered another realm, a realm in which Sam just seemed determined to relax and have a good time. And he loved the company of Billy Sherrill — he loved imparting his wisdom, the lessons he had learned, to someone who was as eager to absorb them as he was to teach them.

Billy had never touched so much as a drop of liquor in his life — but he took to it naturally, he said, it was just part of the ongoing conversation with Sam that seemed like it was never going to end. He had his own situational sense of morality — he had promised his late father, for whom he had played piano at churches and tent revivals, that he would never do anything to embarrass him, but he was confident that such transitory elements as social behavior would do nothing to compromise that pledge. And besides, in Sam he had found someone who provided an altogether original take on just about everything under the sun. They would stay up all night sometimes, just talking — Sally and Billy's girlfriend, Charlene, whom he had recently met through Kelso and to whom, before long, he would propose in the studio, would fall asleep on the couch, as they talked about . . . just everything, Sally said, even with all that drinking, they almost never argued so much as discussed things in infinite, painstaking detail.

"I could never get enough talking," said Billy. "I could never get enough of it. Sometimes we would sing gospel songs. I would play piano and [sing] the melody, and Sam would figure out a way to harmonize and sing the bass. And he would preach, he'd carry on, and we'd argue about the Bible and he'd say this, that, and the other. I'd say, 'No that's not right.' He'd say, 'Well, this so and so happened.' I'd say, 'No, it didn't.' And we'd go get the Bible out, and I'd say, 'Okay, find it.' He'd dig around, and he'd say, 'Well, it's *somewhere.*' He was pretty knowledgeable about the Bible, but [sometimes] he would imagine things that weren't in there."

Mostly they would talk about philosophy, about *life*, said Billy, about Sam's philosophy of life.

> Sam did most of the talking. I did most of the listening. He'd go — I [can't think of] any particular subject, but whatever it was he'd start on it and expound on it and kick back, and we'd have a drink. And he'd say, "I'll tell you another thing, Billy Boy. I don't have a lot of credit around here, but I got more cash than any son of a bitch around." He'd always emphasize that cash. I learned to love Sam. He'd say, "I'll tell you about Moses. Moses is not what people thought he was. And if you read and get in there and get into the mind of Moses — or Jacob for that matter . . ." And a lot of times I didn't even know what the hell he was talking about. But I just loved being around him.

To Billy, a self-proclaimed iconoclast himself who was not particularly drawn to mentors — never was, never would be, even as he invented what came to be called the "countrypolitan" sound of the 1970s and in the process made Nashville one of the recording capitals of the world — Sam was a mentor who defied categorization, and someone to whom he felt an almost filial connection. One of the most striking things about him was that he never dwelled on the past — he wasn't interested in talking about Elvis or any of his celebrated triumphs, and if he ever spoke of Charlie Rich, it was with regard to his intrinsic, not his commercial, qualities. "He'd say, 'You know Charlie don't know who he is. Charlie is a blues singer but he won't admit [it]. Charlie just needs to set down and relax and become what God made him.'

"But Charlie never did, thank God," said Billy, whose highly orchestrated country hits with Charlie in the 1970s were the breakthrough that finally made him a superstar. "We cut some pretty good songs that wasn't blues."

In the end what may have drawn Billy most to Sam was that same combination of absolute certainty and impenetrable mystery that baffled so many others — the sense that even in a matter as cut and dried for most engineers as mastering records, Billy, without any question an astute and highly sophisticated observer, could never be certain that he fully understood him.

"We had a little mastering room back there, and he'd say, 'Now when you master a record and you think you got it right, get everything ready and then go to five thousand cycles and boost that up just a little bit, whether it needs it or not, and that'll give it that edge. Always boost everything up five thousand. That's someway or another in tune with the human ear." And Billy did it on every record he ever made, he said — long after he had left Sam, on all his highly produced, multimillion-selling hits so different in sound and philosophy from Sam's — because in the end he *trusted* Sam, without ever really knowing the reason why.

Sam was just genuinely enjoying himself in a way that Sally had never seen before. He acquired a mynah bird named Inky from Jimmy Velvet, a young singer and Elvis acolyte from Florida, who brought the bird by the studio one day. It was solid black and had been saved from a burning building in town, Jimmy said, whose owner did not survive the fire. Jimmy had paid $125 and wanted to present the mynah bird to Sam. This seemed to Sally a dubious proposition at best, but Jimmy left the bird with them on the theory that it would sell itself, and to her amazement Sam was so taken with Inky that he actually purchased it. Leaving her to take care of it, while Sam entertained himself from time to time by teaching it to speak. Eventually he put it in the car one day and took it back to Memphis, where Becky became its principal caretaker, and in the recollection of Sam's longtime friend and WHER employee Bettye Berger the bird learned to say, "Do you love me?" just like Sam.

Then there was the prominent Nashville businessman who tried to persuade Sam to run for governor, and Sam was intrigued for a while and actually encouraged him, until in the end he decided it was not a realistic ambition. He socialized with industry figures and reconnected with old Nashville friends in a casual manner that he had rarely displayed in

Memphis. But it was through Audrey Williams, the hard-drinking widow of country music legend Hank Williams, who still resided in the house at 4916 Franklin Road, where she and Hank had lived before they divorced, that he really came to know the hillbilly haut monde.

There was a party every night out at Audrey's, and Sam went to most of them. Audrey, a boisterous, outgoing woman who was not universally embraced by the stuffier elements of the country music world, just tickled Sam — she loved to drink, she loved to party, and there was no pretense about her. There was always lots of music, and lots of pretty girls, and through Audrey Sam met Big Ruby Folsom, too, the sister of one of his true heroes, and one of the few outspoken paragons of Alabama liberalism, former governor Big Jim Folsom, as well as her daughter, Cornelia, an aspiring entertainer, who would one day marry another Alabama governor, George Wallace.

"Sam and Audrey just always hit it off," said Sally. "They argued a lot. They drank together a lot. Sam had certain people that he liked to drink with, and Audrey Williams was one of them. They argued about the business: the phonograph record business, the music publishing business, all sorts of things like that. Audrey just never had much business sense, yet she would tell you she was the smartest businesswoman that ever lived. Sam would be there all night long, sitting and drinking with Audrey. He just really enjoyed talking with her. But she never took his advice on anything he ever told her."

One of the pieces of unsolicited advice he offered had to do with the career of her son, Hank Williams Jr., just three years old when his daddy died, whom she had pushed out onstage at the age of eight as the heir to his father's kingdom. Once her son turned fourteen, she started actively campaigning for MGM Records, his father's old label, to sign him — something Sam argued strongly against. He was just too young, Sam told her. It was clear he was talented, but he shouldn't be singing his father's songs, least of all on his father's old label. "Just wait till he gets old enough," Sam told her.

But she didn't listen to him in this any more than she did on anything else — Hank Jr. was recording the sound track to his father's life story before he turned fifteen — and it didn't affect their friendship one bit. Nor did it affect her son's admiration for Sam. Hank Jr., who went on to become an iconic country figure in his own right after finally casting off his father's mantle in his late twenties, would always hold

Sam in high esteem, not only for the help that Sam offered his mother and him but for the vivid example of untrammeled freedom that he set for a twelve-year-old. "I won't forget what you did for us," Hank Jr. declared via videotape at a roast for Sam in the 1980s. But the one image, whether real or mythic, that would remain indelibly etched in his mind, he declared to gales of knowledgeable laughter from an audience of Sam's friends and associates, was of Sam "running buck-naked out of Mother's bathhouse and jumping in the pool in front of fifty guests. I said to myself, 'I want to be just like that when I grow up.'"

THAT SAME UNFETTERED ECCENTRICITY seemed to cross over into his Memphis life, too, now that he was no longer encumbered by the daily duties that had ruled his life for so long. He still signed the checks, he still approved all expenditures, he might supervise or engineer the occasional session, and he still monitored the WHER broadcasts as well as traveled to Florida frequently to check up on his second all-girl station—but for the most part he found himself increasingly unmoored as the drinking, both social and solitary, became more and more a part of his everyday life. It *relaxed* him, he said—he enjoyed it. And who else's business was it if he did?

It was as if his life had become his work, and the unconventional cast of characters with whom he had always chosen to surround himself had now become a substitute for his artist roster. That cast of characters included an ever more dysfunctional Dewey Phillips, for whom, whether adrift in the world or not, Sam would never feel anything but unwavering love. He was still on Memphis radio, but just barely, with the inspired free associations that had once galvanized a city now fueled by the hallucinative properties of painkillers and amphetamines, and old friends for the most part drifting away. But Sam stood unflinchingly by him. When he needed money, Sam supplied it. When the family needed support, Sam was there. Dewey was at this point inclined to address almost everyone as "Elvis" and as likely to come bursting through the studio door hollering, "Call Sam, call Sam" (the mantra of his original *Red Hot and Blue* show) as he was to show up outside the house in the middle of the night, yelling, "There goes Elvis! There goes [movie costar] Tuesday Weld!" But Sam would always usher him in and do his best to calm him down—and he never failed to stress to his sons or anyone else who would listen that this was a man for whom the music *mattered*, that this was a man who may have paid the price for adhering too strictly to the principle of "individualism *in the extreme*" but who never deserved anything less than recognition and respect.

There were many others of nearly equal eccentricity — if considerably less dependency than Dewey — but none more captivating than a new arrival in town, "Sputnik" Rock Monroe. Sputnik was a professional wrestler of considerable renown — he had recently been crowned Tennessee champion after more than a dozen years on the pro circuit, with the scars to show for it — who had gone through a number of names ("Pretty Boy Rock" "Elvis 'Rock' Monroe") and territories before finally arriving in Memphis as "Sputnik," after the first Soviet space satellite, in 1959. It's unclear how exactly he and Sam met, but he naturally gravitated toward the Sun studio, and almost instantly Sam invited him home.

They were truly, as each of them vied to be the first to proclaim, birds of a feather. It would be impossible to enumerate all of Sputnik's notable achievements or his cheerfully exuberant, generally grandiloquent, and invariably attention-getting pronouncements. (He was prone to describing himself in a voice several decibels above the normal range as "220 pounds of twisted steel and sex appeal with the body that women love and men fear," and even adapted a Gilbert-and-Sullivan lyric to express his philosophy of self-promotion: "If you wish in this world to advance / And your merits you wish to enhance / You got to strew it and strump it / And blow your own trumpet . . ."). Suffice it to say that in looking for a way to distinguish himself that was consonant with both character and commerciality, Sputnik hit upon race, proclaiming himself not only a champion of the Negro cause and the Negro people but getting himself arrested in the process — for breaking Memphis' segregation laws by "being in the wrong part of town." He asked the judge "if this was a Communist-run city that [I] couldn't go wherever the hell I wanted to go. Russell Sugarmon [his black attorney] grabbed my hand and said, 'Man, you can't talk like that in a white man's court.' So I got fined $25 anyway."

He was a hero to the black man, a villain to the white — he liked to boast that he practically desegregated Memphis' Ellis Auditorium singlehanded, calling up to his colored fans in the "crow's nest," with a seating capacity of less than one hundred, "Let my people go." Every time he threw an opponent down, he would raise up his hands to his fans, and they would just call back, "Sweet man!" When the promoters objected, he said, "Hey, if their money's no good, just give it to me, and I'll give it back to them," and gradually "colored" seating capacity was expanded until the auditorium was de facto integrated. He and Dewey walked a goose down Beale Street on a leash—"Dewey came up with the goose, I came up with the Chihuahua collar and the leash. The people would holler and hug me and jump up and down. I knocked a white guy out on the corner of Third and Beale one time for calling me a nigger-lover, and a little black guy says, 'Sputnik Monroe, you a mean motherfucker when you drinking, and I believe you drinking a little bit all the damn time.' I've always been for the underdog."

Knox and Jerry were agog when Sputnik started coming out to the house, Jerry even more so than his older brother. Sputnik was more like an overgrown teenager than a sober adult — with no limits to either his daring or imagination. He was to them both not unlike Dewey or Uncle Jud or Jerry Lee. "All those guys," as Jerry saw it, "were one of a kind. That was our environment, and it definitely set a course for [us] to be a little different."

Sputnik encouraged them to dive into the pool off the chimney at the top of the roof. "I don't know whether Jerry taught me or I taught Jerry, but Sam didn't like it, so we got grounded," said Knox. As to whether or not Sputnik himself was willing to accept Sam's authority, "Well, you got to. You know, his kids are involved — not mine but his." But Sputnik was not inclined to challenge Sam in any case — tease him maybe but not challenge him. "Sam was a character studier—he's a guy who studied various and different and sundry things, and he was about a hundred miles ahead of everybody else. I used to sit in his seat behind the board, and everybody'd buzz me — 'Sam don't want nobody in his seat behind the board now, Sputnik.' The doors open, I'm in the seat, and Sam is like a little banty rooster jumping around. He didn't say anything. There wasn't anything for him to say. I respected him, and I think he respected me. Sometimes our pride overcomes our common sense—that's a Sam cliché."

He lifted weights with the boys in the backyard and showed them wrestling holds (he claimed to know thirty-five hundred with ten thousand variations), he attended sessions at the studio and they would attend his matches at the auditorium and outdoors at Russwood Park— he felt like part of the family. But Jerry, a well-built twelve-year-old who wanted nothing more than to be in show business, was the one who

Sputnik enters the ring.
Courtesy of the Sam Phillips Family

assiduously sought his advice. "I was always asking him to show me how to be tough, 'Tell me how to be tough.' And he'd say, 'There's only one way to be tough. Eat raw meat and gunpowder and go out every weekend and start fights, and you'll be tough.' But like he said, every tough guy he knew was either dead or in jail. So I didn't know if I really wanted to be that tough."

"I put my hat on him one time," said Sputnik, "stuck a cigar in his mouth, and we went in a bar. The guy said, 'Who's that?' I said, 'That's a midget.' I think he was about [twelve] years old."

That apparently was the genesis of Jerry's wrestling career. Jerry and a seventeen-year-old friend of his and Knox's, Johnny Dougherty, who later gained mid-South fame as the DJ Johnny Dark, formed a fan club for Sputnik in May of 1960, with Johnny as president, Jerry as secretary, and Knox as the first charter member. Johnny knew a guy named R. J. McCandless, a drywall installer who wrestled as Rex Morgan on the Arkansas circuit and had a wrestling ring in his backyard. At

The World's Most Perfectly Formed Midget Wrestler flexes.
Courtesy of the Sam Phillips Family

Jerry's urging Johnny drove him over there to work out, and R.J. showed him some moves—"of course, Sputnik had taught me stuff already, some dirty trick stuff, you know, which came in handy." R. J. McCandless had a friend, a midget named Fabulous Frankie Thumb, who was looking to break into the business, but there were no locally available midgets for him to wrestle with, so Jerry started working out with him in Rex Morgan's backyard. The details here get a little blurry, but in essence that was how DeLayne (a variation on Jerry's middle name of "Layne") Phillips, the World's Most Perfectly Formed Midget Wrestler, was born.

He wrestled in smoky high school gyms and arenas and auditoriums in Twist, Lepanto, Jonesboro, Tyronza, and Marked Tree—all over Arkansas, and occasionally Tennessee, but never more than a two- or three-hour drive from Memphis, with the evening usually ending at Earl's Hot Biscuits in West Memphis, where wrestling fans, wrestlers with lumps on their heads, and wrestling groupies all gathered together and junior high attendance for Jerry was always a question mark for the next day.

"They said I was from Nashville, because Memphis was too close. Johnny Dougherty was my manager—he had a stick and a hat, he was definitely playing the manager's role, and, of course, Johnny could drive, he had a car. I'd walk into the arena wearing this jacket my mother made for me, with a big cigar—in those days the people would always be there, and you'd have to walk through the crowd, black people on one side, white people on the other, and then there was a bar setup where they were serving beer and drinks, so by the time the matches got started, these people were ready for 'em! I'd just play it up the best I could. It was a taunting thing, you know, you'd walk through there, and they'd yell at you, and Sputnik had taught me how to pull my pants down and tell 'em to kiss my ass, so they hated me pretty good.

"We wrestled fairly regularly. Usually I did a single match with one of the midgets—you know, a preliminary bout—and the main event would culminate in a mixed tag-team deal between big guys and midgets. The big guys would fight, and then the midgets, which, I, of course, was one of them, but when the big guy would get the other big guy down, the midgets would all run and kick the shit out of him. It really irritated the people, because, number one, I mean, these were small towns, and they just didn't like midgets to start with, and they liked me even less, because they kind of knew—somehow they *knew*—that I wasn't a real midget!"

The midgets didn't much like him either. "I don't want to divulge too much of the inner rassling things—but it's called a work when you're up there, you know, you're working with each other, and these guys a lot of times wouldn't work with me. That's where the Sputnik Monroe training came in. He said, 'Look, if they don't work with you, knock the shit out of them. They'll start working with you.' He told me, 'Keep bottle caps in your trunks and get 'em on the ground and make 'em bleed, and talk to them the whole time you're down there doing it—"You motherfucker!"'' So I did—it was just like a rock 'n' roll show, [going] through a series of emotions each night, scared sometimes and feeling great other times, all those things mixed together. It was a little scary to be my age and be involved with this scowling crowd of people that really were capable pretty much of just about anything."

Sam had always been a "rassling" fan up to a point, but now he started coming to the matches with some frequency. "I can remember going over to Arkansas with him," Knox recalled, "and it would be a tag-team deal, and Sam would get so out of control he'd run up to the ring and go, 'Jerry, knock that sonofabitch out. Come on!'" "I mean, he got into it," Jerry agreed. "He'd come over to my corner sometimes and tell me to kick the guy in a certain place, you know, do something dirty — I mean, he knew it was not all totally real, but we never really talked about how the matches were gonna [come out] and, really, when I was wrestling, the referee was the guy that kind of called the shots as far as who might win tonight. But he was just pulling for me, and I think he thought I did a good job."

It all came to an abrupt halt in Twist, Arkansas, as most of the Phillips family remember it. The whole family was there that night — Sam and Becky and Knox — and Jerry knocked his opponent out of the ring, and they were fighting on the concrete floor when a guy emerged from the crowd with a knife, "and he had the strangest look on his face — I mean, the guy was wanting to kill me, [so] we jumped immediately back in the ring, and the bouncers were right on top of him, but [after that] my parents said, 'You know, maybe that's enough.'"

"I WAS ALWAYS A MOTHER that let the boys go their own way," Becky said. "You know, my boys were just nice. I expected them to be good, and they were." And Jerry's wrestling career was so much fun, she said, until it simply became too dangerous. She had complete faith in her boys, but she worried about them. And she had complete faith in her husband, too, she had never doubted his loyalty, his judgment, his devotion to his family — and yet she was increasingly unable to deny the concern she felt about the changes that she observed in his behavior, his growing recklessness, what seemed to be a lack of certainty and direction in his life. She never voiced that concern explicitly, but she had seen Sam spin out of control before, and she was desperately anxious not to see it happen again. So she spoke to their long-time pastor — he knew the family so well, and the boys thought the world of him, Sam, too, even though he rarely attended church anymore — and she asked if he would talk to Sam about his drinking. He came out to the house, and Sam heard him out politely and then explained without rancor that this was *his* life, this was how *he* chose to live it, and as certain as he was that Pastor Barnick was not going to die for him, Sam sure as hell wasn't prepared to let some Lutheran minister — let *anyone else* — live for him now. There were no hard feelings — Sam continued to think well of Pastor Barnick and to help out with all the youth programs that Knox was involved in, supplying a sound system for various church productions and making sure that everything was just right. But for Becky something went out of her heart then; the hope she had so long harbored that the innocent young man she had once known would somehow be returned to her intact slowly shriveled and died, even as the love she felt for him never wavered for one moment.

Sally had known Becky was going to call on the pastor — she had told Sally she was going to do it beforehand. "I just thought this was so wrong. That if she really knew Sam Phillips, she would know this is not the thing to do. This was at a time that so much had happened in the phonograph record business, and [nearly] all of the artists were gone, and Sam, you know, he sometimes just had lulls, not knowing what he's going do, and that's what he does. He thinks about it. Sam would sit around and think more than most people do in their lifetime. And I just thought it was so wrong for Becky to do that. I thought it was really going to backfire on her."

MAYBE THAT WAS IT. Maybe Sam just needed the time to get himself right, to get his equilibrator back in gear. But many of those around Sam were as bewildered as Becky, even some of his fiercest admirers, as the label and the brand-new Memphis studio seemed to mean less and less to him, and while there was no diminution in the certitude of his pronouncements, there was a disturbing lack of certitude in the steadiness of his course.

To Barbara Barnes, who left just before the opening of the new Memphis studio to embark upon an academic career, working for Sam had been "a great turning point in my life, because my attempts to get a toehold in radio-TV had been [so] fraught with limitations. The decline of Sun was a great disappointment, because I loved the business and the music, and I hadn't intended to start teaching so soon. But I sensed things weren't going to turn around." To Roland Janes, whose label, Rita, was languishing after a single big hit and who, with encouragement from Sam, was now thinking about opening a studio of his own, it seemed as though the creative drive had simply fled, and what had once been a small, tight-knit family held together primarily by Sam's charismatic belief in them all, was suffering from what Roland could only imagine was a temporary fitfulness of attention. Jerry Lee Lewis, on the other hand, summed it up pretty much the way most of the artists still left on the Sun roster inescapably felt. Sam had just *abandoned* him, Jerry said bleakly on numerous occasions. "Sam Phillips," he said, with all the conviction of a spurned lover, "screwed everything up."

It was as if the speech he had given at the first ARMADA convention could have served as his farewell address. There was no place in the independent record industry for anybody that was timid, he had said. "I saw it falling apart," he said in later years. "I couldn't live with it, and I couldn't make a living in an honest way. I was a lot better off than I was when I started, so rather than lose respect for myself and cheat people, or trying to compete against certain economic blocs that I just could not control, I had just rather give it up and do what I felt I could do and be satisfied. [So] I just proceeded to do something else."

As Jerry Wexler, a more worldly practitioner of the "insider" game, whose label, Atlantic Records, maintained its status as an independent operation for another seven or eight years, observed, "It's like, how do you follow this? What else can you do? In [just] a decade, he produced a millennium's worth of music."

Wexler never discussed the matter with Sam, though they remained close friends for the rest of their lives. "It's something that I respected him enough not to even question or challenge in my own mind." But he observed the incontestable playing-out of Sam's undeclared withdrawal ("Everything was all happening one day," as Jack Clement noted, "and then it's not") as Sam to all intents and purposes simply stepped off the world stage and disappeared from public view for the greater part of the next two decades.

NINE

"They'll Carry You to the Cliff and Shove You Off"

I MET SAM in February of 1979. It was one of those long-dreamt-of events that you never expect to happen, and when they do — well, I'm not going to even try to generalize. Meeting Jerry Lee Lewis. Conversing with Chuck Berry. Going places with Solomon Burke. Engaging with Howlin' Wolf, Merle Haggard, Aretha Franklin, James Brown. These were things I could never have imagined actually taking place in the Real World, and it required going against what I took to be all of my natural instincts (and my obligations as an aspiring writer) for reticence, existential detachment, and solitary creativity. Every one of which was almost instantly, if shakily, obliterated when I forced myself at twenty-one, despite a predictable attack of excruciating self-consciousness, to seek an interview with the bluesman Skip James for no other reason than that *greatness such as this would not pass my way again.*

In the case of Sam Phillips, the meeting was at least ten years in the making. From the time I first started writing about music — well, from the time I first started *publishing* that writing, about a year after that 1965 Skip James interview — Sun and the blues, sometimes one and the same, were at the center of my universe. I sent stories I published in *Rolling Stone* and elsewhere to Elvis, Solomon Burke, and Sam Phillips, casting them to the wind (since obviously I had no other entrée), with a wistfully worded note that if any of them should ever want to talk to me about their music.... In 1971 I published my first book, *Feel Like Going Home: Portraits in Blues and Rock 'n' Roll,* which had a five-page entr'acte called "Boppin' the Blues: Sam Phillips and the Sun Sound" serving as the vital link between chapters on Howlin' Wolf and Jerry Lee Lewis.

Sputnik and Knox. *Courtesy of the Sam Phillips Family*

("If there is one man without whom the revolution which took place in American music seems difficult to imagine," I wrote from my far-off perch, "that man is Sam Phillips.")

I sent the book to the Sam C. Phillips Recording Studio, 639 Madison Avenue, Memphis, Tennessee, and at some point I received in return an incredibly gracious, incredibly eloquent, and extravagantly complimentary letter from Sam's son Knox, who, as it happened, was just about the same age as me.

I met Knox in person a year or two later on one of my numerous pilgrimages to Memphis, and we rapidly became the best of friends. But it brought me no closer to Sam, because, as Knox apologetically explained, Sam was too busy with his radio stations, Sam wasn't interested in looking back, Sam didn't do interviews, Sam could not be *persuaded* to do interviews — well, not yet anyway, Knox said, with the implicit assurance of someone who was on a mission to make all that change. But, in fact, for the next six or seven years nothing much did change, and there were no interviews to speak of, at least not in the national press. Sam was a legendary figure, to be sure, if only for his discovery of Elvis Presley, but he was also, wrote *Memphis Commercial Appeal* music critic Walter Dawson, one of Sam's few favored local (as opposed to *national*) reporters, "something of a recluse these past couple of decades, at least . . . as far as talking about Sun Records." Not, as he pointed out to Dawson in 1978, because he didn't have a lot to say, but because "I don't want to address myself to that era unless I'm sure in my mind about what I'm saying and I'm sure the person I'm talking to understands. I'd rather go to my grave leaving things unsaid than to feel I have somehow misled somebody."

We were getting closer, Knox offered up encouragingly from time to time, but it was not until early 1979, when I got an assignment from the *New York Times Magazine*, that I had anything more suitable than my own passion for the subject to bring to Sam.

The *New York Times* assignment came about through a serendipity of circumstances — I mean, put like that *(I got an assignment)*, it sounds so much more grandiose and blasé than it really was. I don't know if I need to add that I had never written for the *New York Times Magazine* before, and I never have since — but what had initially provided the opportunity was the elevation of a friend of mine, Ken Emerson, a colleague at the underground weekly the *Boston Phoenix*, to articles editor at the *Magazine*. With his encouragement I had been suggesting a

Knox in Sam's office, May 1981. *Courtesy of Colin Escott and Hank Davis*

series of story ideas (Merle Haggard, as I recall, was one of them, Satchel Paige another), none of which turned out to hold any interest for the hypothetical *Times* reader.

Then rumors began to fly that renegade Nashville record man and entrepreneur Shelby Singleton was about to put out a recently discovered copy of the Million Dollar Quartet session. This was the fabled day in December 1956 when Elvis, Carl Perkins, Jerry Lee Lewis, and Johnny Cash all came together in the Sun studio for what could only have been a moment of exquisite renegade beauty—but since no one in the general public had ever heard it, and as far as I know no one had ever really quizzed the principals about it (well, I mean, Elvis and Sam were not exactly accessible, and no one ever accused Jerry Lee of being an archivist), the tapes were widely believed to have disappeared.

Their rumored reemergence, as it turned out, was not only news—it was of real interest to *New York Times* readers, if only because of the involvement of Elvis Presley, who had died at the age of forty-two just sixteen months earlier. So, with Ken Emerson's tentative commitment, I called up Shelby Singleton in Nashville to make sure I could actually listen to the tapes, and I got in touch with Jack Clement, who was also located in Nashville and had engineered the original session. Jack, whom I had written about and gotten to know over the last two or three years, volunteered to intercede with Johnny Cash for me, and I called Carl Perkins, whom I had interviewed recently and who happened to be at home in Jackson, Tennessee, two-thirds of the way to Memphis from Nashville. That left Sam—and when Knox got back to me with the news that Sam had agreed to the interview, I confirmed the assignment and booked my trip.

Everything about it was a thrill, from the hour or two I spent in one of the little outbuildings behind the Nashville headquarters of SSS International (SSS for Shelby S. Singleton), listening to the roughly twenty-five-minute tape over and over, to the Johnny Cash gospel session that Jack was supervising (or maybe just contributing spiritual energy to) to the Grayline tour of Memphis, which gave me my first glimpse of the recently restored Sun studio at 706 Union. But, really, if I had to single out one thrill above all—well, there's no one who's read this far who doesn't know what it was. So it was with increasing anticipation (and the same trepidation I had felt when I first interviewed Skip James, some fourteen years earlier) that I pulled up to the curb in front of WWEE (WHER's talk-radio successor) and WLVS, Sam's brand-new, format-free stereo FM rock station ("I don't run it just because it's on *Billboard,* and it jumped ten slots this week," Sam told the *Commercial Appeal* sometime later. "I don't give a damn. If I know a record doesn't have it, I'm not going to play it"), at 6080 Mt. Moriah Road in Memphis. He had spent the last two years building the studio, which might best be described as a pyramidally modernistic structure with turrets and a brown cedar-and-stone facade—but when I drove up, the parking lot seemed unusually crowded for an ordinary Friday morning.

I was barely out of my rental car, my cumbersome canvas bag slung over my shoulder, when Knox, ordinarily a person of the sunniest and most indomitable disposition, emerged from the building with a worried look on his face. There had been a flood at the station early that morning, he explained to me, the sprinkler system had gone off and flooded the station before anyone was able to shut it off. Everyone was involved in trying to get the massive cleanup effort under control, and he was afraid we were just going to have to postpone the interview.

Can you imagine how I felt?

ALL RIGHT. I think it's time to take a breath and backtrack a little. I said at the end of the last chapter, "Sam to all intents and purposes simply stepped off the world stage and disappeared from public view for the greater part of the next two decades." Which is certainly true, as far as it goes. But he was by no means idle. To say his life was uneventful would be a misstatement in the extreme — as Sam would have been the first to insist.

Just to take a random example, right after the Bay of Pigs invasion in April 1961, he called Castro. To Sam, Fidel Castro was a genuine hero, a revolutionary in the true spirit of the American Revolution, and he didn't want him to get too discouraged.

Here's Sam's story, which is fully supported by Sally's account of discovering an unprecedentedly large phone bill that summer of 1961 and asking Sam if it was right.

I was sitting right here on this couch and had a few drinks and thought about this thing [with] Castro and the United States. I mean the Bay of Pigs was the stupidest damn thing in the whole wide world. Here was Castro, not only one of the smartest people on this earth but one of the bravest. And don't forget for one minute that Batista wasn't anything in the world but a mobster, starving [all] the people to death — outside of the gamblers in Havana.

I guess it was about eight thirty, nine thirty at night — they kept me on the line so long, getting a little more information, a little more information, [but] finally they put me through. And I just knew I had Fidel. But actually it was Raul, his brother.

This was a great conversation, a *fun* conversation. I explained to Raul that I was just another person that was concerned. I wasn't in sympathy with Communism. I wasn't in sympathy with democracy. I was in sympathy with common sense and people. I didn't know if I could do a thing. And I certainly was not gonna embarrass our government. But I was not gonna back off of [my belief in] how badly Cuba needed us and we needed Cuba.

I had a great time talking, [even though] it didn't take a guy with a few drinks to know that he was going to be monitored every word. I mean, *every word*. And I knew I would be on record the rest of my life. But I just felt that to have a war over Cuba, a wonderful, wonderful little island — I mean, how stupid can you get?

Everybody's gonna say I'm a Communist. I don't care. I'm an American through and through. But I was not going to back off on what I believed. And don't think for one cotton-picking minute that I wouldn't have gone over there, if the State Department would have permitted me. [Which] they probably wouldn't — and I would not have broken the law. But I sure would have done some talking as to why [they should let me go]. Let me fail. Let me fail as a citizen. We've had enough diplomats and Presidents that have failed. And it does not take a professor of history — it just takes somebody with some damn common sense [to understand] that the Bay Of Pigs was the stupidest thing the United States ever did: to start a fight with a man that truly wanted to help his people.

Not long before he called Castro, Sam heard that WSM was planning to scrap the transmitter that had carried the sound of the Grand Ole Opry to the world ever since its early days. He called up an engineer that he knew at the station and went out to the transmitter house to examine it for himself. For Sam it was "the most magnificent piece of equipment you have ever seen in your life," a vast, handcrafted relic of a lost age, and, he announced, he wanted to buy it — who did he see about purchasing this irreplaceable piece of history? Within weeks he had bought it from General Electric for $7,500, arranged for it to be disassembled for shipping, and for the next forty years stored it in pieces, offering it to the Smithsonian and the Country Music Hall of Fame, both of whom turned it down because it was simply too big for any display space they had available. It remains in storage to this day, at an aggregate cost that has by now exceeded its purchase price many times over, but Sam never wavered in his commitment to its preservation, and the preservation of what he always regarded as a precious collective memory.

This was a rare instance of accumulation, though, in a decade of divestiture that took place sometimes with dramatic purposefulness, more often without evident acknowledgment, but never ceased to progress in irreversible fits and starts.

By 1961 he had given up on ARMADA. He carried Jud with him to the convention in Hollywood, Florida, outside Miami, with the thought that Jud, whom he had put back on the payroll once again at $150 a week for unspecified duties, might take a job at the radio station in Lake Worth. But Jud stayed drunk in his hotel room the entire time, and the most memorable thing to occur on the whole trip took place on the drive down. They were traveling in tandem in Sam's two Cadillacs, Sam was in the lead and Knox was driving the purple El Dorado with the white hardtop, with Sun promotion head Bill Fitzgerald and his Uncle Jud as his passengers. They were stopped by a highway patrolman, something of a concern, since Knox was only fifteen, but Jud, who had been drinking in the backseat, struck up a conversation with the policeman and asked if he could show them the way to the local bootlegger. The cop just told them no problem and led them to the bootlegger's house, as Sam's car disappeared out of sight. And Jud even talked the cop out of giving his nephew a ticket. But Sam, not surprisingly, was fit to be tied.

Jud remained, as Sam would occasionally say in a shamefaced moment of candor, "a fucking thorn in my side." He retained an uncanny, and uncommon, ability to get under his brother's skin — and not just when they were drinking either. One example — and it is only one — came about when Sam cut Jerry Lee Lewis doing one of his favorite boogie numbers, Little Junior Parker's "Feelin' Good" (which Parker himself had adapted from John Lee Hooker's "Boogie Chillen"). To take advantage of the twist craze — and possibly to register a new copyright — Sam had him record the song as "I've Been Twistin'," with *twistin'* simply substituting for *boogieing*, but Jud felt compelled to alert Sam's old partner (and his own old nemesis), Jim Bulleit, who Jud knew was likely to feel entitled to half the publishing on "Feelin' Good." A spirited correspondence between Sam and Bulleit ensued, seemingly ending in a draw, with Bulleit windily backing down ("Make your move anyway you wish") and the song not selling enough to make much of a difference anyway. But the whole episode did not exactly engender feelings of warmth or trust on Sam's part toward his brother.

Jud was still functioning off and on as Jerry Lee's manager, and he took him back to England for a May 1963 tour, largely financed by Sam, that turned out to be an unqualified triumph. Jerry Lee had visited England the previous year as well with great success, but this seemed to mark a sea change in his fortunes, and Jud came home with gifts for everyone, including cuff links that lit up, and a new tailored wardrobe for himself, all charged on the Sun credit card.

Jerry Lee and Charlie Rich were the last artists left on the Sun roster that Sam really cared about, and he was expecting Jerry to sign a new five-year contract on his return from England in June, but then

Jerry told the *Press-Scimitar* that he was "thinking seriously of changing labels" when his contract was up in the fall. "I'm open to bids," he said, while Sam was reported to be "not happy with the situation."

Charlie Rich, whose contract had expired in March, was well into the process of leaving. In fact, he had already signed with RCA when Sam telegrammed his new record company that Charlie was in violation of a long-standing verbal agreement with the Sam C. Phillips International Corporation to allow Sam to match any competing offer, and that he would sue if Charlie and RCA did not cease and desist. RCA suspended the contract, Charlie countersued, and the dispute was settled two days after it was joined in chancery court on June 12, with Sam and Charlie forming a publishing partnership that would hold the rights to all Charlie Rich compositions written over the next three years. All proceeds from the new company, Charlie Rich Music, would be split 50-50, after a modest fee for administration, and Sam promised to seek the same 38 percent bonus payment from BMI that he got on his own publishing, with studio time at Phillips Recording to be provided free.

Sam scheduled two last nights of sessions for Jerry Lee, with the second falling on the evening of August 28, by coincidence the same date as the civil rights March on Washington, which he watched with intense excitement on television that afternoon. It would be, he was absolutely certain, the harbinger of a new day. "Sam just thought that this was going to be *the* thing," said his niece Dot West, the only child of his first mentor, Jimmy Connolly, who had visited with her husband the weekend before the march. Not everyone in the family would necessarily have agreed with Sam, said Dot, always a special favorite but even more so since her father's death, of a heart attack at fifty, two years earlier. "Sam thought it was just really going to be something special — and, you know, if you didn't believe in it, if you didn't think it was wonderful, you didn't dare say that around Sam. 'Cause he took two hours telling you why it was going to happen and [what] it was going to mean to the world. And that was just — I never heard anybody really talk like that," said Dot, "about racial [issues] and how this was going to be such a special time in our lives."

But for Sam the oratory and the music (not to mention the dream of social justice) could not help but remind him of his own inspiration as a boy on the sidewalk outside of Armstead Methodist Chapel in Florence, Alabama. As he would later write in his rough draft for a tribute album following Martin Luther King's death: "Dr. King certainly knew of music's power and used it to its highest accord. In the great Spirituals of the church he found his refuge and [left a] legacy made only more powerful from the touching sounds . . . flowing from the windows of the black church." And as if to reinforce a personal reference that no one else could fully grasp, he concluded with an emphatic exhortation: "COME NOW — LET US OPEN THE WINDOWS AGAIN AND *HEAR* THE *MUSIC!*"

The final Jerry Lee Lewis session was scheduled for early evening, from seven to ten. Surprisingly, Sam had engaged a string section led by Memphis Symphony Orchestra concertmaster Noel Gilbert to play live in the studio with a band that included Scotty Moore on acoustic guitar and Roland Janes on electric, with the Hurshel Wiginton Singers. Sam conducted the session with a warmth and engagement that sometimes eluded him these days, and they cut four songs in rapid succession, three of which would not be released for another six years, when they would rise to the top of the country music charts in the midst of Jerry Lee's decadelong-delayed return as a star. After the fourth take of the final number, a jumped-up version of the 1878 African-American-authored "minstrel song" "Carry Me Back to Old Virginia," Sam blamed himself for "messing up" (he had simply gotten too excited, he said) and asked Jerry to give it just one more try. "We're broke, and we're out of tape, so this'll have to be the last one," he said before cutting the master. Ten days later Jerry formally severed his connection with the company, and he signed a five-year contract with Shelby Singleton at Mercury Records shortly thereafter for $25,000 upfront and an additional $25,000 guarantee.

There was more than a little irony in this. At the time that Jerry Lee signed with Mercury, Sam had been engaged in a lawsuit with its vast conglomerate owner, the Dutch-based Philips Electronics, for more than two years. The lawsuit was over the name of the label and corporation he had announced with such pride in 1957, Sam C. Phillips International, which in one variation or another had been applied to nearly all of his operations other than Sun since that time. Sam had been well aware of the Philips company's growing presence in the record business throughout the world since first establishing Philips Records in 1950 — by 1957 the United States was virtually the only major market they had not conquered, and the only one in which the name of their record company had not been trademarked. You just watch, Sam told Sally, they're going to come into the American market and they're going to come after me.

And so they did, in August of 1961, after purchasing Mercury Records, the largest of the American independent labels, earlier that year. It wasn't long before he received the letter he had so long expected, demanding that he cease and desist from any and all uses of the "Sam C. Phillips International" name in any and all of its various iterations. That was when Sam hired a Washington, D.C., patent and trademark attorney named Boynton P. Livingston and, after first suggesting that Philips Electronics would have to take up the issue of his employing his own name with his late mother ("I hope they do not expect me to abandon my birthright to them or anybody else for any consideration," he wrote to his lawyer at one point), he countered with the demand that Philips stop using *his* name, a name on which he had built his reputation in the record business since he had first opened his studio in 1950.

Even as this was all playing out, at least as early as January of 1962, he had entered into separate negotiations with Mercury with the idea of their underwriting his Nashville operation by guaranteeing a certain number of studio hours and being guaranteed in turn free office space, first priority on session dates, and a 30 to 40 percent discount on studio rates. This negotiation, like the Philips lawsuit, proceeded fitfully, with Shelby Singleton, Mercury's Nashville-based head of Eastern and Southern recording, leading the talks, then turning them into a conversation not so much about studio rental as about Mercury purchasing the Sun label.

Sam had known Shelby, a flamboyant thirty-year-old Shreveport-area native, since he had first brought Elvis to the Louisiana Hayride, when Singleton, an industrial engineer at an ammunition-manufacturing division of Remington Rand in Minden, Louisiana, was trying to promote the entry of his wife, Margie, into the country music business. In 1957 both he and Margie, a talented singer and songwriter, signed on with Don Pierce and Pappy Daily's Starday label, so successful as an independent that it was serving at that time, in a cooperative arrangement, as the country division of Mercury. Shelby started out as a "junior" promotion man but soon proved to have a natural aptitude for pitching product, and when Starday and Mercury split in 1958, he remained with Mercury, along with George Jones, Starday's premier country star. Shelby turned out to be nearly as much of a "star," with the ability required of every promo man to freely dispense drinks, cash, and women and, in his own formulation, "stay up for two or three days,

outdrink everybody, [and] still be up when they were all on the floor."
He possessed the same gregarious charm and charismatic personality as
Jud Phillips, whom he very much admired for his promotional flair, but
he had a drive and focus that seemed to elude Jud. He carved out new
territory for Mercury and within two years had fallen into an a&r ("producing") position almost by accident, becoming Eastern and Southern
recording chief and Mercury vice president in 1962 as he shuttled back
and forth between Nashville and New York with a restless energy that
led *Billboard* to call him "a man with a mission . . . one of the busiest — if
not the busiest — a&r men on two continents."

Sam got a big kick out of Shelby — he just plain *liked* Shelby's independent pluck and spirit — and that as much as anything may have been
the reason he continued to talk to him about the label sale. Shelby for
his part was mesmerized by Sam, but he didn't think Sam would ever
cut a deal. He mistakenly assumed that Sam was too irate over the whole
Philips Electronics business — but he clearly liked to talk, and Shelby
always enjoyed his company. So he kept calling on Sam and having
these lengthy, rambling conversations about the *possibilities* of a sale,
the creative opportunities that a sale might open up. He knew how dis-
enchanted Sam was with the whole distribution system ("he thought the
distributors were a bunch of damn crooks"), and suggested to Sam that if
Mercury purchased the masters and took all those business worries off
Sam's hands, then maybe Sam could get back in the studio and produce
some records. Shelby even went so far as to set up a Memphis meeting
between Sam and Mercury president Irving Green in early 1963 (Green
was Mercury's widely respected cofounder and had continued to run
the company after the Philips acquisition), and that dialogue continued
for over a year, but like all the previous discussions, it ended up going
nowhere.

In the meantime Sam sold the Nashville studio. This was precipitated
by two events. The first, and by far the more significant, was that Billy
Sherrill left the company. Billy hadn't really been looking for another
job, but he wanted to *produce* records, not simply engineer them, and
he knew that he would never get that opportunity through Sam, with
Sun recording virtually at a standstill, and the studio, for all its traffic,
functioning almost entirely as a rent-out to other labels.

Billy's chance came at the end of 1963, when Columbia's new Epic
office had an opening for an all-around "shotgun producer," a producer

who, in other words, would work with any artist not already claimed by another, more established a&r man, at a salary of $8,000 a year. Epic was a Columbia subsidiary that had been created in 1953 for music not sufficiently in the pop mainstream for its parent label — which in Nashville translated primarily into country and rhythm and blues. It was just the kind of opportunity, both artistic and financial, that Billy had been hoping for, but for the longest time he didn't know how to broach the subject to Sam. "I like to never got enough courage to tell him. Finally, I got up the nerve. I said, 'Sam, I've really got an offer for a good job at a good salary, about double what you're paying me — which is all right.' He said 'Who?' I said, 'Epic Records.' He said, 'Out of New York?' I said, 'Yeah.' He said, 'Well, you need to do what you got to do, but remember — Sambo, old Sambo is telling you this right now. Them boys up there is not going to treat you like I treat you. Hey, they don't have the heart, the feelings that Sambo has.' I said, 'Well, I'm going to take my chance, you know.' It was the hardest thing I ever did."

With Billy gone, Sam just didn't have much of an impetus to carry on. He could always get another engineer — and he did — but he doubted that he would ever find another conversationalist willing to explore the mysteries of the universe into the wee hours of the morning like Billy. And without any solicitation whatsoever on his part, he already had an ardent suitor, Monument Records label owner Fred Foster, who, sensing the void that Billy's departure had left, redoubled his efforts now to persuade Sam to sell.

Fred Foster was another former promo man, if nowhere near as flamboyant as either Shelby or Jud, whom Sam had originally met coming through Memphis in the midfifties. A transplanted North Carolinian, he cofounded Monument Records in 1958 in Washington, D.C., his adopted hometown. Then in 1960, after taking over the company and on the verge of moving it to Nashville, where he did all of his recordings, he had the hit that would define Monument's success, Roy Orbison's multimillion-selling operatic pop aria, "Only the Lonely."

It was the beginning of a run of unprecedented success for Orbison, a one-hit Sun artist who Jack Clement had predicted would never make it as a ballad singer — though Jack may have been speaking with a certain amount of irony and, in any case, at Sun the proposition was never given a chance. Fred Foster had been recording Roy at the RCA studio on 17th Avenue South almost from the start, but he had begun scheduling r&b sessions for his subsidiary label, Sound Stage 7, at Phillips some six months earlier, and he had fallen in love with the room. He kept pestering Sam, Sally said, almost from the day he started recording there — "just kept after Sam, kept after Sam, and every time he saw Sam he would want to buy the studio, and then after Billy left, Sam's interest [in the studio] kind of went away — so he just sold it to Fred."

Fred might not have put it quite that way. To Fred Foster, dealing with Sam was one of the most excruciating business negotiations he ever engaged in. It may well have lasted no more than four or five days, he said — but it was four or five days of negotiating around the clock. "Sam loved negotiating better than anyone I've ever known. His favorite saying if he thought you were getting the better of him, was, 'Now, wait just a damn minute. Now, let's be realistic.' It was like pulling shark's teeth with a tweezer to get him to commit — but once he did, it was etched in stone."

In the end they made the deal on February 10, 1964, for $175,000 for the studio and all of its physical assets, which were specified, and for its "goodwill," which was not. Sam agreed not to enter into the recording studio business in Nashville for at least five years, and it was clearly understood that the owner of the building, Cumberland Lodge, had the right to terminate the rental agreement according to the terms of its lease with Sam Phillips Recording Studio of Nashville. Which they did just two years later when they sold the building to National Life and Accident Insurance, the owner of WSM and the Grand Ole Opry, which intended to expand its home offices to include both the Lodge and the Clarkston Hotel next door. Foster at least had a grace period, which eventually stretched to almost two years, but then had to resort to doing his recording at various locations around town until he was able to complete construction of his own studio at the end of 1968. Fred had carefully studied the way Sam set up his operation and replicated as many of the details as he could, including a similar sense of spaciousness and a twenty-three-foot-high ceiling, three feet higher than the majestic Masonic Lodge, that Sam always considered one of the keys to its incomparable live feel.

It was just after selling the studio in February of 1964 that he finally reached an agreement with Philips of Holland. He fought them to the very end but more for the sake of principle at this point (and undoubtedly out of his love of battle) than for any great practical purpose. He would not agree to drop the use of his name on *any* competing products, he wrote to his lawyer on March 6, but as he pointed out, he had no intention of putting out any competing products other than phonograph records, and as things looked right now, he would be out of the recording business before long. "They are just straining at a gnat," he wrote — but a very vexatious gnat.

Ultimately he graciously acceded to a check for $45,000, while giving up virtually nothing in return, save for the promise to drop the term "International" from the names of his various enterprises and to cease to employ the name "Phillips" alone, without linkage to his first name and middle initial, and then with the surname to be presented "at all times in lettering of the same style, size and color . . . but in a style differing from so as not to be confusingly similar to that used by N. V. Philips." In addition he agreed not to contest or interfere with Philips International's right to market their products in the United States and to drop the "globe" or "world" illustration from the design of all his products while retaining the right to manufacture anything he liked under the Sam C. Phillips rubric — but only in the United States and Puerto Rico. It was all, as he suggested, highly theoretical, for not only did he never "employ the name in connection with the production, manufacture and sale of products," he never, so far as I can tell, put out another release — or ever intended to — on his own fiercely defended Phillips (International) label.

For Sam it could certainly be seen as a triumph — an unqualified one by any measure, though just how satisfying would be difficult to say. It was a little bit like his victory over the IRS — he was proud of having paid off every penny of the excise tax that they had carried on account when he simply couldn't afford to pay it at the beginning. But then when they came after him on a trumped-up charge, saying that he owed $600,000 or $700,000 because he had set up an intermediary "pass-through" corporation the same way all the majors did (this was so as to be able to pay the 10 percent tax not on the roughly $.40 per record that Sun Record Sales charged the distributor, but on the wholesale pressing cost of maybe $.20 that the "pass-through" company paid the pressing plant and then charged Sun Record Sales), he fought them tooth and nail.

At one point, when he was in a conference with his attorney Roy Scott and an IRS agent, he became so exorcised in his argument that the agent told him, "Well, Mr. Phillips, if you don't like the tax structure, why don't you just leave the country?" Which made Sam so mad he could barely speak. *Leave the country?* He had never heard anybody say anything like that to him before. This was his country. That's what the argument was all about. But then he found a retired IRS agent in Nashville, a Mr. Snodgrass, who knew his way around the agency, and in the end, after several years of disputation, it was determined that rather than owing anything, he was actually owed $60,000. Which he promptly collected — every penny — with deference to Mr. Snodgrass every time he told the story.

He prided himself on his ability as a businessman, he prided himself on his honesty and his good reputation — and there was no question that he relished matching wits with a formidable opponent, whether it was Philips Electronics or the federal government (this was Sam's opportunity at last to be a kind of "country lawyer," advocating if not for the poor for the principle of justice for the "little man" against the machine). But it was a crusade with a limited spiritual return, and there must have been a certain hollowness in expending his emotional and intellectual energies over matters of getting and spending rather than the unmapped voyages of exploration he had undertaken in earlier days.

I F IT WAS NOT ALTOGETHER fulfilling for Sam — and I'm not sure that he would ever have admitted that, given the relish he took in later years in telling the tales — it was unquestionably disappointing for Knox and Jerry, though again they might not have put it quite that way. They had grown up believing in rock 'n' roll — it was a revolution that their father had taught them would never come to an end, because the power of the people, once unleashed, could never be bottled up again. They believed that, they believed it as fervently as they believed that they would one day take their place, *earn* their place in the brave new world into which they had been born.

Knox entered college in the fall of 1963, choosing Southwestern in Memphis (now Rhodes College) because he couldn't bear to be too far from where the action was. He took an active part in campus life, taught a college-age Sunday school class at Ascension Lutheran, where he introduced the writings of Paul Tillich and put on little plays and holiday pageants with Pastor Barnick and his wife, Carol. He was unstinting both in his zeal and in his studies (as Jerry said, "Knox was always a great brother, but he was very studious. I used to come in at two or three in the morning and see him studying, and I thought, 'Boy, what a waste of time, you need to be out partying!')—but in the end his heart was in the studio.

He and Jerry had started out there as little kids, just keeping the tape logs and packaging up samples. They had absorbed mixing and production technique from Sam "by osmosis. Sam didn't say, 'Come on, Knox, I'm going to show you EQ. I'm going to show you about the echo chambers.'" Sam, said Jerry, "always told us that the best way to learn was to just get in there and do it." Sometimes he would specifically tell one or the other of them, "Well, if you're into it, then come on, we're going to do this session tonight, you be my sideman, so to speak." But he never pushed it, and he never made them feel like this was something that was expected of them—just that if they did it, even if they screwed up, they had better not hold anything back.

Knox married his childhood sweetheart, Betty Mustin, who lived just down the street, in July 1964, at the end of his freshman year. There were more than seven hundred guests, and while everyone else was throwing rice, Dewey threw 45s. Knox had been designated as an official Sun Records a&r man earlier in the year, and with free run of the studio he had been fulfilling his a&r duties mostly working with a bunch of bands made up of fellow Southwestern students ("I'd get them in, and they didn't know what they were doing, and I didn't know what I was doing!"), but then he got a little more serious with a popular local band he met through Johnny Dougherty, onetime manager of DeLayne Phillips, the World's Most Perfectly Formed Midget Wrestler, who was now a DJ on WGMM in Millington. He was also managing several local bands, including a group of six high school students (each from a different high school) called Randy (Haspel) and the Radiants. At Johnny's urging Knox went out to see them at the Clearpool on Lamar and was so knocked out he invited them to come into the studio right away.

"They were the first real-deal band that I worked with. I mean, Bob Simon wrote such great songs, and Randy had this unique voice, and their harmonies were terrific. I really thought they were pretty spectacular for a really young band." They all gained confidence, Knox as much as anyone else, from working together in the studio, and after a while Knox got Sam to come in and listen to what they had been doing and even cut a few tracks on them. It was, for Knox, a moment of truth.

"Sam told me, 'You make the studio sound great, Knox. Don't be afraid to bring anyone in here that you feel has heart and talent.'" And from that point on, as Knox recalled it, he never was.

He continued to run the board for all of his brother's sessions, too, with every band Jerry put together, up to and including the Jesters, who would follow the Radiants' two Sun releases with a single release of their own, "Cadillac Man." Perhaps because of the very scarcity of new material (1965 would see the release of only four Sun records), the Jesters would eventually acquire such an outsized reputation, particularly among British collectors, that the liner notes to their first collection, issued in England some forty years after the fact and made up almost entirely of previously unreleased sides, would proclaim it "some of the best rock 'n' roll the [Sun] label produced." Be that as it may, with just one release on a practically moribund label that did virtually no promotion of its own product, there was little opportunity for stardom or chart success. And stardom was clearly what both boys were aiming at, in Knox's case the opportunity to discover previously untried, untested, untapped talent in the same way his father had, for Jerry — with what he could justifiably claim as the requisite looks, musical ability, drive, and *attitude* — to achieve, with the right breaks, Jerry Lee Lewis, Sputnik, and Elvis-styled rock 'n' roll immortality.

That attitude, similar to Sam's in so many ways, so like Sam in the unswerving pugnacity of his determination, was bound, too, to put him at odds with his father, and it did — constantly. "Don't expect anything from me, I'm just along for the ride," was one of Jerry's mantras, and when he dropped out of school after his junior year, just as his father had but for very different reasons, Sam was fit to be tied. Jerry deeply resented Sally, too, and didn't try to hide it. But most of all he refused to be bound by his father's strictures. It wasn't that Sam expected anything in particular from him and Knox — it was just that, as Jerry saw it, he expected *everything*. The catch was that Sam never told you how to achieve it, but at the same time he never neglected to tell you how you had fallen short. "Sam was always, essentially, giving you crap," said Knox, who was willing to put up with it, because he saw it as a test. If you could put up with Sam's withering criticism, then it was almost like you had passed the test, you had proved that you were really *convicted* in what you were doing, and then he was with you 100 percent.

But that wasn't Jerry's style at all. Jerry, as Knox said, was "an oppo-site reactor. He was so combative it was almost unbelievable." Some-times the two of them would practically come to blows, and Knox would have to step in between them. "I mean, I can't tell you how tough it was on me. Here I've got this wonderful brother, gifted, bright, but he has a different frame of mind from Sam. And he's just not going to go too far out of his fucking way."

What was hardest of all, though, for both of them, was watching their father, a father who had never been anything less than fully, passion-ately engaged in something he believed in so much he thought it would change the world, seemingly doing little more than drifting, drinking, and figuratively twiddling his thumbs. Sometimes he just confused them by the careless way he conducted himself both in public and in private.

"One time he really embarrassed me at Southwestern," Knox recalled. "Every year for homecoming there was this fraternity com-petition to build [the best] exhibit — I mean, this wasn't just putting up balloons, this was serious stuff. Well, this was the Viet Nam era, and my fraternity, Sigma Nu, decided to do a Viet Nam exhibit with bombs and music and explosions and whatever. So I got all these big speakers from the studio, and they were supposed to be behind the exhibit for the explosions and the music, but I just couldn't get it to work. So I called my dad and said, 'Look, Dad, can you help us?' So he drives over, and he's a little tipsy. And I'm like, 'Okay, Dad, we have this Viet Nam exhibit' — and he *hated* Viet Nam. But there was a whole mess of crap, and he says, 'Okay, we'll make this work,' and he worked his ass off, stayed there for hours to get the sound perfect, and I think we won the exhibit that year. But as he walked around, and he's doing his thing — I mean, this is *weird Sam,* you know — I'm going, 'Man, I don't even *know* you.' I mean, today I just look at all that stuff as another rock 'n' roll evening. But at the time I'm thinking, 'I don't know. This is not good. How could he do this to me?'"

Knox knew that when all was said and done, Sam couldn't have been prouder of him — and, for all of his doubts, Jerry knew it, too. In his own way Sam supported the boys without hesitation in everything they did, he made it possible for them to pursue their dreams, he even lent a hand at the board on some of their sessions and almost certainly kept the label alive for them, whether or not he was willing to put any money into promoting it. In a way he was giving them the same kind of laboratory to fool around in that had been so essential to his own creative endeavors — but the one inarguable difference was that he no longer believed in it.

It had to be hard on the boys, Sally observed. To deal with a father who had such an intractable, uncompromising view of the world, who was a perfectionist in so many ways. But what stung most was his outright dismissal of the life they had chosen, his utter disbelief in the future of the record manufacturing business to which they had both been drawn not by his exhortations but by the example of the life that he had lived. "They'll carry you to the cliff, then they'll shove you off," he told them over and over again. Meaning: the artists, the distributors, the jukebox operators, the majors and the cutthroat competitors — the whole damn shooting match. It was a warning that quickly grew old — it sounded sometimes like a tired reflection of a Depression-era upbringing — and it inevitably became a refrain that was passed back and forth between Knox and Jerry with more than a hint of mocking forbearance.

On April 1, 1967, Sam announced the "reactivation" of the Sun label with the release of three new singles, two of which were produced by Knox (including the debut release in a new gospel series). Knox and Jerry were named as two of the key players in the revamped company. So was Jud, whom Sam had recently been backing in the first Saab dealership in the Florence area, which came to an inglorious end after many ingenious promotions, when Jud, in order to further sales, gave away all five of his demonstration models. Sam even hired Jud's nineteen-year-old son, Juddy, another Phillips destined to take his place in the music business, and hinted at unspecified plans for expansion. There was a small page-one *Billboard* item headlined "Sun Shines Again," but as the carryover noted in a bittersweet afterthought, "Sam Phillips and the Sun label once played a major role in the record industry through the discovery of a flock of top artists, including Elvis Presley. . . . The 'rockabilly sound' originated in Sun's Memphis studios during the 1950's and influenced the entire course of American music."

Sam did it for Knox and Jerry, Sally noted matter-of-factly. "We were putting some records out, but Sam had no confidence in it at all. He knew that the independent record business was over." And in fact, there was only one more release, another Knox production that did not arrive until eleven months later, on the "new" Sun label.

Everyone attended Knox's graduation at the end of May — a proud

Sam and Becky; Jud and Dean and Juddy; Knox's wife, Betty, and their five-month-old daughter, Kim; even Dewey, on his best behavior. Knox, a political science major who had made the Honors Society and gave the valedictorian speech, had applied to various law schools but had ultimately made the decision to go to Vanderbilt, because, somewhere in the back of his mind, he thought if he could just set up an outpost in Nashville, like the one Sam had built and then sold a few years earlier, maybe he could establish a new Sun presence in the record industry. But then after thinking about it some more, and taking into account his twenty-four-hour access to the studio and a life that seemed little less than idyllic with his little family in the bungalow on McEvers Circle, the first home his parents had ever owned (and one which they would never sell), "I decided, I'm just going to stay here and see how this works out." He left open the option of going back to school someday, but realistically he knew that was pretty unlikely. Sam said to him, "Knox, I'm not so sure you want to do this." But he knew that he did. And as proud as Sam had been of his decision to attend law school, "Sam didn't argue with me about, 'You should go to law school.' Or 'Are you crazy?'" Sam had told him enough times that dedication was more important than results. And he was resolved in his mind that he would never be anything less than 100 percent dedicated.

Six months later Sam announced what sounded like a bold new venture. "Sam Phillips, pioneer of the 'Memphis Sound' in music," reported the *Memphis Commercial Appeal* in March of 1968, "yesterday was named president of the Holiday Inns of America, Inc. record and music publishing companies by Kemmons Wilson, HIA board chairman. 'This is a great challenge to me. During the past few years I have devoted most of my time to my own music publishing companies,' Mr. Phillips said. 'It will be good to return to the actual production end of the industry.'"

There was an exchange of mutual compliments ("'We recognize Mr. Phillips' abilities, talent, and knowledge of the complex music industry,' Mr. Wilson said," and Sam in turn hailed "the 20-million dollar computer system at HIA [that] will be used in 'market analysis'"), expanded opportunities were stressed, and the same team that had been named to head up the revamped Sun label was renamed to the same positions in the new company, thus formally shutting Sun Records down, at least for the time being.

Kemmons had dipped his foot in the record business once before, with an earlier Holiday Inn label that operated from 1961 to 1963 under the direction of his National Contract Sales Manager, D. Wayne Foster, a passionate music aficionado. The philosophy behind the label was easy to understand: with more than a thousand different locations around the country, Holiday Inn had more than a thousand different lounges in which to present, promote, and sell the music — and how better to exploit that market than to create your own stars and manufacture your own product? This early dream of synergy had failed to fully materialize, and the label fell into desuetude when D. Wayne Foster left the company. But to Kemmons, an invincible optimist and indefatigable entrepreneur (his autobiography is cheerfully entitled *Half Luck and Half Brains*), it was mostly lack of experience, and an effective way of getting the word out, that doomed this first attempt to failure. So he hit upon another scheme.

About six months earlier, with not just the radios in every Holiday Inn room across the nation in mind but also all the insomniacs and early-morning risers like himself, he launched a self-syndicated Holiday Inn radio show, buying up time cheap between midnight and six on stations across the country with little else to program (and virtually nothing else from which they might derive advertising income) during those hours. He paid just $12,000 a year, for example, to put the show on the air on WMC in Memphis, with "Dolly Holiday," the sultry-voiced DJ who presided over the program, spinning atmospheric late-night favorites like "Misty" or Julie London's "Cry Me a River" and advertising Holiday Inn nationwide on over sixty stations from Virginia to California. "Dolly Holiday" was in fact WHER's original general manager, Dottie Abbott (she had gone to work for the Holiday Inn home office just two years earlier), and she rapidly became something of a star in her own right, recording the first Holiday Inn album release, a collection of easy-listening favorites called *Nighttime,* just before Sam joined the company.

For all of Dolly Holiday's nominal success, though, Kemmons was convinced that he could do better. All the original reasons that a Holiday Inn label couldn't fail (and it should be noted that the label of every Holiday Inn record carried the square emblem of the Holiday Inn sign, known since its inception in 1952 as "The Great Sign") still held true. The only thing missing, according to the thirteenth of Kemmons' "Twenty Tips for Success" ("No job is too hard as long as you are smart enough to find someone else to do it for you"), was someone with the expertise to carry out the task. Who better than his old friend Sam Phillips, not only the most reliable of partners but one of the shrewdest men in the business? With Sam at the helm, he was absolutely certain Holiday Inn Records couldn't miss.

Sam regarded it a little more skeptically. At first he indulged Kemmons, because he *liked* Kemmons so much — Kemmons was one of his oldest friends, there was no one dearer to him in the world — and he thought maybe he could help him out. He knew it was a crackbrained scheme, but, hell, Kemmons had succeeded with schemes that were just as crackbrained and they had made him one of the richest men in Memphis. And besides, the more he examined the proposition, the more he thought maybe it could serve his own purposes as well. With Kemmons' money behind it, and the whole Holiday Inn apparatus at his disposal, maybe he *could* get this project off the ground, and with his own crackerjack staff already in place (and Knox handling the a&r chores), without too much of an effort on his part either. The deal called for an investment of only $5,000 in exchange for 20 percent ownership and a 50 percent split of the profits, with Holiday Inns of America picking up all expenses, including the salaries of everyone he had on his current payroll. And so, against his own better judgment, he signed on as president, chief executive, and decision-maker-in-chief for the new label.

"It was a total mistake," said Sally, who balefully observed the inevitable result, though she was not about to voice her opinion. "I think Sam in his own mind said, 'Well, hell, this is not going to take too much of my time. I can put so and so out there, and Knox and Jerry can produce'— he thought he could do it, and he wanted to do it, but, man, I'll tell you, you're in the phonograph record business or you're not, it's not something you can do part-time. And, I mean, to start up an independent label [at that time] was stupid, things had changed so much by then, and Sam knew it. But he didn't want to tell Kemmons."

Loyalty was the operative word, not common sense or creativity — loyalty to old friends, loyalty to his family, loyalty to firmly held principles and ideals. But where once it had been about "shooting for that damn row that hadn't been plowed"—that was what it had *always* been about — now, Sally sometimes felt, it was as if he had momentarily lost his way.

H E WAS IN ANY CASE a steadfast friend to Audrey Williams, Hank's first wife and the mother of his only son, when, beset by a sea of legal and personal troubles, largely of her own making, she found herself abandoned by virtually the entire country music community. The climax of her troubles came with the fight over the copyright renewals to the songs in the Hank Williams catalogue. These did not actually begin to be eligible for renewal until 1974 (under the old law, copyrights had a term of twenty-eight years, with a one-time renewal of equal length), but starting around 1960 Hank's sister, Irene, the executor of his estate, had surreptitiously entered into talks with Wesley Rose, whose late father, Fred, had discovered Hank and whose publishing company, Acuff-Rose, held the rights to all of Hank's songs. The upshot was that without Audrey's or anyone else's knowledge (and after Audrey had borrowed heavily against the prospect of the renewal money), Irene made a deal with Wesley Rose for the renewal rights to the entire catalogue for a one-time nonrecoupable bonus payment of $25,000 to the estate, plus $5,000 to Irene. When Audrey found out, she sued, both on behalf of her then-seventeen-year-old son, Hank Williams Jr. (at this point the sole heir to the estate) and as the recipient of half the songwriting royalties herself. The lawsuit, which contended in essence that a priceless heritage had been given away for a bargain-basement price, made its way through the courts and, after a number of judgments in favor of the deal Hank's sister had made, eventually found its way to the circuit court in Montgomery, Alabama, in September of 1967.

Most of the tight-knit country music establishment was prepared to testify for the defense. Wesley Rose was a powerful figure in Nashville, and Audrey was an easy person to disapprove of. She was widely dismissed as loud, erratic, and out of control, a woman with an increasingly serious drinking problem and an independent streak that permitted her to unapologetically choose the company of young men not much older than her own child. Sam didn't give a shit about any of that. He liked Audrey, he had always liked Audrey, and he was sick of all the fucking hypocrites and pharisees throwing bricks through glass windows and banding together to beat a woman out of what she had every reason to believe was rightfully hers.

Going against the testimony of one country music legend after another, he made his views just as plain (if more temperately expressed) in court and, to drive the point home, declared under questioning that he himself would pay half a million dollars for the renewal rights to Hank's catalogue "in a minute."

But it was all to no avail. Not surprisingly, Sam's offer was not accepted, and the judge's decision four months later dismissed Audrey's legal complaint out of hand, leaving the renewals firmly in the control of Fred Rose Music, Inc. Almost simultaneously Hank Jr., emancipated by his eighteenth birthday the previous May, fired his mother as his manager, and though she would live for another seven years, Audrey Williams' life was to all intents and purposes over. Of all of her many so-called friends, wrote her daughter, Lycrecia, the child of her first marriage, "only one . . . came through for her down in Montgomery, Sam Phillips," and she was a scorned and reviled figure in Nashville, where she continued to live in declining health in the same house that she and Hank had bought when they first arrived in 1949. Sam never wavered in his affection or support. "I've never known anyone who was as vilified as Audrey," he told the coauthor of Lycrecia's memoir, Dale Vinicur, "and still I didn't have a better friend, there wasn't anybody I had more respect for, despite her faults." He tried to advise her on her ongoing tax problems, even going so far as to get in touch with Mr. Snodgrass, the same retired IRS agent who had helped him beat the IRS on the excise tax, but Mr. Snodgrass was too sick at this point to be of any assistance. The one thing Audrey vowed she would never allow to happen was for the IRS to take her house, and she died, at fifty-two, the day before they were scheduled to do so. With the result that they couldn't take possession of it — not technically anyway — because for the time being at least, it became part of her estate.

SAM MOVED SALLY into his Mendenhall home in January 1968. There was never any talk of divorce, there would never *be* any talk of divorce, but he bought a house for Becky nearby, which Jerry, unencumbered at nineteen by any pressing obligations or relationships, moved into as well. For Becky it was a crushing blow, challenging her faith in God's works, if not His grace, leading her to seek answers to questions she could not quite bring herself to ask with formulations that in one way or other never failed to put the blame on herself. But whatever her feelings, she was determined to hide them from the boys, as more and more she sought refuge and belief in family. Part of her was convinced that Sam would return to her someday. Part of her knew he wouldn't. She continued to work with Sally and treat her as a friend. She was determined to keep things as much the same as she possibly could, so that if

Sam should ever change his mind, he could come back to her without having to feel he was coming back with his tail between his legs.

For Jerry, on the other hand, the situation was just fucked. He could see how hurt and rejected his mother felt—she still loved Sam, she would *always* love Sam, but she was not the kind of person who was ever going to fight back. She was the one who was expected to keep the family together, she was the keeper of family secrets and family pets, the smoother-over of family disputes, and it was a role that she not only accepted but embraced—because, as Jerry recognized with a mixture of indignation for the way that she'd been treated and love for who she was, *that was her nature.*

It just pissed him off. He was sick of his father's constant criticism. He was sick of his father's bullshit. He was sick of Sam spouting all these high-and-mighty principles that seemed to benefit only him. He could barely contain himself now when it came to Sally. But what was most infuriating of all was that Sam just didn't seem to care. There was never any discussion. There were never any explanations. You either went along with him, or you didn't, he just didn't seem to give a fuck.

For the first time, Jerry's rebellion turned into outright defiance. He'd always known his daddy was weird, but in the past it was something he had been proud of. Their fights accelerated now to the point where Knox couldn't count the number of times he had to intervene ("It was like, gee, you guys, give me a break—I mean I was bigger than both of them"), but it was the intensity of their emotional struggle that was more alarming. In the end, said Jerry, a bright, funny, sensitive man with a gift for analysis that he is in general as reluctant to share as his inner feelings, what may have both driven their relationship to the breaking point and yet still kept it from shattering was the similarity of their natures. "I think one of the things that made him maddest was that I was so much like him. He saw a lot in me that he didn't like, but it reminded him so much of himself that he couldn't really hate me for it."

But he could, certainly, make it difficult for Jerry to successfully mark his own territory. That was what happened with the tattoo. The tattoo may have been intended in Jerry's mind to express a kind of solidarity with the Sputnik credo, expressed in any number of colorful ways. "The higher the monkey gets on the pole," Jerry liked to say, "the more of his ass you can see. I think that sums up my position on life. Sputnik had a bear running to one titty for milk, and a pig running to [the other]. He's got a cherry on his left that says, 'Here's mine where's yours?,' a tattoo that says 'Butch,' and a ring that says 'Puke' on it." Jerry's tattoo was a little more random in its selection. "I got drunk one night and picked it off the wall in a tattoo shop, three roses with my initials underneath. I have no idea why I picked the roses out. The tattoo artist had gotten the flowers off of a funeral announcement of some motorcycle biker's death." Jerry knew it didn't exactly make the grand philosophical statement that Sputnik's did, but still, he felt, it made a statement.

They were all having dinner at Becky's house one Sunday afternoon when Sam got his first glimpse of it and, without even batting an eye, instantly declared, "Man, if you want to be a freak, why don't you just cut your damn arm off?" It was a typically Delphic pronouncement that right away became a part of family lore, the very apotheosis of Sam's oft-repeated and equally inscrutable insistence that "you can be a nonconformist and not be a rebel, and you can be a rebel and not be an outcast"—but whatever it meant, it pretty much put an end to Jerry's dreams of tattoo glory.

Although he had finished high school by now after taking evening classes and was nominally attending Memphis State, Jerry's application to his studies was nowhere near enough to protect him from the draft. He was going out with a girl whose mother was working for the draft board, though, and when she alerted him that his number was about to come up, he quickly enlisted in the reserves. He got married to another girl, Ryta Carol Harris, right after getting back from basic training in Texas and Louisiana, just around the time he turned twenty. Ryta was former Sun artist Ray Harris' daughter (Ray Harris had gone on to cofound Hi Records, a successful Memphis label that was just about to become a lot more successful with the arrival of soul singer Al Green), and Jerry didn't bother telling anybody about the wedding—they just got married at the Florence courthouse, after his Uncle Jud set it up for him, and Jud and his wife, Dean, were the only family in attendance. He had been trained as a combat medic at Fort Sam Houston in San Antonio and was attached to the Field Hospital Unit in Memphis, waiting to be activated, as he read in the news that medics were getting killed in Vietnam every day. But for some reason he never did get called up and just went on with a life that he would be the first to call both aimless in its utter lack of direction and fun for much the same reason.

Dewey died on September 28, 1968. His last years had been spent in a wandering state — it was only through Sam's intervention that he stayed out of jail on DUI, vagrancy, and disorderly conduct charges, and at the end, he was no longer able to hold down any kind of job in radio, as his once-brilliant gift for free association degenerated into incoherent babble. Sam put him on the payroll and took care of his family, arranging for him to be admitted into hospital psychiatric programs on more than one occasion, but Dewey was simply incapable of helping himself. He stopped by the studio to see Sam the day before he died. He was hacking and coughing and told Sam he thought it was pneumonia, but then he shambled off to his mother's house, where he died that night in his sleep. He was forty-two years old, a "lonely man with the heart of a boy," wrote Bob Johnson in a moving tribute in the *Press-Scimitar*. "His last years [were] lived in the past."

"He didn't ask for one damn thing," Sam said. "I did not do anything for Dewey other than I was always his brother, and he knew he could walk in any damn time."

Sam made all the funeral arrangements, helping Dewey's widow, Dot, to pick out the casket and staying with her, according to Dewey's biographer Louis Cantor, from the time of his death right up until the burial. He arranged for the service to be held at the Memphis Funeral Home, and, after a suitable period of suspense, Elvis even showed up with several of his guys, expressing his genuine and heartfelt sorrow to Dot before succumbing to a fit of giggles during the service prompted by everyone's recollection of one or another of Dewey's famous foibles. Burial was in Dewey's birthplace of Crump, Tennessee, and Sam, Knox, and Jerry were among the half dozen pallbearers. Knox and Jerry and their good friend and fellow pallbearer singer Dickey Lee had elected to drive out to the graveside service with Claude Cockrell, one of Dewey's more uninhibited associates, and they lost track of the time when they stopped for lunch in Moscow and got caught up in conversation. They arrived so late that they nearly missed the service altogether, something that everyone agreed Dewey would certainly have appreciated but Sam assuredly did not.

Sam announced his departure from Holiday Inn Records on July 1, 1969, waiving claims to any stock in the company but keeping the publishing. Under other circumstances one might have surmised that he had simply grown tired of a bad business, but in fact the reason was much more surprising. Sam had sold Sun Records. He had divested himself of the last link (save for the publishing, the financial bedrock of the music industry) to the label on which he had labored so long and hard to give birth. And the buyer was not Mercury Records, it was not Columbia, it was not any of the major corporations who had been waiting in line with their offers. It was Shelby Singleton, who had left Mercury when his contract ran out in 1967 and, financed by roughly $100,000 put up by Mercury licensees around the world with whom he had done business, gone out on his own as SSS (Shelby S. Singleton) International. At first he focused on r&b primarily and had a number of fair-sized hits, but then in 1968 he started a country label, Plantation, and, with its third release, struck pay dirt.

He first heard the demo of songwriter Tom T. Hall's "Harper Valley P.T.A.," a homespun fable about the hypocrisy and faux piety of the puffed-up new hillbilly middle class, in June of 1968. He then found an unknown singer, a Music Row secretary named Jeannie C. Riley, to sing it, at just about the same time his ex-wife, Margie, recorded it for another label. The Jeannie C. Riley record hit number 1 on the pop charts in September, going on to sell something like mmmph million copies (Shelby always fudged the number), and, with all the potential sources of exploitation (records, tapes, merchandise, and, eventually, movie rights) figured in, went on to gross somewhere between five and seven million dollars for the company over the next year.

So Shelby was sitting on a pile of money, which he knew very well he was just going to pay out in taxes if he didn't spend it, when Sam called him in December of 1968. Kemmons, Sam said, was growing impatient with the Holiday Inn label's lack of immediate success. He wanted to buy Shelby's company and have Shelby run the combined label for him.

Shelby almost laughed in his face. Didn't Sam understand that he had more than enough money at this point — he didn't need to add to it. What he needed to do was figure out how to spend it. Sam fully understood, but he urged Shelby to come to Memphis for a meeting anyway, and out of respect for Sam ("Sam was my idol almost"), Shelby agreed.

The meeting in January was no more productive than he thought it would be. Kemmons explained his revolutionary new theory of record distribution (they would sell their records in Holiday Inn gift shops, completely bypassing the distributors), and Shelby explained why it would work no better in future than it had to date. Shelby then further described his situation to Kemmons, and he thought the meeting had reached a standstill, until he suggested that maybe Kemmons should just buy Sun Records from Sam, giving him a catalogue to work from. That was a ridiculous idea, Kemmons said, people weren't interested in any of that old stuff—rock 'n' roll had had its day, they wanted "good music." Or something really up-to-date like "Harper Valley P.T.A."

That was when Shelby, ever the entrepreneur, spied his chance. If Kemmons wasn't interested in Sun, Shelby said, he certainly was. And he turned to Sam, expecting to see him laugh in his face. But Sam didn't laugh. "He said, 'Well, okay, I might sell it to you.' I said, 'Well, what do you want for it?' Sam said, 'I don't know. I'll have to think about it.' I said, 'Let me know what you want for it.' So I left and came back to Nashville, and about a week later, I believe, Sam called again and said, 'I've been thinking about what you said. Are you really, seriously interested in buying Sun?' I said, 'Yeah, I'm interested.' He said, 'Well, what kind of price have you got in mind?' I said, 'Well, I don't really know what it's worth. What have you got in mind?' Well, we argued back and forth for over thirty minutes, finally agreed on [a] range, and I told Sam, 'Let me know how many masters you've got and so forth.' Something like that. He gave me a list maybe two weeks later, and I guess we argued about the price. We probably started in January and came to an agreement around the first of June."

Why, one might wonder, would Sam sell to Shelby? Well, here's Sam on the subject. "The reason I sold it to him was because Shelby loved Sun Records, and he was always in the Louisiana Hayride audience and spoke to me every time I went down. He was just such an admirer of [the music], he really was. I had better offers, and I don't know [if] that was the greatest or the worst decision—*but I didn't sell out to a major label.*"

It may have been as simple as that. That's the way Sally saw it, and Shelby in his guilelessly calculated way agreed. "I think Sam sold the company to me because, number one, he liked me, and, number two, I had promised him I would keep the Sun label alive."

And Shelby's motivation? Apart from his cash overload, what was it exactly that prompted him to buy? On the one hand, it might have been little more than a pure gamble, as much of a whim on his part as it was on Sam's. On the other, he had made certain specific market calculations. "Sam had no record-club deals. He had no foreign deals. And with what

I knew about the foreign markets, I knew I could put these records out all over the world and get my money back from foreign releases if I had to. Plus I figured that Johnny Cash was going to get hot. That was my reason for buying Sun, really."

He was certainly right about Johnny Cash. Over the course of the past twelve months, Cash had had one of the biggest-selling pop albums of the year, *Johnny Cash at Folsom Prison*, which would stay on the charts for 122 weeks, while the single that was drawn from it, "Folsom Prison Blues," reached number 1 on the country charts in the summer of 1968. He had had a second number 1 country hit, the Carl Perkins-authored "Daddy Sang Bass," in early 1969; had just recorded another live prison album, *Johnny Cash at San Quentin* (which would itself reach number 1 in August and stay on the charts for seventy weeks); and his summer-replacement ABC television series debuted on June 7, with Bob Dylan and Joni Mitchell as his first guests, becoming an improbable hit that would remain on the air for close to two years. Not only that, Jerry Lee Lewis had experienced a no-less-improbable resurgence on Smash, the Mercury division that Shelby had until recently been overseeing, with four Top 5 country hits in the last year, the most recent, "To Make Love Sweeter for You," arriving at number 1 on March 1, 1969.

Even so, there was no way of calculating the exact worth of the catalogue, as Shelby would have been the first to admit. He had no idea that there were three big Jerry Lee Lewis country hits tucked away among the unreleased tapes from Lewis' last session with Sam—and he wouldn't have cared if he did. ("You can't," as Shelby noted, "make much money off of singles.") He didn't know that Harmonica Frank would become a cult hero, or that Sam's blues recordings would be prized as much around the world as some of Sun's biggest hits. He just knew that Johnny Cash alone had the potential to more than repay the cost of purchase—and that there were new markets to exploit that Sam had never dreamt of. But it might have been difficult at this point for even Shelby to imagine that, after all the success he had enjoyed as both a record producer and a Mercury executive, he had now at last found his true métier, in the role of a mutton-chopped modern-day super-salesman version of P. T. Barnum, the once-and-future merchandising king of the record industry.

R IGHT UP TO THE END Shelby thought Sam would change his mind. But Sam's mind was made up. So many of his longtime col-

leagues had either folded their tents or sold out to the major corporations (Atlantic had been bought by Warner Bros.-Seven Arts for $17.5
million in October of 1967, Leonard Chess had sold his company to GRT
[General Recorded Tape] for $6.5 million in December 1968 in order to
concentrate on the expansion of his rapidly growing radio and television
empire, and Specialty was virtually out of business) — he was not about
to linger any longer. He was certainly prepared to negotiate right up to
the end ("Sam," said Shelby, perhaps a little disingenuously, "was very
shrewd"), but he never wavered. And on July 1, 1969, the deal was signed.

It was for $1 million, with Sam retaining 20 percent of the company.
In Sam's mind this may well have meant that he would retain 20 percent
of the influence as well as 20 percent of the profits, should there be any,
but Shelby's view of a minority shareholder's role was, not surprisingly,
somewhat different.

Knox and Jerry were shocked initially. Neither had any idea that a
deal was in the works. Knox at one time had spoken to both Chess and
Atlantic, each of whom had made overtures about buying Sun before
selling out themselves, and he had been particularly drawn to the idea
of working with Leonard Chess' twenty-six-year-old son, Marshall, who
had grown up in the record business like himself, on an independent
production deal that would offer wide distribution to all the records
Knox was making in Memphis. But nothing ever came of that — Sam just
wasn't interested — and neither Knox nor Jerry was even aware of any
negotiations with Shelby. In retrospect, Knox realized, his first inkling
should have come when Shelby was talking with Sam one day, just like
he always did whenever he was in town, and Knox was working on a cut
by a popular local group, the Gentrys. Shelby came into the studio and
listened for about half an hour, expressing what sounded like genuine
enthusiasm, but Knox didn't think about it again until after the deal was
made, when Shelby licensed the record, "Why Should I Cry?," and put it
out on the new Sun, where it went to number 61 on the national charts.

That was the way the deal should have worked — that was the kind of
deal he had been talking about with Marshall Chess, the kind of binding
deal that Sam might have made with Shelby. But as it turned out, there
was nothing in the contract to compel Shelby to release anything that
Knox brought him. Still, he consoled himself, Shelby seemed open to the
idea, and after all the dead-on-arrival records he had been doing for the
"reactivated" Sun label and Holiday Inn, the sale might at least provide

Sam and Shelby Singleton (center) at the closing of the Sun sale, with SSS executive vice president Nobel Bell. *Courtesy of John and Shelby Singleton*

"an outlet for my stuff for real." He didn't know anything about Shelby other than that he was a longtime record man and an old friend of Sam's, but it was difficult to believe that if Shelby bought something, as a born promoter he wouldn't do everything in his power to sell it.

"I was a little surprised," said Jerry, which might qualify as an understatement in the extreme. "I think I always kind of thought—" But he refrains from voicing the sense of dispossession he clearly felt. Instead, he suggests, "I probably didn't understand all the dynamics of the record business. I was hot to trot, ready to be a star. I mean, we had a thriving studio business, the place was really hot, but as far as putting out records, Sam just wasn't doing that much. So I don't know that we were disappointed—it really wasn't that big a deal."

Maybe not. Or maybe this was just the only way Knox and Jerry had to rationalize their shock. But they were right about one thing: it did offer them an opportunity to finally strike out on their own, an opportunity that was unlikely to come from a father who, as Jerry pointed out, "is not ever gonna hand over the reins to the family business and say, 'Here, guys, have a good time.' I mean, he's not gonna do that. You're going to have to earn it—and he'll be cussing you the whole time!"

There wasn't anything to do about it anyway. It was, as they both knew, a done deal. So Knox got all the tapes together and labeled the boxes, and they were all sent over to Nashville, including the vast repository of early blues tapes, which had been explicitly excluded from the deal. Sam was upset about that, but he worked out a plan with Shelby for the start-up of a new blues label, Midnight Sun, and if that didn't pan out, he figured he could get the tapes back from Shelby any time he liked.

E LVIS CALLED FROM CALIFORNIA on almost the same day that Sam signed the sale agreement. He was going to be opening at the International Hotel in Las Vegas at the end of the month, his first extended live performance in nearly twelve years, and his voice betrayed the kind of nervousness that Sam recalled from their very earliest meetings. He hadn't seen Elvis in quite a while, not from any lessening of admiration or affection, though he took a dim view of the way Tom Parker had treated him, and the way Elvis had allowed himself to be treated, with one silly-ass movie after another.

Elvis talked about his upcoming show — he talked about the song selection, he talked about the band he was putting together, he talked about the big thirty-piece orchestra that would be playing behind him — until finally he got to the reason for his call. He wanted Sam to be there. Well, of course, he'd be there, Sam said — wild horses couldn't keep him away. But what about the fucking rhythm section? Were they just going to get lost among all the strings and woodwinds? "I said, 'Where is the placement of the rhythm section? Is that motherfucker kicking you in the ass?' I said, 'Just put that rhythm out there, baby, just put it out there. That is your *i-den-ti-fi-cation.*'" To which, what else could Elvis do but assent?

Sam wasn't going to fly out to Vegas — he hadn't flown in almost fifteen years now — so he borrowed a limo from Bill Tanner, the Memphis radio "jingles" king, and organized a party that would include Sally and himself, Knox and Betty, Jerry and Ryta, and Elvis' friend Cliff Gleaves, a part-time member of Elvis' group of guys, who had been sent back from California presumably to help Sam with the travel arrangements but really because, as welcome as he was to Elvis for the first few days of any visit, his hyperkinetic charm soon wore off.

Sam and everyone else enjoyed him anyway — he always provided good comic relief — and it was a very companionable journey until, somewhere in the desert, the car developed a bubble on one of the tires. They were lucky to find an isolated service station, where the guy told them he was sorry, the tire couldn't be fixed (hell, Sam already knew that), and then quoted a price for a replacement tire that was totally out of line. Sam tried to bargain with him at first, but then, after realizing the price wasn't going to come down, called him a fucking liar and a thief and told him he could go fuck himself and stick the tire up his ass while he was at it. So they limped along for another thirty or forty miles before finding another service station that offered more reasonable prices, permitting them to roll into Las Vegas on four good tires in style.

The show was sensational. "There was," Sam said, "some raunchy-ass shit, and I never heard a better rhythm section in my life." Which is exactly what he told Elvis when Elvis and all his guys came down to Sam's little suite in the early hours of the morning. He and Elvis went into the bathroom, and Elvis asked him what he thought, and Sam gave him a complete rundown, sitting on the commode with the top flipped down. "I told him, 'Elvis, that was fabulous, but, you know, that song, "Memories," has got to go!' I said, 'Goddamn, didn't that motherfucker bog down the fucking show?' And he said, 'Mr. Phillips, I just love that song.' And of course, he kept on singing it ever since."

THEY ONLY STAYED in Las Vegas for two days, but they saw Tom Parker doing business everywhere, a ubiquitous presence, selling his boy, Sam thought, like he was some damn piece of meat. Ike and Tina Turner were playing the small room at the International, and Sam went to see the show, the first time in years that he had seen Ike, whose 1951 recording, "Rocket 88," was the first full realization of Sam's vision, and the first number 1 hit to come out of his studio. It was a great show, as good in its own way as Elvis', and Sam thought Ike's wife, Tina, was one of the best entertainers he had ever seen. But the impression that really lingered was Ike's reaction when he saw Sam. Ike had a well-earned reputation as an unruly character, from the time that Sam first met him as a combative twenty-year-old, and his actions over the years had done nothing to diminish it. But now he practically lit up when he encountered Sam with Elvis' wife, Priscilla. Sam was equally happy to see Ike, explaining how they had all come out for Elvis' opening as Ike just looked at him, out of those dead lizard eyes and said, "Damn, man, you recording him too?" and they both burst out laughing.

FOR THE TIME BEING Sam was at something of an impasse. He offered Shelby advice, but it wasn't taken. He saw Shelby achieve one success after another with Johnny Cash's Sun material (one single, a live overdub of "Get Rhythm," went to number 23, and there were three charting albums before the year was out) as Cash claimed a virtual lock on the country music market, with a growing hold on the pop spotlight, too. But Sam never had any second thoughts about the sale — he was not one to look back. He simply drank more than he was accustomed to, more than he ever had, because, for the moment, he had no other place to go.

But then he discovered the lake house in Iuka. It was on Pickwick Lake, created in the 1930s by the damming up of the Tennessee River at Pickwick Landing, and he knew the area well — from the lake, you could easily travel forty miles by water, all the way to Florence. But he had never spent any time there, never really had any time to spend, until in the spring of 1970 Jerry told him about the house.

Jerry's wife Ryta's dad, Sam's onetime artist Ray Harris, had built a little cottage at Eastport Marina, right on the water. Jerry had fallen in love with the lake as a teenager — it was a real Mississippi/Alabama backwoods kind of a place, more than two hours removed from Memphis, a great place for him to go with some of his high school buddies to fish and drink. Once he got married, he spent as much time there as he could, and when the house two doors down from Ray's went up for sale, he told Sam about it — at $20,000 it was a real steal. He got Knox and Sam to come down to look it over, and in April of 1970 Sam bought it.

Jerry knew how much Sam loved the water. He had always spoken of the Tennessee River as second only to the Mississippi when Knox and Jerry were little kids. Then six or seven years ago, once he had finished the Nashville studio, he had gotten the boating bug, and the three of them had pursued it pretty much every summer weekend right up until the time Knox got married. Sam bought a sporty, all-aluminum Polar Kraft that they transported out to his old partner C. A. Camp's place on Horseshoe Lake in Arkansas, where Knox and Jerry amused themselves with Mr. Camp's three slot machines and learned to water-ski while Sam piloted the boat with his jaunty captain's hat cocked at a rakish angle. There was no question in either Knox's or Jerry's mind how much their father was going to enjoy the lake.

With the acquisition of the lake house, once again everything changed. It was a modest, unprepossessing structure, strictly functional, almost drab in its layout, but, not surprisingly, Sam was determined to transform it in every way. It was, said Sally, "his biggest project yet." He knocked down walls, put in big picture windows, built a new dock, planted zoysia grass, and totally remodeled the previously windowless boathouse/basement, while purchasing a brand-new supersleek red-and-white AristoCraft with a retractable hardtop ("a real rock 'n' roll-looking boat," said Jerry) that he hauled over from Memphis. He strung the trees with multicolored lights and built a stone-and-cement sea wall to keep the shoreline from eroding while putting down pea gravel to direct the water around the house. He was, as always, strictly his own contractor, but it was a family venture all the way. As Jerry said, "It was work. He was down there ramrodding and working Knox and me — everybody had to be involved, you know, ['cause] Sam never played." And he hired local artisans to do the work, finding them by word-of-mouth or small newspaper ads. "If there was a wino that did Sheetrock," Jerry said, "he'd get that guy. I don't know why he liked to use those kind of guys, but he did. And he'd always have to stay home [to supervise]. He was a character, man. He'd be down there in his white pants working with the backhoe man, not barking orders necessarily, but he knew more than they knew — or at least he perceived himself as knowing more. He had his belt on sideways. I mean, for everybody that ever encountered him, he was just a trip!"

He did this for almost two years. "He just loved building things," said Sally. "I mean, good Lord, it was the biggest project you've ever seen. We hauled stuff down there every weekend. Every weekend. Sam and I stayed down there for I don't know how long. He knew exactly what he wanted, and he got the people to do it. But he was standing right there with them. He practically redid the whole house. It took time, a lot of time." And then when it seemed like he had finished, he started all over again.

But as much as he loved all the planning and building, he seemed to enjoy his change of lifestyle even more. In Memphis they never had people over to the house anymore — Audrey Williams was just about their only houseguest — and Sam had even given up the annual Christmas party that he used to throw at the studio. But here on the lake he and Sally made friends with nearly everyone. As Sally recalled: "It was the whole neighborhood. Everybody just got together — it was just get in your boat and go across here to somebody's house and do something." And, of course, there was always family. "Knox and Jerry were usually down there every weekend — Knox and Betty and Jerry. The people next door — he was a plumber, these were just people who did all sorts of things. It was the whole neighborhood, everybody got together and done something. You'd go fishing, and you'd catch two or three fish off the dock and [maybe] a turtle. And every morning you'd hear the commercial fishermen go out." It was a place, Sally said, where Sam could really unwind, like he never could at home.

Shelby, who appreciated Sam, certainly, but never as anything more than a colorful character touched with some adventitious combination of genius and luck, visited one weekend with his wife, Barbara, and, for all of his own determined eccentricity, was taken aback by the scene.

He called and wanted me to come down to talk. Anyway we get down there, and me and my wife went to bed at maybe ten o'clock. I get up the next morning about six thirty, and Sally was up, and I said, "Well, is Sam up yet?" And Sally's just madder than a hornet. "Well, I don't know. He hasn't been home all night."

So maybe an hour later Sam comes dragging in [and tells] Sally, "Woman, fix me some breakfast." So Sally fixes breakfast, and he says, "You baste them eggs, don't turn them over." He liked basted eggs. And come to find out, Sam had been out in the boat all night with some girl.

So that night he wanted to have a fish fry. Invited all the neighbors, and about six o'clock all these people start arriving. Women still got their hair rolled up in toilet-paper rollers, about half the men had a half pint or a pint of whiskey in their back pocket. They had a band, two or three guitar players and singers and a bass man — there must have been fifty to seventy-five people, all neighbors around the lake, and they had a big dance, and a few guys get in a fight, stuff like that. I told my wife, "I think we better go to bed and get out of here tomorrow. You know there's no telling what's going to happen!" But I remember the next day, Sam's lawyer, Roy Scott, was down there too, 'cause Roy wanted me to go out in the boat with them. And Sam would open that boat up, he'd turn that thing wide open and tell me, "We're going across that water like anything, and I'm going to shake you to death."

MAYBE IT WAS THE DRINKING — maybe shaking Shelby to death was just something that Sam had in mind. Sam always insisted that drinking freed him up, in a good way, though others sometimes saw it differently. "He could take one drink of vodka," said Jerry, "one drink, and you could see the transformation coming. It would sort of get his nose [to] twitching, and you could tell he was in for the long haul. It would always start off, he'd be in a great mood, you know. Great mood, great mood, great mood. And then at some point it would shift over. Into all the things he didn't like about you, or things you were doing wrong — you know, me and Knox, or whoever it might be — and it would always end up in some sort of scene." He said things that Jerry knew he would never have said if he hadn't been drinking, "not that he was afraid to say it, but the alcohol would bring it out of him. And then the next day it was over."

You could see the transformation in other ways as well. All of a sudden this exemplarily dapper, habitually well-groomed, now middle-aged man let his hair grow out, at first continuing to slick it back so it curled up on his neck, then wearing it in a modified Beatles, or pageboy, cut, then, later, adopting a look that created an almost threatening sense of intimidation, a kind of distancing effect that could easily be taken as intentional if you didn't get past the surface. And he grew a beard, too — at first, like the hair, neat and well-trimmed, then gradually elongating and filling out the wolf-man look. He never spoke to Sally about why he grew it, though she didn't really have to ask — she knew Sam's determination not to show his age in any way. He started growing it around the same time she began to dye his hair, using a Clairol product that for years turned his hair and beard reddish after it set for a while until they finally got the mix right, but helping Sam to maintain a remarkably youthful appearance until the end of his life.

Not everyone approved of the new look or manner. His family in Alabama, whom he was able to see again on a regular basis now that he had finally found his way back home, took a particularly dim view — of his drinking, of his appearance, of his domestic arrangements in particular, of which they could no longer choose to be unaware. His two older sisters, while they remained grateful for all the help he had offered them and his other brothers and sisters over the years, said of his behavior, "I'd leave him and clean his clock." Other members of the family declared, not without the same mix of indulgent affection and admonitory disapproval, he was starting to look like a damn hippie. But his favorite nephew, Phillip Darby, who as his oldest sibling Mary's oldest child was not far removed in age from his uncle, always recalled something Sam said to him one time. "He and I were talking about Uncle J.W. [Jud] and Jerry Lee Lewis being together, and he said, 'Well, they'll both have to get in the gutter before they get up.' Of course Uncle Sam almost got in the gutter himself, I think. He really and truly got so bad I don't know how he managed his business as well as he did. But, you know, success changes a lot of people. They grasp the opportunity to be different. Uncle Sam seemed to want to be different about everything. That's just the way he was."

Sally saw it from another perspective. To Sally, Sam's change had come slow. And the drinking was just one of the things that played a part. "There were things that Sam did only when he was drinking. There were those things. He wouldn't have done them if he weren't drinking, you know. But yet he remained so much the same — [maybe] you're with him so much you just somehow or another don't notice. You know, you go through life, and you reach a certain age, and you find yourself with all this knowledge, but nobody wants to know it. And I think that's the way Sam felt. And I think that really bothered him."

Sam might very well have agreed. And yet there was a certain restlessness to his thinking that just wasn't going to be satisfactorily addressed by questions of drinking or not drinking, staying up all night long to record the Wolf or staying up all night long to probe the great philosophical questions, drunk or sober. Maybe he was fooling himself, but it was a point on which he remained constant all his life — and he didn't much care whether his listener bought into it or not. He had set forth on a voyage long ago with the determination to chart his own course and, rough seas or calm, whether land was in sight or not, he was going to enjoy every damn minute of it.

I'm going to give Sam the last word on the subject — although, as I'm sure every reader will have come to recognize by now, he would have insisted on it anyway.

"There are certain focuses that you go through in life. Some of us make changes. Some of us never change. Some change in a very small, or minuscule, way, and some of us change in a dramatic way — may be fast, may be slow, may be gradual. I think that's just part of the engenderment of what you're around, what's around you and how you react to it. From the wind blowing to an in-towner shaking hands with you and looking you in the eye. Or reading a word in the Bible, or listening to a spiritual, or listening to Beethoven's Fifth. It don't make any difference. If people just knew how beautiful this life is from an education[al] standpoint — even if you *didn't* finish school. How much there is out there to learn, and not let yourself become stagnant in the ways of the convenience of the time. [Or] get tied up in the lack of confidence in yourself — and we all go through those stages. But you just can't remain that way. I mean, inside you got to be somewhat of an arrogant bastard — I don't think it's possible [just] to be sweet and nice. Maybe on the surface. But I think there is a certain amount of arrogance that all creative people [possess], and you just stay in trouble by suppressing it all the time."

FOR THE FIRST TIME since his arrival in 1945, Memphis was no longer the unequivocal center of Sam's universe. It was not as if he was about to abandon his adoptive hometown, or that he was not proud of Knox's dedicated efforts to create recognition for Memphis music, both its history and its present-day impact on the industry. (Memphis had recently surpassed Nashville in the number of singles produced and the Memphis music industry was grossing well over $100 million a year, making it the third-largest contributor to the local economy.) At twenty-four, Knox had been instrumental in the formation of Memphis Music, Inc., an ambitious attempt to bond together all the unaffiliated strands of the city's great music tradition, which would culminate just three years later, in 1973, in the selection of Memphis as the sixth regional chapter of NARAS (the National Academy of Recording Arts and Sciences, by now the industry's dominant voice, best known to the public for its annual Grammy awards), on a par with New York, Chicago, Los Angeles, Atlanta, and Nashville. But however proud he might be of his son, and however committed he remained to the promulgation of the Memphis spirit of independence, musical and otherwise, this was not the future for Sam. In fact, in many ways Memphis was becoming more and more of a way station of the past, where he found himself in the unaccustomed (but not entirely unwelcome) role of accepting the plaudits and honors that were finally accruing to him for the revolutionary part he had played in the music.

"Everybody laughed [at] me," he reflected in an uncharacteristically expansive interview in *Billboard*'s 1969 end-of-the-year issue. It had been a bitter struggle at times, he conceded, with more than one of his artists arrested for "too many people in a car." ("I don't mean by this that our Southern people were against the Negro," he said—but he did.) And yet they had come through—people like B.B. King, Howlin' Wolf, Little Junior Parker, and Ike Turner were all getting proper recognition today because they were "great artists."

"Rocket 88" was the first record to pull it all together, he declared, blues and country and pop, and the Sun label had merely extended that pledge "to keep the music to the basics and at the same time to capitalize on the 'feel' of the Memphis area, which is steeped in the blues." And when Elvis came along, it was still tough, "leaving on a Sunday afternoon to visit distributors and radio stations. I'd sleep in my car." And he told the familiar story (familiar today forty-five years later, but virtually unknown in 1969) of being rejected in Houston, driving to Dallas, and having Alta Hayes tell him that, with "'That's All Right,'" he had a hit on his hands.

All the familiar touchstones of the Sun success story were noted— the transformation of "Blue Suede Shoes" with the injection of the phrase, "Go, cat, go," Sun's first certified gold record with Johnny Cash's "I Walk the Line," the "ghost gospel tape" (as he referred to what would become known as the Million Dollar Quartet session) that had meant so much to everyone involved and that was lying around somewhere, he wasn't quite sure where. It was validation at last from an industry that no longer had room for singular, revolutionary voices—it was not lost on Sam that the further that spirit of unreconstructed individualism and pioneering eccentricity receded into the past, the more validation there was to be gained.

The first Memphis Music Awards Dinner, with Knox active in all aspects of the program, was held on May 21, 1971, with Founders Awards to be given to Sam, Stax Records head Jim Stewart, Chips Moman, a brilliant producer who went back to the beginning of Stax and over the last four years had had something like 120 chart hits come out of his tiny American studio, and Elvis Presley. In addition, Sam was to present *Billboard* editor Paul Ackerman with a special surprise award in honor of the inestimable contributions he had made to the recognition of what would come to be called American vernacular music (blues, rhythm and blues, gospel, hillbilly, and rock 'n' roll) and to the recognition of Memphis music in particular.

Sam and Paul Ackerman, September 7, 1972, at a NARAS dinner in Memphis honoring Sam, which Ackerman was finally well enough to attend. *Courtesy of the Sam Phillips Family*

Opposite, left to right: Jack Clement, Paul Ackerman, Charlie Rich, Jerry Wexler, and Margaret Ann Rich (with back to camera), September 7, 1972. *Courtesy of the Sam Phillips Family*

Sam's relationship with Ackerman had grown from one of unabashed wonder that anyone in New York, least of all someone of Ackerman's scholarly bent, should have been such a champion of Sun Records at a time when the rest of the world had barely heard of the label and the grand high poobahs in Nashville were trying to kill it. Sam had not actually met Ackerman until well after Elvis had achieved his earliest success, but in recent years they had seen more of each other at industry events, and their relationship had blossomed to the point that they eagerly sought each other out at any and every available opportunity.

It was the most unlikely of friendships, Sally noted. "Paul just put Sam on a pedestal — and you wouldn't think Paul Ackerman was [that] type of person!" Like everyone else, Paul said at another industry dinner, he felt "privileged to have participated in the Phillips era." Sam for his part was no less adulatory. It was only with Paul, it sometimes seemed, that his restless adolescent need to shock was temporarily quelled. No one else had ever filled this space other than his late brother-in-law Jimmy Connolly, who had taken Sam up when he was just eighteen years old. As Sam never failed to acknowledge, he was not the sort of person to make friends easily, and the people that really counted for him were few and far between. Dewey. Kemmons Wilson. His son Knox would always occupy a special place somewhere between buddy and brother,

with the proviso that if Sam ever got nettled, Knox was demoted a notch to loyal son and lieutenant. But Paul occupied a unique place — and not just because of his passionate espousal of all the things Sam believed in, but because of his intellectual weight as well. I don't think there was anyone else with whom Sam felt that he shared such *instinctual* (Sam's word) intellectual appreciation not just for the music but for life in all its multifarious splendor.

Bettye Berger picked Paul up at the airport. Sam had introduced her to Paul in 1969, when *Billboard* was putting together a special issue on Memphis and Sam had touted her, in her latest incarnation as president of her own booking agency, Continental Artists Attractions, as one of the most dynamic movers and shakers in town. She had started the agency after a brief return to WHER following her divorce from Louis Jack Berger, and for a time her only client was Charlie Rich. This was not exactly a coincidence. Sam had done everything he could to get the two of them together some years earlier when Charlie was separated from his wife and living in a shared apartment just behind the apartment building where Bettye lived. "We were just two of his favorite people," Bettye said, "and Sam kept telling us both, 'You two were meant for each other.' He called me in the middle of the night so many times and put Charlie on the phone, until we both got tired of it." When they finally met, they clicked just as Sam had said they would. And Bettye was already in love with Charlie's music.

Paul was tired and in a low mood when Bettye picked him up at the airport—all he wanted to do was go back to Bettye's office in Kemmons Wilson's brand-new modernistic Midtown Building (just down the hall from WHER's plush new studios) and listen to Charlie Rich records. That seemed to get him out of his mood, and then Bettye took him back to his hotel and got dressed for the event, which was to be held at the Rivermont, Holiday Inn's flagship hotel, on the river.

When she got there, Sally met her at the door and told her Paul had had a heart attack. He was over at Baptist Hospital, and they thought he was going to die.

In his grief-stricken state, Sam still managed to deliver a passionate tribute to his friend. For years, Sam said, he had been looking forward to paying homage to Paul Ackerman, to repaying in some small measure "this blessed man" who loved Memphis so. Now, he said, in light of the gravity of the situation, he didn't know if he was up to the task. "All the words that I had thought up just say: so this just shows what life is all about, and nobody has a lock on life.

> I wish I were eloquent enough to express myself about this man. I wish I could read over the number of things that he has done that nobody really recognized formally but I think that everybody who knew this man recognized informally. . . .
>
> I understand that I'm supposed to be honored here tonight. I can say truly that I am being more honored right now to be able to talk about this fantastic individual . . . and I don't know of any privilege or pleasure that I've had before [that] gives me such great honor. And the only thing that leaves a void is that Paul can't be here. But he knows that we love him . . . and I want every person here—I was going to have him come up here surprised and sit on this stage with me, because you look at the countenance of this man, and you know he's not an ordinary man.
>
> But anyway . . . I [just] want to say, Let's raise the roof of this building so Kemmons Wilson—and bless his heart, he's right out there in front of us, and he'll put the roof back on this thing by five o'clock tomorrow afternoon for that meeting tomorrow night—let's raise this roof for Paul Ackerman and this special award.

P AUL WAS HOSPITALIZED for more than a month. By the testimony of everyone, including Paul and his sister Evelyn, who came down from New York and spent much of her time with Sam and Sally when she wasn't at the hospital, Sam took care of everything. Sam and Sally and Bettye all visited him regularly — when he was a little better, Charlie Rich, an intensely private man who, as far as Bettye knew, had never met Paul before, visited, too, at Paul's behest. On one of her very first visits, when visitors were limited to no more than a minute or two, Bettye just stood by the bed, thinking at first that he was sleeping. But then he reached out for her hand and said in a low, almost indecipherable voice, "Don't ever let the world forget, Sam Phillips was the one who discovered rock n roll."

A S THE LAKE HOUSE neared completion, Sam grew increasingly restive — and, perhaps not coincidentally, he began to grow increasingly irritated with Shelby. He got after him about one thing or another, he couldn't believe the way Shelby was constantly repackaging the same material ("You going to sell them masters so many times," he told Shelby not even half joking, "you're going to wear them out"), he even precipitated a breach-of-faith lawsuit between GRT, the giant tape manufacturer, and Shelby Singleton International, when he voided a deal that Shelby had made for a mass tape release of the Sun masters, on the grounds that contractually it required his approval.

"Sam," said Sally, "pretty much thought he was [still] involved. He tried to tell Shelby what to do and what not to do, and that just wasn't the way Shelby did business." He was, in fact, enough of a thorn in Shelby's side that in a long telegram pointing out his own fifteen-hours-a-day devotion to the job and Sam's unrealistic, absentee-landlord perspective, Shelby invited him flat out to buy back the company, "if you are really unhappy."

But Shelby didn't really mean it. He knew Sam would never buy back the company — that was the last thing he was going to do for any number of reasons, practical, philosophical, financial. His own job, as Shelby saw it, was to educate Sam — to use all the tools that he possessed as a born promo man constitutionally unable to take no for an answer, to bring Sam around to his point of view. When they formed the new corporation, Sam had wanted a 50-50 ownership situation, given the small amount of upfront money involved. But Shelby persuaded him that "because of the tax consequences," they couldn't do that. He had to have 80 percent. Now, as he patiently but implacably explained, Sam had to accept the consequences of minority ownership. He could bitch and grouse all he wanted, but "he only owned twenty percent, so I could outvote him anytime I wanted to. So he really didn't have any say. And I don't know, it might have taken a couple of years for him to realize that—[but] then I think he finally forgot about it." There is an impish gleam in Shelby's eye as he explains how Sam Phillips, a man he had always idolized, in the end came to learn his place. "He always loved me," Shelby reflects toward the end of his life, confident in his inescapable pitchman's way that it's true but with an implied pause that suggests a complicit wink, "[even] though he thought at times he didn't."

This whole extended drama might very well have gone on indefinitely; in another galaxy Sam might just have continued working on the house, building it up and tearing it down; he could easily have found even more reason to challenge Shelby's business practices, as his old artists complained bitterly to him (and even began to initiate lawsuits) over the issue of nonpayment by Shelby's Sun Entertainment Corporation, and Shelby's personal reputation in Nashville grew shakier and shakier (he was busted for taxes, busted for marijuana, there were lawsuits galore, and Shelby, in the midst of a bitter divorce, disappeared for the better part of a year)—but then something happened that brought Sam up short and all at once restored to him the focus that had been missing for most of the last decade. He fell back in love with radio.

Well, that's really not quite right. After all, he had never fallen out of love. And while he was living on the lake, working, drinking, catching up with family and old friends, and generally indulging himself in a way he had rarely permitted himself in the past, even as he drove everyone else crazy in the process, when the reception was right, he started listening to the radio stations of his hometown. Others might well have taken this as an occasion for nostalgia, the idyllic dream they had imagined as kids to be waiting for them at the end of the road—but, as Sam might have said, the hell with idylls. The idyllic life was never going to suit him. Listening to the radio just led him to start thinking about greater possibilities, to enlarging on the ideas he and Jimmy Connolly had talked about from the time he first began work at WLAY. And he started making inquiries.

From what he understood from a local studio and radio engineer named Paul Kelley, there were two stations that were likely to be available: WJOI, WLAY's chief rival in the greater Muscle Shoals market, and its sister FM station, WQLT, a 25,000-watt easy-listening station (no DJs, just reel-to-reel tapes all day long) with an FCC license that would permit expansion to 100,000 watts. (Just by way of comparison, WHER had started out, and remained, "1000 Beautiful Watts," which barely allowed it to be heard outside the Memphis city limits.) He loved the call letters of both (QLT stood for quality, and JOI was the station on which Elvis had made his Muscle Shoals-area debut), and he quickly made a deal with the owners when he approached them in the summer of 1972, just around the time he started thinking seriously about converting WHER to Memphis' first all-talk radio station, WWEE ("We").

He was, once again, thoroughly immersed in his work, and for better or worse (certainly not better in terms of Sam's financial stake in the Sun Entertainment Corp.), from this point on Shelby scarcely heard from him at all. The record manufacturing business, his own personal malaise, the lake house into which he had poured the last two years (he and Sally didn't even stay at the lake house once he began remodeling the stations in the spring—the forty-mile drive was simply too much time to waste when there was work to be done), all rapidly receded into the distance as he flung himself into the new project. "The more he got into it," said Sally, "the more he loved it. That's what he wanted to do." She had never doubted he would find himself —but there must have been times when even she grew impatient, waiting for the change to come.

MY MEETING WITH SAM

SAM'S NEW STATIONS IN FLORENCE went on the air March 1, 1973. He assigned 15 percent ownership to his studio and radio engineer, Paul Kelley, who had scouted out the stations' availability and value for him, and 20 percent to Bill Thomas, the general manager of his Memphis radio stations, whom Knox and Jerry had met at a radio convention in New Orleans the previous year. Thomas now took on the management of all five of Sam's stations, including WLIZ, which still retained its all-girl format, and WHER, which was in the process of changing its call letters and converting to all-talk.

Even as he was undertaking these ambitious new ventures, Sam also agreed to go into business with Jerry's father-in-law, onetime Sun artist Ray Harris, who had by now left Hi Records, the Memphis label that he had helped found, and gotten hold of a studio in his hometown of Tupelo some ninety miles down the road. Sam was currently remodeling and revamping the Memphis recording studio for Knox and Jerry, so Sam simply had Paul Kelley, who was supervising the update, take the old equipment and install it in Ray Harris' new studio, Trace. Aside from his personal liking for Ray, Sam was convinced the new studio couldn't fail because of a development and distribution deal that they had negotiated with *Playboy* magazine's new record division, which guaranteed them $100,000 in the first year of operation. So Sam threw himself into this new enterprise as well, just as he was getting the radio stations in Florence up and running. He was at this point dividing his time between Florence, Tupelo, and Memphis, though not nearly in equal measure. There was no time for leisure now — the lake house was practically forgotten as Sam once again had his eye fixed firmly on the future.

It was, unquestionably, radio that was the centerpiece of this new vision. The Playboy Records deal fell apart by the end of 1973, just three or four months after its first Trace Studio release, a novelty item that Sam for some reason was convinced would be a hit. He and Ray sued Playboy Enterprises for going back on its word, but the trial and the business both came to an inglorious end, and Sam's involvement with Trace didn't last much past Playboy's withdrawal.

Not even the Memphis recording studio, Knox and Jerry were well aware, meant much to Sam at this point — he would probably have sold it in a minute if it hadn't been for them. Instead, he was spending a good deal of time and money simply to support their ongoing ambitions in an industry that, he never missed an opportunity to remind them, had little room left for innovation or individuality. Whereas radio, as he couldn't help but point out, was a growth industry — not only that, it was the kind of family enterprise that could provide a firm footing not just for them but for their children and, if they really dedicated themselves to it, their children's children as well.

"It was all radio," said Sally. "He just — he never gave a flip about TV. The sound of the radio stations was the most important thing in his life — you know, how those stations sounded. He would have arguments with Paul Kelley — with *anybody!* — about the sound of a microphone if it didn't sound right. That was always a big point with him. He did everything he could to get the stations upgraded. He looked for transmitter sites for weeks and months and God knows how long, just to find the right transmitter site to put a tower on. He was always trying to figure out something. And whatever had to be done was going to be done right."

In June of 1975 he applied to upgrade WQLT, his FM station in Florence, to 100,000 watts. That had been his goal from the start. Even though WJOI was performing well (as WXOR now — he had sold the call letters for $35,000) in the prevailing AM market, Sam was convinced album-oriented FM was the future, and he was determined to be the first 100,000-watt FM station in the region. Once he began the upgrade, Florence to all intents and purposes became his primary residence, as he camped out with Sally at the Tourway Inn and Pancake House just down the hill from the station, sometimes for as much as a month at a time.

He delighted in showing her his old hometown. If there was a moment free, "we would ride around and he would [show me] all the places he walked as a child. The hill he walked up to go to the swimming hole where they swam. He knew who lived in every house — we would go by the house he grew up in all the time." He had nothing but the fondest memories of teachers and schoolmates. And when a scholarship was established at Florence State in his old junior high school principal's name, he was one of its primary contributors. But most of all he delighted in his rediscovery of his Florence family, his two oldest brothers, Turner and Horace, both big-rig operators who had worked on huge construction projects ("Turner was like my daddy, push himself back in a rocker on the front porch when he was through with his day's work and philosophize about the conditions of the world"), his sisters Mary and Irene ("the kindest person I have ever known"), and the whole lost (but never forgotten) world of Lovelace Community.

In 1970 the Phillips family, over sixty strong, began a tradition of once-every-five-years reunions, and Sam posed proudly with his brothers and sisters for a picture of "The Magnificent Seven," as the seven siblings called themselves, with the kind of ironic deflection that they all seemed to share. In the photograph, there is no question of his difference (the beard alone would give him away) — but there is no question of his hunger for inclusion either. Or of the pride he took in each and every one of his siblings, all of them, with all of their individual distinctions, shaped by the world of their parents and representative, in Sam's deep-rooted view, of "a good cross section of what the world ought to be."

It was a homecoming I'm not sure he could ever have fully envisioned, and one that most of the world would never get a chance to see, but from the time I first met him, he always insisted, in the face (as I see it now) of my stubborn, unreasoning disbelief, that not only did the whole story start in Florence—if I truly wanted to understand the story, that was its most important part. Whenever he and Sally spent any amount of time in Memphis, he was always looking for a way to hear his stations in Florence. "He tried every way in the world to listen," Sally said, and as they drove the 150 miles from Memphis to Florence, the closer they got, the more excited he would become. "By the time we got to where we could get the stations on the car radio, I mean, he had them blaring wide open."

K NOX AND JERRY were hardly persuaded. It just got old, listening to Sam preach to them with that same indefatigable conviction about how their dreams were going to be dashed against the rocks. But if they were just supposed to follow him blindly, what was all this bullshit he kept talking about independence and individualism in the extreme? Nobody had ever stopped him—nobody *could ever* have stopped him, or could stop him still—from making his own mistakes. Or from taking pride in them either.

With a state-of-the-art mastering facility and two sophisticated modern studios at their disposal, they maintained a brisk mastering business and were producing more and more sessions for both the majors and independents. Knox conducted gospel sessions for Don Robey's Duke and Peacock labels, and he frequently engineered vocal and piano overdubs for Jerry Lee Lewis' hit Mercury recordings. Not to mention all the sessions they conducted on their own.

Jerry still had his own band and continued to entertain ambitions of stardom, and Knox would run the board for his brother whenever he wanted to record. Knox himself was exploring some of the outer peripheries of Memphis' unique brand of individualism. One time two Harleys were imported into the studio for authenticity on a Dan Penn song called "Tiny Hineys and Hogs," nearly asphyxiating everyone in the process. Another time Knox was engineering a Jim Dickinson session on serious local outlaw Jerry McGill, who got so caught up in a Civil War song called "With Sabres in Our Hands" that when he reached the line referring to the noble struggle as a "lost cause" he pulled out his gun and shot out the ceiling. "I didn't know he had a gun," Knox said. "I had the lights down in the studio, lights down in the control room, and Jim and I were sitting there, and at the end of the song, he got so emotional he pulled his gun out and started shooting, and the only thing I could think to do was to duck down and turn the echo up."

For all the high times, there were unquestionably moments — more like a decade in Jerry's case — when they were both tempted simply to leave. Knox decamped for a month in the early seventies, moving briefly to Nashville like he had thought about doing when he graduated from college. But Knox just didn't have it in him to break with his father ("Sam and I were always cerebrally connected. We would fight and scream, but we always kind of came together"), even after he himself had had a big pop hit with the Amazing Rhythm Aces' "Third Rate Romance" in 1975. The Aces were a band he had lovingly nurtured, much to Sam's disapproval ("He let them stay in that studio for six or eight months at no cost"), but it was only after success led to a breach and in the end to Knox selling the Aces' contract that, much against his nature, Knox finally understood the essence of what Sam had been saying all along. "They were such wonderful guys," he says today with a wry appreciation for the vagaries of human nature, "I didn't think they were ever going to push me off that cliff!" But as much as it pained him to admit it, and as often as he would choose to follow his own generous impulses over the years, he couldn't deny the truth of yet another variant on Sam's all-too-predictable advice. "Keep your distance, Knox," he said, "and let your footprint be known — just don't let them get too familiar with your path."

It was the same with the house that Knox bought with the fruits of his Rhythm Aces' success. It was the first house he had ever really owned on his own, out in the country, far beyond the city limits, and he was understandably proud of his purchase. But when he showed it to his dad, Sam exhibited the same kind of challenging skepticism that he seemed unable to suppress, questioning Knox closely about whether the siding of the house was really cedar like the house at 79 South Mendenhall (it was), thereby undermining the very pride that Knox took in his newfound independence. Knox got it — Sam was just trying to teach him a lesson, a lesson that he himself had had to learn the hard way. But why did he have to be such an asshole about it? It was as if he just had to "give you the worst, most horrible scathing advice that you could ever have and then if you could overcome it, [he] was with you."

It pissed Knox off at the time—it *really* pissed him off ("I just wanted him to go, Oh, man, how great the house was")—but at the same time he sort of saw Sam's point.

Jerry was not quite as understanding. In fact, given Jerry's combustible nature, Jerry was not understanding at all. In 1971 he formed a partnership with Stax promotional tyro and longtime friend Eddie Braddock. (Eddie was so hyperkinetic that he was tagged Super Whitey by his black colleagues—he would hit three far-flung urban centers for the company in a single day and have a change of clothes for each.) Eddie approached Knox as well, but Knox, for all of his affection for Eddie, had a deep-seated wariness of anyone he felt might be looking to take advantage of the Phillips family name.

Jerry on the other hand had no such reservations. "I was frustrated. I was disgruntled. And Eddie came along, and he just represented action. But Knox was smarter than I was on that deal."

Jerry and Eddie formed a production company called Hot Water and got a deal with Stax to produce a young white soul singer named Louis Paul at the Phillips Recording Studio. But right away they started spending money on luxury cars and other emblems of conspicuous consumption, before their deal was even in place. Which couldn't help but get Sam's back up as an example of the kind of bullshit that the record business had become. "You know, I think Sam looked at it as Jerry being very young," Sally commented acerbically, no doubt reflecting what she heard Sam say many times. "Didn't know anything about business or anything else. And I think Jerry will tell you that marijuana played a pretty big part in his life at that point, too. They were put on the payroll at Stax for no reason at all, frankly. And here they are paid money—to sit around and do nothing. But I think [the way] Sam looked at it was, They'll learn. Either they'll learn—or they'll be successful. That usually is what happens. And I think Sam felt like it was going to work itself out. Sam felt that way about a lot of things. That it'll work itself out."

And this time Sam took a different approach with his younger son. "Sam would take me fishing," said Jerry. "He really wasn't out there fishing. It was mainly to get me off by myself and talk. And I think this was one of these times Sam really thought I was heading off in the wrong direction, you know. Basically with the wrong people. Not that he thought I was going to be a drug addict or anything. I just think he thought these people may be full of shit. I don't know how much of this you want to put in the book. I wouldn't want to hurt anybody's feelings. Sam never really thought a whole lot of Eddie — I mean, he didn't dislike him, but I think he just didn't like his style. But, you know, I was always kind of the rebel guy, [like] 'Oh no, we're going to change the world,' and at first [when] Eddie and I got together, I thought it was a good relationship, and we accomplished some things, but—"

In the end, probably Jerry's biggest regret was the feeling of being used. He was proud of the Louis Paul record, and he and Eddie had a lot of fun — but in the long run, just like Sam predicted, it didn't work out. The nadir came when Eddie persuaded him that it would be hip to form a new label, Son Records, with the logo much like RCA's familiar image of a dog ("Nipper") looking into the speaker cone of a gramophone, except in their case it was a pig eyeing a radio.

There were no I-told-you-sos afterward, Jerry insists. In fact, later, when Jerry for a time was experiencing anxiety attacks of his own, Sam once again offered the same understanding side of himself. "He told me I came by it honestly. Sam did suffer that mental — well, it's not mental illness, I don't guess you'd say, [but] he was an anxiety-prone person. I mean, he got it under control with Xanax or Valium at [various] points, and, you know, when I was suffering through it — and mine really wasn't that debilitating — he helped me a lot. Because he knew how to talk to you about those things. He'd lived through it and he knew how to ease your mind. Sam Phillips could ease your mind about a lot of things that were bothering you, I don't care who you were. He could make it make sense to you in an authoritative way." Jerry hesitates at his choice of words and corrects himself. No, he says, "Believable. In a believable way."

Which isn't to say that their fights didn't continue with more than occasional ferocity. Or that Knox didn't still have to step in between them on more than one alcohol-fueled occasion. But in the aftermath of his unilateral secession, Jerry came back into the fold, as always on his own terms and, as always, reserving the right to strike out on his own again if he chose — it seemed like he was as prone to quitting on principle as to being fired, essentially, for the same principle. But it never lasted long. "I told him one time when he was kind of down," said Roland Janes, who would come back to work at the Phillips studio in 1982 after having a studio and record company of his own, and of all the former Sun artists and musicians probably remained closest to the entire Phillips family. "I said, 'Jerry, man, you need to settle down.' He was always thinking, 'I'll just leave the company.' I said, 'You need to just back up a little bit [and] hang in there. You've got a vested interest in all this. Just always keep in mind, there's one thing for sure. Sam loves you boys.'"

At some point it finally dawned on him, Jerry said. "When you're in a family business, if you quit the business, you quit the family. That's pretty much what it is. If you decide you don't want to be in it, you know, it's not like a regular employee walking out. You're walking out on a man's life's work. [And] I did that several times."

Undoubtedly one additional element contributory to this increasing sense of the importance of family was his own domestic situation. Both Jerry and Knox had gotten divorced by now and were out on their own. Everyone liked Jerry's wife, Ryta, there were no children involved, and Jerry never made any bones about whose fault it was ("I was just an asshole, she was a great girl"), so the situation was easier to accept. With Knox it was more difficult. He and his wife, Betty, had been together since they were teenagers, and there was, of course, a child. No one was more heartbroken than Becky—but no matter what the issues were, no matter what frictions might arise from the divorce, Becky was determined not to let the domestic balance be disturbed and not to allow her granddaughter, Kim, who was four years old when her parents separated, become in any way a victim of the process. Becky had been taking the little girl to work with her at the station almost since she was old enough to walk—at first she would just "sit on my lap, and I would announce, and she would sit as still as anything. Later she would help pick out my records and set them up." She called Becky "Maw," and Becky was as proud of her as she was of her own boys.

For all of her seeming meekness, she was prepared to go to any lengths to keep the family together—if Sam or Sally needed her for anything, she would always do it gladly, without complaint, and if Knox was feeling low and not worthy of being a proper daddy, as he sometimes did during this time, she was always there to tell him to believe in himself and to *cherish* his little girl. When the marriage broke up, she took Knox's Doberman that Sally wouldn't even allow in the house, she took in *everybody's* pets—and if her former daughter-in-law was feeling victimized or alienated in any way, she embraced her, as she embraced everyone else in the family, no doubt articulating to some degree the philosophy by which she had herself learned to live: "We all have problems in our lives. It's just a part of life. But, I think, more than the problem, it's the

Sam with Knox's daughter,
Kim, 1972. *Courtesy of the
Sam Phillips Family*

way we deal with the problems. The way we let God help us to deal with
our problems. There's a Scripture that says, all things work together for
good, for those who love God. And, I think my life is living proof of that."

They were all, however shakily, working together in a common
enterprise now — Sam and Sally, Knox and Jerry, Becky, who continued
to do her own meticulously prepared show of big-band classics even
after the station went all-talk, before long Knox's ex-wife, Betty, would
go to work at WWEE and even become its general manager for several
years until its eventual sale in 1986. Even as Knox and Jerry continued
to pursue their own place in the music industry (both took on numerous
recording projects, Knox continued to vigorously promote a national
identity for Memphis music, and Jerry joined former Sun artist Billy
Lee Riley's band on bass), they became more and more vested, both in
business and to a lesser extent in belief, in Sam's dream of radio empire.

As for Sam, he never missed the studio, he said. He did occasionally flirt with the idea of diversification: his new physician, Dr. Bernard Kraus, was the owner of the Memphis Blues, Memphis' financially
imperiled Triple A baseball team, and, after soliciting Sam's advice as
to how to get Memphis a major-league baseball franchise, he tried hard

to interest Sam in investing in the team. But for all of Sam's passion for the game, and his high regard for Dr. Kraus, with whom he always enjoyed highly informed discussions about the latest advances in medical research as well as the intricacies of baseball (no appointment lasted less than several hours), Sam never really thought too much about the proposal or, for that matter, got serious about entering into any other field of endeavor. There was simply too much to do in radio.

In accordance with his lifelong philosophy, he never consciously looked back. And yet once in a while, most likely when he least expected it, he was brought up short by the memory of all that he had left behind. "I don't have the feeling anymore that I'm contributing anything," he told a reporter from *Country Music* magazine in 1973, in an entirely uncharacteristic moment of regret. "I miss coming out of the studio and seeing the record break. Back then I felt almost like a preacher feeding the gospel to hungry souls."

I T WAS AT JUST ABOUT THIS TIME, in 1975, two years after putting his new radio stations on the air in Florence, that one of those events occurred that no one could ever have anticipated, least of all, I would suspect, Sam himself. For it was at this point that Sam, a man who had always prided himself on his control of self, people, situations, and events, lost his head — in love, lust, desire, remorse, call it what you will, but it seemed for a time as if he was no longer in command of his own emotional destiny.

There had been women before, of course, and there would be women again — it wasn't that Sam was not capable of having affairs, though by some women's testimony he was more interested in talk, as often as not over the telephone, with the talk almost invariably fueled by drink and more likely to encompass philosophy, grandiloquent self-regard, and global events than romantic chit-chat. But there was something else about it, too. There was a kind of loneliness, an almost desperate need for company that had been with him since childhood and seemed to grow more pronounced, especially late at night, with every passing year.

Bettye Berger always liked to recall the trip she and Sam took to New York during this same time period, prompted by Sam's spur-of-the-moment determination that they needed to see Paul Ackerman, whose health was in precipitous decline, *right away — before it was too late.*

Bettye was caught by surprise, not just by the impulsiveness of Sam's action but by the very idea of flying to New York City, a destination he rarely visited anymore and a mode of transportation that he had only recently resumed after a lapse more than fifteen years. She didn't hesitate to embrace the invitation, though — and she was perfectly happy to accept Sam's generous offer to pay for her ticket, she told him, so long as he understood she was paying for her own room.

It was a wonderful visit, bittersweet with memories and the almost certain sense, on Paul's part and their own, that they would never see each other again. But it was a strange visit in its own way, too — and as well as Bettye thought she knew Sam by now, this time he confounded her yet again.

Sam had told her the day he hired her at WHER, in 1956, that she would never have to worry about his hitting on her or anything like that — he had nothing to do with any of the girls who worked at the station after they went home at night. It didn't bother her when he called her at home that night any more than any of his other flirtatious talk over the years — she was well accustomed to fending for herself. In a way she thought it was just a game with Sam — just his own weird way of making a connection, whether by an insult or a compliment, it didn't really make any difference. When she first opened her own agency, Sam had come by to congratulate her and then announced that he wanted to be her partner. After she turned him down, he told her she could never make it on her own in the business. She got mad at first — she couldn't really interpret what exactly his *point* was — but in the end she decided to take it as just another of Sam's unconventional forms of foreplay. They were never lovers, and she had grown accustomed by now to having him drop by her house in Whitehaven at any hour of the night or day and just go to sleep on the couch — he wasn't going to bother anyone, he told her, he was just going to sleep there until he felt better. He might ask if he could sleep beside her. "He'd say, 'I just don't want to sleep by myself.' I'd say, 'Well go home and sleep, then.' One time she went off to work with him sleeping and butterbeans on the stove. When she came home, she found a note: "Dear Bettye, I took your butterbeans. You can pick up the pan, or I'll bring it home."

It was the same in New York. Even though Bettye told him she had paid for it and she wanted him to stay out of her room, in the end he acted so pitiful her resolve broke down. Sam would sit in the lobby and just talk to people, he seemed so afraid to be alone. "Finally he'd knock, it would be late, and he'd say, 'Just let me come in and read the newspapers.' And, of course, finally he talked me into it. I had two little beds, and he'd sit over there with those newspapers and read a while, then talk, and I'd say, 'I don't want to talk to you Sam.' I was so sleepy. But he wouldn't stop talking."

It was like she always said, she didn't know anyone more hungry for love than Sam—or less able to satisfy that hunger. It was as if there were always limits, whether self-imposed or imposed by circumstance—but with this girl he met in Florence, all of a sudden there were no limits, it was as if, at age fifty-two, with all of the weight of his responsibilities, and for all of the ambition that radio had rekindled, Sam seemed for the first time since he was a very young man to have really and truly fallen under a romantic spell.

H E MET THE YOUNG WOMAN in question, Sylvia Guidry, a twenty-eight-year-old aspiring singer with three children, through his good friend and drinking buddy, longtime Florence newspaperman Ben Knight. Sally knew all about it from the start. Sam was not one to skulk around and hide either his actions or intentions. In fact, over the years Sally often drove Sam to his assignations, dropped him off, and trusted him to get home on his own. But even though she pretended otherwise, Sally sensed right away that this was different from the kind of casual infatuation that quickly wore off or the kind of long-term relationship, like the one with Bettye Berger, whether explicitly sexual or not, that was not going to threaten the stability of the arrangement she and Sam had had for nearly twenty years now. Ordinarily he wouldn't have put up with all the baggage that Sylvia brought to the relationship for a minute—Sam Phillips was not interested in bringing up someone else's kids. With Sam the attention had to be all on him, *that was just the way he was.* But with Sylvia none of that seemed to faze him, he was clearly just taken with her, whether it was her youth and beauty or some other qualities that Sally for one just could not see—and he boasted to one and all that she cooked the best chicken and dressing he had ever had.

It embarrassed Sally deeply, it made her look—well, it might very well make her look to the world like a kept woman. Or, even worse, a *wife.* But she knew it wasn't like that. Whatever anyone else thought, she insists, she never felt threatened. "I mean, it gave me a break," she says, laughing a hollow laugh. "I know nobody believes that, Peter, but

Sam and Sylvia. *Courtesy of Sylvia Smith*

sometimes it was a relief, because Sam and I were together an awful lot. [But] I always knew where I was with Sam. If you want to know where you are with Sam, you just ask. You know? You always know where you are with him. And I always knew."

Even so, it was a real sticking point, not just for Sally but for Knox and Jerry, too. Not because they didn't like Sylvia necessarily, they just didn't like seeing their father behave like a love-struck teenager. As Jerry noted, after wrestling with whether or not he should even talk about the affair and deciding in the end, hell, Sam would have just said, "Tell the goddamn truth," Sylvia wasn't suited to the usual girlfriend role in one essential respect: her independence.

"I mean, this is my take on it. Sam really, really, really liked Sylvia. She was beautiful, number one. I mean gorgeous, gorgeous young girl. And she fell in love with him and all that stuff. But Sylvia didn't fit the let-Sam-do-what-he-wants-to-do mold. [And] that was a problem."

The way Jerry saw it, it was all part and parcel of Sam's almost ungovernable need to be in control while at the same time, deep down, he was unsure of "whether or not he was as in control as he wanted to be. You know what I'm saying? I mean, that anxiety thing, once it takes over, man, you're running wide open. It's got you, and it's hard to get out of it." But no one was ever going to say anything like that to Sam, least of all his sons. No one was ever going to tell Sam Phillips what to do—that was his mantra, drunk or sober—and no one ever did.

Sally, for all of her protestations, as Knox and Jerry both knew, was a mess. She hated the situation, and she didn't like the girl one bit—but she didn't have any choice in the matter. As Jerry put it, "Sam wasn't hiding anything. If Sally wanted to hang around for the ride, [it was like], 'You pretty much can if you want to, but, you know, this is what I'm doing.'" But then Sam took it one step further. He really rubbed her nose in it, and everyone else's too, when, a couple of months after meeting her, he moved Sylvia to Memphis, installed her in an apartment with her mother and kids, and, to cover her expenses, at different times put her on the payroll of one or another of his various corporations. It was at this point that it finally became clear to Sally that the girl had every intention of moving her out of Mendenhall, *she thought she was going to marry Sam Phillips.*

In a way there was nothing all that different about it. "Well, sure, that's what they all think, Peter. There wasn't a one of them that didn't think, 'Well, wait until she finds out about *me*. I mean, if he's dating me, well, certainly, he's going to tell Sally to leave.' But that was not the reason Sam dated [these women]. And I knew that Sam was not gonna run off with a woman with three kids, for Christ's sake. You *know* I knew that. I mean, Sam really liked her—but, you know, he wasn't looking to get married. I mean, if he was going to get married, he would marry me."

And yet all of her brave certainties provided her with little comfort. Sam, she knew for a fact, was certainly not going to marry her or anybody else, because he was still married to Becky—he was never going to *stop* being married to Becky. Which no one else ever seemed to recognize or take into account. But it must have galled her as she wrote Sylvia's weekly checks or delivered Sam to Sylvia's house for the weekend, or when Sylvia came to pick him up for the evening—there was never any mystery as to his whereabouts, she knew where Sam was twenty-four hours a day. But somehow neither knowledge nor experience provided her with the kind of surety she craved as the situation seemed to grow ever more volatile, with Sam's true intentions increasingly difficult to read.

Sam moved Sylvia into Bettye Berger's old house on Claree Drive in Whitehaven in 1979. He had loaned Bettye some money and held a third mortgage on the house, which the bank, which had the first two, was threatening to take. So, to protect his investment, he bought the house, but evidently made no offer to let Bettye stay in it. Bettye's reaction, even thirty years later, was beyond pissed off. Hurt, perplexed, apoplectic—I don't know that I could begin to express it, nor can I say that I fully understand Sam's actions. Unless it was simply to give Sylvia a house. "It was," said Bettye, "a beautiful house inside. It didn't look good out-side, but it was gorgeous inside. Oh, I don't even want to talk about it." I suppose in the end it was just one more twist in a tangled relationship which, for all of her love of Sam (and his for her), remained inexplicable to Bettye—or, in some ways all too explicable—even after his death.

In the end Sally's patience appears to have won out. Or at least this is the commonly accepted version of events. From everybody else's point of view, Sylvia just overplayed her hand. Or maybe, as some might see it, Sam simply came to his senses. Sylvia had a different point of view. A proud, independent woman who fiercely rejected any categorization of herself as a "mistress," or anything less than an equal partner in a shared romantic relationship, she finally came to the conclusion that, because of all the other complications in his life, Sam was never going to deliver on his promise of a music career, a life in the music business if not as a recording artist at least working for one of his companies. It was in any case a messy end to a long and intense relationship in which Sam had played a major role in the raising of three children not his own. "He was," said Sylvia, "the most wonderful man in our lives. My kids adored him. And he literally saved my life." But in the end, she said, "I think it became an obsessive relationship. I think people can be too much in love, and that's what happened to us. It was heartbreaking, but I couldn't keep living like that—I had to get out."

That was not at all the way Sally saw it. This was her view of what she took to be the final act, as it transpired roughly eight years after the relationship began.

"She did everything she could to get Sam's attention. She kept say-ing, 'I'm leaving, I'm leaving,' expecting him to say, 'Oh my God . . .' But she was giving him a lot of problems by then. Then one day she told Sam that she was moving to Texas, and Sam said, 'Okay, let's get a truck and load you up.' So he got this truck that was coming in from Texas and a driver, and he was going to meet out there on Saturday morning to load her stuff up. [When] he got there, she didn't have a damn thing packed. Nothing packed—[not] in a box or nothing. So he got the truck driver and said, 'Okay, you take everything in this house and put it in that truck,' and they left, Sylvia and the three children. And he never would take her calls anymore—he just didn't want any involvement. [But] sometimes she would talk to me and tell me what she wanted, and he would tell me to send her a money order."

That would appear to have been the end of it. And yet it was not. The relationship would in fact go on for another three or four years, with Sylvia returning and then quitting Sam two more times. The third time she left, he told her that she would not get anything further from him, but they remained in touch and he continued to send her money from time to time. She visited just weeks before his final illness in 2002. And when he died she was at the funeral with her three children, mourning the man who had written her passionate love letters on napkins and any scrap of paper he could commandeer. At first she was blocked by the security guards, but then Becky, who had had her to dinner with Sam several times when she was living in Memphis, intervened and told them to let her in, she and the children were family.

JUD AND HIS WIFE, Dean, moved into the house on Claree Drive almost as soon as Sylvia moved out. They had been living in an apartment in Memphis for the past decade, with Jud never far removed from Jerry Lee Lewis' world (from 1976 he listed himself in the phone book as Jerry Lee's manager) but never altogether defined within it. One story that both he and Jerry always liked to tell, about how Jerry Lee came to record "Chantilly Lace," a number 1 country hit for him in 1972, probably comes as close as you can to describing his role, both its intrinsic and extrinsic nature. According to Jerry: "I told him, 'Jud, I don't even know the words to the song'"—but the record was cut at Jud's insistence and direction, even as, according to both men's testimony, Jud was lying dead drunk on the floor. "Jud," said Jerry, "was never wrong," and his faith never wavered in the man he regarded as his spiritual mentor, one of the two brothers uniquely placed by fate to guide his success.

For all of his exuberant personality, though, Jud was, if anything, becoming more eccentric as his drinking increased in both volume and effect. At one point he announced his intention to become a riverboat captain and, with a salt-and-pepper beard and a jaunty captain's hat that made him look even more like a Hollywood version of his younger brother, planned to conduct guided tours of the Tennessee River. Unfortunately, the engine of the well-traveled boat that he hoped to turn into a "sightseeing cruiser" blew up in Natchez as he was bringing it back to the Shoals area from its purchase point in the Gulf, and after several weeks of trying to get the engine repaired in Natchez, nothing more ever seemed to come of this plan.

He was by now entirely dependent on his brother. Sam was housing and supporting him; when Jerry Lee fell on hard times, Knox put Jud on the production payroll; and Dean went to work at the studio as a bookkeeper in 1980, a role she was still fulfilling very capably at the age of eighty-nine, in 2012.

If Jud felt any sense of embarrassment, though, it showed up neither in his utterances nor his actions. He continued to mercilessly goad Sam in private (at one point, he told Bettye Berger, he persuaded Sam's yardman to move all of Sam's meticulously placed plantings around, utterly bewildering, then enraging his brother when he discovered the cause), and far from acting chastened, he seemed to take greater and greater pleasure in claiming public credit for his brother's achievements, often in language virtually indistinguishable from Sam's own. It had been *his* idea to start the label, he would slyly suggest to unsuspecting journalists in his few on-the-record interviews. It was he who had conceived of the idea of translating the black man's music to the white marketplace, he had gotten the idea from traveling around and seeking out the spiritual uplift of the black church, the *presentness* of the black community, where, at some unspecified time in his life he "just went around and watched how they lived and went to their parties and drank with them." Later, when he was peddling records out of the back of his car, he said, he saw the way that young white audiences were responding to r&b records, "digging the heavy beat that these colored people were putting down. But there was so much division and so much prejudice in the country that they couldn't idolize the artist that was delivering the song. So I thought if we could find a white man that had real sex appeal and could deliver this material as nearly like the Negroes were putting it down, then we might have something."

In this narrative, that was what led him to the discovery of Elvis Presley, at a time when he was in fact selling used cars back in Florence. That intuitive sense of a larger white audience, he said, was "the reason that I went through all of this problem of finally getting Elvis Presley signed and putting out the product and . . . all of that." But he couldn't resist adding that in his view Elvis never really possessed the inherent genius that, by inference, an unbridled talent like Jerry Lee Lewis exemplified. The Elvis business, he conceded, "paid off handsomely for everybody concerned. [But] I never did see that Elvis had the depth musically that was required to run the distance, or run the last mile, even though I thought he had the real feel for the type music that we were presenting to him."

E LVIS' DEATH on August 16, 1977, seems to have marked a sea change in Sam's life. Bill Thomas, the general manager of WWEE and all of Sam's other radio stations, called him at home a little after three o'clock in the afternoon, before Elvis had been officially pronounced dead. The hospital was going to hold off the announcement for another hour or so out of consideration for the family. Sam, Sally said, never uttered a word. The phone didn't stop ringing once thc news was out — Sally finally took it off the hook — but Sam refused to speak to anyone. Sally called Knox and told him he had better get down to the studio right away to field all the calls that they would be getting there, and Knox ended up practically living at the studio for the next few days.

At the funeral Sam went up to the bier and patted Elvis on the cheek. "I told him I loved him, [but] I couldn't believe it. Here was this beautiful man, so bloated — I knew all the guys over at Memphis Funeral Home, and I knew they had some very good technicians. I mean, Elvis wanted to look good all the time, asleep or awake — it was just something almost unbelievable to see." It brought home to Sam an almost anguishing sense of guilt. He blamed himself for not having made the time to see Elvis over the last two or three years. What never ceased to gnaw at him was that for Elvis, that most self-directed of all his discoveries, there had been in the end no sense of personal fulfillment. *I could have saved him*, Sam said to me the first time we met, some eighteen months after Elvis' death. And as messianic as it may have sounded (and as messianic as it would continue to sound when Sam repeated it with ever more outlandish insistence over the years), there was as much introspection as self-regard in the statement. We all need someone we can trust, Sam said to a wide-eyed (and probably for the most part uncomprehending) me. We all need someone to whom we can communicate not just our innermost thoughts but our most lacerating self-doubt as well.

Paul Ackerman's death just four months later, on New Year's Eve,

Leaving Elvis' funeral with Sally. *Photograph by Pat Rainer*

only seems to have confirmed his own sense of isolation. "He went to bat for us when our music was so alien that we couldn't get anyone to see it like we felt it," Sam told the *Commercial Appeal,* a sentiment he repeated at the funeral in New York, which he recorded as he had recorded so many other similar sad occasions when he was just starting out on his career. It was for Sam an incalculable loss. He didn't have a lot of close friends, Sam told me one time, musing on his own increasing disconnection in a world of familiar objects. Unlike Knox, he was not the kind of person "who builds close relationships and friends like I wish maybe I could do. Elvis was the same way, in the lack of [ability] to build true friends." They were both, he suggested, "innately loners," and when you lost someone like Paul Ackerman or Jimmy Connolly in your life, for Sam there simply was no replacing them.

And yet, he insisted, he was the last person to dwell on the past — you needed to engage, you needed to go on, and goddamnit, he knew where he was heading, and he was damned if he would dwell on past glories or regrets. From his point of view, there was plenty of glory still to come. And if other people chose to cash in on Elvis, he was not going to join in. He was galled that Marion had spoken to *Rolling Stone* reporter Jerry Hopkins for his biography of Elvis several years ago — but he couldn't be bothered to read what she had said. It incensed him that she had spoken to Hopkins while Elvis was still alive, without Elvis' permission or authorization. That was something, Sam said, he would never do — with any artist, with *anybody*.

In fact, he told Sally, he had no more intention of talking about Elvis now that he was dead than he'd had when he was alive. This despite the fact that Sally was fielding requests from newspaper reporters and radio and television personalities almost daily. "He kept getting calls and calls and calls and calls and, you know, people wanting interviews, and he just refused to do it." For all of his veneration for history, he saw all of these so-called *reporters* feeding on Elvis like vultures on carrion. All they wanted to do, he told Sally, was "to put him down or say bad things about him — and Sam didn't like that at all. [He felt like] people didn't have a right to say those things about him, people didn't have a right to put him down." Sally doubted that he would ever change his mind — he wouldn't discuss the subject with her or anyone else — but then he got past it, and, Sally said, "I think it did him good."

In reality he got past it much sooner than he, or anyone else, would have expected. Just eight months after Elvis' death he found himself talking on the phone to *New York Times* music critic Bob Palmer, a Little Rock native and adoptive Memphian who had long championed the music, for a story Palmer was doing about the recent "rockabilly" revival, which had brought so much attention to the original sound of Sun. I don't know if he even needed to be prompted, but before anyone could say, "Sam, you can't say that" (not that there was a chance in the world he would have listened), he was telling Palmer that Elvis Presley "was positively the greatest human being to walk the earth since Jesus. I'm not talking about as an individual, as an *influence*." And just in case anyone might think he was being misquoted, he unapologetically repeated the same sweeping assertion to *Memphis Commercial Appeal* reporter Walter Dawson several months later, in August of 1978, on the one-year anniversary of Elvis' death. "Elvis almost had a Christ-like ability to communicate and to touch . . . as I see it now," he told Dawson. "And maybe people are gonna accuse me of getting my values all screwed up," he declared—but he wasn't going to backtrack or recant what he said. What he was talking about was Elvis' *impact,* the extent to which he embodied the American spirit, the American dream. Elvis, he said, "probably left more single impressions on people than—now notice this, *'single'*—other people like kings, queens, other entertainers usually will leave a mass impression, but what people feel about Elvis is wide and diverse."

"He speaks with an almost evangelical conviction," wrote Dawson, who over the next few years would become Sam's hometown confidant, filling much the same role that Bob Johnson of the *Press-Scimitar,* who had died five years earlier at fifty-eight, had occupied since Elvis first appeared on the scene. It was that very conviction, Dawson wrote, that had caused Sam to maintain his silence for so long, almost as if he were the repository of a sacred trust, that he for one, as he explained to Dawson, was not going to betray to nonbelievers. I don't doubt for a moment that that was how Sam saw it. I don't doubt that it was true up to a point. But I think there was something else that Sam would have been as unlikely to consider as to express. *He saw it as unseemly, in a sense, to court history.* It was not up to Sam Phillips to declare or evaluate his own role, however strongly he was convinced (as he was) that he had indeed changed the course of history. With Elvis' death, I think, it became clear to him for the first time that history did not write itself. He recognized, without ever fully acknowledging it, what Knox had been telling him all along: that he had to claim his place at the table—something that became more and more evident to him as he saw everyone else claiming theirs, sometimes, in his view, without the slightest foundation in fact.

Which is how the Sam Phillips that the world came to know over the next twenty-five years—messianic and publicly self-proclaiming in a manner that few of his early associates would have recognized—came into being. And how just a short time later, in early 1979, after a decade of trying, I was finally permitted to enter the picture.

DOES ANYONE STILL REMEMBER that intrepid young reporter on assignment from the *New York Times* (well, not all that young, really—thirty-five—and not all that intrepid either) whom we left stranded at the curb in front of Memphis' first free-form album-oriented FM Stereo radio station (named with fortuitous audacity WLVS by the very man who had discovered the late Elvis Presley) at the beginning of this chapter? I really hope so—for all of my faith in extended digression (think *Tristram Shandy*), I hope I haven't stretched the limits of reader patience too much by now. Well, let me just pick up the thread.

I arrived in Nashville and listened to the tape of the long-rumored (but never heard) Million Dollar Quartet for the first and second, and maybe even third, time at Shelby Singleton International on Belmont Boulevard on February 5, 1979. Everyone was suing Shelby by now. Johnny Cash had sued for something like $500,000 in unpaid royalties in 1976. Charlie Rich, who had recently achieved superstardom through the unlikely vehicle of a Billy Sherrill–produced string of sappy country hits on which he didn't even play piano (but that's another story) had sued for $2 million for "fraud and breach of contract" not long before. Carl Perkins, after suing Sam for his publishing (basically, he was looking to acquire the renewal rights to his songs, and in the end for the most part he did), had initiated a complicated series of legal challenges, going back to December of 1977, when the existence of the Million Dollar Quartet tapes first became widely known, seeking to block release of the tapes until it was acknowledged that since the music was recorded during his session (for which Jerry Lee Lewis had been paid $15 to play piano, and at which Elvis was merely a drop-in visitor), he was the legal owner. In some respects his interests coincided with those of RCA (representing Elvis) and Johnny Cash; in others (with respect to ownership, obviously), they were in conflict.

Shelby, on the other hand, was just a happy-go-lucky, equal-opportunity gadfly, seemingly taking as much delight in goading friends, foes, the powers that be, and any and all government offices without ever paying the full cost or even permanently alienating any of those groups. (Sam, for one, had yet to see and, as he was increasingly coming to realize, was never likely to see, anything like a proper return on his 20 percent share of the company—but he *still* loved Shelby.) Shelby in fact had pleaded guilty to income tax evasion just the year before, leaving himself open to fourteen years in prison and a $70,000 fine—but not even the full amount of the fine, as far as I know, was ever levied, as Shelby declared, "It is entirely possible that we had a bookkeeping problem, and this was a result. I make records and promote them, and there are so many things like bookkeeping I don't know anything about." Or, as he told the press in another context, "You're not a success in the record business unless you've been sued ten or twelve times."

Only Jack Clement and Jerry Lee Lewis remained above the fray, Jack because, as a self-proclaimed citizen of Alpha Centauri, he was not about to get caught up in such earthly frivolities. This, despite the great success he had enjoyed as a Nashville producer from the time that, in the spirit of Sam, he had broken Charley Pride as country music's first black superstar a decade earlier. And despite a recent dramatic downturn in his fortunes when, by going where no one but a citizen of Alpha Centauri would dare to go, he had lost all of his publishing and studio empire by investing his own money in a shot-in-Nashville, make-it-up-as-you-go-along gothic horror picture starring Agnes Moorehead called *Dear Dead Delilah*. Jerry Lee Lewis on the other hand just couldn't be bothered. He had never put any stock in the mundane details of cash or career — he just blamed Sam.

There was lots more, believe me — but I knew scarcely any of it at the time, and at this point further detail, which in the end would merely serve to underscore the same convoluted context, would have little bearing on the story. For me at the time the real story was about the music. Like Jerry Lee — but in this regard only — I liked to think I was focused on *nothing but the music*.

Here in brief is the tale of my progress. Jack spoke to me cheerfully and casually about the session. ("I thought all that carrying on ought to be recorded. I just turned on the tape recorder and let it run.") I called Carl in Jackson to set up an interview, and in the course of our brief telephone conversation he told me in no uncertain terms that Johnny Cash had played no role in the session. He had merely stopped by the studio at Sam's request so he could be included in the photograph and then gone shopping with his wife.

Johnny Cash, who was recording a gospel number with Helen Carter for a double album that would be called *A Believer Sings the Truth*, angrily insisted that he *had* sung on the session, aural evidence to the contrary (he thought he must have been singing high bluegrass harmonies, something no one ever gave him credit for being able to do) and was in general edgier than I could have imagined from his gracious stage presence. We talked a little about the black gospel singer Sister Rosetta Tharpe, one of his all-time favorites, but here again, there was an edge to his most innocent remarks, and what I noticed most of all was how jumpy he was, his general jitteriness, how fast the words flew out of his mouth. John had a history of substance abuse (mostly amphetamines) but was

Sam and Johnny Cash, ca. 1961. *Courtesy of the Sam Phillips Family*

thought to have been long since cured — by marriage, by fatherhood, by a religious reawakening prompted by his joining the evangelical church of Hank Snow's son, Jimmie Rodgers Snow.

As it turned out, as newspaper accounts would soon make clear, he was in the midst of a serious relapse ("I've talked to those pills," he would say a decade later, with the same unsparing honesty that he brought to all of his endeavors, musical, intellectual, and emotional. "I want to take amphetamines right now!"), with Sam remaining one of his staunch supporters over the years. When John first got in trouble for amphetamines in El Paso in 1965, Sam called the jail to offer help, and when he entered the Betty Ford Center eighteen years later, Sam wrote right away to reaffirm his faith in "your total integrity and honesty as an individual in a business that sometimes is not always conducive to those qualities." Cash for his part wrote to Sam during this same period about "the hundreds of times your name has come up in conversations over the past years, and I just wanted you to know that I love and respect you as much or more than I did in 1955 when you offered me that first Sun contract."

Carl was an even more admiring and unstinting supporter of his longtime friend. In early 1966, when both he and John were at their lowest ebb (Carl's drinking had accelerated to the point that he could barely function, while John, a big man, was down to 135 pounds), John had sought Carl out and asked him to join the tour. For nearly ten years Carl had had a featured spot on the highly successful Johnny Cash road show, and eventually, Carl said with some degree of hopeful conclusiveness, "he threw away the pills, and I threw away the whiskey." When I visited him in Jackson, Carl was his usual gracious but mournful self (he was caught up in a lawsuit with his latest record company). He didn't falter in his insistence that John had not sung on the session — but he wasn't interested in dwelling on it either. Mostly what he wanted to talk about was the music and where it had all come from (Sister Rosetta Tharpe was, once again, a touchstone) and the creative brilliance that permeated the atmosphere at Sun. He had strong feelings about the tape itself, which he had first heard at the home of Elvis' producer, Felton Jarvis, who seemed to be representing RCA's interests in the matter. "I heard the tape, and see, I had just gotten a little Les Paul guitar, and I had had a little tremolo bar put on it — and I went kind of crazy with that thing. When I heard it, I thought, Well, that's kind of silly, I would [never] have been doing it that much [if I'd had] any idea it was being put on tape. So Felton said, 'Well, what would be wrong with us taking that tape and you [overdubbing] your guitar, 'cause it's still you — but I don't want to fool with it. That's just the way it is, mistakes and all."

As far as what he was going to do with it, if and when the rights were cleared (and by this time he had accustomed himself to the idea that, with Elvis on the label, RCA was the right company to put it out, so long as they all got their proper royalties), he had had a vision, he told me, not long after Elvis died, when he first heard the tape. "I'm telling you, I've never felt any stronger about anything, it was so real, it was not a dream — it was like Elvis was speaking to me from the grave [telling me] to take the money and do some good, set up scholarships for underprivileged kids around the country. That's what I think needs to be done. That's what Presley would want."

I've got to admit, I didn't even try to contact Jerry Lee Lewis — I thought about it, but he was in the midst of a period of escalating calamity and crisis (his cousin, the television evangelist Jimmy Lee Swaggart, pulled him offstage at just about this time, so concerned was he about his cousin's increasingly erratic behavior, not to mention his eternal soul, and the IRS took possession of all of Jerry's worldly property at the end of this same month, February 1979), but I think his attitude can best be gleaned from a typically irreverent, insightful, and pithy summation of the Sun experience. "Nutty as a fox squirrel," he said, referring to Sam. "He's just like me, he ain't got no sense. Birds of a feather flock together. It took all of us to get together to really screw up the world. We've done it!"

Oddly enough, that same exuberant spirit permeated the recollections of every person that I spoke to on this trip. Johnny Cash may have taken a more edgy (and even querulous) tack, Carl a more conventionally sentimental one, and Jack's preferred mode of expression was always affectionate irony—but every one of them without exception bought into Jerry Lee's premise, that it all began with Sun and Sam ("Mr. Phillips," still, to most), and every one in some sense, even in the midst of the Sturm und Drang of lawsuits, historical revisionism, and forensic accounting, saw Sun as a golden age of inspiration and opportunity, which each would gladly have revisited—if only they could have gotten a better royalty rate.

It had all taken place little more than twenty years ago, and I struggled to find my way through thickets of memory and desire, through the miasma of my own unwavering hunger for the music and equally unwavering determination to make sense of a world in which I had clearly not grown up but to which I so desperately sought admittance, as historian, as writer, as fan.

T HERE WAS SO MUCH ELSE, of course, that I didn't know at the time, *couldn't* have known at the time—but in a way it really didn't matter. One particularly significant anomaly that I was unaware of when I arrived in Memphis: Sam had just been in the studio for the first time in over a decade and, as it would turn out, for the last time.

This came about in typically atypical fashion. Knox and Jerry had been working on an album by singer/songwriter John Prine, hailed not without justification as "the next Bob Dylan" when he first emerged as a poet of protest (also sensitivity, also humor) in the early 1970s. Because of the depth of his lyrics, and the keenness of his social observation, insufficient attention had been paid to his *music,* he felt, but now he wanted to explore a different aesthetic ("I wanted to make an album with a certain sound to it, with a sound like human beings were playing. The more producers I talked to, the more I got looked at like I was crazy"), and after working with Jack Clement for several months in

Working with Knox on John Prine's *Pink Cadillac*, ca. January 1979.
Courtesy of the Sam Phillips Family

Nashville and discovering a way to locate a sound of his own and have fun doing it, eventually, through Jack, he found his way to Knox and Jerry and the Phillips Recording Studio in Memphis.

They had *lots* of fun in the studio — sometimes more fun than was strictly legal — and they laid down a hard, rockabilly-based sound that was antithetical to anything John had ever recorded. At some point they even brought in Billy Riley, whom Knox and Jerry had induced to get back in the business after an absence of almost five years, and John recorded Billy's "No Name Girl" with a growliness that effectively set off the raggedy-ass sound of his own voice and roughly matched Billy's muscular second vocal. But Knox felt there was something about the quality of that voice, unadorned, that might genuinely interest Sam. "I said, 'This guy sings so bad I think you'll love him.'" And depending on whose version of the story you prefer, Sam either came by at their invitation to help (Knox and Jerry), or he saw the lights in the studio as he was driving by one night (John), or he was on his way to the bank (John again) and just stopped off to see what was going on.

Whatever the case, they worked all night and well into the morning, finally quitting just before noon the next day. The first thing Sam did was to have John play some of the songs John thought they might like to record, not just the new material that he had brought to the session but "old things that we'd done on the road, just stuff we liked to sing here and there. He wanted to hear *everything*," John said, recalling that at one point he launched into Elvis' first record, "That's All Right," and "Sam just stopped us and said, 'Now that's a *holy* song'—[in other words] you couldn't just go into it at any given time."

John was beginning to think that nothing much was going to come out of all this aimless experimentation other than maybe some great stories, but then Sam got behind the board and started messing around as they played a song they hadn't cut yet called "How Lucky Can One Man Get."

"Sam liked that. He said it was kind of like somebody walking down the street, you know, it was like you were walking down the street and you knew everybody, and you walk up and shake people's hands—and that's how he described it to the band, that's the way he wanted them to play behind me on this song.

"When we got all done with that, Sam said—he played it over a couple times, and he said, 'That's really nice, that's really, really, nice—but let's do something different now, let's do something with some push-ups in it.'"

The song he was referring to (the song with the push-ups in it) was "Saigon," a post-traumatic-stress-syndrome scream of pain ("The static in my attic is getting ready to blow," was its mantra) that they had been recording at the breakneck speed that its subject seemed to demand, except it went out of control every time they thought they were nailing it down. First, Sam had them cut it to half tempo and perform it so quietly they could hear one another without headphones. "Now," he said, "can you do it at half of half speed?" At this point it got so slow, John said, it felt "almost painful." Which was when Sam turned to him and said, "Now can you put some *sexxxx* in it? Can you sing with a little soul?"

This was probably the point at which, as John said, Sam's eyes grew wide, "they were like fire and brimstone, it looked like his eyebrows and his eyes themselves were on fire—they were just wild—and he spoke very clearly, and everything was [moving] slowly, but he started looking like a preacher, you know, like you'd swear that his hair would kind of get curly, and his hands moved like a preacher's would during a sermon, and he'd say, 'Now you boys seem very *nice*'"—John's laugh denotes just how paradoxical Sam's words were, and how emphatic his gestures. "Sam said, 'Think about a Slinky going down the steps—and all of a sudden you're on the next step.' Everything was with his hands. He just hypnotized us."

John would have jumped off a bridge by now if Sam had asked him to, if Sam had told him it would make the song better—but Sam didn't have anything like that in mind. Instead, "he put my guitar player's amp in the echo chamber and turned it up and turned it up, so that it would blow the tubes out in it, because he wanted to have pieces of hot metal flying through the air—that's what he said. The song was about Saigon, so he wanted to have hot metal flying through the air."

It was like he was directing a motion picture, John said, not telling anyone too much, letting everyone play their part, for a result that only he could envision. And when he invited them into the control room to hear what they had accomplished, he didn't play them a rough mix to be refined later, he presented them with a finished two-track that he had mixed down on the spot, just like he cut all of his records.

That was exactly the way it sounded when John took the finished tape out to California to play for the executives at his record company some six months later, a mix of old and new, retooled classics and arresting originals, all guided by the Phillips family dictum, *Do something different (Do something* really *different).* He had never done anything like this before, John said, "but I took it out there myself, because I was just so enamored by the whole record. I thought, 'Boy, they're going to love this,' you know—but [their reaction] was anything but. When the record was done, there wasn't anything said, and I went into one of the head a&r guy's office, and he was telling me really slowly that he didn't think that what I had here was what I wanted [and here John laughs again, with a certain amount of ironic detachment], and I thought, 'What is he trying to say?' You know, 'What I have here is not what I want?' And I said, 'Oh no, all this is what we want.' I said, 'Every bit of noise on this record, we paid for. We stayed up all night to get this noise.' I said, 'This is *exactly* what we want.'"

But Sam's involvement, and Knox and Jerry's dedicated aesthetic, even the free-of-charge PR coup of having the legendary Sam Phillips emerge from self-imposed retirement to further the artistic vision of a major artist like John Prine (a natural hook not lost on the *New York Times*' Robert Palmer, who called the album "Mr. Prine's masterpiece to date," in a feature that focused on Sam)—all of this mattered not one whit to John's label, Elektra/Asylum, who "ended up putting the record out," as John said, "like it was a stray cat. They just let it out of the house one night and never fed it again, just let it go on out there."

But no matter. Eventually John licensed the rights and put the album out himself some ten years later on his own Oh Boy label. It's called *Pink Cadillac* — and it continues to exist in its original, pristine, unvarnished, and unretouched form. So do yourself a favor, as Sam might say. Give it a listen. Who knows what new vistas it might open up?

I N RETROSPECT, I suppose, I found myself in a little bit of the same position in which John Prine found himself on that ill-fated trip to Los Angeles, when Knox, confronted with a flooded radio station, said to me, *"I think we're going to have to postpone."* Knox was not the enemy, it's true — far from it, he was my longtime friend, he was the one who had gotten me this far — but ultimately it was my hopes and dreams that were on the line. Not just a story in the *New York Times* — that was the least of it. *This was my life.*

I looked at Knox, impossibly sunny where Sam, both in photographs and in John Prine's vivid description, could be dark and glowering — the wave of Knox's hair as it curled to his shoulders, its golden sheen, the self-effacing stammer, the air of implacable optimism modified now by the compassionate shrug of empathy that would become emblematic of a Clinton presidency — what choice did I have but to respond in kind with my own form of hesitant (*very* hesitant) optimism, as out of my mouth came the only words that occurred to me at the time (or would occur to me still), *Can't I help?*

That was what I spent the rest of the day doing.

This was not, needless to say, heroic work. I mopped up. I carried buckets of water. I squeegeed, stacked tapes, sponged off equipment, and helped move furniture around, pitching in wherever and whenever I could. I took my place in what seemed like a ragtag army of volunteers, every one of whom was carrying out inscrutable tasks with what looked like confidence and direction. At one point I broke off to grab a sandwich with some of my fellow workers, from time to time we would exchange nodding conversation, mostly words of casual encouragement, with the water soaking up through our shoes. Sam dispatched Knox and Jerry all over town to collect equipment, suction cleaners were brought in, and gradually, over the course of a long, long day, the waters receded.

Every time he passed me in a hallway, Knox would pat me on the shoulder with an almost contagious air of warmth and affability — but mostly I had my eye on Sam as he moved from room to room, group to group, person to person, dealing with contractors, insurance adjustors, employees, the press (the press was out in force), friends and family, with a concentration that I could neither have imagined nor manufactured. There he was, quietly encouraging, exhorting, inciting, cajoling, and commanding. He was still at this point cultivating his Mephistophelean look, with a full, indifferently trimmed brownish-reddish beard, an unlikely fringe of bangs, and those deep-set boring-in blue eyes that compelled the attention of whoever they might happen to focus upon. And gradually I came to realize — and I can't say it took very long — *I was getting to see Sam Phillips produce a session.* In real time. In real life.

So many of the people I would later come to know were there. Knox and his brother, Jerry. Sam's wife, Becky, still a weekly on-air personality at WWEE. Sally, whose role I knew nothing about at the time. Knox's ex-wife, Betty, who worked at the station. For all I know, Knox's long-time girlfriend, Diane Duncan, whom he had met initially at Memphis Music, Inc. and who now was working at the recording studio, and Sylvia, too, might very well have been there, though Sally swears they were not. And I must have just missed Johnny Dougherty, Jerry's ex-wrestling manager and founder of the original Sputnik Monroe Fan Club, who would not come in as DJ and program director under his radio monicker of Johnny Dark for another few months. But I was not really in a position to recognize any of the players other than Knox and Sam. I was just a hapless reporter, mopping up my story, knowing that if it paid off in no other way, I had been given a sidelong glimpse of history that I could never have dreamt I would be vouchsafed.

Probably eight hours after my arrival, with the flood waters finally in retreat and most of that extraordinary army of volunteers gone home, we went back to a waterlogged little office and sat down for an interview that for all I knew might last five minutes or five hours. I was bone tired but ready for anything, but Sam, fifty-six at the time, seemed ready at any moment not just to jump out of his seat but to jump out of his skin to make a point — he seemed almost electrified by an immanence of the spirit brought out perhaps by near-catastrophe.

"I'm very cautious about who I talk to," Sam said. "I'm not sure that everybody has the love for what I feel and what I have felt, so therefore I'm very, very cautious about talking to a quote unquote writer."

Well, I could understand that. I might very well feel that same caution itself. But perhaps I should mention at this point something that I
don't think I've made entirely clear. I've written at some length about
the manifest complications, for all of Knox's tireless advocacy, of simply
setting this interview up. I mean, it took nearly a decade! I think I've
made some of the reasons clear — Sam possessed an almost pathological
aversion to looking back when the future was shining so bright ahead —
and I've theorized a little, too, about what I've come to feel was Sam's
underlying understanding of history, his assumption that, as an abstract
province administered by objective scholars, it simply wrote itself. But
what I haven't mentioned up till now was Sam's belief, stated contem-
poraneously and repeated many times over the years, that this was to
be *his first interview,* the first that he had ever explicitly granted outside
of a very narrow parameter of conditions.

Now, I know on the face of it, that may seem ridiculous, especially
given Sam's availability for the last twenty-five years of his life. But
here's the way I think Sam saw it. Bob Palmer had just written a brilliant piece, "Sam Phillips: The Sun King," based on an epic introductory
interview, for the December cover of *Memphis* magazine. But — and this
is the point that might well escape the casual reader, it certainly escaped
me at the time — the story was written for *Memphis* magazine. It was, in
other words, a <u>Memphis</u> story, something that Sam had agreed to, just
as he had agreed to countless stories by everyone from *Memphis Press-
Scimitar* reporter Bob Johnson to the *Memphis Commercial Appeal*'s
Walter Dawson, because it was going to appear in his own hometown.
Similarly, he had done countless interviews for innumerable news stories and features (well — countable and numerous, but you get the point)
for the trade papers, for *Billboard* and *Cash Box* and, I'm sure, for *Record
World,* too, over the years. But none of these were either for books or
for the national press.

I'm well aware that this may seem like a distinction without a
difference — I certainly wouldn't argue that it's not — and I must admit,
I'm at a loss to explain the handful of other interviews that Sam had
done over the years, unless Sam had simply forgotten about them or
rationalized that they were the product of some other kind of journalistic enterprise existing in a parallel universe not to be confused with our
own. There was, for example, the extensive interview that he did in 1973
for *Radio Times,* the oversized English weekly which, with a circulation

of ten million, could be found in just about every British household in possession of a television or radio. It was called "Rock's Daddyo" and covered his life and philosophy in admirable detail—but for some reason this didn't seem to qualify in Sam's mind as the kind of exposure he was so determined to avoid. Maybe because it was explicitly linked to the launching of a twenty-six-part Radio 1 series on the "history of modern pop music," or perhaps simply because it was for a foreign audience. I know, that doesn't make much sense to me either. Nor do I understand how he could overlook a cover story in *Country Music* magazine that same year on "The Rise and Fall of Sun Records," for which once again he was thoughtfully interviewed—unless it was that the story was more about the label than him.

I guess what it came down to was that from Sam's point of view an interview with a writer from the *New York Times*—what's more, an interview focusing explicitly on an unplanned moment that had taken place some twenty-two years earlier—was something altogether different. And something that took a good deal of convincing, not to mention a good deal of *self*-convincing, to alter his long-held and fiercely enunciated views.

Maybe it was just a natural evolutionary step, as Jerry Phillips would later come to feel. "It was a strange period of time. I don't know exactly what he was doing, but I think he was trying to move on to another dimension." Maybe it was simply Knox's positive determination that won the day. Or maybe it was, as I now believe, that, prodded by Knox's insistence that his legacy could be preserved only with his active participation, he finally came to the conclusion that history was indeed waiting—and might very well choose not to wait much longer.

Whatever else he may have been thinking, Sam instantly made his expectations clear. As to why he had not spoken to anyone in the past, he said, "I [didn't] think that I could express to anyone *genuinely* what took place, and the feelings that transpired, and the rapport—I hate that word—the *feel* between me and the people I worked with in those days. I don't think any ordinary writer could feel this unless they had a feel for what the overall thing was all about, [unless] they were willing to have researched and somehow equated with what was taking place sociologically, economically, the various other forms of deprivation. I don't think it's too possible for me to talk to many people and for what I feel and know about the era to come forth in print as it should"—he scrutinized me carefully here, he fixed me with his gaze, like John Prine I would have jumped off the Mississippi-Arkansas Bridge if he had told me to. *"Not for me,"* he emphasized, "for what I felt and what these artists felt all their lives and, once they were given the opportunity [and] began to know they weren't being used, that the greatest reward wasn't money, which they didn't get a lot of in many instances, but they got a way to say something that they had wanted to, through generations."

I was there. Can any reader who has gotten this far doubt that? Was Sam sizing me up, or was this merely the preamble he would have delivered to any writer who happened to wander into his sight. I didn't know then—I still don't know. It doesn't really matter. He was, clearly, preaching to the converted.

By a strange coincidence Andrew Solt and Malcolm Leo's groundbreaking documentary *Heroes of Rock and Roll,* the first full-scale cinematic treatment of the music, was scheduled to be shown that night in place of the ABC network's prime-time Friday night movie. It started at seven o'clock Central time, and Sam had the sound turned down on the tiny black-and-white television set that was flickering in the corner of his office. Whenever one of his artists came on, though, it was almost as if he sensed it before the image appeared on the screen, and his voice took on a different tone. "Let me tell you something about him," he said when his most famous discovery suddenly leapt into view. "Elvis—you looking at him now, back then he looks so clumsy and so totally uncoordinated. And this was the beauty of it—*he was being himself.*" "Ah, Uncle Gerald," he chuckled appreciatively as Jerry Lee Lewis raked the keyboard. "You think that guy isn't dynamic? That man can play more piano in a minute than anyone I've ever seen!"

Mostly, though, the interview spun out into a consideration of greater matters, not abstractions exactly but themes that rested on a bedrock of unshakable conviction and deep belief. The importance of history. The significance of his own story. The wild-ass premise on which Sun Records had been founded. The infinite promise of untried, unproven talent and the dream of an egalitarian society. The sense of outrage at man's inhumanity to man, at the class and racial distinctions that Sam had witnessed from the time he was a child ("I thought to myself, suppose that I would have been born black, suppose that I would have been born a little bit more down the economic ladder"). The sense of purpose that drove him ("My mission was to bring out of a person what was in him, to recognize that individual's unique quality and then to find the key to unlock it"). The essential innocence, the necessary *hunger* that he felt was at the heart of all true artistic expression. As for the Howlin' Wolf, his greatest discovery: "God, what I would give to see him as he was in my studio, to see the fervor in his face, to hear the pure instinctive quality of that man's voice." And his ultimate goal? To somehow or another protect them — or was it perhaps, ultimately, just as much to protect himself? "This is the void," he declared. "When they get out on the stage of life, the first thing that starts in their mind [is]: *when am I going to be rejected?"*

THIS, AS I WOULD SOON DISCOVER, was the very foundation of Sam's story. This was the text of his lesson. All of it. Freedom. The democratic process. The vast, untapped talents of those who had been ignored, set aside, scorned, and reviled by a world that, without even knowing it, was waiting for the bestowal of their gifts. Most of all, *individualism* — but individualism at any cost, individualism *in the extreme.*

I don't mean to make light of this in any way, for it became my lesson, too. But for those who met Sam over the next twenty-five years — and there were many, for once the doors of history had been opened, they were never again closed — it was not difficult for the suspicion to arise that this was some form of theatrical self-aggrandizement, that this man whom I described from our first meeting as possessing the look of "an Old Testament prophet in tennis sneakers speaking in an oracular tone and language" was putting his listener on, was imposing some kind of crazy, arbitrary rite of journalistic kidnapping, as he insisted upon *his* truth, his narrative, in the face of any and all attempts to get him to focus on a central story. But if some thought that this was in some sense a kind of put-on, they were wrong. Sam felt, passionately, unquestionably, irreversibly, that he had a lesson to impart, and, drunk or sober, cock-eyed or reality-based, he was determined to impart it, come hell or high water.

Sometimes the prologue was as important as the primary text. Sometimes the prologue could go on for as long as two hours, and Sam undoubtedly lost some of his audience along the way. But to Sam the prologue — the theoretical infrastructure — was as significant as the story to be told. The story, as he would insist again and again — often to raised eyebrows or unspoken suspicions of disingenuousness—was not about *Sam Phillips*, it was much bigger than that, it would be just as important, perhaps even more so, if the name Sam Phillips were never mentioned. History, Sam felt, was "the stalwart of everything. History is so much more important than [the] existence of any one life." This was a story about democratic dreams and possibilities.

THE "MILLION DOLLAR QUARTET" TAPES, as it turned out, would not come out officially—or at least *legally*—for another decade, after what appears to have been considerable self-bootlegging and much amusing Shelby Singleton chicanery and double-talk—and they were not restored to their full, unabridged length for another sixteen years after that. The *New York Times'* reaction to the Sam Phillips in my story was about the same as Elektra/Asylum's reaction to John Prine's album. They didn't like either Sam or his syntax. Sam's rhetorical model may well have been Cicero's periodic sentence, but all too often from their point of view (well, from any impatient listener's), he did not reach the promised end. Most of all, they said, their readers would never countenance the use of the word "nigger" in the magazine, even if it was being used to show the endemic racism of a place and time. "At the radio station," I had written, "he was frequently met by fellow workers with greetings like, 'Well, you smell okay. I guess you haven't been hanging around those niggers today.'" But the entire quote was excised to spare their readers' sensibilities.

It didn't really matter. Sam's message got through. And in a sense for the rest of his life that was his mission: to convey that message, to promulgate, to teach and preach that lesson, just as he once had with his brother Jud in the backyard garage of their house on North Royal Avenue in Florence.

"Let me say this," he declared to me, to Knox, to the world at large, at the conclusion of our nearly three-hour first meeting in that small, waterlogged office, "I don't want to come off as the poor ole country boy that made good, or anything like that. I'm just trying to come over with what I know deep in my heart to be the truth, as I relayed it to myself then. I may have some dates wrong, and some facts and figures, but the material aspects of it is not wrong. 'Cause I will see it in my mind's eye until the day I die—and then I'm not so sure I won't see it after that. I'm not looking for any heroism, or anything at all, but I think that music is a part of a very spiritual aspect of people. And I just think that it has gotten out of hand a little bit today, scientifically trying to analyze everything that you do, and if it doesn't have that stamp, then nobody can peddle it. I don't say that there's a thing wrong with [today's music], but when you drive so much of the same thing and people get into too much of a pattern, I want to tell you that if that is giving of yourself in a way that you can be fulfilled, then I just don't have the ability to interpret it in that way. Listen. They're talking about that you've got to have — well, what is the trend now? Well, *Jesus God,* now, if there's anything that we don't need, it's a *trend.*

"One of these days, though, I may not live to see it, maybe you all will, but one of these days that freedom is going to come back. Because, look, the expression of the people is almost, it's so powerful, it's almost like a hydrogen bomb. It's going to get out.

"Now, let me tell you one other thing, Peter, and I'll get out of here. I'm not just saying go back to the fifties and this sort of thing. But if it could be worked — and it *will* be worked — to where just a few like Elvis could break out again, then I would preach, I would become an evangelist if I were alive, saying, For God's sake, *don't* let's become conformists — *please.* Just do your thing in your own way. Don't ever let fame and fortune or recognition or anything interfere with what you feel is here — *if* you feel you are a creative individual. Then don't let the companies get this going real good and buy up all the rights of the individual some way or the other. That's not right. We'll go back in another circle. Till it gets so damn boring that your head is swimming. And I'll tell you, I hope it's not too long coming, because of the fact as we go longer and longer into the lack of individual expression, as we go along, if we get too far we're going to get away from some of the real basic things. All of us damn cats that appreciate not the fifties necessarily but that freedom are gonna forget about the feel. We gonna be in jail, and not even know it."

S AM APPEARED on *Late Night with David Letterman* on May 15, 1986, just four months after being inducted into the newly formed Rock and Roll Hall of Fame. He was one of two nonperformers so honored (Alan Freed was the other), while Elvis, Chuck Berry, James Brown, Ray Charles, Sam Cooke, Fats Domino, Buddy Holly, the Everly Brothers, Little Richard, and Jerry Lee Lewis were all suitably enshrined and (save for the three deceased and Little Richard, who was still suffering the effects of a car accident several months earlier) freely roaming the halls of the Waldorf Astoria in New York.

The television appearance was the result of Sam's newfound (and somewhat precariously attained) celebrity, something it might be difficult to understand in an age of instant Internet notoriety. But Sam Phillips, far from being a household name, was virtually unknown to the world at large when he was voted into this new self-styled Hall of Fame, and it was only through the strenuous efforts of David Letterman's bandleader and sidekick, Paul Shaffer, music director for the Hall of Fame festivities, that he was booked on the show. It was as if this were his long-awaited audition for fame.

"In the 1950s," David Letterman, an inveterate ironist, announced with only a residual amount of irony, and even that held mostly in check, "my next guest owned a company called Sun Records, based in Memphis. He was the man responsible for discovering the likes of Elvis Presley, Jerry Lee Lewis, Carl Perkins, Roy Orbison, and Johnny Cash, and just a few months ago this man was inducted into the Rock and Roll Hall

Photograph by Riss Murray, courtesy of Pat Tigrett

of Fame — you were there that night, Paul?" And then after a moment of demystificating badinage: "Folks, it's a pleasure to have on our program tonight Sam Phillips."

But then Sam did not immediately appear. The camera scans the empty hallway, dollying in on a NO SMOKING sign, and lingering uncertainly as the host sardonically declares, "Sam, come on out in there. We've got to do something here." At last Sam emerges with full chestnut-colored mane and beard, making his delayed entrance in a puffy white overshirt with black hook-up buttons and studded jeans, as he playfully clenches his fists and shouts something indecipherable while slinking over toward his host.

"Hi, Sam, how are you?" Letterman says, meeting him halfway and being greeted in turn by a "Hello there, Mister David," and a firm two-handed handclasp that keeps them both standing, stranded uncomfortably in a no-man's-land far removed from the television host's safe harbor, his elevated desk. When Letterman at last manages to steer Sam to his assigned seat and is about to take his own, Sam not only fails to sit down, he skates around the two-chair setup, as if dancing to an unheard tune, and stands with his back to the audience, at last pronouncing his verdict, "This is a beautiful set here, David." To which Letterman, who, if he is not disconcerted by now, is surely baffled, responds, "Thank you very much. And it's all ours."

The rest of the interview goes pretty much like that. Before David can even ask a question, Sam suggests that perhaps he should have as his guest executive producer Robert Morton, who has been talking to Sam backstage and who, Sam said, "could write a book about anybody." When David indicates he just might do that someday, but "we want to talk about you tonight, Sam," Sam responds with a calculated slowness of speech and gesture. "I see," he says, then tilts his head and leans in toward David until he is so close that it looks like he is trying to put his head on David's shoulder, declaring with that same calculated defusing of expectations, "David, we will try to talk about me just here for a little while." But then rather than even begin to do that, he chooses instead to ask, "Are you going to have your teeth fixed before long?" And when David responds with a laugh and a good-natured joke, Sam simply refuses to be deflected from whatever strange course he is on. "How did you [have] buck teeth and make a million dollars? Now, you know there's not a lot of people can do that." "No, I know, I know, I've been very lucky," David concedes, as artificial thunder rolls. "You're lucky you're inside tonight, Sam," says David, and Sam stares at him for the longest moment, holding his gaze from that strangely lowered subordinate position of the guest on national TV, before at last saying, "Is it that bad?" and then conceding that it does indeed look like it is.

It's hard to guess what exactly he's up to. On the one hand, you might think he was drunk — and every respectable Memphian, glued with horror to his or her television screen, was, of course, certain that he was. On the other hand, you might well think that he was sending up the hipster, which might be akin to conning a con — and I've got to admit that this was certainly my reaction watching it at the time and for many years thereafter. As to what Sam is thinking, as he sits slouched back in his chair until he is practically lying down, looking as if he has not a sleepy-eyed care in the world? To every serious question Sam responds with such misdirection, drawling indifference, or not at all, that Letterman finally asks Paul Shaffer, who must at this point be in fear for his job, to join them. What kind of sound were you trying to establish? Sam is asked. Was there something specific you were looking for, or — and I would say the tone is one of undisguised exasperation by now — "would you just record anybody who came through?"

"Why certainly, David," Sam affably, and perversely, agrees. "You got to work for this a little while tonight, son. You know, I don't give away all of my secrets, because when this show goes under, you might want to start recording. If I give away all of my secrets, what am I going to have to write about in a book and a movie? You could copy me, and you're so young I might drop off dead. . . ."

And to questions about the Million Dollar Quartet, prompted, like some of the previous questions, by big poster-board blowups of the familiar photographs, Sam stares for some time at the iconic picture of all four, begins a response, and then, rolling his eyes upward, returns to the theme of David's studio set. "Our great big studio — it's almost as pretty as this studio . . ." As for the session itself: "Well, Carl Perkins was doing a session, and it just so happened . . . they all dropped by — it just so happened that they all dropped by, and — they all dropped by. So we got together. . . ."

"Well, you're certainly a legend —"

"An interesting guest," says Sam simultaneously.

"You're certainly a legend. You're responsible for the very formation of rock 'n' roll. Don't you think you had a hand in helping the sound of rock 'n' roll evolve from bits and pieces of other influences . . ."

"David, you're getting awfully serious for this show. What are you setting me up for?"

"I'm just trying to think of a real nice way to say good-bye, Sam," David says, as the lightning flashes and the thunder rolls, and Sam laughs and offers a languid handshake, and after six excruciating minutes they go to break, with Sam still slumped back in his chair with the magisterial indifference of someone who is not about to be easily dislodged.

How to interpret it? To this day I don't honestly know. Whether a total debacle, a moment of exquisite truth, or, simply, one more demonstration of Sam's *extreme* refusal to be predictable let alone patronized, it no doubt remains etched in the memory of everyone who has ever seen it, whether at the time or on YouTube, where it continues to serve as an uncanny foreshadowing of actor Joaquin Phoenix's 2009 put-on appearance on the same show. Sam's own reaction, it turned out, may well have been one of mild disappointment — but not for the reasons one might think. Since she was with Sam all through the experience, and I can't really call up any other witnesses to Sam's state of mind, I think I'll just let Sally tell the story.

Sam hadn't been drinking at all, Sally said — and Sally has never been averse to pointing out when he has. But he wasn't drunk that day, just exasperated. "These people had gone over and over and over and over what Sam was going to talk about. I mean, over and over and over. They came to the hotel room. And they said, 'David don't like surprises.' You know. And Sam just walked out there and just surprised everybody! I think that he thought David was going to go along with him. And he was kind of mad that David didn't. I was totally flabbergasted. He had not said a word to me about it. I didn't have any idea that he wasn't going to talk about what he'd already talked to these people about. But he [just] didn't really want to sit there and talk about Sun Record Company — I think he was just tired of talking about it. . . . I mean, they could have discussed something else besides, you know, rock 'n' roll or the music or something. I was just so upset. I said, 'Man, I just don't understand this. I just don't understand why you would have ever done it.' And Sam, I think, got kind of mad at himself and wished he hadn't have done it. But then after he saw it back, he thought it was good. He thought it was

Sam and Solomon, May 22, 1986. *Photograph by Pat Rainer*

good. And every time it came on as a rerun, Sam watched it. But I could never watch that show. I could never watch it."

Just how unembarrassed Sam was became evident to me just one week later when Sam came to a publication party for my book, *Sweet Soul Music,* at the Round Table Bookstore in Memphis. Knox and Jerry were not able to attend — they were out checking the line on their new transmitter in Alabama — but Sam graciously made an appearance, and though I don't think there was a single member of the public at large in attendance (and, quite possibly, not a single book sold), so did many of the people I had written about in the book. Songwriter Roosevelt Jamison was there. So were David Porter (cowriter of "Soul Man" and "Hold On, I'm Comin'"), Rufus Thomas, musician-about-town Jim Dickinson, Solomon Burke, and a filmmaker who wanted to make a documentary about Solomon's life. It was a wonderful party (and I say that as someone who has never been much of a party guy), but for me the highlight was the presence of two of my greatest heroes, Sam Phillips and Solomon Burke, in the same room. Solomon had driven in from either Los Angeles or Atlanta (with Solomon it was always a little difficult to single out his exact point of origin or departure), and I hastened to introduce them, thinking they would have so much in common (among other things their early beginnings in the funerary profession). But rather than warm to each other, in a reaction as inexplicable to me as Sam's appearance on *Letterman,* they just stared one another down, locking gazes in a way that I had never seen anyone else attempt with Sam. Later, they appeared to relax for more casual picture taking, but you could still detect a frosty distance that seemed to me characteristic of neither man.

Toward the end of the party Rufus Thomas, natty in a wide-brimmed gray Stetson, yellow, pin-striped sports jacket with a purple handkerchief peeking out from the breast coat pocket, and sharp brown-and-white correspondent shoes, approached Sam with typical bonhomie. I should probably say here that for all of his public denunciations of Sam in later years for what Rufus saw as his abandonment of black music ("Me and Sam Phillips were tighter than the nuts on the Brooklyn Bridge," Rufus once told me, "[but] when Elvis and Carl Perkins and Cash come along, he just cut it off and went to white: no more blacks did he pick up at all"), he never treated him in person with anything less than the utmost deference, admiration, and respect. In this instance he wanted a favor. He had seen Sam on the Letterman show, and he thought getting on that program could be a big boost to his career. I almost burst out laughing— in a sense I wondered if this might be intended as a not-so-subtle put-down. But it didn't faze Sam in the least, and both men were perfectly serious as Sam told Rufus how wonderful everyone at the show had been to him — how hospitable and *professional,* some of the nicest people he had ever met in his life, they had all just made him feel completely at home, and there was one man in particular, producer Robert Morton, who he thought Rufus should be in touch with, and he'd be glad to contact Morton personally if Rufus would like him to.

Once again I have no definitive interpretation to offer. Such are the vagaries of show business — or, I suppose, of life — in which the human comedy will always prevail. Except: I can't help but feel that that this was all part of Sam's rebellion against ever permitting himself to be pigeonholed, against ever allowing himself to be considered (or perhaps more important, to consider *himself*) conventional in any way — and his concomitant belief that in that refusal he couldn't help but gain the respect of others.

This proposition would be tested yet again the following January, at the second Rock and Roll Hall of Fame induction ceremonies. This time Sam would be asked to induct Carl Perkins, who with Roy Orbison's admittance that same year would make the fourth Sun alumnus out of only twenty-five full-fledged "performer" inductees. By now, though, it had been announced by Hall of Fame chairman of the board and Atlantic Records founder and chairman Ahmet Ertegun, the son of the second Turkish ambassador to the United States and an unfailing subscriber to realpolitik, that the Rock and Roll Hall of Fame would make its physical home in Cleveland, not Memphis — and Sam was practically beside himself with rage.

Quite simply he felt betrayed. More than that, he felt that Memphis had been betrayed, *history* had been betrayed, moreover, he felt that he had been personally double-crossed by Ahmet Ertegun, who had assured him, as he had declared at his own induction the previous year, that "this thing [was] going to be truly, genuinely democratic, fair — no damn politics. . . . Ahmet also told me," he had informed the corporate crowd at the Waldorf Astoria, "we're not going to put this rock and roll hall of fame, the edifice itself, the mortar and the bricks, anywhere that we don't feel that the community is totally behind it. Because it is an American project that represents the greatest creative talent in the world."

Now Sam knew full well that half a dozen cities had been in the running — and he certainly embraced the democratic process. But once that democratic process had run its course, how in God's name could there be any question that Memphis would be selected — Memphis, the damn birthplace of rock 'n' roll. Except Cleveland, with something like $40 million pledged, had come up with the money, and the city had united to get behind the effort in a way that Memphis, with its own long-standing commitment to what could only be described as runaway factionalism, never could — and Ahmet failed to give any credit to the spirituality of the whole damn thing, he was just gonna take the money and run.

"Good people," Sam declared to the tuxedoed crowd at the 1987 ceremony as he embarked upon his induction speech for Carl Perkins, "I want to look out there individually, although I can't see you very well [with] all these beautiful lights in my face. But last year at this time, this great institution, although it's in its infancy, showed me and I think all of us through the leadership of Jann [*Rolling Stone* founder and Hall of Fame executive vice president Jann Wenner] and Ahmet and many, many people that have worked ceaselessly and tirelessly in this effort, it makes me especially proud —" But here he got distracted by his real message.

"I'd be lying if I told you that I wouldn't have liked to have seen it in Memphis, Tennessee."

Shouts, laughter, some boos from the crowd, which will grow in volume. But Sam is not to be deterred.

"By God, we would have *done* something. We would have changed the course of the river!" And now he is off to the races, before long he's preaching to an audience that has little patience with his sermon. "Let me tell you something. I was talking to a young man this afternoon. I met those beautiful people from Cleveland last year, and I'll guarantee you'll be taken with those folks because they are absolutely precious souls. And I believe they mean every damn word they're saying. But I told Mike this afternoon on the radio station in Cleveland that the Rock and Roll Hall of Fame and the music and the institution of spirituality and bringing brotherhood of mankind, black, white, I don't give a damn what color you are. You know, baby, that's what it's all about. . . ."

Eventually he got around to Carl Perkins, whom he embraced as someone who, like himself, had come "from the meager means that so many of us have seen in life, outhouses, bad crops, no damn fertilizer that you could buy at the store" — but if there was anyone in the room who came from such meager means, they didn't seem willing to acknowledge it, and the scorn they felt for anyone so provincial as to go on and on about it, as if it were a badge of honor, could be measured by the palpable restiveness and swelling sounds of disapproval from the crowd. Sam couldn't have cared less — he didn't give a damn. He had said what he had come to say, and fuck all the sorry-ass sidewinders and motherfuckers. It was as if he were back at the 1959 ARMADA convention in Chicago, calling all the independent record men "a sorry bunch of bastards" if they didn't mend their ways — anyone who knew Sam had heard this kind of speech before, but until now his audience had been limited to a select circle of friends, family, fellow Memphians, and industry peers. It was a little like the Letterman show, but here he was in complete command, and in this brief moment he seemed almost to have discovered the role that would sustain him for the rest of his life: teacher, preacher, populist historian, utopian visionary, public scold. This was the voice, these were the lessons that he would invoke again and again over the course of the next fifteen years, no matter the circumstances, no matter the occasion, whether people wanted to hear what he had to say or not.

THE NEWBORN LEGEND OF SUN

MUCH OF THIS newfound sense of direction undoubtedly had to do with the unprecedented international acclaim Sun Records had gotten in the last decade — with much of that having to do with the untrammeled spirit of entrepreneurial adventure of Shelby Singleton, who by now had owned the label longer than Sam had. He had initially released a series of Greatest Hits compilations with great success, then further capitalized on the same material by licensing them on budget lines around the world. At the same time he had had a good deal of success selling Johnny Cash and Jerry Lee Lewis product in the contemporary country market — not to mention, in the aftermath of Elvis' death, promoting an Elvis sound-alike named Jimmy Ellis as a masked singer of indeterminate planetary origin named Orion, with some of the publicity even suggesting that this might be Elvis come back to life following his retreat from the public eye by faking his own death.

It was during this same time period that two recent British university graduates, Martin Hawkins and Colin Escott, whose shared passion for Sun Records went back to their secondary school days, began writing a series of liner notes for the Sun reissue program on the British division of the Philips label, with whom Shelby had made a distribution deal in exchange for a substantial advance. When Shelby simply stopped delivering product with much of the advance still unrecouped, Colin and Martin, who were already working on a book called *Catalyst: The Sun Records Story* (this would metamorphose some twenty years later into *Good Rockin' Tonight: Sun Records and the Birth of Rock 'n' Roll*, their definitive history of the label), sought permission from the Philips subsidiary label to start a Sun reissue series of their own.

They projected seven thousand sales for the first album, *Sun Rockabillys*, which came out in the spring of 1973 and, as it turned out, considerably exceeded all expectations. By now Hawkins had started a career with the British health service and Escott was working full-time for a British record wholesaler in London, but they followed up rapidly with two more Rockabilly volumes and a brilliantly selected Sun survey, *The Sun Story*, and then, under the aegis of Charly Records, Shelby's new British licensee, with thirteen volumes of a Sun *Roots of Rock* series, seven *Sun Sound Special*s, and various other series and stand-alone releases. In 1980, after coming to the realization that Charly just might be "crazy enough to issue whole boxes of this music," they embarked upon an extensively annotated and illustrated succession of boxed sets, culminating in a breathtaking twelve-LP Jerry Lee Lewis package in 1984 and an equally breathtaking nine-LP box, *Sun Records: The Blues Years*, the following year. In all, there would be eight boxed sets, made with Sam's cooperation, in the form of hours of late-night transatlantic telephone calls with Martin Hawkins in which he expounded at length not just about his most famous discoveries but, with equal pride, about some of his most obscure. By 1989 they had issued by Hawkins' count roughly a thousand Sun tracks on the Charly label, and while the dedicated Sun enthusiast might well have suspected the wealth of material that had been recorded at Sam Phillips' tiny 706 Union Avenue studio, not even the most ardent collector could have altogether imagined the breadth that this systematic catalogue release of largely unissued sides would unveil.

It was only then that the full genius of Sam Phillips was revealed to the general public, with an outpouring of praise not just from collectors but from influential critical voices around the world. But even more significant, the most important critical voice of all pronounced himself satisfied. "I think, man, if I had done it myself," Sam told the *Memphis Commercial Appeal*'s Walter Dawson, "I couldn't have done it any better." And it led for the first time to a series of extended interviews for a variety of projects and publications, including a lengthy profile by Robert Hilburn in the *Los Angeles Times;* a 1981 appearance on ABC's *Nightline;* an utterly unself-conscious filmed interview in appreciation of Chuck Berry's genius for Taylor Hackford's concert documentary *Hail! Hail! Rock 'n' Roll;* a full-scale *Rolling Stone* profile by Elizabeth Kaye to celebrate his Hall of Fame induction in 1986; a three-part 1987 interview in the preeminent collector's magazine, *Goldmine,* by Colin Escott and Hank Davis, Escott and Hawkins' colleague in the Charly reissue series; and a two-part radio appearance on the BBC with an in-depth interview conducted by Manfred Mann alumnus Paul Jones for his long-running *Rhythm and Blues* show.

Sam had certain reservations, it's true, about the reissue program. Despite his public (and, I'm convinced, entirely sincere) vote of confidence, he would, he sometimes said, have done things a little differently, been a little more selective perhaps — or maybe just *differently* selective—put the alternate takes on separate discs. ("There could have been such a great story on this," he told British rock historian Trevor Cajiao. "This part of how it's put together. This is the gas pedal, this is the brake pedal, this is the clutch—here we go!") But these were just minor quibbles. His only real quarrel was with Shelby. And not just over the outrageous misrepresentations and transgressions of taste that a promotional fabrication like Orion represented. Over more weighty issues of substance and finance.

To begin with, Sam contended, Shelby had no right to issue the blues material—it was not part of their deal, and it was covered by neither licenses nor contracts. But that, of course, was Shelby's problem in the end. What continued to be Sam's problem was Shelby's sleight-of-hand approach to finances, or slipshod accounting methods, or just general slipperiness, whatever you wanted to call it. But for someone who prided himself on his own meticulous bookkeeping and business integrity (not to mention business acumen), it killed Sam to have his reputation linked to Shelby's, whether in the world's eye or that of his former artists — and to suffer real financial and personal consequences as a result.

Shelby simply failed to pay people in anything resembling "timely" fashion, a truth made evident by the never-ending series of lawsuits against him from nearly every one of the major Sun artists. In fact, just about everyone sued Shelby except for Sam. "Shelby owes me more money right now," he said in 1999, "than he's ever owed any artist." But for some reason Sam never made any move to go after it, perfectly willing, it seemed, to dismiss Shelby as little more than a victim of his own bad judgment. "It's not that Shelby is a crook," Sam said without in any way exonerating Shelby from falling down on his obligations to the artists, who as often as not failed to distinguish between the former owner of Sun Records and the present one in expressing their legitimate grievances. "It's just that Shelby is like [a lot of] people I've known, he's really not a good businessman."

As for Shelby, he just chuckled over what he seemed to consider Sam's surprising naïveté. "Well, I thought Sam was great, you know, and stuff like that, I remained friendly with him throughout the years, [and] he was never bothersome"—but Sam, he said, simply had to learn what it was like to watch another man bring up your baby. I'm not sure just what Sam would have made of this formulation—or, for all I know, did. He contented himself in any case with the occasional payments that Shelby would present him with, sometimes appearing in Memphis in a rented Lear jet with all of the ceremony of a genuine plutocrat but none of the accounting. There continued to be a constant flow of publishing money, to be sure, and sync money for movie licenses (these came direct to Sam, with no place for Shelby as middleman), and it may well have been that Sam had simply come to the pragmatic conclusion that if he pushed too hard, he might very well force Shelby into bankruptcy, thereby putting the catalogue itself at risk. "I made a mistake in selling Sun to Shelby," he would grumble from time to time. But he never made a move to take it back. Nor would he ever have wanted to. For now he had history to contend with.

MEMORY PAIN

B Y AN ODD COINCIDENCE the very acetate that for most people marked the start of the Sun story—the "personal record" that an eighteen-year-old worker on a factory assembly line named Elvis Presley had paid to make at the Memphis Recording Service in the summer of 1953—had turned up after a quarter of a century, during Elvis Week (the annual tribute to Elvis that occurs in Memphis every year on the anniversary of his death) in August 1988, long after it had been thought to be irretrievably lost. Under ordinary circumstances this should only have gladdened Sam's heart—how could it help but solidify Sam's place in history?—but it turned out there was a catch.

In 1970 Marion Keisker had given a series of interviews—wonderful interviews—to *Rolling Stone* contributing editor Jerry Hopkins, then working on his biography of Elvis Presley. Sam had refused to speak to Hopkins—well, Sam was refusing to speak to practically everyone at this time—on the pretext that without Elvis Presley's permission it would be morally indefensible to contribute to the book. I think in retrospect even Sam might have admitted that this turned out to be a shortsighted view.

Hopkins' book was published in the fall of 1971. It was a fine journalistic account, in which the author unearthed all kinds of fascinating, hitherto unknown and often unsuspected information, from Memphis Housing Authority records detailing the Presleys' early days in Memphis to Marion's beautifully nuanced portrait of the Memphis Recording Service from the start, something that only she and Sam could have

With Marion Keisker at Memphis State University, August 16, 1979.
Courtesy of the Sam Phillips Family

described. But Marion also told a very different story about the discovery of Elvis Presley from the one Sam had always told. And it was a story that in his mind had the potential to undermine the very bedrock of the historical place he was now seeking to claim.

For in Marion's elegiac account, reinforced with details that, as she said, changed with the impressionistic intertwining of memory, it was she who had recorded that beautiful eighteen-year-old-boy when he wandered in on a Saturday afternoon to make a record for his mother — not that she was claiming credit for the discovery exactly, it was just that she was the one who happened to be in the office.

Recounted in this manner, it doesn't seem like all that momentous an historical redaction. And in the absence of a single dissenting voice (which logically could only have been Sam's or, if he had chosen to tell his own story, Elvis') this rapidly came to be viewed as settled history. And why not? Marion was a compelling witness, and why should anyone argue over what seemed like little more than a footnote to the whole resplendent chronicle? One might have thought that Sam was happy to see Marion get this little bit of deserved recognition, but in fact, as he concentrated on his burgeoning radio empire, he appears for six or seven years—at least until Elvis' death—to have been altogether unaware of Marion's account. It was only when he spoke to Robert Palmer for the December 1978 cover story of *Memphis* magazine that he responded for the first time. "I hate like the devil taking anything away from Marion," he told Palmer with the ferocious intensity of a man who seems to mean the exact opposite, "but the record has to be set straight." And when he was awarded the first "Memphis State University Award for Distinguished Achievement in the Creative and Performing Arts" on August 16, 1979, two years to the day after Elvis Presley's death, Sam confronted Jerry Hopkins directly when he ran into him at the first annual Elvis conference in the afternoon, then addressed him from the stage toward the end of his acceptance speech at the ceremony that night. "Now, where is Jerry Hopkins?" he called out, explaining that he had never met Hopkins before, because he wouldn't talk to him when Jerry had originally been in town working on his book. "Well, I did not mean to be discourteous to Jerry, and I guess he had to write the best he could with what he had to work with, but, damn, I'm going to tell you one thing, Jerry. In the next edition I would like you to change a few things if you will. 'Cause it is just not historically right, Jerry!"

As for Marion, also present at the award ceremony—"Marion! I want you to stand up and be recognized. I love this dear woman," he declared. "[She] is probably as responsible as anybody, including me, for whatever we did. She has never been given the credit that she truly deserves. . . . We fussed a helluva lot, but she made a great contribution. And I fussed at her about lying about her version of things, and she says I've lied about [my] version. You know, Marion, two damn people getting as old as we are, are liable to tell a lot of things that might not be right on the mark. Now, Marion, I didn't mean that about you. I'm sorry! It's just me getting old. . . ."

But for all of his show of awkward self-effacement I don't think there was a single interview that he gave from that day on in which he didn't in one way or another challenge Marion's story, declaring with a belligerent authority that scarcely served his purpose that Marion didn't even know how to use the damn equipment, that he would never have entrusted the delicate disc-cutting operation to her when the cost of replacing a damaged stylus could virtually put them out of business! "I said, 'Sam, why are you calling me a liar coast to coast?'" Marion declared to me when I first met her in 1981, a refined white-haired lady who won me over with her kindness and astonished me with her candor. "He said, 'I'm not calling you a liar. I always tell everybody I couldn't have done it without you. I tell everybody to write about you.' I said, 'That's not the point.'"

"That damn thing has become the fucking Bible," Sam exploded to me one time on the subject of the Hopkins biography. Maybe, he conceded, he had made an error in not talking to Hopkins — but *Hopkins* had made an error in not totally authenticating his facts (though Sam never suggested how he might have done so without talking to Sam). It was, Sam said, like a dark cloud hanging over him.

But it was a dark cloud that was for the most part absent, and a dispute that remained largely quiescent, until the acetate resurfaced during Elvis Week in 1988. It was at this point that a TWA pilot named Ed Leek, who had met Elvis their senior year in high school, announced that it was in his possession and that it had been in his possession for more than three decades, ever since Elvis had brought it to Leek's grandmother's house so she could hear it and, despite repeated reminders, never bothered to reclaim it. The collectors magazine *Goldmine* broke the story in their mid-August issue, and it went out around the world in an AP dispatch appearing on August 16, nine years after Sam's first public confrontation with the subject.

For reasons best known — perhaps *only* known — to himself, Sam gave an interview to the *Memphis Commercial Appeal* on August 18 in which he declared that he was "99% certain" that the disc Leek had in his possession was *not* the one he had cut in his studio. He had not heard the acetate at this point, he had not even seen it — it had been presented to him only on a videotape made by NBC News with distorted audio and a view of the disc insufficient to make an authoritative judgment — but while he wanted "to make it clear that I'm not in an adversarial position with Mr. Leek, I really hope that he's found the acetate," there were some things that continued to bother him, like the fact that the label appeared to be peeling off. ("We glued [those labels] on there so tightly there was no way you could get those things off unless you sliced them with a razor blade.") More to the point, there was absolutely no way to authenticate a discovery like this without holding it in your hand, without closely examining the groove patterns of the recording and determining whether or not it had been cut on a three-hole, aluminum-based Presto blank, without actually listening to the acetate itself.

But if he thought that would be the end of it (and I think that part of Sam did, the part that believed he could control the world, and what he couldn't control wasn't worth fighting for), his challenge was met when Ed Leek showed up with the acetate in mid-October, and Marion, who had embraced its provenance from the start ("I made that record," she told *Goldmine*, "and Sam said I did not. It has been a source of great pain to me, [but] it was me, I was there"), called to see if she and Ed could come over and play the 78-rpm disc for Sam. When they arrived, Sam realized he didn't have a record player that could play 78s and he had to call Becky to bring one over. From the moment he heard the voice, he *knew*—there was never any doubt—but he remained recalcitrant. He would have to examine the acetate under a microscope, he said, he would have to make absolutely certain that there wasn't any "trip," or offset groove, which he would never have put on any of his noncommercial acetates. And when the *Memphis Commercial Appeal* called the house for confirmation after Marion declared to music reporter Ron Wynn that she was "convinced" of the record's authenticity, "Phillips, who owned Sun and discovered Presley, could not be reached for comment."

By happenstance I spoke to Marion just three weeks after the *Commercial Appeal* story came out. There was no question that she was hurt. And she made, as always, a convincing case for her version of events, pointing out discrepancies not just in Sam's memory but in her own — and in Jerry Hopkins' book as well. She warned me against trying to work with Sam ("What he wants is an amanuensis") and then, much to my amazement, said that Sam had suggested a kind of collaboration between the two of them on the story of the Memphis Recording Service and the birth of Sun Records. "We were there, and we were together — and we did these things together," she said. And yet there was no way that they could ever collaborate. Their perspectives were simply too far removed — each saw the world from an entirely different point of view. "It amazes me when he says certain things, and it amazes him apparently when I say certain things. And they [are] both true. There were many things that he did not tell me, and many things that I did not tell him. For [our] own reasons. Mine were protective. His were just self-protective, as it turned out. So there's no way we can write the book together."

Once again I must confess to being baffled. I honestly can't imagine Sam ever wanting to embark on a collaboration with Marion (in

Sally's version it was Marion who suggested it in a letter) — but neither can I imagine Marion, the soul of intellectual honesty, making it up. All I can offer by way of explanation is Marion's view of memory as a fleeting and fungible thing. "I've really become very much conscious and preoccupied with the subject of memory," she said to me one time. "How subjective it is, how protective it is. It wasn't that we didn't know that things were happening, it's just that there wasn't enough time and energy [to write it down]. So I don't know, it's sort of like, whatever I may have suggested, it's quite possibly not accurate."

Digging up the past, Marion said, was "a little bit like making love. It feels good at the time, you don't think about it while you're doing it" — but you always ran the risk of "waking up the next morning feeling bruised and hurt."

It was an argument that even Sam recognized he couldn't win. But he couldn't give it up either. He had no doubt who held the more sympathetic position. "I have probably looked like I was on the aggressive side for accolades," he grudgingly conceded, he was well aware that all his crusading for what he insisted was the truth "could easily [lead] people to get the wrong idea." But he couldn't stop.

So the battle raged on, not even brought to an end by Marion's death just one year later, at the end of December 1989. When a second Elvis acetate turned up in 1993 under even more improbable circumstances than the first, it was as if from Sam's point of view Marion was challenging him from beyond the grave. There was no rational reason for this — in fact, Marion had always attributed the recording of this acetate, in January of 1954, to Sam's exclusive supervision. (According to Marion, *she* was out of the office this time.) But Sam had no recollection of Elvis making any second "personal" record, and it conflicted with the fully imagined scenario he had constructed in which he had worked patiently with the boy for nearly a year — until in the early summer of 1954 he was ready. In a way I suppose this only goes to show how unimportant all of this was in the greater scheme of things (as Marion said without exaggeration, "It was amazing the Herculean things [we] did there"), but it didn't prevent another needless argument, this time a self-debate almost exclusively, before Sam was finally able to acknowledge, without ever fully verifying the record's authenticity, that whatever the murkiness of its origins it was an almost miraculous gift to the world.

"I just wish that the thing with Marion had not occurred," he said to me with pained sincerity one time, "because she did so damn much for me when I needed it." And after a lengthy and uncharacteristically nostalgic elucidation of all that she had done, he came as close to an apology (though to whom I'm not sure) as he was ever likely to offer. "I want you of all people to know that," he said, "because I know in your mind that probably you have thought at times that maybe I didn't want to do Marion fair or something. I know you had great respect for Marion — and you should. And she did for you, Peter," he added with a gallantry that never entirely failed him, even under the most trying circumstances, "and I'm glad we got to, you know, kind of discuss that. I was going to ultimately get around to talking it over with you."

In the end, what does it come down to? An eighteen-year-old kid walks into a recording studio, plunks his money down, and makes a record to hear the sound of his own voice. If you think of the recording device as a tape recorder, does it really make any difference who pushed the "record" button, particularly since there was never any question, in Marion's account or any other, of who recognized and nurtured the talent?

Well, evidently so. And given that it does, the reader may well inquire, what does the writer think? I was kind of hoping you wouldn't ask, but at the risk of repeating myself, and recognizing that mine is not the sympathetic view — not even to myself — I'm going to draw upon what I wrote after anguishing over the subject in *Last Train to Memphis*, the first volume of my biography of Elvis Presley. In the end I came down on the side of Sam.

Here's why.

The first detailed published account that I am aware of, Bob Johnson's *Elvis Presley Speaks!*, based on extensive reporting by the *Memphis Press-Scimitar* reporter since early 1955, was clearly Marion's version. In it she has Elvis coming in at lunchtime covered with grime from his job as a truck driver for Crown Electric (he had not, in fact, gone to work for Crown Electric at this point, a discrepancy of no real consequence, and in her first interview with Jerry Hopkins she had him "helping to install air conditioners"), with Sam out of the office and Marion taking it upon herself to record him. Sam came in "before the record session was completed. It took about fifteen minutes."

A second story by Johnson, in the September issue of *TV Star Parade* that same year, quotes Elvis as saying, "I walked into Sun Recording

Service and asked Mr. Sam Phillips if I could pay to have a record made. [After making the record] Mr. Phillips said he kind of liked my voice and took my name." (Actually, in an even earlier, less extensive account by Johnson in February 1955, "Elvis lugged his guitar into the studio one Saturday afternoon. . . . Sam listened [and] tucked the name away in his file.") Subsequent newspaper and magazine stories attributed the recording to one or the other, or simply fudged the issue with nonspecific language that could easily have indicated the presence of one or both parties.

Marion never wavered in her account, nor, once he finally gave public expression to it, did Sam in his. Each augmented their story with details that were probably not strictly available through memory. But it was Marion's vividly rendered emotional details (in one version Sam made her cry by his indifference, in another, related version Jud and Jim Bulleit were engaged in a heated argument), which varied from telling to telling but never failed to provide a bright light on the dimmest recesses of the past, that ultimately led me to believe that her view of memory as a creative function (I speak for all of us, myself included) may not have been too far from the truth. Almost always, for example, the waiting room was full of people and she got acquainted with Elvis while others were taking their turn ("While he was waiting his turn, we had a conversation I had reason to remember for many years afterwards"), but if that was the case, then who was recording the others?

Well, look, I'm not going to belabor the case any further. Obviously, in the absence of a hidden camera, no more improbable perhaps than the survival of the two acetates, there is no proof. To test Sam's contention that Marion had never recorded anyone in that studio, I tried without success to find someone she had. I spoke to numerous people familiar with the Sun operation over the years, and all agreed from what they knew of Marion and the technical operation of the lathe, that not only could she have operated it, she probably did. But none could recall ever seeing her do so. I tried to contact her son, who she said was frequently in the studio with her, but was unable to get a response from him. I even asked Marion if she could suggest someone I might talk to, if she could give me the name of someone she had recorded — which I thought could at least settle the equipment question once and for all — but although we remained in frequent contact right up until her death, she never directly addressed the question.

And so I am left with my own discomfiting conclusion. In the absence of absolute truth (a void that in my cosmogony begins with the universe), what I ultimately came to believe was that this was a dispute between two honorable people, one perhaps with more "people-pleasing" skills than the other, who simply were seeking to re-create a scene whose significance they could not possibly have recognized at the time — and then only in very different ways. The reason that I ultimately chose the scenario that I described in *Last Train to Memphis,* in which Sam cuts the disc while Marion performs the initial introduction and continues to champion "the kid with the sideburns," is that not only does it fit the "crowded room" sequence that Marion describes so vividly, it also permits each of the principals to conform to the roles that were surely theirs: Marion, as Elvis always portrayed her, was the one who offered support, encouragement, and advocacy in the ten months between his first appearance in the studio and his callback in June 1954; Sam, as Marion conceded in every word, gesture, and deed, possessed the vision that permitted that wondrously gifted boy to turn his inchoate dreams into reality. "It wouldn't have made a bit of difference [if] she had recorded him," Sam said to me in the midst of one of his attempts to wrestle the subject to the ground, "because all she would have done it for is for me to hear it. It's not of any significance — but," he couldn't help but add (he simply couldn't help himself), *"it's not true!"*

IT WAS AROUND THIS SAME TIME, in the late fall of 1988, that Sam once again waded into the quagmire of history, though this time, if anything, on an even more personal mission. The film *Great Balls of Fire!,* not the life story of Jerry Lee Lewis but the story of his rapid rise and fall as seen through the eyes of his teenage bride, Myra, started shooting in Memphis that November, with Dennis Quaid in the title role. Sam had signed off on his inclusion in the picture in 1983 without giving much thought to its content or even glancing at the book on which it would be based, but he was unquestionably delighted that it was finally scheduled to begin shooting — until he started getting pages of the script. The film had been conceived by writer-director Jim McBride as a kind of live-action Technicolor cartoon — but from Sam's point of view that wasn't the worst of it. In the script, he came off as somewhere between a hick and a crook. "Every night," said Sally, "he would mark it up and rewrite it. Finally he said, 'Where the hell did you get all this?' They said, 'Haven't you read the book?' So Sam had *me* read it. It was all from Jud!"

Here is just a little bit of what Jud had persuaded Myra's writer, Murray Silver, was the real truth behind the Sun story. Aside from his being a thief, an incompetent, and a liar, Sam's "lack of courage in his convictions," Silver wrote in the book, masking his source, "let dozens of discoveries slip away." The only thing that saved him was his big brother Jud, with his "chaplain's compassion" and "his ability to understand human nature and what lies deep in the hearts of poor country boys who come to the big city looking to make their fortune in the music business. . . . Sam was the company's president and figurehead, banker and accountant. . . . Its heart and soul and mind was pure Jud."

Sam was practically spluttering with rage when we spoke in mid November, just two weeks into shooting. I had never seen him like this before, and, to put things into perspective, I didn't really know much about Jud at this point other than his remarkable eloquence (which I had witnessed at first hand on several occasions) and his early connection to the success of Jerry Lee Lewis. "When I read the bullshit that Jud Phillips said about me in this book — which I [still] have not read — that I was the sorriest sonofabitch that ever lived, I mean, the stingiest bastard, sleeping with every whore in every [town], starving my babies, I was just a reprobate and a sonofabitch, couldn't apparently see the nose [in front of my face], had no conception of what it would take to do anything —" Sam could barely finish his sentences. It was the first time — perhaps the only time — that I ever heard him launch into an unqualified diatribe against anyone, let alone his own brother. Sam always had a good word — or at least an *understanding* word — to say about everyone. Even later, when I came to know him better and he might be reciting what he saw as his early betrayals in business at the hands of Leonard Chess or the Bihari brothers, there was always an element of empathy in his account. Not here. But it didn't last long.

With all of his belief in the power not just of positive thinking but of positive action, Sam soon found a different way to address the situation — and one that appeared to give him the kind of quixotic satisfaction that those guided exclusively by the mundane rules of profit and loss could never understand.

One of the oddest approaches that director Jim McBride had taken toward the making of the picture was to publicly forbid each of the principal actors from having any contact with their real-life counterparts—and then to invite the counterparts on the set. "In a sense, we didn't want to be confused by the facts," McBride said somewhat disingenuously. "My operating principle was to keep everybody at arm's length." The result, of course, was just the opposite, which may well have been what McBride intended all along. There grew up what McBride saw as a "nice tension" between script and real life (Jerry Lee Lewis wrote "Lies! Lies Lies" on every page of his script), with each of the actors identifying to one extent or another with his own role model—but none more so than Trey Wilson, the actor who was playing Sam.

Sam seemed to take it as a special challenge, and one to which he was far better suited than rewriting the script. He dedicated himself not just to persuading the actor of his own version of the story, the *true* version of the story, but also to persuading Wilson that he should not allow a poor script to diminish him in his craft. Sam "kind of worked on Trey," McBride said, noting that after a single meeting with Sam the actor was arguing passionately against one of the fundamental premises of the film, that due to his "lack of courage" Sam had opposed the release of Jerry Lee's "Whole Lotta Shakin'," and it was only Jud's unshakable conviction that had saved the day. "The man practically invented rock 'n' roll," protested Wilson, an accomplished actor with recent credits in *Raising Arizona* and *Bull Durham,* in an interview with the *New York Times.* "He discovered Elvis Presley. He took chances on untried people. I chose to go with what he told me. I ended up playing the scene tongue in cheek, so it looked like Sam was playing devil's advocate."

The movie never really did change, but Sam threw himself into trying to make it better—and to convincing at least one human being to break away from the herd and seek his own true, individual path. He came to thoroughly enjoy the making of the picture, if not the picture itself, and, in fact, became such good friends with the forty-year-old actor who was playing him that when Wilson died suddenly of a cerebral hemorrhage just two weeks after the Memphis shooting was done, Sam and Sally and Knox and Knox's longtime partner, Diane Duncan, who was by now a full-fledged member of the family, drove to Houston in Jerry's new van for the funeral. Sam even came to like the movie after it was released—just like with the Letterman show, he would, said Sally wonderingly, go back in the bedroom and watch it every time it ran on TV.

"LISTEN. You see me as a kind, gentle old man," Sam said, although I must admit it had never occurred to me to see him that way at any time. "Let me tell you something, I was a mean motherfucker—*in a way*. Now, I needed everybody's help, but I didn't need myself kissing anybody's ass. Or even their feet. Let me tell you something, if you get too overly acquainted with people, then they don't listen quite as well." Just make sure they heard you loud and clear, he said. "That's what I did with people [back then], and I was not very pleasant to deal with. I wasn't cocky. I was just damn sure, [not] that everything was gonna hit. I was damn sure that by God, this was what we was gonna try to do, and we weren't gonna be badgered into [anything else.]"

I guess it isn't all that necessary to say that this was when I really started to know Sam. "I'm still a weird character," Sam said on more than one occasion, as if challenging me to dispute him.

Well, I wasn't inclined to, particularly when I was being fixed with those piercing eyes. But at the same time, I think he knew I didn't *want* him to be normal—and it didn't seem all that weird to me to be weird. That was the aspiration, or the condition—in widely variant ways—of everyone I admired. Certainly as a writer it was my own quiet ambition.

It was through Sam, at least indirectly, that I got invited to Elvis' manager Colonel Tom Parker's eightieth-birthday party on June 24, 1989. In January of the previous year I had begun working in earnest on my Elvis biography when it was announced that Colonel Parker would be appearing for the first time at the annual Elvis birthday event in Memphis. Colonel Parker was almost universally seen at this point as the villain in the Elvis story, and had never shown the slightest interest in setting the record straight, so I flew down to Memphis solely for the purpose of setting eyes on him, of being in the same room with him, of at least absorbing a little bit of his "vibe," assuming that that was as close as I was ever going to get.

At Knox's invitation I was sitting at the Phillips table when all of a sudden Sam got it in his head that he should go over and say hello to "Tom Parker," as he, virtually alone among the Colonel's acquaintances, insisted on calling him, for the simple reason that he wasn't no damned Colonel. (It might be worth pointing out that the title, while purely an honorific, was a *sought* honorific, which Colonel—the familiar name without the article, by which his friends referred to him—used, much like Sam, to keep *his* distance.) Sam hadn't seen Parker to speak to in close to thirty years, but he thought it would be only polite under the circumstances to seek him out. Being the trained reporter that I was (that's intended to be ironic — nobody could have been less trained, or more self-conscious), I trailed along behind and hovered over the conversation as Sam parenthetically introduced me to Tom in characteristically generous terms. As soon as I got home, I wrote to the Colonel, saying what a pleasure it had been to meet him and trying to imprint my place in the picture as I slid in mention of the biography that I was just embarking upon. I received a letter by return mail, with "All Star Shows, Exclusive Management" embossed upon it (and "Consultation" typed in), expressing his respect for the "honesty" of my request but stipulating that "there have been so many untrue stories involving me in newspapers and books that I decided several years ago there is no need for me to defend myself, as I sleep well at night with a clear conscience, knowing I have done the right things."

A year and a half of correspondence ensued, mostly one-sided, but with each of the Colonel's letters beginning with the salutation "Friend Peter" and eventually signing off, "Your friend, Colonel" — with the words "THE COLONEL" typed below in caps. All of which eventually culminated in my invitation to his birthday celebration.

Sam was there, of course. It turned out to be the beginning of a different phase of their relationship, Sally said, based not on any greater mutuality of interests or respect but simply because at this point "it was all over, they had no reason to argue or fuss about anything. And Sam would never have brought [anything] up, and Tom never would have, so it was just a fun party." Which was certainly true in every significant respect — for Sam it simply represented a gathering of old friends and acquaintances, many of whom he had not seen in years.

For me of course it represented something much more. It placed me in the middle of a roomful of people who were key to the Elvis story, and while I never mentioned my book to any of them that night, in its aftermath I followed up with letters and calls and got more interviews with many of the central players than I could otherwise ever have imagined.

At the end of the party I went up to the Colonel to thank him for inviting me. He was sitting in a bright red armchair with a cowboy hat perched incongruously on his head and a giant ice sculpture of a trumpeting elephant placed on top of a large cake. Sam and Sally were with him as I identified myself and paid my respects. The Colonel nodded graciously. "I put you on the list," he said. "Yes," I said, thinking he must have misunderstood. "Thanks so much for inviting me." But it was I who had misunderstood. "Peter," he said again, more emphatically this time, "I put you on the list." And this time there was no doubt as to his meaning.

But that wasn't the most extraordinary moment of that meeting. For some reason I had walked into a heated debate about history, in this case specifically the selling of Elvis Presley's contract. I don't know what set it off, but my presence, far from interrupting it, seemed only to inflame the tenor of the conversation as Sam and Colonel went at it hammer and tongs, zeroing in not just on days but on hours and sometimes minutes with a ferocity of focus that showed no sign of letting up. The tone was good-natured enough, and they were enjoying themselves thoroughly, as each summoned up an almost eidetic recollection of the moment — or moments — when it all turned, each absolutely convincing in his own right but viewing events from an entirely different point of view. I had to catch a plane, and their conversation broke off anyway as other guests gathered to wish Colonel many happy returns — but I thought I would expire on the spot when Sam issued me an invitation to breakfast the next morning, when they were planning to resume their conversation, and I had to decline, a witness to history no doubt but like every other eyewitness privy to only part of the story.

My own meetings with Sam were full of their own surprises and unexpected forays into history. I went down to the recording studio with him one time for an interview he was doing with Hoss Allen, one of the legendary white WLAC DJs whose r&b show went out all across the country over the late-night airwaves. ("Ain't it a shame," one of soul singer Solomon Burke's fans said to him disbelievingly on being told that Hoss was white, "how white folks do the colored. First they took Amos and Andy away from us. Now they trying to tell us that that white man is Hoss Allen.")

Hoss, the most equanimous of enthusiasts and a 1948 graduate of Vanderbilt University, was seeking out the "pioneers" of the music for a proposed new radio series on its history. ("There are all kinds of books," he said to Sam, "but no one's ever tried to put it down on tape.") Somewhat to his embarrassment, he had a young producer with him whose plodding attempts to keep Sam on track might under other circumstances have led to Sam simply walking out, or at the very least turning more than a withering gaze on the hapless young man. But Sam seemed satisfied with Hoss' apologetic shrugs, and it was fascinating seeing him talk to someone other than myself about his life and philosophy, talk to someone who had actually shared so many of the same experiences — and at the same time, even more fascinating to realize that there was little difference in the telling. For Sam it all remained just as much a source of wonder, just as much a platform for life lessons, as he told all the familiar tales (radio days, electroshock treatment, the Dallas dust storm when Alta Hayes persuaded him to go on, Dr. George W. Truett, the Wolf, his deaf-mute Aunt Emma, who was "the smartest woman in our whole family"). Occasionally Hoss would throw in stories of his own about legendary DJs like Gene Nobles ("Gene," said Sam, "you know, Hoss, in his own peculiar way Gene was a damn genius"), cutting gospel groups ("Nobody," said Hoss, "can cut gospel shit like that unless [they] have a feel"), and the particular pleasures and challenges of working with Leonard Chess. Sam apologized for not having prepared better for what turned out to be a well over three-hour interview ("I wasn't totally aware of this format, or I would have jotted down [some] things, but I don't see a damn thing wrong with this background") — but there was not a single part of the rambling discussion that he did not direct, as much as he paid sincere and dutiful homage to Hoss. ("My son Knox spoke to me about this project, [and] right off I said, 'If Hoss Allen is connected with it' — and this is no smoke, Hoss — I said, 'honestly it will be good. At least it will be authentic.'") And when it was over, it was clear he was pleased with his performance. For he was telling his story in just the way he wanted. It was just another opportunity to get his unexpurgated, unedited, unfiltered message out to the world.

And yet as much as I believed that I was coming to know him in this respect, there were certain ways in which I knew him scarcely at all.

FLORENCE

S AM'S DAY-TO-DAY LIFE, his *present* life, focused more and more on Florence, something that he occasionally tried to tell me but that I chose to disbelieve. Florence was the place that he had left, as the world had come to understand it and I did not dissent. Florence — the Tri-Cities area of Florence, Sheffield, and Muscle Shoals — was the place where, following in the footsteps of Sam Phillips, Rick Hall, who had started out with Billy Sherrill in a homemade studio above the City Drug Store in Florence before Billy set out for Nashville, would — together and separately from the rhythm sections that he put together for his new Fame studio — create one of the touchstones of Southern soul music in the '60s, the Muscle Shoals sound. I had spent a great deal of time in the Muscle Shoals region when I was writing my book *Sweet Soul Music,* and every musician in the area proudly claimed Sam as both their inspiration and a native son. Which was as much as I felt I needed to know. But in fact Sam's real life was being lived out happily in Florence.

The two Florence radio stations had by now become the centerpiece of his radio interests. WQLT, the Album Oriented Rock FM station, had been number one in the area ever since Sam had increased its power to 100,000 watts, and with the new eight-hundred-foot tower he had built on top of Colbert Heights Mountain, it could reach an even larger constituency. He was in the process of selling WLVS and WWEE in Memphis, assigning the LVS call letters to WLIZ in Lake Worth, Florida, while acquiring a new 6,000-watt frequency in Germantown just outside Memphis and keeping an eye on another small station in Olive Branch, Mississippi. And while he had at this point transferred much of the ownership to Knox and Jerry after buying out almost all of his partners in his various broadcasting operations (Sally remained a shareholding participant), he never relinquished his interest or control, personally supervising the building and upkeep of all towers, the complete remodeling in the early 1990s of the Florence stations' headquarters, including as always interior, exterior, and plantings, and the extensive horse trading that the upgrading of power and acquisition of new transmission sites always involved.

In addition, he had a new romance.

Sleetie Mitchell (yes, that was her given name: she was named, she said, as if who could ever doubt it, for her mother's cousin Sleetie Wadell Speck, who owned half of the Cornelian Court Hotel in Decatur, where Sam and Becky had spent their honeymoon night) was a handsome middle-aged woman of considerable refinement and cultivation, as different from Sylvia as it was possible to imagine and unlike any of the "glamour gals" that Sam might have liked the world to assume were hanging on his arm. Sleetie was five years younger than Sam and had met him on a date in 1942 when she was just fourteen, a last-minute

substitute for her older sister, whose boyfriend had shown up unexpectedly on a weekend pass from the army. Her father owned the Spry Funeral Home, just around the corner from the Brown-Service Funeral Home, where Sam and Jud worked. They dated briefly in the period following Sam's father's death in January 1942 up until the time he met Becky at the radio station in the fall, and Sleetie would always remember Sam's devotion to his mother. "The first time I came to town with Sam, when my sister couldn't come, we stopped on Royal Avenue and set up there on the front porch with his mother and rocked. And he said [afterward], 'You know what? She kinda liked you.' I said, 'Well, you didn't give me — I didn't get to say much.' He said, 'Well I was just nervous. I didn't know what you'd be telling her next.'" But he hadn't been in touch with her at all until she moved back to town from Birmingham after her husband, a well-known attorney, fell ill. With her husband's death in the spring of 1988, their relationship, as Sleetie said, "just bloomed."

"Sam knew everybody in Florence, Alabama," Sally said. "He never forgot any of his growing-up life there — we would just get in the car, and he would know every house and everybody that lived there. And for a long time nothing changed.

"When we started spending a lot of time down there, I think Sam just picked up the phone and called Sleetie — like he did a lot of people down there. People that he'd known, or he would run into them and they'd say, 'Well, call me,' and some he did and some he didn't. But it was mainly the older people that he knew when he was living there that he remade contact with. I don't know how it happened, maybe he ran into Sleetie, but she was in the phone directory and her husband had died, and Sleetie's a very knowledgeable person and really knew everybody, who they married, who had died — Sam just really enjoyed Sleetie, they talked about everything and everybody.

"I was usually working at the radio station, doing something, you know, and Sam would go to Sleetie's to eat — she would cook for him, you know, but I wasn't going to go over there, I'd rather, you know, be by myself for a while, and Sleetie understood that. If I needed to talk to Sam, I would just call."

And she would pick him up at Sleetie's house the next day.

At tower site, Levee Road, Memphis. *Courtesy of the Sam Phillips Family*

HE AND SLEETIE would go everywhere together, just as he and Sally had. One time he had her drive him over to Tennessee ("I never liked for him to drive," Sleetie said, "because he didn't pay any attention to what he was doing") to see all the places he had delivered candy to—"and we found them, every one." Another time they drove out Old Chisholm Road, and he told her about the time he hid in the chifforobe—"he said he was so little he got in that chifforobe and hid himself and they put out a community search. He said, 'Then they'd finally get tired, and I'd slip out of the chifforobe and get me something to eat in the kitchen, and then they'd say "Well, there's food missing I know he's somewhere around here."' He said he finally came out and hollered, 'Boo!' and said, 'I told you I'd scare you.' I said, 'That's when I would have got me a leather belt.'"

It seemed, Sleetie said, like he told her everything that had ever happened to him—they talked about the past, he told her about the three-hundred-acre plantation that the family was living on in Oakland when the Depression hit, he showed her the hill he used to climb every day in summer to the swimming hole where he used to swim, he told her all about Aunt Emma and Kate Nelson and how well she had run her "house of ill repute." They drove over to Decatur frequently, where Sam had worked at the radio station and gotten married and had his first nervous breakdown. "We could just say anything to each other," Sleetie said, "we talked all the time about everything.

"He'd call me from Memphis and say, 'I'm heading to Florence.' I said, 'What you gonna do here?' He said, 'Well I'm gonna come and work a little bit. Get my bed ready.' Oh Lord, we had a great time."

He loved her cooking. ("He tried to be bossy, [but] I didn't pay any attention to him; he'd eat everything I'd give him.") And he adored her children. Sally was never anything less than civil to her. She never met Becky, but she was certainly well aware of her. And she traveled to Memphis frequently, often with one or two purposes of her own. Sam would always arrange for her to stay at Wilson World, Kemmons Wilson's latest venture in affordable hostelry since retiring from an active role in Holiday Inn after a heart attack in 1979—she was well aware of how close Sam was to Kemmons and she really enjoyed Kemmons' warmth and sense of humor. One time she even managed to persuade Sam to attend the Catherine the Great "Wonders" Exhibit, a massive showing of rare art and artifacts never before seen outside the Soviet Union

With Sleetie Mitchell at Big River Broadcasting, Florence.
Courtesy of the Sam Phillips Family

put on by the Memphis International Cultural Exchange program at
the Cook Convention Center. Sam grumbled about going, but then they
ran into an old Florentine couple who were living in Atlanta, and they
reminisced for hours.

One of the things that was most on Sam's mind these days was the
purchase and restoration of his boyhood home on North Royal. This was
an idea that had first occurred to him at least ten years earlier, when he
had had the general manager of his radio stations, Bill Thomas, make
inquiries, and Thomas had come back with an asking price of $18,000 —
which to Sam was outrageous. He'd be damned, he told Thomas, if he'd
allow himself to be held up like that. He continued to pursue the matter
over the years — neither the price nor his opinion changed — but it had
become by now, Sleetie said, a real obsession.

"There was a lot of land involved that Sam really didn't know about
until I researched it for him," Sleetie said. "Sam wanted to have the
little house behind it for a museum and a coffee shop. He said, 'They
can come tour my house, walk right through that alley and go up there,'
and he wanted to have a gift shop and a little luncheon thing [with]

takeout foods and all that. Sam and I went all over—you should have seen the places we went to find the things he wanted to refurnish that house with—he wanted a table just like his mama had, and he wanted the house fixed just like [it was]. In fact I got some wicker downstairs I bought to give him." Sleetie even found someone to do an artist's rendering of the house. "Now what was that little girl's name that did the oil paintings? She sat across the street, and I gave Sam one the first Christmas that he was here. He sat in that little den in there and just cried."

It was during this period that Mary Alice Lanier, his eighth-grade teacher, wrote to him. During his darkest days, just before he went into the hospital in the spring of 1951, he had gone to see her at her mother's house in Florence, but she had long since moved away. Now, thirty-five years later, Mrs. Lanier picked up the correspondence after missing a call he had made at her brother's instigation to congratulate her on her fiftieth anniversary. They had had no other contact over the years, but she wrote about the young man that she recalled so well, recounting a story that she had "repeated rather frequently" to friends and family.

I taught you two subjects—English and what was then called Social Studies. In the latter class we studied the Preamble of the Constitution. Then later in the English class we were studying the comparison of adjectives and adverbs. When speaking of the adjectives, I said that some adjectives could not be compared because of their meaning, and as an example I used the word perfect, saying that if something were perfect it could not be more perfect or most perfect. At this moment, your hand shot up and you said, "But Mrs. Lanier, what about "a more perfect union"? I'm sure there must have been a great big pause. But how gratifying to know that you had listened and that you could think. The end of the story is that I think I must have said that I simply could not explain that. At any rate I went home to my family, and we had a most interesting discussion at the dinner table. I called an outstanding lawyer in the town that night and asked him. I don't recall what he said except that he rejoiced with me at having such an alert student.

She was glad, she concluded, "to have the opportunity to put this story down in writing so that your children can learn about it."

Sam was simply delighted to receive the letter and told Sleetie all about Mrs. Lanier. He had had every intention of replying, he told me many years later, but he misplaced the letter and was never able to come up with it again. "You know, I forgive myself for just about everything that I have done wrong," he declared with a typical mix of grandiloquence and sincerity. "And they are so numerous that I forget most of them. But I didn't answer that letter, and that's one I'll never forgive myself for."

It was as if he were searching for something he couldn't quite put his finger on. "What I would give," he said one time to Davia Nelson and Nikki Silva, National Public Radio's Kitchen Sisters, "to look back in the mirror of my father's era. In the real perspective of just people, all the things that they were confronted with, [like] you had a lame mule that morning and you were going to plow all day in order to make crops. . . . I mean, history is a concept. There is not one single thing more important to the future than looking back."

He never did get the house. For all of Sally's and Sleetie's efforts, and the endeavors of Sleetie's son Dewey, the probate judge of Lauderdale County, the price kept rising even as his bids continued to rise (eventually he would offer $100,000, but by then the owners wanted $150,000) — and Sally thought it was probably better this way in the end.

It was through Sleetie's granddaughter Betsy that he got to know Terry Pace, a young reporter at the *TimesDaily* in Florence and the kind of cultural omnivore that every small town ought to have. Betsy, a sophomore at Coffee High School, was a dedicated member of Terry's theater group, and they were working on a production of *A Man for All Seasons*, when Betsy one day volunteered, "You ought to meet my grandmother. She dates Sam Phillips."

All of a sudden, Terry said, a lightbulb went off in his head. He had actually *met* Sam Phillips in passing three or four years earlier, when, as a brand-new, twenty-three-year-old graduate of the University of North Alabama, he had gone to work as news and program director at radio station WVNA ("the Voice of North Alabama"). Sam had had some business with the station owner, Maudie Darby, and knowing how much Terry admired Sam, Maudie had introduced him. They had met once or twice since then, but it was only when the connection with Sleetie was made that he really got to know Sam.

Sam was in town all the time, working on the transmitter, and there were any number of occasions to get together. Sometimes Sam would call from the Holiday Inn, or Terry might initiate the call, and Sally would tell him, "Oh, he's spending the night with Miz Mitchell tonight." Just as often Sam would telephone from Sleetie's at close to midnight to invite him over, and they would be up all night talking, with Sam more thoroughly at home and at ease than Terry could ever have imagined of someone who had played such a mythic role in his imagination. "Of course he was fairly well lubricated by the time I got there."

They talked about anything and everything. Radio, the tough times that the region was undergoing with industry dying and bright young people leaving, Terry's work at the newspaper — or maybe just the redesign that Sam was planning for the control rooms at the station. They would always talk about music. "A lot of things that we spent time talking about were things that sound mundane. I have friends who are close to people in movies or music, and they say, 'We've been friends so long we don't even talk about movies and music anymore.'" He and Sam never got to that point. Sam would always patiently answer his questions about how he had done certain things, and why, and he never hesitated to express his opinions either (he was vehement in his view that Garth Brooks represented the ruination of country music). "Sometimes, though, he would just call me and say, 'Come over and look at the landscaping I'm doing at the radio station.' If he was doing something that required his mental attention, he would just operate on all cylinders. And that landscaping was as important to him [at that moment] as cutting 'Great Balls of Fire'!"

To Terry it never felt like there was any great age difference between them, or that Sam ever treated him as anything but an equal. He was a good listener and a good sounding board, picking up on when Terry was having problems at work and occasionally offering advice ("in a good-friend, brotherly sort of way") but never intruding. He would compliment Terry on stories he had written, often penning letters that expressed his gratitude for coverage that highlighted not just his own achievements but the musical history of the area.

He clearly liked Terry (this is something to which I can unequivocally attest), and he liked his friends, in particular all the pretty girls that Terry seemed to attract through his various theatrical and musical endeavors. He wouldn't let any of them call him "Mr. Phillips" — he was "Sam" to one and all, and he would practically "throw a fit," Terry said, if anyone addressed him otherwise. Sometimes when they dropped him

Sam in his element, in Florence, ca. 1997, with (left to right) Molly McCanless, Alice Ann Bonfield, and Terry's girlfriend Beth. *Photograph by Terry Pace*

off at the motel, they might accompany him to his room, just to make sure he was all right, and he was not unknown to simply fling open the door and announce without preamble, "Wake up, Sally, Terry and so-and-so are here." Leaving Sally to fend for herself and make them welcome. Which she always did, without complaint.

Sam not surprisingly had decided thoughts about all kinds of things. One time Terry shaved off his beard, "and it distressed him no end. I had just gotten tired of it, and Sam said, 'I want to tell you a lesson I learned with my own face.' He said, 'You've got a very handsome face, but you need something to frame it just like I [do]. So it doesn't look like you've got too thick a neck or too small a chin. Because the rest of your face speaks for itself. And let it speak for itself. But you need that frame down there to frame that beautiful face that you've got.' And he just sounded so philosophical and so thoughtful about it. And my girlfriend agreed!"

Sam was crazy about Terry's girlfriend ("He absolutely worshiped her, and she worshiped him"), and when they broke up he was almost as heartbroken as Terry was. "I'll never forget. We were at Sleetie's two nights after we broke up, and he said, 'What exactly was the problem,

Terry?' and I sort of told him—the age difference (there was about fifteen years' difference in our ages), and she's in college, and she's getting restless and she's probably going to be moving on—and then he looked at me, we're sitting there and it's 2:30 in the morning and I've got tears in my eyes, and he says 'What's her phone number?' Had I given it to him, he would have called her right then. I said, 'No, Sam, that would probably not be a good idea.' And I remember, he told me that night, 'All you want to do is say, in the immortal words of Charlie Rich, "After you get rid of me, who will the next fool be."' And I said, 'Exactly, Sam.'"

"Sam was just so involved with that radio station," Terry said. "He really had his finger on the pulse of everything going on radio-wise." But it was clearly something much more than that. To Terry, who would over the next ten years spend a good deal of time with Sam in Memphis as well, there was just something different about Sam in his hometown. "I think he felt a deep inner need to reconnect. It was something that was sacred to him, and in a way private." There had been times in the early days, Sam acknowledged, when he was so busy he had been absent from the region for long periods and failed to stay in touch the way he knew he should. Now, it seemed like he was almost desperate to make up for lost time.

S AM WAS THERE for every member of the family, he always had been in times of crisis, said his nephew Phillip Darby, more like a brother than a nephew with less than five years between them, but it was different now. He was the first one that all of his older brothers and sisters would turn to, and he was the one who would always come through, whether with money or advice. Phillip, a special favorite of his Uncle Jud's, was not an altogether uncritical observer—he felt that Sam did not give Jud the credit he deserved, and, while never less than admiring, he was not prepared to approve wholeheartedly of every aspect of Sam's eccentric lifestyle. But at the same time, Phillip, a hard worker all his life, could not fail to recognize how hard Sam himself had always worked—and still did. Sam just seemed to have a knack for knowing how to do things, said Phillip, a successful contractor who, like his uncles Horace and Turner, had an aptitude for all things mechanical, without your ever being able to figure out how he could have acquired all that knowledge and insight. "That's the funny thing about it. He didn't have any formal training, he just went in there and did [it]." At Sam's invitation Phillip and his wife, Hilda, went up on Colbert Mountain to watch them put up the new tower. "And those people that build towers are another breed of people," Phillip said. But there was Uncle Sam in a yellow hard hat directing the action every step of the way.

He delighted in the Phillips Family Reunions. He was unstinting in the praise (and sometimes scarcely veiled envy) he showered on his brothers and sisters. But however much he may have idealized them, and the world in which they continued to live, there is always something in Sam's pictured visage, whether jovial or unsmiling, that conveys a distance, an inescapable reserve, that he can never fully overcome. You sense that even if he had never left North Florence, he would still have been the one that got away.

Becky always attended the reunions not just as Sam's wife but as a Sheffield native whose family owned the local bus company, whose cousin Lucille was married to Sam's brother Tom. For years Sally would stay back at the hotel, a silent, unacknowledged presence known to all. When she did attend public events, her role was assigned such commonly understood terms as secretary, assistant, or in perhaps Sam's most extravagant designation, for a 1984 Northwest Alabama Press Association roast at the Holiday Inn in Sheffield, "secretary and compatriot extraordinaire since 1955."

"Sam relied on her tremendously," said one of the relatives. "I'll have to say that she was dedicated to him. But I always have to ask the question: was she ever a happy person, really? You wonder. When you're in love with somebody like Sam — and yet she couldn't get him ultimately. He demanded so much from them both [Sally and Becky]. If it was a daytime soap opera, it would be a good one, wouldn't it?"

There was never, it was duly noted by all, any talk of divorce, though many clearly felt there should have been — if only to restore some measure of dignity to Becky. For Becky, though, it would have been unthinkable. She was determined to preserve her marriage, and her family, in whatever manner she could. She never really held anything against Sally; in fact, the two became close friends in the manner of two business associates working in different roles toward the same end. "Sally's my friend," she told me one time, not long after Sam died. "I don't hold anything against Sally. I don't hold anything against Sam. And I understand it myself. Other people don't understand. They say, How could you let a girlfriend — I mean, that's what she was — take your place? But Sam just

Becky and Sally. *Courtesy of the Sam Phillips Family*

required a lot of love, and I couldn't have given him what he needed. So I just let it be that way."

She told the world that Sally was her friend, she explained how wonderful Sally had been to the family, she fell back on her religious faith. And yet there was a part of her that felt she had utterly failed, that her faith had failed her in leaving her prey to the anxiety with which she was increasingly beset — even worse, that she had failed her faith.

She tried in different ways to tell Sam how much he still meant to her. She wrote a portrait of Sam called "Gentle But Tough" (all her life Becky had been writing autobiographical sketches and family portraits, and Sam and their son Knox always said that her meticulous radio scripts were the backbone of the shows that made her one of the best announcers in the business). "Sensitive but with a lot of nerve," it began. "Never afraid of anything new. Never afraid of change. Believes it is never too late for change or improvement. Willing to forgive, but you're not sure if he ever forgets. He wasn't afraid of telling the truth, even if it hurt and sometimes it did, especially in his personal life. His book was open. If you didn't like what was there you had to deal with it." Which, as Becky concluded, was no more than what a man of his stature had the right to expect. "He is a great man, a fair man," she wrote. "He has influenced so many, beginning with the ones who love him most and reaching around the globe. His magnitude seems to be ever growing."

It is a beautiful, beautifully measured and painfully nuanced love poem — but Sam didn't like it, Sally told her, though she never explained exactly why. Maybe it was too flowery, too sentimental, Becky thought. But she tried again on their fiftieth anniversary, December 13, 1993.

"Dearest Sam," she wrote. "Fifty years ago I gave my heart to the man of my dreams. I knew the very moment I saw you, that rainy day in September, that you were the one I would love for the rest of my life. It was truly amazing. Something I was totally sure of without even thinking about it. It was seriously real . . . as I looked at you that first day with the wind and the rain in your hair."

She recalled "indescribable happiness in the beginning. A happiness so excitingly wonderful it made me feel guilty that I could be so happy while others I loved had missed the splendor I found.

> *The years ahead were not always as I imagined, but the times of joy always held together the shattered times. The love has always been there, changing from one of youth and ideals to one of acceptance, respect, understanding, forgiveness and encouragement. Our lives were filled with successes (mostly yours) and failures (mostly mine) suspended in balance. . . .*
>
> *So now we have reached the Gold — not living dreams but good feelings of knowing we will always be there for each other.*
>
> *Sam, you have brought me great fulfillment, you have been an inspiration to our sons and have won the admiration of people around the world. You have made a legacy for your sons and granddaughters that they will forever be proud of. . . . Now, as in my youth, I say it simply as the song proclaimed so beautifully.*
>
> *"There Will Never Be Another You."*

And she signed the letter "With Love Eternal."

Sally could have written much the same letter, allowing for differences of temperament and self-expression. So could Marion, if she had been so disposed. It would be easy to dismiss this, I suppose, as a sad attempt at self-deception, easier still to simply judge Sam in the harsh terms that his brothers and sisters sometimes felt that he deserved, easiest of all to see any attempt to understand the situation, and the complicated needs that gave rise to it, as nothing more than the excuse-making rationalizations of a besotted biographer. But knowing Sam, and Becky, and Sally, and Marion as I do, I have no easy answers. I guess in the end I prefer to see Becky's letter as a heartbreakingly vulnerable reminder of the spirit we all call on — in different ways, and with varying degrees of success — to survive the life of pain we all inevitably lead (in equally different ways, with wildly varying degrees of success).

And as for Sam — I think of the young boy who was not expected to survive childhood, I think of the young man so devastated by depression his doctors thought he would never be able to lead a normal life — he, too, assumed a carapace (Please don't take this as an excuse. You may well not agree, but to my way of thinking we all have carapaces), and like the rest of us, he did the best he could.

H E WAS INCREASINGLY PREOCCUPIED with growing old. At sixty-five he had set aside his kingdom, at least formally, by resigning from the boards of all his corporations and marching down to the Social Security office, where he was outraged to have his benefits claim challenged by a clerk who questioned both his retirement and his need. Didn't she remember Roosevelt? he raged. That money was a promise, goddamnit. "I remember President Roosevelt saying, 'You're going to thank me for this,' when he started Social Security," he told the poor woman, who had a sign up over her desk saying, "With God's help I can do anything I want to do today." He told her, "That nickel or dime that he took out of my paycheck every week *mattered,* it depended a lot on how Mama and me ate that week." He had to go back three times — but he got his benefits in the end.

At the same time, he hardly welcomed age. He saw the whole matter of keeping up his appearance (faithfully dyeing his hair and beard, maintaining his weight) as being as much of an obligation as a vanity. I can't count the number of times I saw him rag Knox, sometimes playfully, more often with unfeigned irritation, at Knox's occasional failure to maintain his own youthful appearance. "Do you want to see an old gray-haired man in the mirror?" he railed at Knox if Knox let so much as a hint of gray creep into his own blond beard. "He was very particular about his hair," said Sally. "It always had to be cut just right and parted just right. He loved to wear clothes that gave him a younger look, always. Anything that looked like an old man he wasn't going to wear it. He would tell you, 'Oh, that looks like an old man'— a shirt or a jacket or a coat. 'Old men wear that.' And he never considered himself an old man."

But it came at a cost, as he himself seemed to recognize. The doctor that he now went to was Dr. Robert Kraus, the son of his old physician, Dr. Bernard, the failed owner of the Memphis Blues baseball team, who had died of heartbreak (both kinds) at the age of fifty-nine in November of 1978. It took Sam over a year to come to his son, who had finished his training and gone into his father's old practice just after his father's death. When Sam finally showed up at young Dr. Kraus' office, he brought with him all his concerns about mortality, which were increasingly at the fore.

Dr. Kraus, barely thirty at the time, had never known anyone even remotely like Sam. Although they had met at his father's funeral ("He came up to me and said, 'There never will be another man like your dad'"), he had no real sense of Sam until their first appointment, which stretched over the course of nearly two hours, knocking out the next two or three spots. That, Kraus swiftly learned, was just the way it was going to be. "You could take a history from Sam, but Sam's always going to give you an additional history that you're not prepared for, both medical and extra medical. And his fund of knowledge, particularly as it related to medicine, was extraordinary."

Not only that, Sam was always going to give him advice.

"At first I thought it was because he loved my dad so much, I thought [he was thinking], 'Dr. Bernard was the greatest, and I've got to help this young doctor, because his dad's gone and I'm going to try to help him.' After a while, though, [I realized] he did it with just about everybody. He knew a lot of things and he would interject himself into your business, into everything you did."

Once he felt comfortable with his new doctor, he talked about his own problems. "Sam had his own ideas [about] the etiology of illness. I don't know where he got his information — he was like that with a lot of things — but most of the time he wasn't far off." His health, Dr. Kraus said, was generally good all through the '80s, but he had certain concerns that bordered almost on fixation. "He was concerned about HIV. When it first came out, he was concerned that he had [it], and that went on for a while. He was concerned about lung cancer, he was concerned about prostate cancer — it almost bordered on a phobia of cancer. And catastrophic illness. And I think it was because any of these things would automatically take him out of control. He went beyond what most people would do when they fear these catastrophic illnesses. He would investigate them to the nth degree when there really wasn't a lot of reason to do so. You know, I did a colonoscopy, and [there was] a little tiny polyp, and I said, 'We better take another look in six months.' [But Sam's reaction was] 'You know, I better do another one. And then maybe another one. And perhaps the next one I do, I ought to go somewhere else and do it.'"

It was his preoccupation with anxiety and depression, however, that gave Dr. Kraus a new appreciation of Sam. He was aware to some extent of Sam's history, but not the degree or seriousness of it. His father, who had drinking problems of his own, had talked to Sam about his alcohol intake when Sam first came to him in 1973, but he had put nothing in his notes to indicate any real cause for worry, and his son had never seen anything over the years to suggest that there was a deep-seated problem. His father had prescribed Valium for Sam to deal with normal anxiety, and Dr. Kraus continued the prescription, along with Librium, which was a common course of treatment at the time. In the back of his mind was the lingering thought that you might have with any celebrity, that with the number of physicians Sam had come to know over the years, and the power of his own persuasiveness, if Sam got it into his head that he wanted a certain kind of palliative, or that he needed a larger supply of a certain type of medication, it would not be difficult for him to obtain it. Dr. Kraus had never seen any evidence that Sam had done anything of this sort, but that was probably why he was a little uneasy when Sam came to him about a new antidepressant drug that had just come on the market and insisted that it would give him exactly the kind of alleviation that he needed.

"Prozac was the first of the chemicals that we call SSRIs, selective serotonin reuptake inhibitors. Sam just walked in one day and said that he'd been under a lot of stress, and he wanted me to give him Prozac. I said, 'Sam, I don't even know what that is. I've never heard of it.' And he said, 'What! You've never heard of Prozac?' I said, 'No, I'm sorry—'" At which point Sam sat down and delivered a lecture, like "he was the CEO of the pharmaceutical company that made it—he presented all the studies that had been done and the results of the studies up to that point." And when Dr. Kraus still expressed reservations about prescribing a drug that he didn't really know enough about, Sam said, "Well, what the hell else do you need to know? I just told you everything about it."

In the end Dr. Kraus capitulated by writing a month's trial prescription, meanwhile reading up on everything he could find about Prozac and discovering that nothing he found added to what Sam had told him. It worked almost from the moment Sam started taking it, Sally said. "Sam thought it was the greatest medicine that ever came along." He had read about it in the medical journals and hospital printouts he subscribed to ("He studied anxiety attacks and read all these medical books in the library and was taking papers from all these institutions like the Mayo Clinic, he was taking five or six or them") and explained it all to her, the complex chemical interreactions, and why Prozac should be of particular benefit to him. But as miraculous as the effect of the drug, from Sally's point of view, was Sam's ability to absorb and comprehend, much less seek out, the answers to questions that didn't even seem to occur to anyone else she knew.

I think that's unquestionably true. It was the wanderings and divagations of Sam's restless, inquiring mind, far beyond the range of what anyone would consider his nominal interests and expertise, that kept him engaged all his life, that led him to the unorthodox conclusions that had spurred him from childhood on. But it was, even more, his ability to confront his own weaknesses and vulnerabilities — not only his refusal to deny them but his insistence on *proclaiming* them — that gave him a different vantage point from which to fathom the needs of others. He never spoke of his own deep-seated insecurities to his recording artists so far as I know, but from my experience I would guess that they could intuit it. Whether it was Howlin' Wolf or Elvis Presley or Charlie Rich, they could sense an empathetic presence, an underlying uncertainty that gave credibility to the cocky bantamweight assurance that he projected to the world at large. It was the one quality that could continue to win over his own son Jerry, with whom he would never cease to have his share of knock-down, drag-out fights, that same unexpected incursion of egolessness with which he could always soothe a troubled soul in what Jerry termed a *believable* way.

M Y OWN INTERVIEWS WITH SAM in the early 1990s were by now following their own predictably unpredictable course. I was fully engaged in the research for my Elvis biography at this point, and our meetings had become increasingly frequent and, in their own way, more intimate.

Knox was always the starting point. Knox was the person who set up the meetings. Knox was always present and sometimes even taped the interviews for their own records. More important (*most* important), Knox was always my champion, just as he had been from the very first — and sometimes to his own detriment. Not because Sam necessarily mistrusted me, or even the process — more than anything, because Sam inevitably needed to declare his independence, and in this case Knox provided the most convenient target, it was Knox who, by choice and by definition, was always on the firing line.

It didn't matter what the issue was, Sam was always going to disagree to begin with, then almost invariably back off in a quasi-embarrassed, loving, and *fatherly* way. It could simply be a matter of interpretation — Knox attempting to explain what Sam had just said. "Now, that's just not right, Knox," Sam might flare up. Or he would object, ostensibly on my behalf, "Aww, Peter knows that," to brush aside Knox's well-meaning translation of something that might, possibly, be misunderstood. "Hey, Knox, shut the fuck up!" he would say occasionally, and then flash his son a grin intended to show that he didn't really mean anything by it. Sometimes it was comical, sometimes it was painful, but it was something that everyone (with the possible exception of Sam) knew had to be got past so that we could get to the heart of the matter. Which was: History. Philosophy. Setting the record straight. To Knox there was no story and no mission that could be more important. As Sam emphasized again and again, as often in Knox's presence as not: "Knox is my best buddy. Well, I mean, Jerry is, too. But Knox is a guy who began to observe what I was doing very early on, when he was just eight or ten years old — he got into my head a long time ago. I don't know what I would do without Knox. I'll tell you, he has taken a lot of crap off of me."

Every interview started out the same. Every one began with a lengthy preamble, reestablishing philosophical context, tone, and, I suppose, control (the longer ones were well over an hour). We positioned ourselves comfortably on facing sofas on either side of the stone fireplace in the den, Sam always with a drink at his side. There was never any hurry, there was never any set agenda — though contrary to what one might think, Sam always carefully prepared for interviews not in the conventional sense of checking facts (for the facts were nearly always present in his mind with great specificity, and when they weren't, he simply said, "I'm not sure about that. I don't know") but, rather, with the aim of putting himself in the proper frame of reference, so that he was focused entirely on time and place and emotional state of mind. He took this retrieval process very seriously (when Sam did something, as should be evident by now, he really *gave himself over to it*), but at the same time, the atmosphere was relaxed, the drinks were never going to run out, nor was Sam's mood (passionate, engaged, but equable) going to change until finally, after four or five hours, he announced that either he or the subject was exhausted for that day.

It was an astonishing experience. This was for me living, breathing history—I don't mean so much the familiar stories of Elvis or Howlin' Wolf or Jerry Lee Lewis (though there were frequently surprises there, too) as the atmosphere that Sam summoned up and the descriptions that he offered of where it all came from, Sam's ice cream-cone route for the Corner Drug Store or the inspiration provided by Armstead Methodist Chapel or his struggles to establish the studio and the Sun label. *How the weather was.*

Sometimes there was real poetry, as Sam would practically sing his sentences with a soft stammer, and their periodic construction (which didn't *always* reach its intended goal) achieved an eloquence befitting any of the great orators, sacred or secular, that Sam so admired. I can't fully describe the thrill of hearing Sam call up "the elements of the soil, the sky, the water, even the wind, the quiet nights, people living on plantations, never out of debt, hoping to eat—'Lights Up the River,' that's what they used to call Memphis. 'Lights Up the River. One of these days I'll get to go there.' That was Memphis." Or his description of the perilous path he had chosen for his quest, "the flip-log" bridges that he had to cross, "sometimes it seemed like you could just see the grease on them—and to know how swift that current was, and how easy it was to fail, and not just fail, but to have a dream, an idea, and [then] to see this unexplored territory locked out." There were so many passionate moments like these—and I don't mean that they were unique to *my* interviews, anyone getting into a conversation with Sam might have been the equally fortunate recipient. But with all the intricacy of narrative and detail, I felt sometimes as if I had been caught up in a torrent of eloquence and insight, balanced by an earthiness that retained the capacity to shock, to a degree that I had never before encountered in my life.

It was, undeniably, a complicated relationship. Sometimes Sam flattered me shamelessly. Not infrequently he gave me advice ("What he quotes to you, kind of brush it a little bit, but don't take it as being a lie," he said of someone we both liked, whereas, he told me, I should always regard Elvis' guitarist, Scotty Moore, as a "completely honest person," even if what he said directly contradicted Sam's memory of events). His sense of himself, perhaps encouraged by vodka, was sometimes little short of grandiose (let's just call it "grandiose"), and here I simply took Sam's otherwise directed advice and brushed it aside. Once in a while, after we had gotten to know each other a little better, Sam incorporated me into the narrative, calling upon a common bond to explain himself in a way that was both seductive and genuinely empathetic. "It's a feel at the touch end of your fingers," he said one time, trying to explain the truth that he was seeking in the studio. "It's the feel that you see mentally — and it's *everything*. It's just like I would imagine as a writer you set down — and you *know* when you've said something." And his hand slapped down on the table. "I believe you know that, don't you?"

"And it's all feel," I said.

"That's right. I mean, I really feel that way. I don't think we're anything. We're nothing. I don't give a damn. It has nothing to do with religion — but we're all spirit."

How could I help but agree?

In the end, Sam constantly challenged me, whether out of canniness or conviction, or most likely both, to dare to tell the truth. The problem, of course, would always be whose truth? But it was a problem that Sam, in his own way, was perfectly willing to acknowledge. "It's up to you, goddamnit," he would say. "Knowing as much as you know, and as much as you care about the thing we are talking about, Peter — which is the music — you better know what is truth, and what ain't." Anyone, Sam said, could keep a calendar. The trick was to discover the "aspectable" qualities of people. After listening to all these voices, it had better be *my* feeling, *my* truth, *my* "interpolation of this swinging thing at the fair." The bottom line, goddamnit, was, "getting it right for history's sake."

Always his own book lurked in the background. It had been there from the time I first met Sam, it was there in the memo that Knox wrote to Sam, which, unbeknownst to me, set up our initial series of interviews. ("I personally believe that a work like [Peter's proposed Elvis biography] would in no way impinge on Sam's own. . . . The facts are out there now, but the intimacy of what a Sam book would be makes it totally different in my mind.") And it came up again and again in the interviews themselves, most frequently in Sam's good-natured signal that our time was at an end: "I done gave away my book." What his book would be, *whether* it would ever be, was another matter altogether. I think Sam envisioned it as the perfect embodiment of the imperfect order of his life, a kind of stream-of-consciousness masterpiece (I don't know that he would have used that term) that would evoke a life in all the random ways that it is lived. "Looking at all the aspects [with] just one eye, the other eye, how you turn your head, how you feel, how the sun goes down to you."

I volunteered to help in any way I could, and I meant it—but the opportunity never arose.

"You know, Knox always loved you, but I didn't," Sam said to me one time, as if to challenge any sense of entitlement that I might be starting to feel, even as he was declaring, "I'm giving you things, Peter, that I wouldn't give anybody [else], that I want in my book someday." It had taken him all this time, he said, not necessarily because of any holdback on his part but because he sensed a holdback on mine. (I didn't bother to disabuse him.) "I mean, I read folks, I have almost all my life, and it took Peter a while—[but] I kind of like the skepticism, the good, honest person that likes to elicit the word from you and then put it down like it is." I nodded mutely. Knox gave me an encouraging look. And once again we picked up Sam's interior monologue. "Do you know where my mind goes?" he said with something very much akin to pride. "I don't." Which I took as just one more sign of his unqualified belief in what Jack Kerouac called "spontaneous bop prosody" and Sam (and I, too, in my own writerly way) assigned to the realm of "spirit feel."

I N THE MIDST OF ALL THIS I tried to get Sam to go back in the studio again. This had to do with Charlie Rich, with whom I had continued to maintain a close friendship ever since we first met in 1970. I had heard him sing the achingly intimate Cindy Walker composition "You Don't Know Me" when Charlie received the third Memphis Music Award in 1981 (more properly, the Memphis State University Award for Distinguished Achievement in the Creative and Performing Arts), where as it happened I first met Marion Keisker. Then Charlie played me tapes of some of his rehearsal sessions with a shifting jazz rhythm section that incorporated some of Memphis' finest jazz and r&b musicians, and I put

588 | How Lucky Can One Man Get

together a rough demo tape with the live version of "You Don't Know Me," which seemed so perfectly to mirror Charlie's mood, along with a number of raw rehearsal tapes incorporating everything from standards like "I Can't Get Started" to surrealistic improvisations that may have had something to do with the atmosphere in the studio. After six or seven years of shopping the idea, I was finally able to place the projected album with my friend Joe McEwen, whom I had met originally through our shared love of the music. (Joe had introduced himself to me at a Lightnin' Hopkins concert some twenty years earlier by coming up and asking, "Did you really mean what you wrote about Solomon Burke in *Rolling Stone*" — and when I said I did, just nodded his head, said "Cool!" and disappeared up the stairs.) He was at this point vice president of Sire Records and had worked out a deal where he could make one album a year of his own choosing with a budget of $75,000 and no need, or expectation, of making any money on it. Charlie Rich would be the first album.

I talked to Sam about it. I talked to Charlie about it. Each seemed intrigued by the idea of working with the other after all these years — but each was wary, too. I couldn't pinpoint the cause of their wariness at first, though gradually I came to realize it clearly had to do with business. (Some of the reasons may very well have become apparent in earlier pages of this book.) When I first brought the subject up to Sam, he seemed almost to be simultaneously trying to talk himself into it and talk himself out of it. "I'm such an admirer of Charlie Rich," he began. "He's got so much inside of him. See, Charlie's a master musician — he was born with the damn piano in his hands. If you get him in and get him a little bit out of his shell — and I can do that with Charlie. There is nobody that I'd [want to] go back in the studio and play around a little bit with but Charlie Rich. I would enjoy that. That would be the type of thing that you do just for fun."

It didn't happen. Maybe it was all for the best, and there could well have been any number of compelling reasons for Sam's reluctance. Memphis musician and iconoclast-about-town Jim Dickinson always posited that the reason Sam never went back in the studio was that you can't just be an occasional genius, and even provided a quote from Sam to vividly underscore the point. "You can't just go up to Picasso and ask him to paint one little picture," Sam was said to have stated to Knox about a proposed B.B. King session of which Knox has no memory — but

Sam, B.B. King, Charlie Rich, and Jerry Lee Lewis, at the fourth annual
Memphis State University Creative and Performing Arts Award, August 16,
1982 (the three previous recipients are there to congratulate the latest, B.B.
King). *Courtesy of Preservation and Special Collections, University Libraries,
University of Memphis*

even if the opportunity never arose and Sam never made the statement,
it's something that could very well represent his position.

He did offer advice, though, on all sorts of things: how important
it was not just to get Charlie's confidence but to get Charlie *confident;*
about setting the right mood in the studio; about the material itself.
"Sure, let him do his jazz thing," Sam said, "I don't blame him," but
make sure you get him back on the blues. Be sure to watch out, too, for
Charlie's tendency to get down on himself. "Charlie Rich is not going to
lead you astray in anything he does. He has eyes all around his head, and
by that I don't mean that he uses that to criticize anybody but himself.
But he can berate himself a little bit every now and then. Sometimes
tongue in cheek, and sometimes not that lightly."

Perhaps his most intriguing piece of advice would always remain a
little inscrutable to me. "He's going to come in and he's going to whistle
a little bit. I mean, you can be talking around him, and you think maybe

he's not hearing or paying attention, and he will do these things to make sure you don't think he's temperamental or is going to make it difficult on the people who are trying to help him cut a record." Charlie, Sam said, was really a very brilliant person, but he never wanted to let on if something was bothering him — the whistle, I gathered, was the tip-off. At least that's what I *think* Sam meant. But Sam also said, "If you wait for it, it'll all come together."

It all went pretty much the way Sam said it would. Charlie even whistled on one or two occasions. The album was recorded at Phillips Recording, which had recently been refurbished and outfitted with a new analog console, and Sun's original session guitarist Roland Janes, who now managed the studio, was house engineer and, along with Knox and Jerry, Charlie's principal source of familiarity and reassurance. I got another friend of mine, Scott Billington, whom I had met around the same time that I met Joe, also through the blues, to produce the album, and I don't think I've ever felt a greater degree of spirituality in the studio, in the "spirit-feel" sense. When the album came out, I sent a copy to Sam, and he called me. . . .

Well, let me just interpolate a digression here, before I get to Sam's reaction. Some time prior to the album coming out — we had changed the name from *You Don't Know Me* to *Pictures and Paintings* by now but didn't yet have final mixes — we sent a rough cassette mix to Charlie. Now I should probably mention, if it hasn't already become clear, that the entire target audience for this album, the one person we wanted to please, was *Charlie*. He had been carrying around a briefcase full of songs, both literally and metaphorically, for close to twenty years, the songs that *he* wanted to record (jazz, blues, originals, pop standards) as opposed to the songs that it was incumbent upon him as a pop star, as a country superstar, to record.

A day or two after he got the tape, he called. I know that might not seem like that big a deal — and it might not have been for some people — but in all the time I knew Charlie, I almost never got any calls from him. Charlie *hated* to use the telephone, someone else always called for him — even if Charlie himself was in the room. "Guess where I am," he said to me. Without hesitation I professed total ignorance. "I'm in my car," he said (this was his Mercedes 190SL), "just driving around. And guess what I'm doing." By now I was beginning to catch on, but I said I really didn't know. "I'm listening to our album. I just been listening to it over and over." I had never heard such a note of jubilation in his voice.

Sam was almost equally enthusiastic — and he even carried on the car theme. "I listened to that CD driving in the car with Knox all the way to Nashville and back," he said. "I just played that damn thing over and over. I'm just so jealous of you, Peter," he went on with his usual gracious exaggeration. But even as great as it was, he said, not quite bringing me back to earth but heading in that direction, it was just the tip of the iceberg, as far as Charlie's talents were concerned.

That wasn't quite the end of it, though. About four years later, in the spring of 1996, a year after Charlie died, I sent Sam a copy of the Dick Curless album, *Traveling Through*, that my son, Jake, had produced. (Dick, who had died at sixty-three just before the album came out, was known as the "Baron of Country Music," a truly great — and underappreciated — artist and one of the few Maine natives to have emerged on the national country music stage.) Whatever I had experienced with Charlie in the studio in the way of spirit feel went double for the sessions that Jake produced on Dick. I saw Sam a couple of weeks later at the Jerry Lee Lewis 40th Anniversary in Show Business $100-a-plate celebration (as it turned out, you got a commemorative plate labeled not suitable for dining, but no food, just a cash bar — and at the end of at least six hours of inspired nonstop entertainment by the honoree himself, some very wrecked people).

"Now, did your son, Jake — now, tell me the truth now," Sam said with that teasing repetition that he called upon for the purpose of both orotund declamation and social discourse. "Now, come on, now, you tell me, did your son *Jake*" — he paused as if to savor the single blunt syllable of the name, then to my utter astonishment lifted me a few inches off the floor in full view of the Jerry Lee Lewis German fan club — "did he *really* produce that album on Dick Curless?" I tried to swallow my surprise and assent to the proposition. "Well, you know how much I liked that Charlie Rich album?" I nodded. "Well, *this* is even better!" I suppose there could have been any number of ways to take Sam's statement, but from my point of view, there couldn't have been *any* way to top it.

LIFE STUDIES

JUD DIED AT HOME in Memphis on July 20, 1992, after a long illness. It was, not surprisingly, a deeply emotional time for Sam. The funeral was in Florence, and the minister, a Sheffield resident, who was familiar with various members of the family, didn't know Jud at all. But there were heartfelt tributes from Jerry Lee Lewis, Charlie Rich, and Rufus Thomas, among others. ("I loved him just as I loved my own mother and father," declared an emotional Jerry Lee to the crowd assembled at the Elkins Funeral Home Chapel.) And Sam consoled Reverend Gamble that it was sinners like Jud and him who kept the church in business. "Jud liked to change directions every now and then," Sam said while pointing to his brother's genius at both preaching and promotion. The service was more in the nature of a celebration, he said, before introducing the various speakers and two of Jud's favorite gospel recordings as rendered by Elvis and Jerry Lee. "We're here to wish Jud a bon voyage," he declared with genuine fervor, "as he drifts off across Jordan, where he can see things from over on the other side."

It would have been sobering enough in any case, but coming as it did in the midst of a series of family deaths (Sam's brother Tom had died five years earlier, while his two surviving sisters, Mary and Irene, would die within the next two years, all like Jud from cancer) and following immediately on the heels of the death of Buster Williams, the influential Memphis distributor and pressing plant operator who had staked Sam when he was starting out, it seemed to really bring Sam up short in terms of both memory and mortality. Sam got up at Buster's funeral when it became evident that the man was being put into the ground without so much as a declaration of his significance. "Wait a minute," Sam declared, "Do y'all know who this man was?" Without Buster, he said, there might never have been not just a Sun Records but an independent record industry. Buster had extended a helping hand to one and all when a helping hand was very likely the only thing standing between you and the poorhouse. He called Jim Kingsley at the *Memphis Commercial Appeal,* insisting that attention must be paid, but the newspaper didn't run anything more than a standard obituary of a successful businessman whose later-life involvement in the oil business had become the foundation of his substantial fortune.

Sam himself suffered the usual insults of the flesh as the decade progressed. He was increasingly concerned about cancer, particularly after Dr. Kraus found a low-grade transitional cell carcinoma of the bladder (a smoking illness), which was treated successfully with chemical injections and which, along with an incipient pulmonary problem, caused Sam to vow to give up smoking once and for all. He had cataract operations and minor heart procedures as well as a small TIA, a so-called transient mini-stroke, with no visible or lasting effects.

The only really serious challenge to his health came in the mid '90s with an esophageal problem called achalasia that made it more and more difficult to swallow and led in turn to an alarming and precipitous loss of weight. (In a short period of time he lost twenty pounds, as his weight dropped to 130.) He saw various doctors in Memphis and finally, after failing to get any form of effective treatment, started researching the subject himself, reading medical papers on the illness, until he came up with the name of a doctor at the Cleveland Clinic, Dr. Joel Richter, who was generally acknowledged as the expert in the field. He called and made an appointment that day, then told Dr. Kraus what he was going to do, and in the face of Dr. Kraus' questions and remonstrations, delivered a detailed description of Dr. Richter's unorthodox course of treatment, which involved a series of Botox injections in the area of the esophageal sphincter. "I'll let you know how it goes," he said, and when he returned with Dr. Richter's notes for follow-up treatment, the condition was at least stabilized, if not cured, though he never did regain the lost twenty pounds.

But by far his most serious medical intervention came in the case of his son Knox. Knox had developed what was initially diagnosed as a sty on his right eyelid and was treated with an antibiotic ointment at around the same time, in 1993 and early 1994, that Sam first began experiencing esophageal problems. In late January, Knox's doctor ordered a biopsy, and a squamous cell carcinoma was found. Treatment called for wide excision and extensive reconstruction of the right upper eyelid, but the surgeon did such a good job you could barely tell there had ever been a problem. No further treatment was recommended, but then some eighteen months later, in the early summer of 1995, Knox experienced further symptoms and another biopsy was ordered. He was working on the radio tower on Colbert Mountain in Florence with Sam and his brother, Jerry — they were installing a new heavy-duty generator — when he got the news that the growth was malignant. Sam offered to go back to Memphis with him, but Knox turned him down. Part of it undoubtedly was an attempt to downplay the gravity of the situation, part of it was a determination to go it alone — but it was, said Knox, one of the loneliest moments in his life.

The cancer was more serious than anyone had imagined. It turned out to be a rare and aggressive form of sebaceous carcinoma originating in the meibomian gland, which had already spread to the lymph glands of his neck. After going back and forth between Nashville and Memphis for a series of interviews and consultations in July, he was operated on in Memphis at the end of the month, and in the aftermath of that operation, Knox was told by his physicians that they were confident they had gotten it all. So far as further treatment was concerned, they had little to recommend other than radiation therapy (chemo was not an option, they said, and the combination of chemotherapy and radiation was not even considered), but Knox had nothing to worry about in his primary physician's view — although, with only forty reported cases corresponding to his diagnosis, there really wasn't a lot of data to go on, Knox was simply going to have to cultivate a positive frame of mind.

This was not, as you might imagine, a prognosis to inspire confidence, accompanied by what appeared to be little more than a faith-based course of follow-up treatment. For Knox, raised to believe in taking action and in the efficacy of rational solutions, it was almost unendurable — but he didn't know what to do. It was, he says, a terrible moment of doubt and fear, not just for him but for the entire family. For Sam, said Sally, "it was just unbearable." Both the professional paralysis and the murky prognosis. He was not going to just let Knox *die*.

Within a matter of days, Sam had thoroughly researched the disease and determined not only that the M.D. Anderson Cancer Center in Houston was the place to go but that Dr. Waun Ki Hong, chairman of the Department of Head and Neck Oncology and a pioneer in chemotherapy treatment for head and neck cancers, was the person to speak to. So he picked up the phone and spoke to Dr. Hong for almost an hour, and then, with Knox and Diane and Sally, and all of Knox's medical records in tow, set off for Houston.

"It was," said Knox, "the best thing that ever happened in my life — and it was all because of Sam. He did the research, he did the homework, and we went down there together, and when we get there, Dr. Hong says, 'Look Knox, I'm sending you through the system.' And Sam says, 'Dr. Hong, we have to have this done today.'"

The first person they saw was Dr. Gary Clayman, one of Dr. Hong's "most promising young surgeons," who had graduated from Case Western as a dentist and then gone on to get his medical degree. Dr. Clayman's examination, to Knox's mind, was more like Sam's method of recording than any treatment he had received to date. It was more intuitive than technical, Knox said, "he just closed his eyes and palpated the neck. It was like he was playing an instrument. He felt around, and evidently he could just feel this little tiny spot, and he said, 'Knox I don't know about that.' So he sent me down to the second floor to have a fine-needle biopsy, and it was positive.

"Now it's like five o'clock in the afternoon, and I've been there all day, and Dr. Clayman says, 'Well, we're going to have pull your teeth [on that side] before we start radiation.' Let's see what we can schedule.' And Sam says, 'We have to do it this afternoon.' I said, 'Wait a minute, Dad, I may want to go back to the hotel and think about this.' But Sam said, 'We need to do this now.'"

That was the first day, and that still wasn't the end of it. "They pulled all eight teeth, and we're paying bills and stuff. And Dr. Clayman's going to give me something — I forget what it was. But Sam said, 'Dr. Clayman, listen —' like he's the expert on all this stuff. He said, 'Listen, Dr. Clayman, I think we're going to need some Percocet, it has a mood elevator in it, and he's gonna need that.' And Dr. Clayman had to go two or three floors down to get his tablet to write the prescription — but he did it."

And lest anyone suspect that this might be an entirely understandable form of filial exaggeration, here's John Prine with his own testimony to the strength of Sam's medical evangelism. In early 1998 John was diagnosed with squamous cell cancer of the neck and was about to undergo surgery in Nashville "when Knox called and told me I had the wrong doctor for the cancer I had. After I hung up, I thought, Why is Knox trying shake my confidence in my doctor — it had taken me so long to find a doctor that I had confidence in, I'd never gone through anything like this.

"The next morning I get a call from Sam (I think Knox knew I didn't exactly take him one hundred percent at his word) — and Sam kept me on the phone for an hour until I promised him that I would go down to Texas the next day and talk to these doctors at M.D. Anderson, he wasn't going to settle for anything less. Because he said he and Knox [had gone] everywhere until they found these people — these were the *right people*. And at the very end of the conversation he said, 'Besides that, John Prine'— he would always call me by my entire name when he talked to me — he said, 'If you don't go down to Houston, Texas, John Prine, I will come to Nashville, Tennessee, and kick your ass every mile of the way.'"

Knox's treatment was long and arduous. For the first time in as long as Sally had known him, maybe for the first time in his adult life, Sam set everything else aside. He remained constantly at Knox's side for the first two weeks of treatment, becoming so conversant in the language of this particular illness that doctors who didn't know him assumed he was another colleague. After that, as Knox went through daily radiation and wrenching chemo every twenty-one days for almost six months, Sam operated more at a remove, always available by phone, in constant consultation with the doctors, but sensitive to Knox's every shift in mood.

"He talked to Dr. Clayman a lot," Sally said. "Knox probably didn't even know sometimes. Sam always knew when he was going in for chemo. That was the roughest time. Knox was so sick after those chemo treatments. He couldn't talk. He couldn't do anything hardly. Sam would talk to Diane just to find out how low [Knox was] — 'Just tell him I called.' Sam never talked to Knox like he really felt — I mean, you know, until a few years to come, you just don't know whether this chemo is going to work or not. But he was always very up-spirited, always available to get on a plane — or do anything. He never was at a point where he couldn't have gone to Houston at the drop of a hat. I mean, Knox was his buddy. Knox was it, as far as Sam was concerned."

B ECKY WENT BACK AND FORTH to Houston. Sometimes she would accompany Knox to chemo, and when he threw up on the hospital floor, "she'd just start cleaning everything up. I'd say, 'Mother . . . the nurses . . . don't worry about it.'" But she was not to be deterred. Jerry visited occasionally, too, and so did Kim, Knox's twenty-eight-year-old daughter, an accomplished dancer and dance instructor who was studying to become a child psychologist. On Knox's fiftieth birthday, it seemed like all of Memphis got together to make a video birthday card for him, with Rufus Thomas singing "Happy Birthday" and the Memphis Horns playing an instrumental version of their own. Kim, who possessed as sunny a spirit as her father, sent a faxed greeting that began, in its own phillipic tradition, "Happy 50th Daddy-O," while exhorting her father not to be "down about turning 50, and if you are then 'SNAP out of it!' . . . Your daughter thinks you are the most handsome fella in the universe. Daddy, I hope you have a terrific day, you certainly deserve it. . . . You are braving the storm with so much strength and courage. You are my hero!"

And when Knox finally came home in January of 1996, Sam said,

"It ranks so far above everything else that, as thankful as I am for every birthday I've had, and all the wonderful things that have been a part of my life, this is the greatest thing that has ever happened to me." As for Knox, when he first walked into the studio, he told the *Commercial Appeal,* he could think of nothing but all the things he had accomplished in that room, and then "I realized I had missed it all so badly. I had missed Memphis so badly."

And he knew his future course. Like Sam's, his eye was inexorably set on history. Sam's history.

THE DOCUMENTARY

W E HAD BEEN TALKING about making a movie about Sam's life for over four years now, and it would take another three before we got to its realization. I had first approached a Los Angeles filmmaker who was interested in doing a feature in 1992, but after a year or two of conversations it never really went anywhere. Then in 1997 Peter Jones, an award-winning documentary director and producer who owned his own production company, contacted me about doing an Elvis documentary, and soon the discussion turned to Sam. Knox was certainly sold on the idea. For that matter Sam was, too. But the trick was to get Sam to actually *commit* to the project.

It took another two years.

Why so long, you might ask, to persuade Sam to do something that he had envisioned long before we had ever met? There was no question in his mind that his was an epic tale — with or without his own name attached. ("This would truly be an amazing story if I read it about somebody else," he said on more than one occasion.) But it had to be done for the right reasons, it had to be done by the right people, it had to be done at the right time. "Watch out for glorification," he said. "Watch out for the monetary enticements and inducements. Watch for the old thing that we all like to see our name in lights. Those lights are going to go out sometime."

I understood what he was talking about — but then again I didn't. It was the same as with his book. He didn't want to give it away, in any sense of the word. But what if his artists had adopted the same point of view? Failure, as Sam said, could loom over the start of any enterprise.

Somehow you had to get past its specter, somehow you had to learn to embrace imperfection.

For over two years we had dinners, long, two-fisted drinking affairs (literally two-fisted, as Sam held forth with a glass of red wine in one hand, white in the other, and frequently never got to the food at all). "Another rock 'n' roll night," Knox would comment cheerfully afterward, whether the conversation had focused on the film, the lessons to be learned from "smelling the sweat of a mule," or some of the deepest mysteries of life. Sometimes Sam could get a little out of hand ("Go to hell, Sally," he might lash out when Sally attempted to intervene. "I'm not going to eat anything, with this good buzz I got going"). Sometimes in an expansive mood he might compliment my wife, Alexandra, on being so pretty she could have been one of Florence madam Kate Nelson's girls. It's hard to say what led him to drink, it's hard to say what exactly the drinking unleashed. As Sam said, "I can get off of everything when I've had enough to drink." "Something almost primitive came out," observed Terry Pace, the young *TimesDaily* reporter from Florence. "I don't mean that in a negative way. But there were no inhibitions whatsoever in what he said or did. And it scared the hell out of [some] people." But whatever happened, whatever direction the evening took, it was always, as Knox said, Big Fun. Well, *almost* always — and even if it wasn't, these were times you would never have wanted to miss. And more often than not we would think at the end of the evening — Knox and Diane, Alexandra and me, I'm not sure what exactly Sally, who bore the brunt of Sam's moods, thought deep down — that we had made real progress toward our goal, that Sam was finally ready to come to a decision as far as the documentary was concerned. But then the next time, it was as if the previous meeting had never occurred, and we were once more back at square one.

Ultimately Sam capitulated to his own desires. It would be hard to say what exactly tipped him over the edge, though Jerry Schilling, a good friend to us all, who had recently become head of the newly re-formed Memphis Music Commission, served as his negotiating intermediary. But I think in the end it was no more complicated than Sam's own recognition of the issues at stake. "The reason that I have been so reticent for so long, I just didn't trust anybody with [the story]. But, hey, you can wait too damn long to do anything, and then I thought, 'My God, you die and they're gonna [do] any damn thing they want to. You stupid son of a bitch, why don't you go on and do something?'"

At Ernestine and Hazel's, the kick-off party for the documentary, September 18, 1999. *Courtesy of the Sam Phillips Family*

In certain ways, Sam conceded, perhaps unnecessarily, "I'm extremely stubborn. I'm not bragging about that. I'm just saying that this was a big decision — and that guy in there is the only reason I'm sitting here right now. I would still be procrastinating, or some bullshit, about this thing right till this day, were it not for Knox Phillips. Not Jerry, not Sally, not Jane or John Doe. I'm just telling you."

We began production in September, and Morgan Neville, the young director Peter Jones had picked for the project (Morgan had produced and directed a number of shows for the company, including ambitious films on Jonathan Winters, John Steinbeck, and Brian Wilson) had a plan. Morgan, a perspicacious, conspicuously bespectacled thirty-one-year-old Elvis Costello study in hipsterish sports jacket and skinny tie, was familiar enough with Sam at this point. He had met him on a number of occasions, and we had been working intermittently on a rough draft for the film for over two years (it was by now scheduled for a two-hour slot in the A&E *Biography* series), so he had every reason to be aware of Sam's penchant for eloquence, loquacity, and Ciceronian circularity of expression. Morgan's plan, in plain terms, was to let Sam talk himself out. To that end he factored in five days of audio interviews before the film crew (cinematographer Craig Spirko and a local audio guy) even arrived.

This made a certain amount of sense in theory. Film was expensive, and Morgan wanted to shoot as much of the documentary as possible on film, not tape. In addition to giving Sam plenty of opportunity to warm up, the audiotapes could also provide us with good voiceover material (at this point we were planning to have Sam narrate the film), and neither of us felt there was any danger of blowing the big scenes through repetition. Sam was too intent on telling his story. It was, we even managed to persuade ourselves, in many ways parallel to Sam's own recording methods. Working this way, without the pressure of delivering anything on time or on budget, could only encourage Sam to feel more at home in a new setting, more at ease when it came time to hone his story down.

Do I even need to confess that our plan was a failure almost before it began? Not out of any lack of effort on Sam's part (quite the opposite), or any lack of commitment on ours. Sam simply couldn't help himself. He threw himself into the project without reservation from the start. But the early audio sessions turned into more of an extended series of pep talks for Morgan and me than any blowing off of steam for Sam. This was going to be *fun,* Sam reassured us — but it was going to be hard work, too. He would do everything in his power to make it happen, and make it happen *right,* Sam said, before we had a chance to ask a single question, but "it's just like when I recorded people. There is no time, ever, that you'll make a mistake — except when you're not trying. And that I don't tolerate very well. . . . I don't give a damn how many wrong chords or missed beats or jumped beats or whatever [so-called mistakes might exist in the documentary process] — that's just fine. That's just fine. But don't hold back anything in an effort to make it quote unquote perfect. That's the type of thing that I feel — the *investment* we ought to make in this."

What alternative did we have but to nod our heads in mute assent?

This was not, Sam insisted, just the Sam Phillips story. He wanted to "strike a chord that makes us all know that this is a story so much bigger than any one individual or any number of individuals that it will in one way or the other be a potential compass by which you can find your way. And I'm not thinking about making it boring. Totally to the contrary. 'Cause it damn sure wasn't boring. But it strikes me as something that will do two, three, or four different things. Maybe things that none of us could even think of as of today."

And this was all within the first few minutes.

Eventually Sam got down to brass tacks — although I'm not sure that from his point of view this opening salvo was not the real brass tacks. Over the next five days he spoke of his family and Silas Payne and his deaf-mute Aunt Emma, he spoke with feeling about Howlin' Wolf and Jerry Lee Lewis and the struggles of starting up the studio and the record company. He talked about just about everything in fact, and gradually two things became obvious. One was that Sam was writing his autobiography, with nothing left out — not his sixth-grade teacher or his first drum lesson or his electroshock treatments or his fifteen-year-old visits to Kate Nelson's house of prostitution. For all of his concern about doing everything that he could to make this a documentary that would rival *Gone with the Wind* in dramatic sweep and focus, in the end he was for all practical purposes ceding the power to us, if only out of his own need to tell the complete, unedited, and unexpurgated story in full, without regard for what might or might not be practically feasible.

The other realization was one that should probably have occurred to me from the start. I had puzzled so long and so hard over what it was exactly that was holding Sam back from committing himself to a project so dear to his heart. I alternated between the hard-nosed business explanation (Sam was not going to give his story away) and the kind of creative insight that Sam himself offered up on so many occasions (the difficulty of embarking on any creative enterprise, the fear of ruining something that was perfect in the abstract with the flawed face of reality: see above). I think both of these were true in their way, but it never occurred to me that there was an altogether different explanation on an altogether different level, consisting of the nature, and cost, of Sam's commitment to *any* project, whether it was a landscaping job or recording B.B. King.

What I mean by that is, for Sam there was no holding back. That may seem self-evident. I mean, we all like to think that when we give ourselves over to a project, we give ourselves over to it completely — and that is undoubtedly true to a greater or lesser extent (some of us even like to cite the old Sister Rosetta Tharpe gospel number "99½ Won't Do"). But with Sam, there was *really* no holding back, and that became abundantly clear long before we even began. Several weeks before we started production, Sam sent us a list of twenty-three "pick and choose" sites in the Florence area, including the Cypress Creek swimming hole

Down by the river with Morgan Neville (left), the author, and cinematographer Craig Spirko (far right), October 1999. *Photograph by Alexandra Guralnick*

where he had swum as a boy and his blind Uncle Ben's General Merchandise Store in Lovelace Community, complete with a map showing the location of each of the sites. He suggested a parade in downtown Florence and mapped out the route, dropping the idea only after Sally vehemently disagreed on the grounds that people would just be pissed off at all that disruption for just a few seconds of screen time. He threw all of his weight and influence behind the show, and once we started shooting, it became evident that every last bit of his attention was concentrated on it. His energy was unflagging. There was no drinking, there were no distractions, there was nothing but a relentless focus on the task at hand.

But there *was* a problem. And it arose directly from something we had never anticipated (and the world that knew Sam only through his unshrinking, larger-than-life public personality might never have credited): his almost naked need to please.

"Folks, y'all should have been there," he would suddenly blurt out, and not just every once in a while, addressing his unseen audience as if by including them he was somehow going to convince them of his point. "Now, folks, I just want y'all to listen to me." "Now, I know you're not going to believe this. The public will not believe this." "So. I mean, I want the world to know how appreciative I am that the A&E network is letting me share this story, and, folks, there's not one ounce, to my knowledge, of falsification." And so on.

It was touching, it was surprising, and there were any number of braggadocious variations. ("I know all the women out there think I'm [no] substitute for Elvis . . . but, boy, I'll tell you, I come so close. . . . I bet they won't miss watching this show over and over and over again!") But clearly it was an issue that had to be addressed.

Probably Morgan and I should have tossed a coin—but we didn't. Instead we talked about it endlessly. (How was this going to affect our plan to have Sam narrate his own story? The answer, I think, is obvious.) And in the end I called upon the privilege of age and long acquaintance to sidestep the issue. (How could *I* confront Sam? I said, as if that were some logical substitute for admitting I didn't have the guts.) And so it was that Alexandra and I stood in the parking lot down by the river on a bitterly cold fall day and watched Sam and Morgan go back and forth, back and forth, their heads bent in concentration, with Sam nodding occasionally in what we could only hope was agreement as we grew chilled to the bone.

After that it was definitely better—but still not fully resolved or, ultimately, resolvable. Sam was simply too irrepressible by nature, on the one hand, and, in what may have been his most evident concession to age, simply too intent on communicating his message to rein in its means of delivery. It was that, more than his sidelong salutes to the unseen multitudes, that ruled him out as the narrative voice—we couldn't separate his passionate belief in his own story enough to create the tone of calm invitation that a trustworthy narrative voice requires. But that was as it should be. To get Sam unfiltered (as opposed to getting Sam to embrace a modulated self-governing, conventionally "respectable" role) was, as Sam might have said, R-E-A-L, and what could be more persuasive, or more beautiful, than reality in all of its diverse, confusing, and disquietingly beautiful dimensions? Sam poured himself into telling his story, and when he wasn't satisfied with the telling ("I don't think I did justice to the Wolf yesterday. He was such an unusual person, and I think I got off on the guy bringing him to me and never hardly got him in the damn studio"), he would go back and tell it again. He declaimed like Lear on the heath, as he stood atop the Shrine Building in downtown Memphis, looking out across the Father of All Waters to Arkansas, with the wind whistling all around him while he saluted the majesty of the river.

There was not a single aspect of the filming that he didn't take seriously, from the absence of a second camera, which he ascribed repeatedly and seriosarcastically to A&E's cheapness, to the various outfits he wore for different venues and different scenes. He studied his own appearance carefully and liked everything about it except for his teeth and the pouches under his eyes. He wasn't sure he shouldn't do something about the pouches, he said — but then again he didn't seem all that inclined to, relying as much on youthfulness of manner as artificial enhancement (hair and beard always excepted) as he snapped his fingers, pirouetted occasionally should the spirit so move him, and every once in a while hummed a few bars of "How Lucky Can One Man Get," pronouncing the lyrics as if they offered a satisfying summation of his life. Throughout it all he never lost the ability to inspire, and the best moments for all of us, including Sam, came when, drawn in by the passion of his conviction, we forgot the camera was even there.

But it was only when we got to Florence, three weeks into the filming, that I realized for the first time the truth of what Sam had been telling me all along: Florence, Alabama, was not just the beginning, it was inextricably linked to everything Sam had ever thought or dreamt of. It may not have been the whole story, but it couldn't, Sam insisted, "in any way be isolated from [what] occurred in Memphis." Whatever he was, Sam declared, Florence had made him.

I knew, of course, through *TimesDaily* reporter Terry Pace, how closely attached Sam had become, how much he had done for the town in recent years. He had become a kind of benefactor of the arts, supporting the local theater community in any number of ways and donating $5,000 so that the Coffee High drama program could take "I Hear America Singing," an original musical revue devised by its director, to the Edinburgh Fringe Festival. He even participated in a panel discussion that Terry had organized to follow his presentation of *Picasso at the Lapin Agile,* comedian Steve Martin's first full-length play, a fanciful exploration of the creative process by way of a meeting between Picasso and Albert Einstein, which is enlivened by the late arrival of an unnamed Elvis Presley. Sam sat there "riveted" throughout the performance, Terry said. "It was the stillest I have ever seen him." And when he was introduced following the performance with his two fellow panelists (suitably enough, an art professor and a professor of physics), he set the tone by declaring, "I am still and always will be a Florentine."

He was. During our brief time in Florence, Sam was infused with a different kind of spirit, whether it was sipping milkshakes and eating egg-and-olive sandwiches at Trowbridge's Creamery downtown (established 1918) or doing his best to find the location of Kate Nelson's whorehouse on South Seminary. Like Sally, like Sleetie Mitchell, like his sons, we got the full tour, as we tooled around town in the beautiful baby-blue 1960 Cadillac convertible that he had had restored as a surprise for Knox upon his return from Houston a couple of years earlier. He was just full of vinegar, determined that the world see Florence through his eyes, as he coached his old band director, eighty-five-year-old Floyd McClure, through an interview designed to do nothing but secure Mr. Mac's place in history and lovingly embraced his ninety-year-old brother Horace in the lobby of a drearily familiar nursing home. "This is the greatest brother anybody could have," he announced to both the nursing-home residents and his prospective national audience as he paid eloquent tribute to Horace's kindness and mechanical brilliance. "You ain't gonna cry over me now," he playfully remonstrated when Horace started to cry, getting a smile out of his brother as he declared, "He's a sentimental fool. Smartest sentimental fool I know."

We visited Armstead Methodist Chapel, the black church from which he had taken so much inspiration as a boy, and you can see Sam throwing aside all reserve and swaying with delight as the choir rocks their repertoire of sturdy old hymns with cheerful abandon. We visited the modest retaining wall that Sam and his classmates had built in 1940 to keep the new junior high school yard from washing away. ("This is very important," Sam said. "Right here next to the building was a big oak tree that was cut down, and [that was] where I made my first stump speech!") Sam was like a proud father showing off the Big River Broadcasting radio studio that he had recently redesigned on the newly designated Sam Phillips Street. And we visited the W. C. Handy Birthplace and Museum, a central exhibit of Florentine farsightedness, even though, as Sam pointed out with an archivist's regret, the birthplace (a log cabin built by Handy's grandfather) had had to be moved from its original location. "To be from the same town, and a small town at that, [as] W. C. Handy," Sam mused. "W. C. Handy is one of my idols. He probably did more for getting whites and blacks together than anybody I know, and he did it in such a way that nobody — *nobody* — lost."

There were many such moments in Florence, both planned and unplanned. Sam's level of excitement and expectation couldn't have been higher. But it was on our first day of shooting, down by the river, in sight of the old railroad bridge where Sam's father had worked at night flagging traffic, that we had our moment of spontaneous revelation. As it happened, Sam was talking about the reason he had developed the slapback sound — to let the music sound as natural and real as possible — when several dump trucks rumbled by and Craig Spirko, the cinematographer, stopped filming. Sam's reaction was instantaneous — and utterly unsurprising.

Why had we stopped filming? he demanded. What the hell were we thinking? Hell, those were the best dump trucks he had ever seen. Those dump trucks were *real,* he said. Did we have any idea how much it would cost to create a sound like the one they made? And then it wouldn't even be the real thing. Didn't we understand that we were in one of the most beautiful spots in Florence, with the river flowing by, *where the real thing could actually happen?* What in the hell was the matter with us!

We sat there, both chastened and amused, as Sam repeated his familiar mantra — and perhaps I should add, it was no less convincing for its familiarity. He loved perfect imperfection, he insisted. And he cited his recordings to prove it — the inspired accident was what you were *always* looking for, so long as it didn't drown out what you were trying to get across.

And when he addressed the Coffee High School Band on the same field on which he and his fellow band members had marched back and forth some sixty years earlier to pack down the newly graded sod, he was no less forceful, and no less fervent, in expressing his beliefs to the ragtag collection of out-of-uniform teenagers who stood looking more than a little bewildered as they cradled their instruments and batons. "It's such a great inspiration," Sam declared with as much genuine belief in their future as in his past, "to know that here I am at seventy-six years old, right here with a group of people that — had it not been for Coffee High School and this band, I can truly say to you that I doubt if I would have had the success in life that I did." But music, he said, was not to be measured as a pathway to success, or anything else for that matter. "Music is not something you *have* to do, even if they kicked you in the butt and said, Hey, you've got to do it. Music is something you *want* to do." That was pretty much the way it had worked out for him, "an average tuba player and drum player," and that was the way he was sure it would work out for them (given Sam's syntax, you've got to take this as a somewhat free translation). The main thing was, whatever course they chose to follow in their lives, music would always enrich it. "Music is something that you will always remember as long as you live. Don't cheat yourself by not getting everything you can out of music — but in the meantime . . . HAVE A HELLUVA LOT OF FUN DOING IT."

That was the note we tried to strike in the conclusion of the film: a combination of unalloyed faith in the future and belief in the possibilities of the democratic dream — if you chose to see the democratic dream as founded on principles of individualism and choice. We were not able to get Sam to deliver the summation (I had always thought it would be something along the lines of his vision — the whole neighboring region's vision — of Memphis as "lights up the river," but, as should be evident by now, there was simply no way to get Sam to deliver anything on cue). Though as it turned out, Morgan managed to piece together an ending that I think was nearly as effective, with interspersed tributes from others and Elvis' exuberant "Mystery Train" playing in the background, as Sam swings jauntily down Beale and along the river.

"Do you know what this country has done — through *hardship?*" Sam intoned. "It's become the seat of the greatest compositions and versatility in music the world has ever known. . . . The power of the feel of the essence of music that originated IN THIS BABY COUNTRY. Two hundred and fifty years old. *That's a baby* — with a bare butt! Look what we've done — *through music.*

"Music," he almost crooned, "music is such an opportunity for everybody. Sit and sing awhile, man. I mean, even if you can't stand yourself, do it! You'd be surprised."

And Elvis laughs that delighted laugh, as his record trails off and the credits roll.

THE FILM PREMIERED at the Orpheum Theatre in Memphis in June of 2000. It was not, strictly speaking, the "world" premiere (that had already taken place at the Museum of Television in New York, for which Sam and Knox and Sally had all flown up), but it was designated as the "premiere screening," and it was a gala affair, bringing out black and white together for once, along with the entire Memphis musical community. Sam, crisp in his double-breasted white dinner jacket, was visibly moved and delighted. "I'm gonna use a Dewey Phillips phrase here," he said at the start, addressing his audience as "good people," then delivering an extraordinarily brief three-minute peroration pointing to "the great Delta of Mississippi and Arkansas [as] the undergirding spirit of this community." As for his own inspiration, he didn't hesitate: it was growing up on a farm in Alabama with poor blacks and whites working together "in the spirit of knowing that we had to love [one another] and recognize that we all have . . . certain gifts that God bestows upon us." With that out of the way, Sam commended the movie to the audience, declaring confidently, "I believe you will like it."

They did. The film was received with all the visible enthusiasm and abandon that you might expect from a hometown crowd of eleven hundred. There were delighted whoops of recognition and surprise all through the film, but the highlight occurred when it came time for the entertainment at the end of the evening. Each of the four billed performers was allotted two songs. Jim Dickinson, who always liked to boast that he was the last Sun performer produced by Sam, delivered a manic "Cadillac Man," while Billy Lee Riley, resplendent in a bright-red jacket and black bow tie that only served to set off his perfectly sculpted white hair, rocked the house with "Red Hot." Next, Ike Turner, looking as youthful as Sam and in the finest of fettle, served up a storming "Rocket 88" forty-nine years, as he was delighted to point out, after the original recording. It was left to Jerry Lee Lewis to close the show, and he did in typical Jerry Lee Lewis fashion, kicking back the piano stool and then clamping his teeth down on his delicately curved pipe. But then it was announced by MC George Klein that there was a surprise in store for everyone — and indeed all four performers looked surprised as he called Johnny Bragg, the lead singer of the Prisonaires, out onstage to join them. Sam wrapped his arms tightly around Johnny, a broad smile brightening his face — but then his expression changed as the band leader asked what key Johnny wanted, and Sam immediately held up his hands to silence the musicians. "A cappella," he said, "a cappella" — and he waved his arms like a conductor, while Johnny sang a verse or two of "Just Walkin' in the Rain" while everyone gathered around him and stood utterly transfixed, with the exception of Ike Turner, who jumped up and down, hugging himself.

Then it was on to London just three weeks after the show's television debut. Sam had declared when we were making the documentary that he had never left North America ("I never had the time"), but he showed little hesitation when the British Film Institute extended its invitation. In fact, he was practically bursting with energy when he entered Home House, the quietly opulent members' hotel that had been built as the eighteenth-century home of the Countess of Home. It was nearly one in the morning, more than thirteen hours since he had left Memphis, and Knox and Diane and Alexandra and I and Jerry were exhausted just awaiting his arrival. Sam, on the other hand, was irrepressible in his enthusiasm for everything he had seen just on his ride in from Heathrow: how clean the streets looked, how up-to-date everything was (in retrospect I wonder if Sam still retained images of London during the Blitz), how *exciting* a prospect we had before us. Throughout his whirlwind six-day visit, his spirits never flagged. He was scheduled for three interviews on the first day, plus a turn-away crowd for a signing at Borders and a late dinner at the Groucho Club. There were at least another four interviews on the second day — but Sam was indefatigable (appearances kept getting added, despite all attempts to remind the British of Sam's age). But the highlight for Sam was his visits to four different BBC studios. He couldn't get over the equipment they had, said Sally, "three times as much as we had at our radio station, and ours is well equipped. But it's the government over there."

This was his first visit to London, he told celebrated BBC host and music historian Charlie Gillett, and his fourth interview of the day, but "I have never seen greater people prepared to ask me questions than they are here." And when Charlie, a champion of world music, played him a cut by Issa Bagayogo, a thirty-nine-year-old Malian artist, Sam's reaction was one of pure delight.

The reception of the film at the sold-out screening, dotted with celebrities and musical devotees, rivaled the reaction at the Memphis premiere. Afterward, British Film Institute exhibition head Adrian Wootton, who had brought us all over and graciously shepherded the media circus, interviewed Sam onstage, while I played the role of superfluous interlocutor. Sam himself couldn't have been more eloquent, measured, and succinct (for *Sam*), and as close to genuinely self-deprecatory as it was possible for him to get — but he was still a bit much for some of his British fans, who had come to worship the legend, not confront the inevitably messy reality that Sam was determined to present them with. Sam's responses were a summary of all his familiar themes ("I wanted to be maybe a teacher of some sort," he said by way of explanation early on), delivered with an easy grace that was only borne out at the late-night private reception back at the hotel. The next day he and Sally and Knox and Diane traveled out to the film location for *Band of Brothers,* which was shooting in Hertfordshire, where they all donned boots to wade through the muddy wartime set and Sam was greeted as nothing less than a rock star by the series' developer and co-executive producer (with Steven Spielberg), Tom Hanks.

THIS WAS SAM'S MILLENNIAL PERIOD. It was a time of honors and recognition. In 1997 *Life* magazine listed the discovery of Elvis Presley (and the birth of rock 'n' roll) at number 99 in a special issue dedicated to "100 Incredible Discoveries, Cataclysmic Events, [and] Magnificent Moments of the Past 1000 Years," just ahead of "Fixing the Calendar, 1582"), while *Time* included it among the "Great Events of the 20th Century." *Entertainment Weekly's* "100 Greatest Moments in Rock Music" placed it at number 3, two slots behind the Beatles' debut on *Ed Sullivan,* a subject of such ire to Sam that he registered his protest in writing, and then immediately regretted it.

There was never any thought given to abandoning radio. Sam worked no less hard, studied the annual *Broadcasting & Cable Yearbook* no less assiduously, and was always on the hunt for new ways to expand the stations' signals, locate new transmitter sites, improve the sound, and generally expand the listenership. But somehow his focus had shifted. Jerry, who was divorced once again and was living at the lake house in Iuka, was more and more in charge of day-to-day operations at Big River now, and though Sam continued to call family business meetings requiring attendance by Knox, Jerry, and Sally with as much, if not greater, frequency, they seemed to have less and less functional purpose. "When he got to drinking," said Jerry, "he never wanted you to leave — I think he liked preaching and holding court, you know, and he was trying to teach us the psychological aspects of business. But some nights it was just ridiculous, sitting there ten hours and listening to him talk."

Shelby Singleton hardly ever heard from Sam anymore — at least not about business. There were scarcely any calls raising questions about the status of Sam's minority share or challenging what Sam felt to be the lack of proper accounting procedures or payments. "In the last ten years before he died," Shelby said, "he never questioned anything I did, he never called me up [and] said, 'Why are you doing this or that?' I think finally he forgot about it." Or, more likely, he had simply reached the point where, as Sally suggested, he just didn't consider it worth his time to pursue. Every once in a while, to Shelby's amusement, Sam would suggest a meeting, and Shelby and his brother, John, would drive over to Memphis without delay, but the way Shelby recalled it (and remember, Shelby genuinely liked Sam), as often as not "Knox would call around nine o'clock [for a ten o'clock meeting at the house] and say, 'We're going to have to call the meeting off.' And we'd say, 'Why?' 'Well, we don't know where Sam is. He hasn't been home in two days.'"

Contrary to Shelby's impression, Sally always knew exactly where Sam was. She had probably driven him there and was simply waiting for the call to come pick him up. Because for all of his accolades, however much he warmed to the world's embrace, Sam remained, as his son Jerry was the first to suggest, a solitary figure, wrapped up in his own enigmatic thoughts, beset by his own familiar demons. He may have seen himself as the world's protector, he may have had solutions to offer, wanted or unwanted, to all of those closest to him, to everyone within reach of his voice, but when it came down to Sam himself, as he might have been the first to concede in an unguarded moment, he had never been able to escape the anxieties that had beset him from an early age, he had never been able to overcome the overwhelming fear of being alone.

For the most part he would just call someone on the phone, "mainly women that he had known for years and years and years," Sally said, "he only did it when he was drinking, and he would just talk all night long."

"This is God," he announced one night to Bettye Berger, probably the most frequent recipient of his late-night calls (he might have called Sleetie Mitchell more often, but Sleetie went to bed early). "He wanted to know what I needed," Bettye laughed. "I said, 'Just pay me my royalties, Sam.'"

Other times, though, he was not as easily satisfied. "People may have thought he disappeared," said Sally, "but he was always around. There were times when he didn't want to deal with things. There was always those times." Some nights he would just announce to Sally at nine or ten o'clock at night that he was going over to so-and-so's house (as often as not Bettye Berger, but certainly not Bettye Berger exclusively), the woman in question was coming to pick him up. Other nights Sally would drive him to his destination. She knew if she remonstrated it would only mean an argument that she couldn't win. And besides, she recognized Sam's need for what it was, a need to *communicate* in whatever way he could, a need that she knew neither she nor anyone else could fully satisfy. Sometimes he would just want to get away to the suite he maintained at Wilson World out by Graceland, whether by himself or with someone else. "At Wilson World I think he was getting into some people maybe that I didn't know, some friends of somebody's. But sometimes maybe he was by himself — if he couldn't get anybody to come join him, then he would just talk on the phone. I would take him over there. Because he didn't want to drive. Sam had got to where he didn't drive hardly at all."

I realize that this may seem anomalous to those who have mythicized Sam — it may even seem disloyal — but this is who Sam was, *"This is who we all are,"* he might have argued, *"when we reveal ourselves as we truly are, naked and unclothed."* From Sam's point of view it was the equivalent of the dump trucks. He was damned if he would see any of his actions or emotions as anything less than, *other* than, human. And if someone was going to tell his story, he made it abundantly clear, he didn't want them to pretty it up. I know that the world at large, the world that Sam by now had so beguiled, would hardly have seen it that way. For Sam's public image had long since overtaken the complicated and contradictory vision of beauty in ugliness, ugliness in beauty that he so prized.

T HERE WERE more and more interviews — it seemed sometimes as if Sam couldn't turn down an interview — and, as spontaneous as his utterances and eruptions appeared to be, he prepared assiduously for each one. He was proud of his place in history and determined to preserve it, and he sought to refamiliarize himself with the ground that each interview was intended to cover, even if he was always prepared to depart from it. (A typical example would be a 1999 onstage interview he did at the Rock and Roll Hall of Fame in Cleveland. As both interviewers and audience became increasingly impatient for him to get to the *point* — whether that point was Sun, Memphis, Elvis Presley, or the rock 'n' roll revolution, depending upon their own personal perspective — Sam dwelt painfully on his first nervous breakdown in Decatur, a subject which as far as I know he never discussed publicly anywhere else. It was only after a full hour's preamble, including his birth, Uncle Silas, possum hunting, Dr. George W. Truett, and Jud's theological training, that he finally arrived at the rental of the vacant storefront location at 706 Union Avenue in Memphis.) Sam could certainly be said to prize the digression, but the heart of his message was never far from his mind, and even in his writings, whether it was a passionate appreciation of Charlie Rich after his 1995 death or the laudatory inscription he wrote without apparent forethought or hesitation at the front of a thrilled Elvis biographer's book, he labored long and hard, through numerous rewrites, to achieve the individuality, jauntiness, and quirkiness of tone that he was seeking.

The list of honors that came his way in the last decade of the twentieth century included everything from the Lifetime Achievement Grammy Award that Knox had been tirelessly campaigning for since 1972 (some other recipients over the years were John Hammond, Duke Ellington, Thomas Edison, Béla Bartók, and, with Sam, Motown's Berry Gordy) to the Chicago Blues Festival's first annual Howlin' Wolf Award, for which he traveled to Chicago for the first time in years, paying a visit to the long-since-shuttered site of Chess Records on Cottage Grove and an empty Wrigley Field. He received an honorary professorship from the University of Mississippi, appeared in an ad for Northwest Airlines complete with what purported to be his own text ("To me Memphis is the greatest place on earth. Part of the reason is our hometown airline, Northwest"), and was shot by provocative fashion photographer Terry Richardson for the September 1997 issue of *Harper's Bazaar* with twenty-three-year-old model Kate Moss sitting on his lap. He inducted Elvis into the Country Music Hall of Fame in 1998 and was himself inducted three years later. As dear to his heart as any other honor was his Hall of Fame award from *Mix* magazine, "the world's leading magazine for the professional recording and sound production technology industry," in recognition of his "Technical Excellence and Creativity" as a producer and engineer — though for all I know he may have taken just as much pleasure in dressing down the audience at the 1995 Blues Ball, where, upon receiving the first annual Memphis Music Pyramid Award, he launched into what the *Memphis Flyer* called "a rambling tale about [blues singer] Sleepy John Estes' false teeth, which was soon lost upon the perimeter tables of the room. Annoyed by the chatter from the back of the hall, Phillips growled at the assembled upscale throng: 'Shut up! I'm trying to tell you some history here.'"

There was never any telling what Sam was going to say—but he was definitely going to say *something*. With Elvis fans during the annual Elvis Week he rarely passed up the opportunity to tell the story of the chancre on Elvis' penis (see chapter 8 for details), no matter how clear they made it that this was not what they wanted to hear. He seemed to delight (forget about "seemed") in saying the unexpected, introducing what might normally be deemed inappropriate subjects or expressions into the conversation, continuing in his own way to challenge the status quo, even if at this point he was for the most part simply challenging expectations.

One of his proudest moments came when the Kitchen Sisters inaugurated their Peabody Award–winning NPR series, *Lost and Found Sound,* a series dedicated to unearthing the sounds of the American century, with shows on both the Memphis Recording Service and WHER in the fall of 1999. This came about indirectly from the time that one Kitchen Sister, Davia Nelson, came to Memphis as casting director for Francis Ford Coppola's *The Rainmaker* a couple of years earlier. She met Knox first on a location preshoot, and then she met Sam when the company returned to Memphis for the filming and they all went out to dinner. Davia never told him where she was staying, "but around three or four in the morning my phone rings, and I pick [it] up and this voice says, 'I think you know something about the acoustics of life.'" Other women might have stood on ceremony here—I know several who went running for the exit—but Davia and her radio partner, Nikki Silva, were intrepid adventurers, and though she was well aware that Sam possessed a sizable "flattery gene"—and that it was very likely to be magnified at three or four in the morning—she nonetheless took Sam's words as "about the most meaningful thing anybody has ever said in terms of grasping what I do and what I care about. He said it in that moment. That's how it began."

The shows that they produced on Sam are a wonderful aural record of two of the lesser-known sides of his career. One was about the Memphis Recording Service's role not as the birthplace of rock 'n' roll but as a destination point where, guided by the motto "We Record Anything— Anywhere—Anytime," anyone, including an eighteen-year-old Elvis Presley, could walk in off the street and pay $3 or $4 to hear the sound of their own voice. Responding to newspaper items prompted by Davia and Nikki's arrival in the city, people brought in acetates and recordings of events both public and private, some dating back almost fifty years. ("We feel like sonic investigators," Nikki told the *Commercial Appeal.*)

A good many of these were aired on the show as the story of Sam's early years in recording, and all the things he had done simply to keep the studio doors open, was explored in a way that it never had been before. The second audio documentary, "WHER: 1000 Beautiful Watts," might have been, if anything, even closer to Sam's heart, offering a way to pay tribute to Becky, who brought in a number of sound-check recordings and was instrumental in leading the "sonic investigators" to close to twenty of the women who had worked at the station at one time or another. Davia and Nikki then organized a pilgrimage to New York that included fourteen of these "jockettes," with Sam shepherding the entire group to a triumphant appearance at the Museum of Television and Radio.

Some five months earlier, at the Kitchen Sisters' request, Sam had addressed National Public Radio's annual conference in Washington, D.C. "Sam went out of his way for us," Davia said. "I mean, he knew he was anointing us. Once we had Sam Phillips, we had the world [for] that project. And he saw his own world in it, that he was being framed in the context of the important sounds of the century that started with Thomas Edison [whose story had inaugurated the series earlier in the year]. He saw himself as part of that continuum."

But Sam, of course, was only going to do it his way. And as he started to veer off course in his remarks to his distinguished audience, Davia made what she knew could be little more than a vain attempt to intervene, suggesting, "I think they might be interested in . . ." She never got any further as Sam gave her a look that as much as said, "Don't try to tell me what to say. I'm just getting warmed up."

The audience loved it. "From his pointy black cowboy boots to black collar stud to smoked glasses hiding blue eyes," reported the *Washington Post*, as if recording the sighting of a rare and exotic bird, "Phillips is a piece of work, a gloriously unreconstructed Southern man, salty enough to make a packed conference room full of public radio adults titter like grade-schoolers hearing a dirty word." Just to underscore the power of sound, Sam pointed out to them that when a girl whispered in your ear and said, "Darling, I love you," that was something that could always just carry you away. On the other hand, "she could show you her tits, she could show you *anything,*" he said, but, so far as intimacy was concerned, Sam insisted with perhaps some degree of exaggeration, nothing could hold a candle to the sound of the human voice.

His expansive speech made quite an impression on everyone, Davia said, but the irony was that in a room full of sound professionals, no one thought to record it.

F OR SAM it was all, in a sense, catch-as-catch-can. Sometimes he lived up to expectations, sometimes he didn't, but he took his singular responsibility very seriously: to be his own bad self at all times. Which was one more way of reasserting his long-standing belief in unreconstructed individualism, in the all-important precept of unpredictable spontaneity.

I remember another event in 1999, when Johnny Cash was being recognized by the Memphis chapter of NARAS (the National Academy of Recording Arts and Sciences, the official voice of the music industry). Sam spoke at the end of a long evening in which he may have had a drink or two at the table we shared with Jack Clement, who was in a weird, noncommunicative mood, possibly stemming from Sam's denial that he had ever fired Jack after Jack cheerfully referred to it at a lunchtime press conference. Sam was wearing his white dinner jacket with a black shirt, black leather pants, and a black leather vest, and the crowd was growing restive even before he started to speak. After bestowing compliments galore on each of the previous speakers and NARAS in both its national and regional manifestations, Sam settled briefly on a celebration of the role that experience played in creativity and, beyond that, the messianic role that creativity — specifically *music* — could play in the affairs of man.

"If we hadn't have picked cotton and hoed cotton on our knees, baby," he told a roomful of people, some of whom clearly had not been near a cotton field in their life, "we wouldn't know what the hell music is all about. That is an absolute resolute fact. I can also say to you that it is very easy to condemn the public officials of this city and this county and this area. I don't believe in that. I can understand the frustration we all feel. But let me tell you something — educating people to understand and just to see how powerful the elements of music are to bring us not only enjoyment but to bring us together. Not just in this area, not just in the United States, but around the world, folks. All the ambassadors in the world, all the damn wars that have been fought have in no way come within [one] thousandth of the potential of the understanding that the human race can get from music. And a lot of it started here and all over this great beautiful nation of the USA."

But then he arrived at his main theme, which turned out to be Memphis, and his purpose, which turned out to be to get the damn NARAS Hall of Fame and Museum located in Memphis, in the very Pyramid, built on the river just like Memphis on the Nile, in which this evening's ceremonies were being held. A sentiment that was greeted with a modicum of applause until he got diverted once again into musing about what might happen if Jesus Christ came back to earth and had a chance to visit Memphis. There were a considerable number of murmurs by now, but Sam was undaunted. When Jesus Christ came back to earth, he said, now, let me tell you something, he told an audience that didn't want to be told anything at this point, "when Jesus comes back, he might want to hang around for a while." And if he did, there was no question of where he would be staying: he would certainly want to spend a night at the Hotel Peabody. And "if he saw and heard what I did tonight," Sam declared with suitable pauses for dramatic emphasis, "he might stay at the Peabody for a few days, you know."

"Some people," said NARAS chapter head Jon Hornyak, "said it was the greatest speech they ever heard. Some people said it was the greatest disgrace." It was, clearly, a "dividing line in Memphis."

It was as if somehow Sam had placed his faith, *almost literally,* in the power of the spoken word, not simply to convey meaning but to rearrange molecules, move mountains, and bring Jesus and the Rock and Roll Hall of Fame (in the form of the Grammy Hall of Fame) back to Memphis. There's no denying that Sam had come by now to revel in his eccentric public role — it seemed the one thing that gave him the opportunity to express that invincible optimism at the core of his belief, an optimism at direct odds with that part of his makeup that forced him at times simply to "disappear." He fought valiantly against the anxieties that had plagued him since childhood, but there were times, sadly, when words simply failed him, as they must inevitably fail us all.

The first time I ever saw Sam look old was at the funeral of his granddaughter Kim (Knox's only child), shortly after we finished shooting the documentary, in December of 1999. Kim was thirty-two years old, a bright, vibrant young woman just a month away from getting her master's degree in child psychology at Pepperdine, who simply went to sleep one night and failed to wake up, the victim of an undiagnosed heart infection mistakenly treated as flu.

It was, it need hardly be said, an unutterably sad occasion. I think only someone who has lost a child can imagine the grief that Knox and Kim's mother, Betty, felt, though Knox as always conducted himself with grace and gallantry, barely revealing the bruised quizzicality that has characterized his life ever since the inception of his illness. Sam looked completely stricken. For the first (and maybe only) time in our long acquaintance, I saw him just look defeated, shoulders slumped, eyes almost imploring, like a man who has lost faith in the rationality of the universe. "My grandfather," Kim had written as a senior in high school, "believes in being an individual. In many people's eyes he is an eccentric, but [he was] a man ahead of his time. . . . I have always looked up to him, [but] there are many stories I know that reporters do not that place him higher in my heart. He always helps the people close to him in need. He has morally and financially helped his many sisters and brothers and his children without ever mentioning a word to anyone." "Grandpa could write a book," Sam wrote in a heartbroken note to Terry Pace two days before the funeral, "of her talents and genius."

But then Sam pulled himself together. I don't know what it was that caused the transformation, but all of a sudden it was as if he remembered the role that had been thrust on him, the role that he had embraced ever since he was a young man, and he straightened his shoulders and greeted each and every one of the people who had come to mourn with the same compassionate gallantry that he had once shown Elvis on the death of his mother, the same patient understanding that he had extended to the mother of the little girl in Russellville, Alabama, when he was working for the Brown-Service Funeral Home almost sixty years before, the young mother who couldn't bear to give up her daughter's body.

At the restaurant to which the family repaired after the service Sam was still struggling for meaning, still looking for a formulation that could give some surcease from suffering. "In a tragic situation," Becky had written of her husband, "[Sam] always is the first to lend a hand." He might be "hurting inside," she wrote in a kind of poetic shorthand, but he always presented "the appearance of strength." It was from Sam, Knox said, that he had learned to "always hold your head high," no matter what his personal trials and tribulations. "I might be down, but if Kim came to me with a problem, I had to show her: *there's a way out.*" If that was true — and Knox had no doubt that it was — "My first thought when I learned of her death was: 'I'm going to do a good job with it. I'm not going to fall apart. Kim wouldn't want me to. I have to do this in her honor.'"

Sam was oblivious now not just to the presence of other diners but to the existence of family and friends, as he almost desperately sought a transcendent note and his voice swelled in both volume and intensity, so that no one in the room could ignore the words of this man so obviously in pain but struggling to rise above it. I don't remember all the words now, but Sam's voice rose and rose until in the end he confronted the final contradiction of faith. "She hasn't gone to a better place," he roared indignantly at some imagined preacher's false syllogism. "She's gone to *her* place," he thundered. And then after a momentary pause: "She's gone to her place," he repeated. And we all sat there stunned — almost persuaded.

THE BOOK became more and more of an issue over the next couple of years. Sam's book, that is. He talked about it constantly. He let me know in no uncertain terms that he was furious at me for wasting my time on a biography of Sam Cooke when I could be working on a book about him (he was kidding, kind of — but not really). I told him he was selling the other Sam short — he was probably thinking only of pop songs like "You Send Me" — but he was not about to be mollified. I made a tape for him composed mainly of Sam's gospel recordings with the Soul Stirrers, together with great gospel-influenced numbers like "Bring It On Home to Me" and "Lost and Lookin'." Not surprisingly, I never heard Sam's reaction, but Knox loved it.

I say "not surprisingly," because, as should be evident by now, when Sam was focused on something, he didn't play. I never doubted his affection for me at this point, or his regard — but I knew he was never going to let up. He might flatter me, comparing my work as a writer, and my feel for my subject, with his feel for the artists he worked with. Sometimes he exerted gentle pressure. ("Let me quote one thing that will be in my book if Peter will ever write it. He's trying to get out of it," he confided to a public audience in my presence on more than one occasion.) Sometimes he just unloaded, making clear his impatience, or exasperation, or just plain frustration, whatever you want to call it. (I tended to regard it as a moment of theater.) But one way or another he knew, and I did, too, that I would ultimately capitulate, however great my reluctance — not out of cowardice, not out of fear, but out of affection, respect, and a refusal to turn away from someone who had so enriched my own and so many other lives, in my case in a personal way I could never fully repay.

Let me explain my ambivalence. For one thing, I didn't really believe Sam wanted to do this (we're speaking here of autobiography). He had talked about it for so long and imagined it in so many guises ("I may write a book about the Wolf") that it was almost as if he had wrung all spontaneity from the enterprise, that he would never be satisfied with "the thing itself," as opposed to all the expectations he had put on it. More to the point, though, I didn't see how a full-scale collaboration could ever work. Sam was no more a "partner-type" person now than he was when Marion first made the observation fifty years earlier. I told him again and again I would help in any way I could — with publishers, with editorial ideas, I even suggested that he do it with Terry Pace, who, in addition to all of his many other attributes (including Sam's unreserved affection), had the advantage of being close by.

We were in Seattle, in May of 2001, to do a program at the Experience Music Project, when I finally gave in. It wasn't a very good trip — well, it wasn't a very good program (it was a *great* trip!). For the onstage interview Sam wasn't anywhere near as focused, or as confident, for want of a better word, as at the British Film Institute appearance the year before. And then he got drunk at the celebratory dinner the following night — which was understandable enough, given that we sat around at the restaurant for almost two hours with only hors d'oeuvres and drinks to consume while awaiting the arrival of key EMP personnel who had been scooped up for a meeting by their CEO. But what I didn't know then — and in fact didn't find out until well after Sam's death — was that Sam was experiencing serious pulmonary problems at the time as well as increasing back pain, to the point that he needed an oxygen tank in his room and wasn't embarrassed to request a wheelchair at the airport. But I had no sense of this at the breakfast meeting Sam had so carefully planned — I had no sense of it over the next year, and outside of Sally (and probably Becky) I'm not sure how many others did either, Sam was so determined to present a positive aspect to the world. As Knox said, "He always showed you strength. He never appeared weak. We didn't even know he was sick." Whatever he may have been feeling, he seemed as jaunty as ever, as irreverent in his attitudes ("I never cared what people thought about me," he was as likely as not to blurt out. "I didn't go around as a child espousing my fascination [or worrying] what some of the unconventional things I thought would show"), and as eccentrically — as *electrically* — spiffy in his appearance.

It became obvious from the start that Sam had a definite agenda for our meeting. Alexandra and I met Sally and him in the hotel dining room — Sam made it clear that *he* was paying, which was not in the least unusual but seemed in this case part of the whole setup — and he laid out the plan he had come up with. He had been talking with Alex Ward, a longtime oldies DJ and proprietor of Professional Video Systems near Overton Park in Memphis, about digital audio recorders, and he thought he had the right one picked out. We each would have our own recorder, which would function, I believe, as a means to share and edit digital information — this was long before "cloud" storage systems like Dropbox were developed to share this information much more easily — and in this way we would be able to minimize the issue of distance, which I had suggested might inhibit the easy flow of collaboration. Don't ask me to explain all this — I didn't take notes, but it made sense at the time, and Sam had worked it all out anyway, except for the final decision as to which particular model might best serve our purpose.

Clearly I had no choice in the matter but to assent. Unequivocally. Or *unequivocably,* as Sam might have said. As soon as I finished the Sam Cooke, I said, we would begin in earnest — and in the meantime there was no reason we couldn't make a start. Sam was jubilant, and when I called Knox on the phone, he was, too. (Knox had broken his ankle just a week before and so wasn't able to make the trip.) Neither of us voiced our underlying doubt.

I suppose I ought to make it clear at this point that there would have been no holdback on my part if we had ever gotten started. For all of my reservations, I wouldn't have hesitated to write the book, and I would have done the very best I could to surmount the obstacles that stood in the way, both personal and professional — *but* (and I doubt that this even needs to be said) by now it had as much to do with my affection for Sam — hell, why not just come right out and say it, even if it raises all sorts of questions about that mythical quality of "objectivity" — I loved Sam, and I had come to recognize more and more a kind of fragility on his part that needed support as much as it did opposition. Ultimately, I wondered if throwing himself wholeheartedly into an endeavor of this sort might not be too much of an unretractable admission of mortality for Sam to bear.

Sally clearly shared my doubts — though I know she wouldn't put it quite that way. "Sam always said he wanted to write his book," she told me after Sam died. "But, you know, Peter, I don't think Sam ever wanted to write a book. He didn't want to do the A& E documentary, but after he did it, he was proud that he did. But to sit down and write a book—he never really started. Do you know that? He got a tape recorder—he told Alex Ward what kind of machine he wanted, and Alex got him stuff and would bring it out here—but he never turned [it] on and he never said a word into it to start his book."

E VEN WITHOUT KNOWING FOR SURE how this whole book project would turn out, for me this marked a real change in our relationship. I don't mean to say that all of a sudden I started feeling sorry for Sam—I didn't in any way. Sam was still Sam, the same person that Jack Clement described in the documentary as "the most dynamic person I've ever seen, he's almost fearsome at times," someone with the continuing power to inspire, intimidate, actuate, and lead. He was, unquestionably, still that Sam. And believe me, I never thought of Sam as *old*—no one did, least of all Sam. Nor did his energy seem the least bit diminished on those occasions when you saw him in public, or in private. But the occasions were fewer. And, without meaning to suggest any of the sharpened focus of hindsight, one had an almost inescapable sense of his vulnerability. There were a couple of ill-advised documentary projects that he embarked upon at this time—ill-advised because he simply no longer had the capacity to protect himself, or his point of view, with the single-minded ferocity of vision that Jack cited in his description, or with that invincible sense of self-certainty either. And yet at this point he simply seemed incapable of saying no to any opportunity he was offered to tell his story.

There was one moment in the second documentary, Dick Pearce and Robbie Kenner's *The Road to Memphis*, in the seven-part Martin Scorsese Blues series, where he got lost in a story he had told a thousand times before, about the racial remarks he encountered at WREC for "fooling around with a bunch of niggers." His fellow conversationalist, Ike Turner, seventy years old and dressed to kill in bright, mustard-colored pants, a purple shirt with yellow accents, and a chain around his neck, just cackled. The exchange turns serious, however, when Sam tries to make a point that is one of the cornerstones of his beliefs: that his white artists, too, were authentic originals, that they may have borrowed from the African-American tradition, but they brought just as much of their own experience to it. Ike shakes his head in vehement disagreement. "No, no," he says with little regard for social niceties, "just then you said that they didn't copy the black style—they *dead on it.*" Sam, clearly disturbed, goes on trying to make his point, with painfully diminishing results, until at last he throws up his hands and demands almost imploringly, "Do you love me? Or have you fallen out of love with me?" And with a tenderness that not even his admirers might credit, Ike simply declares, "You know I love you. Ain't gonna never change."

"Making fun of me," Sam grumbles, staring balefully into the camera. "Do you believe that?" And Ike kisses him on the forehead as he gets up to go, leaving Sam looking sadly disgruntled until he rises from his seat and starts to sing "That's All Right, Mama." And Ike comes back into the room and, speaking into the camera himself, says without a trace of anything but genuine affection, "That's the first time I ever heard him sing in my life!"

Ike was one of the few of his old artists with whom he continued to stay in touch. He had always maintained a highly congenial relationship with Jack Clement, and his love for Johnny Cash had survived betrayal, personal disaster, and even lawsuits, perhaps because, as much as anything else, in some ways the relationship never really changed. Sam had stood by John in his darkest hours, and the intensity of their underlying feeling for each other had never wavered, even if it took on a ceremonial cast at times.

But for all of his bonhomie and the deep-seated pride he took in the accomplishments of each of his discoveries, Sam kept a nervous distance from most. He never had anything but the most positive things to say about them all ("If there [was] one damn shit-ass, I'd tell you—but even if there was, it still wouldn't have anything to do with me thinking that if he had talent it deserved to be expressed"), and he had learned to express those superlatives in different ways for each and every one. (Jerry Lee possessed the greatest innate talent, Elvis was the most charismatic, no one else could tell as profound a story in as universal a manner as Johnny Cash, Roscoe Gordon had developed his own inimitable rhythm, and Howlin' Wolf and Charlie Rich remained two of the deepest human beings he had ever encountered, with gifts that were both incalculable and immeasurable—*they* were the artists Sam would have chosen to work with until the day he died.) And yet in almost every instance it was at this point an arm's-length relationship. Sam was ill at ease, as he

"I'll Always Love Yea." *Courtesy of the Sam Phillips Family*

explained to the BBC's Paul Jones, with managing the expectations not just of the fans but of the artists themselves. "I don't think I'm timid, but I'm uncomfortable. I don't like to extemporaneously answer questions and things on the run," he said with an honesty that was barely masked by indirection. And so for the most part reunions were limited to formal occasions, with intimacy neither risked nor rejected.

With Ike Turner it was, for some reason, different. Maybe it just came down to Ike's own irreverent (and irrepressible) personality. The relationship had been rekindled at the 1998 opening of the new Rock and Roll Hall of Fame inductees' display at the museum in Cleveland, when they shared a limo to the exhibit and Sam was knocked out by Ike's green shoes. Not long afterward Sam went down to the Lady Luck Casino in Lula, Mississippi, to see Ike play (this was an almost unheard-of event for Sam, who had rarely gone to see any of his old artists, including Howlin' Wolf, and who had no use whatsoever for gambling). Sam took the occasion to present Ike with an autographed picture of the two of them in the backseat of the limo in Cleveland, and Ike in turn inscribed a copy of the same picture, "To My Real Love SAM I'll Always Love Yea."

Ike, who had only recently gone back to playing piano (he was known for his guitar-playing in all his years directing the Ike and Tina Turner Revue), stormed through "Rocket 88," pointing out to the audience "the man who introduced Elvis, me, and a lot of others." Afterward, Sam showed no hesitation in critiquing the show, and Ike accepted Sam's suggestions that he incorporate more blues into his set with good humor and humility, I'm sure, and very likely a dollop of caustic delight.

One of the few artists with whom Sam felt similarly at ease was Jerry Lee Lewis. With Jerry Lee, who just like Ike was always indomitably himself, for better or worse, Sam seemed to feel equally unburdened. He used to go to Jerry's famous birthday parties at Bad Bob's Vapors and as often as not delivered long, detailed critiques, which were received with a surprising degree of filial attentiveness and appreciation. Then one night in early March 2002, Jerry Lee showed up at Sam's door in the pouring rain. It was ten-thirty or eleven, and Sam and Sally were in their pajamas, but Jerry appeared agitated, he seemed to have something he wanted to get off his chest, and there was no more hesitation about inviting him in than there would have been forty-five years earlier, when he was twenty-one years old and just starting out in the business.

That was what he wanted to talk about. To Sally's astonishment, he had come to offer an apology, of all things. "First time," Sally said, "I ever heard this man say anything was his fault. But he said it. About Myra. He said, 'I should have never taken her to London.' He must have been here for two hours, telling Sam all the mistakes that he'd made. He just set there and talked and talked and talked. But, you know, I think he felt better by doing it. I really do. I think he felt like this was something that he really wanted to tell Sam." And meanwhile, the phones of the two associates who had accompanied him kept ringing and ringing. Evidently, Sam and Sally were finally able to deduce, he was supposed to be in Ferriday that night for the grand opening of the Delta Music Museum, which was in essence dedicated to him and his two cousins, country star Mickey Gilley and televangelist Jimmy Lee Swaggart. But he didn't like the plane the governor's office sent, and he didn't like the weather. So he just stayed, pouring his heart out to a man whose admiration for his talent was exceeded only by his own and whose loyalty and affection remained undiminished.

As Jerry Lee once said in another, but no less revealing, context: "I always wished that my mind was as swift as my piano playing. There's no telling how things might have turned out. Can you imagine thinking that fast? But that's not the way it is. Time just eats you up, and there's nothing that you can do about that. It'll always win. Nobody's that fast."

S AM COULDN'T HAVE put it any more eloquently. He was, by nature, a solitary man. This was something he had always known, it was something that he volunteered without prompting the first time that we met, even as he expressed regret that this was so. "I have a lot of friends," he said. "I really do." But, he said, he had to "build friends" carefully — often overcoming a degree of initial suspicion that he was unable to escape — in his own way.

In many ways he was no more interpretable than the most individuated of his artists, than Jerry Lee Lewis, or Howlin' Wolf, or Charlie Rich, for that matter — and no more accessible either. At times Sam's determined removal of himself from anyone else's expectations but his own could create an impregnable wall that even those closest to him could not breach. ("You know," Sally said with a solemn sigh, "Sam will say anything to anybody at any time.") Dewey was gone, Jimmy Connolly was gone, Paul Ackerman was gone — perhaps the only ones whose unconditional love Sam had sought and rewarded with a reciprocal love of his own.

Of all his old friends, only Kemmons Wilson was left — and yet, as Sally said, even with Kemmons there was a gulf. "Sam considered Kemmons one of his closest friends, he was just one of the best friends that Sam ever had, someone he really loved — and yet they didn't talk or see each other a lot. Sam would always take Kemmons' calls, it didn't matter where he was or what he was doing, [they just] didn't socialize a lot."

After Kemmons' wife, Dorothy, died in early 2001, Sam made it his business to see more of him — he and Sally would take Kemmons out to dinner occasionally, and then they would all share in the sugar-free chocolate chip ice cream that Kemmons, a diabetic, stocked up in his freezer in gallon containers, which he hastened to assure Sam he got at a very good price. ("A day without ice cream," Kemmons was frequently given to expound, "is like a day without love.")

But Kemmons, for all of his appreciation of Sam, had his own view of their friendship. He was himself in many ways as energetically eccentric a figure as Sam in Memphis' fabled pantheon of eccentricity (Kemmons in the 1990s had taken to printing billion- and trillion-dollar bills

With Kemmons at the Blues Ball. *Courtesy of Kemmons Wilson Companies*

engraved with the faces of himself, his late mother, Doll, and his wife, and giving them out to friends and passing strangers alike. The back of the bill declared, "This certificate is backed and secured only by confidence in the American dream"), but he considered himself a family man first and foremost. After all, it was the $2 fee for each of his five children tacked on to the $6 room rate that he encountered on their 1951 drive to Washington, D.C., that first gave him the incentive to create a *family* motel chain, and it was his wife of sixty years who, after his mother, had been his constant inspiration.

"Sam's a guy pretty much like me," he could unhesitatingly declare. "He knew what he wanted, and he wanted to do it his way. And if you didn't do it his way, he didn't like it. And I'm pretty much that way. But I was happily married, I had five kids and stayed home. Sam just had a different kind of life — I guess that's the reason we didn't see much of him."

Besides, said Kemmons, a pink-cheeked, fresh-scrubbed Rotarian go-getter, even as an old man, he just didn't know about Sam's beard. "I say a man's hiding—[are there] any beards here?" he inquired of his interviewers. And after taking a quick look around and ascertaining that there were none among the small group who had come out to film him for Sam's A&E documentary at his airplane hangar, he declared with a certain amount of conflicted reluctance, "Well, a man that hides behind a beard has got something he's trying to hide. He don't want to be out there."

THE TAO OF SAM

"I'M NOT TRYING to be ugly or discourteous," Sam said one day, trying to explain his steadfast refusal to be pinned down. "[But] I'm weird. To you I look pretty normal, [but] you don't know." I knew I didn't know — but I was *supposed* to. As Sam kept hammering away at me, I needed to both feel the weight of history and then wriggle free of it — if I were to prove myself worthy of this task. "You understand," Sam sometimes said, after issuing a particularly enigmatic pronouncement, but whether the statement was declarative or interrogative I was never quite sure.

On the other hand, Sam did not really want to be understood, even by himself. He deeply mistrusted understanding over feeling. As he said to me one time, "I don't want to know what I am, Peter. Maybe somebody else can figure it out sometime. I never, never wanted to know what I am. I have just wanted to know that I never looked out on one day of my life, no matter how bleak it was, and didn't have —" Here he broke off into what seemed like a digression. But his point was, simply, that it was all part of the life experience, the Sam Phillips experience, the Peter Guralnick experience, it didn't matter, "all of these things, as multitudinous as they are, is to me experience, I look back on it as one experience" — and it was all to be *cherished.*

Not everyone bought into this. Some of Sam's oldest acquaintances saw him as no more than a colorful "character," and more than one could dismiss him for his egregious lack of humility. "I'm not like Sam," said one prominent record producer. "I don't claim to have invented the wheel."

But Sam genuinely enjoyed his life. Sally thought he even "got to enjoying it a little more, you know, than when the responsibility was always on his shoulder. I mean, back then, there was a lot of things going on" — with the concomitant fear of "not wanting to lose those things." He remained as busy as ever — his philosophy, as his son Jerry pointed out, continued to be "work hard all the time, no hands on the clock. He's the one that's going to be staying up late, getting up early. He's gonna be the one that's educating himself to what he's trying to get done." And if he weren't, one might implicitly be given to understand, his attention could be drawn all too easily to the fleeting passage of time.

More and more his attention was drawn now to ceremonial occasions and expressions of support, both financial and spiritual, for old friends and new. Weddings, funerals, birthdays — Sam invariably made it his business to attend, and his presence was always deeply felt. "When my son Greg was killed in 1997," said fellow Florentine Kelso Herston, who had managed Sam's publishing business in Nashville in the early 1960s and directed him to the Nashville studio in the Cumberland Lodge Building, "he was one of the first people to call. He said, 'I was in a business meeting when I heard. Sally and I are going to come over right away.' I think they came that afternoon, and he was really kind. You know, he went up to the casket with me and talked to [my son] and everything. Of course he'd known Greg when he was a young kid. He didn't have to do that, but he did." It was the kind of intimacy with which Sam, who had seen very little of Kelso in recent years, was comfortable — in time of need he was always there, and unstinting in his emotional generosity, but, just as with his former artists, he seemed to feel far less comfortable with everyday social intercourse. The connection was never lost but never fully sustained either.

Like many public figures (and Sam was certainly a public figure by now), you were not going to see Sam out in public with anything less than an upbeat mood. But it was a mood that was bolstered as much by philosophy as by temperament. "No matter what happens to you in this world," he told *Rolling Stone* reporter Elizabeth Kaye, "if you don't make it your business to be happy, then you may have gained the whole world [but] lost your spirit and maybe even your damned soul." Or, to put it another way, on another occasion: "Hell, I'm not talking about utopia. Not at all. It's not necessary to talk about utopia. [This] *is* utopia. Period. I guarantee you. It doesn't mean every day you're going to wake up and the sun's gonna shine. If it did we might have a dry planet. I'm just telling you, there is so much that you can do. And I am living proof."

HIS NEPHEW PHILLIP, just four years younger and probably as close to him as anyone in the Lovelace Community family, thought Sam would live to be a hundred. "In fact," Phillip said, "he planned things that way."

"He acted like he was going to be around forever," echoed his doctor, who, despite abundant evidence to the contrary, tended to think so, too. "He acted like he had a handle on everything, and he could control everything," said Dr. Kraus, who was doing everything he could to treat Sam's worsening pulmonary condition and his increasingly severe osteoporosis. "There weren't many people that gave me advice the way Sam did. He always was good at it."

For his part, Sam remained determined to focus on the future. And yet at the same time, there were elements of the past that never ceased to draw him back. He loved the marches of John Philip Sousa and prided himself on his ability to recall every one. His boyhood days in Florence remained a source of constant wonderment and fascination. And, of course, Beale Street was always calling. "Oh God, what I wouldn't give to just walk down that street just one more time when it was really Beale Street," he told the BBC's Paul Jones. "I think I'd give up a goodly portion of the rest of my life to get to do it."

Beale Street was heaven, he told one and all. And when Knox was asked by a Memphis lifestyle magazine to name his dream vacation in 2003, he went back to "Beale Street in 1952, a land of promise and imagination, in the company of my then twenty-nine-year-old brilliant, intuitive, and perceptive father, Sam, who wouldn't hear of taking the trip without bringing along the most outgoing ambassador of enthusiasm, energy, and goodwill that either of us ever met, legendary Memphis DJ Dewey Phillips. In other words, this would be a family vacation, for even if Dewey was not related by blood, he was, as my father always said, a true brother."

Sam was very ill by then, and he might have rejected the sentimentality, if not the sentiment ("By the light of day," Knox went on, "Beale Street might not have looked so glamorous, but it was *shining* with the hopes and aspirations and beliefs of all the people who thronged to its sights") — but I don't think so. It was in keeping with his own view of his life, which never lost its capacity to entertain and instruct. To Sam it was in a sense like a great epic novel, and his enthusiasm for the tale never flagged. Uncle Silas was at the epicenter of the narrative, Uncle Silas and Beale Street called up everything in which Sam ever believed, with little distinction made between myth and reality, because it was, for all of its remarkably vivid eidetic detail, in the end as much a creation myth as a straightforward narrative.

When he was firing on all cylinders (and he was *frequently* firing on all cylinders), you were treated to a supernova of free association in which there was no telling what you might get. It never failed to feature deep, often imponderable philosophical thoughts ("Do you realize how beautiful total chaos is?")—but it could just as easily incorporate Sam's own autologous observations on his interaction with the natural world. ("A dog won't bite me," he was as likely as not to proclaim, while insisting that "Nobody talks to a frog but me.") You just never knew where the conversation might go—even old tales took on entirely new hues, as Sam's interest was drawn to a digression (not a correction, an expansion) that might never have occurred to him before. It was like his recordings: the melody, the rhythm, the chord changes provided a form, a *structure*, from which the greater truth might take off.

So far as conventional truths went, Sam remained cheerfully theosophic—he never ceased to assert his belief in a higher spirit, but in the end I would say he subscribed to the church of himself. Certainly he had little interest in religion as presently "organized." He believed in prayer—but primarily as it was reflected in the unselfishness of one's prayer for another. Most of all he believed in the here-and-now. "We don't have to wait for the hereafter," he might declare in one of his frequent sermons on the transformative nature of the imagination, of music in particular. "How beautiful it is to be alive today, to see this peak, this mountain top, all the little things that went [into it], the dirt and the pushing and the pulling and the storms and the wind and the tide and the rain and the snow and the sleet—all of it spiritually coming together for us to get up to where we can see and know and appreciate, that beautiful valley, the contours of life's earth—not the physical, but *LIFE'S* earth."

Every story taught a lesson, every observation suggested a template for a higher plane. For Sam above all considered himself a teacher. However much he may have loved to shock, he was intent even more on delivering his message: of free-thinking, of the necessity for a hard-headed approach to the practicalities of life, of the equal necessity for a dream to undergird those practicalities, and, ultimately, of never failing to strive for the ideal of individualism and freedom.

"I prepared myself for other avenues," Sam said, coming as close as he could to summing up this unquantifiable mix as he spoke of the vision he himself had originally pursued. "And I certainly had no idea I could do it with economic success. So I had hopefully approached it from the standpoint of doing it — and I hate to [use] this word — as an 'avocation.' But instead of trying to do something just to relieve my mind — like playing something, and I loved baseball — I put it in my mind, 'Look, prepare yourself, and if the best comes, fine, if it doesn't, please don't be disappointed — but make sure, wherever you get with your mission, complete it. *Complete it.* Wherever you go, if you've seen that you can go no further, just make sure that up to that point you were satisfied."

That was the lesson — well, one of them anyway — he delivered to me the first time we met. And he never failed to reiterate it in a multiplicity of versions every time we met thereafter. "He'll dispense advice without being asked," Knox said with wholehearted admiration. "He is a teacher, and he perceives himself as that, and he tries to give you, you know, his heartfelt, total thought." It didn't matter who he was talking to — his sons, his yardman, his artists, his employees — he was always intent on delivering his message, whether personal or pragmatic. It could be something as urgent and practical as offering informed medical advice. One time I came in as Sam was in the midst of delivering an impassioned lecture to his yardman, Al, a trusted family friend and employee, on the importance of diet in the treatment of hypertension, an illness that ran in his family. Another time, Sally said, some men came out to cut down a tree in front of the house. "The tree was dead or dying, and Sam said, Yeah, they could cut it down. But then I have this picture of him out there telling them, the tree people, how to cut it down and get it out of the way. 'I mean, if you want to cut the tree down, that's fine, but I'll tell you how to do it.' And he would know *how* to do it, Peter, that's the thing, and you would think he was right. Even somebody [who] had been doing it all their life. He could tell them better how to do it."

O NE OF THE MOST frequently asked questions of a biographer — well, *this* biographer anyway — is, What did you discover in all your years of research and rumination that surprised you most? The "Rosebud" moment, in other words, the previously unknown element, or incident, or revelation, that provides the key to character, the motivation for a life's work? Well, I don't know about that, I'm not very big on revelations — and in a certain sense the most honest answer is that *everything* is surprising. Not because the story is not known — usually the broad outlines of the generally accepted narrative are not going to change—but because context puts them in an entirely different light. And if you proceed with the same impulse as any other kind of writer—setting aside knowledge of outcome as you explore the particulars of event—you can't help but be surprised by that outcome. And you hope the reader will be, too, however familiar that conclusion may be.

But with Sam I did experience a genuine revelation—and I'm not sure in describing it I'm not displaying my own naïveté, but so be it. Some years after Sam died, Knox and Jerry discovered at their mother's house a trunk full of letters and papers, many of which bore directly on Sam's experience of mental illness. I don't know why I should have been surprised. Sam had never hidden anything about that experience—the two "nervous breakdowns," the electroshock treatments—from me or anybody else. In fact, one of the first times we talked, he called Becky up to determine the exact dates of his hospitalization in 1951. "I don't know why you want to be telling that man about that," said Becky, whom I had barely met at this point but who then dutifully provided the information. He spoke less frequently of his hospitalization in Birmingham in 1944, but Becky had painted a vivid picture for me, of how she hid under the bed when visiting hours were over and stayed there all night to keep Sam company, sneaking out of the sanitarium at dawn.

I imagined it, I guess, as a *story*, a *fable*, in which Sam was the Sam I knew, and the incalculable depth of Becky's love, selfless, devoted, romantic beyond measure, could not help but protect her young husband from harm. Wasn't that the meaning of the stories that Becky told me, and Sam, too, of how, when they first met, there were times he was simply unable to shut off his thoughts, to keep his mind from racing away from him, and he had to pull over by the side of the road and lay his head in Becky's lap, until he was able to calm down?

It wasn't that the letters told a different story exactly—it was just that they told so much *more* of a story, so much rawer and realer and messier a story, just as Sam always insisted (and I would always have concurred, with or without Sam's prompting) real life always does. Even knowing Becky as I did, I don't think I could ever have fully imagined the naked intensity of her feelings, her willing abandonment not just of propriety but of her own sense of self-regard for this beautiful, idealistic young man with the wind and the rain in his hair.

"Dearest Sam," she wrote, just months after they first met, "I'm writing this letter to tell you my deepest feelings. I might begin by telling you that you are my dream boy. You're my first sweetheart and I might add the only one I will ever want. All my heart is filled with love for you. There is no room for another love."

I feel a little guilty at invading the privacy of this very private, gentle, and self-effacing woman, but it was, in stark contrast, her immoderation, the terrible ferocity of her love that stands out most in this real-time record of that turbulent period in her life. "'I love you,'" she went on in the same early letter. "I only dreamed that I would ever hear you say this to me.

> And when you did, I knew the beginning of my dream was coming true, and as time went by each time I saw you made me have an even deeper feeling for you. You called me darling, yes, and you kissed me, and when you did I seemed to vanish to another world. A world where there is no pain, sorrow, and unhappiness. I was in a world with you. We stood out under the moon and stars with all the rest of the world around us, but I wasn't thinking of the rest of the world but only of our own together. . . .
>
> Perhaps you think I am very foolish to write you a letter like that, and I suppose I am foolish, but please don't laugh at me. I believe you will understand that I only want you to know my true feelings. I don't want to interfere in any way with your life. I don't want you to think I am trying to make you love me, because I wouldn't want a made love. I only want you to know that wherever you are, whatever you are doing I will be thinking of you and loving you every minute. Forgive me if I shouldn't have written you this letter, but please believe it, for every word is from my heart.

> With all my love,
> Rebecca

And it is Sam's own naked need, the utter helplessness he showed in the face of so bewildering a loss of control, so much at odds with his conception of himself and his plans for the future, that is as much of a shock. "It's a dreadful day for me," he writes to Becky, as his troubles begin to mount in June of 1944, just six months after their marriage, when she is in Decatur, trying to hold down their increasingly precarious positions at the radio station, and he is stuck at his mother's house in Florence, paralyzed with fear, unable to make the fifty-mile journey back to her. On the following day: "I just absolutely feel lost without my darling. It seems so unrealistic to be away from her, even though necessary as it is. I live in trust that it won't ever have to be this way anymore. My hope, courage and faith is centered around you, you only!" And he signs it "with seas of love, Samuel." Two days after that, he seems to have firmed up his resolve to make the journey. "I know that it's been extremely hard on you," he writes, "but it's absolutely unavoidable. Maybe I can be on the job consistently from now on. Mama is coming with me to stay a while with us. I sure am glad that she's able to go back with me."

The doctors try everything. Dr. Bayles in Florence tells Sam he thinks the problem is low blood sugar ("hyper-insulism"), and he treats him with a series of shots, but evidently they do little good, and Dr Bayles expresses his dismay to a colleague in Birmingham, Dr. Seale Harris, whom he practically implores to get Sam admitted to Hill Crest Sanitarium. "I'm sending you Mr. Sam Phillips for diagnosis and treatment," Dr. Bayles writes. "He has been to so many different doctors without obtaining any relief from his symptoms that it is probably best to put him through your clinic and give him a complete examination. . . . So many of us have already failed to give this man relief, but I know that you can find his trouble and I believe give him relief. I've told him to disregard everything that the rest of us have told him and listen to you and you would cure him. Fraternally yours . . ."

I have gone into so much detail not out of any ghoulish fascination with Sam's "problems," but to illustrate just how serious those problems were. At Hill Crest, Sam had eight convulsive electroshock treatments, and in Memphis seven years later, Sam was sent home from the Gartly-Ramsay psychiatric hospital after eight more doses of electroshock with a series of pamphlets mapping out a course of self-treatment that prescribed such daily forms of "therapeutic relaxation" as "Bibliotherapy" 7:45-8, during which the patient reads or recites TR material only; 8-8:30 "Educative Therapy"; 8:30-8:45 "Reflective Therapy"; and at some point reciting the mantra "Feeling fine" twenty times in a row.

When Sam told the story in later years, he expressed indignation that his employers at both the Decatur and the Memphis radio stations didn't have greater sympathy for his plight, that they should have so failed to understand that mental illness was an illness like any other, one from which the patient was as likely to recover as from any other hospital stay. In Sam's telling, his story was always a triumph over adversity — as indeed it was — and he laughed off the suggestion that he was sent home from both hospitals with little expectation that he could ever again lead a "normal" life. When Dr. McCool stipulated that he really shouldn't be pressured or overexcited after his release from Gartly-Ramsay, not then, maybe not ever, Sam always said he took it as the best form of therapy he could have gotten. It was a challenge, and he rose to it.

But he might very well not have. That's my point. He might very well not have. "I could have ended up in Bolivar, Tennessee," Sam said from time to time in later life, referring with a specificity that no one in his audience could have grasped, to the West Tennessee Hospital for the Insane, at one time the largest such institution in the state. And for all of Sam's pep talks, however persuasive his sermons might be, the triumph of mind over matter is never one that is easily assured. For any of us. One could very well see much of Sam's later bravura as a kind of whistling in the dark, not so much an impersonation of an alternative, more heedless self as compensation for the fear, the sense of lurking disaster that continued to haunt him in one way or another for the rest of his life. It makes it so much easier to understand Sam's mixed feelings toward his brother Jud, for example, his alternating adulation and resentment of Jud's indomitable self-assurance. ("Jud," Sam always said, "had an absolutely overwhelming personality.") I'm not much inclined to psychobiography, and I recognize the limitations that a facile summary of any sort inevitably imposes. At the same time, for me this unexpected glimpse into raw, unmediated feeling only makes Sam's remarkable story even more remarkable. It is, as I've now come to view it, one of the principal factors that makes that story so heroic, while at the same time underscoring the solipsistic isolation that Sam seemed to see as his only defense against the looming void.

F AMILY WAS, IN A SENSE, his last refuge against doubt. There were, naturally, tensions between Sally and Becky, which Sam chose to ignore. Sally had her dry-eyed view of things, and Becky, for all of her faith and all of the ways in which she so desperately sought to bind everyone together, could confess on occasion, "I don't have peace of mind. I love so hard that I can't [stop worrying] if there's anything wrong with any of my family. I mean, that's a lack of faith, but I don't mean it to be that way."

Sam, Becky, Knox, and Jerry. *Courtesy of the Sam Phillips Family*

With his granddaughters, Becky said, Sam might not "throw out a lot of hugs and kisses, [but] he likes for them to shower *him* with all of that." They called him "Pop" and Grandpa, and he showed his love, Becky said, in lots of different ways. "He listens to them, he encourages them, he listens to their talent if they want to sing him a song, he [just] likes to be with them and do things with them," something that is abundantly clear in all the pictures that show Sam with them — on a scooter, in a silly party hat, or just looking as proud as any grandpa grinning at a one-year-old with a stuffed bear. When Jerry's older daughter, Halley, was born in 1986, Sam got a jigsaw puzzle of the comet for which she was named (Halley's Comet appears once every seventy-six years), and set it aside for her twenty-first birthday, which he fully intended to be around for. Knox's daughter, Kim, who as the first-born was always especially close to her grandfather, sent Sam a card every Father's Day with the salutation "Happy Pop's Day." "We're just a very close family," Becky said, "and we're very proud of that."

Knox and Jerry had each worked things out in their own way. Knox at this point was devoting himself almost exclusively to the mission he had first undertaken some three decades earlier. "My life has always been about trying to make sure that Sam's story was accurately told," he invariably volunteered, even as he continued to seek recognition for Memphis' ongoing cultural contributions to the world. And while this might on occasion lead friends to start a two- or three-person movement to "Let Knox Be Knox," he rarely seemed to chafe under the constraints of pursuing an underlying purpose other than his own. Living on the lake, forty miles from Florence, Jerry remained focused on the radio stations, but he never gave up on his dream of making his own mark on the music industry. In 1998 he started a music publishing company, Power Diamond, and with his partner, Jim Casey, leased a building on the edge of Hillsboro Village in Nashville from which they broadcast a live weekly music hour over KIX 96 in Florence. They got some good cuts on their songs and even revived the Midnight Sun label for a short time, but eventually the office and the operation were closed down, with the radio show replaced by an ambitious once-a-month "Muscle Shoals to Music Row Live" broadcast from the Marriott Shoals Conference Center in Florence.

From the time I first met him, Sam was fully aware of what he had taken away from his sons, not so much in terms of legacy as in terms of belief. "I talk to them," he told me back in 1979, "and I tell them not to be discouraged, but Knox and Jerry feel like—and there's no jealousy here—'Well, Daddy believed in something, and it happened, and I believe just as strongly not in what he did necessarily but in [my own] creativity, in the basic creativity of the artist'—but nobody will listen. And if they listen, they don't hear." But he saw no way around it, then or later. From his point of view, there was no room for the independent spirit in an industry that had put the independents out of business, there was no way for the little man to make any real money in a world of international conglomerates, and his opinions only strengthened over the years. Radio and song publishing, he remained convinced, were the only two sure sources of income in the business, they were the one way to guarantee the future.

"He just thought that if you wanted to be in business, radio was one of the best businesses that you could be in, even today," Sally said. "It's always been good. He wasn't looking to—I don't think he ever wanted to leave Knox and Jerry in charge of anything that they [would think] he wanted them to keep for the rest of their lives. He knew that they've got sense enough to know what is good for them and what's not. Leaving a bunch of stuff was not something that he really cared about. He was just thinking about making money. How to do it."

By now he had transferred nearly all of his radio ownership to Knox and Jerry, and to a lesser extent to Sally, too, but for all of his unquestionable attention to the financial end of the business, he remained, Sally said, just as fascinated by the radio airwaves as he had been from the time he was eighteen years old. He never stopped looking for new ways to improve and upgrade the signal of his stations in Florence. There was no way to really monitor the stations from Memphis, but Sleetie Mitchell, whom he saw less frequently now that the three-hour drive to Florence had become something of a chore, continued to report to him about problems from time to time. "She wasn't telling on anybody, really," Sally said, "she would just tell him, 'Well, I was listening to the radio station today and blah blah blah,' and then Sam would say to us, 'Well, now, Sleetie says—'" It had long since become a kind of running joke between Sally and Jerry. "Jerry would get so mad at Sleetie, and we got to mocking her. Jerry would say, 'Well, Sleetie says.' Finally one day I said to Sam, 'Do I have to hear everything that Sleetie says?' You know, you just get to where you want to scream."

Sleetie for her part took it all in stride. She and Sam continued to be good friends. Even if they didn't see each other as often, they remained in frequent contact on the phone, and Sleetie still came to Memphis sometimes. One of the last times she saw Sam in Florence, she told him teasingly, "You know, you just using me. You sleep in my bed. I cook for you night and day. I make all your favorite things. What do you ever do for me?" Sam just stared at her out of those blue, unblinking eyes. "Well," he said with a verbal shrug, "everybody got to use somebody."

Toward the end of his life, Sam gave serious thought to selling the radio stations. Clear Channel, one of the largest media conglomerates in the country, was buying up stations in every market, sometimes at more than double their worth, and Sam was beginning to have real doubts about the future of traditional radio in the face of such aggressive satellite competition. But he never seriously pursued the matter, perhaps in part because while Knox might very well appreciate the advantages of getting out ahead of the impending crash, Jerry, for whom radio had become a way of life, plainly could not. Not to mention what Clear Channel was doing to the radio stations they bought up.

"I don't know if he would have ever sold," Sally said. "[Because] these people who were taking over all the radio stations, the minute they took over, there were not people on the air anymore. I mean, everything is front intro and back intro, your payroll drops fifty percent [because] you have one or two people that run the radio station all the time, and everything is done at a location somewhere else. Sam just never wanted that. If somebody came in and did that to [our] radio stations, it would be a disaster for the market — for the people."

In fact, Sam was busy putting another station on the air right up until the time of his death. In this case, putting the new station on the air was not really the point. Seven years earlier, in 1995, Sam had acquired a second major radio station in Florence, WXFL, with the idea of boosting its signal from 6,000 to 50,000 watts and establishing it as the Shoals area's leader in FM country.

The expansion was almost immediately blocked by Mike Self, the present owner of WLAY, the Florence station where Sam had gotten his start. WLAY was already offering FM-country programming in the area, and, presumably for self-protection, Self obtained an FCC permit to build a new station in Clifton, Tennessee, which lay within the protective circumference mandated by the FCC to prevent one station from "short-spacing" another's signal. Sam was still fuming about this when we made the documentary in 1999, he was so angry that he could barely bring himself to utter the name of his first employer, and he was insistent that the call letters on the microphone in an early still be blurred on the screen.

In the end, after Mike Self sold WLAY, Sam bought the Clifton frequency from him, and WXFL-FM started broadcasting from its new site in March of 2000 as "KIX 96," to this day the leading country station in the area. But he still had to build the station in Clifton, to which he had now assigned the call letters WLVS (these had migrated from Memphis to his onetime "all-girls" station in Florida and were returned to Sam when he sold the Florida station at just around the time that "KIX 96" went on the air).

Work on the Clifton station proceeded slowly over the next two years, under Jerry's on-site supervision but never without Sam's active consultation. He purchased the property on the phone and got regular field reports from Jerry and Greg Pace, their tower man. "They put that station on the air on the telephone with Sam," said Sally. "It was his last radio station, but do you know, he never saw it? He never went to Clifton. He just wasn't able to."

O N MARCH 28, 2002, the Memphis chapter of NARAS kicked off what promised to be a year of celebration of the fiftieth anniversary of Sun. It was fifty years almost to the day since the pressing of the first Sun record, and the local chapter, which Knox had brought to the city against overwhelming odds some thirty years earlier, had organized a gala celebration at the Orpheum Theatre, with a shower of Sun stars (Jerry Lee Lewis, Billy Lee Riley, Sonny Burgess, and Jack Clement were all billed, and only Jerry Lee failed to show up) and national president of NARAS, Mike Greene, in attendance.

Sam was obviously in good spirits when Terry Pace, the young Florence reporter and dramaturge, first spotted him across the room, but he seemed somehow a little "detached," Terry felt, as he spoke with well-wishers and reporters, "more quiet and restrained than usual." With Sam's visits to Florence sharply curtailed, Terry hadn't seen him in a while — he hadn't even spoken to him much on the phone, with Sally generally telling what she told so many callers lately: that Sam just really didn't feel like talking. For the first time he hadn't even heard from Sam himself in advance of his visit. Ordinarily Sam made sure he had a ticket and a place to stay, but this time Jerry called at the last minute to offer him a ride up in the radio station van, and a ride back the same night. "I don't ever hear from you anymore," Sam mock-complained as he wrapped Terry in a big hug. "I guess you've just gotten too damn important — trying to keep me away from all those women of yours."

He was presented with eight different Grammy Hall of Fame certificates over the course of the evening (for "Blue Suede Shoes," for "Rocket 88," for "Whole Lotta Shakin'" and "That's All Right"), and when he got up to give his acceptance speech, NARAS dignitary Mike Greene, a man to whom punctuality and order were nearly as important as honors, told chapter director Jon Hornyak, "We just may have to go out onstage if he runs over."

They had scheduled Sam early in the evening as a precaution, but as it turned out, he delivered a brief, eloquent, and surprisingly emotional address. At its extemporaneous heart was an extended tribute to his wife, Becky, for standing by him so loyally all these years, for providing him with the kind of support he needed at a time when he so desperately needed it, when, if she hadn't been there to provide it, he might very well have fallen by the wayside. "My wife, Becky," he declared, "the most beautiful woman in the world . . . would have gone with me *in death* if [she] believed I wanted to do it. That's the type of person Becky is."

Terry was deeply moved. He had never heard Sam speak like this in public before, he couldn't remember ever hearing Sam talk about Becky in this way. But when he went backstage to congratulate Sam, Sam just said, "Well, you know, I really fucked up. I am in deep shit, brother. I may need you to give me a ride home." It didn't take long to figure out why. "You know, I got out there," Sam said with his own unique combination of gusto and chagrin, "and I started talking about Becky, because all these people know Becky, and they love her, and Becky—I just wouldn't have been anything without Becky. But then I walked backstage, and I looked at Sally and I think if she had had a cannon, she would have shot me."

Terry could certainly sympathize, but at the same time he almost had to laugh, as he recognized that Sam, however much he had fucked up, was determined now to simply square his shoulders and set it right. "He said, 'I've got to go back out there and fix it.' I went back into the audience, and at some point whoever was MCing announced that Sam had something else he would like to say. He brought Sally out onstage and went on to praise her to the heavens. She stood there by him the whole time and never said a word. He finished, and the audience politely applauded, and they went back through the curtain."

A MONTH LATER he flew to New York for a *Vanity Fair* photo shoot with Ahmet Ertegun, the founder of Atlantic Records, and still (thirty years after its acquisition by Warner Bros.-Seven Arts) its powerful chairman. Ahmet was almost exactly the same age as Sam—they went back to the beginning of the independent era—but Sam had never much liked him, and liked him even less after the way he felt that Ahmet had double-crossed Memphis in the selection of a site for the Rock and Roll Hall of Fame. He couldn't help but be resentful, too, of the way that Ahmet was putting himself front and center on the PBS American Masters television tribute to Sun, *Good Rockin' Tonight* (Ahmet was credited as producer of the accompanying album, featuring musical tributes from such luminaries as Paul McCartney, Bob Dylan, Eric Clapton, and Jimmy Page and Robert Plant), whose premiere broadcast on August 3 was the occasion for the photo session. It was all a lot of nonsense from Sam's point of view—he would have been much more comfortable with

Ahmet's onetime Atlantic Records partner, Jerry Wexler—but on the other hand he was not about to be left out, and the picture ran as an elegant full-page portrait opposite Ravi Shankar (Sam and Ahmet were dubbed "The Pioneers") in the November issue of the magazine.

It was on this trip that Knox for the first time began to be aware of just how debilitated his father really was. Despite their almost daily contact, and Knox's participation in virtually every aspect of Sam's life, he had failed to grasp the extent of Sam's weakened condition, as much as anything because every time he saw his father falter, Sam embraced the moment with such an air of jaunty confidence, you couldn't help but believe that he not only recognized the challenge, he was *glad of it*. There were a couple of times on this trip, though, when they might have to walk a couple of blocks, "and Sam would, you know, show a little trepidation, and I couldn't quite understand why, but he had a difficult time [with his breathing]. It was sort of a deteriorating situation, and I didn't realize it. Now, Sally probably did. But the truth of it was, he never wanted anybody to know that he was weak in any way. And he really wasn't—spiritually, mentally, effectively—it was just his body laying down a little bit."

There were other honors, other events, most notably a Blues Awards show in Memphis that reunited Sam with some of his earliest artists, with B.B. King, Little Milton, Roscoe Gordon, and Ike Turner all in attendance. Ike sang "Rocket 88," and all four gave an impromptu performance together onstage to the delight of the crowd. Then in August Sam geared himself up for a whirlwind of activity commemorating not only the fiftieth anniversary of Sun but the twenty-fifth of Elvis Presley's death, which would culminate in Memphis in the annual gathering of Elvis fans from around the world during the week of August 16.

At the beginning of the month, Sam and Sally flew to New York, where they met Shelby Singleton and his brother, John, to publicize the premiere broadcast of the American Masters documentary on public television and the release of a new two-CD *Sun Records 50th Anniversary Collection* on Sony / BMG.

It was a great trip, Sam really enjoyed himself, Sally said, even though the company that was supposed to deliver the oxygen tank to his hotel failed to do so and, when Sally called to complain, said they couldn't provide a substitute tank on short notice. It could have been a real setback, Sally said, because Sam needed oxygen all the time now, but evidently he was so energized by the nonstop schedule that he never had a chance to slow down. He never let on to Shelby, who was as bemused as ever by what he took to be Sam's stubborn eccentricities (he was as offended by New York City portions and prices as he was by the very idea of bottled water), not to mention his unvarnished impatience to get on with it — even if that meant making idle threats of exiting a company limo in the middle of a traffic jam. Over the course of the three-day trip, Sam did numerous radio and television interviews, visited BMG, and went out to dinner with the record-company people. ("Are you trying to wear out an old man?" he demanded of Rob Santos, the enthusiastic young BMG Heritage director of a&r, who worried that Sam might be serious, although he worried even more that he might be cited for breaking New York's new antismoking ban, until the maître d' came over and said, "Here's an ash tray, Mr. Phillips.") He did the *Charlie Rose* show as well as an interview for Sirius satellite radio, on top of the McGraw-Hill Building, across the street from Radio City, where, to his great delight, he ran into Harry Belafonte and spent ten minutes telling him how much he admired him and even serenaded him with a verse or two of "The Banana Boat Song."

But undoubtedly the highlight of the visit (after an in-store speech and signing at J&R Music World and a press reception at the Rodeo Bar and Grill earlier in the evening) was his impromptu address to the Music Monitor Network Convention, a group of independent record stores, distributors, and labels, on August 5. I'm not going to quote from it too much, because you've heard it all before — but still I can't refrain altogether from quoting from it, because it expresses so perfectly Sam's continued belief in the invincibility of the human spirit, his determination to deliver a sermon no less uplifting, no less *inspiring* to this latest generation of independent entrepreneurs, than the message he conveyed to all of his artists, his children, and anyone else who would listen, over the past fifty years.

He was bound and determined, he told them, to come over and say hello if his schedulers at BMG would permit "an old cat like me" to break away from the busy agenda they had set for him. The reason it was so important to him should be almost self-evident — because "you people

Courtesy of the Sam Phillips Family

have got to be the bravest people and the smartest people in the retail business, to compete with what is out there today. And I really do have nothing against big business, but when it comes to the idea of something as intimate as music, something that has changed the face of this earth for better . . . to think that the U.S. and the world would live without you people. I mean, it makes me want to cry."

Not, he said, that he was predicting their demise, "but I do know what you're confronted with." And he hoped and prayed to God that "you don't give up the ghost.

"I know it is so tough, but there's nobody, *nobody* smarter than you are. I'm being honest about that. Nobody is smarter than you are, because if you have remained in business, in the retail record business, I can tell you [that] you have got something that very few of us have. That is brains, that is hard work, that is guts, and that is an attitude that they're going to have to whip my ass good before I give up.

"Now I do want to repeat this. There would be no Elvis. There would be no Johnny Cash. There would be no B.B. King. There'd be no Roscoe Gordon. There'd be no Howlin' Wolf. There'd be no Carl Perkins. There'd be no Jerry Lee Lewis. There would be no Roy Orbison. I can just tell you—we owe all of that to the independents. . . ."

Their business, he said, was not just another business. It was something that, no matter how many records you sold, you had to feel passionate about—it was something, he knew, that was intimate to each and every one of their souls. He wished, he said, with all the forcefulness he could muster:

"I wish there was some way that I could do more. And if I wasn't eighty years old, I can tell you one damn thing. I would travel this country like I did before—like when I started Sun Records—sixty to sixty-five thousand miles a year, after I got through with a session working with people that had no opportunity, had no chance in the music business. They wouldn't have *happened* had I not got on that road and [had the help of] the independent distributors and the independent retail outlets—had it not been for you folks. You would not have heard of Sam Phillips in this day, and the people I named, and many more. God bless you. I love you, and I'm delighted to be in your company."

And with that he applauded the entire gathering with a benign expression that might at one time have been hard to come by, and mixed and mingled with a crowd of true believers at the end of a very long day.

H E GOT HOME ON AUGUST 7, just in time to leave for Jackson, Tennessee, the next day for the inaugural International Rockabilly Hall of Fame festivities. In special recognition of the Sun anniversary (not to mention the dominant role the label would have played at the event in any case), Shelby had designed a special Sam-Sun award, which he submitted to Sam for approval and presented to various distinguished Sun alumni at the ceremony, including Sally.

The following afternoon Sam and Sally drove down to a sweltering tin storage shed in South Memphis to review the float that he would be riding in the Beale Street parade, which was scheduled to kick off Elvis Week the next day. This was the first time the city itself would play an official role in the memorial celebration, and all logistics, organization, planning, and execution had been placed in the hands of Pat Tigrett, a social dynamo, high-end events organizer, fashion designer specializing in antique lace, and 1964 Miss Tennessee, whose late husband, John, an international financier some thirty years her senior, had been a close associate of Sir Jimmy Goldsmith and Armand Hammer in various entrepreneurial ventures.

Pat Tigrett, as enterprising in her own business, social, and philanthropic activities as her husband, had started the Memphis Blues Ball in 1994 as a high-society salute to the city's cultural heritage, with Sam the recipient of its first Pyramid Award. (John Tigrett had been the driving force behind Memphis' "Great American Pyramid," situated on the banks of the Mississippi, with a giant statue of Ramses the Great presiding over its fortunes. Upon its completion in 1991 the Pyramid had taken its place for a little more than a decade as the city's premier sports and performance arena and the seventh-largest pyramid in the world.)

Pat had met Sam as a student at Memphis State in the early 1960s, but it was only through the Blues Ball that she had really come to know him, and when she called him to take a look at his float — well, here, let Pat tell the story:

> Jack Soden [the head of Graceland] called and said, "The fans have been coming here for twenty-five years, and we really need to thank them — the city of Memphis needs to thank them. Would you help us?" And I agreed. But I said, "Parades kind of to me mean floats and tiaras and girls waving — and that's not what I think we should do for Elvis." I said, "Why don't we create something that

really represents him and do something that has a theme from each of his movies or a period of his life?" For example, his army time really transformed his life. So I said, "Why don't I call the Pentagon and get some Humvees and things down?" And Jack said yes, and so we got them — the artillery howitzers and the machine guns and the Humvees and the jeeps with roll bars. And separate from that, we had the rock climbing wall, ten thousand American flags, uniformed soldiers — we just did a ton of stuff.

And that was just for starters. In addition Pat enlisted Disney to supply characters from *Lilo & Stich,* their popular animated feature with an Elvis character and an Elvis sound track; she had Hawaiian hula dancers and race-car drivers, twenty-four baying hound dogs, hundreds of motorcyclists and vintage cars, an air show featuring the "missing man" flight formation highlighted by red, white, and blue flares, a fireworks display timed to detonate spectacularly from the rooftops of various buildings along the parade route, and, of course, a float saluting Memphis' new pro basketball team, the Grizzlies, and proclaiming, "I Just Want to Be Your Grizzly Bear," with the Grizzlies Dance Team gyrating to Elvis' "Teddy Bear."

The float she had built for Sam had a big Sun label and jukeboxes ("It was," said Pat, "a real rock 'n' roll sort of fifties thing"), but when she called to tell him about it, he jumped into the conversation with both feet. "Oh, Pat," he said, "I know *exactly* the way I want my float to look."

This took her a little aback, since the float was already constructed.

"But I said, 'Oh, okay, terrific. Tell me exactly what you want.' He said, 'I envision a rocket — a big rocket. And I want it to say: "Sam Phillips and Sun Records launched rock 'n' roll"'— I can't remember the exact verbiage, it was just this whole rocket launch thing—'and we've sent it to the skies.' I said—I just took a deep breath, and I said, 'Absolutely. I'm absolutely all over it. That's precisely what it should be.' So then I said, 'Maybe you can come down at the end of the week.'

"I went out to Home Depot the minute I got off the phone. And you know those big aluminum vent things that you have for building? That was the only thing that I could quickly think of. So we totally took his float down and rebuilt it with his rocket — we worked twenty-four / seven to get it completed, and it looked like a big phallic symbol! And when he came down, oh, my gosh, he was so excited. He said, 'Pat, you did it again.

Riding the Rocket, August 10, 2002. *Courtesy of Pat Tigrett*

I thought I had you this time.' He was so funny. He said, 'Just tell me exactly what you want. And I said. 'Our parade, our grand marshal is the governor, and he will go in front of your float.' And he said, 'By God, he won't either.' He said, 'I will lead the parade.' I said, 'Of course you will.'"

Sally was deeply worried. There was another full week of events scheduled after the parade, and Sam just seemed to be getting weaker and weaker. "He had [all these] things to do, and I think he just felt like he had to get through them. I was scared for him to be on that float by himself. I really was. I told him, I said, 'I won't do anything. I'll just sit there — but I need to be there.' But he said, No, he was fine."

He wore his white suit with a red shirt and a scarf pinned back like a cape, with stars and wavy stripes in patriotic red, white, and blue. At first he sat on the chair Pat had provided for him that was set at the base of the rocket's erection. But when the parade finally got moving, he stood up and waved to the crowd, brandishing the little flag that he held in his hand. At the end of the five-block route, he disembarked a little shakily and walked over to where Shelby was sitting with Knox and Sally.

To Shelby it was clear that Sam, for all of his cheerful bonhomie, was unsettled and out of sorts. "You know, the sons of bitches want me to straddle that damn thing," he had muttered to Shelby with that singular mix of humor and bravado before the parade had even begun. "I knew he was sick," Shelby said, "but I didn't know how sick. They never let on. Anyway, when he got through, he came over to the stand and said, 'Knox, let's go.' Knox just kept talking to whoever he was talking with. He said, 'Goddamnit, Knox, I said, Let's go.' And he kind of looked at me and said, 'That son of a bitch will talk to anybody that'll talk to him.' He was ready to go."

THE LAST TIME I saw Sam was on August 15, 2002, when we both appeared at Professor of Communications John Bakke's annual Elvis seminar at the University of Memphis. Sam looked weary beyond words — it was evident, as Sally said, that he was simply doing the best he could to get through — and for the first time he didn't offer Alexandra a hug, saying, "I've got this damn congestive thing, and I don't want to give it to you." He put on a good front anyway, giving interviews to ABC's *World News Tonight,* and Memphis' channel 5, and even managing to drag himself through another one or two Elvis-related events over the next two days (even though he was sick as a dog, he told the fans at the "Farewell Tribute Concert" on Saturday night, "I knew I had to get up and get down here to talk to you people before you all left"), as well as appearing on both *Nightline* and the *Today* show. Then he went home and went to bed.

Sally grew increasingly alarmed at his condition. By the end of the following week he was practically comatose. "He just got to where he couldn't breathe. He didn't have the strength to do anything and Dr. Kraus wanted him to come in to see him and I said, 'Man,' I said, 'Robert, he's just not able.' I said, 'He can't get up.' He was in bed. He didn't eat. He wasn't drinking anything, water or anything, so I called Robert and told him. I said, 'Look, Sam hasn't had anything to eat for two days. He is just—he can't, you know, maneuver.' So Robert says, 'Well, put him in an ambulance and bring him to the emergency room.'"

Sam arrived at the hospital on the afternoon of August 23 in acute respiratory distress—but he was also exhibiting symptoms that puzzled Dr. Kraus. Once his doctor had gotten him stabilized, Sam provided him with the explanation. "Sam had been going to a pain management [clinic] for about a year and a half, and he was on pretty good doses of narcotic medication—Hydrocodone, Vicodin—for chronic compression fractures of his thoracic spine from the osteoporosis. He told me he stopped on his own. He'd made his mind up he was going to take care of it himself right after Elvis [Week], just went cold turkey and came into the emergency room in full blown withdrawal. Same as somebody that was a heroin addict and just suddenly stopped."

Dr. Kraus treated him the same way he would any other patient under similar circumstances. He gave him just enough medication to settle Sam down and told him, "Well, let's try to do this the right way." Which entailed working with the hospital's pain management clinic and psychiatric service to help wean him off the narcotic drugs, while continuing to maintain a cautious approach to his breathing problems—Dr. Kraus didn't see any reason why, following that plan, they shouldn't be able to keep him functioning reasonably well for years to come. "So I called the psychiatrist who normally helps us with our narcotic addiction in the hospital to see the patient, but it was Sunday afternoon and he wasn't on call." Nor, as a result, was Sam moved to the psychiatric floor, remaining instead in Intensive Care, where he was inadvertently put on routine protocol by a physician unfamiliar with his history.

"Routine protocol included a very strong Phenobarbital substance— you just switch over to Phenobarbital for the narcotic. And he immediately quit breathing. Probably within thirty minutes of giving him his first dose of Phenobarbital. It was enough sedation to cause him to have respiratory arrest. It just basically put him to sleep, turned his respiratory center off in his brain and said, You don't have to breathe. The Harvey team came down and immediately put him on a respirator—we tried to reverse it, but it was already too late. And he never really got off the respirator. That was in August of 2002. And he stayed on a respirator until he died [almost a year later]."

S AM TRIED GOING HOME off and on over the next few months, but, Sally said with sorrowful resignation, "he was never able to do anything. He came home and he was just really depressed. You can't—you just can't imagine what it's like. And there is not a thing you can do to make it any better."

At the beginning of February he went back into the hospital for good. All of Dr. Kraus' efforts to wean him off the ventilator had failed; Sam needed the machine all the time now, and within a few days of going back into the hospital he had a tracheotomy to alleviate some of the cumbersomeness and pain of having a twelve-inch tube down his throat twenty-four hours a day. The idea was that he would be able to speak without too much effort. A tracheotomy involves making a small hole, or tracheostomy, in the neck connecting to the windpipe, which ordinarily allows the patient to speak by breathing through his mouth and nose and closing off a speaking valve, but Sam simply didn't have enough breath to close the valve and was reduced almost entirely to writing notes. Dr. Kraus dealt with the depression with Effexor (along with Xanax, to allow him to tolerate being hooked up to a respirator twenty-four hours a day), in addition to regular psychiatric consultation. But, really, the only thing that kept Sam going was his unrelenting focus on finding a cure.

He read all the medical papers and journals—he was, said Dr. Kraus, engaged in every aspect of his treatment, "every step, every medication, every dose. Everything that was going on, he knew what was going on, and he questioned what he didn't think was right. He would write notes, and sometimes he'd write the notes before I made my rounds, and he'd have them written [when I came in]. I'd say, 'Now, Sam, we're going to do this today,' and he would go into a lengthy dissertation—'I'd like to do it this way.' Then you'd have to say, 'Now, Sam, if we do it this way, we'll have these problems.' He'd say, 'Well, we're going to try this.' He was in control, he wanted to hear [everything]—it would take forever. There was never any time that he was out of it. And I did that with him for ten months on an everyday basis. It was an amazing learning experience."

He was no longer interested in anything else. Sally never tried to talk to him about business—it just didn't matter anymore. He didn't want to see anyone, and he didn't want anyone to see him—not even his family in Alabama was aware of his condition. And for the first time he gave no thought to his appearance—he let his hair and beard go gray. "He was convinced," said Dr. Kraus, "that he was going to get well. All he wanted to do was get better. He never gave up. He never stopped." As Knox remembered it, when Sam was asked one time, as things continued to worsen, if he might at some point choose to discontinue treatment (the trigger may have been no more than a standard "Do Not Resuscitate" form), his reaction was no less than Olympian in its thunder. "Are you fucking kidding?" he wrote furiously on his notepad. "You've gotta be fucking crazy."

S ALLY AND BECKY were with him every day — Sally stayed with him in the room every night. Sally was the one person who could always interpret his gestures and his strangled attempts at speech, but Knox would come in and talk to him almost every day. Sam brightened at his visits but, rather than write notes, signed to him instead in the manner he had long ago learned from Aunt Emma. Becky tried to cheer him up by recalling happy moments from the past, but Sam made it clear he wasn't interested. At Easter she wrote an impassioned six-page letter calling on him to embrace Christ. "I have wanted so long to talk to you about Jesus," she wrote, "but the time hasn't been right until now. . . . I know, Sam, that you are a spiritual person and have been all your life. But I have a very great need in my life — to know that I can help you to have eternal security. I must do that for you and you must let me." It's a profoundly heartfelt letter, springing from the deepest wellsprings of Becky's faith — but it's almost painful (forget "almost") to imagine Sam's reaction. "So much beauty surrounds us," she concluded,

> and so much awaits us later. I don't want to miss it, and I don't
> want you to miss it. Jesus is with me. He has helped me write these
> things and I thank Him. I thank you, Sam, for letting me share
> them with you.
>
> I Love you
> and Jesus loves you,
>
> Becky

Finally at the end of May Sally decided it was time to go home. It wasn't a question of giving up, they just weren't making any progress here, and Sam needed to be at home, she knew he would be happier that way. Dr. Kraus said he could get by with a small portable ventilator — it couldn't do the same job as the big hospital respirator, his lungs were just filling up too fast. But he could come into the hospital every few days and get hooked up to the respirator, and then he'd be all right again for a while.

Knox knew that this was going to present them all with a real challenge — but he was determined that just as Sam had done for him, he would now do for Sam. The first hurdle was to get a generator that wouldn't fail, no matter what, if the power went off at home. "I just went into Sam mode. I knew I had to get the greatest generator in the history of the world, so I researched it, and the best people to install it — once I realized the level of seriousness of the whole thing, I just kind of became Sam. It was almost frightening. I wasn't going to leave any stone unturned. But I wasn't successful."

This seemed like a terrible (and terribly undeserved) self-indictment to me. Nobody, I said to Knox, could have been "successful" under these circumstances.

"Yeah," Knox reluctantly agreed. "Nobody could have."

There was no question that Sam was happier at home. He had two TVs stacked up, one on top of the other, both of them on all of the time, and mostly he watched baseball. The Cardinals had always been his favorites, but the telecast of their home games was blacked out in the Memphis area whenever there wasn't a sellout, so mostly he watched the Cubs now, who were carried by the Chicago superstation, WGN. Baseball had always provided an opportunity to Sam not just for relaxation but for reflection as well. "Oh, God, I love it," Sam said to me early in our acquaintance. "It's such a *skilled* game." Often he used it as a metaphor for the way he brought many of his artists, like Elvis, along. For example, he said, he would sometimes slow the tempo down to where the musicians could hardly stand it, "and then when I finally let them pick it back up and they locked in and sang their ass off, it felt just like they'd hit a home run — I mean, you hit that ball solid, man, with the bat in your hand, you *know* you got it."

Sally hired a nurse to come in four hours a day to spell her a little and allow her to take care of some of the press of ongoing business — but she might just as well have not hired the woman at all, she said, because Sam had gotten to the point where he just couldn't stand for her to be out of his sight. He wasn't even writing notes much anymore ("His lungs were taking all [his strength] away from him") — most of the time she could understand pretty much what he wanted just by looking at him. Dr. Kraus would come by from time to time to check on Sam's well-being. "It's very difficult for people to live on a home respirator. It takes a lot of skill, maintenance, and know-how, by the people caring for him, [but] Sally learned quickly and she was very good at it." Becky came over and sat with Sam every day. Knox always came by to talk to him and watch the ballgame.

On Father's Day, June 15, both of his sons sent Sam a card. "Dad," Knox's began:

> *Every Father's Day, I reflect on my feeling that you have been the best Father ever. You know everyone else knows you as this great man and this great revolutionary that made such a difference in the world, but for me your most amazing asset is your greatness as a teacher — teaching Jerry and me, your artists, and all you have come in contact with to be ourselves, trust our hearts, and be the best individual human beings we could possibly be in our own way. That is the most wonderful gift any father can give. Thank you and special love on this Father's Day.*

"Dad, I love you," Jerry wrote. "You have made it possible for our whole family to have a wonderful, comfortable, and completely secure life. You are the greatest, most honest and fair man I have ever known.

"Somebody call Sam!"

WHAT VERY QUICKLY came to be known as Hurricane Elvis by native Memphians (it was more like a freak onslaught of straight-line winds of up to one hundred miles per hour, lasting no more than a few minutes) struck at dawn the morning of July 22. It knocked out power for 306,000 of 450,000 Memphis Light, Gas and Water customers, both business and domestic, many of whom would not get their electricity or phones back for over two weeks. Dr. Kraus' first thought was of Sam. He hopped in his car — he lived just two miles away — and arrived to find that a tree had blown down across the house, but the generator was humming and the portable ventilator "never missed a lick."

Over the next week, the generator stayed on, and Sally's cell phone worked intermittently, but the air-conditioning never came back on and Knox brought ice for Sam every time he came, with weather just as hot and humid as it had been before the storm. Sam's condition was clearly worsening. The little ventilator just couldn't keep his lungs clear. The only alternative, Sally knew, would be to go back in the hospital, to go back on the big machine—"and he would have never gotten off of it, you know. He would have just had to stay there. It would have not been a good life at all."

Sam was watching the Cubs the afternoon of July 30. He was drowsy, and Sally had been having trouble with the ventilator all day. She had been trying for some time to get someone at the hospital who could give her advice, and when her cell phone rang, she assumed it was the hospital calling back. But it turned out to be Becky, who was going to pick up some prescriptions for Sam and just wanted to find out if there was anything else she could do—but after speaking to Sally, she decided to come straight to the house.

Sally tried to tell Sam that Becky was coming over, and when she couldn't rouse him, she called 911, which put the call through to the local fire station—they were well aware of Sam's condition and had answered other calls with a fire truck and an ambulance when she was having trouble with the ventilator. But by the time they arrived it seemed clear there wasn't much anyone could do. It happened almost exactly like Dr. Kraus had said it would. The doctor had told her that when the time came, "Sam would just go to sleep and that you would not be able to wake him up and that this would be because all of the gases in his body would change. I knew he was going to sleep, and Becky knew it, too. She was talking to Sam while I was trying to talk to the paramedics. When they put him on the stretcher to carry him out, I knew that he was dead. He looked peaceful and asleep. They kept trying to [resuscitate] him, but I knew there was no way to ever get him back again."

Sally rode with him to the hospital in the ambulance. Becky followed in her car, after first calling Knox and Jerry so they wouldn't have to learn it from the news. "You know, it was time," Sally said. "It was just time. 'Cause taking him back there and putting him on that machine— man, I mean, nobody can live that way. And I wouldn't have wanted to see him live that way anymore. But, you know, Sam always thought he was going to get well. He never thought he was going to die. He *did* not think he was going to die. But it didn't surprise me. Sam's lungs had nothing left. There just [was] nothing left."

AND DEATH SHALL HAVE NO DOMINION

S AM LOOKED GOOD IN HIS COFFIN. So good in fact that when they had the viewing one week after his death, Knox and Jerry chose to disregard their father's wishes and opt for an open-casket ceremony not only for family but for the public at large. Sally had carefully dyed his hair and beard ("I would not let him be buried with gray hair. I just wasn't going to do it"), and he was wearing his favorite tinted "Elvis" glasses with a Sun pin on the lapel of his jaunty double-breasted blazer, as more than a thousand people stood in line and solemnly — or not so solemnly — filed by.

Knox, Jerry, Becky, and Sally served as the official greeters. Becky fussed over Sam, speaking to him from time to time, as Elvis' first record, "That's All Right," and Howlin' Wolf's "How Many More Years," along with a succession of Sun hits, played loudly over the funeral home's PA system. ("We couldn't have a visitation without Sun playing," said Jerry.) The overall mood could not have been less "morose," as Knox pointed out, it was intended to mirror the same joyful irreverence that Sam had always embodied in life, it was intended to evoke the same air of unforced celebration that would mark the memorial service at the Cannon Convention Center for the Performing Arts in Memphis' new convention center (built on the site of the old Ellis Auditorium) the next day. "Sam would have loved seeing all these people he loved in the same room," said Scotty Moore, Elvis' original guitarist. "I keep expecting him to get up and start hugging people and talking their ears off."

Knox had enlisted Pat Tigrett to help coordinate the memorial planning, and she brought to it that unmistakable penchant for precise execution that she brought to every event she organized — but it was in the end, as Knox said, the spirit of Sam that was directing the show, with a series of characteristically offbeat video interview clips interspersed throughout the program ("When you're talking about music," announced the cover of the printed playbill, "now, that's my soul") and the 1960 baby-blue Cadillac in which we had driven around Florence for the documentary sitting center stage.

The general public entered to the sounds of Sun, leading off with "Rocket 88," while the honorary pallbearers and ushers marched in to the exuberant strains of Jerry Lee Lewis' recording of "I'll Fly Away."

(Jerry Lee was originally scheduled to perform but was too overcome with emotion to do so.) In the only explicitly religious note of the afternoon, longtime Memphis civil rights leader and former NAACP head Rev. Benjamin Hooks gave a stirring invocation in which, after quoting the first three verses of "O God, Our Help in Ages Past," the Isaac Watts hymn, he cited "the exuberant spirit with which You endowed him and which he used to help lighten the load of so many." Then Knox welcomed everyone with a brief talk that reaffirmed his father's credo.

The family had thought about having the usual respectful, reverent service for his father, Knox said, "but then we kind of looked around at each other and said, 'Nah. Not for Sam.' And we kind of decided we'd better not do anything politically polite. We thought we had to do something this afternoon that would give you a sense of Sam's *style*. You know, after all, he is the guy who taught Elvis. And he just wasn't a quiet, restrained guy. He was more of a flamboyant, irreverent type, you know? I mean, look at the center of the stage," he said, addressing the inescapable presence of the blue Cadillac, its spotless whitewalls and fins gleaming brightly behind him. It was a metaphor for Sam, he said. "It's open to the sky, it's open to the air and all the sounds all around. It's very bright, and you—you know, you can hardly miss it."

Above all, he saluted Sam for his unreconstructed commitment to individualism. *Trust yourself* was his dad's first lesson. And if other people didn't like it, he said, using Sam's words to address every one of his congregants. "Well, THEY CAN JUST KISS YOUR ASS."

That set the tone for the fifteen hundred gathered at the Cannon Center and all those who would listen to the service on the radio the following day. There were moving tributes from Little Milton and Jack Soden of the Elvis Presley Estate; there were video testimonials from B.B. King and Atlantic Records' Jerry Wexler, Sam's old compadre in the independent wars; and Johnny Cash, too sick himself to attend, recorded an eloquent (and typically humorous) audio salute. Renegade country singer (and Sam disciple) Marty Stuart even contributed an original song with a swinging gospel beat and a chorus that proclaimed "Precious memories rattle and roll / Deep in my heart I got a country soul." But I think it was Jack Clement who, after performing an ironically elegiac version of "Ballad of a Teenage Queen" ("Sam always hated that song," Jack said, grinning cherubically. "We oughta do it then," said Marty Stuart—and they did) best summoned up the spirit of Sam.

"Sam Phillips," he said, adjusting his reading glasses to read from a brilliantly begun but never-to-be-finished autobiography, "is someone you have to see to understand. It is a unique experience to have Sam Phillips really love some music you have made. He tells you how great it is in that certain way of his, and you believe him. About half the time I thought Sam was full of shit, but I still wanted to please him. I think the centerpiece of Sam's genius was his ability to make people want to please him. And all he had to do was to act naturally, using his considerable charm. . . .

"Sam fired me one day," he said to a lot of knowing laughter, "but nothing changed. It wasn't long before I figured out I didn't want to lose touch with Sam. I felt a need for his musical ingredient. It was always profound — even when it was full of shit. Whatever it was, it was strange, surprising, and unique, a voice I'd always wanted to hear, whether I liked it or not. I could always count on Sam to be Sam. Forty-something-odd years later, nothing has changed." And here, Jack, who always liked to keep things light, was unable to keep the emotion out of his voice, as he continued to read from his memoir. "He still calls me sometimes in the middle of the night, preaching to me for an hour or more. Nonstop. No bathroom breaks. Few words in edgewise. I love it. Sam loves the fact that I let him do it. I decided to do it to him one time a few years ago. I did it, and he let me. . . . I think Sam misses not having me around to fire."

Throughout it all, there was Sam playfully sharing a secret with all of us (but never *the* secret — his greater point was, there *was* no secret), glorying in all of his vivid self-contradictions, proclaiming all of his emphatic contrariness, whether we liked it or not. And my eulogy, preaching the sermon of perfect imperfection, can be gleaned from this book. Perhaps its more naked inspiration was expressed in a letter I wrote to Sam shortly before he died.

I was sure, I began, that Knox had passed on to him how much I missed him, how much I thought of him, how much I wished that I could be of more help.

And, you know, I think so often of how much, and how generously, you have helped me through the years, both in ways that I'm sure you can recognize and in other ways that you might not — as a kind of model for the type of person that I'd like to be: aware, impassioned,

dedicated in a single-minded but at the same time broad-minded way,
an implacable enemy of bullshit.

    I'm sure I told you, after we first met almost twenty-five years ago
now, I used to think of you as an example for the way that I wanted
to run [the summer camp that I ran], in trying to bring out the
best in every kid, and every camp counselor, in that three-hundred-
member community, trying to recognize the particular talent that
each individual had to offer and then create an environment in which
they were able to offer it, above all in trying to make it FUN. Because
as you have so often said about Sun, if it wasn't fun, it wasn't worth
doing. Anyway, you gave me a very high bar to aim for.

    Those were just a few of the lessons that you imparted to me. And
I have been a very imperfect student, I know. But I've tried — believe
me, I've tried! . . .

    I think you know how much Alexandra and I love the whole
Phillips family — you and Sally and Becky and Knox and Diane and
Jerry, and let's not forget the extended family, which I won't even begin
to name — and for Alexandra and me it's just been a privilege and
a pure pluperfect pleasure, as Rufus [Thomas] might say, to travel
with you to England and Seattle and Grisanti's, among many other
excursions of the world and the mind.

    So I'll just keep having my daily dialogue with you. And if you and
Knox ever do decide to take that vacation (to Beale Street, with Dewey,
in 1952), I hope you'll consider taking me with you.

That Sam almost certainly never read this letter in no way diminishes the truth behind it or the fact that it infused everything I have ever said or written about Sam.

It didn't matter what I, or anyone else, said at the memorial anyway. This was Sam's day, and Sam ended in typically oracular and upbeat fashion.

"I've been so blessed, man, you know, if I'd have never made a dollar out of it, hey, it was *so well spent,* and I am the best-rounded human being that there could be for *my* abilities because of all of these things. I didn't teach those people these things. *I got into their head,* though, and they learned on their own. *There's a difference.* They learned, I got into their head — I like that. Yeah. Then it ultimately, I mean, you dig a little deeper, and you might be down there where that soul is stirring around, you know, and then the aspects of confidence that can come from underneath, without being overly confident. I mean, what an interesting *'profession'* I've been in for a *long* time.

"HOW LUCKY CAN ONE MAN *BE?*"

And with that, a still of Sam flashed on the screen, his hair and beard redder than they would appear in later life, his expression sober but reassuring, his thumb and forefinger joined as if to say, *It's gonna be all right.* And then the ringing sound of Little Junior Parker's "Mystery Train" announced that Sam's sermon was at an end. And everybody left feeling good. Just as Sam would have wanted.

Notes

THE MAJORITY OF THE INTERVIEW MATERIAL is my own, but I am indebted to Colin Escott and Martin Hawkins, John Broven, Patrick Carr, the Country Music Foundation, Alex Gibney, Robert Gordon, Holger Petersen, Cilla Huggins, the Kitchen Sisters, David Less, Eric Olsen, Terry Pace, the Rock 'n' Roll Hall of Fame, the Smithsonian Institution, Charles White, and Peter Wolf, among others, for sharing their raw, and in many cases unpublished, tapes and transcripts, which are specifically acknowledged in the notes themselves. I have also drawn on Jerry Hopkins' interviews for his 1971 biography, *Elvis,* which are housed in the Mississippi Valley Collection at the University of Memphis (MVC/MSU) and which were made available with Jerry's kind permission and through the helpful efforts of Dr. John Bakke.

Many others generously contributed their time and resources. And I have tried to indicate my thanks and indebtedness in both these notes and the acknowledgments that follow.

What I have not done is to provide source notes for my own interviews, simply because in some cases I have interviewed people as many as fifteen or twenty times (or more) over the course sometimes of nearly as many years, and to attempt to separate out each strand of conversation would amount to a deconstruction of text, and an accumulation of source notes, that might equal the length of the book itself. So, where a quotation is not sourced, it can be assumed to come from one of my own interviews.

ONE | "I DARE YOU!"

5 the 323-acre farm at the Bend of the River: Strictly speaking, the farm was not at the Bend of the River, which is in Waterloo, thirty miles away, where the Tennessee River bends northward. Sam, however, seems to have applied the term broadly and symbolically (mythically and heroically, too) to the rich alluvial floodplain created by the river's many twists and turns, which, as he proudly pointed out, provided northern Alabama with its best farming land. Just to show how different perceptions can be, Sam's nephew Phillip, who later lived on the very same farm, never thought to refer to its location in that manner and was a little mystified when he heard Sam talking about the Bend of the River, since, strictly speaking, the farm wasn't anywhere near the river at all.

6 What if I had been born black?: This comes not only from Sam's frequent statements but from various older family members who did not necessarily share Sam's views.

8 the one record they were able to afford: In another version of the story that Sam told, the family was given two records with their purchase. Sam didn't remember the name of the other.

18 "Father of the Blues" W. C. Handy: W. C. Handy was known as the Father of the Blues because he was among the first to formally recognize and codify the form. A schooled musician, he arrived in Memphis with his band in 1909 at the age of thirty-five and quickly established himself there by writing a campaign song for mayoral candidate Edward "Boss" Crump, who would run Memphis for the next forty years. That song, under its revamped title "Memphis Blues," became the template for the new three-line, twelve-bar form, a conscious adaptation of an observed folk tradition. The runaway success of "Saint Louis Blues" (perhaps most familiar from Bessie Smith's majestic 1925 version) and his establishment of one of the first black-owned song publishing companies, assured his unique position in the evolution of American popular music. He lived in New York City for the last forty years of his life but remained a revered figure in Memphis until his death in 1958.

24 one of Sam's first acts was to lobby Mr. Powell once again for new uniforms: I wouldn't want to swear to the exact chronology of all this band business. I am going primarily by Sam's testimony, which at this point I think I have parsed past the point of parsing, as well as scrutinizing the 1941 and 1942 Coffee High School yearbooks (*The Coffee Pot*). I've also called upon the research of *TimesDaily* reporter Terry Pace and Lauderdale County historians Lee Freeman and Billy Warren. In most cases, in the absence of hard facts, I've gone with the trajectory of Sam's account, but, of course, in the end the responsibility is mine. Also, as a point of more than casual interest, Sam's brother J.W. would bring in the John Daniel Quartet in February 1942 for their third highly successful appearance in the area and would go on to become the quartet's promoter and manager after the war.

33 an old poem called "Would Anybody Care?": By a strange twist of fate, a recording of this recitation turned up many years later, in 1999, when Sun researcher Hank Davis found a tape box labeled only "Sam's poem — Do not erase." He listened to it, was unable to identify the voice, and asked Sam who it was. Sam said he was the speaker and told Hank about Mary Lois Crisler, and what happened afterward. "Mary Lois went off and got married to a guy in the Air Force. He was killed quite young and she moved around a bit, finally settling in Texas. Years later, after I came to Memphis, I got to thinking about Mary Lois and all that had happened to her, so I decided to surprise her with that tape. I recited the poem in my best 'announcer's voice' and sent it to her. That was around 1950 [and] she was delighted with it." The funny thing is, even after knowing the story, I still cannot hear Sam's voice, nor could his son Knox. Sally Wilbourn, his close companion for nearly fifty years, admits that she feels the same way — but, she said with a shrug, Sam definitely identified the voice as his own. You can hear the recording on *Sun Gospel* (Bear Family BCD 16387).

34 Highland Baptist Church burned down: "Fire Destroys Church Sunday," *Florence Times,* December 15, 1941.

35 nothing but bafflement at what he considered to be the irresponsibility of his choices: In Sam's account, J.W.'s marriage and his enlistment seem to have taken place at virtually the same time, though that could well be my misunderstanding. Jud in any case got married on January 10, 1942, and enlisted on August 23, either one of which by itself might have led to Sam feeling that he had no choice but to quit school. Listening to the emotionally fraught way that Sam told the story, I sometimes wondered if, with all the events that subsequently transpired, Sam might not be exaggerating the sense of acute betrayal that he said he felt at the time — but the letter that Jud wrote seventeen months after his enlistment (which I only discovered after Sam's death) on receipt of the news of his brother's marriage indicates that Jud was just as aware of the irresponsibility of his choices. "Your very nice letter arrived today," Staff Sergeant J. W. Phillips wrote from the Pacific Theater on January 29, 1944, in response to a letter Becky had written on behalf of both Sam and herself. "What I have to say in the following will not be empty words but they will be just as full of sincerity as could ever be spoken. . . . In the future it is my will to be so fixed that you and Sam will have nothing to worry about but your own future. In that I mean I want to take all the outside responsibilities into my hands." And in praising both Sam and his new wife (whom J.W. had never met) to the skies, he reflected on his own situation as well. "Sam has been more fortunate in that respect than myself," he wrote. "Sometimes we too hastily call unto ourselves a companion that is nothing but one that will offer misery in the days where happiness should be."

TWO | RADIO ROMANCE

44 he didn't seem able to decide on a date: Just how uncertain Becky was of that date can be gleaned from a fanciful marriage announcement she wrote on WLAY stationery during this time in which she speculated as to the bride and groom's attire, and had the Reverend Hacker presiding over the ceremony in Florence on November 6, while naming two prospective best men, neither of whom made the final cut. As to Sam's state of mind, his letters seem to reflect desperate loneliness coupled with almost crippling indecision.

45 he would no longer have a job: Letters from Melvin Hudson to both Sam and Becky dated January 1, 1945, regretting their December 30 "decision." "I am very sorry," he wrote, "that conditions are such that it makes it necessary for you to resign." Interestingly enough, Sam's best man, and their best friend at the station, John Slatton, wrote to the couple two months later that he had been fired under different circumstances but for what he considered to be equally unjust reasons. ("I got the same kind of deal you got, Sam.")

45 He was firmly convinced that mental illness was no different: Along with my own conversations with Sam (and many other interviews that he gave), his cousin Christine Gentry (not to mention Sally Wilbourn, Marion Keisker, Becky, and his two sons) made it clear that Sam made no secret of his nervous attacks. "He'd tell anyone."

48 the first station he had put on the air: The best background on the Wooten brothers' early dedication to radio that I have found comes from the *Memphis Press-Scimitar,* January 27, 1932, "Wooten Brothers Form Own Station," by James R. Lee, along with another early clip, "Ask the Press-Scimitar" (also dated January 27, but with no year indicated). See also Robert Johnson, "Wooten Sells T-V, Radio Stations," *Memphis Press-Scimitar,* November 3, 1958.

51 *Time* magazine reported: *Time,* "City & County Crowd," August 17, 1936.

51 the black population could no longer be bought off with "gifts": The primary source for this account is Scott Bayer's 2006 "Black Vote's Impact on the Descent of Boss Crump" (https://dlynx.rhodes.edu/jspui/handle/10267/23954), which quotes Randolph's letter to Crump of April 6, 1944, as well as a story from Memphis' black newspaper, the *Memphis World*, of April 4, 1944, in which Randolph made the comment about "well-kept slaves."

52 "In every progressive community or organization": Sam's letter, titled "Crump Does a Good Job for City and I Admire Mrs. Richardson's Initiative," appeared in the *Memphis Press-Scimitar* on October 2, 1945. The positive outcome of this exchange was recognized by Mrs. Richardson herself on the following day. "You are to be commended for expressing your personal, unbiased opinion," she wrote to Sam at home, echoing the quote from Euripides that served as a banner to this citizen forum. "I am sure that citizens such as you and I, even tho we differ in opinion, serve to encourage others in this community who have been deprived of their freedom of speech."

54 It was John Daniel who christened him "Jud": Jake Hess, with Richard Hyatt, *Nothin' But Fine: The Music and the Gospel According to Jake Hess*, p. 35. By a strange coincidence, Jake Hess was so impressed with Rebecca Burns, whom he met during an early stint at WLAY, that years later he would name his daughter Rebecca in explicit recognition of Becky's many fine qualities, not least of which was the kindness she showed to others.

57 no standardized equalization curve yet existed: The RIAA curve didn't come into common use until 1953, although there was a strong impulse toward standardization from at least 1950 on.

58 newcomers like Eddy Arnold: Just to show how deep some of these roots and interactions extended, at the request of John Daniel, Sam had booked Eddy Arnold on a WLAY-sponsored Daniel Quartet concert in Tuscumbia in the summer of 1943, before Arnold had even made any records. This was a casual, but valued, relationship that would continue at sporadic intervals for the rest of Sam's life.

60 A 250-watt Memphis radio station: The principal source of information not just on the start but on the continued operation of WDIA is Louis Cantor's seminal work, *Wheelin' on Beale*.

61 "And when they stuck the microphone out there": Ibid., p. 42.

62 "I don't know what made me say that": Stanley Dance, "Interview (1967)," in Richard Kostelanetz, ed., *The B.B. King Companion: Five Decades of Commentary*, p. 38.

67 Mr. Plough, the owner: This was Abe Plough, yet another in a long line of Memphis independent spirits and entrepreneurs, who started his own patent-medicine company in 1908 at the age of sixteen and went on to found the pharmaceutical giant Plough, Inc.

68 "I treated the ceiling with an inverted V": This quote, and much of the technical talk that follows, is from Fetzer Mills Jr.'s graduate thesis in Southern Studies at the University of Memphis, "The Room That Shook (Rattled and Rolled) the World: The Memphis Recording Service and Sun Records at 706 Union Avenue, Memphis, Tennessee" (2000). Fetzer's work is groundbreaking in its attention to detail, but if you want to understand it further, you're going to have to read a treatise on audio engineering. Sam's essential point is captured in the summation at the end.

70 he acquired the equipment he would need: Once again it's hard to say the exact order of things here, particularly with respect to tape recorders and microphones. Sam spoke in some interviews about getting a Crestwood recorder first, then a Bell, then another—but I've gone with his description to the Kitchen Sisters, Davia Nelson and Nikki Silva, which is quite detailed, about the progression.

70 "I wanted it to sound big": Sam's interview with the Kitchen Sisters, April 2, 1999.

71 She . . . took a picture of Sam out front: This is from Colin Escott with Martin Hawkins, *Good Rockin' Tonight: Sun Records and the Birth of Rock 'n' Roll*, p. 14. My language mirrors theirs because, mostly, I couldn't figure out another way to say it. I never saw the photograph, and Colin no longer has a copy. It was originally in the scrapbook that Becky assembled for her husband, as she would for each of her sons as well—but though I've seen the picked-apart remnants of all three, much of their contents has scattered to the journalism- and fan-driven winds.

THREE | THE PRICE OF FREEDOM

73 the strength of his belief that . . . there was great art to be discovered in the experience of those who had been marginalized: If there is any doubt that this was his contemporary purpose, you can hear Sam voicing almost exactly the same sentiments in Robert Johnson, "Thru the Patience of Sam Phillips—Suddenly Singing Elvis Presley Zooms into Recording Stardom," *Memphis Press-Scimitar*, February 5, 1955, and in *Elvis Presley: His Complete Life Story, Prepared by the Editors of TV Radio Mirror*, July 1956, p. 20, among others.

75 "Man, that's just what we need here in Memphis": Martin Hawkins unpublished interview with Sam about Joe Hill Louis, May 1, 2000. See also Broven, Hawkins, and Dave Sax liner notes to Joe Hill Louis, *Boogie in the Park* (Ace CDCHD 803).

78 a faux-African herbal faith healer: This was Dr. Samuel Shokumbi, who passed himself off as an Oxford-educated Nigerian and would be convicted of fraud in November 1950, five months after Sam recorded the radio spots. See Hank Davis, Colin Escott, and Martin Hawkins' book accompanying the magisterial Bear Family box set *The Sun Blues Box* (Bear Family BCD 17310), p. 72.

79 Overall the conventions probably brought in the most money: For information and insight into Sam's early business strategies I have relied on the Kitchen Sisters' interviews as well as my own.

80 Dewey Phillips, playing records over a crude PA system: Ida Clemens, "'Phillips Sent Me' Has Become Vital Part of City's Lexicon,'" *Memphis Commercial Appeal*, June 9, 1950.

80 "one of the top five most profitable departments": Louis Cantor, *Dewey and Elvis: The Life and Times of a Rock 'n' Roll Deejay*, p. 39. This, and much of the factual material on Dewey Phillips, comes from Louis Cantor's painstaking biography.

82 "'Phillips Sent Me' Has Become Vital Part of City's Lexicon": Clemens, as above.

82 "Memphis' radio wonder boy": two stories with different titles but virtually the same text, *Memphis World*, June 9 and June 13, 1950.

84 Hampton reciprocated: *Memphis World*, June 16, 1950. It seems unlikely that the record actually existed at this point. According to Martin Hawkins, it was recorded at exactly this time, perhaps even in Memphis during this engagement (as "Phillips Sent Me") by Hampton's sax player, Jerome Richardson, for the Nashville label Bullet, but a copy has never been found.

85 The Bihari Brothers had from the start: For more on these and many other connections, not to mention the full story of Modern Records, see John Broven's comprehensive *Record Makers and Breakers: Voices of the Independent Rock 'n' Roll Pioneers*.

86 "we would be very interested in working out some arrangement with you": Joe Bihari to Sam, May 12, 1950.

87 He had met Bill McCall: For more about 4 Star, see John Broven, *Record Makers and Breakers*.

88 "I never did see anything particular about either Buck or Slim's band": "Sam Phillips Talking About Country Music on Sun to Martin Hawkins: March 13, 1985," in the book accompanying *The Sun Country Box* (Bear Family BCD 17311), p. 12.

88 The Bihari brothers came to town toward the end of July: By triangulation it is clear that they have come (and only recently gone) by July 27.

89 "quiet-spoken" and "unassuming": "From Itta Bena to Fame," *Tri-State Defender,* March 29, 1952.

91 His uncle had married a sister: Charles Sawyer, *The Arrival of B.B. King,* pp. 39–40.

92 "looking like a million bucks. Razor sharp": B.B. King with David Ritz, *Blues All Around Me: The Autobiography of B.B. King,* p. 2.

92 "He could have been a con man": Ibid., p. 25.

92 "he seemed to measure each pick precisely": Jerry Richardson and Rob Bowman, "Conversations with B.B. King," in Richard Kostelanetz, ed., *The B.B. King Companion: Five Decades of Commentary,* p. 118.

92 the ability "to connect my guitar to human emotions": Ibid., p. 127.

92 "By trilling my hand, I could achieve something": Ibid.

93 This was not the way they had left it: This is the way Sam remembered it — vividly, if reluctantly, and no one else has ever weighed in with a narrative recollection of comparable detail. It remains, of course, inferential to a considerable degree, dependent to some extent upon the date of the first assigned master numbers (B.B.'s first record didn't come out for at least another month, although this wouldn't necessarily impinge upon Sam's memory of what he was *told*), Sam's vivid memory of the sequence of what occurred in the aftermath of his recording B.B., and how quickly he withdrew the Joe Hill Louis sides on which he was pinning so much hope. It is also dependent upon Sam's memory, which was for the most part extraordinarily sharp, and with the exception of his start in the business, almost uniformly positive. I should add that this chronology, like a number of others, has been worked out through extensive e-logue with John Broven and Dave Sax, as well as Roger Armstrong and Jim O'Neal. Perhaps needless to say, none of us agree on every particular or interpretation — how could we?

94 "I mean, I was *hot*": I should make it clear that Sam said all of these things with reference to the two older brothers, Jules and Saul. Sam regretted his words almost as soon as they came out of his mouth. Both Jules and Saul were dead, he said — they couldn't defend themselves. And the sentiment itself went against everything he believed about maintaining a positive spirit, never harboring bitterness. "I'm wasting my time here," he said to me. But in this instance he just couldn't help himself, becoming almost apoplectic as he spoke, some fifty years later, with the same fury and resentment that he must have felt at the time.

96 "I have the three outstanding race disc jockeys in the South": Letter to Howie Richmond, August 8, 1950, echoed in an August 23 letter to ASCAP and no doubt others for which I have no text.

96 close to six thousand records a day: Lydel Sims, "First It's a Hot Black Mess, and Then It Gives Out Music," *Memphis Commercial Appeal,* March 23, 1950. Again I would recommend Broven, *Record Makers and Breakers,* for more extensive background.

97 "a negro quartet that is far superior": Letter to ASCAP, August 23, 1950, in which he is inquiring about how to obtain licensing for both "Jezebel" and "Your Red Wagon." This was almost certainly the Gospel Travelers track — it is definitely the same title — that Sam had sent to Modern in July.

97 he would soon be broadcasting from his hospital bed: Clark Porteous, "3 Memphians Die in Mid-South Traffic," *Memphis Press-Scimitar,* September 4, 1950.

97 how little he knew: This was just one more extension of his utter ignorance of the rules of the game, evidenced by his correspondence with ASCAP and various song publishing companies at the same time about how to license a song—or even find its publisher. It must have humiliated Sam, who prided himself on his straightforwardness in business, to discover that his one established artist was still signed to another label.

99 "High-pitched warbler does okay": *Billboard,* September 23, 1950.

99 It was with very mixed feelings that he got back in touch: The communication between the two parties from this point on is a study in disingenuousness. Sam couldn't be more accommodating to Jules Bihari's every whim, and he is an unfailingly upbeat salesman for the talent in which he so much believed. But there is an absence of candor, and an abundance of caution always to be read between the lines, while at the same time Jules reveals a thinly veiled contempt for someone he clearly sees as a hapless naïf. Perhaps the single moment of candor on Sam's part occurs when, just after meeting Leonard Chess in the spring of 1951, he writes to Jules how essential it is that the artists he has just signed "receive their accounting without fail every three months. . . . I am sure you realize that it's not that I feel that you are in any way lackadaisical, but the fact remains that if I am to keep all these personalities happy—and that certainly is a necessary requirement—I will have to have your assurance in every way that whatever I tell these artists from time to time they can depend on." Jules' constantly reiterated theme, as perhaps best expressed in a letter of February 15: "Sam, I realize that I am putting a lot of responsibility on you and there is not too much compensation, but after looking over our last year's situation and our recording costs out here on the West Coast were so prohibitive that we were unable to make money. . . . This is the reason we are so pleased with your association with us. Our record [i.e. what they had to pay Sam for studio rental charges and "scouting"] has been exceptionally low, and also our talent cost the same, and I feel that as time goes on we will be doing considerable more and more business with you." It was a strange relationship.

99 Joe's one-year contract with Columbia had finally run out: A notation in Marion Keisker's loose-leaf notebook indicated that Joe was released by Columbia on November 1 "by mutual consent." Sam sent the Biharis the formal release on December 16.

100 "I was just walking around one day": Interview with Walter Horton by Jim O'Neal and Jim Themelis, May 7, 1981. Sam says in a letter to Jules Bihari, January 17, 1951, that Joe Hill Louis brought Horton in for an audition. I leave it to history to judge.

100 his playing represented just what Sam was looking for: Sam was in fact so taken with his sound that not long afterward he brought Becky in to sing a blues, with Walter's harmonica providing the principal melodic backing.

100 Roscoe Gordon was twenty-two years old: Although he was billed on his early recordings as "Roscoe," the "e" in his name was later dropped and appears to have been Sam's addition.

102 the very day that Sam sent off his new sides: Letter from Sam to Leonard Chess, March 3, 1951, establishes their meeting as two days earlier, the same day that Sam sent Modern Records six new sides by Walter Horton, four by Roscoe Gordon.

103 "the first thing I gave him": It was not in fact the first thing. As early as September 20, 1950, Sam had sent Leonard dubs by both Charlie Burse and the Gospel Travelers, presumably the same cuts he had been planning to put out on The Phillips several weeks earlier. Sam sent him "Rocket 88" and the other cuts by Jackie Brenston and Ike Turner on March 7.

102 at Buster Williams' suggestion he changed the name of the company: Nadine Cohodas, *Spinning Blues into Gold: The Chess Brothers and the Legendary Chess Records,* p. 56.

104 The drive to Memphis was not without incident: The principal sources for information on Ike and the Kings of Rhythm, as well as their first recording session (needless to say, not always in total agreement), are: Morgan Neville's December 1999 interview with Ike Turner for the A&E documentary on Sam; Cilla Huggins, "Ike Turner in the Beginning," *Juke Blues* 37 (spring 1997); Bill Greensmith, "We Got a Song Called 'Rocket 88,'" *Blues Unlimited,* 135–136 (July/September 1979); Jim O'Neal, "Jackie Brenston," *Living Blues,* spring 1980; plus numerous interviews with Sam.

104 they subsequently had a flat tire and then went and dropped the guitar amp on the pavement: There are various versions of the amp story—in some it fell off the roof of the car—but this is the one Ike consistently told.

106 he wrote to Jimmy Connolly on March 11: The date of the recording session has always been somewhat in dispute. It is usually given as March 5, but Sam sent the record to Leonard Chess on March 8, a day after recording it. To show how fast things were happening, and how eager Sam was to *make* them happen, Sam sent Chess rough sketches for four different ads for "Rocket 88" with endorsements from three leading DJs, Bob Umbach, Gene Nobles, and Dewey Phillips, who with the exception of Dewey had yet to hear the record (but I'm sure loved it when they did).

107 an "iron-clad" agreement with Leonard Chess: Sam to Leonard Chess, March 26, 1951, in which he further characterizes the agreement as one "that will strictly be give-and-take in equal portions." This took a little while to work out, with Leonard submitting a signed and notarized agreement on March 14 and Sam sending back a revised version (with a number of small but significant protections) on March 26.

107 "Rocket Becomes Flying Disc, Spins Toward Record Glory": Lydel Sims, *Memphis Commercial Appeal,* March 28, 1951.

110 McGee confessed to the good people of Memphis: Mike McGee, "One Can Really Learn About 'Rocket 88' If One Tries," *Memphis Commercial Appeal,* April 15, 1951.

110 how the altogether unanticipated success of "Rocket 88" might imperil their relationship: Success seemed to affect everyone's understanding of the nature of that relationship. Sometimes it even divided individual recollections from themselves. According to blues historian Jim O'Neal, in the draft for his liner notes for *The Modern Downhome Blues Sessions,* vol. 1 (Ace CDCHD 876), Jules Bihari himself offered conflicting views of the origins of their disagreement. "'I told Leonard to get in touch with Sam Phillips,' Jules Bihari recounted in a 1981 interview, 'that he had a lot of good masters and maybe he could get himself a hit. He contacted Sam Phillips and the first thing that came out of the box was "Rocket 88" by Brenston, and that really got Chess started on his way.'" But in an earlier interview, Jules took a less beneficent view. "Phillips would scout talent as they came into the studio. I had a deal to pick up all the stuff he made. But I only got three or four masters from him until Leonard Chess came in the area. The first thing Chess got was 'Rocket 88,' which turned out to be a big hit. That sure blew the deal with Phillips. I was so mad then." Which was pretty much his brother Joe's perspective, according to Jim O'Neal, albeit in a more good-natured way. "What actually happened," said Joe, "he was getting ready to send 'Rocket 88' to us, then Leonard Chess happened to be in Memphis. Heh-heh! He sold it to Leonard without sending it to us.

Well, that severed our relationship with Sam." And, of course, Sam, needless to say, didn't see it that way at all.

111 they were the best psychiatric hospital: Just as a side note, according to Frederick R. Karl, *William Faulkner: American Writer* (New York: Grove Press, 1989), p. 845, William Faulkner was hospitalized at Gartly-Ramsay on September 18, 1952, for eight days, for acute alcohol poisoning.

112 "'Eyesight to the Blind' [by Sonny Boy Williamson] was a song that was very popular": Sam quoted in liner notes to Joe Hill Louis, *Boogie in the Park*, from Martin Hawkins' unpublished interview with Sam, May 1, 2000.

FOUR | "WHERE THE SOUL OF MAN NEVER DIES"

115 By the end of August it would sell over one hundred thousand copies: I was amazed — but that's what the royalty statements say.

116 Chess had already given the publishing to its lawyer: This only further emphasizes how little Sam or Leonard Chess seemed to know about how to exploit the value of a song. Song publishing has always been the most lucrative (and predictable) part of the music business, but neither Sam nor Leonard had his own publishing company at this point, and for the next three years Chess Records would turn over all of its publishing to its in-house lawyer, John Henry Burton, in lieu of legal fees. According to Nadine Cohodas, *Spinning Blues into Gold: The Chess Brothers and the Legendary Chess Records*, pp. 78, 79, it was Burton, under the name of John Henry Burton Ltd., who sold the song to Hill and Range, with the date of the assignment confirmed by Marshall Chess. In similar fashion, Chess would assign the authorship of "How Many More Years," Howlin' Wolf's big hit later that year, to Carl Germany, a Midwestern dance promoter, apparently with a good deal of influence, who was about to debut a new radio show in Chicago. Interestingly, Sam wrote to Leonard Chess consistently, and persistently, that he felt that all the artists he recorded should receive not only record but songwriting royalties, too. (I would say this is just one more proof that, as Marion Keisker pointed out, Sam was not cut out to be a partner — certainly not a junior partner.) "My first wish," he wrote on April 2, "is to give the artists all we can in royalties." Perhaps as a sop to Leonard, perhaps as an indication of his own good business sense, he always stipulated that he and Leonard should "make something out of the song-writing end [if] possible," though the practicalities seem to have eluded him. But the view that he articulated over and over again was that only if the artists felt some real commitment to them would they put forth their best efforts. As he wrote to Leonard on November 12, "Let's do our best to play this thing wisely, even though it is more trouble for all of us, and send them some money all along (at least every three months) and I'm sure we'll be able to make it profitable for all of us."

117 "Modern Inks Seven Artists to Pacts": *Billboard*, July 28, 1951, with a July 21 dateline.

117 "I had a deal with Phillips to pick up all the stuff he made": Jules Bihari interview with Frank Scott, Bruce Bromberg, Pete Welding, and Gary Paulsen, May 1968, published in *Blues Unlimited* 68 (December 1969). This was never exactly the case. There were various deals, and various attempts at deals, none with any suggestion of either exclusivity or right of "first refusal." As far as I can determine, the best deal that Jules Bihari was prepared to offer in response to Sam's outlining of his "partnership" arrangement with an unnamed "Chicago record firm" was $25 per accepted side plus a 5 percent royalty on all records sold. Jules was highly skeptical of the Chess proposition and warned Sam that a partnership based on net profits was a chimera. ("Even Einstein himself could not figure out the net profit on certain recordings," he wrote on March 27. "As long as I have been in the record business . . . it took a staff of accountants 10 months to give an actual cost on records manufactured.") Following which, Jules suggested that Sam propose his own terms for a new deal with Modern. Sam maintained his disingenuous posture for as long as he could (he had in fact already made his deal with Chess), but in the end Jules agreed that Sam needed to do what was in his own best interests. "Nothing ventured is nothing gained and believe me when I say I have ventured on many occasions," he wrote on April 9. "All I can say is if your deal doesn't work out satisfactory . . . I am always open to negotiate a deal with you." In the meantime, while he was fully aware of how busy Sam was going to be, he hoped that Sam would still find the time to record B.B. King, Joe Hill Louis, Walter Horton, and Roscoe Gordon for Modern and that "this new business venture will not have any bearing upon our relations." It must have given Sam some small measure of satisfaction to be able to respond, politely, on April 12, that while "I do not know how much time or talent I will be able to offer your concern, I am sure we can handle the four artists' recording from time to time." He only stopped cutting records for Modern when Jules stopped paying him for a time, in mid-July, after things had finally blown up between Chess and Modern, and even after the bill was paid three months later, there were no more business relations (though no evidence of overt hostility either) between the two of them.

118 "the soul of man never dies": Robert Palmer, *Deep Blues*, p. 233. Everyone since then, including me, tried to get Sam to repeat, or expand upon, that quote, but this is where it originated.

118 "My grandfather was one of them away-back guys": Pete Welding, "'I Sing for the People': An Interview with Bluesman Howling Wolf,'" *down beat*, December 14, 1967, p. 22.

119 a broad pneumatic vibrato: This is taken from Jerry Portnoy's and Kim Field's descriptions in James Segrest and Mark Hoffman, *Moanin' at Midnight: The Life and Times of Howlin' Wolf*, pp. 95, 96.

120 "He would set in the middle of the studio": This is constructed from several interviews in which Sam struggled to describe what he ultimately believed to be an ineffable thing. He never saw Wolf perform. He didn't have to, he said.

121 "Pt. is a mental defective": This was first revealed in the Segrest and Hoffman biography. The records are most readily available on their site www.howlinwolf.com/docs, which includes many other interesting elements as well.

121 It was something of which he was deeply ashamed and almost never spoke: In most interviews, if he referred to his army service at all, he spoke of having served till the end of the war. Oddly enough, the first time I formally interviewed him, in 1970, having no idea of the circumstances of his army experience, I asked if it had "changed [his] outlook any, getting out of Mississippi for the first time." No, he responded gravely. "One thing about it, they drilled us so hard they just naturally give me a nervous breakdown." I thought, of course, that he was speaking metaphorically, as he so often did, about yet another of the many burdens that life had placed on him. And I never found out otherwise until I read the biography.

123 his uncompleted memoir, *Success Was My Downfall*: Portions of this were published in *Blues World Special Edition* 46/49 (1973), as "A Lifetime in the Blues: Johnny Shines," by John Earl.

125 This time he got Roscoe Gordon's mentor, Billy "Red" Love: There remains considerable controversy in the blues world over just who played piano on this recording. Ike Turner always said he did and demonstrated his knowledge of the part in the documentary we did on Sam in 1999. In the aftermath of the breakup of his band, the Kings of Rhythm, Ike moved to West Memphis in the summer of 1951, and at some point he started playing with Wolf, as evidenced by his presence on Wolf's recordings for the Biharis that fall. But the crudeness with which he played on those records (and on "Rocket 88," for that matter) does not support his presence on this one, and Sam was adamant that Ike never played with Wolf in the Memphis Recording Service studio. In addition, the evidence for Billy Love is compelling (you have only to listen to him play the same figure on Willie Nix's "Lonesome Bedroom," sent to the Biharis on July 9), not just in the fluidity of the playing but in his near-constant presence in the studio on his own and others' recordings at exactly this time.

125 the "blue yodel" of Jimmie Rodgers: This was perhaps the most surprising of many surprising things that Howlin' Wolf told me and others, and I'm still not sure how much to credit it. To me, Tommy Johnson, one of the most influential of all the great Mississippi blues singers and for all I know one of the chief inspirations for Jimmie Rodgers himself, always seemed like the clear source for his howl. But for Wolf it was always Jimmie Rodgers, and sometimes Tommy Johnson—and perhaps, if he were to consider the matter further, the Mississippi Sheiks. So I'll leave it at that.

125 "I can take one damn record like 'Moanin at Midnight'": Segrest and Hoffman, *Moanin' at Midnight*, p. 90.

126 Sam put down $1,000 for a bus: All of Sam's payments are recorded in Marion's notebook. His letter to Leonard Chess on November 12, 1951, does not seem to fully reflect the depths of his outrage (though it comes pretty close)—perhaps he just muted it for diplomatic reasons.

127 Leonard's lack of any real belief: As Sam wrote to Leonard on December 19, 1951, "It takes time and numerous sessions—not just one or two, as a rule—to get outstanding numbers and I don't believe in putting just another release by an artist on the market. I think they should <u>always</u> be the very best that can possibly be gotten out of them."

130 a virtual shutdown of new Memphis Recording Service releases: One additional contributing factor was the health relapse Sam suffered in October (he was hospitalized for over a week, and the effects lingered into November). While the illness was never named ("Sam is a very sick boy" was as close as Marion would come to specifics in a letter to Jules Bihari on October 12), one can only surmise it was related to his breakdown five months earlier. "I am sorry that I was so unsettled about whether to go into my own label or just what to do," Sam wrote to Leonard Chess on September 29, two weeks before this second hospitalization, "but believe me, my anticipation of starting a label (if and WHEN I ever do) will not affect in any way my immediate supply of talent to you." And he was energetically back in harness by November 6, "hoping to be completely well in the next two or three weeks [but] in the meantime . . . strictly beatin' the bushes for the talent down here."

130 it had "inked a term disk contract": *Billboard*, September 15, 1951.

130 the colored YMCA on Lauderdale and Linden: This has always been referred to as Lauderdale and Vance, about a block and a half away—but that was the location of the black YWCA. Since both Joe Bihari and B.B. speak of the session taking place at the black YMCA, I have given the location in this way.

130 "We rented a room in the black YMCA": Joe Bihari Oral History, pp. 101–2. Completed under the auspices of the Oral History Program at ULCA, interview conducted by Steven L. Isoardi. Used by permission. Ike had much the same memory about an unnamed piano player "playing jazzy chords" in his interview with Morgan Neville for our A&E documentary on Sam. Still, there are a number of problems with this story. To begin with, Ike had met at least some of the Biharis in July when he signed a contract with them in Memphis. In addition, he had been playing live gigs with Howlin' Wolf since moving to West Memphis that summer and is generally believed to have played on Wolf's first Modern session, which almost certainly preceded B.B.'s. And Joe Bihari at one point has Ike taking him to meet Wolf for the first time. In addition, the editing of the story in this fashion ignores the fact that B.B. knew Ike from years before in Clarksdale and had in fact introduced Ike to Sam. In B.B.'s variant, in his autobiography, there is no mention of the "3 O'Clock" session in particular, and in fact B.B. has the story almost reversed, with Ike bringing him first to the Biharis and, through them, to Sam Phillips. I mention these details not with the aim of finally unraveling the true story (I think these are all true stories) but to point out once again the *Rashomon*-like nature of memory and subjective truth. And I would suggest that while some details may be literally problematic, there is no question in my mind of their many poetic truths.

132 "I hired Ike": Joe Bihari Oral History, pp. 103–4.

134 had filled in very effectively: Rosco tells the story – very effectively – in John Floyd, *Sun Records: An Oral History*, p. 19.

135 He was still managing and announcing his little gospel quartet: In fact Sam had submitted sides he had recorded on the Sun Spot Quartet to Modern as early as February 14, 1951, when Jules first broached the idea of recording hillbilly talent. "I have run across this Gospel Quartet (White Male)," he wrote to Jules, "which I think can be commercial as well as good to listen to." And when he didn't hear back, he brought them up again to Jules a month later, without ever mentioning the fact that their manager was his brother.

136 "Frank Floyd was a beautiful hobo": interview by Paul Jones, *Paul Jones R&B Show*, BBC, 1988–1989. The quote has been edited and arranged.

136 He was "a very fascinating character": Ibid.

136 their new hillbilly series: It's hard to say where exactly the idea originated. When Leonard Chess mentioned it at the very beginning of their association, Sam responded with language that almost exactly mirrored the words Jules Bihari had been using for the past month or so to describe his own plans for a hillbilly line. "The types of Hillbilly that I'm interested in," Jules wrote in a letter of March 2, "is Hillbilly-Boogie, Blues, Jump, and occasional ballads with a heavy rhythm beat using electric guitar and rhythm guitar on almost everything." These were exactly the types of music that Sam discussed with Leonard in a letter of March 26, "hillbilly numbers with a good solid BEAT!...We will not attempt to compete with the major companies with run-of-the-mill types of hillbilly music [but] I do see a definite steady business from coin [jukebox] operators alone on the type of rhythm-with-a-beat numbers that we plan to do." I don't know. Maybe it was just something that was in the air.

136 the label took out an ad: *Billboard*, August 4, 1951. The quote is cited in *First Pressings 1951*, p. 76, in the aggregated "Notes from the R&B Beat" and appears to have come from *Cash Box*.

138 the formation of a new label: *Billboard*, February 16, 1952 (dateline February 9).

139 Mrs. McMurry hit the Biharis with a $1.001 million lawsuit: The lawsuit, as reported in *Billboard*, February 16, 1952, did not actually name Elmore James and Sonny

Boy Williamson (Leroy Holmes and His Darktown Boys was the group named), but it arose out of the same dispute and had the same inhibiting effect.

139 "stick a microphone out there and let them play": *Blues Unlimited* interview quoted in Arnold Shaw, *Honkers and Shouters: The Golden Years of Rhythm and Blues*, p. 203.

141 Everyone talked: Most details from Phillips Family 1995, *In Memoriam* "Yearbook," as well as a letter from Aunt Emma to Sam shortly after her sister's death.

142 "I wish I could be there with you": Marion Keisker to Sam, January 20, 1952.

142 an item in *Billboard: Billboard*, February 23, 1952, which makes reference to a February 16 story. Marion's notebook shows Roscoe's rights signed over to Modern, in agreement with Chess, on February 15.

143 "[Sam] fell in love with what we were doing": *The Sun Blues Box*, pp. 60-61.

144 who should he run into but an old schoolmate: Michael Lollar, "True Rock's Rays," *Memphis Commercial Appeal*, July 2, 2004, a feature on Jay Parker, as well as numerous interviews with Sam.

145 "Sellin' My Stuff": In Marion's notebook, "Stuff" was crossed out and "Whiskey" written in, as though, as Colin Escott has noted, a title change might make the record more palatable to a contemporary audience.

145 "he found the sound that he wanted": *The Sun Blues Box*, p. 61.

147 his teeth . . . went flying across the room: *Paul Jones R&B Show*

147 a couple of hard blues sides: The record, "Bad Woman Blues," backed with "Hydramatic Woman," did not come out until 1954, on Big Town Records.

148 "I don't think they wanted to take the time": *Paul Jones R&B Show*.

148 Leonard Chess did his best to get the Wolf to quit Memphis: This was a problem Sam had foreseen for some time. At the heart of his disagreement with Leonard over Jackie Brenston was Leonard's insistence on recording Brenston in Chicago in late 1951. "I feel that I have got to have your full cooperation in getting [these artists] to record here [in Memphis]," Sam wrote on December 19, 1951. "I don't mean to question your ability in supervising a session [but] you are going to find that these sessions [in Chicago] are not going to pay off."

148 "Howlin' Wolf came to me": 1981 interview with Les Bihari by Jim O'Neal, published as "Lester Bihari of Meteor Records" in *Living Blues*, October 2004. Martin Hawkins writes about this, too, in his feature for the Swedish magazine *American Music*, published in fall 2014, "Meteor Records: 'A better record — a finer label.'"

148 "I turned my farming business over to my brother-in-law": Interview with Dave Booth, quoted in Colin Escott liner notes, *Howlin' Wolf Memphis Days*, vol. 1 (Bear Family BCD 15460), and elsewhere. In that interview Wolf said he left Memphis in 1952 or 1953, as he had earlier told me, but there seems no question, from Memphis radio listings and evidence of his Chicago club bookings as well as the date that Muddy Waters purchased the house in which Wolf stayed when he first came to Chicago, that he did not arrive until early 1954.

148 an "entirely different approach to rock 'n' roll": *Moanin' at Midnight*, p. 103, from Bill Wyman with Richard Havers, *Bill Wyman's Blues Odyssey: A Journey to Music's Heart and Soul*, p. 297.

148 "the counterpart of Elvis": Bill Ellis, "For the Record," *Memphis Commercial Appeal*, January 9, 2000.

151 in June they formalized their plans: I am working backwards from the instrument of incorporation, dated September 29, 1952, which references a partnership that has been going on for some time. By a process of triangulation, I have estimated that the partnership went back to June, but I have no piece of paper that gives the specific date.

153 Alburty's replacement, Clarence Camp: It's hard to say exactly how Clarence Camp became involved. He seems to have become recently interested in radio — in fact, at the beginning of May, it had been reported in *Cash Box* that he and Leonard Chess and Buster Williams were bidding to buy a station in Memphis. Over the years, he and Sam would maintain an ongoing friendship — with both Knox and Jerry recalling visits to Camp's home on Horseshoe Lake in Arkansas, where they would go boating and play the pinball machines in his living room — but it was never the kind of intimate association that Sam had with either Jimmy Connolly or Dewey Phillips, or with future business associates like Kemmons Wilson and his attorney, Roy Scott.

156 He was soon promoted: This, and much else about Jim Bulleit and the whole Nashville recording scene, comes from Martin Hawkins' masterful *A Shot in the Dark: Making Records in Nashville, 1945-1955*, along with the Country Music Foundation's extensive 1976 oral history interviews with Bulleit, conducted by Doug Green.

157 a headlong hegira of sales and promotion: In addition to my interviews with Sam and Marion Keisker, other sources include Martin Hawkins, *A Shot in the Dark*, both Hawkins' and Doug Green's interviews with Jim Bulleit, and Daniel Cooper, *Lefty Frizzell: The Honky-Tonk Life of Country Music's Greatest Singer*, pp. 76ff.

158 Charles Thomas, whom Sam touted as possessing a style "a lot like Johnnie Lee Hooker's": Sam letter to Jim Bulleit, November 17, 1952. Charles Thomas (né Thompson) would later resurface in Chicago as Maxwell Street Jimmy and have a well-regarded debut album of his own on the Elektra label in 1966.

158 at the same time brought up the idea of a potential partnership: Sam to Jim Bulleit, November 17, 1952: "I wrote Mr. Camp informing him of our phone conversations"; Jim to Sam, December 1: "I can't forget the deal between us and Camp, and I still think it is a good one," as well as subsequent correspondence.

158 his timing was never quite right: Bulleit alludes to this several times in the course of his interviews with Doug Green.

159 he wrote that after thinking it over: Sam to Bulleit, January 15, 1953.

160 "reserved, [almost] stand-offish": This and the subsequent quote are from the Country Music Foundation oral history.

160 45s were making rapid inroads: Jim Bulleit to Sam, January 29, 1953.

162 "the essence of what America has always been about": Alex Gibney interview with Sam, 1995.

163 it reflected . . . something "very personal to him": Sam to Martin Hawkins, May 1, 2000.

163 "a little aviatic": Lee Jackson quoted by Jim O'Neal in "An Aviatic Afternoon: Willie Nix — The Memphis Blues Boy in Mississippi," *Living Blues*, summer 1979, p. 9.

163 Nix had come to Sam's attention: Sam recalled possibly running into Willie at the Home of the Blues record shop on Beale a little earlier, but it appears to have been the radio show that brought him to the forefront of Sam's consciousness.

163 "fantasizing about things that could never be": Jim O'Neal obituary for Nix, *Living Blues*, January/February 1992, p. 36.

164 "Willie was not the subtlest of drummers": Escott and Hawkins liner notes to CD-3, *Sun Records: The Blues Years, 1950–1958.*

165 "one of them good ones that didn't have a telephone ringing": Sam often assigned the telephone to a Little Junior Parker record—but this is where you'll hear it.

166 "I could discern things that were different": 1992 Smithsonian interview, conducted by Pete Daniel and Peter Guralnick for the Rock 'n' Soul exhibit.

167 He had by now acquired an old RCA 76-D radio board: The exact date of this acquisition is indeterminate. I haven't been able to find an invoice or a bill of sale, and Sam himself only referred to its "early" acquisition, but Stuart Colman, Matt Ross-Spang, and Tom Eaton, whom I consulted extensively, and independently, on audio matters, all felt there was a marked improvement in "tone, volume, and overall quality" (to quote Stuart) between Willie Nix's "Baker Shop Boogie," say, in October 1952 and Walter Horton's "Easy" in February 1953. But, of course, for the time being at least, this remains purely theoretical.

167 "of course that was a lot of money": Jim Cogan and William Clark, *Temples of Sound: Inside the Great Recording Studios,* p. 90.

167 "I'm not one who likes to look back": Interview with Hoss Allen, October 26, 1990.

168 $2,000 he had been able to set aside: Actually Sam made quite a bit from his short lived partnership with Chess—almost $10,000 in fact over the course of the first seventeen months of their association. It was a very healthy infusion of cash, and it allowed him to spend more freely on both the studio and the artists. But in the end his dissatisfaction clearly resided elsewhere.

170 "who always follows his own lead": Becky Phillips, "Gentle But Tough," one of Becky's many handwritten autobiographical (and biographical) sketches and portraits.

172 "to regard the answer as an 'original'": "Pubbers Train Legal Guns on Tail-Riding Indie Labels," *Billboard,* April 4, 1953.

172 "a wild thing called 'Bear Cat'": Rhythm and Blues Notes, *Billboard,* March 28, 1953.

172 "releasing is the life of this business": undated letter from Jim Bulleit during the period of turmoil in the spring of 1953.

173 "I wouldn't nor haven't": Jim Bulleit to Sam, June 15, 1953.

173 a check to Lion Musical Publishing Company for $1,580.80: This is the figure entered in the Sun expense ledger, kindly supplied by Terry Stewart and the Rock 'n' Roll Hall of Fame. Colin Escott points out that this would represent a sale of thirty-one thousand copies, a very healthy sales figure if Sam were forced to pay the penalty rate of $.05 a side. But I would suspect that Sam paid the statutory $.02 rate, which would indicate sales of something like seventy-nine thousand records.

173 The Prisonaires were a quintet: In addition to my own interviews with Sam and Johnny Bragg, other principal sources include Clark Porteous, "Prison Singers May Find Fame with Record They Made in Memphis," *Memphis Press-Scimitar,* July 15, 1953; Hawkins, *A Shot in the Dark;* Colin Escott with Martin Hawkins, *Good Rockin' Tonight: Sun Records and the Birth of Rock 'n' Roll;* Martin Hawkins and Doug Green interviews with Jim Bulleit; Martin Hawkins interviews with Red Wortham; John Dougan's various writings on the group; and Jay Warner, *Just Walkin' in the Rain.*

174 "the hopes of tomorrow": Porteous, as above.

175 Eventually Wortham agreed: There are several versions of this story. This is Red Wortham's version, as recounted in one interview with Martin Hawkins. Wortham told Hawkins another story, in which he assigned all the credit to himself, but if I had to choose between the two, this one seems more credible to me on the basis of Wortham's self-interest alone.

175 "a bit of a finagler": Hawkins interview with Red Wortham.

175 He got Jim Bulleit to set up an appointment: Once again there are various contradictory versions: Jim Bulleit insisted in his interviews with Hawkins (see *A Shot in the Dark*, p. 112) that he was the one that persuaded Governor Clement to allow the group to record — but with little supportive detail. Red Wortham told Martin Hawkins that it was *his* recording of "Just Walkin'" that was issued on record — but this seems contradicted by all other accounts and by auditory evidence. From here on in, perhaps I should simply say that it needs to be understood that there are competing stories from credible sources on nearly every detail, and the reader should simply trust that I have made the best choices that I could — and who knows, in future those choices could change, given additional evidence.

176 "Oh, that man!": Hank Davis liner notes, *Sun Gospel* (Bear Family BCD 16387), p. 6.

176 "Howard unpacked his guitar": Ibid.

178 he was scheduled to be paroled: As it turned out, according to Warner, *Just Walkin' in the Rain*, pp. 113, 116, 127, he didn't get his parole, but by that time, Marcel Sanders had already refused to be released and stayed in prison a full year past his release date.

179 an ambitious promotional push: Jim Bulleit to Sam, June 16, 1953. The label on this first release was simply credited to "PRISONAIRES," although all subsequent releases were more dramatically titled "PRISONAIRES, Confined to Tennessee State Prison, Nashville, Tenn."

180 for the first time all of Memphis: Just to underscore how keenly Sam felt this exclusion, he was often at pains to describe the kindness of Mr. O. F. Soderstrom, the executive vice president of the Memphis Chamber of Commerce, who alone extended the hand of friendship.

181 the Wolf's piano player, Bill Johnson, known to all the musicians as "'Struction," had brought in a young harmonica player: This is according to Floyd Murphy's account in Brian Baumgartner, "Eddie Snow and Floyd Murphy: Partnership in the Blues," *Juke Blues*, p. 20. As to the name "'Struction," this appears to be the general pronunciation of his name. However, Marion spelled it "Strutcher" in the Sun ledger book, and in Pete Welding's interview with Howlin' Wolf he is referred to as "Destruction."

181 "that raw stuff": Baumgartner, as above.

183 whatever "civic affiliations": Sam to Jimmy Connolly, October 13, 1953.

184 Sam could certainly see his ongoing value: One other odd side note: Jim Bulleit had convinced Sam that Sam owed his job at WLAC in Nashville to Bulleit because Bulleit had just turned down the job himself, which he informed Sam of when Sam came to audition at WSM. In fact, Bulleit left a very temporary job at WLAC to go to work at WSM on December 7, 1943 (Hawkins, *A Shot in the Dark*, p. 26), just as Sam was about to get married in Decatur, Alabama, but such was Bulleit's power of persuasion that he convinced Sam that this was how it must have happened and Sam believed it to his dying day.

184 "We have wanted to get together for so long": Jud to Sam, July 28, 1953.

185 "Should you need me before Saturday": Ibid.

185 "You wouldn't even know": Jim Bulleit Oral History interview, Country Music Foundation, p. 53.

187 "10 to 25 letters every day": Jud to Sam July 28, 1953, with periods and commas supplied, as Jud employed dashes exclusively.

188 "I have nothing personal against Jud": Jim Bulleit to Sam August 29, 1953. As to the deferred recompense (in other words, Jim would give—or maybe even sell at a bargain-basement rate—half his stock to Jud, while retaining half in expectation of a payday down the line), this is my interpretation of Jim's turndown of a deal that is not spelled out except in the language of his rejection. In this same letter, Jim writes: "You and I understand each other, as do you and Jud,"—but "any other combination," he wrote, "I am afraid . . . would be fatal in some way."

188 a price of $1,600: Sam always contended that it was he—or the business—that put up the money for Jud's share, and the Sun financial ledger would appear to bear this out.

189 "Jud, I am sorry": Sam to Jud, September 3, 1953.

190 "Just Walkin' in the Rain" stalled at thirty thousand copies: The November issue of *Ebony* cited sales of 225,000. The generally accepted figure has always been 50,000. But based on royalty payments to Red Wortham, who held the publishing, the *Nashville Banner*'s report at the end of September that sales stood at approximately 30,000, and Sam's letter to Jim Bulleit a year later (August 16, 1954) that after returns net sales on all Prisonaires product had declined to 36,512, it seems clear that "Just Walkin' in the Rain" was more a *succès d'estime* than a sales blockbuster—and yet it was a blockbuster success nonetheless.

190 "Walkin' in the Rain" cover versions: Johnnie Ray did in fact cover the song and had a number 2 pop hit that was on the charts for twenty-eight weeks in 1956—but by then Wortham had sold the rights to Gene Autry's Republic Music.

190 He was no less proud: If only to show his continuing faith in the group, Sam took out trade ads on August 12 and September 28, at a cost of $125.67 for the first, $200 for the second.

190 *Life* magazine assigned a photographer: The story never ran, but the pictures, taken by photographer Robert Kelley, which appear to date from September 1 and 2, 1953, are available on both the *Life* magazine (Time.com) and Getty Images websites.

190 *Jet* ran a short piece: August 13, 1953, according to Jay Warner, *Just Walkin' in the Rain*, p. 112.

190 "Jim promised . . . free Sun records": Jud's second letter of the day to Sam, from the Hotel King Carter in Richmond, November 13, 1953.

191 "You know how I can ask questions": Jud from the Hotel Adolphus in Dallas, August 11, 1953.

191 "Hope I've made it clear": Jud from the Captain Shreve Hotel in Shreveport, August 10, 1953.

191 "Met Hot Rod [Hulbert]": Jud from the Hotel Mayfair, Baltimore, November 18, 1953.

193 Rufus Thomas evidently announced to Sam: See Martin Hawkins liner notes for *Rufus Thomas: His R&B Recordings 1949-1956* (Bear Family BCD 16695), p. 41. Hawkins points out that in the November 7, 1953, *Billboard* announcement of WDIA's annual Goodwill Revue the "diskeries" for all of the participating artists are mentioned with the conspicuous exception of Sun. The newly formed Starmaker label, closely "affiliated" with WDIA, according to a *Billboard* item two weeks later, is among the labels included, and with at least one of the WDIA "personality jocks," Moohah, and another Memphis DJ, Dick "Cane" Cole, already signed. Hawkins speculates that "perhaps Rufus was planning to record for [the] new label." This is strictly inferential, obviously, but I think it makes perfect sense.

194 sixteen coaches long: In previous recorded versions eighteen was the most common number of coaches cited (Blind Lemon Jefferson, Peg Leg Howell, and Lucille Bogan all used that number), though both Furry Lewis and the Carter Family had it sixteen.

195 Jud met with three IRS agents: Jud to Sam from the Willard Hotel, November 17, 1953.

195 He got sick in Cleveland: Jud to Sam, December 1, 1953.

195 forced to share a $15 hotel room: From the Hotel Barnes, Indianapolis, December 2, 1953.

195 a real SOB in Pittsburgh: From the Hotel Statler, November 27, 1953.

195 "difficulties with going ahead": Martin Hawkins, "Sam Phillips Talking About the Blues Years to Martin Hawkins" in the book that accompanies *The Sun Blues Box* (Bear Family BCD 17310), p. 14.

196 "Right now we do not have that much": Sam to Jud, February 9, 1954.

196 it was reported in *Cash Box* on November 7: Galen Gart and Roy C. Ames, *Duke/Peacock Records*, p. 60.

196 Sam immediately made a person-to-person call: The *Houston Informer*, April 10, 1954, reported on most of these details. In addition, Sam's March 29, 1954, letter to *Cash Box* editor in chief Sid Parnes refers in some detail to his original letter of December 26 regarding the previous week's coverage of the dispute in the magazine.

196 Jud had promised him the Sun publishing: Correspondence between Sam and Jud with reference to this issue, with Sam writing Jud February 9 and Jud responding on February 12, 1954; also numerous letters between Sam and Jim Bulleit between February 21 and April 14, 1954.

196 "Now if you want to . . . call in your lawyer": Sam to Jim Bulleit, March 11, 1954.

197 a down payment of $750: Sam received an allowance of $895 for his six-year-old Hudson, with $2,250 to pay on time.

197 on the back of his bicycle: Bengt Olsson, *Memphis Blues*, pp. 88–89, Studio Vista "Blues Paperbacks."

198 "some of those great Negro artists": "Man Behind the Sun Sound," *Melody Maker*, ca. 1957, as cited by Mike Leadbitter in "Memphis," *Blues Unlimited*, Collectors Classics 13.

199 a new label, Cat Records: *Billboard*, April 10, 1954.

199 "Southern bobbysoxers": Jerry Wexler and Ahmet Ertegun, "The Latest Trend: R&B Disks Are Going Pop," *Cash Box*, July 3, 1954.

199 "They'd tell me, 'These people are ruining our white children'": Hank Davis and Colin Escott, "Sam Phillips: America's Other Uncle Sam, part 2," *Goldmine*, August 14, 1987, p. 18.

200 "Give me the banjo": Background on Hardrock Gunter primarily from Al Turner, liner notes to *Gonna Rock 'n' Roll, Gonna Dance All Night* (Roller Coaster Records), available on the Hardrock Gunter website; also "Birmingham Bounce," in Jim Dawson and Steve Propes' *What Was the First Rock 'n' Roll Record?*, pp. 69–72.

201 "a chemist in a lab": "Sam Phillips Talking About Country Music on Sun to Martin Hawkins," in the book that accompanies *The Sun Country Box* (Bear Family BCD 17311), p. 12.

201 "I said, 'Well, what *are* you interested in?'": Smithsonian Institution interview with Malcolm Yelvington for the Rock 'n' Soul exhibit, conducted by Pete Daniel, Peter Guralnick, and Charlie McGovern, 1992.

202 The hearing was scheduled: *Houston Informer,* April 10, 1954; interviews with Sam Phillips; Sam Phillips letter to *Cash Box* editor in chief Sid Parnes, March 29, 1954.

202 following the experiments: Bill Putnam is generally credited with being the first to use reverb, or artificial echo, with his recording of "Peg o' My Heart" by the Harmonicats at his Universal studio in Chicago in 1947 ("I used the men's room for an echo chamber"). His friend Les Paul followed suit, and sometimes jumped ahead, with his multitrack recordings at almost the same time. According to sound engineer, writer, and musician Stu Colman, early experiments in the kind of "repeat echo" that Sam was drawn to included many of the comic effects in the Looney Tunes/Merrie Melodies cartoons of the late forties (Bugs Bunny, Daffy Duck, et al.), overseen by Warner Bros. sound editor Treg Brown, as well as the tape-delay experiments of electronic composer Karlheinz Stockhausen.

202 he had experimented with the technique: With respect to Kings of Rhythm saxophonist Raymond Hill's first solo session, on October 6, 1952, it was noted in Marion Keisker's comprehensive session book: "!!! 2 'Echo' harmony dubs on Ampex 1-Hr. tape."

203 sound without artifice: It's hard (for me anyway) to resist a comparison to Hemingway's creation of dialogue that, by the selective use of artifice, suggests a kind of naturalism that is "realer than real."

203 an amp that he called the EchoSonic: See Dave Kyle, "An Interview with Ray Butts," available on www.scottymoore.net/Ray_Butts_interview.html. In 1963, Butts would come to work for Sam briefly in his Nashville studio.

204 "that would give me a [very] slight delay": Tetzer Mills Jr., "The Room That Shook (Rattled and Rolled) the World: The Memphis Recording Service and Sun Records at 706 Union Avenue, Memphis, Tennessee," graduate thesis in Southern Studies at the University of Memphis, (2000), p. 38. I have changed the tenses slightly.

207 "Over and over I heard Sam say": Jerry Hopkins interview with Marion Keisker (MVC/MSU), ca. 1970.

207 And he would always laugh: This was always a sore point with Marion, even when, in later years, she was most at odds with Sam — that, in fact, contrary to the way most people took her "billion-dollar" quote, Sam was never in it for money. "I take a pause [in the Hopkins interview]," she told me, "and it's obvious on the tape that it's hyperbole — I wasn't really quoting him." Marion's right, Sam never hesitated in articulating his belief that this was the only way that real music, that the real gutbucket blues, was ever going to break through — for the black man *and* the white man. The publicity release, for example, introducing his Phillips International label to the world in 1957, said as much, as did his statement to the *Memphis Press-Scimitar* in Edwin Howard, "He's Made $2 Million on Disks — Without a Desk," April 29, 1959: "But there was something in many of these youngsters that resisted buying this kind of music. The Southern ones, especially. . . . They liked the music, but they weren't sure whether they ought to. . . . So I got to thinking how many records you could sell if you could find white performers who could play and sing in this same exciting, alive way."

207 a kid who had stopped by the previous summer: Elvis Presley had actually come in just a few weeks after the Prisonaires story in the *Memphis Press-Scimitar,* very likely drawn in by the promise of the article. There was a myth in later years that he met and was encouraged by Johnny Bragg in the studio, but nothing other than the recollections of Johnny Bragg, which tended toward the fanciful, has ever come forward to support the story, and although Elvis befriended Johnny Bragg in later years, neither Sam nor Marion, nor Elvis himself, suggested anything that might indicate a prior acquaintance.

208 before Miss Keisker hung up the phone: 1972 interview with Elvis for the film *Elvis on Tour* inter alia.

208 "his insecurity": Robert Palmer, "Sam Phillips: The Sun King," *Memphis* magazine, December 1978, p. 32.

208 "I guess I must have sat there at least three hours": Robert Johnson, *Elvis Presley Speaks!*, p. 10.

210 Scotty called Sam at home the following evening: The audition with Scotty and Bill, the session the following night, and the narrative of the next few days are all extensively sourced in Peter Guralnick, *Last Train to Memphis: The Rise of Elvis Presley*. The detail and chronology are based primarily on numerous interviews with Sam Phillips and Scotty Moore, as well as interviews with Bobbie Moore and Evelyn Black.

212 "this song popped into my mind: Ibid., plus *TV Star Parade*, September 1956, p. 24.

212 a slap beat and a tonal beat: I got the concept from Colin Escott, liner notes to a Bill Black Combo album.

213 He didn't even use his new discovery of slapback: Contrary to most received opinion, as well as my own firmly held assumptions over the years, there is no slapback to be heard here. The reason that our ears deceived all of us over the years (or at least those of us who were not listening to the original Sun 45s and 78s) is the electronic echo that RCA added to all of its recordings at that time, "enhancing" the sound of Elvis' Sun recordings in this fashion from the time they started rereleasing them in December 1955. Slapback was clearly a matter of choice for Sam at this point, as evidenced by the fact that while you can hear the effect on the Starlite Wranglers' and Raymond Hill's recordings in April, it is noticeably absent from both James Cotton's and Billy "Red" Love's sessions in May.

213 "we couldn't believe it was us": Johnson, *Elvis Presley Speaks!*, p. 10.

213 "It just sounded sort of raw": Trevor Cajiao interview with Scotty Moore for "We Were the Only Band Directed By an Ass," *Elvis: The Man and His Music* 10 (March 1991), p. 19.

213 "We thought it was exciting": Jerry Hopkins interview with Scotty Moore, ca. 1970 (MVC/MSU).

214 Dewey played it on the air the next night: Much of the information, and *all* of the color, about this epochal appearance comes from Stanley Booth, "A Hound Dog to the Manor Born," *Esquire*, February 1968.

214 "I was scared to death": Elvis interviewed on Dewey's death in the *Memphis Commercial Appeal*, September 29, 1968.

214 They went back into the studio the following night: I had always assumed until very recently that several nights intervened between the first and second sessions. That's the way Scotty remembered it, certainly. But discovering a letter from Sam to ASCAP on July 8 urgently requesting copyright information on "That's All Right" and "Blue Moon of Kentucky" led me to the inescapable conclusion that "Blue Moon of Kentucky" must have been recorded on July 7, following Elvis' appearance on Dewey's show on July 6, the night after the first session.

214 "Then Bill jumped up": Jerry Hopkins interview with Scotty Moore (MVC/MSU).

215 "May we please call your attention": Sam to Bob Rolontz, July 21, 1954.

215 "He was very hard to interview": Bill E. Burk, *Elvis: A 30 Year Chronicle,* p. 7. The article itself appeared in the *Memphis Press-Scimitar* under the heading "In a Spin" on July 28, 1954.

216 "I was scared stiff": Paul Wilder interview, August 6, 1956.

218 a sound he hadn't heard before: Malcolm Yelvington, Smithsonian interview, conducted by Pete Daniel, Peter Guralnick, and Charlie McGovern, 1992.

219 "I got this man": Charles Raiteri liner notes to the Dewey Phillips airchecks album, *Red Hot and Blue,* on the Zu-Zazz label; also Colin Escott with Martin Hawkins, *Good Rockin' Tonight: Sun Records and the Birth of Rock 'n' Roll,* p. 67.

220 "Mr. Phillips, I wish I could play your record": Trevor Cajiao, "The Most Important Man in the World: Sam Phillips Talks to *Now Dig This,* part 2, *Now Dig This,* 84 (March 1990), p. 20. The rest of the account is from my own interviews with Sam. But he told this story many times, in almost exactly the same fashion.

221 "too racy": Marvin Lieber, Pan American Distributing Corp., to Sam, September 24, 1954; Sam's reply is from his letter to Lieber six days later. He had originally written to Lieber on August 10 to try to enlist him in the crusade: the record, he said was going "ALL THREE WAYS . . . everybody from young white teenagers to old colored people are buying it with equal zest."

222 "He made a tremendous showing": October 6, 1954, letter to Bill Sachs at *Billboard*'s office in Cincinnati.

224 "everyone was trying very hard: Jerry Hopkins interview with Marion Keisker (MVC/MSU).

225 "I still remember": Ibid.

228 "I took my hat and started out the front door": This is almost entirely from Carl's 1992 interview by a Smithsonian team at the New Daisy Theatre, of which I was part. There is a single phrase from Carl's autobiography, *Go, Cat, Go!,* and one or two even slighter amplifications from my own interviews with Carl, all painting exactly the same scene.

229 "That thing was going to move": Larry Nager interview with Sam for NARAS archives, 2000.

229 and helped put together a group that became known as the Blue Seal Pals: Bill Cantrell's origin story about the Blue Seals, as told to Martin Hawkins and Colin Escott, was virtually the same as Quinton's, except that he was there first. On a website devoted to Edgar Clayton, who was broadcasting at WLAY before any of the others, the foundation of the group was attributed to Clayton and Quinton, with Bill Cantrell and Dexter Johnson joining very soon thereafter.

231 "What do you boys think": Dialogue from Carl Perkins and David McGee, *Go, Cat, Go!,* p. 98; transcribed from *The Classic Carl Perkins,* Bear Family 5-CD box (Bear Family, BCD 15494).

233 "the rhythmic beat of 'That's All Right Mama'": *Tri-Cities Daily,* January 12, 1955. On July 28, with another show coming up, the *Tri-Cities Daily*'s entertainment column, "The Marquee," referred to the January show as "one of the biggest hits ever to show at the [Sheffield Community] Center."

235 "Elvis sells": Just to quantify this a little for the reader, "That's All Right"/"Blue Moon of Kentucky" was by far not just Sun Records' but the Memphis Recording Service's best-selling record to date. According to Sam in Elton Whisenhunt, "Another Tennessee Boy Has Hit Song Going," *Memphis Press-Scimitar,* February 27, 1956, it had sold 138,000 copies by the end of 1955, which Sam specified was Elvis' biggest seller on Sun.

SEVEN | SPIRITUAL AWAKENINGS

237 "Milkcow Blues Boogie" didn't sell any better: In a January 25, 1955, letter to his Chicago distributor, Al Benson, Sam boasted that every one of Elvis' records had sold better than seventy-five thousand — but in fact, whereas "That's All Right" had sold well over one hundred thousand copies at this point, according to Elton Whisenhunt, "Another Tennessee Boy Has Hit Song Going," *Memphis Press-Scimitar*, February 27, 1956, clearly neither of its follow-ups came anywhere near matching it.

237 a five-date regional tour: This turned out to include seven dates over two weeks before Elvis entered into a week of east Texas bookings previously arranged by Tom Perryman.

238 he took an immediate dislike to him when they met between shows: This account has been put together primarily from interviews with Sam Phillips and Scotty Moore, together with Oscar Davis' colorful, if somewhat confused, description to Jerry Hopkins (MVC/MSU).

238 "We don't want you to feel": letter to Al Benson, Bronzeville Distributing Company, January 25, 1955.

239 a local distributor was "of the opinion": Nate Duroff to Sam, March 21, 1955.

239 almost certain to be his biggest seller yet: It is worth noting that just four months after Nate Duroff's letter, "Rock Around the Clock" became the first record labeled as "rock 'n' roll" to hit number 1 on *Billboard*'s pop charts, where it remained for the next eight weeks, while simultaneously sparking the rock 'n' roll revolution in England.

242 A tall, lanky boy named J. R. Cash: Much of the detail on Cash's early life comes from a plethora of trustworthy but often contradictory sources: Christopher Wren, *Winners Got Scars, Too: The Life and Legends of Johnny Cash*; Johnny Cash with Patrick Carr, *Cash: The Autobiography*; Robert Hilburn, *Johnny Cash: The Life*; and Steve Turner, *The Man Called Cash: The Life, Love, and Faith of An American Legend*, among others.

242 he had first started coming around the studio: In what appears to be a self-penned publicity bio from 1957, "This Is My Story," Cash speaks of calling Sam in March and telling him that he had two original religious songs and that he would like an audition. Two weeks later, according to this chronology, "after Mr. Phillips told me [very politely] he wasn't interested," he got that audition. Many other accounts have this first meeting considerably earlier, some as far back as late 1954, but this seems to me the most likely time frame. Cash linked the impetus for his original contact with Sam to seeing Elvis, and meeting Scotty, at the Katz Drugstore opening at which Elvis performed on September 9, 1954, then subsequently going to see Elvis play out at the Eagle's Nest. But his initial contact with Sam by his own account came considerably later.

244 "I stood up and I said, 'I'm John Cash'": This is from a 1980 interview I did with Cash. He was also at pains to make the point in the same interview that "Sam Phillips didn't come out and tap me on the head and say, 'Come on, son, let's go to make a record. I had to fight and call and keep at it and just push, push, push." I should point out that in this, as in every other recollection and account that I've come across, I'm sure that time has shrunk and events have become conflated. Sometimes in the way both he and Sam told it, he presented himself initially as strictly a religious singer, but then Sam listened to his music, both standards and originals, and was sufficiently impressed to invite him back. There's no telling, really, which version is true, but in any case, Sam clearly heard something original in him. He sang with the conviction of gospel pioneer V. O. Stamps, Sam said, and gospel singer or no gospel singer, "I heard a depth in him."

244 "He was so nervous he couldn't play": This is from an unpublished Patrick Carr interview with Johnny Cash. Once again, it seems entirely possible that there might have been two audition sessions, or more.

244 "Marshall, when you play": Marshall Grant with Chris Zar, *I Was There When It Happened: My Life with Johnny Cash*, p. 36.

245 a poem that John wrote: In "This Is My Story," p. 3, Cash says that he wrote the poem "on my way home"; in Bill Flanagan, "Johnny Cash, American," *Musician*, May 1998, p. 100, and elsewhere, he says, "I was in the Air Force when I started writing songs."

245 "Go home and write me an up-tempo weeper": Flanagan, as above.

245 listening to Smilin' Eddie Hill: "This Is My Story," p. 3.

245 he wrote it originally as "You're Gonna Bawl": "This Is My Story," p. 3; also Christopher Wren, *Winners Got Scars, Too*, p. 93, though there it's "Squall and Climb the Walls."

246 "Johnny" Cash sounded better than "John": Steve Turner, *The Man Called Cash*, p. 53; also Christopher Wren, *Winners Got Scars, Too*, p. 95.

246 Mr. Phillips could "see something happening": Carr interview with Cash.

246 with artist royalties split: Colin Escott with Martin Hawkins, *Good Rockin' Tonight: Sun Records and the Birth of Rock 'n' Roll*, p. 100.

246 "I said, 'One of these days I'm going to walk in here'": Carr interview with Cash.

247 "I might can make a living at it": Ibid.

247 "I thought my world had ended": Colin Escott booklet biography, p. 8, *Johnny Cash and the Tennessee Two: The Sun Years* (Charly Records Sun Box 103, a 5-LP set).

247 "Mr. Phillips would listen to anything": Carr interview with Cash.

248 "taking off big": Sam to Nate Duroff, July 8, 1955.

248 on the show that Ernie's Record Mart sponsored on WLAC: It was scarcely coincidental that Ernie Young owned the Excello label, on which Arthur Gunter's "Baby Let's Play House" was released.

248 "I'm Left, You're Right, She's Gone": The ordering of the words in the title would frequently be confused. The song was in fact originally copyrighted as "You're Right, I'm Left, She's Gone" but was re-copyrighted in December with "I'm Left" going first in the sequence, as it did on the label.

250 "Oh, forget it": Jerry Hopkins interview with Bob Neal (MVC, MSU). Different figures have been quoted at different times, often by the same people.

250 his new partner: By the beginning of the summer, Colonel Parker was not only booking the vast majority of Elvis' dates, he and Neal had come to an understanding that was formally realized on August 15, designating Parker as the sole person empowered "to negotiate all renewals on existing contracts."

251 a license to operate: The station actually restricted itself to twenty hours a day at first, according to Louis Cantor, *Wheelin' on Beale*, p. 100.

251 his station's emphasis would necessarily have to change: Sam to Miss Mary Jane Morris, Secretary, Federal Communications Commission, October 6, 1954.

252 when "Carl's voice moved up in tempo": Larry Nager interview, NARAS.

252 Be sure to have a supply of records: This is adapted from Perkins with David McGee, *Go, Cat, Go!*, p. 157, where Carl quotes the precise advice Sam gave to both Cash and him.

252 "Johnny Cash . . . was simply great": "The Marquee," *Tri-Cities Daily,* ca. August 3, 1955.

253 "Country Rhythm Fills a City Park": *Memphis Press-Scimitar,* August 6, 1955.

253 he was as quick a learner: These were some of Sam's thoughts in interviews we conducted for the A&E *Biography* documentary and in an insightful interview he did with Charlie Gillett for the BBC in June of 2000.

253 He had conceived of "Folsom": Actually, part of his conception was never acknowledged at the time. In addition to seeing the movie *Inside the Walls of Folsom Prison,* which he frequently said was his initial inspiration, he had evidently listened to a 1953 "concept" album by arranger-composer Gordon Jenkins, *Seven Dreams,* which contained a song called "Crescent City Blues," a mirror image of his own later composition. As to the piece of paper underneath the strings, I don't hear it in the finished version — though it may well be there. But it definitely surfaces in "I Walk the Line," recorded some six months later.

253 "We just weren't versatile enough": Colin Escott booklet biography, p. 9, *Johnny Cash and the Tennessee Two: The Sun Years* (Charly Records Sun Box 103, a 5-LP set).

254 "That was a part of Sam Phillips' brilliance": Carr interview with Cash.

255 "the best song" he had ever written: This is from a letter by Cash to his friend Ted Freeman on September 30 or October 1, 1955, and quoted in Turner, *The Man Called Cash,* p. 57. Just a note about the dating of this session: July 30 has always been given as the date for his recording of both "I Walk the Line" and "So Doggone Lonesome," but this letter two months later refers explicitly to the recording of "I Get So Doggone Lonesome" the previous Monday night. Bass player and Cash historian Marshall Grant always recalled cutting both sides very close together, just before a brief tour with Elvis, and while Grant attached it to the four-day tour that ended at Overton Park on August 5, they went out on another six-day tour with Elvis October 9-14. Also, in the notes for LP-1 in the boxed Johnny Cash set on Charly, Cash says of "So Doggone Lonesome," that he "finished [it] just a week or two before we recorded it." The possibility, of course, still remains that he recorded the master for "Folsom Prison" two months prior to cutting "So Doggone Lonesome" — but both chronology and the logic of the Sun release schedule would argue against it. Both songs were copyrighted November 30, 1955.

255 "Don't listen to the music on the record": from letter to Ted Freeman (always addressed as "Fenrod," a takeoff on his given name of Fenton), ca. November 26, 1955.

258 Marshall's bar mitzvah: This was something of an industrywide event, including everyone from Chess artist Muddy Waters to most of the prominent r&b DJs and independent record industry figures. It took place on April 17, 1955.

262 Jud . . . refused to cash the checks: Sam wrote to Jud on July 12, 1955, pressing him to sign the agreement and cash the two checks. Jud replied on July 14 that he had used his stock as security for a $2,000 bank loan, and should "they decide to take it, one accountant and one lawyer will come to Memphis and check the thing all the way through [and then] it will be put in the hands of a trust officer at one of the banks to operate their interest."

262 He had . . . never taken a drink in his life: This is according to the testimony not just of Sam but of Becky, Marion Keisker, and Sally Wilbourn, who initially went to work as Sam's secretary in November of 1955. Sam freely acknowledged that he more than made up for it.

262 his nine P.M.-to-midnight shift: The times of Dewey's show seemed to shift without much evident rhyme or reason. So maybe nineish would be more accurate.

263 he had called Kemmons Wilson: In addition to my own interviews, many of the details come from the Kitchen Sisters' interviews with Kemmons Wilson and Sam Phillips for their *Lost and Found* NPR documentary, *WHER: 1000 Beautiful Watts,* as well as their wonderful, privately printed book, *WHER: 1000 Beautiful Watts, The First All-Girl Radio Station in the Nation.* I've also gotten great help from Lauren Young and Dottie Bonds of the Kemmons Wilson Family Foundation and Kemmons Wilson Companies respectively.

264 "glamour, sparkle [and] spice": Advertisement in the *Memphis Press-Scimitar,* October 28, 1955.

267 Sam applied to the FCC: Sam wrote to the FCC on August 31, and the request was granted on September 13.

267 "Wanted: Fresh, friendly, female voice": Sam letter to Classified Advertising, *Broadcasting-Telecasting,* August 27, 1955.

268 "He said, 'I've just got this idea'": This, and all subsequent quotes by Denise Howard, are from the Kitchen Sisters' interview in February 1998.

270 "Mystery Train" forged ahead of it: *Billboard,* September 17, 1955.

270 they had been scheduled to go on the air: Robert Johnson, "WHER: All-Lady Station," *Memphis Press-Scimitar,* October 14, 1955.

272 He had in the end been able to persuade Jud: A letter and "sight" draft of payment (to be redeemed after all paperwork was completed) was sent on October 14, 1954, with specific instructions as to how Jud needed to deal with his bank. "Thanks for your co-operation, and with all best wishes, I am, Sincerely, Sam C. Phillips," the letter concludes.

272 "ladylike tardiness": *Memphis Press-Scimitar,* October 28, 1955.

272 Evidently by coincidence: Sam never saw any evidence of collusion, he said. I'm not so sure there wasn't.

272 they would also be licensed: The contract went into effect on November 17, 1955.

274 awarded unspecified damages: *Billboard,* December 10, 1955, refers to a "recently handed down" court decision, with damages still to be assessed.

274 cumulative damages . . . were set at $17,500: Undated clip ("Phillips Wins Damages") almost certainly from a Memphis newspaper, in Colin Escott and Martin Hawkins, *Sun Records: The Discography,* with additional anecdotal material from Sam, Marion Keisker, and Sally Wilbourn.

277 he couldn't even remember Elvis' name: Marion liked to say in later years that she had stated this fact on the air, but I would imagine this was probably more in the realm of the "like" world ("I, like, said"), and it might in fact be read more as a character judgment than an historical fact. Marion was ordinarily a very polite person, who whatever the sharpness of her opinions, always observed the amenities in public.

279 "There are few boundary lines left in music": "Boundaries Between Music Types Fall; Deejays Spin 'Em All," *Billboard,* November 12, 1955.

279 on the morning of Saturday, December 17: The session was logged and mastered on December 19. In most of Carl's accounts, he wrote the song in the early morning hours after a gig in his hometown of Jackson, Tennessee, and called Sam that morning.

279 it finally reached number 14: *Billboard,* November 26, 1955.

280 "I don't care what you do": Steve Turner, *The Man Called Cash,* p. 59.

280 Just a few nights later: I should note that Carl told several different versions of this story, with both the time and sometimes the place of its original inspiration occasionally shifting. The one constant was that Johnny Cash always provided the suggestion, and in almost every case Elvis was on the show. According to Ernst Jorgensen's *A Boy from Tupelo*, his definitive day-by-day account of Elvis' eighteen months on Sun, the December 13 Amory concert is the only date that fits the bill.

280 a nursery rhyme introduction: Colin Escott points out that Bill Haley used the same rhyme to introduce his 1953 number "Whatcha Gonna Do," the flip side of "Crazy Man Crazy," with Haley's ending, "Three to get ready, and here I go."

280 His older brother, Jay, was still having a little trouble: Perkins with McGee, *Go, Cat, Go!*, p. 132 — though in this account Carl wrote the song in October.

281 a "RUSH job": Letter to Jack Rosen, December 19, 1955. Sam was at this point so carried away by the potential that he now saw in Carl that he not only sent masters for the two-sided "rocker" with which he intended to announce to the world the arrival of his new star (the other side was "Honey Don't," a classic "boogie" number), he included the masters for a country single as well. That single had Carl's brother Jay singing lead on one side and was intended to be credited to the Perkins Brothers Band. Originally the two records were meant to be issued simultaneously, but with the tidal wave of success that "Blue Suede Shoes" instantly enjoyed, Sun 235 by the Perkins Brothers was never issued. See Colin Escott and Bill Millar booklet liners, *The Classic Carl Perkins* (Bear Family, BCD 15494).

281 After gross sales of $45,000: These sales figures are derived from excise-tax statements.

283 "a morbid mess": Sam was quoted in the *New York Post*, October 3, 1956. This certainly is not how the record struck many people. I particularly like Ian McEwan's description, provided by Colin Escott: "It spoke only of loneliness and irresolvable despair."

283 that was what Steve Sholes . . . told Sam: With respect to the time and purpose of the call, there seems to be considerable ambiguity. Sholes had had real problems directing Elvis in any manner and had most likely recorded "Blue Suede Shoes" simply because of Elvis' enthusiasm for the song. According to Sam, he tested the waters even further by inquiring if Sam might be interested in producing Elvis' sessions for RCA, strictly on a freelance basis, an almost-unheard-of concept at the time. As far as Sholes' job security was concerned, there seems general agreement. Sholes had faced withering criticism from his superiors when he returned to New York with tapes from the first Nashville session. "They told me it didn't sound like anything; I'd better go back and record it again." As if to underscore the record company's lack of faith, Elvis didn't even perform his new single until his third appearance on Jimmy and Tommy Dorsey's nationally televised *Stage Show*, on February 11, and then only with the Dorsey brothers' orchestra joining in for a highly unconvincing big-band arrangement (he sang "Blue Suede Shoes" on the same show). But it should be noted, for all of Sam's personal distaste, the public was not in the least put off in the end, either in terms of the verdict of the market or history.

284 "I told him, 'Well, Steve, I can't keep you from covering it'": Nager interview, NARAS. Just one final note on Elvis' version of "Blue Suede Shoes." Elvis in Sam's view — and I would tend to agree — rushed his version. He never did get the vamp, or the two-beat stop-time that marked the Perkins original, and it was Sam's opinion that this was Steve Sholes' fault. "Steve was the greatest guy in the world," he said, "but he was no fucking producer." A view with which history (and Elvis) would ultimately concur, as Elvis in effect took control of his own sessions from July 1956 on.

284 the "growing trend for the country and western, pop and rhythm and blues fields to merge into one big 'Mongrel music' category": "C.&W. Talent Hit Spots on B.S. Pop Chart," *Billboard*, March 10, 1956.

285 "It has already been suggested": "Don't Lose That Kid," *Billboard* editorial, March 17, 1956.

285 the provocative names assigned: Memory seems at times to have assigned different names to different rooms, but there's no question that all of these names were used.

285 "It was easy to sell": Smithsonian interview with Becky Phillips, conducted by Pete Daniel and David Less, December 1999.

286 "I'm having the time of my life": Becky to her sisters, Earline and Erin, Halloween, 1955.

286 a type of programming "that wasn't offered": Kitchen Sisters interviews with Sam and Becky, both together and separately, 1998, 1999.

286 "the power of communication": Kitchen Sisters interview with Sam and Becky, 1999.

287 "And, also, he *listened*": Bettye Berger interview with Kitchen Sisters, 1998.

287 WHER, the home of "beautiful music," gradually infiltrated: *Billboard*, June 1, 1959.

287 "Man, you know I've been listening to this all morning": Kitchen Sisters interview with Sam. And for those of you not in the know, Sadie Hawkins Day was the creation of cartoonist Al Capp in his popular hillbilly strip, "Lil' Abner," one day out of the year when women took control from the men with respect to dating, dancing, and marrying. Daisie Mae was Lil' Abner's beautiful and hopelessly-in-love girlfriend and, eventually, wife.

289 she followed Sam to Shreveport: This was on June 16, 1956, when Sam took a rare day off from the studio to be present at Roy Orbison's Hayride debut. The course of Sam and Sally's affair, and Marion's and Becky's feelings, is drawn from numerous interviews with Sally, Marion, and Becky. Sally said that at one point Marion's suspicions centered on Alta Hayes. She thought that Sam might be meeting Alta in Shreveport. And when he didn't meet anyone there, she came back even more frustrated than ever.

289 he had had sell-out crowds: the Big D Jamboree was a weekly Saturday-night program in Dallas, which, like the Louisiana Hayride, occasionally sent its troupe out on the road. The February 18, 1956, program book for Carl's appearance details both the blizzard and the number of encores two weeks earlier, with Lee Cotten, *Reelin' and Rockin': The Golden Age of American Rock 'n' Roll*, specifying the sell-out dates in San Antonio and Odessa as February 3 and 4.

291 "I was just about to go out on the stage". Once again Carl's memory, and his warmth as a storyteller, ascribes a little more to the scene than the bare facts do — but not much. Because while Sam may not have flown from Memphis and would never have hidden his fear of flying, everything else rings true and, more important, captures the emotion that both men clearly felt.

291 the unexpected upshot: Perkins with McGee, *Go, Cat, Go!*, p. 154.

291 he never had any doubt: Robert Johnson, "Crash Taught Carl Perkins, 'Don't Drive When Tired,'" *Memphis Press-Scimitar*, April 11, 1956.

292 his prime-time national television debut: To be absolutely precise, Carl had appeared on Red Foley's *Ozark Jubilee*, the first network (ABC) television show to feature "America's top country music stars," a week earlier, on March 17 — but *The Perry Como Show*, not to mention the Dorsey Brothers' *Stage Show*, reached a far larger mainstream audience.

293 he went into Southern Motors: Johnson, as above.

293 The Chrysler rolled over four times: The language of this account closely mirrors the language of Perkins with McGee, *Go, Cat, Go!*, p. 178.

294 "Reason #1": letter to Ted Freeman, October 4, 1955, in Turner, *The Man Called Cash*, p. 58.

294 "somber, melancholy ballads": Stars Inc. publicity bio, late 1956.

294 "reverse the usual country progression": Escott with Hawkins, *Good Rockin' Tonight*, p. 103.

295 While Cash was stationed in Germany: This whole narrative comes from a direct quote from Johnny Cash in Ed Salamon, "Johnny Cash Tells the Stories Behind His Songs, *Country Music*, July/August 1980, quoted in Escott with Hawkins' *Good Rockin' Tonight*, p. 103.

295 "there was two women": letter to Vivian Liberto, December 19, 1953, as quoted in Vivian Cash with Ann Sharpsteen, *I Walked the Line: My Life with Johnny*, pp. 216–17.

295 "Not me, buddy": This is the way Michael Streissguth tells it in *Johnny Cash: The Biography*, p. 78. In Steve Turner, *The Man Called Cash*, p. 59, Johnny tells Carl that "he wanted to write a song about being true . . . to himself, to Vivian, to God. He thought he might call it 'I'm Still Being True' or 'I'm Walking the Line' [and] Carl pounced on the idea." In his own contemporaneous autobiographical sketch, "This Is My Story," p. 4, "the words 'because you're mine' kept running through my mind . . . and Carl suggested I make a song about it." "I Walk the Line," he said, simply fit as the next line. There are, needless to say, many other variants, but Carl Perkins, Gladewater, Texas, and the twisted tape are the prevailing constants.

296 The old man "was taking it real slow and easy": Flanagan, as above, p. 100.

298 "The most outstanding record label": *Billboard*, July 7, 1956.

300 a minor hit . . . with a novelty song called "The Chicken": According to Rosco's royalty statement through the end of the year, reproduced in *The Blues Box* book, p. 132, the record sold 40,500 in the last six months of 1956, with a 25 percent reserve bringing the number on which royalties were figured down to 30,375.

301 "He was the kind of character": Escott with Hawkins, *Good Rockin' Tonight*, p. 184.

301 Earls was an eccentric figure: My two principal sources are Craig Makie, "Jack Earls Interview," *Blue Suede News* 40; and Colin Escott and Hank Davis notes for *The Sun Rock Box* (Bear Family BCD 17313).

302 to make Jack Earls a little money: Earls said he received $2,500, which would mean the record sold something like one hundred thousand copies. In fact, it seems to have sold moderately well only in certain "spot" markets, like Memphis, Atlanta, and Houston, without ever breaking out to national recognition.

302 He had his heart set on a career in baseball: Much of the biographical information on Sonny Burgess comes from the 1999 Smithsonian interview, conducted by Pete Daniel and David Less for the "Rock 'n' Soul" project. Other key sources include Ken Burke, "'We Wanna Boogie!' Sonny Burgess and the Legendary Pacers," *Blue Suede News* 51; and Billy Miller, "Sonny Burgess & the Pacers: 'We Mighta Been a Little Too Crazy for the Big Time!'" *Kix* 6.

302 "he was just the best we had ever seen": Burke, as above.

302 "We just went up there": Ibid.

303 Jack Nance . . . had a trumpet: Elijah Wald, "Sonny Burgess Relives the Rise of Rockabilly," *Boston Globe*, July 6, 1996.

303 "What he wanted [us] to do in that studio": Burke, as above.

303 "They were a working band": Martin Hawkins introduction and interview, *The Sun Rock Box* booklet.

303 a "jumping, pounding boogie": *Billboard,* September 1, 1956.

304 One time he got the idea of dying his hair white: Burke, as above. The red clown reference is from Hawkins and Escott's liner notes to the two-LP set *Roy Orbison: The Sun Years* (Charly CDX4), in which Sonny, referring to a disastrous show with Roy Orbison in Albuquerque, says sardonically to Roy: "They'll always remember us in Albuquerque as the Wink Wildcat and the Red Clown."

304 "The music just made you feel good": Smithsonian interview with Sonny Burgess, conducted by Pete Daniel and David Less.

304 "Sam would listen to the playbacks": This combines separate interviews by Colin Escott and me.

305 "He couldn't sing": Escott with Hawkins, *Good Rockin' Tonight,* pp. 173-74.

305 he was an albino: There is some debate over this. Orbison's second wife said he was an albino; other sources have argued more persuasively that he was not.

305 "To lead a western band": Quoted in Escott book for *Orbison,* an 8-CD box set (Bear Family BCD 16423), p. 7.

306 on the roof of their frat house: Escott notes for *The Sun Rock Box,* plus various other Colin Escott and Martin Hawkins writings. Unless otherwise noted, the sources for all Roy Orbison quotes and much of the biographical information come from the various Escott and Hawkins writings. See also "Recollections of Cecil Holifield Jr." on the Scotty Moore website (http://www.scottymoore.net).

306 One of the first people he took it to: See "Recollections of Cecil Holifield Jr.," above.

306 "some of the novelty hits": Escott with Hawkins, *Good Rockin' Tonight,* p. 148.

307 someone else might have been tempted: it should be noted that Weldon Rogers claimed that Sam *did* try to purchase the master because he couldn't get the right sound in his studio (see *Orbison* book for 7-CD box set, p. 15)—but to say that this doesn't sound like Sam begs the question.

307 "Roy was a perfectionist": Hawkins and Escott liner notes, *Roy Orbison: The Sun Years.*

307 "it was so tight": e-mail exchange with Dave Sax, 2009.

307 a spiffy half-page ad: *Billboard,* June 2, 1956.

308 "the back shack sound": *Billboard,* October 20, 1956.

308 "go out and learn how to sing": Hank Davis, "Barbara Pittman: Sun's Teen Queen," *Goldmine,* June 14, 1989.

308 Hayden Thompson: All information on Hayden Thompson comes from Martin Hawkins' notes to *Rock-A-Billy Gal: Hayden Thompson, The Sun Years, Plus* (Bear Family 16131).

309 "These guys would come in there by droves": Martin Hawkins interview CD with 8-CD set, *A Shot in the Dark: Nashville Jumps* (Bear Family BCD 15864).

309 "Sam Phillips' contribution": Hawkins and Escott liner notes, *Roy Orbison: The Sun Years.*

309 Sam quite simply "encouraged me": Carr interview with Cash.

309 "He made you comfortable": Billy Riley, Smithsonian interview, conducted by Pete Daniel and Charlie McGovern, with Peter Guralnick, 1992.

309 "The studio was like a hole in the wall": Colin Escott interview with Conway Twitty.

311 "I just hated high school": Smithsonian interview, conducted by David Less, 1999.

312 "One night, it was Christmas Eve": Ibid.

313 "My brother-in-law was a meat-cutter": This has been condensed from John Floyd, *Sun Records: An Oral History,* pp. 64–65.

314 "At first I was like a lot of other people": Billy Riley Smithsonian interview, 1992.

315 there "just seemed to be something pulling me": Roland Janes Smithsonian interview, conducted by David Less.

315 "We just got into the studio": Billy Riley Smithsonian interview, 1992. There is some disagreement over which song was cut where and when, and in what order, but I'm not going to get into that. Roland Janes had the most clear-eyed memory, and I'm sticking with that.

316 It was June 15: Okay, by now you must be sick of this, but June 15 was a Friday, and Jack said he had Wednesday afternoons off. Just for the historical record, Jack's first Sun paycheck was issued Saturday, July 14, 1956, at $65 a week.

316 "Sam was sitting out in the front office by himself": Jack Clement Smithsonian interview, conducted by David Less.

317 "The musicians we were working with": Ibid.

318 "I wanted them to know": Dave Hoekstra, "Recalling Sam Phillips/Sun Records," *Chicago Sun-Times,* October 6, 2008 (an edited version of his 1987 story).

320 "Johnny could be bought": In addition to Sam's letter, there is an undated *Memphis Press-Scimitar* clip from mid-July in which Sam "admitted there had been discussions and that $50,000 was the figure he had set as rock bottom.... Phillips said Steve Sholes ... had called from New York. 'I told him $50,000 was my lowest figure ... but that first I would have to talk to Johnny,' said Sam. 'But Johnny, when I talked to him about it said he didn't want it, that he wanted to stay with Sun, [where] he was getting personal attention in his recording sessions that he couldn't expect elsewhere, and that he likes our sound.'"

319 "I thought he and his band were kind of pissy," Jack Clement in John Floyd, *Sun Records: An Oral History,* pp. 78, 79.

320 "He called me into his office": Carr interview with Cash.

321 Golden, a former Lipton tea salesman: Dewey Webb, "Goodness Graceland! Elvis' Interior Decorator Tells All," *Phoenix New Times,* July 28–August 3, 1993; also Shelley Ritter interview with George Golden, 1993.

324 "They put that tape on": Robert Palmer, "Sam Phillips: The Sun King," *Memphis* magazine, December 1978.

324 his cousin J. W. Brown: J.W.'s mother, Jane, and Jerry's father, Elmo, were brother and sister (Elmo was six years younger), though Jerry Lee was not particularly well acquainted with his Memphis-based cousin.

325 "We came in," said Roland: This account includes material from my own interviews with Roland Janes, David Less' 1998 interview, and Rob Bowman and Ross Johnson, "Roland Janes: Behind the Scenes at Sun," *Journal of Country Music* 10 (3), 1985.

326 "Crazy Arms"... currently at the top of the country charts: Ray Price was in fact scheduled to headline at Ellis that very weekend, on November 16, with Sonny Burgess on the bill.

326 "With His Pumping Piano": On all subsequent Sun records (except "Whole Lotta Shakin'," which omitted subtitles altogether), "With" was changed to "And," but the first single employed the more modest accompanying preposition.

327 "I mean, Jerry Lee played the piano": Carl Perkins Smithsonian interview, 1992, conducted by Pete Daniel and Charlie McGovern, with Peter Guralnick.

327 He may have been cocky: Perkins with McGee, *Go, Cat, Go!,* p. 224.

327 "Pickers — no one has to tell them": Ibid.

328 "a sad story with a happy beat": Robert Hilburn, "Sam Phillips: The Man Who Found Elvis and Jerry Lee," *Los Angeles Times,* April 19, 1981. (I've taken the liberty of reversing the order of the comparison). The subsequent quote is from my 1991 interview with Sam. It is worth noting that the "Hound Dog"/"Don't Be Cruel" session marked the moment that Elvis became his own producer, a position that, leaving aside the movie sound tracks, he never relinquished to the end of his life, with the sole exception of the American Studio sessions in Memphis in 1969, which were brilliantly produced by Chips Moman.

328 Bob Johnson reported: *Memphis Press-Scimitar,* December 5, 1956. "Isle of Broken Dreams," too, was mentioned in another write-up by Johnson as well as various other songs by various other participants, including "Strange Things Happening," which like the other variants never turned up on tape.

329 with Smokey Joe Baugh, the gravel-voiced half of "Split Personality," on piano: It has been said by many critics and writers, including me, that Elvis ceded the piano chair to Jerry Lee Lewis, but careful listening — with extra-careful listening by Jerry Lee Lewis aficionado Cal Morgan — leads one to the inescapable conclusion that for the most part it is neither one. Elvis does play on a few tracks, it's true, and Jerry Lee gives a virtuoso recital at the end — but on most of the selections I am certain it is Smokey Joe Baugh, whose presence in the studio is confirmed by voice and photographs.

329 "this guy in Las Vegas [with] Billy Ward and His Dominoes": This turned out to be future rhythm-and-blues and soul star Jackie Wilson, though Elvis didn't know it at the time.

330 "Me and Elvis knew the words to every song": Elvis and Jerry Lee both grew up in the same Pentecostal shouting-and-testifying, speaking-in-tongues tradition of the Assemblies of God church in their respective hometowns.

331 Sam told British journalist Roy Carr: Roy Carr, "The Man Who Rolled the World," *New Musical Express,* February 16, 1980.

EIGHT | "I'LL SAIL MY SHIP ALONE"

333 "the magic door swings open": Robert Johnson, "Gleason Signs Cash for 10 Guest Spots," *Memphis Press-Scimitar,* January 7, 1957.

333 "With Johnny Cash": Interview with Charlie Gillet, BBC, 2000.

334 "as deft as a concert pianist": Helen Bolstad, "Jerry Lee Lewis: New Memphis Skyrocket!," *TV Radio Mirror,* January 1958, p. 62.

334 he followed B.B. King's music "quite desperately": This combines a phrase from an interview done for the A&E documentary on Sam ("quite desperately") with a longer passage ("Man, if I could play guitar like B.B. King . . .") from John Grissim, *Country Music,* p. 286.

334 his mother brought him meals at the piano: Michael Tisserand, "Jerry Lee's Legacy," *OffBeat,* August 1993, p. 31.

335 "an informal person": Colin Escott with Martin Hawkins, *Good Rockin' Tonight: Sun Records and the Birth of Rock 'n' Roll,* p. 207.

336 "he just jumped straight up": Smithsonian interview with Billy Riley, conducted by Pete Daniel and Charlie McGovern, with Peter Guralnick, 1992. Other sources on Billy include Martin Hawkins, liner notes to *Red Hot Riley: Billy Lee Riley & The Little*

Green Men (Charly 2-LP set, CDX 9); John Floyd, *Sun Records: An Oral History;* and my own interviews with Roland Janes and J. M. Van Eaton, among others.

336 one time, in Jonesboro, Arkansas: Walter Dawson, "Billy Riley's Still Looking for Some Rafters," *Memphis Commercial Appeal,* June 3, 1979. See also Smithsonian interview. Dawson, a fine critic and reporter, noted that "like so many of the artists on Sun, Riley has an ambiguous touch of arrogant humility."

336 the suits . . . became so heavy with sweat: Smithsonian interview. See also various interviews with Roland Janes, including, especially, David Less'.

337 "he was playing drums and singing": Andrew Solt interview of Jerry Lee Lewis for Time-Life's *The History of Rock 'n' Roll,* March 15, 1994. Jerry has the performance taking place at the Wagon Wheel. In *Hellfire* Nick Tosches has Jerry playing with Littlejohn — and quotes from Littlejohn — at the Blue Cat, post Wagon Wheel. In *Feel Like Going Home,* based on my own 1970 interview with Jerry, I had him first encountering both Littlejohn and the song at the Wagon Wheel, where Littlejohn was singing with the group Jerry played drums for on weekdays and piano on the weekend. "Then," he said, "I started doing it."

337 Memories differ: There are at least as many variations to this story as any other in this book. In Jack Clement's version, which is certainly the way it *should* have happened, there was just one take, and it wasn't even planned — it was just a way to break the monotony they had fallen into doing take after take of Jack's composition "It'll Be Me." "Blap, and that was it," said Jack. In *Feel Like Going Home,* I quote Jerry in an interview from the *24-Hour Radio History of Rock 'n' Roll* declaring that after a run-through, there was just one take, and Jack was at the controls. But after talking to Roland Janes and J. M. Van Eaton at considerable length about the sequence of events, I am convinced that this is as close to a true account as you can get. Jerry confirmed in 2011 that both Sam and Jack were in the studio, engineering and directing the session. And you have only to listen to the various takes — and to their subtle and not-so-subtle differences — to confirm for yourself that the illusion of spontaneity (the *reality* of spontaneity) came from hard work, exuberance, application, and (what Sam would often say was fully as important as anything else) precise microphone placement.

341 as Bob Johnson reported: Robert Johnson, "Marion off into Wild Blue Yonder," *Memphis Press-Scimitar,* August 21, 1957.

342 he begged Sam to push the other side: Johnny Cash with Patrick Carr, *Cash: The Autobiography,* p. 122.

343 a lead "Spotlight" review: *Billboard,* February 16, 1957.

343 a half-page ad: *Billboard,* March 2, 1957.

344 Carl's record at number 82: *Billboard,* "The Top 100," March 30, 1957.

344 "I saw something in Jerry Lee Lewis": Jud Phillips in a 1973 taped-response interview format with Martin Hawkins (in other words, Martin sent the questions from England, and Jud provided the taped responses, the equivalent of an interview by e-mail today). Jud's wife, Dean, an accomplished pianist herself, had just as vivid a memory of the occasion in her interviews with me.

345 Jud came back into the company: Jud's first paycheck of $125 was issued on June 21, 1957. Sally thinks it's possible that he was paid a week or two earlier, but this is the first actual record of it. He received $125 through the end of the year, then was raised to $150 in 1958.

345 with understandable misgiving: As one of their older siblings wrote to Sam at this time: "I hope you can give J.W. a job all the time. Poor thing, looks like everything he tryes to make a living with goes against him."

345 "The platter is taking off like wildfire": *Billboard,* June 3, 1957.

345 Jud came up with his idea: Jud's idea is well documented by Jerry Lee Lewis in John Pugh, "The Greatest Live Show on Earth," *Country Music,* January 1973, pp. 25-26, and by Jud himself indirectly in Walter Dawson, "The Killer on the Rocks," *Country Music,* June 1977, p. 46 — as well as in many other places (including below).

346 he and Jerry flew: Terry Pace, "Phillips Brothers Inspired Millions," *Florence TimesDaily,* July 24, 1992, included in *In Fond Memory of J. W. "Jud" Phillips: A True Unsung Hero* (A Remembrance Book), p. 23, and Jud Phillips, "The Story of Whole Lotta Shakin' Goin' On," ibid., p. 30. Most of the following two paragraphs comes from one or the other account, along with Sam's extensive recollection of the event.

346 "The man," recalled Jerry, "looked at Jud like he was crazy": Pugh, as above, pp. 25-26 (slightly condensed). In Andrew Solt's interview for the Time-Life series, Jerry recalled that "I took my bubblegum out of my mouth and laid it up on the piano."

346 the Coney Island roller coaster: Helen Bolstad, "Jerry Lee Lewis: New Memphis Skyrocket!," *TV Radio Mirror,* January 1958, p. 4.

347 With the record at number 30: *Billboard,* July 15, 1957. Jud, who deserves all the credit in the world for his entrepreneurial zeal, liked to recast the story considerably in later years. In his version, Sam had given up on the record, he was afraid of it for one reason or another, and it was only Jud who, using Sam's money, even gambling the future of a company in which he had no investment, showed the requisite faith to make the record a success and Jerry Lee Lewis a superstar. It is taking nothing away from Jud to say that these are not the facts of the matter.

348 a million singles a quarter: At the peak of the success of "Blue Suede Shoes," in the first and second quarters of 1956, Sun had gross sales of $240,000 and $350,000 (representing approximately 865,000 record sales), pulverizing a previous high of $45,000 in sales in the last quarter of 1955. After a fall-off of nearly 50 percent in the first quarter of 1957, and even more in the second quarter, the success of "Whole Lotta Shakin'" in the third and fourth quarters of 1957 topped even the "Blue Suede Shoes" figures.

348 spot announcements: Ren Grevatt, "On the Beat," *Billboard,* November 18, 1957.

348 "more general in its repertoire": "Sam Phillips to Go Global with New International Label," *Billboard,* August 5, 1957.

350 how "simple, yet basic and savage" the music was: Martin Hawkins interview with Bill Justis, 1974, quoted in booklet for *The Sun Rock Box.* All subsequent quotes come from this interview, as well as much of the information on Justis.

350 "Bill's orchestra has been playing": Robert Johnson, "T-V News and Views: Bill Justis to Be on *Ed Sullivan Show*": *Memphis Press-Scimitar,* November 21, 1957.

350 Sam offered him a job: Bill Justis went on the payroll on Friday, July 19, 1957, according to Sally Wilbourn's payroll records, with his starting salary of $90 a week topping Jack's by $25.

351 "enthusiasm in everything he did": John Pugh, "The Rise and Fall of Sun Records," *Country Music,* November 1973, p. 29.

351 "stop bugging the mike": From my interview with Billy Sherrill.

351 That was the reason: Martin Hawkins interview with Bill Justis, 1974, quoted in booklet for *The Sun Rock Box.*

352 five different melodies: Ibid.

352 "it just blew me away": Trevor Cajiao, "The Most Important Man in the World: Sam Phillips Talks to *Now Dig This*," part 3, *Now Dig This* 85 (April 1990), p. 2.

352 he had said to the fellows: Robert Johnson, "T-V News and Views," *Memphis Press-Scimitar,* November 21, 1957.

353 "someone else is getting a chance to tell the story": The disingenuousness of tone might be further called into question by an additional authorial declaration: "I am in no way affiliated with Sun or Phillips International. I am . . . more than anything else one of the great public to which the record company at 706 Union owes its almost unbelievable success."

353 "a shotgun hole-in-the-wall": Barbara Sims, "Sun Records: An Insider's View," reprint of a talk delivered at the sixth annual convention of the Popular Culture Association in April 1976.

354 "the chicken coop nested in Cadillacs": This comes in various forms from Jerry Hopkins, *Elvis: The Biography,* p. 107; Hopkins interview with Marion Keisker (MVC, MSU); and Barbara Barnes Sims, *The Next Elvis: Searching for Stardom at Sun Records,* p. 7.

354 "while their eyes were closed": Hank Davis and Colin Escott, "America's Other Uncle Sam," part 2, *Goldmine,* August 14, 1987.

354 "We could have probably sold twice what we did": Ibid. In fact, Sam prided himself on what he said was the lowest return rate in the business.

357 "Well, being an old country boy": This narrative is an amalgamation of various, virtually identical accounts, including the transcript of a television appearance that appeared in *Kix* magazine, various other public appearances, and interviews with me, the Kitchen Sisters, and Eric Olsen in September of 2000. Sam *loved* to tell the story!

358 Lorene Frederick: "Florence's Sam Phillips," *Florence Times,* ca. March/April 1957.

358 a letter he wrote: Exchange of letters May 11 and May 14, 1957. Interestingly, Dr. Cloyd is quoted in the Lorene Frederick article with respect to Sam's dedication to religion as a young boy. "He could pray as fine a prayer as the best theologian," Dr. Cloyd said. "He put so much time into his church work and Bible study that I had to bear down on him for neglecting his school work. He was getting into subjects way over his head before he had the English to support it."

360 it was well on its way: This is from "Sam Phillips Opens WLIZ: Second All-Femsee Station," *Billboard,* June 1, 1959.

361 "No Sun record": *Billboard,* July 22, 1957.

361 a policy "dictated not by personal taste": *Billboard,* June 1, 1959.

363 he and Earl Daly: To get an idea of some of the informal business machinations necessary to maintain multiple ownerships in the same territory, Earl Daly and Mrs. Rebecca Phillips of 1028 McEvers (a house that she and Sam still owned, and would continue to own fifty years later), were cited as co-owners of the Millington station, WHEY, in an undated late 1957 newspaper clipping.

364 $2.00 at first, then $3.00: Colin Escott points out that if they had been working in Nashville they would have been getting the AFM rate of $41.50 for a three-hour session, scheduled to produce four sides. But then again, if they had been living in Nashville, they almost certainly wouldn't have been working.

364 "He could make you feel": Billy Riley Smithsonian interview, conducted by Pete Daniel and Charlie McGovern, with Peter Guralnick, 1992.

365 "Let me hear what you've got": Rob Bowman and Ross Johnson, "Roland Janes: Behind the Scenes at Sun," *Journal of Country Music* 10 (3), 1985.

366 "John was the last one": Jack Clement Smithsonian interview.

366 "Let's go to Taylor's": Ibid.

367 in the middle of October: The official release date has always been listed as September 23, but I can find no evidence of any sales prior to October 14.

367 Sam looked the word up in the dictionary: In one of a series of telegrams to Dewey, addressed to Dewey "Stone" Phillips and dated September 24, 1957, the day after the record's release, Sam wrote: "Webster's International Unabridged Dictionary raunchy means clumsy. Harvard's index department concurs [Signed] Librarian 'Stone' City Memphis Cossitt." I can't fully interpret this. Except to say that Cossitt was the original Memphis Public Library and to confirm that I found a secondary definition of "grimy; unkempt" in the *American Heritage Dictionary*.

368 a red-and-black half-page ad: All ads were in *Cash Box* as well.

368 "PLEASE TAKE JUST A MINUTE": *Billboard,* November 11, 1957; *Cash Box,* November 16, 1957.

369 "'Great Balls of Fire' was the toughest song to start": Elizabeth Kaye, "Sam Phillips: "The *Rolling Stone* Interview," *Rolling Stone,* February 13, 1986, p. 86.

372 He designed a one-sheet: This is the language of the one-sheet, which was mirrored in the subsequent ad.

372 a glowing lead review: *Billboard,* November 11, 1957.

372 a full-page ad: *Billboard,* November 25, 1957.

372 "I tried to make him feel welcome": Perkins with David McGee, *Go, Cat, Go!,* p. 221.

373 he had been offered "Great Balls of Fire" first: Ibid., p. 251.

373 "you got Jerry Lee Lewis of the brain": Ibid., p. 253. This quote is somewhat compressed, and I would say it represents more of a "like" than a literal conversation, with Sam desperately trying to persuade Carl to stay at the company. But it's true, "Glad All Over," Carl's last single for Sun, released just after he left, or at least simultaneously with his leaving, *did* come accompanied by the tag.

373 he and John were about to register: Both signed with BMI under the new mandatory arrangement on October 1, 1957. As an interesting side note, Elvis Presley, with priceless cowrites on compositions like "Don't Be Cruel" and "Love Me Tender," which had been negotiated for him in return for his recording the songs, never signed a writer's agreement with BMI and never received any writer's royalties during his lifetime.

374 Columbia Records would not be able to pay any advance: Despite what has been written and generally understood (by Sam, among others), Columbia's contractual records clearly indicate that Cash got no advance for signing with the company.

374 if John had any concerns: Cash's point of view about Columbia comes largely from Patrick Carr's interviews with Johnny Cash, though there are many additional sources that touch on his dissatisfaction with Sam, including my own 1980 interview.

374 when each of their present contracts ran out: Carl's ran out January 12, John's not until the following summer. As an additional inducement to sign with Columbia: according to a 1973 Bob Neal interview cited in the Cash LP box set, p. 17, Cash's Columbia contract guaranteed him a 100 percent rate on mechanical royalties for any song that he had written. Mechanical royalties represent the licensing royalty paid by a record label to a song publisher (who then splits the sum with the songwriter) and were customarily discounted at this time to the 75 percent rate paid by "self-dealing" independents like Sun (which owned its own publishing companies) or, in most boilerplate agreements offered by the majors, on self-written songs by the recording artist.

375 an article about himself: Steve Turner, *The Man Called Cash: The Life, Love, and Faith of An American Legend,* p. 74.

375 guitar and bass drum: John Floyd, *Sun Records: An Oral History,* p. 80. I can't say that I hear the drum.

375 "I brought in a barbershop quartet": Martin Hawkins interview with Bill Justis.

375 "Attention, DJ's": *Billboard,* November 11, 1957.

376 "we just made a real wild, Little Richard-type thing": Billy Riley Smithsonian interview, 1992.

376 no orders coming in: If you look at the distributors' orders, it appears highly doubtful that the record could have sold more than twenty-five thousand copies total.

376 he started yelling at Sally: Robert Palmer's account in "Sam Phillips: The Sun King," *Memphis* magazine, December 1978, p. 44, is the earliest and most temperate version of the incident, but it still includes Billy's claims that Sam deliberately canceled orders for the record ("I stood right there in the office and heard him do it") and that when he came into the studio, drunk and, so to speak, gunning for Sam, he "kicked a hole in the bass fiddle."

377 Sam just waited him out: These are all constructed arguments from Billy's and Sam's various accounts.

377 "Sam got there": Palmer, as above. As an addendum to the incident itself, in Billy's later, increasingly fanciful versions of the story, the record was breaking when he was on tour in Canada, and Alan Freed was told to drop "Red Hot" in favor of "Great Balls of Fire" (this would in fact have been impossible as "Great Balls of Fire" was not released until November 11, long after "Red Hot" had stopped selling) — but the essential point always remained. He felt betrayed by Sam. No one else remembers the incident the way Billy did, not Sally Wilbourn, who asserts quite convincingly that she thinks she would remember if it happened that way, not Jack Clement, who says that there was no console wrecking (one of Billy's latter-day additions), not Roland Janes, who concedes "Riley could get a little out of hand at times but not like this." And not Sam, who said, "There's no way I would ever lose a record intentionally." But no one denies that Billy had a right to his feelings, least of all Sam, who was the first to admit that many of his artists had reason to be disappointed, because as a one-man operation he simply did not have the time to devote himself to them the way he should. (Charlie Rich was always a prime example.) If he had the opportunity to redo one aspect of his character, he said, it would have been to learn how to better delegate authority. "Riley was just a damn good rocker," he told Colin Escott and Martin Hawkins in *Good Rockin' Tonight,* p. 177. "But, man, he was so damn weird in many ways. He interested the hell out of me."

378 the perfect realization of a long-held dream: Sam made this entirely unsolicited point to me at our first meeting in 1979.

378 "the most sensational performer": Ren Grevatt, "On the Beat," *Billboard,* January 6, 1958.

379 A magazine reporter, spotting their ducktails: Bolstad, as above.

380 So they went out there: This is based on multiple interviews and multiple sources drawing on the recollections of both John and Sam. The details may differ, most notably in the number of times that Sam confronted John before getting an admission from him, but on one point there was no disagreement: John found it almost impossible to admit the truth to Sam. Ultimately there is no way to know how many times Sam broached the subject to John or Bob Neal, or how the ultimate confrontation took place, on the phone, in person, or simply by attrition — and ultimately, of course, it doesn't really matter.

381 "I've apologized to him many times": Patrick Carr interview with Cash.

381 "as if we were petting Jerry Lee": Hank Davis and Colin Escott, "Sam Phillips: America's Other Uncle Sam," part 2, *Goldmine*, August 14, 1987, p. 20.

383 a request at the end of March: To give an idea of Jerry's financial situation at this time, Jerry's June 30, 1958, statement shows 1.4 million singles sales, paid at a royalty of 4 percent on 90 percent of sales, as per record-company custom, adding up to $41,000 for singles sales, plus another $1,123 for EPs and LPs. He had drawn $22,000 in advances, including $3,000 for Judge McCormick and $17,000, unspecified, on March 27.

383 At first Jay wanted to kill him: This is from Myra's account in Jerry Lee Lewis and Charles White, *Killer! The Baddest Rock Memoir Ever*, p. 44. For all you genealogists out there, because of the sibling relationship of Jerry's father and Myra's grandmother, Jerry and Myra were first cousins once removed.

383 one of the principal reasons Sam had gone to New York: Clark Porteous, "Memphis Singer Married to His Cousin," *Memphis Press-Scimitar*, May 23, 1958.

384 it was picking up full sponsorship: *Billboard*, March 3, 1958; see also John A. Jackson, *American Bandstand: Dick Clark and the Making of a Rock 'n' Roll Empire*, pp. 106ff., for a full account.

385 the salvation of a good friend: Robert Johnson, "Dealings with Dick Clark Explained by Sam Phillips," *Memphis Press-Scimitar*, December 2, 1959. Sam is quoted here, presumably on the authority of his brother, since he barely knew Clark himself: "Clark needed help, and I wanted to help him. It was a good-will thing for all of us." Jud for his part totally discounted the sales success of the record prior to the Clark "gimmick," telling Jerry Lee Lewis biographer Nick Tosches in *Hellfire: The Jerry Lee Lewis Story*, pp. 144–45, that "sales had tapered off because the song had a broken beat and it was difficult to dance to," and expanding even more on his role (and Sam's haplessness) in Myra Lewis with Murray Silver, *Great Balls of Fire: The Uncensored Story of Jerry Lee Lewis*, pp. 140–41.

385 it was just about to hit number 15: *Billboard*, March 17, 1958. It was number 26 the week before.

385 thirty-eight thousand copies: Sam detailed these figures in Robert Johnson, "Dealings with Dick Clark Explained by Sam Phillips," *Memphis Press-Scimitar*, December 2, 1959, whose impetus seems to have been the payola investigations that were then taking place and had predictably swept Clark up in their web. Sally Wilbourn spoke of the ongoing sales, while June Bundy, "Mail Pull Rates Clark a Topper in TV Promotions," *Billboard*, November 10, 1958, indicates that there were "two TV pitches by Clark," with forty-eight thousand total sales cited.

386 "he did whatever he wanted to do": Roland Janes–J. M. Van Eaton Smithsonian interview, 1999, conducted by David Less.

386 "A lot of the antics just depended on the mood": Roland Janes interview, 1998, conducted by David Less.

386 "Chuck and my daddy kept mumbling": White, *Killer!*, p. 47 (shortened slightly). In my 2011 video interview with Jerry Lee in New Orleans, Jerry describes the same scene, with himself running as fast as he could after the two of them and hoping to God he didn't catch them.

387 Did he really do it?: Roland, who was never anything less than forthright, was insistent in several of our conversations that if any of these events actually happened, he had missed them—and he didn't miss much. After telling Robert Palmer both stories—the piano burning and piano drowning—in Palmer, "The Devil and Jerry Lee," *Rolling Stone*, December 13, 1979, pp. 58, 60, Jerry later asked the reporter, "Did you believe I was telling the truth when I said I pushed that piano in the ocean? If I did, I swear I don't remember it. A lot of times people make up things, and I just go along with them." On the other hand, there is a fully detailed account in *Billboard,* March 10, 1958, in Ren Grevatt's "On the Beat" column of Jerry Lee interrupting his act when the "tired-looking piano . . . cracked up under his special kind of pounding. . . . Lewis informed the audience, 'Well, man, I guess this piano's had it,' while assistants rushed on stage to try to repair the damaged strings."

387 "My mama . . . thought Chuck Berry was the king": White, *Killer!,* p. 47; also Taylor Hackford interview for the Chuck Berry documentary *Hail! Hail! Rock 'n' Roll!*

387 a riot . . . that led to serious charges: John A. Jackson, *Big Beat Heat: Alan Freed and the Early Years of Rock and Roll,* pp. 194–201.

387 Freed's almost instantaneous dismissal: Ibid., pp. 204–5.

389 a kind of byzantine partnership: In a revised January 3, 1958, agreement, Oscar Davis was named as the recipient of the first $25,000 of the Corporation's "net receipts," with no salary or minimum compensation specified, and agreed to fold Jerry Lee Lewis Enterprises, which appears to have been a booking agency formed in partnership between Davis and Jim Denny, whom Sam told me, somewhat confusingly, he had brought together in a social gathering with their wives at his house. Even more confusingly, this was preceded by a 50-50 sharing arrangement between Jerry and his soon-to-be-father-in-law, J. W. Brown. Perhaps needless to say, no one got rich off of their business dealings with Jerry Lee, least of all Jerry himself.

389 grossing close to $100,000: Jerry Lee was asked upon his departure from England by *Daily Mail* reporter Hugh Medlicott if "his British tour was worth $100,000," and he professed not to know, while Oscar Davis claimed in the same story that they were still owed $23,000.

390 his site of operations: *Billboard,* June 23, 1958.

392 even at the airport: This account is primarily from the *Memphis Press-Scimitar* story, May 23, 1958, and clippings from the British newspapers as well as Myra Lewis with Murray Silver, *Great Balls of Fire;* Tosches, *Hellfire;* and White, *Killer!*

392 "Baby snatcher": Hugh Moran, "We Hate Jerry, Shout Ex-Fans," *Daily Mail,* May 27, 1958. There is another story, "CLEAR OUT THIS GANG," that says, "And the girl is not, as he has said, fifteen years old. She is THIRTEEN YEARS AND TEN MONTHS OLD and she is his cousin"—but for the most part this appears not to have been mentioned during his British stay.

392 another *Daily Mail* reporter caught up with a disconsolate Jerry Lee: Hugh Medlicott, "Rock Star Flies Out As Ranks Cancel His Tour," *Daily Mail,* May 28, 1958.

393 "I told Jud [Phillips] Myra was my wife": White, *Killer!,* pp. 61, 62.

393 "Everybody thinks I am a ladies' man": unlabeled clip from a British daily, May 27, 1958, in the booklet accompanying the Bear Family 8-CD box set, *Classic Jerry Lee Lewis* (Bear Family, BCD 15420).

393 "point the finger of scorn": Hank Davis and Colin Escott, "Sam Phillips: America's Other Uncle Sam," part 2, *Goldmine,* August 14, 1987.

393 "So many people," Sam said, "wanted to do in rhythm and blues": John Pugh, "The Rise and Fall of Sun Records," *Country Music,* November 1973.

394 he composed: Although he wrote this with the help of Barbara Barnes (see Barbara Barnes Sims, *The Next Elvis: Searching for Stardom at Sun Records,* p. 82), it bears the unmistakable mark of his thinking and the language of his thought.

395 "From the very start it didn't look like a good match": Ren Grevatt, "Jerry Lee Mismated in N.Y. Club Debut," *Billboard,* June 16, 1958.

395 filing for bankruptcy: *Billboard,* June 23, 1958.

396 a good in-house joke: George Klein with Chuck Crisafulli, *Elvis: My Best Man,* pp. 119–20. This is reinforced by what both Sally Wilbourn and Jack Clement had to say.

396 "We think it's a cute record": *Billboard,* June 23, 1958.

396 "a very cowardly act": Jackson, *American Bandstand,* p. 111.

397 "Jerry's a very, very proud man": Trevor Cajiao, "Roland Janes," *Now Dig This* 247 (October 2003), p. 5.

397 "What could I do?": Cliff White, "The Killer Speaks," *New Kommotion* 24 (1980) (originally published as "Jerry Lee Lewis: Meet the Killer" in *New Musical Express,* November 25, 1978; more recently reprinted in *Now Dig This* 346 [January 2012]).

398 a resurgent demand for "authentic rhythm and blues": Bernie Asbell, "Sam Phillips Notes R&R Fading but Imprint Permanent," *Billboard,* May 18, 1959.

398 a former Midas Muffler shop just around the corner: By coincidence 639 Madison was the former home of S. D. Wooten's W&W Distributing Company, where Sam had bought much of his studio equipment, and just across the street from the Clarence Camp property that provided the transmitter site for WHER.

398 It had room for two studios: Edwin Howard, "Plush Phillips Studios Open Tomorrow," *Memphis Press-Scimitar,* September 16, 1960, along with many interviews with Knox.

398 custom-built reversible wall panels. Much of this description comes from Rick Clark's sidebar, "The Sun Space," in Barbara Schultz, "Sam Phillips: The *Mix* interview," *Mix* magazine, October 2000.

399 *"concentrating everything on sound":* "New Phillips Studio About Ready to Roll," *Billboard,* November 2, 1959.

400 "Sun Records has patiently recorded": This appears on p. 19 of the booklet for the Charly Johnny Cash LP Box Set. The clipping is undated, but in the October 1958 edition of Barbara Barnes' new in-house publication, *Sun Liners,* it is described as having been published recently in both *Billboard* and *Cash Box.*

402 In the end he agreed: he signed over seven songs, with the final agreement dated October 23, 1959. "Sam taught me a lot about business and contracts — *afterward,"* Roy is quoted in the book for the Bear Family 7-CD *Orbison* box set, p. 22. And yet, he said, when he signed his contract with Wesley Rose in the immediate aftermath of leaving Sun, he didn't bother to read it, because Wesley told him, "Hank Williams never looked at a contract. He always just signed them."

403 Just before he was scheduled to leave for his new job: Much of this account from Dewey's perspective comes from Louis Cantor, *Dewey and Elvis: The Life and Times of a Rock 'n' Roll Deejay,* p. 200.

403 "exactly what the mortician's field of work was": Sam told this story many times. This quote is from Escott with Hawkins, *Good Rockin' Tonight,* p. 90, where the initial conversation seems to have taken place in the kitchen — though in other versions, when speaking to me, or in Charles Raiteri's account, it was exclusively by the pool. He told Eric Olsen, "It was a nice night, very cool for August."

403 "I was so hungry to get back in Memphis": Robert Johnson, "T-V News and Views," *Memphis Press-Scimitar,* August 7, 1959.

403 a revamped WHHM: One of the new owners of the station was a partner of Sam's in WHEY; another was Harlon Hill, an NFL All-Star and MVP for the Chicago Bears. Hill was originally from Killen, Alabama, just outside Florence, and would soon become yet another of Sam's eccentric band of brothers. Later in life he went back to school, got his master's in Education, and became the high school principal in his hometown.

404 Bill Jay reported: Bill Jay, "This 'N' That About Entertainment: We Made It! Everything Set for Saturday Night," *Florence Times*, n.d., but the story was filed September 5, 1958.

404 "with a spontaneity born of necessity": September 1, 1958, letter going out under Ewart Abner's signature as co-chairman of the Temporary Organizing Committee.

405 Jack Wiener: Wiener seems to have accepted the alternate spellings of "Weiner" and "Wiener." I'm going with "Wiener," because it's the name on his contract with Sam, though not on his correspondence.

406 "he had that *abandon*": Taylor Hackford interview for the Chuck Berry documentary *Hail! Hail! Rock 'n' Roll!*

407 a yet-to-be-established publishing company: The agreement called for a guarantee of one side per single, EP, or LP to be published by Jerry Lee's own company. If Jerry Lee didn't come up with a song, Sun would assign 50 percent of its own interest in a song mutually acceptable to both parties to Jerry's publishing company. Unfortunately Jerry Lee never seems to have gotten around to forming his company.

407 he told journalist Chet Flippo: Flippo, "Pride: Jerry Lee Lewis and the Elvis Demon" in *Everybody Was Kung-Fu Dancing: Chronicles of the Lionized and the Notorious*, p. 162.

407 To encourage renewed sales interest: Hank Davis, booklet for *The Original Sun Singles*, vol. 3 (Bear Family BCD 15803), p. 48; also Escott with Hawkins, *Good Rockin' Tonight*, p. 203.

407 "Mathilda": The original song title and group name are recorded in John Broven, *South to Louisiana: The Music of the Cajun Bayous*, p. 187; it became *His* Cupcakes and "Matilda" on Judd, where it first charted, on the pop charts, in January 1959.

407 Jerry Lee's would advertise "The Great Ball of Fire": This is the way Tom Phillips' son, Johnny, remembers it, parked out in front of their house.

408 he went out first as Jerry Lee's road manager: Information on Tom's ambitions and business activities comes primarily from interviews with Tom, his sons Johnny and Skip (now back to his given name of Sam), as well as Walter Dawson, "Record Shop Losing a Hit with Owner in Retirement," *Memphis Commercial Appeal*, ca. December 1980, and Leigh Ann Roman, "Phillips' Family Business Still Rolling in Music Industry," *Memphis Business Journal*, September 13-19, 2002.

410 "he told me I'd have to learn to play the piano": Bill Williams, "Charlie Rich: The Silver Fox," *Billboard* Supplement ("Section sponsored by associates and friends of Charlie Rich"), September 14, 1974.

410 "I thought from the start he was a real good talent": Ibid.

410 "you could hear the music": Terry Gross interview, *Fresh Air*, September 3, 1992.

411 "one of the best-looking men": Hank Davis in booklet accompanying *Charlie Rich: Lonely Weekends*, a 3-CD Bear Family set (BCD 16152), p. 41.

412 "I loved to hear Charlie play": Barbara Sims, written reminiscence.

412 with the explicit aim of getting him on Dick Clark's . . . *American Bandstand*: Hank Davis notes, *Charlie Rich: Lonely Weekends*, p. 8.

414 a second all-girls station: Just to show how serious Sam was in his radio ambitions, there was a story by Henry Mitchell in the *Memphis Commercial Appeal*, ca. May 20, 1959 ("Two Shelby Broadcasters Seek 50-Kilowatt Station"), which details the efforts of Sam and Earl Daly to establish a 50-kilowatt station. Should he get the license, Sam said, he would give up WHER, as FCC rules required. It was unquestionably his "first love" in broadcasting, but "love or not, you don't turn down a chance to get a 50-kilowatt station — you just can't hardly get those any more." In addition, in January 25, 1960, *Billboard*, there was a little squib headlined "Sam Phillips Plans 7-station Radio Chain."

414 a 32 percent partner: Sam, Kemmons Wilson, and C. A. Camp each had 32 percent of Tri-State Broadcasting Service, with 4 percent going to Roy Scott in 1955 for his legal work. In fact, it's possible that Mr. Camp held on to 7 percent of his investment, according to the terms of the September 10, 1958, agreement.

415 "Well, boys, I'm a millionaire": Martin Hawkins, Bill Justis interview, *The Sun Rock Box*.

416 an ordinary promotion trip: Tom recalled to his sons how Jud flagged down a cab to go to Roulette Records, just three blocks from the hotel. "Dad said, 'We could just walk.' Uncle Jud said, 'We gonna arrive in style.'"

418 Jud would be "joining NRC's offices": *Billboard* and *Cash Box*, October 5, 1959.

422 "Last week, a certain rule-buster": *Billboard*, June 1, 1959.

422 he offered a ringing defense of capitalism: Typed draft of Sam's statement for the "Hearings Before the Subcommittee on Communications of the Committee on Interstate and Foreign Commerce . . . on S.2834, a bill to provide that a license for a radio or television broadcasting station shall not be granted to, or held by, any person or corporation engaged directly or indirectly in the business of publishing music or of manufacturing or selling musical recordings." The draft is undated, but the statement was delivered in hearings held between April 15 and 17, 1958.

423 "we are moving into a period of greater variety in taste": Bernie Asbell, "Sam Phillips Notes R&R Fading but Imprint Permanent," *Billboard*, May 18, 1959.

424 "it did not have the air of carnival": Bob Rolontz, "Lusty Start for ARMADA Meet; Much Accomplished," *Billboard*, June 15, 1959.

429 the work would not be completed: "New Phillips Studio Ready to Roll," *Billboard*, November 2, 1959.

429 Why not write a new song: This is from drummer J. M. Van Eaton, as quoted by Hank Davis in the booklet accompanying *Charlie Rich: Lonely Weekends* (Bear Family BCD 16152).

429 in the manner of many Sam Cooke songs: Colin Escott points out its similarity as well to Don Gibson's work, to Gibson's beautifully evocative "Oh Lonesome Me" in particular, which was a Top 10 pop hit in 1958.

430 "I think he liked the sound": Charlie Rich Smithsonian interview, 1992, conducted by Pete Daniel and Charlie McGovern.

430 "a little Cape Canaveral of the recording business": Edwin Howard, "House That Rock 'n' Roll Built: Plush Phillips Studios Open Tomorrow," *Memphis Press-Scimitar*, September 16, 1960.

432 "a large new recording studio": Ibid.

433 Not much was happening in the Shoals area: The partnership of Rick Hall, Billy Sherrill, and Tom Stafford, which had begun in a homemade studio above the City Drugstore in Florence and served as a magnet to aspiring singers, pickers, and songwriters throughout the area, had recently broken up, and Hall's success with a reconstituted FAME studio in Muscle Shoals was still a couple of years away.

434 Billy Ray Cooner, had rented it from the Lodge: "I came up from Haleyville with Bill Cooner in 1960," said Billy Sherrill in "Phillips Studio Counts Its Hits," *Music*

Reporter, ca. June 1963. "We started a dub studio on the third floor, [which] dwindled for about six months. Then Sam Phillips walked in."

435 "chaotic [and] confusing": Bob Rolontz, "Knotty Problems Strew ARMADA Future Path," *Billboard,* June 20, 1960.

435 "Many people who attended were disappointed": "ARMADA Makes Headway into Industry Problems," *Cash Box,* June 25, 1960.

439 "The lights dim": Charlie Lamb, "Mood Lighting Is Artist Aid at Phillips Studio," *Music Reporter,* June 12, 1961.

442 "Charlie wasn't a demonstrative type": Hank Davis notes, *Charlie Rich: Lonely Weekends,* p. 10.

445 the bird learned to say, "Do you love me?": Everyone seems to have been fond of Inky. Sally cited various other sayings by Inky ("This child's taking off," and "I looove you," among others), but not the exact phrase that Bettye recalls. When Becky moved, she took Inky with her, but Sam and Sally took care of him when Becky visited her family in Sheffield. When he died, Becky had him stuffed and mounted.

446 paragons of Alabama liberalism: Folsom famously stated at the height of the States Rights crisis in 1949, "As long as the Negroes are held down by deprivation and lack of opportunity, the other poor people will be held down alongside them."

446 he shouldn't be singing his father's songs: This was an argument between Sam and Audrey that went on for probably two years but didn't come to a head until the summer of 1963, when Buddy Lee, just then making the transition from professional wrestler to music promoter, booked mother and son on what Audrey seemed to regard as an audition tour for a record contract. The tour was a success, but according to Lycrecia Williams and Dale Vinicur, *Still in Love with You: The Story of Hank and Audrey Williams,* pp. 142–43, before MGM would sign Hank Jr., they required further proof, and Buddy Lee booked a second sixteen-city tour in the fall. In December Hank Williams Jr. (really Randall Hank) signed a three-year, $300,000 contract, and cut his first single, "Long Gone Lonesome Blues," number 1 for his father in 1950, number 5 for Hank Jr. on the 1964 charts. But Sam was right in a way. For all of his profligate talent, it took Hank Jr. fifteen years to establish an identity of his own.

448 before finally arriving in Memphis: Robert Johnson, "T-V News and Views," *Memphis Press-Scimitar,* August 7, 1959. "One of the phenomena of the year is the revival of interest in wrestling, with television providing the push. Channel 5's Saturday afternoon wrestling show is clobbering the competition. . . . Marveled an executive from a competing station: 'This Sputnik Monroe is the new star of the kids.'"

448 "If you wish in this world": The actual lyric: "If you wish in the world to advance / Your merits you're bound to enhance / You must stir it and stump it / And blow your own trumpet / Or trust me, you haven't a chance."

452 "I don't want to divulge too much": Robert Gordon interview with Jerry Phillips. Although I have spoken extensively with Jerry about his teen stardom, there is no question that Robert did the definitive wrestling interview with him, which in turn formed an integral part of Robert's *It Came from Memphis.*

453 It all came to an abrupt halt: Chronology gets a little confused, and confusing, in the Phillips family accounts, but Jerry's wrestling career appears to have come to an end sometime in the fall of 1962, shortly after his fourteenth birthday — at least judging by the dates of some of his mother's pictures.

453 "he had the strangest look": Robert Gordon interview with Jerry Phillips.

455 "Sam Phillips . . . screwed everything up": Chet Flippo, *Everybody Was Kung-Fu Dancing,* p. 161.

NINE | "THEY'LL CARRY YOU TO THE CLIFF AND SHOVE YOU OFF"

458 at some point I received: Ironically, this may be one of the more speculative statements in my story. Some years ago I misplaced Knox's letter, and this is the most plausible construction for what prompted it that either Knox or I have been able to come up with. I guess I'll just have to save any corrections for the reemergence of the letter.

458 "something of a recluse these past couple of decades": Walter Dawson, "Presley and Phillips Had Nothing to Lose By Being Different," *Memphis Commercial Appeal*, August 13, 1978.

459 the tapes were widely believed to have disappeared: The first tape had actually surfaced one or two years earlier and, as it later turned out, there were a number of copies floating around. But the *New York Times* was certainly not aware of it, nor for that matter was I, and Shelby, with his unerring instinct for showmanship, arranged for what amounted to a grand unveiling. There seemed little question that this was the "true gen," though with Shelby's reputation for good-humored scammery (he had recently put out a series of doctored duets of Jerry Lee Lewis and "Orion," whom he exuberantly encouraged the public to believe might be Elvis Presley), that question could always be considered to be in the air.

460 "I don't run it just because it's on *Billboard*": Walter Dawson, "If You Ain't Country," *Memphis Commercial Appeal*, spring 1980. Sam was referring here to the country format he had switched to the previous fall, several months after my visit to Memphis, but it applied just as much to the highly idiosyncratic approach he described to me. As he told Walter Dawson, further expanding on the subject, "I am not going to be a follower — I don't care, I'd rather be dead."

462 the transmitter that had carried the sound of the Grand Ole Opry: This was the original transmitter installed at the WSM transmitter site in Brentwood in 1932. For more detail on its unique construction, check out Craig Havighurst's book on WSM, *Air Castle of the South: WSM and the Making of Music City*, pp. 52ff.

462 Within weeks he had bought it: He purchased the transmitter on March 27, 1961, and, after considerable prodding from its owners, moved it sometime that summer.

463 "Make your move anyway you wish": Jim Bulleit to Sam, February 24, 1962.

464 "thinking seriously of changing labels": Elton Whisenhunt, "Jerry Lee Lewis May End Tie-Up with Sun Record Co.," *Memphis Press-Scimitar*, June 12, 1963.

464 Sam telegrammed his new record company: This and all subsequent details are from the June 12, 1963, *Memphis Press-Scimitar* story above and the follow-up story on June 14. The agreement is dated June 14.

465 "Dr. King certainly knew of music's power": Sam's writings, Notes for a Tribute album to Dr. King. I don't know if the notes were ever finished, or used. In *Spinning Blues into Gold: The Chess Brothers and the Legendary Chess Records*, p. 287, Nadine Cohodas writes about a memorial record, with proceeds earmarked to SCLC, and names a number of record companies involved, though Sun is not mentioned.

465 $25,000 upfront: *Billboard*, October 5, 1963, has him getting a $10,000-a-year guarantee for five years. Colin Escott writes that Mercury committed $25,000 upfront, as does Myra Lewis in *Great Balls of Fire: The Uncensored Story of Jerry Lee Lewis*, p. 274, saying that the second half was to be paid at the end of three years.

466 "I hope they do not expect me": Sam to Boynton P. Livingston, February 4, 1964, and passim; re Sam's demand that Philips "discontinu[e] further use of the name Philips," see Boynton P. Livingston to Roy Scott, October 15, 1962.

466 "stay up for two or three days": John Broven, *Record Makers and Breakers: Voices of the Independent Rock 'n' Roll Pioneers,* p. 290.

467 "a man with a mission": "Whirling Busily, Shelby Singleton Spreads Gospel of Country Music," *Billboard,* June 23, 1962.

467 Billy's chance came at the end of 1963: Billy's last paycheck from Sam C. Phillips Recording was November 15, 1963. Some of his earliest productions for Epic were blues and soul singer Ted Taylor, the Staple Singers, bluegrass duo Jim & Jesse, Stan Hitchcock, country crooner David Houston, and veteran country singer Charlie Walker.

470 "They are just straining at a gnat": Sam to Boynton P. Livingston, March 6, 1964.

470 Ultimately he graciously acceded: The five-page document, accompanied by a single exhibit, was signed April 8, 1964.

470 the 10 percent tax not on the roughly $.40 per record that Sun Record Sales charged the distributor, but on the wholesale pressing cost of maybe $.20: As John Broven had it explained to him in his comprehensive *Record Makers and Breakers,* p. 516, the majors had long ago developed this scheme: "The tax was 10% of the first 'arms-length' transaction. The transaction had to be accomplished by the proprietor of the label. [Early on] the accountants got the idea that if they established . . . an intermediary entity which would buy the records from [the pressing plant] and then sell them to the [record company's] distributing company, it would halve the taxable cost."

475 the "reactivation" of the Sun label: *Billboard,* April 1, 1967.

475 "Sun Shines Again": Ibid.

476 "Sam Phillips, pioneer of the 'Memphis Sound'": James Kingsley, "'Memphis Sound' Pioneer Heads HIA Music Venture," *Memphis Commercial Appeal,* March 8, 1968.

477 $12,000 a year: Kemmons Wilson Kitchen Sisters interview, 1999.

477 over sixty stations: *Billboard,* February 10, 1968, cited sixty stations as of February.

477 a collection of easy-listening favorites called *Nighttime:* Without any distribution system, *Billboard*'s Memphis Supplement, March 29, 1969, pointed out, the album had achieved ten thousand sales.

479 Hank's sister, Irene . . . had surreptitiously entered into talks: Principal sources include Colin Escott, with George Merritt and William MacEwen, *Hank Williams: The Biography,* pp. 293, 294; interviews with Sally Wilbourn; various *Billboard* stories between November 1966 and February 1968; and Lycrecia Williams and Dale Vinicur, *Still in Love with You: The Story of Hank and Audrey Williams.*

479 When Audrey found out, she sued: See Escott with Merritt and MacEwen, *Hank Williams,* pp. 288–89, for terms of the divorce.

479 half a million dollars: *Billboard,* October 7, 1967; *Nashville Tennessean,* October 29 and 30, 1967. In an account that only reinforces the value of the copyrights but also underscores Audrey's lack of providential thinking, Colin Escott tells the other side of the story in *Hank Williams,* p. 294, pointing out that according to court records, by 1968 "the estate's total earnings since Hank's death were in excess of $1.6 million. Half of that amount had gone to Audrey, and she had spent it all."

480 "only one . . . came through": Williams and Vinicur, *Still in Love with You,* pp. 163, 164.

480 "I've never known anyone who was as vilified": Ibid., p. 165.

480 they couldn't take possession of it: Ibid., pp. 189–93.

481 he just didn't seem to give a fuck: It must be recalled that this was Jerry at nineteen. As Jerry would say, looking back on it, "I thought he just didn't give a shit about his family, that it was all about him. But, it wasn't. I know that now." At the same time, it must also be acknowledged that Jerry is no more the kind of person to disavow past feelings than his father was.

481 "The higher the monkey gets on the pole": Robert Gordon interview with Jerry Phillips.

483 only through Sam's intervention: Louis Cantor, *Dewey and Elvis: The Life and Times of a Rock 'n' Roll Deejay*, pp. 204, 212, 213.

483 Sam put him on the payroll: Sally Wilbourn, payroll records; she says there were at least two psychiatric hospitalizations. See also Cantor, *Dewey and Elvis*, pp. 240ff.

483 hacking and coughing: Cantor, *Dewey and Elvis*, p. 216.

483 a "lonely man with the heart of a boy": Robert Johnson, "Good Evening," *Memphis Press-Scimitar*, October 1, 1968.

483 staying with her, according to Dewey's biographer Louis Cantor: Cantor, *Dewey and Elvis*, p. 219.

484 SSS (Shelby S. Singleton) International: According to Walt Trott, "Shelby Singleton: Memoirs of a Music Man," *Country Music People*, May 2005, p. 58, there was a period of several months in early 1967 when the business, functioning as a production company but not a label, was called Shelby Singleton Productions, but it was SSS International by the end of the year.

484 at just about the same time his ex-wife, Margie: There is some question about the order of recording. Colin Escott suggests that the reason for the rushed release of Riley's version was that there was another recording—most likely by Alice Joy, who had demoed the song—waiting in the wings. He articulates the case in his notes to *Dim Lights, Thick Smoke, and Hillbilly Music: Country & Western Hit Parade, 1968* (Bear Family BCD 17263).

486 *Johnny Cash at Folsom Prison:* Ironically the omnipresent success of the album and single for the first time invited the attention of Gordon Jenkins, a distinguished songwriter, producer (the Weavers), and arranger (for Frank Sinatra, among others), whose 1953 album, *Seven Dreams*, had included the song "Crescent City Blues"—which, as mentioned earlier, suggested not just the inspiration for but the very essence of "Folsom Prison Blues." Jenkins sued, and eventually Cash settled for a one-time payment of $100,000, which settled all prior claims and allowed Cash both to retain authorship and to collect all future royalties on the song. In fairness, it should be pointed out that the alterations that John made to the original, like the alterations that so many adaptive geniuses like Bob Dylan have made to less copyright-protected material, gave "Folsom Prison Blues" its unique tone, flavor, and snarl.

489 the start-up of a new blues label, Midnight Sun: James Kingsley, "Phillips Forms Label Keyed to Blues Mart," *Billboard*, September 6, 1969. In addition to the new label's first release, "Frank, This Is It," produced by Jerry Phillips, the story cited "other artists that Phillips recorded, including Rufus Thomas, Howlin' Wolf, Little Junior Parker, Doctor Ross, Rosco Gordon, and Ike Turner [who] will be released on the new label. Phillips said: 'I have so many of those good blues songs on tapes. They are much more valuable now that the blues is hitting all over the world again.'" He was planning to "go heavily" on albums, he said. But as far as the label working out, it didn't. And he never got the tapes back either. Although in the end that may have been fortuitous, as Colin Escott suggests, because eventually Shelby put them all out, and Sam, who was more concerned about niceties like contracts and artist releases and song publishing, might very well never have seen his way clear to releasing many of them.

490 "'that song, "Memories," has got to go'": Elvis did in fact continue to sing the song off and on for another year or so, but according to Ernst Jorgensen he subsequently dropped it, with "Can't Help Falling in Love," which had also been in the show from the beginning, better able to fulfill the same function by itself.

494 grateful for all the help he had offered them: As just one of many examples of how close he had always remained to his family, one of his older siblings wrote in 1957: "Sam I guess you think I was ugly not thanking you for sending me the money. But I can't talk about it without crying . . . so I thought it was best. But you will never know how much I thank you."

496 Memphis had recently surpassed Nashville: James Cortese, "Elvis and New Studio Boost Zooming Industry," *Memphis Commercial Appeal,* January 11, 1970. In "Memphis Gets Earful of the Memphis Sound," *Memphis Press-Scimitar,* March 27, 1968, it was reported that the music business had generated something like $100 million the previous year, making it the third-largest industry in the Memphis economy.

496 "Everybody laughed [at] me": Claude Hall, "Phillips, Presley, Cash, Sun," *Billboard,* December 27, 1969, 75th Anniversary Section, p. 110.

499 Sam had done everything he could to get the two of them together: This comes from both my interviews with Bettye and the Kitchen Sisters' interviews.

500 "All the words that I had thought up just say": *Billboard,* June 5, 1971.

501 he even precipitated: *Nashville Banner,* March 18, 1970. The suit (or it may well have been a countersuit, or a defensive anticipatory suit) appears to have been initiated by Sun International over the release of the tapes by GRT—but Shelby made clear his unhappiness with Sam in a subsequent telegram, which declared, "I have done nothing regarding contracts without [at least] a verbal discussion with you. . . . It is of utmost importance you think about all of your own actions."

501 Shelby invited him flat out to buy back the company: Shelby telegram, December 2, 1970.

503 in the process of . . . converting to all-talk: This was something of a long-drawn-out process, beginning with the introduction of regular newscasts and "Feminine Forum," a sex talk show, in the spring of 1972, and leading up to the adoption of the new call letters in late 1973. The Kitchen Sisters' book, *WHER: 1000 Beautiful Watts, The First All-Girl Radio Station in the Nation,* pp. 173-75, gives a good picture of the process.

504 The Playboy Records deal fell apart: The demise of the deal came with the departure of Larry Cohn as head of the label in December 1973. Larry, a passionate blues aficionado, had made the deal with a full knowledge of Sam's history, but no one else at the company evidently was much impressed.

505 he camped out with Sally at the Tourway Inn and Pancake House: The Tourway Inn was owned by Jud's wife Dean's cousin, Billy Hensley, and, Sally said, they got a very good deal.

506 two Harleys were imported: Robert Gordon did a wonderful unpublished interview with Jim Dickinson on this subject and covers the shoot-out in *It Came from Memphis,* pp. 229-30. In addition, Knox shared his vivid memories of the sessions.

510 she would just "sit on my lap": Becky Phillips, Smithsonian interview, conducted by Pete Daniel and David Less, 1999.

510 "We all have problems in our lives": Ibid.

512 Sam never really thought too much about the proposal: Sam proved to be right. The team eventually ruined Dr. Kraus, a beautiful dreamer—that and his general manager (soon to be managing partner), Denny McClain.

512 "I don't have the feeling anymore that I'm contributing anything": John Pugh, "The Rise and Fall of Sun Records," *Country Music*, November 1973. This was a cover story and interestingly enough may have been Sam's first extended domestic interview for any publication outside Memphis other than the trades.

513 a mode of transportation that he had only recently resumed: Sam had gotten over his fear of flying just as suddenly as he had acquired it. He was in Florida and had no other way to get back in time for the funeral of his brother Horace's oldest son, Leon, in Florence. So he and Sally flew on one of the new superjets from Miami to Atlanta and "loved it," Sally said, and he soon became an enthusiast for flying in all its most up-to-date forms (he was a particular fan of the Boeing 777).

513 "He'd say, 'I just don't want to sleep by myself'": Bettye Berger, Kitchen Sisters interview, 1998.

518 he announced his intention to become a riverboat captain: *In Fond Memory of J. W. "Jud" Phillips: A True Unsung Hero*, p. 9. As Sally recalled, the boat blew up in Slidell, and Jud was stranded there for close to a month, even after Sam wired him the money for its repair.

519 he "just went around and watched": Elvis Memorial, Memphis State University, August 16, 1979.

519 "digging the heavy beat that these colored people were putting down": Hawkins interview.

519 "the reason that I went through all of this problem of finally getting Elvis Presley signed": Ibid.

520 "I told him I loved him": This is a combination of Trevor Cajiao, "The Most Important Man in the World: Sam Phillips Talks to *Now Dig This*," part 4, *Now Dig This*, 86 (May 1990), and Robert Hilburn, "Sam Phillips: The Man Who Found Elvis and Jerry Lee," *Los Angeles Times*, April 19, 1981.

520 no sense of personal fulfillment: Walter Dawson, "Presley and Phillips Had Nothing to Lose by Being Different," *Memphis Commercial Appeal*, August 13, 1978.

522 Elvis Presley "was positively the greatest human being to walk the earth since Jesus": Robert Palmer, "The Punks Have Only Rediscovered Rockabilly," *New York Times*, April 23, 1978.

522 he unapologetically repeated the same sweeping assertion: Dawson, as above.

524 Johnny Cash had sued: Mike Pigott, "Shelby Singleton Admits Guilt," *Nashville Banner*, October 29, 1976. Here the figure is listed as $200,000, but Johnny Cash scholar Mark Stielper says it was closer to $500,000. According to Stielper, Cash sued initially in March of 1976, and accepted a settlement of $175,000 in December of 1977.

524 "fraud and breach of contract": "Shelby Singleton Admits Guilt," *Nashville Banner*, October 29, 1976.

524 after suing Sam for his publishing: This is from court records kindly supplied by David McGee, along with further explanation in his biography of Carl, *Go, Cat, Go!*, pp. 340ff.

524 a complicated series of legal challenges: This comes from my interviews with Carl in 1978 and 1979; Susan Thomas, "RCA, Cash, Perkins Seek to Block Presley Album," *Nashville Tennessean*, December 7, 1977; Carl's deposition from the lawsuit on December 12, 1977; and Paul Hendricksen, "Ol' Blue Suede's Back," *Washington Post* (as published in *Orlando Sentinel-Star*, December 28, 1978).

524 Shelby in fact had pleaded guilty: *Nashville Banner*, October 29, 1976. Shelby had also been sued by RCA for putting out an Elvis Presley album immediately after

Elvis' death (*The Sun Years — Elvis Presley* [Sun 1001], including outtakes from the Sun sessions, which were indisputably owned by RCA. (See Bill Hance, "Ruling Halts Production of Elvis Albums," *Nashville Banner,* December 6, 1977.) As in so many of his other bold (some might say semipiratical) ventures, Shelby would appear to have suffered no more serious consequences than to be told to take his album off the market. The following are just some of the stories touching on this controversy, all of which (and a good many more) I received from Shelby at the time: Ed Newland, "Once Again RCA Suing Singleton," *Nashville Banner,* January 23, 1978; Kirk Loggins, "Singleton Must Turn Elvis Tapes Over to RCA," *Nashville Tennessean,* n.d.; Kirk Loggins, "Rulings Won by Singleton," *Nashville Tennessean,* February 12, 1978.

525 he had lost all of his publishing: Perhaps needless to say Sam had unbounded admiration for Charley Pride — both the man and the idea — and he had nothing but boundless affection for Jack, whimsicality and all, with the proviso that Jack had no head for business.

525 Johnny Cash, who was recording a gospel number: The song was "I'll Fly Away." It was not released on the album — in fact, I'm not sure that it was ever released.

526 "I've talked to those pills": Bill Flanagan, "Johnny Cash, American," *Musician,* May 1988, pp. 106, 107.

526 Sam called the jail: Michael Streissguth, *Johnny Cash: The Biography,* p. 128; Johnny Cash, *Man in Black,* p. 123.

526 "your total integrity": handwritten letter, misdated December 21, 1982. (The year was 1983.)

526 "the hundreds of times your name has come up": Cash to Sam, July 20, 1981.

527 "he threw away the pills": Hendrickson, as above.

527 Jimmy Lee Swaggart pulled him offstage: Robert Palmer, "The Devil and Jerry Lee," *Rolling Stone,* December 13, 1979, p. 58.

528 "Nutty as a fox squirrel": John Grissim, *Country Music,* p. 283.

528 "I wanted to make an album with a certain sound to it": Robert Palmer, "Pink Cadillac — A Rite of Passage," *New York Times,* September 23, 1979.

529 they worked all night: Ibid.

530 "can you do it at half of half speed?": Ibid.

533 Knox's longtime girlfriend, Diane Duncan: I feel guilty that I haven't mentioned Diane before. She and Knox have been together from the time they first met (their first date was September 28, 1972, and she started working at the studio in 1974), and she has been an underlying part of the story ever since I first met Knox. But not a *public* part of the story.

534 the extensive interview he did in 1973 for *Radio Times:* The story was written by Ray Connolly and appeared in the September 27, 1973, issue. It announced the beginning of a twenty-six-part history of modern pop music on the BBC's Radio 1 and opened with Sam's ringing declaration: "Until rock 'n' roll music came along the grossest of all racial discrimination in America was in music."

535 a cover story in *Country Music* magazine: John Pugh, "The Rise and Fall of Sun Records," *Country Music,* November 1973.

538 The "Million Dollar Quartet" tapes, as it turned out, would not come out officially: According to "Random Notes," *Rolling Stone,* October 29, 1981, the first LP release originated in Holland at Christmas of 1980, though Jim Van Hollebeke, "For Elvis Fans Only," *Goldmine,* July 1981, pointed to Germany as the source — and some accounts have a European bootleg surfacing as early as the summer of 1979. In August 1981, according to *Rolling Stone*, this bootleg might almost be said to have been "bootlegged" by Shelby's English licensee, Charly, which, as *Rolling Stone* pointed out, was "a highly respected English reissue label [with] a licensing agreement to the U.K. rights to the Sun catalogue." "We just got it as part of our normal licensing deal," said Charly spokesman Cliff White, perhaps inadvisedly commenting that "Shelby decided to go with it after it had been bootlegged." RCA, which due to the participation of Elvis was the largest single copyright holder, mightily protested, to which Shelby sweetly replied that the Cliff White quote was "bullshit. It's not an official release. In fact . . . we've put them on notice, and we've asked RCA Victor to do something about it." And that was the end of the matter. The British release was never withdrawn, in fact it was reissued and reconfigured, but there was no official American release of the album until 1990, when RCA put out a licensed version, updating it and upgrading the sound with newly discovered tapes in 2006.

TEN | HOW LUCKY CAN ONE MAN GET

544 an uncanny foreshadowing of actor Joaquin Phoenix: As an interesting side note, Cher had a similar reaction to the host that same year, calling him an asshole on the air for what appeared to be his inordinate commitment to comic smugness at the time. Interestingly enough, Letterman really seemed to be stung by Cher's reaction, as he was not at all by Sam's implicit judgment. It's on YouTube.

547 only twenty-five full-fledged "performer" inductees: In addition to Sam, six additional "non-performers," including Leonard Chess, Ahmet Ertegun, and Jerry Wexler, were recognized in the first two years, as well as six "early influences" like Robert Johnson, Jimmie Rodgers, and Hank Williams.

547 $40 million pledged: Michael Goldberg, "Cleveland Affirms Rock Hall of Fame Deal," *Rolling Stone*, October 8, 1989.

549 They projected seven thousand sales: According to Martin Hawkins, each of the *Sun Rockabillys* sold over thirty thousand copies.

550 "I think, man, if I had done it myself": Walter Dawson, "The Uncle Sam of America's Music," *Memphis Commercial Appeal*, March 29, 1981.

551 "There could have been such a great story on this": Trevor Cajiao, "The Most Important Man in the World: Sam Phillips Talks to *Now Dig This*," part 3, *Now Dig This* 85 (April 1990).

551 Shelby had no right to issue the blues material: To quote Colin Escott (again), in a brief after note he wrote to *The Sun Blues Box*: "If Sun had gone to Columbia or another major, its riches would have remained squirreled away in a remote tape vault. Singleton kept the Sun name alive. He kept himself in business in the process, so it wasn't an act of altruism, but there was a generosity of spirit in him that transcended commercial motives."

555 it had been in his possession: Many have questioned whether or not the full story of the record's rite of passage might not be a little more circuitous. Elvis referred to the acetate in a March 1956 interview, saying he still had it at home. In the course of the Million Dollar Quartet session in December 1956, he says, "I recorded the sonofabitch . . . when I [first] come in here, and [I] lost the dub on it." George Klein, in his memoir, *Elvis: My Best Man*, written with Chuck Crisafulli, recalls Leek reminding Elvis in the spring of 1957 that it was in his possession, and Elvis telling him to hold on to it, "Keep it safe for me."

555 *Goldmine* broke the story: The *Goldmine* issue was dated August 26. The AP in its story of August 16 cited "this week's edition of *Goldmine*" as its source.

555 Sam gave an interview: Ron Wynn, "Recording Called First by Elvis, Doubted," *Memphis Commercial Appeal*, August 18, 1988.

556 when the *Memphis Commercial Appeal* called the house: Ibid. Marion's notarized statement of authenticity is dated October 10, 1988, as per a Jerry Osborne story in *DISCoveries*, January 1989, an anomaly for which I can offer no explanation.

557 Marion was challenging him from beyond the grave: As an example of how deeply this latest discovery stung Sam in wholly unmanufactured terms, one has only to look at undated notes he made for a response that was never delivered, in which, totally misunderstanding the issue (he seems to have thought at this point that unnamed persons were attempting to suggest that this second acetate was one made earlier than the first and recorded somewhere other than his studio), and in emotionally wrought language and handwriting uncharacteristic of his compositional style, he speaks of how "they are conspiring to tread on and capitalize on my Life Long Profession and Good Name . . . over a life time [of] Hard Work and high reputation in the Music Industry which to me next to life is the most important thing I have or ever will have."

558 The first detailed published account: Robert Johnson, *Elvis Presley Speaks!*, pp. 6–8.

558 "helping to install air conditioners": Hopkins interview with Marion, ca. 1970 (MVC/MSU).

558 "I walked into Sun Recording Service": Robert Johnson, "Elvis Himself!" *TV Star Parade*, September 1956, p. 24.

559 "Elvis lugged his guitar into the studio": Robert Johnson, "Thru the Patience of Sam Phillips — Suddenly Singing Elvis Presley Zooms into Recording Stardom," *Memphis Press-Scimitar*, February 5, 1955.

559 "While he was waiting his turn": Jerry Hopkins, *Elvis: The Biography*, p. 64. In either that or another of her interviews with Hopkins, Marion describes the scene in which a sailor and his mother are among the multitude sitting in the small waiting area "while Elvis was making his record [and the mother] got up and was listening to him and said, 'Who is that?'" And when Marion told her, this "middle-aged lady" declared that "he just made the goose bumps" come out on her skin.

560 "Every night . . . he would mark it up": This is borne out by McBride speaking in Robert Palmer, "Simmer Down, Son," *American Film*, June 1989, p. 31, of getting daily rewrites from Sam.

561 Sam's "lack of courage in his convictions": Myra Lewis with Murray Silver, *Great Balls of Fire: The Uncensored Story of Jerry Lee Lewis*, p. 43.

561 his "chaplain's compassion" and "his ability to understand human nature": Ibid., p. 73.

562 "In a sense, we didn't want to be confused": Susan Korones, "Jerry Lee Lewis Can Still Stir Things Up," *New York Times*, January 15, 1989. See also Robert Palmer, "Simmer Down, Son," *American Film*, June 1989.

562 a "nice tension": Korones, as above.

562 Jerry Lee Lewis wrote "Lies! Lies Lies": Steve Pond, "Whole Lotta Shakin' Going On," *Rolling Stone*, July 13–27, 1989.

562 Sam "kind of worked on Trey": Both this and Trey Wilson's quotes come from Korones, as above.

564 "there have been so many untrue stories": Colonel Parker to me, February 9, 1988.

567 The two Florence radio stations: Primary information on all radio activity comes from a detailed radio guide that Sally Wilbourn painstakingly put together. In addition, both Knox and Jerry contributed extensive information and insight. See also Bernie Delinski, "Sweet Sounds of Hometown Success: Big River Celebrating Anniversary," *Florence TimesDaily,* March 2, 1997.

570 he told her all about Aunt Emma and Kate Nelson: Just one additional note about Kate. Sally told me, "We tried to find her house. Sleetie told Sam it was still there. But we drove around looking for it for a long time and never could find it. Sam said, 'I'm just going to have Sleetie come down and show me where it is.' He told me he would usually [go there] on his way home after a date. He said that he did it because he didn't want to mess up a girl that he was going out with. And he did it often, I think."

572 his eighth-grade teacher: In her letter Mrs. Lanier recalled it as ninth grade.

572 "I taught you two subjects": The letter was written December 17, 1985, and has been condensed here. It was kindly offered by her daughter, Andrea Craig, a great music fan.

573 "What I would give": Kitchen Sisters interview.

578 a portrait of Sam called "Gentle But Tough": This has been condensed from a nine page handwritten document.

583 Sam's ability to absorb and comprehend: Knox and Becky also confirmed Sam's medical knowledge and expertise.

586 "I personally believe": I didn't discover this memo until I was well into the writing of this biography, but it is certainly in line with everything that Knox told me at the time. "I knew once Sam fell in love with you and had confidence in you and the process," Knox said on the phone one time, "he would be hard to shut up."

591 The funeral was in Florence: See Terry Pace, "Jud Phillips Remembered as Music's Unsung Hero," and "Phillips Brothers Inspired Millions," *Florence TimesDaily,* July 24, 1992.

592 "Wait a minute. . . . Do y'all know who this man was?" This comes from both Nadine Cohodas, who wrote about Buster Williams in her comprehensive history of Chess Records, *Spinning Blues into Gold: The Chess Brothers and the Legendary Chess Records,* and Sally Wilbourn, who was with Sam at the funeral.

592 which . . . caused Sam to vow to give up smoking: He was sincere but not entirely successful in this. You could always tell when Sam had been drinking, because after a certain point he almost always lit up a cigarette—but he never returned to the heavy smoking that had been customary for most of his adult life.

593 He was working on the radio tower: Interviews with Knox, Becky, Jerry, Sally, and Diane; Knox's medical records; Michael Kelley, "Lasting Legacy: Phillips Clan Rocks On, Hangs On, Keeps Going On," *Memphis Commercial Appeal,* June 30, 1996.

597 "It ranks so far above everything else": Bill Ellis, "Happy Birthday to You—and Thanks," *Memphis Commercial Appeal,* January 4, 1997.

597 "I realized I had missed it all so badly": *Memphis Commercial Appeal,* June 30, 1996.

605 Trowbridge's Creamery: This was Sam's original term of reference for what is today called Trowbridge's Ice Cream and Sandwich Bar.

613 "To me Memphis is the greatest place on earth": The half-page ad ran in the *Memphis Commercial Appeal* on September 9, 1996, with pictures of Sam, past and present at the board. See also Jody Callahan sidebar, "Luminaries, Locals Celebrate Memories, A Musical Legacy," in the *Memphis Commercial Appeal,* August 8, 2003, in which

John Moore, vice president for state and local affairs for Northwest, declares: "He rejected the script. He just did his own thing."

613 "a rambling tale": Bruce Van Wyngarten, "Big Balls in Blues Town," *Memphis Flyer*, October 12, 1995.

614 "We feel like sonic investigators": John Beifuss, "Memphians' Link with Mystique of Sound Is Feature on NPR," *Memphis Commercial Appeal*, September 17, 1999.

615 with Sam shepherding the entire group: The event took place on October 30, 1999. *People*, November 29, 1999, had the number of "jockettes" as twelve, the *New York Times*, October 30, 1999, as fourteen.

615 Sam had addressed National Public Radio's annual conference: In addition to Davia's firsthand testimony, Frank Ahrens, "He Laid Down the First Rock," *Washington Post*, May 18, 1999, gives a good account. Sam reiterated his point about intimacy, if in less salty language, in the *Memphis Commercial Appeal* story of September 17, 1999.

618 "In a tragic situation": Becky Phillips, "Gentle But Tough."

620 "I never cared": from Eric Olsen's 2000 interview with Sam, slightly reconfigured.

623 "If there [was] one damn shit-ass": Hank Davis and Colin Escott, "Sam Phillips: America's Other Uncle Sam," part 2, *Goldmine*, August 14, 1987.

624 "I don't think I'm timid": Paul Jones interview, *Paul Jones R&B Show*, BBC, 1988–1989.

625 "the man who introduced Elvis, me, and a lot of others": Bill Ellis, "Ike Turner Keeps It Hummin' in his '88,'" *Memphis Commercial Appeal*, May 30, 1998.

625 detailed critiques, which were received: Terry Pace described one to me. "Sam dissected Jerry Lee's performance. It was as if he were producing a session. Jerry Lee just said, 'Yes, sir. Yes, Mr. Phillips.' A couple of years later, when I asked Jerry Lee who he would like to go in the studio with, he didn't hesitate. 'Sam Phillips.'"

625 "I always wished that my mind was as swift as my piano playing": Michael Blowen, "Great Balls of Fire!" *Boston Globe*, June 25, 1989.

626 "A day without ice cream": Ed Weathers, "The Last Tycoon: Is This Man America's Happiest Millionaire?" *Memphis* magazine, September 1985.

626 Kemmons . . . had taken to printing billion- and trillion-dollar bills: After being shut down by the government for his initial printing of million-dollar bills because they looked too much like legal tender, Kemmons didn't stop at a billion but raised the ante with each successive printing, going all the way up to a duodecillion. "He handed them out to EVERYONE, EVERYWHERE!" explained Dottie Bonds, Kemmons' longtime secretary and employee of the Kemmons Wilson Companies. "He used them as his calling card around the world — with some very humorous results, as you can imagine. He had a ball with them! They represented, as stated on the bill, confidence in the American dream."

629 "No matter what happens to you in this world": Elizabeth Kaye, "Sam Phillips: The *Rolling Stone* Interview," *Rolling Stone*, February 13, 1986, p. 88.

630 "Oh God, what I wouldn't give": Paul Jones interview, *Paul Jones R&B Show*, BBC, 1988–1989.

631 "Do you realize how beautiful total chaos is?": Kitchen Sisters Sam and Becky Phillips interview, 1998.

631 "A dog won't bite me": Smithsonian interview, 1992.

631 "Nobody talks to a frog but me": Kitchen Sisters Sam and Becky Phillips interview. Sam also spoke of his ability to communicate with crickets and squirrels in the same vein. His point, beyond interspecies communication, was, "There's no substitute for the intimacy of sound."

633 "Dearest Sam": This was written January 9, 1943 (when both Sam and Becky were at WLAY), on blue stationery in a blue envelope that is not addressed.

634 "It's a dreadful day for me": June 13, 1944.

635 "I just absolutely feel lost without my darling": June 14, 1944.

635 "I know that it's been extremely hard on you": June 16, 1944.

635 "I'm sending you Mr. Sam Phillips for diagnosis and treatment": Dr. L. E. Bayles Jr. to Dr. Seale Harris, June 29, 1944.

635 a series of pamphlets: "Some General Considerations of Therapeutic Relaxation." Somewhat later: "Mechanical Group Therapy," reprinted from *Science*, February 1, 1952, by Ernst Schmidhofer, Veterans Administration Kennedy Hospital. In addition, more recently I came into possession of the most ghastly recording, which Phyllis Hill retrieved from the Sun Entertainment Corp. archives, with an affectless voice repeating over and over (I would say in an "om"-like way, except for the grating tunelessness of the recitation), such simple mantras as: "Relaxing more, relaxing more . . . I can rid myself of any symptoms more quickly and easily every day," "I feel good, I feel fine — concentrate, concentrate — make a mental pic-ture," and "All my fears and doubts are gone, all my fears and doubts are gone, they're all gone, they're all gone — gone, gone, gone." The entire recording lasts for approximately half an hour.

636 the solipsistic isolation: After writing this I was rereading Donald Spoto's *Hitchcock*, and it occurred to me that Sam, like Hitchcock, had created a myth of himself, perhaps for much the same reason. "It's easier for someone who's shy and repressed to live as a myth," screenwriter Jay Presson Allen is quoted by Spoto. "He didn't do it deliberately, but it was a wonderful defense mechanism."

637 "We're just a very close family": Smithsonian interview.

644 Sam did numerous radio and television interviews: In addition to Sally's and John Singleton's memories of this trip, Rob Santos' recollections, photographs, and videos were enormously helpful.

647 John Tigrett had been the driving force behind Memphis' "Great American Pyramid": The Pyramid, John Tigrett's vision of the resurgent spirit of the city, was mired in controversy from the start, from its siting to its acoustics to its inconsistent plumbing and incompetent management by larger-than-life entrepreneur (most Memphians would say that's too polite a way of putting it) Sidney Shlenker, and the endless amounts of civic investment it seemed to drain. Suffice it to say that after ten years of sitting empty, and with a new civic center built by FedEx on the downtown site where many had originally wanted the Pyramid to go, in 2015 it became the home of a Bass Pro Shops hunting, fishing, and outdoor megastore complex, including a "wilderness-themed hotel."

647 "Jack Soden . . . called": This account is almost entirely from my interview with Pat Tigrett, with some clarification from Michael Donahue, "Universal Launch: Opening Parade Thanks Fans Very Much," *Memphis Commercial Appeal*, August 10, 2002.

648 In addition Pat enlisted Disney: Besides the two sources listed above, see also Michael Lollar, "With All the King's Flair, Event Gurus Stage Kick-Off," *Memphis Commercial Appeal*, August 4, 2002, and Donnie Snow, "Elvis Week Kick-Starts with a Rockin' Parade," *Memphis Commercial Appeal*, August 11, 2002, as well as the official program for the "Elvis Presley 25th Anniversary Celebration of Life Parade."

650 "I knew I had to get up and get down here": Cindy Wolff, "TCB Band Helps Elvis 'Family' Close Out Week," *Memphis Commercial Appeal*, August 18, 2002.

651 He'd made his mind up he was going to take care of it himself: Sally seems to have been the only person he told of this decision.

657 Elvis' first record, "That's All Right," and Howlin' Wolf's "How Many More Years" . . . played loudly: Descriptive details and quotes come from Terry Pace, "A Lifetime of Musical Landmarks," *Florence TimesDaily*, August 15, 2003; Michael Donahue, "Phillips's Visitation Is Light-Hearted," *Memphis Commercial Appeal*, August 7, 2002; and Bill Ellis, "Laughter, Loving, Music See Phillips Off," *Memphis Commercial Appeal*, August 8, 2002, as well as my own interviews and observations.

659 "Sam Phillips," he said, adjusting his reading glasses to read from a brilliantly begun but never-to-be-finished autobiography: From the partial manuscript for Jack's book, used with permission.

660 "I've been so blessed, man": Larry Nager, NARAS interview.

Bibliography

Albert, George, and Frank Hoffmann. *The Cash Box Country Music Charts, 1958-1982*. Metuchen NJ: Scarecrow Press, 1984.

Amburn, Ellis. *Dark Star: The Roy Orbison Story*. New York: Lyle Stuart, 1990.

Barlow, William. *Voice Over: The Making of Black Radio*. Philadelphia: Temple University Press, 1999.

Bearden, William. *Memphis Blues: Birthplace of a Music Tradition*. Charleston, SC: Arcadia Publishing, 2006.

Berry, Chuck. *Chuck Berry: The Autobiography*. New York: Harmony Books, 1987.

Blumhofer, Edith L. *Restoring the Faith: The Assemblies of God, Pentecostalism, and American Culture*. Urbana: University of Illinois Press, 1993.

Booth, Stanley. *Rythm Oil: A Journey Through the Music of the American South*. London: Jonathan Cape, 1991.

Bragg, Rick. *Jerry Lee Lewis: His Own Story*. New York: Harper, 2014.

Branch, Taylor. *Parting the Waters: America in the King Years 1954-63*. New York: Simon and Schuster, 1988.

Broven, John. *Record Makers and Breakers: Voices of the Independent Rock 'n' Roll Pioneers*. Urbana: University of Illinois Press, 2009.

———. *South to Louisiana: The Music of the Cajun Bayous*. Gretna, LA: Pelican Publishing, 1983.

———. *Walking to New Orleans: The Story of New Orleans Rhythm & Blues*. Bexhill-on-Sea, Sussex, England: Blues Unlimited, 1974.

Burton, Thomas G., ed. *Tom Ashley, Sam McGee, Bukka White: Tennessee Traditional Singers*. Knoxville: University of Tennessee Press, 1981.

Cantor, Louis. *Dewey and Elvis: The Life and Times of a Rock 'n' Roll Deejay*. Urbana: University of Illinois Press, 2005.

———. *Wheelin' on Beale*. New York: Pharos Books, 1992.

Capers, Gerald M. Jr. *The Biography of a River Town: Memphis: Its Heroic Age*. 2nd ed. 1966. Reprint, Memphis: Burke's Book Store, 2003.

Cash, Johnny. *Man in Black*. New York: Warner Books, 1975.

Cash, Johnny, with Patrick Carr. *Cash: The Autobiography*. New York: HarperCollins, 1997.

Cash, Vivian, with Ann Sharpsteen. *I Walked the Line: My Life with Johnny*. New York: Scribner, 2007.

Cash, W. J. *The Mind of the South*. 1941. Reprint, New York: Vintage Books, 1991.

Cogan, Jim, and William Clark. *Temples of Sound: Inside the Great Recording Studios*. San Francisco: Chronicle Books, 2003.

Cohn David. *Where I Was Born and Raised*. Notre Dame: University of Notre Dame Press, 1967.

Cohodas, Nadine. *Spinning Blues into Gold: The Chess Brothers and the Legendary Chess Records*. New York: St. Martin's Press, 2000.

Coles, Robert, and Dorothea Lange. *Dorothea Lange: Photographs of a Lifetime*. Millerton, NY: Aperture, 1982.

Conaway, James. *Memphis Afternoons*. Boston: Houghton Mifflin, 1993.

Cooper, Daniel. *Lefty Frizzell: The Honky-Tonk Life of Country Music's Greatest Singer*. New York: Little, Brown, 1995.

Cotten, Lee. *Reelin' & Rockin': The Golden Age of American Rock 'n' Roll*. Vol. 2, *1956-1959*. Ann Arbor, MI: Popular Culture Ink, 1995.

——. *Shake, Rattle & Roll: The Golden Age of American Rock 'n' Roll*. Vol. 1, *1952-1955*. Ann Arbor, MI: Pierian Press, 1989.

——. *Twist & Shout: The Golden Age of American Rock 'n' Roll*. Vol. 3, *1960-1963*. Sacramento: High Sierra Books, 2002.

Danforth, William H. *I Dare You*. St. Louis: American Youth Foundation, ca. 1931.

Daniel, Pete. *Breaking the Land: The Transformation of Cotton, Tobacco, and Rice Culture Since 1880*. Urbana: University of Illinois Press, 1985.

——. *Lost Revolutions: The South in the 1950s*. Chapel Hill: University of North Carolina Press, 2000.

——. *Standing at the Crossroads: Southern Life Since 1900*. New York: Hill and Wang, 1986.

DeCosta-Willis, Miriam, and Fannie Mitchell Delk, eds. *Homespun Images: An Anthology of Black Memphis Writers and Artists*. Memphis: Wimmer Brothers, 1989.

Dollard, John. *Caste and Class in a Southern Town*. New Haven: Yale University Press, 1937.

Dowdy, G. Wayne. *Hidden History of Memphis*. Charleston, SC: The History Press, 2010.

——. *Mayor Crump Don't Like It: Machine Politics in Memphis*. Jackson: University of Mississippi Press, 2006.

Dundy, Elaine. *Ferriday, Louisiana*. New York: Donald I. Fine, 1991.

Escott, Colin. *All Roots Lead to Rock: Legends of Early Rock 'n' Roll*. New York: Schirmer Books, 1999.

——. *The Grand Ole Opry: The Making of an American Icon*. New York: Center Street, 2006.

——. *Roadkill on the Three-Chord Highway: Art and Trash in American Popular Music*. New York: Routledge, 2002.

——. *Tattooed on Their Tongues: A Journey Through the Backrooms of American Music*. New York: Schirmer Books, 1996.

Escott, Colin, with Martin Hawkins. *Good Rockin' Tonight: Sun Records and the Birth of Rock 'n' Roll*. New York: St. Martin's Press, 1991.

Escott, Colin, and Martin Hawkins. *Sun Records: The Discography*. Vollersode, West Germany: Bear Family Records, 1987.

Escott, Colin, Martin Hawkins, and Hank Davis. *The Sun Country Years: Country Music in Memphis, 1950-1959*. Vollersode, West Germany: Bear Family Records, 1987.

Escott, Colin, with George Merritt and William MacEwen. *Hank Williams: The Biography*. Rev. ed. New York: Back Bay Books, 2004.

Evans, Walker. *Walker Evans, Photographs for the Farm Security Administration, 1935-1938*. New York: DaCapo, 1973.

Federal Writers' Project of the Works Progress Administration. *The WPA Guide to Tennessee*. Knoxville: University of Tennessee Press, 1986.

Field, Kim. *Harmonicas, Harps, and Heavy Breathers: The Evolution of the People's Instrument*. New York: Simon and Schuster, 1993.

Flippo, Chet. *Everybody Was Kung-Fu Dancing: Chronicles of the Lionized and the Notorious*. New York: St. Martin's Press, 1991.

Floyd, John. *Sun Records: An Oral History*. New York: Avon Books, 1998.

Gart, Galen, comp. and ed. *First Pressings: The History of Rhythm and Blues: Special 1950 Volume*. Milford, NH: Big Nickel Publications, 1993.

——. *First Pressings: Rock History as Chronicled in* Billboard *Magazine*. Vol. 1, *1948-1950*. Milford, NH: Big Nickel Publications, 1986.

——. *First Pressings: Rock History as Chronicled in* Billboard *Magazine*. Vol. 2, *1950-1951*. Milford, NH: Big Nickel Publications, 1986.

——. *First Pressings: The History of Rhythm and Blues*. Vols. 1-9, *1951-1958*. Milford, NH: Big Nickel Publications, 1991-2001.

Gart, Galen, and Roy C. Ames. *Duke/Peacock Records: An Illustrated History with Discography*. Milford, NH: Big Nickel Publications, 1990.

Gentry, Linnell. *A History and Encyclopedia of Country, Western, and Gospel Music*. Nashville: Linnell Gentry, 1961

Gentry, Robert, comp. *The Louisiana Hayride: "The Glory Years — 1948-60."* Vol. 1, *1948-1955*. Many, LA: Robert Gentry, 1998.

——. *The Louisiana Hayride: "The Glory Years — 1948-60."* Vol. 2, *1956-1960*. Many, LA: Robert Gentry, 1998.

Gillett, Charlie. *Making Tracks: Atlantic Records and the Growth of a Multi-Billion-Dollar Industry*. New York: Dutton Books, 1974.

Goff, James R. Jr. *Close Harmony: A History of Southern Gospel*. Chapel Hill: University of North Carolina Press, 2002.

Gordon, Robert. *Can't Be Satisfied: The Life and Times of Muddy Waters*. Boston: Little, Brown, 2002.

——. *It Came from Memphis*. Boston: Faber and Faber, 1995.

Grant, Marshall, with Chris Zar. *I Was There When It Happened: My Life with Johnny Cash*. Nashville: Cumberland House, 2006.

Greenfield, Robert. *The Last Sultan: The Life and Times of Ahmet Ertegun*. New York: Simon and Schuster, 2011.

Grissim, John. *Country Music: White Man's Blues*. New York: Paperback Library, 1970.

Gruber, J. Richard, organizer. *Memphis: 1948-1958*. Memphis: Memphis Brooks Museum of Art, 1986.

Guralnick, Peter. *Last Train to Memphis: The Rise of Elvis Presley*. New York: Little, Brown, 1994.

Haley, John W., and John von Hoelle. *Sound and Glory: The Incredible Story of Bill Haley, the Father of Rock 'n' Roll and the Music That Shook the World*. Wilmington, DE: Dyne-American Publishing, 1989/1990.

Hall, Rick. *The Man from Muscle Shoals: My Journey from Shame to Fame*. Clovis, CA: Heritage Builders Publishing, 2015.

Handy, W. C. *Father of the Blues: An Autobiography*. New York: Macmillan, 1941.

Havighurst, Craig. *Air Castle of the South: WSM and the Making of Music City.* Urbana: University of Illinois Press, 2007.

Hawkins, Martin. *A Shot in the Dark: Making Records in Nashville, 1945–1955.* Nashville: Vanderbilt University Press and the Country Music Foundation Press, 2006.

Heilbut, Anthony. *The Gospel Sound: Good News and Bad Times.* New York: Simon and Schuster, 1971.

Hemphill, Paul. *The Nashville Sound: Bright Lights and Country Music.* New York: Simon and Schuster, 1970.

Hendricksen, Paul. *Hemingway's Boat: Everything He Loved in Life, and Lost.* New York: Knopf, 2011.

Hess, Jake, with Richard Hyatt. *Nothin' but Fine: The Music and the Gospel According to Jake Hess.* Columbus, GA: Buckland Press, 1995.

Hilburn, Robert. *Johnny Cash: The Life.* New York: Little, Brown, 2013.

Hinson, Glenn. *Fire in My Bones: Transcendence and the Holy Spirit in African American Gospel.* Philadelphia: University of Pennsylvania Press, 2000.

Holmes, Richard: *Footsteps: Adventures of a Romantic Biographer.* New York: Viking, 1985.

Hopkins, Jerry. *Elvis.* New York: Simon and Schuster, 1971.

Hoskyns, Barney. *Say It One More Time for the Broken Hearted: The Country Side of Southern Soul.* London: Fontana Paperbacks, 1987.

Jackson, John A. *American Bandstand: Dick Clark and the Making of a Rock 'n' Roll Empire.* New York: Oxford University Press, 1999.

———. *Big Beat Heat: Alan Freed and the Early Years of Rock and Roll.* New York: Schirmer Books, 1991.

Johnson, Robert. *Elvis Presley Speaks!* New York: *Rave* (Magazine) Publishing Corporation, 1956.

Jorgensen, Ernst. *A Boy from Tupelo.* Denmark: Follow That Dream Books, 2012.

Killen, Buddy, with Tom Carter: *By the Seat of My Pants: My Life in Country Music.* New York: Simon and Schuster, 1993.

King, B.B., with David Ritz. *Blues All Around Me: The Autobiography of B.B. King.* New York: Avon Books, 1996.

King, B.B., with Dick Waterman. *The B.B. King Treasures: Photos, Mementos, and Music from B. B. King's Collection.* New York, Boston: Bulfinch, 2005.

Kingsbury, Paul, ed. *The Encyclopedia of Country Music.* New York: Oxford University Press, 1998.

———. *The Grand Ole Opry History of Country Music: 70 Years of the Songs, the Stars, and the Stories.* New York: Villard Books, 2005.

The Kitchen Sisters. *WHER: 1000 Beautiful Watts, The First All-Girl Radio Station in the Nation.* San Francisco: self-published (but beautiful), 2009.

Kostelanetz, Richard, ed. *The B.B. King Companion: Five Decades of Commentary.* New York: Schirmer Books, 1997.

Lewis, Jerry Lee, and Charles White. *Killer! The Baddest Rock Memoir Ever.* London: Century, 1993.

Lewis, Linda Gail, with Les Pendleton. *The Devil, Me, and Jerry Lee.* Atlanta: Longstreet, 1998.

Lewis, Myra, with Murray Silver. *Great Balls of Fire: The Uncensored Story of Jerry Lee Lewis.* New York: Quill, 1982.

Lewry, Peter, with introduction by Mark Stielper. *I've Been Everywhere: The Definitive Diary of America's Greatest Country Performer,* http://www.johnnycashfanzine.com/e-book.html.

Lornell, Kip. *"Happy in the Service of the Lord": Afro-American Gospel Quartets in Memphis.* Urbana: University of Illinois Press, 1988.

Lydon, Michael. *Rock Folk: Portraits from the Rock 'n' Roll Pantheon.* New York: Dial, 1971.

Mazor, Barry. *Meeting Jimmie Rodgers: How America's Original Roots Music Hero Changed the Pop Sounds of a Century.* New York: Oxford University Press, 2009.

McCloud, Barry. *Definitive Country, The Ultimate Encyclopedia of Country Music and Its Performers.* New York: Perigee, 1995.

McIlwaine, Shields. *Memphis Down in Dixie.* New York: Dutton, 1948.

McKee, Margaret, and Fred Chisenhall. *Beale Black and Blue: Life and Music on Black America's Main Street.* Baton Rouge: Louisiana State University Press, 1981.

McNutt, Randy. *We Wanna Boogie: An Illustrated History of the American Rockabilly Movement.* Hamilton, OH: HHP Books, 1988.

Millar, Bill. *Let the Good Times Rock!: A Fan's Notes on Post-War American Roots Music.* York, England: Music Mentor Books, 2004.

Miller, William D. *Mr. Crump of Memphis.* Baton Rouge: Louisiana State University Press, 1964.

Moore, Scotty, as told to James Dickerson. *That's Alright, Elvis: The Untold Story of Elvis's First Guitarist and Manager, Scotty Moore.* New York: Schirmer Books, 1997.

Murray, Albert. *South to a Very Old Place.* New York: McGraw-Hill, 1971.

Nager, Larry. *Memphis Beat: The Lives and Times of America's Musical Crossroads.* New York: St. Martin's Press, 1998.

Newborn, Calvin Jr. *As Quiet As It's Kept! The Genius of Phineas Newborn, Jr.* Memphis: The Phineas Newborn Jr. Family Foundation, 1996.

O'Neal, Hank (text). *A Vision Shared: A Classic Portrait of America and Its People 1935–1943.* New York: St. Martin's Press, 1976.

Palmer, Robert. *Blues & Chaos: The Music Writing of Robert Palmer.* New York: Scribner, 2009.

———. *Deep Blues.* New York: Viking, 1981.

———. *Rock & Roll: An Unruly History.* New York: Harmony Books, 1995.

Passman, Arnold. *The Deejays: How the Tribal Chieftains of Radio Got to Where They're At.* New York: Macmillan, 1971.

Perkins, Carl, and David McGee. *Go, Cat, Go! The Life and Times of Carl Perkins, the King of Rockabilly.* New York: Hyperion, 1996.

Poe, Randy. *Music Publishing: A Songwriter's Guide.* Cincinnati: Writer's Digest Books, 1990.

Porterfield, Nolan. *Jimmie Rodgers: The Life and Times of America's Blue Yodeler.* Urbana: University of Illinois Press, 1979.

Raichelson, Richard M. *Beale Street Talks: A Walking Tour Down the Home of the Blues.* Memphis: Arcadia Records, 1994.

Reagon, Bernice Johnson, ed. *We'll Understand It Better By and By: Pioneering African American Gospel Composers.* Washington, DC: Smithsonian Institution Press, 1992.

Rowe, Mike. *Chicago Breakdown.* London: Eddison Press, 1973.

Russell, Wayne. *Foot Soldiers and Kings.* Vols. 1 and 2. Brandon, Manitoba: Wayne Russell, n.d.

Ryan, Marc W. *Trumpet Records: Diamonds on Farish Street.* Jackson: University Press of Mississippi, 2004.

Sanjek, Russell. *American Popular Music and Its Business: The First Four Hundred Years.* Vol. 3, *From 1900 to 1984.* New York: Oxford University Press, 1988.

Sawyer, Charles. *The Arrival of B.B. King.* Garden City, NY: Doubleday, 1980.

Seaman, Ann Rowe. *Swaggart: The Unauthorized Biography of an American Evangelist.* New York: Continuum, 1999.

Segrest, James, and Mark Hoffman. *Moanin' at Midnight: The Life and Times of Howlin' Wolf.* New York: Pantheon Books, 2004.

Shaw, Arnold. *Honkers and Shouters: The Golden Years of Rhythm and Blues.* New York: Macmillan, 1978.

Sigafoos, Robert A. *Cotton Row to Beale Street.* Memphis: Memphis State University Press, 1979.

Sims, Barbara Barnes. *The Next Elvis: Searching for Stardom at Sun Records.* Baton Rouge: Louisiana State University Press, 2014.

Smith, Wes. *The Pied Pipers of Rock 'n' Roll: Radio Deejays of the '50s and '60s.* Marietta, GA: Longstreet Press, 1989.

Stambler, Irwin. *Encyclopedia of Pop, Rock, & Soul.* New York: St. Martin's Press, 1977.

Streissguth, Michael. *Johnny Cash: The Biography.* Cambridge, MA: Da Capo Press, 2006.

Stribling, T. S. *The Forge.* Tuscaloosa: University of Alabama Press, 1985.

———. *The Store.* Tuscaloosa: University of Alabama Press, 1985.

———. *Unfinished Cathedral.* Tuscaloosa: University of Alabama Press, 1986.

Swenson, John. *Bill Haley: The Daddy of Rock and Roll.* New York: Stein and Day, 1982.

Taylor, David L. *Happy Rhythm: A Biography of Hovie Lister & The Statesmen Quartet.* Lexington, IN: TaylorMade WRITE, 1994.

Terrell, Bob. *The Music Men: The Story of Professional Gospel Quartet Singing.* Asheville, NC: Bob Terrell Publisher, 1990.

Tigrett, John. *Fair and Square: A Collection of Stories from a Lifetime Among Friends.* Nashville: Spiridon Press, 1998.

Tobler, John, and Stuart Grundy. *The Record Producers.* New York: St. Martin's Press, 1982.

Toll, Robert. *Blacking Up: The Minstrel Show in Nineteenth-Century America.* New York: Oxford University Press, 1974.

Tosches, Nick. *Country: The Biggest Music in America.* New York: Stein and Day, 1977.

———. *Hellfire: The Jerry Lee Lewis Story.* New York: Dell, 1982.

———. *Unsung Heroes of Rock 'n' Roll.* New York: Charles Scribner's Sons, 1984.

Tucker, David M. *Lieutenant Lee of Beale Street.* Nashville: Vanderbilt University Press, 1971.

———. *Memphis Since Crump: Bossism, Blacks, and Civic Reformers, 1948-1968.* Knoxville: University of Tennessee Press, 1980.

Turner, Steve. *Hungry for Heaven: Rock 'n' Roll and the Search for Redemption.* London: W. H. Allen, 1988.

———. *The Man Called Cash: The Life, Love, and Faith of an American Legend.* Nashville: W Publishing Group, 2004.

Wade, Dorothy, and Justine Picardie. *Music Man: Ahmet Ertegun, Atlantic Records, and the Triumph of Rock 'n' Roll.* New York: W. W. Norton, 1990.

Wald, Gayle F. *Shout, Sister, Shout! The Untold Story of Rock-and-Roll Trailblazer Sister Rosetta Tharpe.* Boston: Beacon Press, 2008.

Ward, Brian. *Just My Soul Responding: Rhythm and Blues, Black Consciousness, and Race Relations.* Berkeley: University of California Press, 1998.

Warner, Jay. *Just Walkin' in the Rain.* Los Angeles: Renaissance Books, 2001.

Werner, Craig. *A Change Is Gonna Come: Music, Race & the Soul of America*. New York: Plume, 1999.

Wexler, Jerry, and David Ritz. *Rhythm and the Blues: A Life in American Music*. New York: Knopf, 1993.

Whitburn, Joel. *Joel Whitburn's Top Pop Singles, 1955-1993*. Menomonee Falls, WI: Record Research, 1994.

——. *Joel Whitburn's Top Pop Albums, 1955-2001*. Menomonee Falls, WI: Record Research, 1993.

——. *Joel Whitburn's Top Country Songs, 1944-2005*. Menomonee Falls, WI: Record Research, 2006.

——. *Joel Whitburn's Top Country Albums, 1964-1997*. Menomonee Falls, WI: Record Research, 2008.

——. *Joel Whitburn's Top R & B Singles, 1942-1988*: Menomonee Falls, WI: Record Research, 1988.

——. *Pop Memories, 1890-1954: The History of American Popular Music*. Menomonee Falls, WI: Record Research, 1986.

White, Charles. *The Life and Times of Little Richard: The Quasar of Rock*. New York: Harmony Books, 1984.

Williams, Lycrecia, and Dale Vinicur. *Still in Love with You: The Story of Hank and Audrey Williams*. Nashville: Rutledge Hill Press, 1989.

Wilson, Kemmons, with Robert Kerr. *Half Luck and Half Brains: The Kemmons Wilson Holiday Inn Story*. Nashville: Hambleton Hill Publishing, 1996.

Withers, Ernest C. *The Memphis Blues Again: Six Decades of Memphis Music Photographs*, selected and with text by Daniel Wolff. New York: Viking Studio, 2001.

Withers, Ernest C., et al. *Pictures Tell the Story: Ernest C. Withers Reflections in History*. Norfolk, VA: Chrysler Museum of Art, 2000.

Wolfe, Charles K. *A Good-Natured Riot: The Birth of the Grand Ole Opry*. Nashville: The Country Music Foundation Press and Vanderbilt University Press, 1999.

The WPA Guide to 1930s Alabama. Introduction by Harvey H. Jackson III. Tuscaloosa: University of Alabama Press, 2000.

Wren, Christopher S. *Winners Got Scars Too: The Life and Legends of Johnny Cash*. New York: A Country Music/Ballantine Book, 1971.

GENEALOGY

I would be remiss if I didn't credit Jimmy David and Barbara Ann Moomaw's Phillips Family Genealogy, compiled in 1995, which together with the Phillips Family Directory (the last I have is from 2006) gives a pretty complete picture of the births, deaths, marriages, and present-day activities (if applicable) of the entire extended Phillips clan.

A FEW VIDEO AND AUDIO POINTS OF REFERENCE

All Day and All Night: Memories from Beale Street Musicians, 1990. Robert Gordon and Louis Guida video documentary.

Sam Phillips: The Man Who Invented Rock 'n' Roll. Peter Guralnick and Morgan Neville video documentary.

Sam Phillips and the Early Years of the Memphis Recording Service. Kitchen Sisters audio documentary.
Shakespeare Was a Big George Jones Fan: Cowboy Jack Clement's Home Movies. Robert Gordon and Morgan Neville video documentary.
Sister Rosetta Tharpe: The Godmother of Rock and Roll. BBC video documentary.
WHER: 1000 Beautiful Watts. Kitchen Sisters audio documentary.

LINER NOTES

And then there are the liner notes and accompanying books and booklets, which in many cases offer the authoritative word on the subject. Here are just a handful.

Broven, John, and Colin Escott. *B.B. King: The Vintage Years* (Ace ABOXCD 8).
Broven, John, Martin Hawkins, and Dave Sax. *Joe Hill Louis: Boogie in the Park* (Ace CDCHD 803).
Davis, Hank. *Charlie Rich: Lonely Weekends* (Bear Family BCD 16152).
Davis, Hank, Colin Escott, and Martin Hawkins. *The Sun Blues Box* (Bear Family BCD 17310).
———. *The Sun Rock Box* (Bear Family BCD 17313).
Escott, Colin. *Classic Jerry Lee Lewis* (Bear Family, BCD 15420).
———. *Orbison* (Bear Family BCD 16423).
Escott, Colin, Martin Hawkins, and Hank Davis. *Johnny Cash and the Tennessee Two* (Charly Sun LP Box 103).
———. *The Sun Country Box* (Bear Family BCD 17311).
Escott, Colin, and Bill Millar. *The Classic Carl Perkins* (Bear Family BCD 15494).
Hawkins, Martin. *Rufus Thomas: His R&B Recordings 1949-1956* (Bear Family BCD 16695).
———. *A Shot in the Dark: Nashville Jumps* (Bear Family BCD 15864).
Hawkins, Martin, and Colin Escott. *A Shot in the Dark: Tennessee Jive* (Bear Family BCD 15854).
O'Neal, Jim. *The Modern Downhome Blues Sessions.* Vols. 1-3 (Ace CDCHD 876, 962, 1003).

A Brief Discographical Note

VERY BRIEF, given the vast array of reissues available (almost any of which could be well worth exploring), and virtually unique in my brief discographical experience in that with one glaring exception (and a few obvious tips to Sony for Elvis Presley and to the British Ace label for a variety of pre-Sun recordings by Sam), I could just turn you over to the Bear Family catalogue (bear-family.com) for a complete overview of Sun, from individual artist collections to 10-CD box sets.

Let me get to that glaring exception first, with the explicit warning that this is an equally glaring example of something located somewhere between synergy and shameless self-promotion. I have put together and annotated a 2-CD, 3-LP, 55-track set called *Sam Phillips: The Man Who Invented Rock 'n' Roll* (Yep Roc 2453 for both), which includes everything from Joe Hill Louis' 1950 debut on Sam and Dewey's (very) short-lived label, The Phillips, to Sam's first big r&b hits, "Rocket 88" and Howlin' Wolf's "Moanin' in the Moonlight," to a 1979 cut by John Prine, "How Lucky Can One Man Get," from Sam's last studio date. It's not by any means a Greatest Hits package. It includes just as many near-misses and never-wases. It's not a collection of Sam Phillips' own favorites either. (Well, they were *all* his favorites in a way, they were all his children.) This is a selection of my own personal—what can I call them? I guess *favorites* will have to do, but I need to specify: they're my own idiosyncratic favorites, they're my own favorites of the moment, they're my favorites because it tickles me to see them all gathered together here and sequenced without regard to category, across time and space, not because this represents some sabermetric pantheon of aesthetic values to which I'm asking everyone to subscribe, but as a ringing affirmation of Sam's democratic principles, his championing of the unique, the personal, the strikingly unconventional (what Gerard Manley Hopkins called "all things counter, original, spare, strange"), as well as a companion piece to the book.

Okay, with that out of the way, where to start?

One place would be Bear Family's *The Complete Sun Singles* series Vols. 1-6 (Bear Family BCD 15801-15806, each a 4-CD set). You can go as far as you like with this, but I would say for the casual Sun fanatic Vols. 1 and 2 would suffice, including everything from all the Sun-label blues sides and Elvis' five Sun singles through Carl Perkins' and Johnny Cash's greatest hits. With Vol. 3 you move into Jerry Lee's Greatest (following "Whole Lot of Shakin'"), not to mention some wonderful Cash, Warren Smith, and Billy Riley, among others—but there are many other ways to acquire these tracks, and only a commitment to completeness would necessitate the purchase of Vols. 4-6. Each volume comes accompanied in typical Bear Family fashion by a full-scale, lavishly illustrated and documented booklet, which not only complements the music but adds appreciably to its understanding.

But, all right, let's get to the real jewel in the crown. No record collection should be without the truly epochal *The Sun Blues Box* (Bear Family BCD 17310), a 10-CD masterpiece of historical research, sound restoration, and presentation (textual, pictorial, and musical)—hey, forget anything negative I've ever said about the mania for completeness (and I've said a lot)—if you want to grasp not just what Sam Phillips was all about but what he was talking about when he said, "This is where the soul of man never dies," this is the place to start.

There are in addition the 6-CD *Sun Country Box* (Bear Family BCD 17311) and the 8-CD *Sun Rock Box* (Bear Family BCD 17313), and they are well worth buying, too, though I'm not going to repeat the unconditional claims that I made for *The Sun Blues Box*. Each is invaluable in its own way, however, and each is a tribute to the dedicated, way-above-and-beyond-the-call-of-duty efforts of label head Richard Weize as well as producers and annotators Martin Hawkins, Colin Escott, and Hank Davis.

There are any number of fine individual albums on Bear Family by artists like Billy Riley, Billy "The Kid" Emerson, Rufus Thomas, Warren Smith, Sonny Burgess, Joe Hill Louis (you don't want to miss the Ace compilation, *Joe Hill Louis: Boogie in the Park* [Ace CHD 803], either), Dr. Ross, the Prisonaires, et al. There's a lovingly compiled 3-CD Charlie Rich set, *Charlie Rich: Lonely Weekends: The Sun Years 1958–1962* (Bear Family BCD 16152) that bears repeated listening, but while Sam placed Charlie alone in the same pantheon as Howlin' Wolf, he was always the first to admit that, due to time constraints, distractions, and autumnal discontents, he never did full justice to Charlie's talents in the studio. You will find many glimmers of that talent here, and with Charlie, even a glimmer can suggest pinnacles that most artists will never reach. Which is the reason I feel no hesitation in recommending the set—but with a condition attached. You need to commit yourself to the exploration of the many other sides of Charlie Rich available on his RCA, Hi, Smash, and Epic recordings over the next ten years, as well as on the album he made toward the end of his life, *Pictures and Paintings* (Sire 26730), a "personal statement" that I tried to get Sam to produce and over which Sam's presence hovers, despite the fact that he was never in the room.

So far as other individual artists go, here are some of the unmissable albums and box sets (up there with *The Sun Blues Box* in terms of intrinsic essentiality).

HOWLIN' WOLF

Howlin' Wolf: Memphis Days — The Definitive Edition, Vols. 1 and 2 (Bear Family BCD 15460, 15500); *Howling Wolf Sings the Blues* (Ace CDCHM 1013). The first two represent pretty much all of Sam's recordings of the "most profound and different" artist he ever recorded. The third continues the story with Joe Bihari's recordings of Wolf for the Modern/RPM label in the fall of 1951, when the Chess-Modern wars were on. While perhaps not quite as transcendent as Sam's recordings—well, hell, I wouldn't want to be without these either. As Sam said of his first encounter with Wolf in the studio, "I was totally blinded by the sound of his voice. I'm not sure that I heard anything in the way of instrumentation. I mean, I was sure enough that I knew I didn't have everything quite right. But his distinctiveness was so overwhelming to me that I couldn't find a way to make a suggestion!"

B.B. KING

B.B. King: The Modern Recordings, 1950-1951 (Ace CHM2 835). This is a wonderful collection of all of Sam's recordings of B.B. for the Bihari brothers, as the twenty-four-year-old "Singing Blues Boy" gradually begins to develop a style of his own. That style emerges full-blown with "3 O'Clock Blues," the first recording King made after the Biharis' split with Sam in the fall of 1951 (he recorded it under Joe Bihari's supervision at the "colored" YMCA in Memphis), which is included here along with two other songs from his first post-Sam session. You should definitely go on to the next chapter, though, which is beautifully represented by *B.B. King: His RPM Hits 1951-1957* (Ace CHD 712), wherein that familiar B.B. King style flourished and developed into one of the most distinctive voices in the blues. And if you're feeling ambitious (and with B.B. King, why shouldn't you be?), don't hesitate to acquire the extensively annotated and illustrated 4-CD box set, *B.B. King: The Vintage Years* (Ace ABOXCD 8), which includes pretty much all of the tracks that appear on the two individual albums above, plus a great deal irreplaceably more.

THE MILLION DOLLAR QUARTET

The Complete Million Dollar Quartet (Sony/BMG 82876 88035). Well, you certainly can't miss this one, in which Elvis, Carl Perkins, and Jerry Lee Lewis (the quartet was rounded out by Johnny Cash only for the picture-taking) come together more or less by happenstance for what Sam described as "a good old-fashioned jam session. It was totally extemporaneous. Everything was off mike — if it was on mike it was by accident. But I think this little chance meeting meant an awful lot to all those people not because one was bigger than another [but because] we all started out at this place, every person in that room was electrified by the fact that we were together." They sang gospel (mostly gospel), country, blues, and rock 'n' roll, and for all of the shock of its revelation (it was talked about for nearly twenty-five years before it ever saw the light of day), it would be a mistake to think of it as apocalyptic — it's just too damn charming. Maybe the best way to look at it, aside from the uplifting spirit of the music, is that it offers the closest clue we will ever get to the free-and-easy spirit, the *revolutionary* spirit, that was Sun. And speaking of that quartet, here are the individual members, each represented in his own shining and reflective light.

ELVIS PRESLEY

What you really need for a full immersion in Elvis' Sun period is Ernst Jorgensen's sumptuous *Elvis Presley: A Boy from Tupelo: The Complete 1953-1955 Recordings* (Follow That Dream), which, in addition to the two earlier acetates, includes virtually everything that he recorded over the roughly sixteen months that he was on the label, both in the studio and in live performance, along with a complete photographic and anecdotal record of every date he played in the oversize 527-page book that accompanies the 3-CD set (or maybe it's the other way around). But if for purely practical reasons this is beyond the range of your readiness to commit—and for the moment it's out of print anyway, though Sony/Legacy promises a somewhat truncated version in future—by all means pick up *Sunrise* (RCA 67675) or *Elvis at Sun* (BMG 28766 12052). The first includes all the Sun titles, most of the alternate takes and studio conversations, the two original acetates, all the experiments and all the dogged failures, plus six rare Hayride sides and two additional r&b numbers (recorded at a Lubbock radio station) on a 2-CD set. *Elvis at Sun,* on the other hand, is a compact 19-track collection, limited pretty much to complete masters, with truer sound (producer Ernst Jorgensen has stripped the sound back to Sam Phillips' original "slapback" approach, discarding the RCA echo-enhanced version that has been almost exclusively available until recently) and the added bonus of a personal reminiscence by Knox Phillips to introduce the liner notes.

CARL PERKINS

Carl Perkins: Up Through the Years, 1954-1957 (Bear Family BCD 15246); *The Classic Carl Perkins* (Bear Family BCD 15494-95). The first is a wonderful 24-track survey of the Sun years. The second, a 5-CD box, is Carl close to complete through 1964, including all of his post-Sun Columbia and Decca recordings as well. Carl is creative enough (and more than antic enough) to sustain this kind of attention.

JOHNNY CASH

I'm in a little bit of a quandary here. *Johnny Cash: The Man in Black, 1954-1958* (Bear Family BCD 15517), a 5-CD set, offers the usual meticulously annotated and presented body of Cash's Sun work, with an introduction to his earliest recordings on Columbia and a fifth CD devoted to the entirety of a 1958 Columbia session. It's a terrific tribute to the breadth and diversity of Johnny Cash's talents, but I'm not sure this would be my first recommendation—and if you're looking for completeness, you should also consider *Johnny Cash at Sun* (Sony/Legacy), an 88-track collection confined exclusively to Sun selections (masters, demos, alternate takes, outtakes, and undubbed masters), but available only as a download. On the other hand, you might simply select *Johnny Cash: Up Through the Years, 1955-1957* (Bear Family BCD 15247), a 24-track, single-CD selection of the most essential Sun material. Put that together with *Johnny Cash: The Outtakes* (Bear Family BCD 16325), a 3-CD set that includes four alternate takes of "Folsom Prison Blues" and "Get Rhythm," one of "Big River," three of "Guess Things Happen That Way," etc., and you'll have as complete an introduction as you could ever want to the Cash creative process from the start. Just bear in mind that there is still an entire body of work to come, with all the Columbia hits, theme albums like *Ride This Train* and *Bitter Tears* and the live ones recorded at Folsom Prison and San Quentin, along with all sorts of creative sidetracks, including books, documentaries, and a wonderful 2-DVD set, *The Best of the Johnny Cash TV Show 1969-1971* (Sony/Legacy 88697040269), which definitely lives up to its title. So, as I'm sure you've noticed by now, I think I'm just going to sidestep the adjudication process here—the decision is entirely up to you.

JERRY LEE LEWIS

Classic Jerry Lee Lewis: The Definitive Edition of His Sun Recordings (Bear Family BCD 15420) is the only multi-CD box set I would put on the same level as *The Sun Blues Box*. If we can say that *The Sun Blues Box* is the one box set that no blues collection should be without, this is the one box set that no rock 'n' roll collection should be without (and no self-respecting "roots" collection should be without, either)—an 8-CD, 246-song set, complete with some of the most amazing music, thematic variations, and incidental dialogue ever recorded. Jerry Lee Lewis said at one time that he had recorded enough material at Sun for forty separate albums to be issued, and he may well have. But this will have to serve for now. I could offer as a compromise solution (and by now I think we all know how Sam and Jerry Lee both felt about compromise) *The Essential Jerry Lee Lewis: The Sun Sessions* (RCA/Legacy 88883706092). It's a wonderful selection, with 40 tracks on 2 CDs, and it could certainly serve as a form of introduction—but I swear, if you're looking for transcendence, don't wait, don't hesitate, go out and buy *Classic Jerry Lee Lewis: The Definitive Edition of His Sun Recordings* right now.

And I think that's the note I'll go out on.

Acknowledgments

IN WRITING A BOOK over so long a period (and one that stretches back far beyond its formal start), one incurs debts that one can never repay. Literally hundreds of people have helped me with my research and my interviews, and I thank them all. The following are just some of the people who gave me a hand over the weeks, months, and years:

Mark Albert, Hoss Allen, Roger Armstrong, Bill Austin, John Bakke, the Balton Sign Company, Saul Belz, Bettye Berger, Joe Bihari, Steve Bing, Bar Biszick-Lockwood, Dottie Bonds, Johnny Bragg, John Broven, Del Bryant, Paul Burch, Tony Burke, Trevor Cajiao, Little Milton (Campbell), Louis Cantor, Patrick Carr, Johnny Cash, Marshall Chess, Quinton Claunch, Rose Clayton, Jack Clement, Nadine Cohodas, Jim Cole, Brenda Colladay, Stuart Colman, the Country Music Foundation, Andrea Lanier Craig, T. Tommy Cutrer, Pete Daniel, Phillip and Hilda Darby, Hank Davis, Walter Dawson, Jim Dickinson, John Doyle, Diane Duncan, Janine Earney, Tom Eaton, Bill Ellis, Colin Escott, Giovanni Luca Fabris, Charlie Feathers, Donn Fileti, Fred Foster, Dale Franklin, Lee Freeman, Donnie Fritts, Galen Gart, Gregg Geller, Christine Gentry, Peter Gibbon, Alex Gibney, Robert Gordon, Rosco Gordon, Michael Gray, Bill Greensmith, Pete Grendysa, Bob Groom, Rick Hall, Allan Hammons, Ray Harris, Henry Harrison, Randy Haspel, Martin Hawkins, Josh Hecht, Kelso Herston, Jake Hess, Bob Hilburn, Phyllis Hill, Mark Hoffman, Jon Hornyak, Howlin' Wolf, Cilla Huggins, John Jackson, Roland Janes, Jim Jaworowicz, Sebastian Jeansson, Jimmy Johnson, Peter Jones, Ernst Jorgensen, Marion Keisker, Emily Kelley, Stan Kesler, Buddy Killen, the Kitchen Sisters (Davia Nelson and Nikki Silva), George Klein, Howard Kramer, Dr. Robert Kraus, Kurt Kurosawa, Joe Lauro, Andy Leach, Eric LeBlanc, Dickey Lee, David Less, Michael Letcher, Jerry Lee Lewis,

Peter Lewry, Don Light, Colin Linden, Kenny Lovelace, Ellen Mandel, Michael McCall, Floyd McClure, Ronnie McDowell, David McGee, Charlie McGovern, Bob Merlis, Bill Millar, Devin Miller, Fetzer Mills, Sleetie Mitchell, Sputnik Monroe, Scotty Moore, Cal Morgan, Joe Mulherin, Larry Nager, Morgan Neville, Nikki Nobles, Eric Olsen, Jim O'Neal, Terry and Anita Pace, Robert Palmer, Victor Pearlin, Judy Peiser, Carl Perkins, Stan Perkins, Holger Petersen, Dean Phillips, Halley Phillips, Horace Phillips, Johnny Phillips, Jud Phillips Jr., Skip (Sam) Phillips, Tom Phillips, Barbara Pittman, Randy Poe, John Prine, Bill Putnam Jr., Pat Rainer, Charles Raiteri, Richard Ramsey, Allen Reynolds, Charlie Rich, Margaret Ann Rich, Sue Richards (Maggie Sue Wimberly), John Richbourg, Billy Lee Riley, the Rock 'n' Roll Hall of Fame, Jeff Rosen, Matt Ross-Spang, Fred Rothwell, Mike Rowe, James Roy, Bob Santelli, Rob Santos, Dave Sax, Jerry Schilling, Zenas Sears, Billy Sherrill, Johnny Shines, John Shore, Dick Shurman, Barbara Sims, John Singleton, Shelby Singleton, Ronald Smith, Sylvia Smith, Jack Soden, Andrew Solt, Chris Spindel, Terry Stewart, Mark Stielper, John Tefteller, Rufus Thomas, Pat Tigrett, Henry Turley, Ike Turner, Steve Turner, J. M. Van Eaton, Slim Wallace, Billy Warren, Steve Weiss, Richard Weize, Dot West, Jerry Wexler, Charles White, Kemmons Wilson, Peter Wolf, Adrian Wooton, Malcolm Yelvington, Lauren Wilson Young (Wilson Family Foundation), Warren Zanes.

I owe an inestimable debt to the Phillips family. Knox, Jerry, Becky, Diane Duncan, and Sally Wilbourn all gave themselves over unstintingly to the book from the start. Each and every one of them flung themselves into every aspect of the work, digging up photographs, unearthing documents, giving more than generously of their time and spirit, and freely making themselves available for lengthy interviews (and lots of them). All in the service of an enterprise in which they all believed without looking to influence the outcome in any way except (in the spirit of Sam) in the interests of the truth, whatever that turned out to be. Knox, of course, was captain of the ship, Becky showed an unfailing generosity of spirit, but it was Sally who turned out to be not only the keeper of the records but a researcher extraordinaire who knew both where to look for the relevant information and what else to look for to fill out the picture.

The photographs would be another case in point of cooperative enterprise. Becky took almost all of the early photographs, Sally many of the later ones. Becky put together scrapbooks for Sam and the boys, while Sally also maintained (along with Sam) an extensive record of his early life. Diane was tireless — and resourceful — in seeking out the best prints that she and Knox could lay their hands on. And even Jerry's daughter Halley, who is carrying on the family tradition in both radio and recording, maintained a rich repository of her grandmother's pictures.

I should also acknowledge the above-and-beyond-the-call-of-duty help I got from Martin Hawkins and Colin Escott, who for years — *many* years — suffered all my annoyingly unanswerable questions and did their best to answer them. They also read the book in toto in manuscript, as did Gregg Geller. So, too, did Susan Marsh (several times), whose primacy as a designer is firmly founded on text. Researchers and historians Robert Gordon, Jim Cole, and David Less provided invaluable help in Memphis, while Terry Pace, Robert Palmer, Lee Freeman, and Billy Warren did the same in Florence. Both Shelby and John Singleton made all the Sun Records archives at their command freely available to me. In audio matters (that's close listening), I relied on the educated ears of Colin Linden, Stuart Colman, Matt Ross-Spang, and Tom Eaton (not to mention Cal Morgan on every question of Jerry Lee Lewis pianistics) for finely tuned counsel and advice. And I would be remiss if I didn't cite the invaluable insights and historical and personal perspective of Marion Keisker, Scotty Moore, Jack Clement, and Roland Janes, participants and keen-eyed observers all. For all matters blues (and beyond) I turned to Jim O'Neal. And for anything to do with the record business (and much more) I consulted John Broven. And that's only a start at singling out all the invaluable contributions of friends, fans, scholars, writers, and historians (frequently one and the same) along the way.

Kit Rachlis once again offered the most scrupulous, irritatingly perceptive, and noninvasively confrontational editorial advice, and Alexandra Guralnick patiently read, transcribed, debated, and imagined the details of the story every step of the way. As always, thanks to Jake and Nina for their incalculable contributions. And thanks once again to Pamela Marshall not just for her cheerfully stringent approach to copyediting but for her occasional willingness to forsake consistency for feel — and, of course, for her continued sensitivity to the ongoing role of the enclitic in Latinate speech. Working with Susan Marsh, whose passionate commitment to elegance of form and unswerving dedication to the text have guided the design of every book I have written since 1979, was, as always, an unalloyed pleasure. And I could say much the same about my editor, Michael Pietsch, whose honesty, loyalty, editorial insight, and friendship have served as guideposts for the last twenty-three years.

Thanks to all, and to all those not named, from whom I drew encouragement, sustenance, and inspiration, not to mention the courage (and enthusiasm) to go on!

Index

About the Author

Peter Guralnick has written extensively on American music and musicians. His books include the prizewinning Elvis Presley two-volume biography *Last Train to Memphis* and *Careless Love;* an acclaimed trilogy on American roots music, *Feel Like Going Home, Lost Highway,* and *Sweet Soul Music;* the biographical inquiry *Searching for Robert Johnson,* the novel *Nighthawk Blues;* and *Dream Boogie,* a biography of Sam Cooke. He splits his time between Nashville and Massachusetts.